Charles Hardwick

A History of the Christian Church

Middle Age

Charles Hardwick

A History of the Christian Church
Middle Age

ISBN/EAN: 9783337162146

Printed in Europe, USA, Canada, Australia, Japan

Cover: Foto ©Lupo / pixelio.de

More available books at **www.hansebooks.com**

A HISTORY

OF THE

CHRISTIAN CHURCH.

Middle Age.

WITH FOUR MAPS CONSTRUCTED FOR THIS WORK
BY A. KEITH JOHNSTON.

BY

CHARLES HARDWICK, M.A.

FORMERLY FELLOW OF ST. CATHARINE'S COLLEGE, AND ARCHDEACON OF ELY.

FOURTH EDITION, REVISED.

EDITED BY

W. STUBBS, M.A.

REGIUS PROFESSOR OF MODERN HISTORY IN THE UNIVERSITY OF OXFORD.

London:
MACMILLAN AND CO.
1874.

[All Rights reserved.]

Cambridge:
PRINTED BY C. J. CLAY, M.A.
AT THE UNIVERSITY PRESS.

TO

THE MASTER AND FELLOWS

OF

ST. CATHARINE'S COLLEGE,

𝔗𝔥𝔦𝔰 𝔙𝔬𝔩𝔲𝔪𝔢

IS RESPECTFULLY AND AFFECTIONATELY

INSCRIBED

AS A MEMORIAL OF HAPPY YEARS SPENT IN THEIR SOCIETY.

ADVERTISEMENT TO THIS EDITION.

IN the preparation of the present Edition no further alterations have been made than seemed necessary in order to maintain the character of the Book. With this view I have carefully revised both text and notes, re-writing several of the latter and one or two passages of the former, on which recent research has shed new light. All the alterations are corrections of matters of fact, dates and the like; and the doctrinal, historical and generally speculative views of the lamented Author have been preserved intact whether or no they happened to be my own.

WILLIAM STUBBS.

KETTEL HALL, OXFORD,
  May 4, 1872.

PREFACE TO THE SECOND EDITION.

A FEW words will explain the circumstances under which the Second Edition of a portion of the late Archdeacon Hardwick's Work has been prepared for the press by another hand. The Author had made preparations for a revised edition of this volume. These additions and alterations have been inserted in their place.

The editor has verified a large proportion of the original references. A few additional references are also given, *e.g.* to the *Chronicles and Memorials of Great Britain and Ireland*, now in course of publication under the sanction of the Master of the Rolls, and to Dean Milman's *History of Latin Christianity;* and some others, which it is hoped will make the work more useful to the Students, for whom this Series of THEOLOGICAL MANUALS is mainly intended.

PREFACE TO THE FIRST EDITION.

ALTHOUGH this volume has been written for the series of THEOLOGICAL MANUALS projected by the present Publishers five years ago, it claims to be regarded as an integral and independent treatise on the Mediæval Church.

I have begun with Gregory the Great, because it is admitted on all hands that his pontificate became a turning-point, not only in the fortunes of the Western tribes and nations, but of Christendom at large. A kindred reason has suggested the propriety of pausing at the year 1520,—the year when Luther, having been extruded from those Churches that adhered to the communion of the pope, established a provisional form of government and opened a fresh era in the history of Europe. All the intermediate portion is, ecclesiastically speaking, the Middle Age.

The ground-plan of this treatise coincides in many points with one adopted at the close of the last century in the colossal work of Schröckh, and since that time by others of his thoughtful countrymen; but in arranging the materials I have frequently pursued a very different course. The reader will decide upon the merit of these changes, or, in other words, he will determine whether they have added to the present volume aught of clearness and coherence.

With regard to the opinions (or, as some of our Germanic neighbours would have said, the stand-point) of the author, I am willing to avow distinctly that I always construe history with the specific prepossessions of an Englishman, and, what is more, with those which of necessity belong to members of the English Church. I hope, however, that although the judgment passed on facts may, here and there, have been unconsciously discoloured, owing to the prejudices of the mind by which they are observed, the facts themselves have never once been seriously distorted, garbled, or suppressed.

It is perhaps superfluous to remark, that I have uniformly profited by the researches of my predecessors, ancient, modern, Roman, and Reformed. Of these I may particularize Baronius[1], and, still more, Raynaldus (his continuator), Fleury[2], Schröckh[3], Gieseler[4], Neander[5], Döl-

---

[1] BARONIUS: best edition, including the *Continuation* of Raynaldus, and the *Critica* of Pagi, in 38 volumes, Lucæ, 1738.

[2] FLEURY: in 36 volumes, à Bruxelles, 1713 sq. The Continuation (after 1414) is by Fabre.

[3] SCHRÖCKH: in 43 volumes, Leipzig, 1768—1808.

[4] GIESELER: translated in Clarke's *Theological Library;* 5 volumes, Edinburgh, 1846—1855.

[5] NEANDER: translated in Bohn's *Standard Library:* 9 volumes.

linger[1], and Capefigue[2]. Others will be noticed as occasion offers in the progress of the work. But more considerable help was yielded by the numerous writers, whether English or Continental, who have dedicated single treatises to some peculiar branch of this inquiry. I must add, however, that I do not pay a servile deference to any of the second-hand authorities; while in those portions of the history that bear upon the Church of England, nearly all the statements I have made are drawn directly from the sources.

One may scarcely hope that in a subject where the topics to be handled are so vast, so various, and so complicated, errors will not be detected by the learned and sagacious critic. As my wish is to compile a useful and a truthful hand-book, every hint which he may furnish, tending to remove its blemishes, will be most thankfully received.

---

[1] DÖLLINGER: translated by Cox, 4 volumes.

[2] CAPEFIGUE: in 2 volumes, à Paris, 1852.

Excepting where a given work has not been printed more than once, which happens frequently among the great historical collections (*e.g.* those of Twysden, Petrie, Bouquet, or Pertz), the particular edition, here made use of, has been specified in the notes.

CONTENTS.

FIRST PERIOD.

FROM GREGORY THE GREAT TO THE DEATH OF CHARLEMAGNE.

590—814.

CHAPTER I.

	PAGE
§ 1. *Growth of the Church.*	
In England	6
In Germany and parts adjacent	16
In Eastern Asia	26
In Africa	28
§ 2. *Limitation of the Church.*	
Muhammedanism	29

CHAPTER II.

CONSTITUTION AND GOVERNMENT OF THE CHURCH.

§ 1. *Internal Organization*	34
§ 2. *Relations to the Civil Power*	49

CHAPTER III.

STATE OF RELIGIOUS DOCTRINE AND CONTROVERSIES.

Western Church	56
Eastern Church	64
The Paulicians.	78

CHAPTER IV.

STATE OF INTELLIGENCE AND PIETY . . 85

SECOND PERIOD.

FROM THE DEATH OF CHARLEMAGNE TO POPE GREGORY VII.

814—1073.

CHAPTER V.

PAGE

§ 1. *Growth of the Church.*
- In the Scandinavian kingdoms 100
- Among the Slavic or Slavonian races . . . 111
  - Moravian Church . . . . . . *ib.*
  - Bohemian Church 114
  - Polish Church 116
  - Wendish Church 117
  - Russian Church 119
  - Bulgarian Church 121
  - Other Slavonic Churches . . . 124
  - Hungarians 126
- In Central Asia 128

§ 2. *Limitation of the Church.*
- Ravages of the Northmen 130
- Persecutions in Spain 132

CHAPTER VI.

CONSTITUTION AND GOVERNMENT OF THE CHURCH.

§ 1. *Internal Organization* 134
§ 2. *Relations to the Civil Power* 149

CHAPTER VII.

STATE OF RELIGIOUS DOCTRINE AND CONTROVERSIES.

- Western Church 156
- Eastern Church 176
- Separation of East and West . . . 181
- Eastern and Western Sects . . . 187

CHAPTER VIII.

STATE OF INTELLIGENCE AND PIETY . . . 191

THIRD PERIOD.

FROM GREGORY VII. UNTIL THE TRANSFER OF THE PAPAL SEE TO AVIGNON.

1073—1305.

CHAPTER IX.

		PAGE
§ 1.	*Growth of the Church*	
	Among the Finns	206
	In Pomerania	207
	Among the Wends	209
	Lieflanders and other tribes	212
	Prussians	214
§ 2.	*Vicissitudes of the Church in other regions.*	
	Eastern Asia	217
	Spain and Northern Africa	219
	Among the Jews	220

CHAPTER X.

CONSTITUTION AND GOVERNMENT OF THE CHURCH.

§ 1.	*Internal Organization*	221
§ 2.	*Relations to the Civil Power*	243

CHAPTER XI.

STATE OF RELIGIOUS DOCTRINE AND CONTROVERSIES.

Western Church	257
Eastern Church	272
Relations of the East and West	276
Eastern and Western Sects	282
Bogomiles	ib.
Cathari and Albigenses	286
Petrobrusians	290
Waldenses or Vaudois	291
Apostolicals	294

CHAPTER XII.

STATE OF INTELLIGENCE AND PIETY . . 296

FOURTH PERIOD.

FROM THE TRANSFER OF THE PAPAL SEE TO AVIGNON UNTIL THE EXCOMMUNICATION OF LUTHER.

1305—1520.

CHAPTER XIII.

Growth of the Church.

	PAGE
Among the Lithuanians	312
Samaites and Lapps	314
Kumanians	ib.
In the Canaries and Western Africa	315
In America	316
Compulsory Conversion of Muhammedans and Jews	318

CHAPTER XIV.

CONSTITUTION AND GOVERNMENT OF THE CHURCH.

The Papacy	321
Other Branches of the Hierarchy	340

CHAPTER XV.

STATE OF RELIGIOUS DOCTRINE AND CONTROVERSIES.

Western Church	351
Eastern Church	362
Relations of East and West	364
Reformatory Efforts	371
Wycliffites	374
Hussites	400

CHAPTER XVI.

STATE OF INTELLIGENCE AND PIETY . . 414

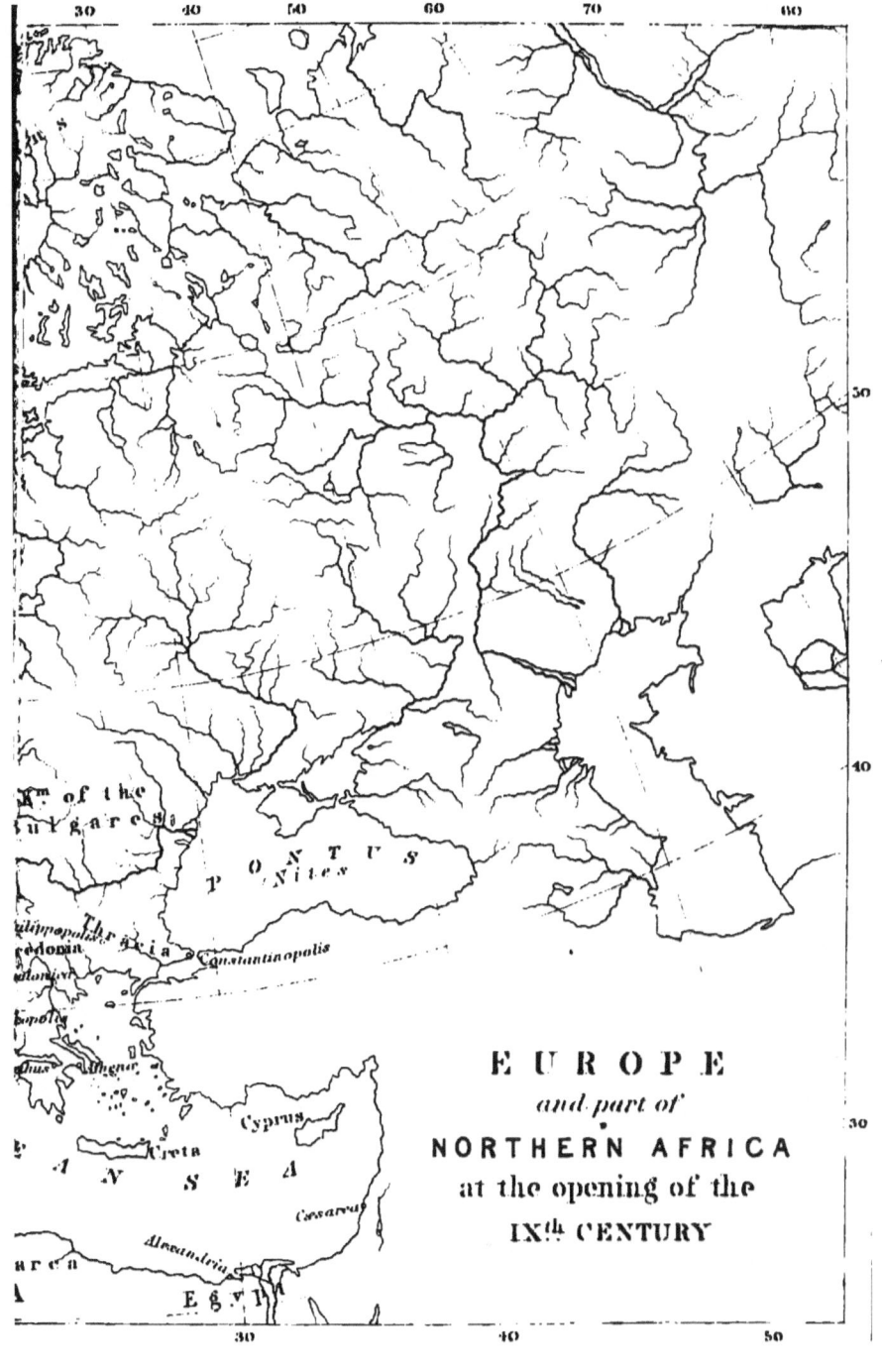

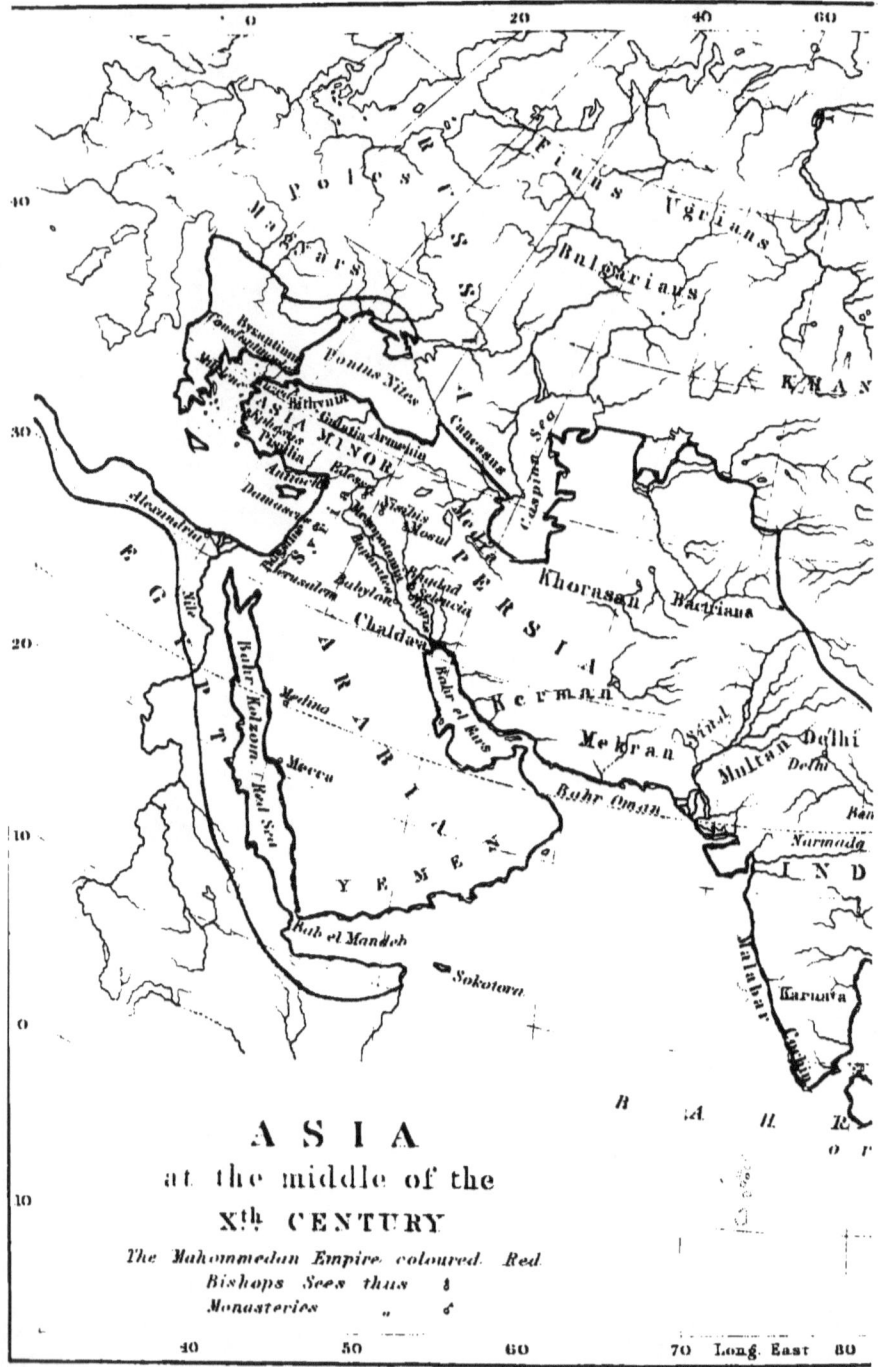

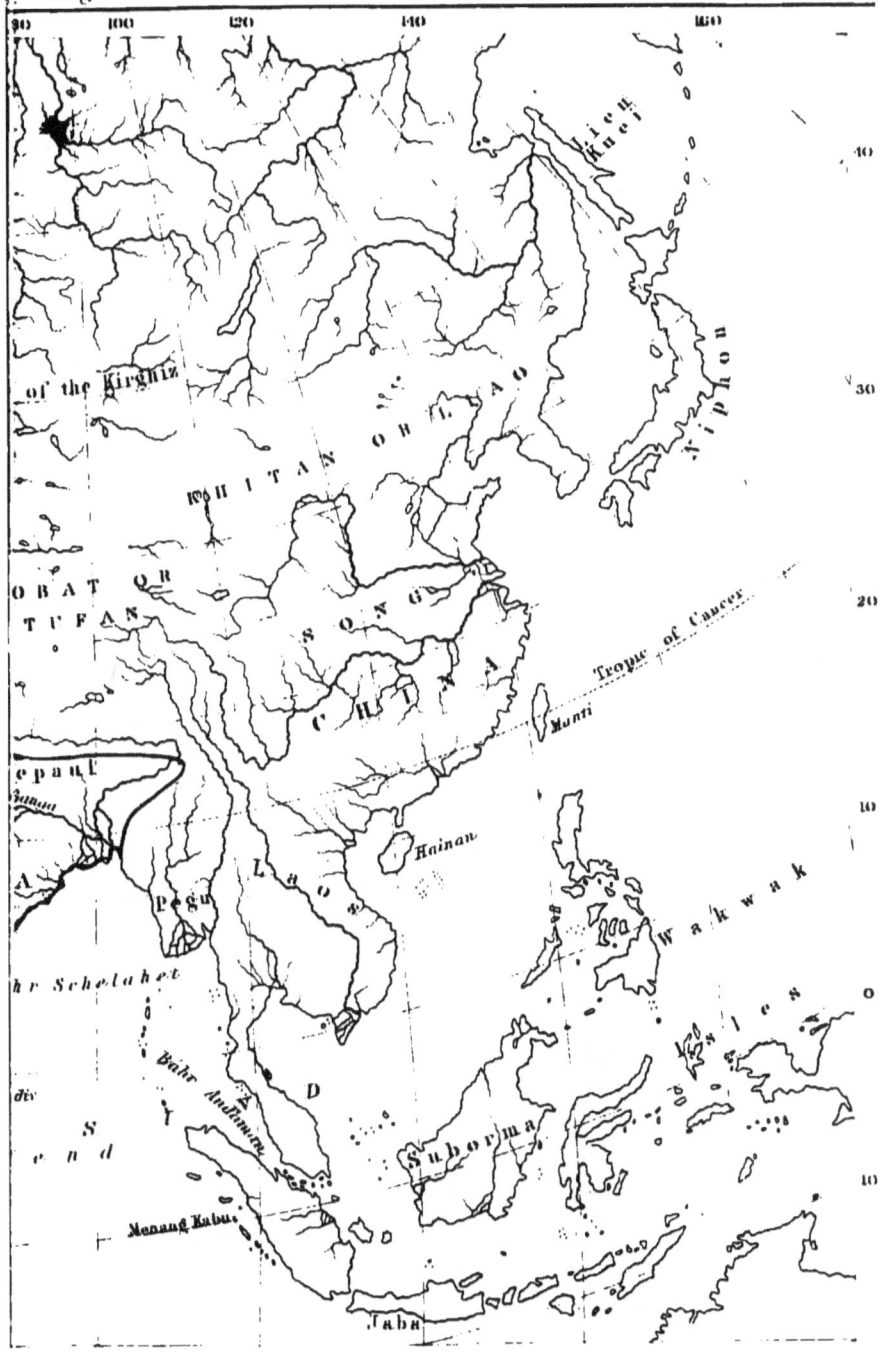

PLATE 2

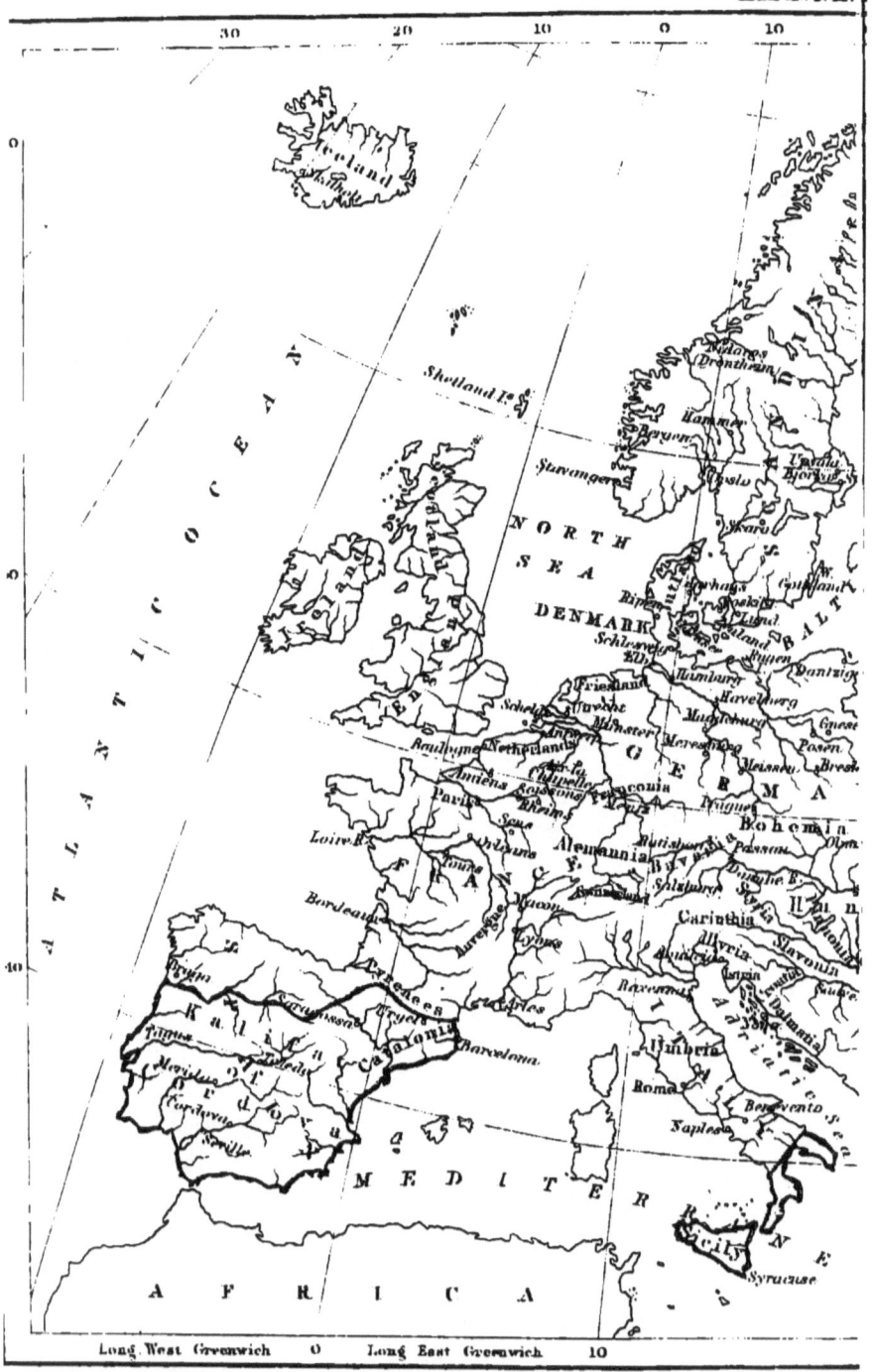

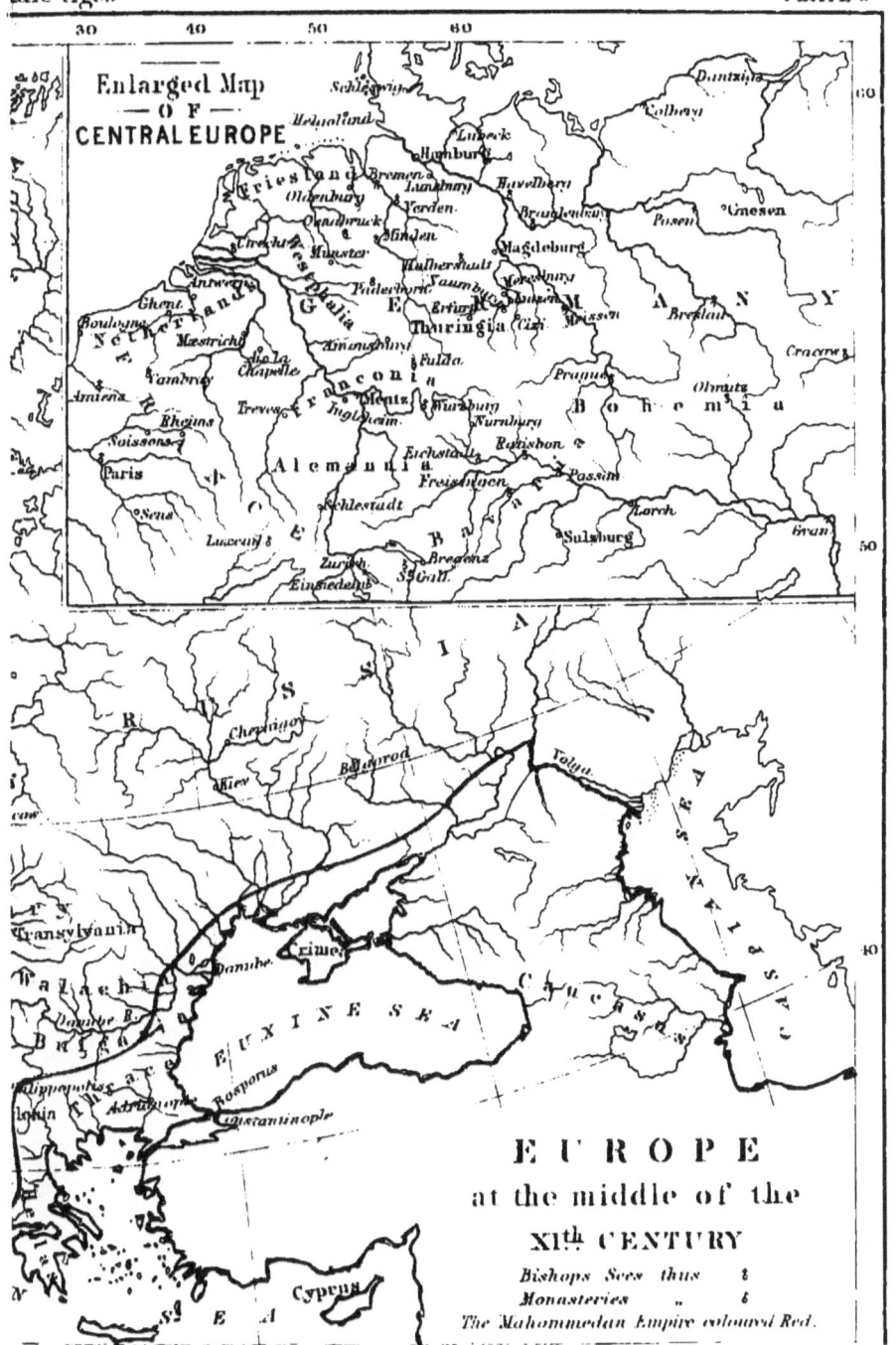

A HISTORY
OF THE CHRISTIAN CHURCH.

Mediæval Period.

THE period of the Church's life, to be considered in the following pages, will exhibit a variety of features with which the student has been familiarized already in the history of earlier times.

The foremost article of faith, the Incarnation of our Lord, after a long struggle with Rationalism on the one side and Spiritualism on the other, was finally elucidated and established at the Council of Chalcedon (**451**): and although we shall hereafter notice sundry forms of misbelief on this and kindred tenets, they are frequently no more than reproductions or recurring phases of the past. It should also be observed, that not a few of the characteristics of the Church in her ritual, constitution, and relations to the civil power, had been permanently fixed at the opening of this period; and most of the external changes afterwards effected are the natural fruit of principles that had long been ripening within. The same is true in a considerable measure of the mediæval Church-writers. Generally speaking, they trod in the steps of their immediate predecessors, epitomizing what they had no longer the ability to equal, and, with bright exceptions in St Bernard and some of the leading schoolmen, showing little or no depth and originality of thought.

It is true the degree of intelligence was different at

Introduction.

Comparative sameness in the aspect of the Church.

2 History of the Christian Church.

<small>INTRODUCTION.</small>

Decay of intelligence and of piety.

different points of the Middle Ages, and varied also in the several branches of the Church. Perhaps the lowest point for western Christendom at large was the sixth and two following centuries, when society, everywhere depressed by the recent inroads of barbarians, had not been able to rally from its languor and to mould its chaotic elements afresh. To this, among other causes, we may assign the deterioration of piety as well as of arts and letters, which is painfully prominent in the records of that period: and to the same source is due the admixture of unchristian feelings and ideas that had been blended with the life of the Mediæval Church, clouding the sense of personal responsibility, or giving birth to a servile and Judaizing spirit, that continued, more or less, to keep its hold upon the faithful till the dawn of the Reformation.

Growth of the papal power in the West.

Synchronizing with the decay of literature, the degeneracy of taste, and an obscuration of the deeper verities of the Gospel, is the growth of the Papal monarchy, whose towering pretensions are in sight through the whole of the present period. It may have served, indeed, as a centralizing agent, to facilitate the fusion of discordant races; it may have proved itself in times of anarchy and ignorance a powerful instrument, and in some sort may have balanced the encroachments of the civil power. Yet on the whole its effect was deadening and disastrous: it weakened the bonds of ecclesiastical discipline by screening the mendicant and monastic orders from the jurisdiction of the bishops: it perpetuated the use of Latin Service-books when the mass of the people could no longer understand them: it crippled the spirit of national independence as well as the growth of individual freedom: while its pride and venality excited a bitter disaffection to the Church, and opened a way for the deep convulsions at the middle of the sixteenth century.

Eastern Church different from the Western.

But this remark, as well as the former on the altered phases of society, must be confined to the Western or Latin Church, which was in close communion with the popes. In the Eastern, where the like disturbing powers had operated less, the aspect of religion was comparatively smooth. Islamism, which curtailed it on all sides, but was incapable of mingling with it, did not waken in its members a more primitive devotion, nor inject a fresh stock of energy and health: it had already entered, in the seventh century, upon the calm and protracted period of decline which is continuing at the present day.

Yet, notwithstanding the stagnant uniformity in the general spirit of the age, a change had been gradually effected in the limits of the Christian kingdom. True to the promise of the Lord, the Church of God multiplied in all quarters, putting forth a number of new branches in the East and in the West, and, in spite of the dimness of the times, bearing witness to its heavenly origin and strength. As it had already triumphed over the systems of Greece and Rome, and had saved from the wreck of ancient civilization whatever they possessed of the beautiful and true, it now set out on a different mission, to raise the uncultured natures of the North[1], and to guide the Saxon, the Scandinavian, and eventually the Slave, into the fold of the Good Shepherd.

Proofs of surviving energy in the whole.

---

[1] All Science and art, all social culture, and the greatest political and national movements, received their impulse from the Church, and were guided and ruled by her spirit, however imperfect the form may have been under which Christianity then existed.

First Period of the Middle Ages.

THE CHRISTIAN CHURCH FROM GREGORY THE GREAT TO THE DEATH OF CHARLEMAGNE.

590—814.

CHAPTER I.

§ 1. *GROWTH OF THE CHURCH.*

IN ENGLAND.

<small>ENGLISH CHURCH.</small>

STEPS had been already taken for the evangelizing of the Goths in Germany, the Burgundians and Franks in Gaul, and the Picts[1] in Scotland; in all which provinces the labours of the missionary had been very largely blessed. But a race of men, who were destined above others to aid in converting the rest of Europe, was now added to the Christian body. The Anglo-Saxons had been settled on the ruins of the British Church for at least a century and a half, when a mission, formed by Gregory the Great[2], appeared in the isle of Thanet. It was headed by his friend Augustine, a Roman abbot, whose companions were nearly forty in number[3]. Although the Germanic tribes were bordering on the British Christians[4], whom they had driven to the west, and had extended their conquests as

<small>Roman mission to the Anglo-Saxons, A.D. 596.</small>

---

[1] Columba, after labouring 32 years, breathed his last at the time when the Roman missionaries landed (*Annales Cambriæ*, in *Monument. Britann.* p. 831; see also his life by Adamnan, ed. Reeves, Dublin, 1857, pp. 228—230, 310; and in Canisius, *Lectiones Antiquæ*, v. pt. II. p. 559).

[2] The pious design had been conceived many years before, while Gregory was abbot of a monastery in Rome. Beda, *Hist. Ecc.* II. 1: and from his own letters we learn that intelligence had reached him of a desire on the part of the English themselves for conversion to the Christian faith. Lib. VI. ep. 58, 59.

[3] 'Ut ferunt, ferme quadraginta.' Bed. I. 25. They were at first deterred by the hopelessness of the undertaking, and only reassured by an earnest letter from the Roman bishop: Gregor. *Ep.* lib. VI. ep. 51.

[4] Though much depressed, the British Church was far from extinguished. Bede (a warm friend of the Roman missionaries) mentions 'septem Brittonum episcopi et plures viri doctissimi,' II. 2; and the monastery of Bancornaburg (*Bangor-ys*-Coed), under its abbot Dinoot, was large and flourishing. This applies of course only to the Western side of the island.

far as the Church that was already planted in the north[1] by a mission from the sister island, they had lost very little of their zeal for Woden, Tiw, and Fricge[2]. It is not indeed unlikely that some of them may have gained a slight knowledge of the Gospel from their numerous Keltic slaves; yet the only Christian of importance in Kent on the landing of Augustine was the Frankish queen of Æthelberht, whom he espoused on condition of allowing her the free use of her religion[3]. The system, therefore, which the Roman missionaries founded was entirely of extraneous growth, was built on the *Roman* model of the period; and as it differed[4] not a little from that of the British

---

[1] Bed. III. 4; v. 9. Saxon Chron. ad an. 565. Ninias, 'the apostle of the southern Picts' (between the Firth of Forth and the Grampians), had been educated at Rome, and died early in the fifth century. His see was at 'Candida Casa' (in Sax. Chron. *Hwiterne*). It afterwards came into the hands of the 'Angles' (Bed. III. 4). Columba and his successors had their original establishment among the northern Picts (the Gaël) at Hycolumbcille, or Iona.

[2] For an account of their mythology see Turner, *Anglo-Saxons*, Append. bk. II. c. III., and Kemble, *Saxons in England*, I. 327—445.

[3] In her retinue was a Frankish bishop, Liudhard, who officiated in the church of St Martin near Canterbury, preserved from the time of the Romans. Bed. I. 25, 26.

[4] The *first* point of difference was in the reckoning of Easter. The British and Irish were not indeed Quarto-decimani (Bed. III. 4): they uniformly solemnized that festival on a Sunday, but in some years (owing to their use of the cycle which up to 458 had been employed at Rome) on a Sunday different from that observed by the rest of the Church. (Bed. II. 2. 19; Ideler, *Chronol.* II. 275 seq. *Councils and Ecclesiastical Documents*, ed. Haddan and Stubbs, I. 152, 153.) The second was in the administering of baptism, the exact point of which is uncertain. It appears however that the defect was not the omission of Chrism or Confirmation, which although disused in the Irish Church at a later period (*Ep. Lanfr. Opp.* ed. Bened. p. 320), are mentioned in St Patrick's letter to Coroticus. It is more probable that the practice was that of single immersion. (Kunstmann, *Pönitent. Bücher der Angelsachs.* p. 2. *Councils and Eccl. Doc.* I. 153.) Other points which emerged later than Augustine's time were the form of clerical tonsure (Ussher, *Antiq. Brit.* 477), a practice of consecrating bishops by a single bishop (*Counc. and Eccl. Doc.* I. 155), peculiar ritual at ordination (*ibid.*), and consecration of churches. The question of the Marriage of the Clergy, which is sometimes alleged as a disputed one, does not seem to have arisen; nor is there any reason to suppose that the state of opinion respecting it was at this moment in Britain at all different from that of the other Western Churches. The real question that prevented union was no doubt Augustine's claim to superiority. (See below, pp. 8, 9.) Augustine consented to waive the other differences for the present, if three points were conceded: 'Quia *in multis quidem nostræ consuetudini*, imo universalis ecclesiæ, contraria geritis: et tamen si in tribus his mihi obtemperare vultis, ut pascha suo tempore celebretis; ut ministerium baptizandi, quo

ENGLISH CHURCH.

First steps of the Roman mission.

Disagreement with the British Church: A.D. 603.

and the Irish Churches, its advancement could not fail to place it in collision with those bodies.

The field of Augustine's earlier labours was the kingdom of Kent. Softened by a Christian consort, the king was himself baptized; and in his chief city (Durovernum =Canterbury), Augustine was acknowledged as archbishop of the English, being consecrated in 597, by Virgilius of Arles[1]. This fact was announced to Gregory the Great by two members of the mission, Laurentius and Peter[2], who bore a detailed account of its success; and Gregory[3] was able to inform an Eastern correspondent, that on Christmas-day, 597, no less than ten thousand 'Angli' had been baptized by their brother-bishop. Still, in spite of this glowing picture, the conversion of the people was afterwards retarded: numbers of them, only half-weaned from paganism, relapsing to their former state[4]. As the sphere of the Roman mission widened, the unfriendly posture of the native Christians would be more and more perplexing. A conference[5] was accordingly procured by the help of Æthelberht, with the hope of disarming this hostility and of gaining the cooperation of the British: but the haughty manner of Augustine, threatening an invasion of their freedom, was the signal for a harsh and spirited resistance; they instantly rejected his proposals, and declared that nothing should induce them to accept him as their archbishop[6]. A similar divergency of usages,

Deo renascimur, juxta morem sanctæ Romanæ et apostolicæ ecclesiæ compleatis; ut genti Anglorum una nobiscum verbum Domini prædicctis, cætera quæ agitis, quamvis moribus nostris contraria, æquanimiter cuncta tolerabimus.' · Bed. II. 2.

[1] Bed. I. 27, and Pagi, *Critic.* ad an. 596, § 5.

[2] Ibid. They carried also a string of questions from Augustine, touching matters in which he was himself at a loss. The answers of Gregory are preserved in Bede, *ib.*

[3] Gregor. *Epist.* lib. VIII. ep. 30. Bede attributes the success of the missionaries to the 'simplicitatem innocentis vitæ ac dulcedinem doctrinæ eorum cœlestis,' I. 26, though Augustine is said to have wrought miracles (I. 31: cf. Greg. *Epist.* VIII. 30).

[4] e. g. in Kent itself, Eadbald, the next king, restored the heathen worship.

[5] Bed. II. 2: cf. Palgrave, *Engl. Common.* I. 238 seq.

[6] 'At illi nil horum se facturos neque illum pro archiepiscopo habituros esse respondebant.' Bed. *ibid.* A very spirited protest, granting that the Britons owed to the Roman bishop, in common with all Christians, the deference of love, but denying that any other obedience was due to him, is ascribed to Dinoot abbot of Bangor, who is mentioned by Bede on this

combined with this independent spirit, had produced a similar estrangement in the Irish missionaries, who were stationed in the north of Britain. Laurentius[1], the successor of Augustine at Canterbury, with Mellitus of London and Justus of Rochester, endeavoured to secure their friendship, about 605, complaining that a prelate of their communion (Daganus) would not even eat bread with the Anglo-Roman party: but this, like the former application to the Britons, was at present void of fruit.

Meanwhile the two bands of workmen were proceeding in their labours, and though parted from each other felt the blessing of the Lord. At the death of Augustine[2], the English Church had been organized in *Kent* and brought into close communion with the Roman; the pope, however, leaving its founder at liberty to select a ritual for it from the Gallican and other 'uses[3],' instead of copying the Roman rules entirely. On the accession of Eadbald, the son of Æthelberht, in 616, the prospects of the Church were darkened by the restoration of the pagan worship: and only when Laurentius was on the point of giving up the mission in despair[4], did the king retrace his steps, and bow the knee to Christ.

A similar reverse occurred in the neighbouring state of *Essex*. Its king, Sæberht, was the nephew of Æthelberht of Kent: he had received the Gospel[5] early from

---

same occasion. See Spelman's *Concil.* I. 108. But although the authenticity of the document in which this is contained has been accepted by some critics (Lappenberg, *Hist. of England*, ed. Thorpe, I. 135), it is generally regarded as apocryphal, and exists only in very late MSS. (*Councils*, &c. I. 122, 142.) A passage in Bede (II. 20) proves that the feeling of repugnance on the part of the Britons grew up into bitter hatred: 'Quippe cum usque hodie moris sit Brittonum fidem religionemque Anglorum pro nihilo habere, neque *in aliquo eis magis communicare quam paganis.*'

[1] Bed. II. 4. The form of address is remarkable: 'Dominis *carissimis, fratribus episcopis,* vel abbatibus per universam Scottiam.'

[2] A.D. 604 or 605. This date, though very important, cannot be accurately ascertained. See Smith's note on Bed. *Hist. Eccl.* II. 3. Wharton, *Ang. Sac.* II. 89—91.

[3] 'Non enim pro locis res, sed pro bonis rebus loca amanda sunt. Ex singulis ergo quibusque ecclesiis, quæ pia, quæ religiosa, quæ recta sunt elige, et *hæc quasi in fasciculum collecta, apud Anglorum mentes in consuetudinem depone.'* Bed. I. 27.

[4] Bed. II. 6: cf. Neander, *Church Hist.* V. 24, note.

[5] Bed. II. 3. Gregory had designed London as the seat of the southern metropolitan, *Epist.* lib. XI. ep. 65: but Boniface V. in 625, confirmed the selection of Canterbury. Wilkins, *Concil.* I. 32.

ENGLISH CHURCH.

the hands of the Roman missionaries and established a bishopric in London, his chief city. On his death, however, in 616, his sons, who had clung to their heathen habits, made light of the Christian faith, and the refusal of the bishop (Mellitus) to give them a share of the Eucharistic bread was followed by his expulsion[1] from their kingdom. A gloomy interval succeeded, the faith either languishing in secret, or being utterly subverted[2], till the reign of Sigeberht the Good (653—660). His friendship with Oswiu, king of Northumbria, led the way to his own conversion, while on a visit to that court[3]. He was baptized by Finan, one of the Irish missionaries, and took back with him Cedd[4] and others, by whom the whole kingdom of Essex was at length added to the Church.

Conversion of Wessex.

In *Wessex*, the Christian faith was planted by Birinus[5], sent over by pope Honorius in 634. He succeeded in converting Cynegils, the king, and was bishop of Dorcic (Dorchester) till 649 or 650; but much of his success may be attributed to a visit of Oswald, king of Northumbria, whose brother Oswiu (also of the Irish school) did further service to the Wessex-mission[6]. The successor of Cynegils, Cenwealh, a pagan, was driven from the throne in 643, but afterwards converted at the court of East Anglia. He was distinguished by his Christian zeal. On his

[1] Bed. II. 5.
[2] Bed. III. 22. Justus, through the influence of Eadbald, was restored to Rochester, from which he had retired (Bed. II. 5), but the pagan inhabitants of London would not receive their bishop Mellitus (*Ibid.* II. 6). In the following year (619) he succeeded Laurentius at Canterbury, and was in his turn succeeded by Justus in 624 (II. 7, 8).
[3] Bed. III. 22; Florent. Wigorn. *Chronicon* ad an. 653.
[4] Afterwards consecrated by Finan and two other Irish prelates as bishop of the East-Saxons. Bed. III. 22. A short relapse ensued on the death of Sigeberht, but the new faith was permanently restored by the zeal of bishop Jaruman. Bed. III. 30.
[5] Bed. III. 7.
[6] Wharton's *Anglia Sacra*, I. 192. Through the influence of Oswiu, a Gaul named Agilbert, who had 'spent not a little time in Ireland *legendarum gratia Scripturarum*,' was chosen to succeed Birinus (Bed. III. 7), but his imperfect knowledge of the English language displeasing the king, he returned into France. His successor was an Anglo-Saxon, Wini (664); but he also incurred the displeasure of the king, and migrating to London (666) was placed in that see by the king of Mercia. His post was filled for a time by Leutherius, nephew of Agilbert, who was consecrated in 670, by Theodore, the seventh archbishop of Canterbury. Bed. *ibid.* The first Anglo-Saxon raised to the episcopal dignity appears to have been Ithamar of Rochester: Florent. Wigorn. *Chron.* ad an. 644.

restoration, therefore, the extension of the faith was a primary concern, and Wessex, destined to become the leader of the English race, continued from that time faithful to the Church.

Sussex, like its neighbour Kent, was converted by the Roman party. The task had been reserved for a native of Northumbria, Wilfrith, who combined with his devotion to the pope the earnestness and prudence which are needed for the work of the evangelist. Banished from his diocese in the north of England[1], he was able in five years (681—686) to organize the church of the South-Saxons, who had previously resisted the appeals of a small Irish mission[2]. The king, indeed, Æthelwealh, was a Christian already, having been baptized in Mercia, but paganism still kept its hold upon his people, in whose hearts it had found its last entrenchment.

The conversion of *East Anglia* was early attempted by the Roman Mission. Rædwald, the king, had been instructed at the court of Æthelberht of Kent, but afterwards, through the influence of his wife and friends, the strength of his faith relaxed[3]. The assassination of his son (Eorpwald) in 628, was a further check to the progress of the Gospel, which, at the instance of the king of Northumbria, he had cordially embraced: and for three years it was almost everywhere suppressed[4]. At the end of this interval, however, his brother, Sigeberht, who had been Christianized in Gaul, was able to restore it; and with the aid of Felix[5], a native of Burgundy, the see of Dumnoc (Dunwich) was founded for the prelate of East Anglia. But the completion of their work is due to the efforts of an Irish monk, named Fursey[6], whose missionary

---

[1] Bed. IV. 13.
[2] Ibid. They had a 'monasteriolum' at a place named Bosanham. Wilfrith's monastery or mission station was at Selsey.
[3] Bed. II. 15. To satisfy both parties he reared the altar of Christ at the side of the ancient 'arula ad victimas dæmoniorum.'
[4] Ibid.
[5] He received his mission from Honorius, the fifth archbishop of Canterbury, and presided over the see of Dunwich 17 years. Bed. *ib.* Under his advice Sigeberht founded a school on the plan of those he had seen in Gaul: 'Scholam, in qua pueri literis erudirentur......eisque pædagogos ac magistros juxta morem Cantuariorum præbente.' Bed. III. 18.
[6] III. 19. The date of his arrival in England was 633. Bede gives a glowing picture of his sanctity and zeal.

ENGLISH CHURCH.

Conversion of Northumbria.

tours, extending over a period of fifteen years, are said to have produced a marvellous effect on the heathen and the faithful.

The kingdom of *Northumbria* consisted of two parts, Deira (from the Humber to the Tees), and Bernicia (from the Tees to the Clyde). They were forcibly united at the opening of this period, under the sway of an enemy to the Christian faith. His defeat led the way to the accession of Eadwine, who on mounting his paternal throne at York (**616**), was permitted to annex the kingdom of Bernicia. His second wife was a daughter of Æthelberht of Kent, whom he espoused in **625**; but notwithstanding a residence among the British clergy[1], he was still disaffected to the Gospel. Several circumstances had conspired, however, to impress it on his mind[2], and in **627**, through the influence of Paulinus, who had accompanied his queen to Northumbria, he was baptized with a concourse of his people[3]. His death followed in **633**, Penda, king of Mercia, the last champion of the English pagans, ravaging the whole of his dominions and subverting every trophy of the Gospel[4]. But the arms of his kinsman Oswald, made a way for its permanent revival in the course of the year **635**; and since Oswald had been trained by the Irish missionaries[5], he sent to their principal station at Iona for clergy to evangelize his people, himself acting as interpreter. Aidan was the chief of this band of teachers, and from his see in Lindisfarne (or Holy Island) he guided all the movements of the mission[6]. He expired

---

[1] See Lappenberg, *Anglo-Saxons*, I. 145.

[2] Bed. II. 9—12. Among other predisposing causes was a letter from Boniface V. (625), accompanied by a present, and the 'benedictio protectoris vestri B. Petri apostolorum principis,' but his conversion did not occur till two years later.

[3] See the very interesting circumstances in Bed. II. 12. Coifi was the last of the pagan high-priests. The scene was at Godmundham, in the East Riding of Yorkshire. So great was the success of Paulinus in Deira, that on one occasion he was employed for thirty-six days in baptizing on one spot. Bed. II. 14.

[4] Bed. II. 20. Paulinus, with the widowed queen, sought refuge in Kent. He succeeded to the see of Rochester.

[5] 'Misit ad majores natu Scottorum, inter quos exulans baptismatis sacramenta.........consecutus erat.' Bed. III. 3.

[6] Bed. III. 3. His field of labour extended as far as Scotland, embracing York, abandoned by Paulinus. York did not regain its archiepiscopal rank till 735. *Saxon Chron.* ad an. The archbishops of York

in 651, after an episcopate of seventeen years, the admiration of his Roman rivals[1]. His mantle fell on Finan, who lived to see religion everywhere established in the northern parts of Britain, and died in 661 or 662.

To him also *Mercia* was indebted for its first bishop Diuma, in 655. His master Oswiu, king of Northumbria, having signalized himself by the overthrow of Penda, was finally supreme in Middle England as well as in the north, and urgent in promoting the conversion of the natives. Addicted in his earlier years to the principles of his instructors, he established a religious system of the Irish cast, and three of the Mercian prelates in succession owed their orders to the Irish Church[2].

The planting, therefore, of the Gospel in the Anglo-Saxon provinces of Britain was the work of two rival bands, (1) the *Roman*, aided by their converts and some teachers out of Gaul, (2) the *Irish*, whom the conduct of Augustine and his party had estranged from their communion. If we may judge from the area of their field of action, it is plain that the Irish were the larger body: but a host of conspiring causes[3] gradually resulted in the spread and ascendancy of Roman modes of thought.

The ritual and other differences, obtaining in the various kingdoms, came painfully to light on the intermarriage of the princes; and it was an occasion of this sort[4] that

subsequently claimed to exercise metropolitan jurisdiction in the whole of Scotland: see Spotswood, *Hist. of Ch. of Scotland* (Lond. 1677), pp. 34, 36, 38. From this claim the Scottish church was released by the popes, who towards the end of the 12th century made the bishops immediately subject to Rome. The see of St Andrew's was not made archiepiscopal until 1472.

[1] 'Hæc autem dissonantia paschalis observantiæ, vivente Ædano, patienter ab omnibus tolerabatur, qui patenter intellexerant, quia etsi pascha contra morem eorum [*i. e.* the Irish party], qui ipsum miserant, facere non potuit, *opera tamen fidei, pietatis et dilectionis, juxta morem omnibus sanctis consuetum*, diligenter exequi curavit.' Bed. III. 25.

[2] Bed. III. 21.

[3] *e. g.* The political predominance of Wessex, which had been entirely Romanized by Birinus and his followers, the activity, organization, and superior intelligence of the Roman missionaries (such as Wilfrith), the apostolical descent of the Roman church (one of the *sedes apostolicæ*), and the prestige it had borrowed from the Roman empire.

[4] Bed. III. 25: 'Unde nonnunquam contigisse fertur illis temporibus, ut bis in anno uno pascha celebraretur. Et cum rex pascha Dominicum solutis jejuniis faceret, tunc regina cum suis persistens adhuc in jejunio diem Palmarum celebraret.'

ENGLISH CHURCH.

served in no small measure to shape all the after-fortunes of the Church in the northern parts of Britain. The queen of Oswiu, the Northumbrian, was a daughter of Eadwine and brought up in Kent; with Ealhfrith his son[1], the co-regent, she was warm in her attachment to the customs of the south. Oswiu, on the other hand, continued in communion with the Irish, over whom he had placed the energetic Colman as the third bishop of Lindisfarne. The controversy waxing hot in 664, Colman was invited by the king to a synod at Streoneshealh (the *Whitby* of the Danes), to meet the objections of an advocate of Rome, in the person of the rising Wilfrith[2]. The end was, that Oswiu and his people[3], persuaded by the agents of the queen, and dazzled by the halo which encircled (as they dreamt) the throne of the 'chief apostle,' went over to the Roman party; while the clergy, who were slow in complying with the changes of the court, withdrew from the scene of conflict into Ireland[4].

Conference at Whitby, 664.

Withdrawal of the Irish Clergy.

Influence of Theodore.

But it was not till the time of Archbishop Theodore (668—690) that the fusion of the English Christians was complete[5]. The two leading rulers, of Northumbria and Kent, agreed in procuring his appointment[6], and advancing his designs in the other kingdoms. By the aid of a Roman

---

[1] Eddius, *Vit. S. Wilfridi*, c. VII. apud Gale, *Scriptores*, xv. p. 54.
[2] Bed. III. 25.
[3] The king was afraid lest St Peter should finally exclude him from heaven; and after his decision in behalf of Wilfrith, 'faverunt adsidentes quique sive adstantes, majores cum mediocribus.' *Ibid.* The balance of argument however, it is but fair to state, was on the side of Wilfrith.
[4] Bed. III. 26. For the after-life of Colman, see Bed. IV. 4. Others, however, like Bishop Cedd the brother of St Chad, conformed to the Roman customs. *Ibid.* The next bishop of Lindisfarne, Tuda, had been educated in the *south* of Ireland, where the Roman Easter had been adopted as early as 634. Bed. III. 26. cf. III. 3 (p. 175, A, in *Monument. Britan.*). This conformity was afterwards increased by the labours of Adamnan (687—704), v. 15. The Picts accepted the Roman Easter in 710, the monks of Iona in 716; the tonsure was received by the former in 710 and by the latter in 718. The Britons of Wales conformed later, between 755 and 809. (*Councils*, &c. I. 203, II. 106.)
[5] Bed. IV. 2: 'Isque primus erat in archiepiscopis, cui *omnis Anglorum ecclesia* manus dare consentiret.'
[6] Deusdedit died July 14, 664, and after a vacancy of two or three years Oswiu and Ecgberht sent a presbyter, Wigheard, elected by the church of Canterbury, for consecration at the Roman see. Wigheard died at Rome; and after some correspondence with the two chief kings of England, Vitalian sent, at their request (Bed. III. 29; IV. 1), a prelate for the vacant see.

colleague and through the exertions (often conflicting with his own) of the ever-active Wilfrith, he was able to reduce the Irish school to insignificance[1]; and while giving to the Church a high degree of culture, he was unwittingly binding it more closely in allegiance to the popes[2]. At his death the island had been *Romanized*, according to the import of the term in the seventh century: but the freer spirit of the Early Church still lingered in the north. When, for example, an attempt was made to enforce the *mandates* of the pope, as distinguished from his fatherly advice, it met with a vigorous repulse[3] from two succes-

ENGLISH CHURCH.

Disregard of the papal claims.

---

[1] So far as culture goes Theodore was not in opposition to the Irish; they attended his schools in large numbers (Aldhelm, *Epist.* 4; ed. Giles, p. 94): but in reference to discipline he directed that the imperfection in the orders of persons ordained by Scottish or British bishops should be remedied by imposition of hands of a Catholic bishop; churches consecrated by them are to be purified and "confirmed;" they are not to receive the Eucharist or Chrism without expressing their wish to be united with the church; and if any doubt about their baptism, they may be baptized. Theod. *Poenit.* II. c. 9. (*Councils,* &c. III. 197.)

[2] Bed. IV. 2. He was seconded in 673 by a synod held at Hertford; Wilkins, *Concil.* I. 41. *Councils* &c. III. 118. The English sees at the close of the present period were the following: *Province of Canterbury*—(1) Lichfield, (2) Leicester, (3) Lindsey (Sidnacester), (4) Worcester, (5) Hereford, (6) Sherborne, (7) Winchester, (8) Elmham, (9) Dunwich, (10) London, (11) Rochester, (12) Selsey. *Province of York*—(1) Hexham, (2) Lindisfarne, (3) Whithern. Kemble, *Anglo-Saxons,* II. 361, 362. At a later period some of these perished altogether, as Hexham, Whithern and Dunwich; while others were formed, as Durham in succession to Lindisfarne, Dorchester for Lincoln, and in Wessex, Ramsbury (Hræfnesbyrig = ecclesia Corvinensis) for Wilts, Wells for Somerset, Crediton for Devonshire, and during some time, St Germans and perhaps Bodmin for Cornwall. It was only in the 12th century that the whole Cambrian Church was brought under the jurisdiction of the see of Canterbury: Williams, *Eccl. Hist. of the Cymry,* pp. 162, 163; Lond. 1844. *Councils,* &c. ed. Haddan and Stubbs, vol. I. pp. 302 sq.

[3] When Wilfrith, on his deposition from his see, brought his grievance to the pope, the sentence in his favour in 679 was so far from reversing the decision at home, that on his return Ecgfrith of Northumbria threw him into prison, and afterwards banished him. Bed. IV. 12, 13. Aldfrith, on a like occasion, having readmitted him into the kingdom, was no less opposed to his Romanizing conduct. Having made a fresh appeal to Rome, and obtained from John VI. a favourable sentence (in 704, see *Vit. S. Wilfrid.* c. 48—52), the bearers of it to the king were addressed in the following terms: 'Se quidem legatorum personis, quod essent et vita graves et aspectu honorabiles, honorem ut parentibus deferre, cæterum *assensum legationi omnino abnuere,* quod esset contra rationem homini jam bis *a toto Anglorum concilio damnato* propter quælibet *apostolica scripta* communicare.' A compromise, however, was effected at his death, and Wilfrith was transferred to another see. W. Malmesb. *Gesta Pontiff.* ed. Hamilton, p. 239. It should be remem-

sive kings, assisted by their clergy, who thus stand at the head of a line of champions in the cause of English freedom.

IN GERMANY AND PARTS ADJACENT.

Although the cross had long been planted, here and there[1], in the heart of the German forests, as well as in the cities which had owned the Roman sway, it was not till the present period that religion could obtain a lasting basis and could organize the German Church. The founding of the work was due to foreign immigration. Ireland was at this time conspicuous for its light[2]: it was full of conventual houses, where the learning of the west had taken refuge, and from which, as from missionary schools, the Gospel was transmitted far and near.

The leader of the earliest band who issued to the succour of the continent of Europe, was the ardent Columbanus[3], (reared in the Irish monastery of Bangor). With twelve young men, as his companions, he crossed over into Gaul, at the close of the sixth century; but the strictness of his Rule[4] having rendered him obnoxious to the native clergy, and at length to the Burgundian court[5], he was compelled to migrate into Switzerland (610), working first in the neighbourhood of Zürich and next at

bered that in this struggle Theodore took a most active part against Wilfrith, and whilst he could hardly be expected to declare his contempt of Rome, maintained the independence of the Church as much as did the kings.

[1] See an interesting account of the labours of Severinus and other solitaries in Neander, *C. H.* v. 34, seq. Bohn's ed.

[2] 'Hibernia quo catervatim istinc lectores classibus advecti confluunt:' a saying of Aldhelm; the contemporary of Theodore; *Epist. ad Eahfridum, Opp.* p. 94, ed. Giles: Ussher's *Epist. Hibern.* p. 27; *Opp.* IV. 451, ed. Elrington. 'Antiquo tempore,' says Alcuin at the end of the next century, 'doctissimi solebant magistri de Hibernia, Britanniam, Galliam, Italiam venire et multos per ecclesias Christi fecisse profectus.' *Ep.* CCXXI. (Al. CCXXV.) *Opp.* I. 285.

[3] See a life of him by Jonas, a monk of his foundation at Bobbio, in Mabillon, *Acta Sanct. Ord. Benedict.* sæc. II. pp. 2—26.

[4] Among his other works in *Biblioth. Patrum,* ed. Galland, tom. XII.; cf. Neander, *C. H.* v. 41, 42. The *XVI. Instructiones* of Columbanus are well worth reading.

[5] Three great settlements had grown out of his labours in Gaul, the monasteries of Luxeuil, Fontaine (Fontanæ) and Anegray; besides the impulse he had given to religion generally.

Bregenz. From thence in **613** he was driven over the Italian frontier, and founded the monastery of Bobbio, where he died in **615**. Columbanus was attached to the customs of his mother-church, and the struggle we have noticed in the case of England was repeated in his lifetime. The freedom of his language to the Roman bishops[1] is a proof that he paid no homage to their see, though his final residence in Italy appears to have somewhat modified his tone. He had a noble fellow-worker in his countryman, Gallus[2], the founder of the monastery of St Gall, who, with a perfect knowledge of the native dialects, promoted the conversion of the Swiss and Swabians, till **640**.

and of Gallus 590—640.

Yet these were only drops in a long stream of missions that was now bearing on its bosom, far and near, the elements of future greatness and the tidings of salvation. At the end of the series of evangelists, contributed from Ireland, one of the more conspicuous was Kilian[3] (**650—689**), who may be regarded as the apostle of Franconia, or at least as the second founder of its faith. The centre of his labours was at Würzburg, where some traces of the Irish culture are surviving at this day[4].

Kilian in Franconia.

Meanwhile the ardour of the native Christians was enlisted in the spreading of the German Church. Thus, a Frankish synod, about **613**, wakened to a sense of duty by the earnest Columbanus, made an effort to evangelize the neighbouring heathen[5]. Emmeran, a prelate out of Aqui-

Native missions;

---

[1] See one to Gregory the Great, Gregor. *Epist.* lib. IX. ep. 127. A more important testimony is supplied by his fifth letter, *ad Bonifacium IV.*, where he administers some salutary warnings to the Church of Rome: cf. W. G. Todd's *Church of St Patrick*, pp. 118 sq. Lond. 1844. In one passage he admits that a church, instructed by St Peter and St Paul, and honoured by their tombs, is worthy of all deference; but he reserves the first rank for the church of Jerusalem: Roma orbis terrarum caput est ecclesiarum, *salva loci Dominicæ resurrectionis singulari prærogativa*. § 10.

[2] The Life of Gallus, in its oldest form, is printed in the *Monument. German. Histor.* tom. II. 5—31, ed. Pertz: cf. Neander, v. 47—49.

[3] See a Life of him in Canisius, *Lect. Antiq.* III. pt. 1. pp. 175—179, ed. Basnage; also a *Passio SS. Kiliani et Sociorum ejus*, ibid. 180—182. Kilian applied to the pope for his sanction of the undertaking.

[4] Lappenberg, *Ang.-Sax.* I. 183.

[5] They made choice of Abbot Eustasius, the successor of Columbanus at Luxeuil, for the director of the mission. See his Life by Jonas, the monk of Bobbio, in Mabillon's *Acta Sanct. Ord. Benedict.* sæc. II. pp.

GERMAN CHURCH.

success in Bavaria.

tania¹, and Ruprecht² of Worms, left their sees in the seventh century to share in the holy conquest now advancing on all sides. By them, and the Frank Corbinian, the foundations of a church were laid, not only in Bavaria, but also on the banks of the Danube as far as Pannonia. A multitude of sources were thus opened for the speedy propagation of the faith in the whole of southern Germany.

Eligius, Amandus, and others, in the Netherlands.

In the north, where the pagan system³ had a firmer hold upon the people, the promoters of the Gospel were continually resisted. Notwithstanding, zealous bishops like Eligius⁴ won their way in the midst of the savage Frieslanders, whose empire at the opening of this period had extended also to the Netherlands. There, it is true, religion had been planted long before, but the inroads of those heathen tribes had left scarcely any vestige of the Church. The sword of Dagobert I., who wrested many districts from their grasp, had made a way for the reconversion of Batavia (**628—638**), while missionaries out of England afterwards engaged to soften and evangelize the barbarous invaders. Ground was already broken by the enterprising Wilfrith⁵, who, in his flight from his diocese in **678**, was driven to the coast of Friesland, where he seems to have reaped a harvest of conversions.

English missions to Friesland, and the neighbourhood.

His work was resumed by Willebrord⁶, an Englishman,

116—123: one also of Agil, a companion of Eustasius, *ib.* pp. 316—326, cf. Neander, *C. H.* v. 51—53.

¹ Life in Canisius, *Lect. Antiq.* III. pt. 1. pp. 94 sq., though from its date (the tenth or eleventh century) it is not trustworthy throughout.

² The oldest account of him is printed in Kleinmayrn's *Nachrichten von Juvavia* (the ancient Salzburg). A Life also of Corbinian may be seen in Meichelbeck's *Hist. Frising.* (Freising), tom. I, pp. 1 sq. ed. 1724.

³ For a good account of Paganism in those regions, see Mone's *Geschichte des Heidenthums in nördlichen Europa*, Leipzig, 1823; and J. Grimm's *Deutsche Mythologie*, Göttingen, 1844.

⁴ Or St Eloy (born 588, died 659), appointed, in 641, bishop of Tournay and Noyon. See an interesting Life of him by a pupil, in D'Achery's *Spicilegium*, tom. II. p. 76, and Dr Maitland's *Dark Ages*, pp. 101 sq. Eligius was preceded by Amandus, ordained (630) without a diocese (episcopus regionarius) to labour in the neighbourhood of Ghent and Antwerp, but appointed in 648 to the see of Mästricht (Trajectum), where he died in 679. Life in Mabillon's *Acta Bened.* sæc. II. 679—706. Contemporary with him was Audomar (St Omer), out of the Irish monastery at Luxeuil, who preached from the neighbourhood of Boulogne as far as the Scheldt.

⁵ Florent. Wigorn. ad an. 677: Eddius, *Vit. Wilf.* c. XXVI—XXVIII.

⁶ His Life was written by Alcuin; *Opp.* tom. II. 183: but a still older account of his labours is in Bede, *Hist. Ecc.* v. 10 sq.

who, though a student for twelve years in Ireland[1], was marked, like the other Anglo-Saxons of the period, by the warmth of his devotion to the Roman see[2]. The field of his principal success was the neighbourhood of Wilteburg (Trajectum=Utrecht), where he died, after a long episcopate, in **739** or **741**. He is said to have been assisted in his labours by Wulfram[3], bishop of Sens, who migrated with some attendants into Friesland; and the work was enlarged by a native, Wursing[4], as well as by other pupils of Willebrord; one of whom, Swithberht[5], in the life-time of his master, appears to have penetrated even into Prussia.

But meanwhile a fresh actor had come forward in the same hopeful cause. This was a Devonshire-man, Winfrith, who, under the title BONIFACIUS[6], is known as the apostle of Thuringia, and of some of the neighbouring districts. He was to Germany what Theodore had been to England, binding all the members of the Church together, and imparting to it new stability and life. Crossing over into Friesland (**716**), he joined himself to Willebrord at Utrecht; but, retreating, for some cause or other, to his native country, he remained in his cloister at Nursling two years. He then went to Rome, commended[7] to the pope by Daniel of Winchester, and in **719** was formally deputed[8] by Gre-

GERMAN CHURCH.

Willebrord (692—741).

Wulfram.

Wursing.

Swithberht.

Labours of Winfrith or Bonifacius:

---

[1] 'Ibique duodecim annis inter eximios simul piæ religionis et sacræ lectionis magistros, futurus multorum populorum prædicator erudiebatur.' *Vit. S. Willebrord.* lib. I. c. 4.

[2] He visited the pope in 692, 'ut cum ejus licentia et benedictione desideratum evangelizandi gentibus opus iniret.' Bed. v. 11. In 696 he was sent by Pepin of Heristal, who as mayor of the palace of Austrasia had subdued some of the Frieslanders, to be ordained, by the pope, archbishop of that region. Ibid.: cf. *Annales Xantenses* (in Pertz), A.D. 694.

[3] Life in the *Acta Sanctorum* for March 20, ed. Bolland.

[4] See the interesting account of him in the *Vit. S. Liudgeri*, c. 1—4: *Monum. German.* ed. Pertz, II. 405, 406.

[5] Bed. v. 11. He also mentions (c. 10) a mission of two English brothers, Niger Hewald and Albus Hewald, who perished in their attempt to evangelize the foreign Saxons (provinciam antiquorum Saxonum).

[6] The best Life of him is that by a presbyter, Willibald: Pertz's *Monumenta*, II. 334 seq. Jaffé, *Monumenta Moguntina*, pp. 422—471. Cf. *Bonifacius der Apostel der Deutschen*, by Seilers, Mainz, 1845.

[7] *Vit.* § 14.

[8] *Bonifacii Epist.* II.; I. 26. ed. Giles. But notwithstanding his profound respect for the papal chair, his independent spirit more than once breaks out in the course of his correspondence. Thus in 742 he quotes the tradition of his native land, as reckoned from Augustine, against a reported decision of the ruling pope, *Ep.* XLIX. p. 103; and it is clear from the same letter (p. 105) that he did not allow the right of any pope to dispense with the 'decreta canonum.'

GERMAN CHURCH.

in Friesland:

gory II. 'to inquire into the state of the savage Germans' eastward of the Rhine. The first fruits of his zeal were gathered in Thuringia; but news out of Friesland drew him thither, and he taught for three years in conjunction with Willebrord[1]. His next missionary station (**722**) was at Amöneburg, in Upper Hessia, chosen with the hope of converting the Hessians, and after them the Saxons. Summoned by the pope, who had heard of his success, he undertook a second journey to Rome (**723**), where, together with the name of Bonifacius[2], he received ordination as a missionary bishop, and made himself, by oath, the vassal of the Roman Church. He was thus armed with a new authority; and, seconded in many cases by the civil power[3], was able to extend the sphere of his operations, and to bear down all opponents, whether heathen, or disciples of the freer Christian school[4], that had its birth in Ireland. At the same time he was constant in imparting, to the utmost of his power, the salutary doctrines of the Gospel. Famed for his preaching[5], his diffusion of the Scriptures[6], and his

in Thuringia:

zeal in the founding of monastic schools, which he fed by a number of auxiliaries[7] from England, his work could not fail to prosper in a neighbourhood which was the field of his missionary zeal for no less than fifteen years. In

---

[1] *Vit.* § 16.
[2] § 21.
[3] 'Tuo conamine et *Caroli principis*,' was the language of pope Gregory III. to Boniface (Oct. 29, 739); Bonifacii *Opp.* ed. Giles, I. 97; yet the power of Charles Martel was not uniformly on the side of the missionaries. It was only under Pepin and Carloman that Boniface could feel himself supreme.
[4] Neander discovers traces of this early *protestantism* in the records of his preaching: *e. g.* in a letter of Gregory III. to the bishops of Bavaria and Alemannia, after urging them to adopt the Roman uses, as taught by Boniface, he warned them to reject 'et gentilitatis ritum et doctrinam, vel venientium Britonum, vel falsorum sacerdotum, et hæreticorum, aut undecunque sint.' Bonifacii *Opp.* I. 96: cf. Neander, v. 67 (*and note*). Neander's notion of the freedom of the Irish school is somewhat visionary. It can hardly be denied that the accusations brought against these teachers by Boniface are countenanced by the half mystic half sensuous views of religion which appear in the best authenticated legends of the ancient Irish. Boniface himself (Ep. XII.) draws a gloomy picture of the state of the clergy and deplores his inability to hold communion with them.
[5] 'Evangelica etiam doctrina adeo præcipuus extitit, ut apostolorum tempora in ejus prædicatione laudares.' *Annales Xantenses*, A.D. 752.
[6] Epp. XVIII, XIX. *Opp.* I. 52, 53.
[7] Willibald, *Vit. S. Bonifac.* § 23.

738 he is said to have baptized a hundred thousand natives[1]. A third visit to Rome (**738**) resulted in his mission to Bavaria, where he laboured in the twofold task of organizing the Church, and counteracting a large class of teachers, who, here as in Thuringia, were opposed to 'the tradition of the Roman see[2].' With the sanction of the duke of Bavaria, his territory was distributed afresh into the dioceses of Salzburg, Regensburg (Ratisbon), Freising, and Passau[3]: and the death of Charles Martel[4], which followed soon after the return of Boniface (**741**), allowed him to advance more freely with his centralizing projects. In **742**, the founding of the bishoprics[5] of Würzburg, Erfurt, and Buraburg (in Hessia), to which Eichstädt may be added, conduced to the same result. He was now also urged by Carloman to revive the action of the Frankish synods, which had long been discontinued[6]: and presiding at the first of them (**744**), in his capacity of papal vicar[7], he took the lead in promoting what he deemed 'a reformation of the Church[8].' One of

GERMAN CHURCH.

in Bavaria:

founds several bishoprics.

Revival of Synods in the Frankish Church.

---

[1] Such was the report that had reached Gregory III. Oct. 29, 739: Bonif. *Opp.* I. 96. His felling of an oak, which had long been sacred to Thor, made a very deep impression, *Vit. Bonif.* § 22, 23.

[2] Bonif. *Ep.* XLVI: *Opp.* I. 97. He found only one bishop in the whole province, and of him (Vivilo) the pope speaks but dubiously: 'Hic si aliquid excedit contra canonicam regulam, doce et corrige eum juxta Romanæ ecclesiæ traditionem, quam a nobis accepisti.' Ibid. The following is the account given by Willibald (§ 28) of the state of religion there: 'Veræque fidei et religionis sacramenta renovavit, et destructores ecclesiarum populique perversores abigebat. Quorum alii pridem falso se episcopatus gradu prætulerunt, alii etiam presbyteratus se officio deputabant, alii hæc atque alia innumerabilia fingentes, magna ex parte populum seduxerunt:' cf. *Annales Xantenses*, ad an. 752, and Aventinus, *Annales Boiorum*, 254, ed. Gundling.

[3] *Vit. Bonifac.* § 28.

[4] He had patronized what Boniface describes as the 'false,' 'erroneous,' 'schismatical priests' (?) the old Frankish clergy. See *e.g.* Bonif. *Epist.* XII; but they were now driven from the court at the instance of pope Zacharias: Ib. *Ep.* XLVIII: cf. *Ep.* LIV. p. 116; LX. p. 127.

[5] *Ep.* XLIX. p. 101; *Vit.* § 31.

[6] *Ep.* XLIX. p. 102.

[7] He had received the pallium as early as 732, *Vit.* § 23, but was still without a fixed see.

[8] The aim of pope Zacharias in advocating a yearly synod may be seen in Bonif. *Ep.* XLIV. In a letter addressed (Nov. 5, 743) to Boniface himself (*Ep.* LV.), he speaks of his anxiety 'pro adunatione et reformatione ecclesiarum Christi,' and charges his vicar 'ut quæ repereris, contra Christianam religionem vel canonum instituta, ibidem detineri, ad normam rectitudinis studeas reformare.' See also a remarkable letter of Boniface (A.D. 748) to Cuthbert, archbishop of Canterbury (*Ep.* LXIII.), where he

GERMAN CHURCH.

Controversy with Adelbert and Clement.

the leaders of the school whom Boniface had strongly reprehended was a Frankish bishop, Adelbert[1], belonging to the anti-Roman party. He was revered by the people as a saint, though much that is imputed to him savours of the mystic, and betokens an ill-regulated mind. On the suit of his rival, Boniface, who had secured his condemnation[2] at Soissons (**744**), he was excommunicated[3] by a Roman synod in **745**, together with a fellow-bishop, Clement. The latter had been trained in the schools of Ireland, his native country, and had there imbibed an extensive knowledge of the Scriptures; but the tone of his theology, so far as we can judge, was sceptical and indevout[4].

*Later acts of Boniface (**744—755**).*

The silencing of these opponents left the missionary course of Boniface almost wholly unobstructed: but his own anxieties increased as he was verging to his end. Disappointed in the hope of placing his metropolitical chair at Cologne (**744**), where he would have been near to his Frisian converts, he was, on the deposition[5] of Gewillieb, constrained[6] to accept the archbishopric of Mentz (Moguntia). He there found a more definite field of duty in **748**. One of the latest acts in his eventful life was the part he took (**752**) in favour of Pepin, who superseded his imbecile master, Childeric III. Boniface, at the instance of the Pope, administered the rite of unction. The measures he

---

urges the necessity of a reformation in England. His letter has been regarded as leading the way to the reforms of the synod of Clovesho of 747; but it must have been written after that council was held. (*Councils, &c.* III. 383.) Wilkins, *Concil.* I. 94.

[1] Willib. *Vit. Bonif.* § 29: also an account in a second *Life of Boniface* in Pertz, II. 354; Bonif. *Opp.* II. 40—46: cf. Walch, *Hist. der Ketzereyen,* x. 46 sq.

[2] Pagi, ad an. 744, §§ VII, VIII.

[3] Zacharias, two years later, was induced in spite of Boniface to reopen the question, and summoned both Adelbert and Clement to his own court at Rome, but the issue is not known exactly. Neander, *C. H.* v. 77—86.

[4] 'Per suam stultitiam sanctorum patrum scripta respuit, vel omnia synodalia acta parvi pendit, etc.' Bonif. *Opp.* II. 46. Among other errors he is said to have taught 'multa horribilia de prædestinatione Dei contraria fidei catholicæ.' *Ep.* LVII. p. 123. Boniface found other adversaries in two Irishmen, Samson (*Ep.* LXXI. p. 171) and Virgilius, or Feargal (*Ibid.* pp. 172 sq.): but the latter was acquitted by the pope, and died bishop of Salzburg: cf. Todd's *Church of St Patrick,* pp. 59 sq.

[5] Pertz, II. 354.

[6] See the Letter of Zacharias, *Bonif. Epist.* LXXI. p. 174.

had taken to secure his conquests were now rapidly completed, and in 755 he set out, with a large band of fellow-workmen, for the scene of his early enterprise in Friesland; where, after preaching to the heathen tribes with eminent success, he died as a martyr at the age of seventy-five[1].

A man with his strength of character, his learning, and his saintly life, could not fail to have attracted a number of disciples. One of them, Gregory[2], as abbot of Utrecht, was at the head of a missionary-college, and at the same time assiduous in his efforts to promote the conversion of the Frieslanders. Another of the more remarkable was the abbot Sturm[3], who had been also trained under the eye of Boniface, and stationed in a monastery at Fulda, of which he was himself the romantic founder[4]. Aided by no less than four thousand inmates, he was able to disseminate the arts, and augment the conveniences of life, while he softened the ferocious spirit of his neighbours.

With some casual exceptions[5], the evangelizing of the German tribes was hitherto conducted on pacificatory principles[6], like those which had prompted and consolidated the first missions of the Church. A fresh plan, however, was now adopted in dealing with the rude and warlike Saxons[7] (from the Baltic to the confines of Thuringia and

Gregory of Utrecht d. 784.

Sturm of Fulda d. 779.

---

[1] Willibald. *Vit. Bonif.* §§ 33—37. The day of his death was June 5; the place, on the banks of the Bordne (Bordau), not far from Dokkum. His remains with those of his fellow-martyrs, being rescued by the Christians, were interred at Fulda, his favourite monastery.

[2] A Life of him was written by his pupil Liudger, in *Act. Sanct. Ord. Bened.* sæc. III. p. ii. 319 sq. The way in which he was fascinated by the zealous missionary is most strikingly narrated. Though not a pupil of Boniface, Willibald, the early English traveller, was ordained by him in 739; and after a short mission to Thuringia, was consecrated bishop of Eichstädt, one of the dioceses formed by Boniface. See the interesting Life of Willibald, by a nun of Heidenheim, in *Act. Sanct. Ord. Bened.* sæc. III. p. ii. 365 sq.

[3] Life by his pupil, Eigil, in Pertz's *Monument. Germ.* II. 365 sq.

[4] Ibid. p. 367.

[5] *e.g.* The case of Amandus in Belgium, who procured an order from the Frankish monarch, compelling all persons to submit to baptism. Boniface also invoked the 'patrocinium principis Francorum;' but his aim was to quell irregularities among the clergy and religious orders. *Epist.* XII. p. 39.

[6] See the excellent advice given to Boniface by Daniel of Winchester. *Bonif. Ep.* XIV.

[7] Boniface had been already urged to undertake this mission in the years 723, 733; *Epp.* IX, XXVIII; and even earlier (690—740) some im-

GERMAN CHURCH.

Compulsory conversion of the Old Saxons

Hessia), who had forced their ancient idolatry once more across the Rhine. Fierce as they were in their hatred of the Gospel, the repugnance would be naturally embittered by the medium through which it was presented to their notice: for they viewed it, in the hands of a Frankish teacher, as an agent for promoting their political depression. He came in the wake of invading hosts, by which Charlemagne was endeavouring to effect their subjugation (772—804): and although numbers of them did accept the ritual of the Church, it was unquestionably in many cases by compulsion[1]. Alcuin, at the impulse of his Christian feelings, would have fain placed a check[2] on the rigour of the Franks. But his protests were unheeded; Charlemagne still persisting in his plan of breaking the indomitable spirit of the Saxons by forcing the conversion of the vanquished, and establishing himself on the basis of the Church[3]. A long and bloody war, attended by an edict[4] of the Frankish court, which made the rejection of the Gospel a capital offence, resulted in the permanent disarming of the Saxons and their annexation to the Western Church[5]. A way was in the mean time opened for the

Opposed by Alcuin, but in vain.

pression had been made on the Saxons by the labours of Lebwin, a Yorkshire monk. See his Life in Pertz, II. 361 sq.

[1] 'Congregato iam (? tum) grandi exercitu [A.D. 772], invocato Christi nomine, Saxoniam profectus est, adsumtis universis sacerdotibus, abbatibus, presbyteris, et omnibus orthodoxis atque fidei cultoribus, ut gentem quæ ab initio mundi dæmonum vinculis fuerit obligata, doctrinis sacris mite et suave Christi jugum credendo subire fecissent. Quo cum rex pervenisset, partim *bellis*, partim *suasionibus*, partim etiam *muneribus*, maxima ex parte gentem illam ad fidem Christi convertit.' Vit. Sturmi, l. c. p. 376: cf. Alcuin. *Ep.* III. *ad Colcum Lectorem in Scotia: Opp.* I. 6.

[2] Epist. XXXVII. (Al. XLII.) *ad Megenfridum* (a privy-councillor of Charlemagne). Of many striking passages this may be a sample: 'Fides quoque, sicut sanctus ait Augustinus, res est voluntaria, non necessaria. Attrahi poterit homo in fidem, *non cogi*. Cogi poteris ad Baptismum, sed *non proficit* fidei. Nisi infantilis ætas aliorum peccatis obnoxia aliorum confessione salvari poterit. Perfectæ ætatis vir pro se respondeat, quid credat aut quid cupiat. Et si fallaciter fidem profitetur, veraciter salutem non habebit. Unde et prædicatores paganorum populum *pacificis verbis et prudentibus* fidem docere debent.' *Opp.* I. 50; see also his letter (Ep. LXXX, Al. XCV.) written to Charlemagne himself: I. 117.

[3] The chief ecclesiastical establishments were at Osnabrück, Münster, Paderborn, Verden, Minden, and Seligenstadt. The last see was afterwards transferred to Halberstadt.

[4] See the *Capitulare de Partibus Saxoniæ*, I. 251, in Baluze's *Capitul. Reg. Fran.*, Paris, 1677: and cf. Schröckh's *Kirchen-Geschichte*, XIX. 264 sq.

[5] Einhard. *Vit. Karoli Magn.* c. 7; apud Pertz, II. 447.

deeper planting of the Gospel, by means of the numerous schools and churches founded by the Franks, and still more by the holy and commanding character of members of the Saxon mission. Such were Sturm, Willehad, and Liudger. The first, whom we have seen already, spent the evening of his days in this field of labour[1]. The second (Willehad) was a native of Northumbria[2], whom the hopeful letters of the English missionaries had excited to cast in his lot among them. He set out for Friesland with the sanction of the Northumbrian king and the blessing of a synod[3]. Banished from the neighbourhood of Gröningen, which had been already stained by the blood of Boniface, he found shelter at the court of Charlemagne, who sent him (780) to aid in the missions then attempting to evangelize the Saxons. In 787, after an eventful term of suffering and success, he was raised to the episcopal dignity, his chair being placed at Wigmodia (Bremen): but a sudden illness cut him off two years later, while engaged in a visitation-tour.

GERMAN CHURCH.
Fresh measures for the conversion of the Saxons, and other northern tribes.
Willehad d. 789.

Liudger[4] was a noble Frieslander, who had been trained in the school of Utrecht, and afterwards by Alcuin at York. For a long time distinguished as a missionary to his own people, and afterwards as the apostle of Heligoland, which Willebrord quitted in despair, he was sent by Charlemagne, on the subjugation of the Saxons, to Münster, where he toiled in the spirit of a true evangelist[5] till 809.

Liudger d. 809.

A fresh accession to the Church was the tribe of the Carentani, who had settled in the early part of the seventh century in Styria and Carinthia. The Gospel reached them through Bavarian channels, first[6] at the instance of

The Gospel in Styria and Carinthia.
(?) 766— 800.

---

[1] Vit. Sturm. *ubi sup.*
[2] A Life of him, written by Anskar, bishop of Bremen (middle of the ninth century), is printed in Pertz, II. 378 sq.
[3] Ibid. § 1.
[4] For a Life of Liudger by his second successor, Altfrid, see Pertz, II. 403 sq. He is said to have left York 'bene instructus, habens secum copiam librorum.' lib. I. § 12.
[5] 'Itaque more solito cum omni aviditate et sollicitudine rudibus Saxonum populis studebat in doctrina prodesse, erutisque idolatriæ spinis, verbum Dei diligenter per loca singula serere, ecclesias construere, et per eas singulos ordinare presbyteros, quos verbi Dei cooperatores sibi ipsi nutriverat.' Ibid. § 20. We are told in the following paragraph that he had hitherto declined the 'pontificalem gradum.' His reluctance, however, was at length overcome by Hildebold, archbishop of Cologne.
[6] See the Life of Virgilius in *Act. Sanct. Ord. Bened.* IV. 279 sq. The

GERMAN CHURCH.

Virgilius of Salzburg, and afterwards of Arno, his second successor. Arno, on ordaining a 'missionary bishop' for these parts (800), intended, if possible, to make his way as far as the neighbouring Slavonians¹.

Mission to the Avares in Hungary. **796.**

He had been also employed by Charlemagne, whose sceptre was now stretching over Hungary², to organize a mission for the barbarous Avares³. In **796**, one of their chiefs, Tudun, having been baptized at the Frankish court⁴, his return was viewed as a propitious moment for planting further outposts of the Church in the same distant regions. But it seems that the mission was not worked with corresponding vigour⁵.

IN EASTERN ASIA.

The zeal and perseverance that were shewn in the converting of the German tribes had been confined in this period to the bosom of the Western Church. Owing partly to domestic troubles, but still more to their lack of expansiveness and health, the churches of the East were now feeble and inactive. At the death of Justinian I.

Missionary zeal of the Nestorians.

(**565**) they seem to have abandoned the propagation of the Gospel to those numerous offshoots from the patriarchate of Antioch, who continued to reject the council

---

Carinthian chieftain had allowed his son to be educated as a Christian at the court of Bavaria. This, on his accession to the throne, paved the way for the evangelizing of his subjects.

¹ See the treatise of a priest of Salzburg (written at the close of the ninth century), *De Conversione Bojariorum et Carentanorum*, in *Script. Rerum Boic.* ed. Oefele, I. 280 sq.: also a *Life of Rupert* (first bishop of Salzburg) in Canisius, *Lect. Antiq.* III. pt. II. p. 348.

² Einhardi *Fuldenses Annales*, A.D. 788, 791: apud Pertz, I. 350.

³ See Pray's *Annal. Vet. Hunnorum, Avar. et Hungar.* 269 sq., ed. Vindobon. 1761.

⁴ Einhard, A.D. 796. A second case occurred in 805. Ibid. The projected mission to the Avares or Huns drew many excellent remarks from Alcuin, who was fearful lest the policy pursued in the case of the Saxons should be repeated there. In a letter to Charlemagne (796), Ep. xxviii. (Al. xxxiii.) he says, 'Sed nunc prævideat sapientissima et Deo placabilis devotio vestra populo novello prædicatores, moribus honestis, scientia sacræ fidei edoctos, et evangelicis præceptis imbutos,' etc. He recommends, as a model for the missionary, St Augustine's treatise *De Catechizandis Rudibus*: *Opp.* I. 37, 38. The same care and tenderness are impressed on archbishop Arno in Ep. xxx, xxxi, lxxii, (Al. xxxiv, xxxv, lxxxvii; *Opp.* I. 39, 40, 105), his eye being still fixed on the recent failure in the missions to the Saxons.

⁵ Alcuin, Ep. xcii. (Al. cviii.) p. 135.

the name of Nestorians[1] or Chaldæans.   ASIATIC MISSIONS.
their expulsion from the Roman empire,
r with their fellow-Christians in Persia,
e united by a common misbelief. Here
exclusive toleration, though it did not
them from the rancour of the heathen
he sixth to the eleventh century, when
 Nestorians may be said to have cul-
e peculiarly distinguished by their mis-
he head of their system, known as the
bsequently (**498**) as the *patriarch*, pre-   *Vast area of their settlements.*
es in Chaldæa, Persia, Media, Mesopo-
icts far beyond the Tigris, in Bactriana
ee[4] was originally at Seleucia, and after-
nd Babylon, where he might have vied
stern pontiffs in a plenitude of power:
his patriarchate embraced no less than
politans[5], nearly all of whom were located
ntries they had rescued from the yoke of
theus[7], who was the Nestorian patriarch   *Timotheus; and the missions to India and China.*
nay be mentioned as the warmest advo-
He sent out a large band of monks from
eth-abe in Mesopotamia, to evangelize
ho roved in the neighbourhood of the
l some of them penetrated as far as
, either planting or reviving in those

this title (J. S. Asseman, *Biblioth. Orientalis*, tom.
but retained the terminology, and, with few excep-
enets, condemned by the Church at large. See
e *Church*, I. 319, 320, 3rd edit.
, pt. I. p. 109, pt. II. c. v. § 2. This section gives an
tion under the successive Persian kings, from 488
ry was invaded by the Muhammedans.
1. They were materially assisted by the favour of
mbers of them always in his service.
 The see was eventually transferred to Mosul,

astern Church, Introd. I. 143. A 'Notitia' of all
eman, pp. 705 sq.
nspicuous for their love of learning. Their great
which rose out of the ruins of the school of Edessa
 Asseman, tom. III. pt. II. pp. 428, 927. A whole
l to similar institutions.
58 sq.
ces of Christianity in India, see Neander, *C. H.* III.

ed as a bishop ordained for China by the patriarch

distant parts a knowledge of the Gospel. Two of the episcopal members of the mission, Cardag and Jaballaha, transmitted a report of their success to the Nestorian patriarch, who urged them to perpetuate the impression they had made by ordaining other bishops to succeed them[1].

It was also in this period, though the date is not exactly ascertainable[2], that a distinguished Syrian, Mar-Thomas (it would seem a merchant[3]), prevailed on the community of Christians, already stationed on the coast of Malabar[4], to place themselves under the jurisdiction of the Nestorian catholicos. By this step he led the way to a further propagation of the Nestorian creed: and in the ninth century[5] two bishops of that communion, Sapor and Peroses, are said to have planted the cross to the south-west of Cochin in the kingdom of Diamper.

IN AFRICA.

The only progress to be noted in this corner of the Christian kingdom, is due to the sect of the Alexandrian Jacobites (Monophysites), who had already in the lifetime of Justinian found admission into Nubia[6]. In the

---

Timotheus; Asseman, ibid. part II. p. 82. It is by no means improbable that the Gospel had reached this country at a still earlier date. (See De Guignes, *Untersuchung über die im 7ten Jahrhunderte in Sina sich aufhaltenden Christen*, ed. Greifswald, 1769.) Among other evidence is a Syro-Chinese inscription, brought to light by the Jesuit missionaries in 1625, and purporting to belong to 782 (in Mosheim, *Hist. Eccl. Tartarorum*, App. III. and elsewhere). According to it, Olopuen, a Nestorian priest, visited China in 635 from the western frontier of the country. See Kesson's *Cross and Dragon* (Christianity in China), pp. 16 sq. Lond. 1854.

[1] The lack of a third prelate to assist in the consecration of the new bishops was to be supplied by a copy of the Gospels. Asseman, *ubi sup.*
[2] Ibid. part III. p. 443: Neale, *Eastern Church*, Introd. I. 146.
[3] This, however, is denied by Asseman, p. 444, who concludes his argument as follows: 'Habemus itaque Thomam non Armenum mercatorem, neque infra sextum Christi seculum, sed circa annum 800, sub Timotheo Nestorianorum patriarcha a Jaballaha et Kardago Ghilanæ et Dailamæ metropolitis ex monacho cœnobii Beth-Abensis ordinatum episcopum atque in vicinam Indiam missum.'
[4] Cf. Neander, III. 166: Lassen, *Ind. Alterthum*, II. 1101, 1102; Bonn, 1852. The present Christians of Malabar boast of their descent from this Mar-Thomas.
[5] Asseman, *ubi sup.* p. 442.
[6] Ibid. tom. II. p. 330: cf. Letronne's *Christianisme en Egypte, en Nubie, et en Abyssinie*, à Paris, 1832. The Christian priest-kings of

-688) of Isaac (a Jacobite) there is further
xion between that country and Alex-
rposing his authority to settle a dispute
or of Ethiopia and the king of Nubia¹.
teresting notice of an application² made
India to Simon, successor of Isaac
ing at his hands episcopal consecration;
proper or Ethiopia is here meant, has
d³.

AFRICAN MISSIONS.

ITATION OF THE CHURCH.

hich had formed the cradle of the Church
ts earlier triumphs, were now destined
scuration and extinction. Persia, for
esting many Christian provinces out of
astern emperor (604—621), among others
and Egypt, set on foot a most bloody
whom the sword of Kesra (Chosroes)
forced into union with the hated Nes-
tempest, though terrific, was of short
us being able (621—628) to repair his
the distractions of the Church.

Invasion of the Eastern Church from Persia.

rever, had been scarcely rescued from
en a message⁵ was dispatched to the
nviting him to join the Moslems, and to
ophet. Born⁶ at Mecca in 569 or 570,

Rise of Muhammedanism.

nedans only in the 14th century: Lepsius, *Disco-*
259, Lond. 1852.
Patr. Alexand. p. 178.
Le Quien, *Oriens Christianus*, II. 454.
sup. 451 sq.—It is needless to dwell on the efforts
or the conversion of the Jews, in the west by the
and in the east by the Emperor Leo, the Isaurian;
e nearly always *coercive*, and on that account abor-
n the subject in Schröckh, XIX. 298—326.
onographia, pp. 199 sq., inter *Scriptores Byzantin.*
). 213 c, *ibid.* is the following entry: Ἠνάγκαζε δὲ
αι εἰς τὴν τοῦ Νεστορίου θρησκείαν πρὸς τὸ πλῆξαι
ιε emperor]. This seems to have been the policy of
ut in tolerating the Nestorian body.
the Saracens, p. 51, ed. Bohn.
ife of Mahomet, and, for his religious system, Sale's
liminary Discourse, and Forster's *Mahometanism*
Other views may be obtained from Weil's *Mu-*

MUHAM-
MEDANISM.

of the stock of Ishmael, Muhammed[1] seems in early life to have been possessed by the persuasion that he was an agent in the hands of God to purify the creed of his fellow-countrymen. The texture of his mind was mystical, inclining him to solitude and earnest contemplation[2]: but the spirit of enthusiasm, thus fostered and inflamed, was afterwards corrupted by the lust of worldly power[3]. Some of the more intelligent around him were monotheists already, having clung to the tenets of their father Ishmael; but others, a large section of the Arab tribes, were sunk in idolatry and superstition[4]. We learn also that on the rise of Islamism many Jews had been long settled in Arabia, where they gained some political importance[5]; and that heralds of the Gospel on its earliest promulgation made very numerous converts; though the Christians at this time were for the most part Jacobites[6], who had come from the neighbouring lands in quest of an asylum. It is clear, therefore, that materials were at hand out of which to construct a composite religion like that now established by Muhammed; and when he ventured to unfold his visions to the world in **611**, it was easy to discern in their leading features a distorted copy of the Bible[7]. While Islamism was the foe of all creature-worship, while it preached with an emphasis peculiar to itself the absolute dependency of

Materials out of which it was constructed.

Its essential errors and impieties.

hammed der Prophet, ed. Stuttgart, 1843, and Döllinger's *Muhammed's Religion nach ihrer inneren Entwickelung, etc.*, ed. Regensburg, 1838. The last writer looks upon Muhammedanism as a kind of preparation for the Gospel in the southern and eastern world. Möhler's work, *On the Relation of Islam to the Gospel*, has been translated by Menge; Calcutta, 1847.

[1] = Μαχουμὲθ, from which the common form *Mahomet* was derived.

[2] He retired for a month every year into a mountain-cavern, abandoning his mercantile employments. It was not till his fortieth year (609) that the archangel Gabriel (according to his statement) announced to him his mission from on high. Abulfeda, quoted in Ockley's *Saracens*, p. 11. According to the second writer, Muhammed was assisted in compiling the Koran by a Persian Jew and a Nestorian monk. His own followers maintain that it was shewn to him at once by the archangel, though published only in detached portions during the next 23 years.

[3] Cf. Maurice's *Religions of the World*, pp. 18, 19, 2nd edit. Others would regard Muhammed as an impostor from the first; *e.g.* White in his *Bampton Lectures* for 1784, *passim*.

[4] Sale's *Preliminary Discourse*, pp. 24 sq.

[5] Ibid. p. 28.

[6] pp. 29, 31. The Nestorians also had one bishop. Ibid.

[7] Traces also of a Gnostic element have been found in the Koran. Neander, *C. H.* v. 118.

man and the unity and infinite sublimity of God, its teaching even there was meagre and one-sided: it was a harsh and retrogressive movement; it lost sight of what must ever be the essence of the Gospel, the Divinity and Incarnation of the Saviour, the original nobility of man, and his gradual restoration to the likeness of his Maker. It was, in fact, no more than the Socinianism or Deism of Arabia. Clouding over all the attributes of love, Muhammed could perceive in the Almighty nothing more than a high and arbitrary Will, or a vast and tremendous Power,—views which had their natural result in fatalism, and in fostering a servile dread or weakening the moral instincts[1]. His own tribe, the Koreish of Mecca, startled[2] by his novel doctrine, were at first successful in resisting the pretensions of 'the prophet;' but his flight (*i. e.* the *Hejrah*, July 16, 622), while it served as an epoch in the annals of his followers, entailed a terrific evil on the world. It imparted to the system of Muhammed, hitherto pacific[3], all its fierce and its persecuting spirit. On his arrival at Medina, where he acted in the twofold character of prince and prophet, he was able to enlarge the circle of his influence, and to organize a sect of religious warriors,—so gigantic, that in the tenth year of the Hejrah every part of his native land, including Mecca[4], trembled at his word. His death followed in 632, but the ardour he had roused descended to the caliphs, and increased with the number of his converts. Dropping all their ancient feuds, exulting in

MUHAM-MEDANISM.

Flight of Muhammed,

and his appeal to force in propagating his religion.

---

[1] The way in which Islamism was regarded by the Church, in the eighth century, appears from a *Dialogue* between a Christian and a Moslem, ascribed to John of Damascus or to his disciple, Theodore Abukara: in *Biblioth. Patrum*, ed. Galland, XIII. 272 sq., and (somewhat differently) in *Biblioth. Patrum Parisiens.* XI. 431 sq. We there learn that the points insisted on against Muhammed were the Divinity of Christ, and the freedom of the human will.

[2] Sale, *ib.* p. 58.

[3] He was at first tolerant of other systems (*Koran*, ch. II. v.), but he now opened what was called 'the holy war,' for the purpose of exterminating all idolaters, and of making Jews and Christians tributary to the crescent. *Ib.* c. IX. LXVII: Ockley, p. 32. These ends were continually kept in view by the Moslem conquerors. See Milman, *Latin Christianity*, Bk. IV. ch. I.

[4] He took this stronghold of his enemies in 630, and by way of conciliating the Arabs he adopted their national sanctuary (the Kaaba) as the chief temple of Islamism. Ockley, p. 18. This was not the only stroke of policy by which he circumvented the more superstitious of his countrymen.

MUHAM-
MEDANISM.

Probable reasons of its predominance in the Christian districts.

a fresh and energizing faith, or maddened by the sensual visions of the future, the adherents of the crescent fought their way through all the neighbouring states. Though some of their progress may be due to the corruption and distractions of the Church[1], and more to their simple or accommodating tenets, very much was effected by their craft in dealing with the Christian body. It was the aim of the caliph, by conciliating the heretical communities, Nestorian and Monophysite especially, to use them as his agents in diminishing the number of the Catholics, who, firm in their allegiance to the emperor, were branded with the name of Melchites[2]. Joining thus the devices of the politician with the fire of the enthusiast, the fortunes of Islamism rapidly advanced. Its second caliph, Omar, took Jerusalem in **637**, and was master of the whole of Syria in **639**. Egypt was annexed in **640**. Persia bowed its head beneath the crescent in **651**. Under the Ommiades (caliphs of Damascus), Islamism had subdued the northern coast of Africa (**707**), and in **711** it had been established everywhere in Spain, with the exception of a small Gothic kingdom in the mountains: while the Byzantine metropolis itself was made to shudder (**669, 717**) at the sight of the Moslem armies. Restless even at the foot of the Pyrenees, they spread into France as far as the Loire; but in **732** were finally repulsed and humbled by the arms of Charles Martel. In **734** they threatened to extend their ravages to the interior of Italy; and after they had occupied many of the neighbouring islands, Rome[3] was with difficulty rescued from their grasp in **849**.

Its rapid and extensive conquests.

However much of good eventually resulted from the Saracenic conquests, they were fatal to the present welfare

The desolation of the Christian

---

[1] 'The sense of a Divine, Almighty Will, to which all human wills were to be bowed, had evaporated amidst the worship of images, amidst moral corruptions, philosophical theories, religious controversies.' Maurice, *Religions of the World*, p. 23. Overcoloured as this statement is, it is too near the truth: (cf. the language of the emperor Heraclius in 633, when the Moslems were now advancing upon Syria: Ockley's *Saracens*, p. 95).

[2] In Egypt, for example, the Jacobites were the more numerous body, and though not wholly exempted from persecution were for the most part favoured by the Moslems. Neale, *Eastern Church*, 'Alexandria,' II. 72. The Nestorians in like manner were protected by the caliphs of Bagdad, who owed to them much of their taste for literature. Schröckh, XIX. 396 sq.

[3] Gibbon, *Decline and Fall*, v. 209 sq. ed. Milman.

of religion and the progress of the Church. Though tending to promote the interest of letters[1] in a period when the other kingdoms of the world were comparatively dark, they have desolated many a region where the Gospel was supreme, and obliterated all the traces of its earliest propagation. At the time when Boniface[2] and his companions were engaged in evangelizing the Teutonic tribes, they heard that the famous churches of the East, the special husbandry of Christ and His Apostles, were the prey of the antichristian armies of Muhammed. The defenceless patriarchates[3] of Jerusalem, of Antioch, and Alexandria, deprived of their rightful pastors, and curtailed on every side, are moving illustrations of the general ruin; and out of four hundred sees that once shed a salutary light on Africa, four only were surviving in the eleventh century[4]. The rest had been absorbed into the vortex of Islamism.

MUHAMMEDANISM.

Church in Africa and in the East

[1] Abulfeda, *Annales Moslemici*, tom. II. pp. 73 sq. Leipz. 1754. See a chapter on the 'Literature of the Arabians' in Sismondi's *Literature of the South of Europe*, I. 48 sq. The Moslems of Spain began to endow schools about 736: Conde, *Dominacion de los Arabes en Espana*, I. 110, Barcelona, 1844. On the literary taste of Alhakem (A.D. 964 sq.) see II. 14—16.

[2] He speaks with alarm of the Saracenic invasions in *Ep.* XXXII. The 'tribulatio Saracenorum' was in like manner present to the mind of Zacharias, in 745, when he contemplated the growth of the Church among the Frisians: Mansi, XII. 336.

[3] The patriarchs were driven into the Greek empire. In Alexandria the Church was partially restored by the election of Cosmas in 727 (Neale, *ibid.* II. 107); but none of the Eastern Churches have to this day recovered from the blow inflicted by Islamism. In the fifth century they contained as many as 800 bishoprics.

[4] Wiltsch, *Atlas Sacer*, p. 12, Gothæ, 1843.

CHAPTER II.

CONSTITUTION AND GOVERNMENT OF THE CHRISTIAN CHURCH.

§ 1. *INTERNAL ORGANIZATION.*

INTERNAL ORGANIZATION.

The transmission of the episcopal power and privileges.

THE model that was followed from the first in the organizing of the Christian body, had continued to pass over to the churches newly planted. Active members of a mission, if not consecrated in the outset[1] of their course, were advanced to the rank of bishops when their labours had succeeded[2]. With a staff of inferior clergy, who were taken very often in this age from some of the monastic orders, they were foremost in dispensing all the means of grace as well as in the closer supervision of their flocks. While acting[3] as the champions of the wronged, the guardians of the foundling and the minor, and of all who were either destitute or unprotected, they were placed in more intimate relations to the clergy, who had learned to regard their bishop as the centre of all rightful action, and the source of the authority deposited in them.

[1] Under the title 'episcopus regionarius:' see above, p. 18, n. 4; p. 25. Birinus had at first no see: Bed. III. 7.

[2] The case of Liudger (p. 25, n. 5) is a solitary exception; but even he was obliged to conform.

[3] *e.g.* Codex Justin. lib. I. tit. IV. *De Episcopali Audientia*, §§ 22—24, 27, 28, 30, 33. The sphere of their duties was extended (560) to the oversight of the administration of justice: Clotarii *Constitutio Generalis,* § VI, in the *Capitul. Regum Francorum,* ed. Baluze, I. 7. The following extract from Canon XVIII. of the Council of Toledo (A.D. 589) is a further instance of this power: 'Sint enim prospectores episcopi, secundum regiam admonitionem, *qualiter judices cum populis agant:* ut aut ipsos præmonitos corrigant, aut insolentias eorum auditibus principis innotescant. Quodsi correptos emendare nequiverint, et ab ecclesia et a communione suspendant.'

But the acts of the diocesan, if arbitrary and unlawful, might be checked by appealing to another bishop, whom the canons of the Church, in union with the civil power, had raised to superior eminence of rank. This was the metropolitan or primate[1], who presided in a synod of provincial bishops, regulated their election, authorized their consecration, had the power of revising their decision, or of carrying it for judgment to a conclave of his brother-prelates; and lastly, among other rights inherent in the primate, he was the public organ of communication with the State,—the channel for enforcing its enactments or distributing its bounty.

INTERNAL ORGANIZATION.

How affected by the metropolitan constitution of some Churches.

It is true that as the metropolitan constitution of the Church had grown out of the political divisions of the empire[2], it had also felt the shock by which the empire was subverted; and that, compared with its vigour in the former period, it was now very often inefficient, if not altogether in abeyance. Prelates of remoter dioceses, which they were engaged in reclaiming from the heathen, not unfrequently regarded the appointment of a primate as a clog on the freedom of their action. This[3] was peculiarly apparent in the Franks; nor is it hard to discern in their impatience of control a link in the chain of causes which was tending to consolidate the empire of the pope. They bowed to his legates and supported his pretensions, to evade what they deemed a vassalage at home.

The decline of metropolitans at this period.

Its effect on the growth of the papal power.

Yet, in spite of the wide-spread disaffection to the government of primates, it was able, here and there, to perpetuate its hold, and even to secure a footing in the newly founded churches. When Boniface was brought into collision with the bishop of Cologne[4], he strenuously

---

[1] See Bingham, Book II. ch. xvi. §§ 12 sq. and authorities there.

[2] This statement may be seen expanded at great length in Crakanthorp's *Defensio Eccl. Anglican.* ch. XXII. §§ 64 sq.

[3] Cf. Neander, v. 88 sq. 153, 154. The provincial synods, which were calculated to become the strongest agent of the metropolitans, had been discontinued in France for no less than eighty years: see the letter of Boniface, above, p. 21.

[4] *Ep.* XCIV. A.D. 753: 'Et modo vult Coloniensis episcopus sedem supradicti Willibrordi prædicatoris [*i. e.* Utrecht] sibi contrahere, ut non sit episcopalis sedes, *subjecta Romano pontifici*, prædicans gentem Fresonum. Cui respondebam, ut credidi, quod majus et potius fieri debeat præceptum apostolicæ sedis, et ordinatio Sergii papæ, et legatio venerandi prædicatoris Willibrordi, ut et fiat sedes episcopalis subjecta Romano

INTERNAL ORGANIZATION.

Metropolitans established in the recently converted countries; but with a Romanizing bias.

resented every act of interference in the spirit of the Frankish prelates: but in other parts he laboured from the first to organize the metropolitan system, and to use it as the special instrument of Rome. In his view[1] every prelate of a district should be placed in a close dependence on the metropolitan, and the metropolitan in subservience to the pope, on whom the correction of the evils, that might baffle a domestic synod, should be finally devolved. After manifold obstructions[2], the design of Boniface was partly carried out. A council at Soissons[3] (**744**) enabled him to fix one metropolitan at Rheims, and a second in the town of Sens. Mentz was awarded to himself; and at the close of the century two others, Arno of Salzburg and Hildebold of Cologne, were added to the list of primates. In England[4] also we have seen that the Roman mission were in favour of the same arrangement, choosing for their purpose Canterbury[5] and York[6], but the dignity

pontifici prædicans gentem Fresonum, quia magna pars illorum adhuc pagana est; quam destructæ ecclesiolæ fundamenta diruta, et a paganis conculcata, et *per negligentiam episcoporum* derelicta. Sed ipse non consentit.'

[1] 'Decrevimus autem in nostro synodali conventu, et confessi sumus fidem catholicam, et unitatem, et *subjectionem Romanæ ecclesiæ*, fine tenus vitæ nostræ, velle servare: sancto Petro et vicario ejus *velle subjici:* synodum per omnes annos congregare: *metropolitanos pallia ab illa sede quærere*, etc. ... Decrevimus, ut metropolitanus qui sit pallio sublimatus, hortetur cæteros, et admoneat, et investiget, quis sit inter eos curiosus de salute populi, quisve negligens servus Dei... Statuimus quod proprium sit metropolitano, juxta canonum statuta, subjectorum sibi episcoporum investigare mores et sollicitudinem circa populos, quales sint ... Sic enim, ni fallor, omnes episcopi debent metropolitano, *et ipse Romano pontifici,* si quid de corrigendis populis apud eos impossibile est, notum facere, et sic alieni fient a sanguine animarum perditarum.' *Ep.* LXIII. A.D. 748 (addressed to Cuthbert, archbp. of Canterbury).

[2] 'De eo autem, quod jam præterito tempore *de archiepiscopis* et *de palliis a Romana ecclesia petendis,* juxta promissa Francorum, sanctitati vestræ notum feci, indulgentiam apostolicæ sedis flagito: quia quod promiserunt *tardantes non impleverunt,* et adhuc differtur et ventilatur, quid inde perficere voluerint, ignoratur, sed *mea voluntate* impleta est promissio:' *Ep.* LXXV. (to pope Zacharias, A.D. 751): cf. Neander, *C. H.* v. 89.

[3] Labbe, VI. 1552.

[4] It is remarkable that in Ireland there were no metropolitans, or none at least who wore the pallium, till 1151. (R. Hoveden, *ad annum.*) But neither was there any diocesan system.

[5] See above, p. 9, note 5. The primacy of Canterbury, which had been endangered by Offa's erection of an archiepiscopal see at Lichfield, was recognized by Leo III., and settled in a provincial synod, 803. Wilkins, I. 166.

intended for the latter was a long while in abeyance. In all cases it was now the custom to create a metropolitan by sending him the pall or pallium, as a decorative badge. At first[1] it implied that all, thus distinguished by the pope, were prelates in communion with the Roman see: but in after-times it grew into a symbol of dependence.

INTERNAL ORGANIZATION. The grant of the pallium.

Much, however, as the papacy had gained by these centralizing changes, it was equally indebted to the conquests of Islamism. While they tended to unite the Christians of the west, they shook the dominion of the Eastern patriarchs; and three of these we must regard as virtually dethroned[2]. They all, in the former period of the Church, had exercised a constant check on the pretensions of the pope; for like him[3] they had extensive powers and were invested with precedence over other bishops: in proportion, therefore, as the sphere of their influence was narrowed, that of the larger patriarchates would be suffered to increase; and the struggle for priority of place among them would be confined to the Roman and Byzantine sees. The envy and ambition of these pontiffs led the way to a multitude of evils; and resulted, at the close of the

The papal power advanced by the Saracenic conquests.

---

[6] See above, p. 12, note 6. St Gregory directed that the metropolitans of England should receive consecration from each other: but until York had regained its archiepiscopal rank in 735, the prelate-elect of Canterbury was sometimes consecrated in Gaul, and sometimes by a conclave of his own suffragans. Kemble, II. 381.

[1] One of the earliest instances of such a grant from the pope is that of Cæsarius, bishop of Arles, to whom Symmachus is said to have permitted (513) 'speciali privilegio, pallii usum.' *Vit. S. Cæsar.* in the *Acta Sanctorum*, August. VI. 71. For another example of nearly the same date, see a letter of Symmachus to Theodore, archbishop of Lorch, in Ludewig, *Scriptores Rerum German.* II. 352: but Jaffé, *Regest. Pontif. Roman.* (Berolini, 1851), places it among the 'Literæ Spuriæ.' In the Eastern Church all bishops, as such, had worn a pallium (ὠμοφόριον): Pertsch, *De origine, usu, et auctoritate pallii archiepiscopalis*, pp. 91 &c. Helmst. 1754: Neale's *History of Eastern Church*, Introd. p. 312. In the west also, after it came into use, it was given to simple bishops as well as to primates. Pertsch, *ib.* 134 sq.

[2] It is true the Nestorians and Jacobites kept up the patriarchal system (see Asseman, *Biblioth. Orient.* tom. III. part ii. pp. 643 sq., and Neale's *Eastern Church*, II. 98 sq., where the forms of election are given in the two cases respectively): but as they were not in communion with the Church at large, they had no weight in counteracting the encroachments of the popes.

[3] The Roman patriarchate was originally small, confined to the ten provinces of middle and southern Italy and Sicily. See De Marca, *Concordia Sacerd. et Imperii*, lib. I. c. 7.

INTERNAL ORGANIZATION.

Struggle between Rome and Byzantium.

following period, in a deep and irreparable schism between the Greek and the Latin Christians. It is true there had long been a feeling of respect (in some, it may be, allied to veneration) for the Church that was thought to have been planted by St Peter in the mother-city of the world[1]. This feeling was diffused in countries very far from the Italian pale; it was shared even in the Eastern patriarchates, where the many were disposed to grant a primacy of order to the sister-church of Rome. But when the court with its prestige had been transplanted from the west, Constantinople was exalted to a parity of rank[2], and laboured to secure its prominent position.

The title of 'Œcumenical patriarch.'

An example of the contest is supplied at the close of the sixth century. John the Faster (ὁ νηστευτής), patriarch of Constantinople, had begun[3] (about 587) to make use of the title 'Œcumenical bishop,' in accordance with the pompous language of Justinian[4]. This was peculiarly offensive to the Roman prelate, Gregory the Great (590—604), who instantly denounced[5] the conduct of his rival.

---

[1] *e. g.* Valentin. III. A.D. 455: 'cum igitur sedis apostolicæ primatum B. Petri meritum, qui est princeps sacerdotalis coronæ, et Romanæ dignitas civitatis, sacræ etiam synodi firmarit auctoritas' *etc.*: ad calc. *Cod. Theodosian.* tom. VI. p. 12: cf. the language of Columbanus, above, p. 17, note 1.

[2] See Concil. Constantinop. A.D. 381, can. III.: Concil. Chalcedon, A.D. 451, can. XXVIII, which confirms the decision of the earlier council: τὰ ἴσα πρεσβεῖα ἀπένειμαν τῷ τῆς νέας Ῥώμης ἁγιωτάτῳ θρόνῳ, κ.τ.λ., on the ground that Constantinople was the seat of the empire. The Council *in Trullo* (691) repeated the decree in still clearer terms: can. XXXVI: τῶν ἴσων ἀπολαύουσαν πρεσβείων τῇ πρεσβυτέρᾳ βασιλίδι Ῥώμῃ. These canons were signed by the emperor and the four Eastern patriarchs: the pope, however, obstinately refused, and some of the decisions were afterwards reversed by synods in the west. In the *Codex* of Justinian, lib. I. tit. ii. c. 24, the Church of Constantinople is entitled πασῶν τῶν ἄλλων κεφαλή; but he used the same language in regard to the Church of Rome. *Ibid.* lib. I. tit. i. c. 7, and elsewhere. The incursion of the Lombards into Italy (568) weakened the connexion between the empire and the popes, and left them more at liberty to follow out their centralizing projects. Even then, however, the obstructions they encountered were not few. The archbishop of Aquileia and the Istrian prelates had suspended all communion with the court of Rome in the controversy on the Three Chapters, and were not reconciled till 698: see J. F. B. M. de Rubeis, *Monimenta Ecclesiæ Aquilejensis,* ed. 1740, and Gieseler, II. 129.

[3] It is clear from Gregor. *Ep.* v. 18, that Pelagius II., his predecessor, was offended 'propter nefandum elationis vocabulum.'

[4] Cf. *Codex*, lib. I. tit. i. 7: *Novell.* III. v. and elsewhere.

[5] See, among others, a letter addressed to John himself (595), v. 18, and one of the same date to the emperor Maurice, v. 20.

For his own part also he was ready to disclaim an appellation of that nature[1], on the ground that it detracted from the honour of his colleagues. Yet in spite of these disclaimers, it is obvious that to him, far more than any of his predecessors, the foundation of the papal monarchy is due[2]. He seems to have been possessed by an idea[3] that the source of all authority for every province of the Church was lodged, by some special grant, in the successors of St Peter: and the vigour of his mind[4], united with his many Christian virtues, had enabled him to propagate his tenets far and near, not only in the ancient Roman dioceses, but in every province of the west. In contrast with the misery at home[5], a field of increasing glory was presented to his view in the mission to the Anglo-Saxons, the conversion of the Arian Visigoths in Spain[6], and the respect with which his coun-

INTERNAL ORGANIZATION.

Progress of the papal power under Gregory the Great.

---

[1] A.D. 598, in a letter to Eulogius, patriarch of Alexandria, who, in the style of the Eastern Church, had called Gregory 'universalis episcopus.' Gregor. *Ep.* VIII. 30. It continued, however, to be given to the see of Constantinople, and Phocas, the murderer of Maurice, who ascended the imperial throne in 602, rewarded the countenance he had received from the pope (cf. Gregor. *Epist.* XIII. 31), by advocating his pretensions to supremacy: 'Hic (Phocas), rogante papa Bonifacio, statuit sedem Romanæ et Apostolicæ ecclesiæ caput esse omnium ecclesiarum, *quia* ecclesia Constantinopolitana primam se omnium ecclesiarum scribebat.' Beda, *Chronicon*, A.D. 614. The communication of the Roman prelates with the court was kept up by an agent (apocrisiarius) at Constantinople. Gregory the Great and two of his immediate successors had each held this office in their earlier years.

[2] 'Upon the whole, the papal authority had made no decisive progress in France, or perhaps anywhere beyond Italy, till the pontificate of Gregory I.' Hallam, *Middle Ages*, ch. VII: I. 519; ed. 1841. For a minute account of its inroads and possessions at the beginning of the seventh century, see Wiltsch's *Handbuch der Kirchlichen Geographie und Statistik*, I. 67 sq. Berlin, 1846.

[3] 'De Constantinopolitana ecclesia,' he asks, *Epist.* IX. 12, 'quis eam dubitet sedi apostolicæ esse subjectam?'—but this might imply no more than the priority of Rome as *one* of the *sedes apostolicæ*: see the whole of his letter to Eulogius (VII. 40), where he seems to argue as if Antioch and Alexandria, which had also been indebted to St Peter, stood on a level with the Roman church.

[4] This was shewn by his letters, of which 840 have been preserved, and by his theological Treatises.

[5] Gibbon, ch. XLV: IV. 267, ed. Milman.

[6] In a letter to Rechared, king of the Visigoths, A.D. 599, *Epist.* IX. 122, he praises the zeal of that monarch in reclaiming 'all the nation of the Goths' from the heresy of Arius, and forwards a pallium to Leander, bishop of Seville, at his own request. Ibid. IX. 121. In 701—710, however, Witiza the king endeavoured to restore the independence of the

INTERNAL
ORGANIZA-
TION.

His successors.

sels were accepted by the Frankish kings and prelates[1]. He was followed in a quick succession by Sabinian (**604**), Bonifacius III. (**607**), Bonifacius IV. (**608**), Deusdedit (**615**), Bonifacius V. (**619**), Honorius I. (**625**), Severinus (**638 ?**), John IV. (**640**), Theodore I. (**642**), Martin I. (**649**), Eugenius I. (**654**), Vitalian (**657**), Adeodatus (**672**), Donus (**676**), Agatho[2] (**678**), Leo II. (**682**), Benedict II. (**683 ?**), John[3] V. (**685**), Conon (**686**), Sergius I. (**687**), John VI. (**701**), John VII. (**705**), Sisinnius (**708**), Constantine I. (**708**), Gregory[4] II. (**715**),—whose advocate in forwarding the papal power was Boniface, the Englishman,—Gregory[5] III. (**731**), Zacharias (**741**), Stephen II. (**752**), Stephen[6]

Spanish Church, and forbade all appeals to a 'foreign' bishop; but the conquests of the Saracens soon after put an end to this freer movement. For a careful statement of the evidence respecting Witiza, see Gieseler, II. 189 sq.

[1] *e. g.* Gregor. *Epist.* XI. 55, 56, 59, 60, 61, 62, 63, 69. In the last, dated like the others, 601, he asks leave of Brunechild, the Frankish queen, to send a legate into Gaul, with the hope of restraining such priests as lived 'impudice ac nequiter.' This intercourse was, however, weakened during the political disturbances of the seventh century, and only re-established under Pepin and Carloman. Gieseler, II. 187.

[2] In apologizing for his delay in sending legates to the Council of Constantinople (680), he thus speaks of the growth of his dominion in the west: 'Primum quidem, quod numerosa multitudo nostrorum usque ad oceani regiones extenditur, cujus itineris longinquitas in multi temporis cursum protelatur: sperabamus deinde de Britannia Theodorum, archiepiscopum et philosophum, ad nostram humilitatem conjungere: et maxime quia in medio gentium, tam Longobardorum, quamque Sclavorum, necnon Francorum, Gallorum, et Gothorum, atque Britannorum, plurimi confamulorum nostrorum esse noscuntur.' Mansi, XI. 294.

[3] It is remarkable that this pope and six of his immediate successors were either Greeks or Syrians, which is to be ascribed to the want of theological scholars in Rome, or still more to the influence of the Byzantine court. Döllinger, *C. H.* III. 110.

[4] The following passage from a letter to the emperor Leo (729) is very remarkable: 'Nos viam ingredimur in extremas occidentis regiones versus illos, qui sanctum baptisma efflagitant. Cum enim illuc episcopos misissem et sanctæ ecclesiæ nostræ clericos, nondum adducti sunt, ut capita sua inclinarent et baptizarentur, *eorum principes,* quod exoptent, ut eorum sim susceptor ($\grave{\epsilon}\mu\grave{\epsilon}\ \grave{\epsilon}\pi\iota\zeta\eta\tau o\hat{\upsilon}\nu\tau\epsilon s\ \gamma\epsilon\nu\acute{\epsilon}\sigma\theta\alpha\iota\ \alpha\mathring{\upsilon}\tau\hat{\omega}\nu\ \grave{\alpha}\nu\acute{\alpha}\delta o\chi o\nu$). Hac de causa nos ad viam, Dei benignitate, accingimus, ne forte damnationis et incuriæ nostræ rationem reddamus.' Mansi, XII. 981. Another specimen of his extravagant language occurs, *ibid.* 971: $\tau\grave{o}\nu\ \mathring{\alpha}\gamma\iota o\nu\ \Pi\acute{\epsilon}\tau\rho o\nu\ \alpha\acute{\iota}\ \pi\hat{\alpha}\sigma\alpha\iota\ \beta\alpha\sigma\iota\lambda\epsilon\hat{\iota}\alpha\iota\ \tau\hat{\eta}s\ \delta\acute{\upsilon}\sigma\epsilon\omega s\ \Theta\epsilon\grave{o}\nu\ \grave{\epsilon}\pi\acute{\iota}\gamma\epsilon\iota o\nu\ \grave{\epsilon}\chi o\upsilon\sigma\iota$.

[5] In a letter to the English bishops (cir. 731) he informs them that he had constituted Tatwin, archbishop of Canterbury, primate of all Britain and his vicar. Wilkins, I. 81. But the genuineness of the letter is questionable. 'See *Councils,* &c. III. 312.

[6] At his prayer (755) the Franks were induced to rescue his possessions

III. (753), Paul I. (757), Constantine II. (767), Philip (768), Stephen IV. (768), Hadrian I. (772), Leo III. (795—816). But although we may trace encroachments in the conduct of these prelates, and a growing boldness in their tone, especially in Gregory II. and in Zacharias, it was not until the papacy[1] of Hadrian I. that a claim to the pastorship of all the Christian Church was fully brought to light. The Eastern patriarchates, it is true, continued to resist this arrogant demand as firmly and successfully as ever: but it gained a more general acceptance in the west. This will be found especially in regions now brought over to the Gospel, and in tribes of Teutonic blood. A large portion of the extant rescripts[2] issued at this period were directed to the rulers of the Church of England. While they shew us how profoundly she was moved by sentiments of gratitude and veneration[3], they bear witness also to the servile spirit of her children, notwithstanding[4] some

INTERNAL ORGANIZATION.

Further increase of the papal power: its establishment among the Anglo-Saxons:

from the Lombards (*Scriptores Franc.* ed. Duchesne, III. 707), and in this way Italy was lost to the enfeebled emperors of the east, who could no longer keep it in their grasp. The crowning of Charlemagne (Dec. 25, 800) with the imperial diadem, in the church of St Peter, gave fresh vigour to the inroads of the popes. He added also to their landed property, and made them temporal princes: on which see Hadrian's letter to him (777) *ubi sup.* 766; Neander, v. 168; and De Marca, *De Concordia*, lib. III. c. 12.

[1] 'It cannot, I think, be said, that any material acquisitions of ecclesiastical power were obtained by the successors of Gregory (the Great) for nearly one hundred and fifty years.' Hallam, *Middle Ages*, I. 520. Hadrian I., however, says distinctly (782): 'Sedes apostolica caput totius mundi et omnium Dei ecclesiarum,' *Codex Carolin.* ed. Cenni, I. 389: 'Cujus sollicitudo, *delegata Divinitus*, cunctis debetur ecclesiis:' and other similar expressions are quoted by Neander, v. 166, 167 (notes). On the circulation of the pseudo-Isidore Decretals (at the close of the eighth century) these notions were apparently supported by a continuous chain of testimony reaching up to the Apostles. *Ibid.* VI. 2—8.

[2] See the useful index of Jaffé (Berlin, 1851) entitled *Regesta Pontificum Romanorum.*

[3] This led to the foundation of an English college at Rome entitled 'Schola Saxonum.' See Lappenberg, *Anglo-Saxons*, I. 205—207. It was afterwards converted into a hospital 'Xenodochium Sancti Spiritus,' for the entertainment of English pilgrims who, from 720 to the close of the century, were very numerous. Bed. *Hist. Eccl.* v. 7: *Chronicon*, in *Monument. Hist. Britan.* p. 101 A. Others, like the youthful monarch Ceadwalla (689), and his successor Ine (725), took up their permanent abode in Rome, 'ad limina beatorum apostolorum.' Bed. *Hist. Eccl.* v. 7.

[4] See Wilfrith's case, above, p. 15, n. 3. Alcuin, also, led astray by a spurious document (*Ep.* XCII, al. CVIII, *Opp.* I. 134, cf. Neand. v. 168), arrived in the year 800 at the conclusion, that the see of Rome was 'judiciariam, non judicandam;' and in 796 he addressed the pope (*Ep.*

INTERNAL ORGANIZATION

and the Germans.

occasional assertions of their freedom. And the same must be conceded in the case of Germany, as soon as the Irish school was silenced and subverted. In the council[1] at which Boniface presided (742), in his character of Roman legate, he was able to anticipate the fervent wishes of his master. Every scheme he then propounded for the organizing of the German Church was based on subjection to the popes. This tendency indeed was balanced for a while by the action of the royal power; but as soon as the diadem of Charlemagne had descended to his weaker and more pliant offspring, the aggressive spirit of the papacy unfolded all its might.

The growing consideration of the Monks.

A second feature in the changes of this period was the growing reputation of the monks. Being now not unfrequently admitted into orders, and distinguished for their missionary zeal, their swarming numbers, their superior learning, and the strictness of their mode of life, they won the applauses of the multitude as well as of the courts[2], eclipsing the parochial clergy, and evading the exactions of the bishops. It is true, they were subject in most countries[3] to the censures of their own diocesans, but in the course of the seventh century they strove to be exempted from this rule, which had sometimes grown exceedingly oppressive[4]; and the favour they enjoyed at Rome[5] enabled many convents of the west to realize

xx, al. xxiv, *Opp.* I. 30) in the following terms: 'Sanctissime Pater, pontifex a Deo electus, Vicarius apostolorum, hæres patrum, princeps ecclesiæ, unius immaculatæ columbæ nutritor,' etc.; though much of this language is to be regarded as empty rhetoric.

[1] *Ep.* LXIII. Carloman, who prompted this synodal action, withdrew from his court in 748, 'ad limina beatorum apostolorum pervenit,' and assumed the monastic habit. *Annales Laurissenses Minor.* in Pertz, I. 115.

[2] In England alone nearly thirty kings and queens retired into convents or reclusion during the seventh and eighth centuries. Döllinger, II. 58. And the same, though to a less extent, is true of other countries. Schröckh, xx. 10—12. The monastic life was the realization of the ideal of the mediæval mind. Buckingham, *Bible in the Middle Ages*, p. 82.

[3] There was an exception in the case of Africa, where some of the convents placed themselves under the protection of distant bishops. *Concil.* ed. Mansi, VIII. 648. In the seventh century exemptions had commenced in the patriarchate of Constantinople. They were denoted by the erection, at the cloister, of a patriarchal cross. Döllinger, II. 285.

[4] On the despotic powers of the bishops at this period and the opposition (*conjurationes*) they provoked, see Guizot, *Hist. of Civilization, &c.*, II. 55 sq., 94 sq., ed. *Lond.* 1846. The *conjurationes* of the monks were perhaps akin to the clerical 'gilds' in England. Alfred's *Works*, I. 445.

their wishes[1]. They were made to contribute in this way to the fixing of the papal power. The Rules[2] of Columbanus, Isidore, and Cæsarius of Arles, like the older systems of St Basil, Cassian, and the rest, were gradually supplanted in the Western churches by the order of St Benedict. He was a native of Umbria, and in 529 established the great model-abbey of Monte Cassino. His chief aim was to mitigate the harshness and monotony that characterized the Eastern systems, though in one respect he made his institute more rigid,—by the vow, which, after a noviciate of one year, he claimed of every person who retreated to his cloisters. It was not, however, till some time after his death (543) that the order was extensively adopted: but in the course of two hundred years it was everywhere diffused in Gaul, in Italy, and Spain; and it followed in the track of Benedictine monks who laboured in Great Britain and the northern parts of Europe[3]. Much as this order, by its union and its growing

INTERNAL ORGANIZATION.

The importance of the Benedictine order.

---

[5] See Gregor. I., *Epist.* VIII. 15, addressed (598) to the bishop of Ravenna. A Roman Synod (601) drew up constitutions in their favour; there is also a decree attributed to a Roman Council of 610 allowing monks in priests' orders to execute all priestly functions; but this is probably spurious. (*Councils*, &c. III. 63, 64.) Cf. Council of Seville (618) can. 10, 11; Epist. Jóhan. IV. apud Labb. *Concil.* v. 1773.

[1] The early and less questionable exemptions simply relieve the monks from the interference of bishops in the economical management of the monasteries. This privilege is greatly expanded in the forged documents of a later period; a ludicrous instance is that of Medeshamstede, in which the pope is made to appoint the abbot his legate for all England. Wilkins, I. 48.

[2] See L. Holstein's *Codex Regularum Monasticarum*, etc. 1759, and Heylot's *Histoire des Ordres Religieux*, etc. ed. 1792. Monasticism retained its variety of form in the Eastern patriarchates. For some idea of its spirit in those regions, see Moschus (Johan.), Λειμών (compiled about 610) in *Auctarium Bibliothecae Patrum Ducæanum*, Paris, 1624, tom. I. 1057 sq. The numerous conventual establishments of the Nestorians are described in Asseman, *Biblioth. Orient.* tom. II. part ii. The Jacobites at this period introduced monasticism into Ethiopia, where 'the sons of Teklahaimanot' are said to have equalled the Benedictines of the west. Neale, II. 74.

[3] It has been questioned whether the early monasticism of the Anglo-Saxon Church was purely Benedictine. On the whole it seems most probable that Augustine and the Kentish mission introduced the modified or lax practice then in vogue at Rome, and that even this was modified still further by the association of secular priests with monks in the episcopal and missionary settlements. As the character of the church became less distinctly missionary, and as the reforms of the Benedictine rule followed one another, the monks became more strict and separated from the secu-

INTERNAL ORGANIZATION.

Institution of collegiate Canons.

numbers, interfered with the freedom of the local churches, and facilitated the incursions of the popes, it must notwithstanding be regarded as a patron of the arts[1], and as contributing to fan the embers of religion[2].

The corruptions which prevailed in the eighth century among the major and the minor clerics, as distinguished from the monks, appear to have suggested the idea of binding them together by a rule, analogous to those obtaining in the convents. The design is attributed to Chrodegang, a pious bishop of Metz (742–766), who founded[3] what was known as the order of cathedral or collegiate 'canons.' It is clear that the members of his chapter differed little from the Benedictine monks, except in their enjoyment of some personal estate, arising from a periodical division of the funds of the cathedral. They used a common dormitory and refectory; at fixed (or 'canonical') hours they met in the church for worship, and in the chapter-house to hear the exhortations of the bishop. Chrodegang's institute was sanctioned, with some changes, at the council of Aix-la-Chapelle (816), and was copied[4] very soon in other countries.

---

lar clergy (e. g. under Benedict Biscop and later under Boniface) but also diminished in numbers and influence, until at the date of the Danish invasion pure monasticism was nearly extinct. That invasion destroyed the remains of the primitive system, and the English monachism of the tenth century was a new institution. In Germany it was otherwise; Willebrord, Boniface, and most of the German missionaries were also Benedictines. It was natural, therefore, that the German synods should insist upon conformity to the institute under which they had themselves been trained. Helyot, II. 58.

[1] The impulse in this direction appears to have been communicated by Cassiodorus. See his treatises 'De institutione Divinarum litterarum' and 'De artibus ac disciplinis liberalium litterarum' (*Opp.* Rothomagi, 1679), both of which were much esteemed by the mediæval monks.

[2] See Mabillon's *Acta Sanctorum Ordin. Benedict.* passim. The Benedictines and their offshoots were peculiarly devoted to the study of the Bible: see, for instance, the *Antiquiores Consuetudines Cluniacensis Monasterii*, in D'Achery, I. 650, (ed. 1723), where we find the order of reading the whole Bible once a year.

[3] Chrodogangi *Regula Sincera*, apud Mansi, *Concil.* XIV. 313. Strictly speaking, Chrodegang was not the author of the rule. It was akin to the canonical institute of St Augustine: Helyot, II. 64 sq. *Canonesses* also are first mentioned at the Council of Châlons-sur-Saone (813): *Ib.* II. 59.

[4] *Ib.* p. 68. Paul Warnefrid (*Gesta Episc. Mettensium;* Pertz, II. 268) has left a contemporary account of Chrodegang and his active life. Charlemagne was so pleased with the new institute that he wanted all the clergy to be either monks or canons. *Capitular.* A.D. 789, c. 75 (Baluze,

But in addition to the city clergy, whom it was thus attempted to reduce more fully under the inspection of the bishop, every diocese included many others, who officiated in rural districts. These were the *seculars*, comprising (1) the parish-priests[1] and their assistants; (2) the roving or itinerant clergy[2], who had no proper cure and no fixed employment; (3) a large band of chaplains[3], who obeyed all the movements of the court, or were attached to the castles of the gentry. To correct excesses in these quarters, and to mitigate the evils, on the part of laymen, that grew out of their abuse[4] of the right of patronage, it was needful that the prelates should secure a closer supervision of their flocks. An order had indeed been given at the end[5]

INTERNAL ORGANIZATION.

The secular clergy.

I. 239). There are traces of an attempt to introduce portions of the system into England as early as 813; *Councils, &c.*, III. 575; Kemble, *Cod. Dipl.* cc: monastic institutions being then on the wane. But neither the discipline nor the name of *canons* was really planted here before the 11th century and then the rule of Chrodegang was almost universally rejected.

[1] See Bingham, bk. IX. ch. VIII. In most other countries the division into parishes was very ancient, but in England the introduction of the system is a matter of great obscurity. The monastic stations founded by the original missionaries seem to have long supplied the wants of the people. The original parish priest would be the minister of the village community or chaplain of the lord of a franchise, and the parish in most cases would coincide with the territory of the community or franchise. In Bede's letter to Egbert traces of an incipient system of the kind may be found. The process in a thinly populated and unsettled country was naturally slower than on the continent where it was only necessary to adopt the ancient local divisions. Theodore has been named as the founder of the parochial system, but it was probably growing up gradually from his time to that of Alfred.

[2] These had grown up through a relaxation of the ancient laws which provided that no clergyman should be ordained except to a particular church. Charlemagne laboured to abate the evils that had flowed from their disorderly proceedings. *Capitular.* A.D. 789: *ib.* A.D. 794. The former, among other things, decrees 'ut in diebus festis vel Dominicis, omnes ad ecclesiam veniant, et non invitent presbyteros *ad domos suas ad missas faciendas,*' c. 9.

[3] The trouble they created for the bishops may be gathered from the 14th canon of the Council of Chalons (649). The principal chaplain of the court (archicapellanus) became a kind of 'minister of religion' for the whole kingdom: see Planck, *Geschichte der Kirchenverfassung,* II. 147.

[4] *e. g.* Bonifacii *Opp.* II. 22: 'Ut laici presbyteros non ejiciant de ecclesiis, nec mittere præsumant sine consensu episcoporum suorum: ut laici omnino non audeant *munera exigere* a presbyteris, propter commendationem ecclesiæ cuique presbytero.' This prohibition was renewed (813) at Arles, c. 5.

[5] Concil. Bracarense III. (of Braga, 572) can. I.

INTERNAL ORGANIZATION.

Episcopal visitations.
Archdeacons, and rural chapters.
Synods.

of the former period (572) that the bishop should inspect his diocese in person every year. This practice was continued in the following centuries[1]; and the effect of it was extended by the larger powers of the archdeacon[2], and the rise of many rural chapters[3] (or associations of adjoining parishes).

But the organization of the Church is due still more to the influence of Synods[4], which had long been in the Western Church the ordinary courts for determining all controverted questions. The proceedings of the synods[5] of this epoch, with exceptions to be noticed in the following chapter, did not turn habitually on points of doctrine, but related to the conduct of the clergy or the people, the external welfare of the Church, and the wider propagation of the Gospel. They forbad all ministrations of a cleric who was unacquainted[6] with the language of the country; they insisted on a more extensive knowledge of the Bible[7];

Their main objects at this period.

---

[1] *e. g.* Bonifacii Epist. LXIII. p. 141: Synod of Clovesho, 747, can. III.; Wilkins, I. 95. In the Frankish empire these visitations were connected with the establishment of *sends* (? synodi), or spiritual courts: see Neander, v. 148, 149. The bishops in all cases attempted to extirpate the numerous remains of heathenism as well as open vices.

[2] Bingham, bk. II. ch. XXI. § 9: Neander, v. 152, 153. In some of the recently converted districts there was a great lack both of presbyters and bishops. See the excellent letter of Bede to archbp. Ecgberht (734), where he urges the necessity of further subdivision in that prelate's field of labour. As the power of the archdeacon was enlarged, the *chorepiscopi* were all abolished. Giesler, II. 249.

[3] The 'capitula ruralia' were presided over by *archpresbyters*, or, in more modern language, rural deans: see Ducange, *sub voce*, and Dansey's *Horæ Decanicæ Rurales*, 2nd edit.

[4] See above, p. 36, and cf. Guizot, *Civilization*, *Lect.* XIII. In Spain the synods were chiefly *national*, and, in defect of such, *provincial* councils were to be assembled every year. See Council of Toledo (633), c. 3: Merida (666), c. 7. The former of these gives directions touching the *mode* in which the synods should be held, can. 4. In England, under Theodore and subsequently, it was usual to hold *provincial* synods, at least in the southern province, though not, as he directed, twice a-year. Kemble, II. 367.

[5] See an abstract of their acts, chronologically arranged, in Guizot, Append. to Vol. II. For specimens, at length, see those of Clovesho (747), and Cealchythe (787): Wilkins, I. 94 sq.; 145 sq. The object of the annual synod is thus stated by pope Zacharias (Bonif. *Epist.* XLVIII.): 'ad pertractandum de unitate ecclesiæ, ut si quid adversi acciderit radicibus amputetur, et Dei ecclesia maneat inconcussa.'

[6] *e. g.* Bonifacii *Statuta*, § XXVII: *Opp.* II. 24: cf. Charlemagne, *Capitul.* A.D. 813, § 14; I. 505.

[7] *e. g.* Council of *Toledo* (633), c. 25: (653), c. 8: of *Arles* (813), c. 25.

they prescribed the routine of public worship[1], and endeavoured to produce a greater uniformity[2]; in short, they were the legislative and judicial organs of the Church; although their movements might be checked and overruled by the voice of superior councils, by the arbitrary measures of the State, or, at times, in the churches of the west, by the fiats of the Roman court.

INTERNAL ORGANIZATION.

The marriage of the clergy *proper*[3], interdicted though it were by emperors and kings, by western synods, and emphatically by the popes, was not generally suppressed in the seventh century. In the eastern patriarchates, a council held at Constantinople, 691, (the Council in Trullo), while forbidding[4] *second* marriages of priests or deacons, and reflecting on all marriages contracted after ordination, is opposed to the canons of the west. It vindicates[5] the right of married clergymen to live as before with their proper consorts, on the ground that the holy ordinance of matrimony would be otherwise dishonoured. In the Latin Church, however, where the Trullan regulations were not all adopted, we observe a more stringent tone in the synodal decisions[6]; and when Boniface had been successful in his German mission, he expended not a little of his ardour in discrediting the married clergy[7]. This

Marriage of the clergy.

---

[1] *e. g.* Council of *Rome* (595), c. 1, prescribing what parts of the service shall be chanted, and what read.

[2] *e. g. Toledo* (675), c. 3, ordering all bishops of the province to conform to the ritual of the metropolitan church; as an older canon of Toledo (633), c. 2, directed that the same order of prayer and psalmody should be observed throughout the kingdom.

[3] This distinction is important: for a multitude of persons now submitted to the tonsure without passing to the higher orders of the Church. See Guizot, *Lect.* XIII. p. 38.

[4] Can. III: Mansi, XI. 941.

[5] Can. XIII.

[6] *e. g.* Council of *Toledo* (653) can. V. VI. VII. It seems that Witiza, the reforming king of Spain, in the eighth century, rescinded the decrees relating to the celibacy of clerics. Gieseler, II. 191, note.

[7] The following is the language of his patron Zacharias: 'Qui clerici etiam ab uxoribus abstinere debeant, ex concilio Africano, cap. XXXVII. ita continentur: Præterea cum de clericorum quorundam (quamvis erga proprias uxores) incontinentia referretur, placuit episcopos et presbyteros seu diaconos, secundum propria statuta, etiam ab uxoribus continere: quod nisi fecerint, *ab ecclesiastico officio removeantur.* Cæteros autem clericos ad id non cogi, sed secundum uniuscujusque ecclesiæ consuetudinem observari debere.' Bonif. *Ep.* LXV: *Opp.* I. 155.

INTERNAL ORGANIZATION.

antipathy was shared by his countrymen at home[1]: yet, in spite of the admonitions of the bishop, and the legislation of the Witan (or state-council), very many of the English seculars, like those of other lands, continued to bring up the issue of their marriage[2].

Income of the clergy.

With regard to the income of the clergy, it accrued as before from the endowments of their churches, and the voluntary offerings of the faithful[3]. The revenues thus obtained were thrown into a common stock, which it was usual, in the Roman church[4] and others, to distribute in four portions; of which one was allotted to the poor, a second to the parish priests, a third to the fabric and expenses of the church, and the remnant to the bishop of the diocese. The administration[5] of the property was left entirely in his hands.

Tithes.

Another source of church-revenue were the tithes, which, although they had been claimed on moral grounds at a far earlier date[6], were not uniformly paid by Christians of the west until the close of the sixth century[7]. A special law of Charlemagne[8], 779, enforced the payment on all subjects of the empire, and his neighbours for the most part followed his example[9]. Like the voluntary offer-

---

[1] There are however hardly any references to clerical marriages in the genuine Anglo-Saxon laws or canons of this period.

[2] See Kemble, II. 444 sq., where the chain of testimony is shewn to be almost unbroken.

[3] The French clergy at the end of this period had become extremely rich. See Guérard, *Cartulaire de l'Eglise de Notre Dame de Paris*, Pref. p. xxxvii; Paris, 1850.

[4] Bed. I. 27. In Spain, and perhaps elsewhere, the bishop had a third of the revenues: see Council of *Braga* (560), can. VII; of *Toledo* (633), can. XXXIII.

[5] Council of *Orleans* (511), can. XIV. XV: cf. Guizot, *Lect.* XIII. p. 53. The Council of *Braga* (675) complains of the injustice and extortion of some of the bishops.

[6] Bingham, bk. v. ch. v.

[7] The councils of *Tours* (567) and of *Mâcon* (585) endeavoured to procure a more regular payment.

[8] *Capitular.* A.D. 779, c. VII. The severity with which this law had been enforced was regretted by the gentle Alcuin: see *Epist.* LXXX. (al. XCV.) *ad Domnum Regem: Opp.* I. 117. In *Ep.* LXXII. (al. LXXXVII. *Opp.* I. 105) he gives the following advice to Arno: 'Esto prædicator pietatis, non decimarum exactor.'

[9] The history of tithe in England has been complicated both by controversial misstatements and by the existence of the antedated or fabricated penitential literature. The establishment of the right grew up here in very much the same course as on the continent. (1) Setting

ings which preceded them, the tithes were intended for the clergy and the poor; the bishop of the diocese at first prescribing the allotments, even where he was not himself entitled to a portion.

RELATIONS TO THE CIVIL POWER.

§ 2. *RELATIONS OF THE CHURCH TO THE CIVIL POWER.*

The Church has been hitherto regarded as an independent corporation, organized entirely on a model of its own, expanding with the vigour it inherited from heaven, and governed, in the name of its holy Founder, by the prelates who derived authority from Him. But after the imperial coinage bore the impress of religion, and the sovereigns of the east and west were 'patrons' of the Church, its history involved another class of questions: it had entered into an alliance with the State, and, as a natural result, its path was in future to be shaped according to the new relations. This alliance did not lead, as it might have done, to an absorption of the secular into the sacerdotal power, nor to a complete amalgamation of the civil and ecclesiastical tribunals: yet its strength was often injured by the action of opposing forces, either by the Church aspiring to become the mistress of the State, or by the State encroaching on the province of the Church and suppressing her inherent rights. The former of these tendencies predominated in the west, the latter in the east. The one was diverging into *Romanism;*

General character of the alliance between Church and State.

aside the statements of the spurious penitentials, it is clear from the genuine penitential of Theodore, that the duty of giving tithe to sacred purposes was regarded by him as part of the common law of the church; Pœnit. II. c. ii. § 8; c. XIV. §§ 9, 10. The same was the opinion of the early lawyers who refer the introduction of the custom to St Augustine. Leges Eadw. capp. vii. viii. Thorpe, i. 445. (2) The legatine Council of 787, whose decrees were accepted as binding by the kings and witan of Mercia and Northumbria, and probably by the witan of Wessex also, enacts in the seventeenth canon, "ut omnes studeant de omnibus quæ possident decimas dare:" and on this is perhaps based the statement that Offa gave a tithe of all his property to the church. Beyond this canon there is no extant enactment declaring the *legal* obligation of tithe; but it appears as an established law in the time of Edward the Elder; Thorpe, i. 171. "If any man withhold tithes let him pay *lahslit* among the Danes, *wite* with the English." On the story of Ethelwulf's gift of tithe, see *Councils*, &c. III. 637.

M. A. E

RELATIONS TO THE CIVIL POWER.

Romanism and Byzantinism.

the other, to dictation of the civil power in adjudging controversies of the faith,—or, in a word, to *Byzantinism*.

It is true that the claims of the Roman pontiffs, who evoked the aggressive spirit of the Church, were not urged at the present epoch as they were in after-ages. Till the middle of the eighth century Rome was itself dependent on the Eastern empire[1], and its voice in all *civil* questions[2] was proportionately humble. On the contrary it will be found that the court of Byzantium was unwilling to abandon the despotic powers that had been wielded by Justinian. All the Eastern patriarchs, and not unfrequently the Roman[3], were its immediate nominees; it laid claim to a quasi-sacerdotal[4] character, and, as we shall see at large, affected to decide in religious controversies of the very gravest kind.

Deference of the Western kings to the ecclesiastics, in questions of doctrine.

The Western princes, who, until the time of Charlemagne, stood far lower in their mental training, were accustomed to defer entirely[5] to the wisdom of the synods, if the faith of the Church was thought to be imperilled: and in cases even where the kings, the bishops, and the nobles were com-

---

[1] Gibbon, IV. 479, ed. Milman.

[2] Thus Gregory II., one of the stoutest champions of the papacy, writes to the Emperor Leo (729): 'Scis sanctæ ecclesiæ dogmata non imperatorum esse, sed pontificum: idcirco ecclesiis præpositi sunt pontifices *a reipublicæ negotiis abstinentes*, et imperatores ergo similiter ab ecclesiasticis abstineant, et quæ sibi commissa sunt, capessant.' Mansi, *Concil.* XII. 969: cf. *ibid.* 977, where he admits that the bishops have no right 'introspiciendi in palatium, ac dignitates regias deferendi.'

[3] See Schröckh, XIX. 408 sq. But in the case of the Roman bishop there was generally some kind of election, though it was seldom *bona fide*. Gregory the Great, like many of his successors, seems to have owed his elevation to his former appointment, as 'apocrisiarius' at the court of Byzantium. He was consecrated by the command of the emperor Maurice, after his election by 'the clergy, senate, and Roman people.' Johan. Diacon. *Vit. Gregor.* I. 39, in Gregor. *Opp.* ed. Bened. IV. 36: Gregor. Turonensis, *Hist. Franc.* lib. x. 1. Some idea of the excitement caused by these popular elections may be derived from the example of Sergius I. (687), who is said to have been chosen 'a primatibus judicum, et exercitu Romanæ militiæ, vel cleri seditiosi parte plurima, et præsertim sacerdotum atque civium multitudine.' Two other candidates, Paschalis and Theodorus, were elected by different factions. *Vit. Sergii*, in Vignolii *Lib. Pontif.* I. 303, 304, ed. Rom. 1724.

[4] 'Imperator sum et sacerdos' was the claim of the emperor Leo (729): Mansi, *Concil.* XII. 975. One of the charges brought against Anastasius, a disciple of Maximus, in the Monothelete controversy, was that he refused to recognize the emperor as a priest, and as possessed of spiritual jurisdiction. Maximi *Opp.* I. 30: ed. Combefis.

[5] Cf. Guizot, as above, II. 30. The precedents in which the royal power was most freely exercised have been collected in the great work entitled *Preuves des Libertez de l'Eglise Gallicane*.

bined in one assembly—an arrangement not unusual in the Frankish empire[1] and continuing in England till the Norman Conquest[2]—there was still a disposition to refer not a few of the civil questions[3] that emerged to the ultimate decision of the prelates.

It was different, however, in respect of a second class of questions, where the temporal and ecclesiastical provinces appear to interpenetrate each other. We shall there find the Church compelled to surrender a large portion of her ancient rights. A prominent example is supplied in the filling up of vacant sees. The bishop was at first elected, as a rule[4], by the voices of the clergy and the people; but in the Frankish empire, as well as in other parts, this custom had been suffered to die out, amid the social changes of the times. The arbitrary will of barbaric princes, such as Clovis, Chilperic, and Charles Martel, was able to annihilate the canons of the Church. They viewed the bishoprics as a sort of ministerial benefice[5], and as investing their possessors with political importance: it is not surprising, therefore, if we find a series of such kings bestowing them at random on the favourites of the court. These lax and iniquitous proceedings[6] were not, however, always unresisted by the clergy. Several councils[7], in succession, tried in vain to

<small>RELATIONS TO THE CIVIL POWER.

Points in which the civil power encroached.

Discontinuance of episcopal elections.</small>

---

[1] See the list of persons present at the Councils, in Labbe, or Mansi: and cf. Caroli Magni *Capitul.* lib. VI. c. 111.

[2] *Ancient Laws, &c.*, ed. Thorpe, I. 495. Before that time the bishop took his place at the side of the ealdorman in the county-court (scirgemót). Kemble, II. 385.

[3] For an abstract of the varied duties of a bishop at this period, see *Ancient Laws, &c.* II. 310 sq.

[4] The exceptions, under the old Roman empire, were the bishoprics of the more important cities, which in the east and west alike had been generally filled by the royal nominees. Neander, v. 127.

[5] Gieseler, II. 153. Hence the demand of military services, which some of the bishops rendered in person. Gewillieb (above, p. 22) is a striking instance of this usage, though it was less common in the eighth than in the former centuries. Charlemagne (in 801) absolutely forbade all priests from taking part in a battle. Mansi, XIII. 1054.

[6] Gregor. Turon. *Hist. Francor.* VI. 39: 'Cum multi munera offerrent,' etc. *De S. Patrum Vit.* c. 3. *de S. Gallo:* 'Jam tunc germen illud iniquum cœperat pullulare, ut sacerdotium aut venderetur a regibus aut compararetur a clericis.' Cf. Neander, v. 127 sq.; Gieseler, II. 154, n. 9. The abuse had been manifested also in Spain, where the council of Barcelona (599) forbade the elevation of *laymen* to bishoprics 'aut per sacra regalia, aut per consensionem cleri vel plebis:' can. 3: Mansi, X. 482 sq. Gregory mentions a case of this sort in *Hist. Francor.* VIII. 22.

[7] *e. g.* that of Auvergne (533), c. 2; that of Paris (557), c. 8. The

RELATIONS TO THE CIVIL POWER.

Efforts to revive the older system;

favoured in some measure by the Carolingian princes:

stem the growing evil. They were seconded by Gregory the Great[1], and in 615, a synod held at Paris had the courage to reiterate the ancient regulations. It declared[2] that all episcopal elections which have been made without the consent of the metropolitan and bishops of the province, and of the clergy and people of the city, or which have been made by violence, cabal, or bribery, are henceforth null and void. This canon was at length confirmed by Clothaire II., but not until he had so modified its meaning as to be left in possession of a veto, if not of larger powers[3]. It was afterwards repeated in 624 or 625 at Rheims, with the addition[4], 'that no one shall be consecrated bishop of a see, unless he belong to the same district, have been chosen by the people and the bishops of the province, and have been approved by a metropolitan synod.' Under Charlemagne, and the rest of the Carolingian princes, who were anxious to revive the canons of the Early Church, those efforts of the Frankish prelates to regain their independence were more uniformly carried out. The freedom of episcopal elections was, at least in words, conceded[5], and the Church was not unwilling in her turn to grant a confirmatory power to the sovereign[6]. It resulted, therefore, that a prelate, after his election, could not officiate in his

---

latter employs the following language, after directing that the elections should be made by 'the people and the clergy:' ' Quodsi per ordinationem regiam honoris istius culmen pervadere aliquis nimia temeritate præsumserit, a comprovincialibus loci ipsius *episcopus recipi nullatenus mereatur, quem indebite ordinatum agnoscunt.*'

[1] *e. g. Epist.* (A.D. 601) XI. 59, 60, 61, 63.

[2] Can. I: Labb. v. 1650.

[3] His proviso runs as follows: 'Episcopo decedente in loco ipsius, qui a metropolitano ordinari debet cum provincialibus a clero et populo eligatur: et si persona condigna fuerit, *per ordinationem principis* ordinetur: *vel certe si de palatio eligitur,* per meritum personæ et doctrinæ, ordinetur.' *Ibid.* 1653.

[4] Can. III; XXV.

[5] *e. g.* Capitul. Aquisgranense (A.D. 803), c. 2: 'Ut sancta ecclesia suo liberius potiretur honore, adsensum ordini ecclesiastico præbuimus, ut episcopi *per electionem cleri et populi, secundum statuta canonum,* de propria diocesi, remota personarum et munerum acceptione, ob vitæ meritum et sapientiæ donum, eligantur,' etc.

[6] Something like this had been already conceded in the council of Orleans (549), c. 10; where the election is appointed to be made *cum voluntate regis:* cf. above, note 3. 'The contest between election and royal nomination was often reproduced: but in every case the necessity of [the royal] confirmation was acknowledged.' Guizot, II. 31.

sacred calling till he had received the approbation of the secular authority. But, as we shall see hereafter, even where the princes were most friendly to the Church, they were loth to be deprived of so strong an engine as the privilege of naming bishops must have placed within their grasp. They seem indeed to have employed it, in some special cases, with the open acquiescence of the clergy; for a canon of the council at Toledo[1], **681**, enacted, with conditions, that a primate was at liberty to consecrate those persons whom the king should appoint to the vacant sees: and in England, where the clergy, and the people also, had a voice in the royal council (in the 'witena gemot'), the nomination of a prelate by that body, though in theory an act of the sovereign himself, approximated to the primitive election[2].

RELATIONS TO THE CIVIL POWER.

but royal nominations still common.

A second point in which the civil and ecclesiastical authorities might have come into collision was the gathering of church-assemblies. In the former period, *general* councils had been summoned by the kings, while the provincial and diocesan were held at the pleasure of the bishops. But distinctions of this kind were no longer kept in view, at least in the administration of the newly-planted churches. Numbers of the earliest and most active converts, both in Germany and in England, were connected with the royal households; and in this way it would naturally occur that measures which related to the organizing of the Church would emanate directly from the king. His power was in fact exhibited not only in the founding of episcopal sees, but in a general supervision of the clergy, and in the convocation of assemblies whether legislative or judicial. In those countries, synods (as already noted) were most frequently combined with the civil diets; though the prelates, under Charlemagne, held their sessions in a separate chamber[3]; and even where they met to determine a

Right of calling Synods

exercised by kings.

---

[1] c. VI: Labb. VI. 1221.
[2] See Kemble, *Saxons in England*, II. 377, where it is also shewn that English prelates were sometimes both appointed and displaced by a mere act of the royal will, and that bishoprics were frequently bestowed on royal chaplains. It is clear however from Alcuin's letters to the clergy of York, and from other sources, that in the latter days of the Heptarchy the right of election was recognized and really exercised by the clergy.
[3] *e. g.* this was the usage at the council of Mentz (813): cf. *Capitul.* A.D. 811, c. 4; I. 478, ed. Baluze.

RELATIONS TO THE CIVIL POWER.

Mutual confidence of the civil and ecclesiastical authorities.

doctrinal question, they were acting, for the most part, in obedience to the royal will[1].

It is indeed remarkable, that so long as kings were esteemed the real patrons of the Church[2], she felt no wish to define exactly her relations to the civil power: the two authorities, in some way parallel and independent, laboured to enforce obedience to each other[3]. This was manifested more especially in Charlemagne and the Anglo-Saxon princes, who seem to have maintained, with few exceptions, a most friendly bearing to the Church, and to have everywhere infused a mutual confidence into the courts, the bishops, and the people.

Effects of this on society.

Gifted in this manner with peculiar powers[4] in virtue of their close alliance with the State, the clergy, and especially the prelates, were enabled to exert a salutary influence on the daily temper of the kings, and on the administration of the laws. Their frequent intercessions in behalf of criminals, and the asylums[5] opened in their churches for

---

[1] 'Orta quæstione de sancta Trinitate, et de sanctorum imaginibus, inter orientalem et occidentalem ecclesiam, id est, Romanos et Græcos, rex Pippinus [A.D. 767], conventu in Gentiliaco villa congregato, synodum de ipsa quæstione habuit.' Einhardi *Annales:* Pertz. I. 145. In like manner, numerous councils were convoked by Charlemagne ('jussu ejus'). *Ibid.* I. 38, 87, 181, 196, 200.

[2] Alcuin, writing to Charlemagne (799) a letter (*Ep.* LXXX. al. XCV.) in many ways remarkable, thus speaks of his relation to the Church: 'Ecce! in te solo tota salus ecclesiarum Christi inclinata recumbit. Tu vindex scelerum, tu rector errantium, tu consolator mœrentium, tu exaltatio bonorum.' *Opp.* I. 117. He had just been deploring the evils of the times, and especially the insurrection of the Romans against Leo III.: cf. *Annales Lauresham.;* Pertz, I. 38. There can indeed be no doubt respecting the extent of the royal prerogative, as it was wielded by the hands of Charlemagne. Though he exempted the clergy more than ever from the jurisdiction of the civil courts (*Capit.* A.D. 801, c. 1) he retained the highest judicial power in all civil causes, even where the litigants were bishops (*Capit.* A.D. 812, c. 1). By means of the *missi* (two extraordinary judges, a bishop, and a count), he was able to keep a continual check on the administration both of ecclesiastical and of civil officers: *Capitul.* III., A.D. 789, c. ii. and elsewhere: cf. Gieseler, II. 241 sq.: Guizot, II. 319, 320.

[3] 'L'Eglise était tellement identifiée avec l'état, qu'il y avait alors plutôt confusion que rivalité entre eux.' Guérard, *Cartulaire de l'Eglise de Notre Dame*, Pref. p. xxi. Cf. Ranke, *Reformation,* I. 6, 7; Lond. 1845.

[4] How multifarious were the rights and duties of the bishops may be seen from the Anglo-Saxon *Institutes of Eccl. Polity;* Thorpe, II. 312 sq. Doubtless one result of their position was to secularize their spirit; and of this Alcuin frequently complains: *e. g.* 'Pastores curæ turbant sæculares, qui Deo vacare debuerunt:' *Ep.* CXII. (al. CLI.) *Opp.* I. 163.

[5] The abuses of the right of sanctuary were checked by the inter-

the persecuted and the friendless, were effectual in subduing the austerity of justice, and impressing on a rude, impetuous and revengeful age the sacredness of human life. A singular effect of the alliance now cemented in the west, between the Church and civil power, was the drafting of a large body of the serfs into the ranks of the working clergy. It was usual for the free-men of a country to assist in the military service; but as all were exempted who had taken orders, many persons were now anxious to be numbered with the clerics, for the sake of evading the injunction of the State. A law was accordingly passed, forbidding any free-man to become a priest (or even to retire into a convent), until he had secured the acquiescence of the king[1]. It happened as an immediate consequence, that prelates[2] were constrained to levy their recruits from a different class of men; and as the serfs were almost everywhere enfranchised as a step to ordination, this enactment of the civil power was tending in a high degree to humanize and to ennoble the most abject of our race[3].

RELATIONS TO THE CIVIL POWER.

How the relations of Church and State affected slaves.

position of the civil law. Thus the *Capitulare* of Charlemagne, A.D. 779, cap. 6, forbids any bishop or abbot to give shelter to a thief or murderer. In England, however, if the criminal took refuge in a church enjoying the privilege of asylum, a law of Ine (688—725) provided that his life should be spared, but that he should make the legal 'bot,' or satisfaction, § 5; Thorpe, I. 104.

[1] See can. 4 of the council of Orleans (511): Baluzii *Capitular*. II. 386. In 805, *Capitul.* c. 15, the law is extended to all free-men 'qui ad servitium Dei se tradere volunt,' *i.e.* who wish to become either clerics or monks.

[2] In the rule for canons, sanctioned by the council at Aix-la-Chapelle (816) it is stated that many of the prelates selected their clergy *exclusively* from the serfs (can. CXIX.), and did so in defiance of the laws requiring them to be manumitted before ordination: *e. g.* Council of Toledo (633), can. LXXIV. The object was to keep them more entirely under the lash of episcopal discipline (severissimis verberibus): Mansi, XIV. 230.

[3] See Neander's remarks on this point, and on the general feelings of the Church with regard to slavery: v. 133—139. Another remarkable instance of the change produced by Christianity is seen in the Anglo-Saxon *Institutes*, &c., ed. Thorpe, II. 314, where the lord is enjoined to protect his thralls, on the ground that 'they and those that are free are equally dear to God, who bought us all with equal value.' Perhaps no feature of the Middle Ages is more striking than the influence of the Church in teaching the equality of men, and opening a way to preferment for the humblest of her members. Any one might be received into a monastery: he could then be ordained, and if possessing superior qualifications might advance to the very highest eminence in Church and State. In this manner some of the evils, arising out of the hereditary character of feudalism, were largely counteracted; and the Church became the champion and promoter of popular rights.

CHAPTER III.

ON THE STATE OF RELIGIOUS DOCTRINE AND CONTROVERSIES.

WESTERN CHURCH.

WESTERN CHURCH.

Veneration for the Holy Scriptures.

A FEW of the minor discrepancies[1] in the lists of the Scripture-canon had come over to the present period; but in every quarter of the Church a cordial veneration for the teaching of the Bible had continued as of old. It was the treasury of supernatural wisdom and the fountain of religious truth. A personal investigation of it was accordingly required[2] in those who had learned to read, although the number of such persons at this epoch would be relatively small; while ignorance or meagre knowledge of its pages was regarded as a bar to holy orders[3].

[1] See Schröckh. xx. 191 sq. and Bp. Cosin, *Hist. of the Canon*, ch. IX. x.

[2] Thus the English canons of Clovesho (747), after complaining that too many 'rather pursued the amusements of this present unstable life than the assiduous study of the Holy Scripture,' proceed as follows: 'Therefore let the boys be confined and trained up in the schools to the law of sacred knowledge, that being by this means well-learned, they may become in all respects useful to the Church of God.' *English Canons*, ed. Johnson, I. 246, *Oxf.* 1850. Cf. the language of Aldhelm, in Wharton's *Anglia Sacra*, II. 5 (*Opp.* ed. Giles, p. 334); and *De Laudibus Virginitatis*, § 4, p. 4. One of the motives of Charlemagne in forwarding the restoration of letters was a fear lest the prevailing ignorance should lead to misconceptions of the Bible: 'ne sicut minor in scribendo erat prudentia, ita quoque et *multo minor in eis, quam recte esse debuisset, esset sanctarum Scripturarum ad intelligendum sapientia.*' *Capitul.* ed. Baluze, I. 201.

[3] *e.g.* Council of *Toledo* (633), can. xxv; *Arles* (813), can. I. Alcuin (797) thus exhorts the people of his native land (*Ep.* LIX. al. LXXIV. *Opp.* I. 78): 'Primo omnium qui in ecclesia Christi Deo deserviunt, discant diligenter, quomodo Deo placeant, quomodo fidem catholicam, quam primum doctores nostri in eis fundaverunt, obtinere firmiter et prædicare valeant; quia *ignorantia Scripturarum ignorantia Dei est*...Adducite vobis doctores et magistros *Sanctæ Scripturæ, ne sit inopia* apud vos Verbi Dei, etc.' In confuting misbelievers, it was usual to insist on that

From their mode of interpreting the Scriptures, it is plain that the Latin doctors sympathized with St Augustine, and were generally disposed to follow in his steps. Of his more eminent disciples we have one in the Roman bishop, Gregory the Great, who forms the transition-link in our descent from the early to the mediæval schools of thought. He had imbibed the predominating spirit of the west: he clung to the authoritative language of the councils with implicit and unreasoning belief[1]. His writings, therefore, stand in some way contrasted with the subtler and more independent labours of the Eastern theologians, where, especially in men like John of Damascus[2], we may trace a continual effort to establish the traditions of the past on dialectic grounds. So far, indeed, was Gregory the Great from prying into speculative matters, that he seems to have confined himself exclusively to one (the more practical) aspect of the Augustinian system[3]. Like his master, he was strongly conscious of the vast and all-holy attributes of God, the depth and malignity of evil, and the moral impotence of man un-

WESTERN CHURCH.

Theology of Gregory the Great.

The practical bent of his teaching.

---

interpretation of the Scriptures, which accorded with the teaching of the Fathers; *e. g.* 'Tantum Divina voluit providentia, ut rescriberetur in evangelicæ celsitudinis auctoritatem, sanctorumque patrum probabilibus literis, quantum ad nostram sufficere salutem censuit. Illis utamur nominibus de Christo, quæ in veteri novoque Testamento inveniuntur scripta. Sufficiat nobis apostolicæ auctoritatis doctrina, et catholicorum Patrum longo tempore explorata fides.' Alcuin, adv. *Elipandum*, lib. IV. c. 14; *Opp.* I. 914.

[1] Thus at his consecration, he wrote a synodal letter to the other patriarchs (591) testifying his reverence for the Œcumenical councils. Mansi, IX. 1041. Several Spanish Councils (*e.g.* Toledo, 653) did the same: and the English synod of Cealchythe (787) particularizes the Nicene and six General Councils. Wilkins, I. 146.—The only case in which the Western Church appears to vary from this rule relates to the important clause *Filioque*, added to the Niceno-Constantinopolitan creed. The addition can be clearly traced to Spain (Council of Toledo, 589: Mansi, IX. 981). It excited the displeasure of the Greeks about 767 (see *Annales Lauriss.* ad an.: Pertz, I. 144); but the dispute did not come to a head till 809. The clause was everywhere inserted (in the west) at the bidding of Pope Nicholas I. (867): Mansi, XV. 355. See Neale's *Eastern Church*, 'Introd.' pp. 1147 sqq. The defenders of it relied on the 'Athanasian Creed,' now quite current in the Latin Church. Waterland, *Hist. of Athan. Creed.* ch. VI.

[2] Scholasticism properly so called, had its starting-point in him. See below on the 'Eastern Church.'

[3] Neander, *C. H.* v. 197 sq. whose criticism on Gregory the Great is generous and just. The influence exercised by Gregory on the government of the Church has been pointed out already: see p. 39.

WESTERN CHURCH.

The errors he was instrumental in spreading.

quickened by the Blessed Spirit; yet was careful to explain at large the power of self-determination, or the freedom of the human will[1]. He urged on all around him[2], and especially on those who were occupied in teaching[3], their own need of internal holiness and purity of conscience. Although placing a peculiar stress on the liturgic element of worship[4], and on a stern and ascetic training of the body, he was far from losing sight of the essence of religion, or from exalting human merit into rivalry with Christ's[5]. The work that presents him to our view in a less favourable light, is made up of a series of *Dialogues*, in which he has betrayed an excessive credulity. It is there also that the doctrine of a purgatorial fire, which had been long[6] floating in the western churches, gained a fuller and more definite expression. It is principally based upon the evidence of disembodied spirits[7]; and as their pains are said to have been mitigated by the 'oblation of the salutary host'[8], the views which men took

---

[1] 'Quia præveniente Divina gratia in operatione bona, nostrum liberum arbitrium sequitur, nosmetipsos liberare dicimur, qui liberanti nos Domino consentimus,' etc. *Moralia in Job.* lib. xxiv. § 24. This work, in thirty-five books, consists of a practico-allegorical exposition of the book of Job, and furnishes a clear view of Gregory's ethical system. He wrote also twenty-two *Homilies* on Ezekiel, and forty *Homilies* on the Gospels.

[2] e.g. *Moralia*, lib. xix. § 38.

[3] See his *Regula Pastoralis*, which is a fine proof of his ministerial earnestness, and was largely circulated in the west.

[4] His *Liber Sacramentorum* (or Sacramentary) was adopted in the countries which received their Christianity from Rome, and has been substantially preserved ever since. For an account of the liturgical changes due to him, see Palmer's *Origines Liturg.* I. 113 sq., 126 sq., 4th edit.: Fleury's *Histoire Eccles.* liv. xxxvi. § 146.

[5] *Homil. in Evangel.* xxxiv.: 'Habete ergo fiduciam, fratres mei, de misericordia Conditoris nostri, cogitate quæ facite, recogitate quæ fecistis.' Largitatem supernæ pietatis aspicite, et ad misericordem Judicem, dum adhuc expectat, cum lachrymis venite. Considerantes namque quod justus sit, peccata vestra nolite negligere: considerantes vero quod pius sit, nolite desperare. *Præbet apud Deum homini fiduciam Deus homo.* Est nobis spes magna pœnitentibus, quia Advocatus noster factus est Judex noster.' *Opp.* I. 1611. ed. Bened.

[6] See Schröckh, xvii. 332 sq. Neander iv. 442, 443. St Augustine viewed the doctrine of a purgatory in the mediæval sense as somewhat doubtful: 'Incredibile non est, et utrum ita sit, quæri potest.' *Ibid.*

[7] *Dialog.* lib. iv. c. 35, 39, 46, 51, 55. It should be stated that some writers have questioned the genuineness of this treatise; but Mabillon (*Act. Sanct. Ordin. Benedict.* tom. I. § 2) and the Benedictine editor of Gregory's *Works*, appear to have the better of the argument.

[8] *Ibid.* c. 55: 'Si culpæ [i.e. *leves* culpæ, c. 39] post mortem insolu-

henceforward of the sacrament itself would be distorted in the same proportion.

Gregory was succeeded in the west by Isidore of Seville (Hispalensis), who died in **636**. He was a large and intelligent contributor to the literature of Spain. In addition to his other writings, he has left a minute description of the Mozarabic (or Old Spanish) liturgy[1]; but his chief treatise in the sphere of dogmatical theology consists of a train of thoughts[2] on Christian faith and practice. They are drawn, however, in most cases, from the fertile works of St Augustine, and from the *Moralia* of Gregory the Great.

In England[3] one of the ripest scholars[4] that the Roman mission to the Anglo-Saxon had produced was the Venerable Beda (Bede). At the age of seven years he found his way into the monastery of Jarrow[5], in whose cloisters

WESTERN CHURCH.

Isidore of Seville. (595—636).

Venerable Bede. (672—735).

biles non sunt, multum solet animas etiam post mortem sacra oblatio hostiæ salutaris adjuvare,' etc.
  [1] *De Officiis Ecclesiasticis:* cf. Palmer's *Origines Litur.* I. 172 sq.
  [2] *De summo Bono* or *Sententiarum Libri Tres.* Isidore was followed in this line by Tajo of Saragossa and Ildefonsus of Toledo. On the canons attributed to him, see Blondel's *Pseudo-Isidorus*, and above, p. 41, n. 1, &c.
  [3] Famed as were the 'magistri e Scotia' (Ireland), and high as that country stood in literary merits, it produced no distinguished writer at this period. Columbanus (see above, p. 16) is the solitary theologian: for Adamnan (d. 704) though perhaps of Irish extraction, composed no more than a treatise *de Situ Terræ Sanctæ*, and a *Life of St Columba*.
  [4] Others were Bp. Aldhelm (656—709), chiefly known by his poem and prose treatise *De Laude Virginitatis*, (*Opp.* ed. Giles, Oxon. 1844); Eddius, the biographer of Wilfrith; Boniface, the missionary, author of fifteen popular Sermons, and the Letters so often quoted in the last chapter. To this number we may add Archbp. Theodore (668—690), whose mission into England was the opening of a new era in the cultivation of all kinds of learning (Bed. *Hist. Eccl.* IV. 2), and whose *Penitential* furnishes an important collection of disciplinary canons. Of this famous work there were many imitations at an early period, and under its name some later treatises of a much more extensive character passed current. It is given in its genuine form by Wasserschleben, in *Die Bussordnungen der Abendländischen Kirche*, Halle, 1851; and in the *Councils and Ecclesiastical Documents*, ed. Haddan and Stubbs, III. 176 sq. The book published under the title in the *Ancient Laws*, by Thorpe, is a work of much later date and of Frankish origin. A still older example of the class is a work of John the Faster, patriarch of Constantinople (585—593), published in the Appendix of the *Hist. de Disciplina Pœnitent.* by Morinus, Paris, 1651. Compare also the *Liber Gildæ de Pœnitentia*, which is still earlier. *Councils*, &c. I. 119.
  [5] This was the foundation of Benedict Biscop, who aided more than any other person in the civilizing of the north of England. His last anx-

Ecgberht (? 678— 766).

he continued till his death, absorbed by the offices of tranquil worship, or engaged in collecting and communicating knowledge. So ardent was his thirst for learning, that it urged him into almost every field of mediæval study; but he has himself informed us, that he found a special satisfaction in the pages of the Bible[1]. His expository works, comprising Sermons and Commentaries, evince a knowledge both of Greek and Hebrew; in their style and spirit, and in much also of their material, they resemble the more ancient writings of the Fathers, and especially of St Augustine[2].

A bosom-friend of Beda, who transmitted the impression he had made on the whole of the Western Church, was Ecgberht, archbishop of York, where he founded a noble school and library[3], and was distinguished for his patronage of letters[4]. In the crowd[5] of enthusiastic pupils, whom his talents had attracted to the north of England, was a native of his mother-city, Alcuin or Albinus, who was destined to become the master-spirit of the age.

iety was for his books, 'bibliothecam quam de Roma nobilissimam copiosissimamque advexerat.' See Beda's Life of him in *Vit. Abbatum Uuiremuth.*, (at the end of the *Hist. Eccl.* ed. Hussey), pp. 316—325.

[1] ......' cunctumque ex eo tempus vitæ in ejusdem monasterii habitatione peragens, omnem *meditandis Scripturis* operam dedi, atque inter observantiam disciplinæ regularis et quotidianam cantandi in ecclesia curam, *semper aut discere aut docere, aut scribere dulce habui.*' *Hist. Eccl.* v. 24. Nothing can be more simple and pathetic than the narrative which a disciple (Cuthbert) has left us of his last hours. See Wright's *Biogr. Brit. Literar.* I. 267, 268. He had only just completed a translation of St John's Gospel into Anglo-Saxon, when he died, in the midst of his weeping scholars, with a 'Gloria Patri' on his lips.

[2] This connexion is most obvious in the *Commentaria in omnes Epistolas S. Pauli*. The other works of a decidedly theological cast are, *Explanatio in Pentateuchum et Libros Regum; in Samuelem; in Psalmos, in Esdram, Tobiam, Job, Proverbia, et Cantica; in Quatuor Evangelia, et Acta Apostolorum; in Epistolas Catholicas et Apocalypsin;* besides a number of *Sermones de Tempore*, and others.

[3] See an account of its contents in Wright's *Biograph. Liter.* I. pp. 37, 38.

[4] His own genuine works are, a *Dialogus Ecclesiasticæ Institutionis* (in Latin) and a Penitential published first in its integrity by Wasserschleben in his "Bussordnungen" and in the *Councils, &c.* III. 416 sq. The penitential works commonly ascribed to him, printed in Thorpe and Wilkins, are of much later date and foreign origin.

[5] 'Erat siquidem ei ex nobilium filiis grex scholasticorum, quorum quidam artis grammaticæ rudimentis, alii disciplinis erudiebantur artium jam liberalium, nonnulli *Divinarum Scripturarum*, etc. *Vit. Alcuini*, c. II. composed in 829, and prefixed to his *Works*.

His fame having reached the court of Charlemagne, he was pressed to take part in the projects of that monarch for securing a more healthy action in the members of the Frankish church. Directing the scholastic institutions, prompting or tempering the royal counsels, foremost in the work of domestic reformation, and conspicuous for the breadth and clearness of his views with regard to the management of missions[1], Alcuin carried to his grave the admiration of his fellow-countrymen, and of the whole of western Europe. His theology, as it survives in his expository works[2], is like that of Gregory and Beda, with whose writings he had been familiar from his youth: it bears the common Augustinian impress. He has left, however, certain systematic treatises[3] on fundamental truths of revelation, as well as on absorbing questions of the day: and in these he has exhibited, not only his entire acceptance of the teaching of the past, but an acute and well-balanced mind.

Alcuin (? 735—804.)

From Alcuin we pass over to a controversy in which he bore a leading part,—the controversy known as the *Adoptionist*, but in reality a phase of Nestorianism revived[4]. It is the one formidable tempest[5] of this period which had its birth-place in the Western Church. The authors of it were two Spanish prelates (in the latter half of the eighth century), Elipandus of Toledo and Felix of Urgel (a town of Catalonia), who, as it would seem, in their anxiety to

Rise of the Adoptionist heresy:

---

[1] See above, pp. 24, 26.
[2] These are, *Questions and Answers on the Book of Genesis*, Commentaries on the *Pœnitential Psalms*, the *Song of Solomon, Ecclesiastes*, St John's Gospel, and three *Epistles of St Paul*.
[3] The chief are *De Fide Trinitatis* (a body of Divinity), *De Processione Spiritus Sancti* (defending the Western view of it), and his contributions to the Adoptionist controversy (see below, pp. 62—64).
[4] 'Ecce pars quædam mundi hæreticæ pravitatis veneno infecta est, asserens Christum Jesum Deo Patri verum non esse Filium, nec proprium, sed adoptivum: et *Nestoriana hæresis* ab oriente...longum postliminium reviviscens, latitando fugit in occidentem'...Alcuin, *Libellus adv. Hæresin Felicis*, § 2. It is not clear, however, that the authors of the movement were acquainted with the writings of the Nestorian school. For a complete history of it, see J. C. F. Walch, *Hist. Adoptianorum*; Neander, v. 216—233; and Dorner, *Lehre von der Person Christi*, II. 306—329; Berlin, 1853.
[5] For minor struggles in England and Germany, see above pp. 8, 22, 23. It is clear also from Alcuin, (*Epist.* CCXXI. al. CCXXV. *Opp.* 1. 285). that other classes of dissentients ('adversarios Apostolicæ doctrinæ') were not wanting.

WESTERN CHURCH.

its essential resemblance to Nestorianism.

make the truth of the Incarnation less offensive to Muhammedans[1], maintained[2] that our blessed Lord, *as man*, was the proper son of David; or, in other words, that in respect of His humanity, He was only the *adoptive* Son of God ('Deus nuncupativus et adoptivus Filius'). In support of their position[3], Felix, the more learned misbeliever, ventured to reoccupy the ground of the Nestorian, though their arguments were put in a somewhat different form. They seized on the expressions of the Bible which unfolded the subordinate relations of the Son, in His mediatorial work; and while admitting, that, *as God*, He was truly and eternally begotten of the Father[4], they inferred that the humanity of Christ was so dissociable from the Godhead as to be no more than a Temple for the Logos[5],—no more than a creature chosen to become the organ of the Lord, in a way not essentially unlike[6] the adoption of all Christians as the family and instruments of God. The creed of Felix did not recognize in the Incarnate Saviour any true assumption of man's nature into fellowship with the Divine: he was accordingly most scrupulous in his distinction of the predicates belonging unto each; and even went so far as to impute the prayers, the sufferings, and the death of Christ to a necessity inherent in His manhood[7], and not to a voluntary condescension of the Godhead with which humanity was made indissolubly

---

[1] Neander, *ibid.* p. 219.

[2] ...'dicentes, Deum esse verum, qui ex Deo natus est, et Deum nuncupativum, hominem illum, qui de Virgine factus est.' Alcuin, *adv. Elipand.* lib. IV. c. 5. They made an appeal to older authorities (see the *Epist. Elipandi ad Albinum;* Alcuin, *Opp.* II. 868 sq.), especially to the language of the Mozarabic (old Spanish) Liturgy, then in use, where the term 'adoption' is employed to denote the assumption of our nature into unity with God. Alcuin reproached Elipandus with substituting 'adoptivi' for 'assumpti.'

[3] The main authorities are to be found in the works of Alcuin, (1) *Libellus adversus Hæresin Felicis Episcopi*, (2) *Contra Felicem Urgellitanum Episcopum;* to which may be added, (3) the treatise quoted in the last note.

[4] 'Deum Dei Filium ante omnia tempora sine initio ex Patre genitum, non adoptione sed genere, neque gratia sed natura, etc.'

[5] Alcuin, *contra Felicem*, lib. VII. c. 2.

[6] He compared the adoption of Christ with that of Christians, admitting, however, that the relation constituted in the former case was higher in degree ('excellentius'). Alcuin, *contra Felicem*, lib. II. c. 15, sq., and especially the language of Felix himself, lib. IV. c. 2.

[7] *Ibid.* lib. VII. c. 15.

one. Adoptionism, in other words, if carried to its logical results, would have resolved the connexion that subsisted in the two-fold natures of our Lord into a moral and extrinsic union: it was fatal, therefore, to a truth which, of all others, will be found to lie the nearest to the core of Christianity,—the Incarnation of the Saviour.

After lighting up a controversy in the Spanish church[1], Adoptionism extended into Gothia (the adjacent parts of France), where it had soon to encounter a decisive overthrow. It was examined, at the wish of Charlemagne, by the synod of Ratisbon[2] (792), where Felix, as belonging to the Frankish empire, had been summoned to appear. On witnessing the condemnation of his tenets, he renounced them on the spot, and, as a penance, was sent to the court of Rome[3] to repeat his abjuration. But no sooner was he lodged, on his return, in the Saracenic provinces of Spain, than he relapsed into his former errors[4]. Elipandus[5] in the mean time represented the injustice of the recent acts, and earnestly desired the emperor to call another synod. His request led the way to the convoking of a more numerous council in 794, at Frankfort[6], where the verdict of the former synod was confirmed. Soon after this decision, Alcuin, who was personally known to Felix, opened a more friendly[7] correspondence with the champions of the system there exploded; and although

Opposition to Adoptionism.

Its condemnation.

---

[1] Two ecclesiastics were its chief antagonists, Etherius, bishop of Osma, and Beatus, a priest. The latter had employed himself in expounding the Apocalypse, and was the author of the fragment *Adversus Elipandum*, in Canisius, *Lect. Antiq.* II. 279—375, ed. Basnage. Elipandus, on the other side, denounced his antagonism as the work of Antichrist. *Ibid.* 310.

[2] Cf. Schröckh, xx. 465, 466, respecting the accounts of earlier proceedings.

[3] Pertz, I. 179. In the following year (793) the pope (Hadrian I.) wrote a letter to the Spanish clergy, threatening to proceed against Elipandus. Mansi, XIII. 865.

[4] Alcuin, *adv. Elipand.* lib. I. c. 16.

[5] See *Epist. Episcop. Hispan. ad Carolum Magn.* in Alcuin. *Opp.* II. 567.

[6] A Roman Council (799) appears to have affirmed the last decision. Labb. VII. 1150. Pagi, however, places this Roman Council earlier, ad an. 792: Mansi, XIII. 857.

[7] 'Cui [*i. e.* Felici] in has adveniens partes caritatis calamo epistolam exhortatoriam, ut se catholicæ jungeret unitati, dirigere curavi.' *Adv. Elipand.* lib. I. c. 16. The letter alluded to is in his *Works*, I. 783.

WESTERN CHURCH.

and suppression.

by Elipandus, who did not live in the Frankish empire, all his arguments were met with bitterness and scorn, upon the other he was able to produce at least a transitory change[1]. They had a long interview in the synod held at Aix-la-Chapelle, 799, when Felix, vanquished for awhile by his opponent, promised to abandon the delusion, and in future to be guided by the teaching of the Church. But as few of the prelates were induced to rely upon this promise, they delivered him, with the approval of the emperor, into the custody of Leidrad, archbishop of Lyons. At his death, which occurred in 816, it was plain from an extant paper that he still adhered to his former creed on almost every point[2]. It fell, however, into silence and oblivion ere its vacillating author had been taken from the scene of conflict.

EASTERN CHURCH.

Monotheletism:

its nature.

EASTERN CHURCH.

As the heresy of Nestorius had been reawakened in the Latin Church, that of Eutyches (or the Monophysite) recurred, in the opening of the present period (633—680), to engage the more speculative doctors of the East. It was held, notwithstanding the definitions of Chalcedon, that our belief in the union of Two Natures in the Person of the Son of God involves, as one of its consequences, our belief in His singleness of will and operation. (In the reasoning of this party, known as the *Monotheletes*[3], the actions of our Lord, both human and Divine, must be ascribed to a single energy within Him ($\dot{\epsilon}\nu\acute{\epsilon}\rho\gamma\epsilon\iota a\ \Theta\epsilon a\nu$-$\delta\rho\iota\kappa\acute{\eta}$); they were said to spring from the Logos only, as the one proper source, although the human element in Christ was *not* verbally denied, but viewed as the passive agent of His Godhead[4]. It resulted, therefore, that

---

[1] Alcuin was assisted by a committee of inquiry, whom Charlemagne sent on two occasions into the districts (chiefly Languedoc), where Adoptionism had gained a footing. *Epist.* XCII. al. CVIII. p. 136. He had also a coadjutor in Paulinus, patriarch of Aquileia, who wrote two Treatises, *Sacrosyllabus* and *Adversus Felicem*, in refutation of Adoptionism: *Opp.* Venet. 1737.

[2] See the *Liber adv. Dogma Felicis*, by Agobard, who succeeded Leidrad as archbishop of Lyons: *Agobardi Opp.* ed. Baluze, 1666.

[3] = Μονοθελῆται, a name which was not given to them till the following century.

[4] See the Fragments of Theodore of Pharan in Mansi, XI. 567 sq. He asserts that in our Lord εἶναι μίαν ἐνέργειαν· ταύτης δὲ τεχνίτην καὶ

the current usage of distinguishing between the natures of our Lord was founded on no difference or duality in Him, but on abstractions of the human mind.

EASTERN CHURCH.

The author of this heresy was an Arabian bishop, Theodore of Pharan, who brought over to his views no less a personage than Sergius, the patriarch of the Byzantine capital. He was supported also by the emperor, Heraclius, who thought he could discover in the school of Theodore an apt and auspicious medium for disarming the hostility of the Monophysites, and winning back the Armenian provinces, which by their help had been transferred to the rule of Persia. At his desire a Formulary was composed, which in the hands of the pliant Cyrus[1], formerly of Phasis. but now translated to the see of Alexandria (630), effected a reunion of the Monophysites, or Jacobites, with the Melchites, or the Church (633). It was cemented by nine Articles of concord[2], in the seventh of which the heresy of Theodore was formally acknowledged. A monk of Palestine, Sophronius, happening to be then at Alexandria, foresaw the disastrous issues of the compromise, and set out immediately for Constantinople to unburden his dismay to the patriarch in person. Though the protests he there entered were unheeded, he was placed in the following year, by his election to the patriarchal chair of Jerusalem, in a more commanding station. Sergius, now (as it would seem) afraid of his opposition, attempted to enlist the influence of the Roman bishop on the side of the Monotheletes, and in that he was eminently successful. The surviving letters of Honorius (634) leave no doubt as to

The author of it.

Its growth promoted by political influence.

The compromise with the Jacobites in Egypt.

Resistance of Sophronius.

δημιουργὸν τὸν Θεόν, ὄργανον δὲ τὴν ἀνθρωπότητα. The difficulty of the Monotheletes, as we see most plainly in the case of Honorius, bishop of Rome, was in admitting that a two-fold will could subsist, in one and the same subject, without conflict and opposition. They placed great stress on a phrase μιᾷ (or, as others read, καινῇ) θεανδρικῇ ἐνεργείᾳ, which occurs in the writings of the Pseudo-Dionysius (*Ibid.* 565). On the vast influence exercised by this author in stimulating the dialectico-mystical tendencies of the East, see Neander, v. 234 sq.; and Dorner, *Lehre von der Person Christi*, 2ʳ Theil, 196 sq.

[1] He at first seems to have hesitated, but his scruples were removed by Sergius. *Cyri Epist. ad. Sergium*, Mansi, xi. 561.

[2] Mansi, xi. 563. In the 7th Art. it was stated: τὸν αὐτὸν ἕνα Χριστὸν καὶ υἱὸν ἐνεργοῦντα τὰ θεοπρεπῆ καὶ ἀνθρώπινα μιᾷ θεανδρικῇ ἐνεργείᾳ. The Monophysites, who were numerous and powerful in Egypt, looked upon the concordat as a triumph: while not a few of the Melchites quitted the communion of Cyrus. Neale, *Eastern Church*, ii. 63.

M. A.   F

EASTERN CHURCH.

Publication of the Ecthesis, 638.

Opposed in the Western Church.

his approval of the policy adopted by the Eastern emperor, and signify his full agreement with the novelties of Sergius[1]. They produced, however, no effect on the patriarch of Jerusalem, who strenuously maintained his ground[2] until 637, when the cloud of Islamism which had gathered over Syria shut him out from all further notice. In 638, the emperor, assisted as before, put forth an expository edict[3] ("Εκθεσις τῆς πίστεως), in which it is peremptorily ordered, that while the doctrine of one Person must be held in accordance with conciliar definitions, nothing more is to be said or published on the single or the two-fold mode of operation (μίαν ἢ δύο ἐνεργείας). But in respect of the second point, it ventured to determine that there is in Christ one only will, and that the teaching of the other school leads necessarily to the idea of two *antagonistic* wills (δύο καὶ ταῦτα ἐναντία θελήματα),—an assumption, it will be remarked, as arbitrary as it is unfounded. The appearance of this edict, though it roused no active opposition either at the seat of power, or in the patriarchate of Alexandria, was differently regarded by the Christians of the west. At Rome, a successor of Honorius, John IV., deliberately rejected the imperial edict, first[4], in a synod (641), and next in the letters he addressed to Constantine[5], the son of Heraclius, and to Pyrrhus[6], who now occupied the chair of Sergius. Still their edict kept its ground

---

[1] 'Unam voluntatem fatemur Domini nostri Jesu Christi:' Mansi, XI. 539. 'Utrum autem propter opera Divinitatis et humanitatis una, an geminæ operationes debeant derivatæ dici vel intelligi, ad nos ista pertinere non debent: relinquentes ea grammaticis, qui solent parvulis exquisita derivando nomina venditare.' *Ib.* 542: cf. a second letter of the same kind, *ib.* 579. He even explains away the text, 'Father, not My will, but Thine be done,' as if it were spoken merely for the instruction of the faithful, and was no index of the human will of Christ. On these accounts the name of Honorius was placed among those whom the sixth general Council (680) anathematized. Some Romanists have attempted to evade or deny this fact: but see, among others, Bossuet, *Defensio Declar. Cleri Gallicani*, II. 128.

[2] See his γράμματα ἐνθρονιστικά (a circular issued when he entered on his office), in Act. XI. of the Œcumenical Council (680): Mansi, XI. 462 sq.

[3] Mansi, X. 992. It is borrowed, in some parts word for word, from an epistle of Sergius to Honorius of Rome; *ibid.* XI. 529.

[4] Theophanes, *Chronograph.* I. 508: ed. Bonn.

[5] Mansi, X. 682.

[6] *Ib.* XI. 9.

in spite of the denunciations of the west[1], and Paul, who succeeded Pyrrhus[2] in 642, adhered in like manner to the Monothelete opinions.

EASTERN CHURCH.

But they had soon to encounter a severe antagonist in Maximus, the Confessor (? 580—655), one of the most eminent writers of the period, and distinguished by a clear and profound perception of the true humanity of Christ[3]. Originally an important personage at court, he had afterwards embraced the monastic life, and risen to the post of hegumenos, or abbot, of Chrysopolis (on the Asiatic side of the Bosphorus). But as he was opposed to the ruling party in his view of Monotheletism, he retreated into Africa, where his erudition and acuteness[4] were employed in making converts; and in 649 we find him at the Lateran, enkindling the zeal of pope Martin I.

Maximus, the Confessor.

In the previous year (648), the emperor Constans II., anxious to restore tranquillity and order, had determined to withdraw the 'Ecthesis' and to replace it by another edict of a less dogmatic character, entitled 'Type of the Faith' (Τύπος τῆς πίστεως). It forbad[5] all kinds of disputations on the willing and the working of our Lord, and that under heavy penalties; confining the dissentients, whether lay or clerical, within the terms of the older councils of the Church. But, politic as it might seem, this measure was peculiarly offensive to the champions of the truth. In their eyes it was harsh, one-sided, and despotic; and, still more, was calculated to engender disbelief with regard to a cardinal point of their religion[6]. In the west, therefore, Martin I. immediately convoked

Publication of the Type.

---

[1] Thus, Theodore, bishop of Rome, after a long correspondence with the Monotheletes, undertakes (648) to deprive the Byzantine patriarch. *Vit. Theodor.* in Vignolii *Lib. Pontif.* I. 257.

[2] Pyrrhus abdicated on account of his unpopularity, fled into Africa, abjured his Monothelete opinions (645) at Rome, but speedily fell into them afresh and recovered his see in 654.

[3] Cf. Neand. v. 250—254. Some of his works are collected by Combefis in 2 vols. *Par.* 1675. For an account of the rest, see Smith's *Biogr. Dict.*

[4] See his *Disputatio cum Pyrrho: Opp.* II. 159—195.

[5] Mansi, x. 1029...θεσπίζομεν...μὴ ἄδειαν ἔχειν πρὸς ἀλλήλους ἀπὸ τοῦ παρόντος περὶ ἑνὸς θελήματος ἢ μιᾶς ἐνεργείας, ἢ δύο ἐνεργειῶν καὶ δύο θελημάτων, οἱανδήποτε προφέρειν ἀμφισβήτησιν, ἔριν τε, καὶ φιλονεικίαν.

[6] See *Epist. Abbat. et Monachor. in Synodo Lateran.* apud Mansi x. 904. These were Oriental monks and abbots who had fled to Rome for an asylum.

EASTERN CHURCH.

Conduct of Martin I.

a synod (649), which condemned the heresy of the Monotheletes as well as the 'Ecthesis' and 'Type,' and anathematized[1] its principal abettors, Theodore of Pharan, Sergius, Cyrus, Pyrrhus, and Paul, at that time patriarch of Constantinople. Though the emperor was not personally touched by the fulminations of this council, the proceedings had aroused his deepest indignation. He instructed the Byzantine exarch (his governor in Italy) to enforce compliance with the 'Type,' and ultimately (653) to proceed to the attainder of the pope, who had made himself obnoxious to the charge of high treason. The command was punctually obeyed; and on June 17, 653, Martin was transported to the seat of government, like an ordinary criminal. He did not reach Constantinople till Sept. 17, 654. At his trial he was loaded with indignities, and finally banished to the Crimea, where he died in the following year[2]. A still heavier doom awaited Maximus[3] and two of his disciples: they were at first sent into Thrace; but on refusing to accept the 'Type' were dragged back to Constantinople, anathematized in a synod over which Peter, the new patriarch, presided, and after scourging, mutilation, and a public mockery were banished (662) into the Caucasus, among the Lazians. Maximus survived only a few days, and with him all the zeal of the eastern Duotheletes appears to have been extinguished[4].

His attainder, and death.

Fate of Maximus.

In the next ten years we meet with few if any traces

---

[1] *Ibid.* x. 1158. The fourteenth canon will illustrate their view of the controversy: 'Si quis secundum scelerosos hæreticos cum una voluntate et una operatione, quæ ab hæreticis impie confitetur, et duas voluntates pariterque et operationes, hoc est, Divinam et humanam, quæ in ipso Christo Deo in unitate salvantur, et a sanctis patribus orthodoxe in ipso prædicantur, denegat et respuit, condemnatus sit.' The encyclic letters of the pope and synod contain the following violent expressions: 'Impios hæreticos cum omnibus pravissimis dogmatibus eorum *et impiam ecthesin vel impiissimum typum* et omnes, qui eos vel quidquam de his, quæ exposita sunt in eis, suscipiunt aut defendunt, seu verba pro eis faciunt in scripto, anathematizavimus.' *Ibid.* 1175: cf. Martin's letter to the emperor, giving him an account of the proceedings, p. 790.

[2] See the *Commemoratio* and other documents in Mansi, x. 853.

[3] See the *Life of Maximus* and other ancient documents prefixed to the edition of his works by Combefis.

[4] The new pope Eugenius, appointed by the exarch, is said to have trodden in the steps of Honorius: at least his agents (apocrisiarii) at Constantinople, had subscribed the 'Type' and had persuaded Maximus to yield. Vitalian also (657—672) acquiesced, or made no public stand against the court. Schröckh, xx. 435, 436.

of resistance in that quarter, though it is probable that in the Latin Church the disaffection to the 'Type' was silently increasing[1]. Constans left the throne to Constantine Pogonatus (668—685), who does not seem to have ever been devotedly attached to the reigning school of doctrine. On the contrary a letter[2] which he wrote to Donus, bishop of Rome, 678, expressed an earnest wish to heal the distractions of the Church by summoning a general council. On the arrival of the letter Donus was no more, but it came into the hands of Agatho his successor, who immediately adopted the suggestion, and, convening an assembly of the western bishops[3] to deliberate upon it, sent a deputation of them to Constantinople. He also contributed materially to the successful issue of the council, by his full and lucid exposition of the controverted truth[4]. The sessions, which were eighteen in number, lasted from the 7th November, 680, to the 16th September, 681, the emperor himself presiding not unfrequently in person. After a minute and somewhat critical review of the authorities which had been alleged on either side, Monotheletism was left with an almost solitary champion[5] in the person of Macarius, patriarch of Antioch, who for adhering to his old opinions was eventually deposed by his brother-prelates (March 7, 681). A definition of the true faith[6] and an anathema

EASTERN CHURCH.

Reaction in the Eastern Church.

The convocation of the Sixth Œcumenical Council, 680.

---

[1] In the year 677, the communion between the Churches of Rome and Constantinople was entirely suspended, Theodore the Byzantine patriarch proposing to strike the name of Vitalian, as well as of the other Roman bishops after Honorius, from the diptychs, or sacred catalogues of the Church. *Ibid.*

[2] *Constant. ep. ad Donum* in *Act. Conc.* VI. *Œcumenic.* Mansi, XI. 195.

[3] Held at Rome, March 27, 680; Mansi, XI. 185: cf. Eddius, *Vit. Wilfrid.* c. 51.

[4] He wrote to the emperor in his own name and that of the synod, containing 125 delegates: Mansi, XI. 286. He cites passages from the Gospels which prove the co-operation in our Lord of the human and Divine wills: dwelling among others on S. Matth. xxvi. 39, which his predecessor Honorius had explained away. The letter was read in the 4th session of the ensuing council.

[5] At the opening of the synod, George I., patriarch of Constantinople, took his side, but afterwards declared himself a convert to the opposite party. In the 15th session, Polychronius, a fanatical monk of Thrace, endeavoured to establish the truth of Monotheletism by raising a dead man to life, but after whispering some time in the ear of the corpse, he confessed his inability to work the miracle. He was accordingly deposed from the priesthood. The same penalty was inflicted on a Syrian priest at the following session (Aug. 9).

[6] Mansi, XI. 631—637...τὸ ἀνθρώπινον αὐτοῦ θέλημα θεωθὲν οὐκ ἀνῃρέθη.

pronounced on all who were infected with the heresy of the Monotheletes (Honorius[1] in the number) brought the sittings of the council to a close, and renewed the communion of the Greek and Latin Churches. Their solution of the controversy was as follows: that in Christ 'there are two natural wills and two natural operations, without division, without change or conversion, with nothing like antagonism, and nothing like confusion,'—yet they were careful to add a precautionary clause, to the effect that the human will could not come into collision with the Divine, but was in all things subject to it.

Their definitions, though confirmed anew by the voice of the Trullan Council[2] (691), did not immediately suppress the Monothelete discussions. On the contrary, a later emperor, Bardanes, or Philippicus[3], commanded the erasure of the recent creed from the Acts of the General Councils, and proceeded (711) with the help of a creature of the court, whom he placed in the see of Constantinople, to revive the exploded errors. But his own dethronement in 713 put an end to the agitation.

A small remnant of Monotheletes continued to subsist for ages in the fastnesses of Lebanon. These were the

σέσωσται δὲ μᾶλλον...δύο δὲ φυσικὰς ἐνεργείας ἀδιαιρέτως, ἀτρέπτως, ἀμερίστως, ἀσυγχύτως ἐν αὐτῷ τῷ κυρίῳ ἡμῶν...δοξάζομεν. There is some variation in the statements as to the number of bishops present. The subscriptions do not exceed one hundred.

[1] See above, p. 66, n. 1. Attempts had been made to vindicate the orthodoxy of Honorius (e. g. by Maximus, Mansi, x. 687), and his acquiescence in the creed of Sergius had been studiously passed over in the proceedings of the Roman synods, but here at Constantinople the clause καὶ 'Ονώριον τὸν γενόμενον πάπαν τῆς πρεσβυτέρας 'Ρώμης, κ.τ.λ. was thrice added to the list of the anathematized. Mansi, xi. 556, 622, 656. Leo II., in notifying his acceptance or confirmation of the council (682), adds a clause to the same effect: he anathematized 'et Honorium I., qui hanc apostolicam ecclesiam non apostolicæ traditionis doctrina lustravit, sed profana proditione immaculatam fidem subvertere conatus est.' Ib. xv. 731. The case of Honorius has occupied a considerable place in recent controversy, in connexion with the action of the Vatican Council of 1869—70 on Papal Infallibility.

[2] Mansi, xi. 921. On the displeasure which this council had excited in the west, see above, p. 88, n. 2; p. 47; p. 51; and cf. Gieseler, ii. 178 sq.

[3] Theophanes, *Chronograph.* 319 sq. ed. Paris: Combefis, *Hist. Hæres. Monothel.* § ii. 201 sq. Paris, 1648. Philippicus, with the same object, ordered the removal of a picture ('imaginem, quam Græci votaream vocant, sex continentem sanctas et universales synodos') from St Peter's church at Rome; but his mandate was rejected by Constantine I. (712): *Vit. Constantin.* in Vignolii *Lib. Pontif.* ii. 10.

Maronites[1], the followers of a civil and ecclesiastical chieftain, John Marun, who is said to have flourished in the seventh or eighth century. It is not clearly[2] ascertained at what time the Monothelete opinions were accepted by this tribe, but we learn that somewhat earlier than 1182 about forty thousand of them recognized the jurisdiction of the Latin patriarch of Antioch, and passed over to the Church of Rome[3].

It has been mentioned that the task of vindicating orthodoxy at this period had been consigned in no small degree to Maximus. But his works are not all devoted to polemics[4]. He was the representative of a tendency to dialecticism, which had been long prevailing in the Greek communion. Both his learning and his spirit were transmitted to another student, John of Damascus (fl. 740), who has left behind him logical investigations of nearly all the earlier controversies, and of the Monothelete[5] among the rest. His work, entitled[6] *An Accurate Exposition of the Orthodox Faith*, is tinctured with the Aristotelian philosophy, and exercised an important influence on the culture of the Eastern churches from that day to our own. It was in truth the starting-point of their scholastic system, although the materials out of which it grew were borrowed in most cases from the Fathers, and especially from Gregory of Nazianzus.

But the pen of Damascenus did not dwell entirely on this class of theological discussions: it invested a less specu-

---

[1] See the *Biblioth. Orientalis* of J. S. Asseman (himself descended from this body), tom. I. 487 sq., and a different account in Combefis, *Hist. Hæres. Monothel.*, p. 460: cf. also Gibbon, IV. 383—385, ed. Milman.

[2] John of Damascus (*Libellus de Vera Sententia*, c. 8: *Opp.* I. 395, ed. Le Quien) already (cir. 750) numbers them among the heretics. He also describes a Monophysite addition to the Trisagion (*Ibid.* p. 485) by the term Μαρωνίζειν.

[3] Schröckh, xx. 455. The chief authority for this statement is William of Tyre; but at a later period Abulpharagius (who died 1286) speaks of the Maronites as still a sect of the Monotheletes. *Ibid.*

[4] See a review of his theological system in Neander, v. 236 sq.

[5] Περὶ τῶν ἐν τῷ Χριστῷ δύο θελημάτων καὶ ἐνεργειῶν καὶ λοιπῶν φυσικῶν ἰδιωμάτων.

[6] Ἔκδοσις ἀκριβὴς τῆς ὀρθοδόξου πίστεως. On his system of religious doctrine, see Schröckh, xx. 230—329: Ritter, *Geschichte der Christl. Philosophie*, II. 553; Dorner, *Lehre von der Person Christi*, II. 257 sq.; and, for a list of his multifarious writings, Smith's *Biograph. Dictionary*.

EASTERN CHURCH.

Rise of the Iconoclastic controversy.

lative theme with all the subtleties and nice distinctions of the schools[1]. This was the question of image-worship[2], which in the reigns of Leo the Isaurian, and his successors (726—842), convulsed every province of the Church. It was already an established custom to make use of images and pictures, with the view of exciting the devotion of the people, or of instructing the more simple and unlettered; but the Western Church, at least until the close of the sixth century, had not proceeded further than this point[3]. A different feeling was however common in the Eastern, where the softer and more sensuous Greek was frequently betrayed into a blind and superstitious veneration for the images and pictures of the saints[4]. It was, accordingly, at the seat of the Byzantine empire that a series of reactions now commenced.

Conduct of Leo the Isaurian.

Leo, the Isaurian, of a rough and martial temper, was the first of the Iconoclastic princes. Influenced[5], it is said, by the invectives of Muhammedans and Jews, who had stigmatized the use of images as absolute idolatry,

---

[1] In his discourses, Πρὸς τοὺς διαβάλλοντας τὰς ἁγίας εἰκόνας: *Opp.* I. 305 sq. He viewed the Iconoclastic movement as an attack upon the essence of the Gospel; and the dread of idolatry as a falling back into Judaism, or even into Manichæism. Cf. Milman, *Latin Christianity*, II. 107.

[2] It is a great misfortune that the surviving authorities are nearly all on one side,—in favour of image-worship. The council by which it was established, in their fifth session, commanded that all the writings of the Iconoclastic party should be destroyed. On this account the records of the opposition made by an earlier synod (754) have to be collected from the Acts of the Council of Nicæa, and from the *Libri Carolini;* on which see below.

[3] *e. g.* the very remarkable letters of Gregory the Great to Serenus, bishop of Marseilles (599); *Epist.* lib. IX. ep. 105: 'et quidem zelum vos, ne quid manufactum adorari posset, habuisse laudavimus, sed frangere easdem imagines non debuisse judicamus: idcirco enim pictura in ecclesiis adhibetur, ut hi, qui litteras nesciunt, saltem in parietibus videndo legant, quæ legere in codicibus non valent:' cf. lib. XI. ep. 13.

[4] See the instances adduced by Neander, V. 277, 278.

[5] One of his advisers was Constantine, bishop of Nacolia: another was of senatorial rank, named Beser, who had passed some time in captivity among the Saracens. See Mendham's *Seventh General Council*, Introd. pp. xii—xiv. Other attempts to explain the antipathy of Leo may be found in Schlosser's *Geschichte der bilder-stürmenden Kaiser*, pp. 161 sq. Frankf. 1812: cf. Mansi, XII. 959. It is not unlikely that a wish to reabsorb the Muhammedans into the Church was one of the leading motives.

he ordered[1] (726), that the custom of kneeling before them should in future be abandoned. The resistance of the aged patriarch[2], Germanus, and a fiery circular[3] from John of Damascus, who was now residing in a convent at Jerusalem, incited Leo to more stringent measures. He accordingly put forth[4] a second edict (729 or 730) in which images and pictures were proscribed, and doomed to unsparing demolition. It extended to all kinds of material representations, with the sole exception of the cross[5]. The speedy execution of this peremptory order drove Germanus from the helm of the Oriental Church, and forced into the vacant place his secretary Anastasius, a devoted servant of the court. The rest of the non-conforming clergy were now silenced or ejected: but the cause of image-worship, hopeless though it seemed, had still a most vehement defender in John of Damascus, whom the terrors of the empire could not reach.

EASTERN CHURCH.

Triumph of the Iconoclasts.

The shock which this controversy had occasioned in the east was rapidly transmitted far and near. The Roman bishop, Gregory II., nominally subject to Byzantium, bade defiance to the royal edict (? 730), in a letter full of scorn and sarcasm[6]: and, in order to elude the vengeance of the

Resistance of Gregory II.

---

[1] The edicts on image-worship are collected in Goldastus, *Imperialia decreta de cultu Imaginum*, ed. Francof. 1608.

[2] Mansi, XIII. 99: cf. his *Liber de Synodis*, etc. in *Spicilegium Romanum*, VII. 99 sq. Rom. 1842. For the probable nature of his interview with Leo at the opening of the controversy, see Neander, v. 281—283. He seems to have first struck out the distinction of a *relative* worship (προσκύνησις σχετική), as addressed to the images of Christ: and affirms that with regard to the Virgin and the saints no worship (λατρεία) is due to them, much less to material representations of them. It is plain, however, that the idea of giving some honour to the pictures of the saints (*e.g.* praying and placing lights before them) had been worked into his creed, and to abandon it appeared equivalent to a renunciation of the Gospel.

[3] See the first of his *Orations*, above referred to; p. 78, n. 3.

[4] Goldastus, *ubi sup.* note 1: cf. Theophanes, *Chronograph.* pp. 336, 343.

[5] On removing an image of our Lord from a niche in the imperial palace, he erected the symbol of the cross in its place. See *Analecta Græca*, ed. Benedict. I. 415.

[6] Mansi, XII. 959 sq.: cf. his letter to Germanus, *Ibid.* XIII. 91. His successor, Gregory III., held a council at Rome (Nov. 1, 731), in which it was decreed, 'ut si quis deinceps sacrarum imaginum depositor atque destructor et profanator, vel blasphemus exstiterit, sit extorris a Corpore et Sanguine Jesu Christi, vel totius ecclesiæ unitate et compage.' *Vit. Gregor. III.*, in Vignol. *Lib. Pontif.* II. 43, 44.

EASTERN CHURCH.

Proceedings of Constantine Copronymus.

exarch, threw himself for help into the arms of the Lombards.

At the death of Leo, 741, his policy was vigorously carried out by Constantine (Copronymus), his son: but it is plain that a large section of the people, and especially the 'monks[1], were ardently attached to the interdicted usage. It must also be confessed that, in the acts of Constantine, still more than in the life-time of his father, we may notice an extreme but salutary dread of superstition in alliance with fanatical dislike of art, and a fierce and persecuting spirit[2]. Having quelled an insurrection which the image-worshippers excited in his absence[3] (743), he determined to convoke a synod in the hope of bringing the dispute to an amicable issue, or at least of fortifying the position of the Iconoclastic party. It assembled in 754 at Constantinople, and was composed of three hundred and thirty-eight bishops of Europe and Anatolia[4]. The deliberations were continued for the space of six months, and led to a unanimous decision[5]. It declared that the

Council of Constantinople, 754.

---

[1] περισσοτέρως δὲ τῶν τῷ μοναχικῷ ἀσκουμένων τάγματι θεοσεβεστάτων ἀνδρῶν. Germanus, *de Synodis*, etc; ubi sup. p. 61. The majority of the artists at this period were inmates of religious houses, and as their craft was endangered by the measures of the court, nearly all of them were found in the ranks of the recusants. They were loud in denouncing Constantine as a blasphemer and a renegade: which would naturally inflame the hatred he already bore to monachism in general. See a good picture of the state of feeling in the life of the monk Stephen (of the grotto of Auxentius), in the *Analecta Græca*, ubi sup.: and cf. Neander, v. 303 sq.

[2] The impiety and profligacy of Constantine may have been very much over-coloured by the monastic chroniclers, *e. g.* Theophanes, 346 sq., but his cruelty it is impossible to question: see the evidence in Schlosser, *Geschichte der bilderstürm. Kaiser*, pp. 228—234.

[3] It was headed by his brother-in-law, Artavasdes; Theophanes, p. 347.

[4] None of the patriarchs were present at this council. The see of Constantinople was vacant: the heads of the churches of Antioch, Alexandria, and Jerusalem were subject to the Saracens, and were deterred by the jealousy of their masters from public communication with the Christians of the empire; while the Church of Rome was invaded by the Lombards, and devoted to the use of images. Constantine II. (767) informs Pepin of France 'qualis fervor sanctarum imaginum orientalibus in partibus cunctis Christianis immineat.' *Hist. Franc. Scriptores*, ed. Duchesne, III. 825. A Roman council (769) under Stephen IV. confirmed the 'veneration of images.' Mansi, XII. 720. It is clear also that the proceedings at Constantinople (754) were repudiated by the patriarch of Jerusalem (Mansi, XII. 1135), who was joined by the patriarchs of Antioch and Alexandria. The president of the council was Theodosius, metropolitan of Ephesus.

[5] Mansi, XIII. 205.

worshipping (προσκυνεῖν καὶ σέβεσθαι) of images and pictures was a relapse into idolatry, excited by the malice of the Tempter; and that consequently emperors were bound, in imitation of the Apostolic practice, to destroy every vestige of the evil[1]. At the same time, not a single prelate manifested any wish to vary from the standard language of the Church[2]. They opened the proceedings by acknowledging the doctrine of the Six General Councils, and abjuring every phase of misbelief which had there been examined and condemned.

EASTERN CHURCH.

Its decision.

A long and triumphant reign (741—775) enabled Constantine to carry out the wishes of his party: and his successor, Leo IV., surnamed Chazarus (775—780), though more lenient than his father, steadily enforced the oath[3] which had been issued by that king against the worshipping of images and pictures. Leo was espoused to the artful and unscrupulous Irene, who at his decease administered the business of the State in the name of Constantine VI., her minor son. She had been educated in a family opposed to the Iconoclasts, and was tinged with the superstition of the age: no sooner, therefore, was she mistress of the empire, than her leanings to the monks were frequently betrayed in her distribution of the church-preferment. It was not, however, until the sixth year of her administration, that she ventured to proceed more freely. Hitherto the soldiers, who revered the memory of Constantine and took the side of the Iconoclasts, had operated as a formidable check upon her zeal: but

Accession of Leo IV.

The empress Irene:

her zeal in behalf of images.

---

[1] μηκέτι τολμᾶν ἄνθρωπον τὸν οἱονδήποτε ἐπιτηδεύειν τὸ τοιοῦτον ἀσεβὲς καὶ ἀνόσιον ἐπιτήδευμα. Mansi, xiii. 328. Their prohibitions extended not only to all kinds of images composed 'by the pagan and accursed art' of the painter, but even to the figures (hitherto preserved) upon the sacred vestments and church-plate (Mansi, *ib.* 332); although to check any further outbreaks of individual fanaticism, it was now ordered that the permission of the patriarch, or of the emperor, should be procured to warrant alterations in the ecclesiastical ornaments.

[2] They even pronounced an anathema on all who do not confess τὴν ἀειπάρθενον Μαρίαν κυρίως καὶ ἀληθῶς θεοτόκον, ὑπερτέραν τε εἶναι πάσης ὁρατῆς καὶ ἀοράτου κτίσεως; and on all who do not ask for the prayers of her, and of the other saints. Mansi, xiii. 345, 348.

[3] It seems to have been administered to every citizen of Constantinople, if not in all quarters of the empire: cf. Neander, v. 307, 308. Leo, however, permitted numbers of the exiled monks to shew themselves in public, and thus laid a train for the explosion that ensued.

EASTERN CHURCH.

Second Council of Nicæa, 787.

Its sessions,

and decree.

the election of Tarasius[1] to the patriarchal chair enabled her to make arrangements for the convocation of a synod, which she trusted would reverse the policy adopted in the former reigns. The Roman bishop, Hadrian I., most cordially invited by Irene, sent a deputation of the Western clergy to assist her; but the efforts of Tarasius, who was anxious to secure a like concurrence on the part of the Oriental patriarchates[2], were not equally successful. Very many of the delegates assembled at Constantinople, Aug. 1, 786; but, owing to an insurrection[3] of the military, their proceedings were suspended for a year. They next met at Nicæa in Bithynia, to the number of about three hundred and fifty prelates, and immediately resumed their labours (Sept. 24, 787). In less than a month the business of the Synod was completed: and as soon as their 'definition' had been formally proclaimed (Oct. 23) in the royal city, images were almost universally restored. A multitude of bishops, who had been hitherto distinguished as Iconoclasts, alarmed in some cases by the evidence[4] in favour of the use of images, or anxious to retain their mitres and their incomes, signed a humble recantation[5] of the tenets now exploded. The decision[6] of the Council

---

[1] His predecessor Paul, on the point of death, retired into a monastery. Tarasius was secretary to the emperor, and the irregularity of his election, together with his use of the title 'Œcumenical patriarch,' scandalized the Roman bishop Hadrian I. (Mansi, XII. 1056, 1077): but in consideration of his zeal for images, the anger of the pope was speedily disarmed. See a Life of Tarasius by his pupil, in the *Acta Sanctorum*, Febr. tom. III. pp. 576 sq.

[2] The messengers of Tarasius, on reaching Palestine, were informed by some monks whom they met with, that the Moslem authorities would not tolerate a general council, and that it would be fruitless to proceed any further on their errand: but in order that they might secure at least a show of representatives, they brought back two Palestinian monks, with the style and title of Legates of the East. On this account, the synod has no claim to be called *Œcumenical;* cf. Palmer, *Treatise on the Church*, II. 151, 152; 3rd edit.

[3] Mansi, XII. 990 sq.

[4] The inaccuracy of the quotations from the older writers, as betrayed in the proceedings of the Nicene Council, and the utter want of criticism evinced by the prelates in adducing spurious works, are painfully astounding: *e.g.* the story of a miraculous image at Berytus was attributed to the great Athanasius, and urged as an authority: cf. Mendham, *Seventh General Council*, Introd. pp. lii. sq.

[5] Cf. Neander, v. 318—320.

[6] Mansi, XIII. 377. The προσκύνησις would include the offering of lights and incense (θυμιαμάτων καὶ φώτων προσαγωγήν) as well as bowing

ran as follows: it enjoined that 'bowing and an honourable adoration (ἀσπασμὸν καὶ τιμητικὴν προσκύνησιν) should be offered to all sacred images; but this external and inferior worship must not be confounded with the true and supreme worship (τὴν κατὰ πίστιν ἡμῶν ἀληθινὴν λατρείαν) which belongs exclusively to God.'

In the time of Irene and her son, as also of Nicephorus I. and Michael Rhangabe, this decision of the council was unsparingly enforced; although an insurrection of Iconoclasts in 812 bore witness to their strength and formidable numbers[1]. But a milder and more lasting opposition took its rise in the west of Europe. It appears, that soon after the conclusion of the synod, Charlemagne had received from Rome a Latin version of the 'Acts,' which was transmitted for the sake of gaining his concurrence[2]. Startled by the language of the Eastern prelates, he determined, with the aid of his clerical advisers[3], to compose an elaborate reply. It came out under the title *Libri Carolini*[4]. In the course of one hundred and twenty chapters, he examined and confuted all the arguments on which the Council of Nicæa rested. But in spite of an occasional display of bitterness in criticizing his opponents, he was far from a heated partizan. He occupied a kind of middle place[5]; and while strenuously denouncing the impieties connected with the worshipping of pictures, did

Eastern Church.

Opposition to image-worship in the West.

The Libri Carolini.

down and prostration. The *degree* of reverence is the same as many of the Iconoclasts were not unwilling to bestow on the sign of the cross and on the volume of the Gospels (τῷ τύπῳ τοῦ τιμίου καὶ ζωοποιοῦ σταυροῦ καὶ τοῖς ἁγίοις εὐαγγελίοις καὶ τοῖς λοιποῖς ἱεροῖς ἀναθήμασι).

[1] For an account of the reaction, under Leo the Armenian, and the final triumph of the image-party in 842, see the following period: 'State of religious doctrine,' &c., in the 'Eastern Church.'

[2] It appears that the question was already mooted at Gentilly in 767, under Pepin, but the verdict of that synod is not known. Labb. VI. 1703. Cf. above, p. 54, n. 1.

[3] One of the principal was most probably Alcuin: Lorenz, *Alcuins Leben*, p. 132; Neander, v. 324, note.

[4] In Goldastus, *Imperialia Decreta de Cultu Imaginum*, pp. 67 sq. Neander (v. 325—335) has left a careful analysis of the *Libri Carolini*.

[5] *e. g.* 'Adorationem soli Deo debitam imaginibus impertire aut segnitiæ est, si utcunque agitur, aut insaniæ, vel potius infidelitatis, si pertinaciter defenditur:' lib. III. c. 24. 'Imagines vero, *omni sui cultura et adoratione seclusa*, utrum in basilicis propter memoriam rerum gestarum et ornamentum sint, an etiam non sint, nullum fidei catholicæ adferre poterunt præjudicium; quippe cum ad peragenda nostræ salutis mysteria nullum penitus officium habere noscantur:' lib. II. c. 21.

not fall into the track of the fanatical Iconoclasts, who were proscribing all the imitative arts as the invention of the Devil. His treatise very soon elicited an answer[1] from Pope Hadrian I., which, as it fell innocuous on himself, made no impression on the bishops of the empire. They assembled at Frankfort (**794**), to the number of three hundred, and determined in the presence of the papal legates, that the recent council of the Greeks had no claim whatever on their notice[2]; adding, that all acts of worship, such as many were not indisposed to offer to the images of saints, invaded the prerogatives of God. And as the English Church[3] appears to have united with the Frankish in the passing of this memorable protest, very few of the Western Christians, those of Italy excepted, were committed to the fatal principles established at Nicæa.

THE PAULICIANS.

But while the strength of the Christian Church was tried to the utmost in the midst of domestic conflicts, she had also to encounter a fresh form of thought which threatened her dominion in the East. This was the creed of the Paulicians[4]. Like the other mediæval sects, they

---

[1] Mansi, XIII. 759.

[2] Mansi, XIII. 909. The following is the entry of Einhard, *Annales*, A.D. 794 (Pertz, I. 181): 'Synodus etiam, quæ ante paucos annos in Constantinopoli sub Herena (Irene) et Constantino filio ejus congregata, et ab ipsis non solum septima, verum etiam universalis est appellata, ut nec septima nec universalis haberetur diceretur\e, quasi supervacua in totum ab omnibus abdicata est.'

[3] Simeon of Durham, following a contemporaneous authority, (*Scriptores* x. col. 111, ed. Twysden), thus describes the correspondence between Charlemagne and the English: 'Anno 792, Karolus rex Francorum misit synodalem librum ad Britanniam, sibi a Constantinopoli directum, in quo libro (heu! proh dolor!) multa inconvenientia, et veræ fidei contraria reperientes; maxime, quod pene omnium orientalium doctorum, non minus quam trecentorum, vel eo amplius, episcoporum unanimi assertione confirmantum *imagines adorare debere; quod omnino ecclesia Dei execratur*. Contra quod scripsit Albinus [*i.e.* Alcuin] epistolam ex authoritate Divinarum scripturarum mirabiliter affirmatam; illamque cum eodem libro *et persona episcoporum, ac principum nostrorum*, regi Francorum attulit.' *Mon. Hist. Brit.* p. 667: cf. Twysden's *Vindication*, pp. 206 sq., new edit.

[4] Παυλικιανοί, otherwise called Παυλιανῖται. Some have looked upon the name Παυλικιανοί as equivalent to Παυλοιωάνναι (Photius, *adversus recentiores Manichæos*, lib. I. c. 2: in J. C. Wolf's *Anecdota Græca*, tom. I. and II. ed. Hamb. 1722); arguing that the founders of the sect were

were distinguished by their opposition to the whole of the ecclesiastical system, and not merely to peculiar articles of faith. They seem to have been an offshoot from the Marcionites, who lingered[1] in the regions of Armenia Prima, where the founder of Paulicianism appeared at the middle of the seventh century (657—684).

THE PAULI-CIANS.

Its founder.

His former name was Constantine, but at the outset of his mission in behalf of what he deemed the genuine teaching of St Paul, he chose the expressive title of 'Sylvanus.' Though addicted to the study of the sacred volume, and especially the writings of the great Apostle, whom his predecessor, Marcion, held in equal honour, he was notwithstanding governed all his life-time by the principles of *dualism*, in which it is likely he was reared. He argued that the Maker of the human body and the Lord of the sensible creation, was to be distinguished from the perfect God, the Author of the world of spirits[2]. In his view, matter, as the agent of the Demiurgus, was the source of every evil; while the soul of man, originally wedded to Divinity itself, had been seduced into union with the body, where she dwelt in a doleful prison[3]. Her deliverance out of this enthralment was the work of the

Glaring instances of misbelief.

two Manichæans, Paul and John, sons of Callinice: but there are strong reasons for doubting the truth of this account. See the Essay of Gieseler in the *Theolog. Studien und Kritiken* for 1829, Heft I. pp. 79 sq. He maintains that the name *Paulician* (Παυλικοί leading to Παυλικιανοί) was given to them on account of the exclusive value they attached to the writings of St Paul. Neander also has shewn that their tenets were not, strictly speaking, *Manichæan*, but are to be classed under the phase of Gnosticism put forth by Marcion and his party: v. 337 sq. The oldest treatise on the heresy of the Paulicians is an Oration of John of Ozun, patriarch of the Armenians (718—729): *Opp.* ed. Venet. 1834. But the fullest statement of their errors is to be found in the work of Photius (above cited), and the *Historia Manichæorum* of Peter Siculus (about 800), ed. Ingolstadt, 1604, and elsewhere.

[1] Neander, v. 339.
[2] Πρῶτον μὲν γάρ ἐστι τὸ κατ' αὐτοὺς γνώρισμα τὸ δύο ἀρχὰς ὁμολογεῖν, πονηρὸν θεὸν καὶ ἀγαθόν· καὶ ἄλλον εἶναι τοῦδε τοῦ κόσμου ποιητὴν καὶ ἐξουσιαστήν, ἕτερον δὲ τοῦ μέλλοντος, κ.τ.λ. Pet. Siculus, *ubi sup.* pp. 16 sq. Photius, *ubi sup.* lib. II. c. 3, 5.
[3] See the investigation of Neander on this point, v. 356 sq. They had a firm belief in the possibility of redemption, which they rested on the known affinity subsisting between God and their spirits: Οὐδὲ γὰρ οὐδ' οὕτω κατεκράτησεν οὐδὲ τῶν ἑκόντων προδεδωκότων ἑαυτοὺς τῆς ψυχῆς ὁ ἐχθρός, ὡς μηδαμῇ πρὸς μηδεμίαν ὅλως τῆς ἀληθείας αἴγλην τοὺς ἐσκοτισμένους ἐπιστρέφεσθαι, ὅτι ὁ ἀγαθὸς Θεὸς ἦν ἀεὶ καί ἐστι καὶ ἔσται. Photius, lib. II. c. 3.

THE PAULI-CIANS.

Views of the Sacraments:

of the Scriptures:

Redeemer. He descended from the presence of the Highest God, invested with a heavenly body[1]; for, as matter was essentially corrupt, the Saviour did not take our human nature, but was born of His Virgin Mother only in appearance[2]. A denial of the Incarnation led the way to other forms of blasphemy and misbelief. It was held by the Paulicians that the sufferings of Christ were equally unreal, that in virtue of His higher nature He was incapable of death, and that His cross in particular was nothing more than a sign of malediction[3]. Firm in a belief that matter is the seat of evil, they rejected all the outward means of grace, and more especially the Sacraments. They held that the Baptism[4] which our Lord intended was a baptism only of the Spirit, resting on the passage where He pointed to Himself as the one 'living water.' The Communion, in like manner, was divested of its symbols[5] and its meaning; for, according to the creed of the Paulicians, it is not the material elements but only Christian doctrines that can possibly become the vehicle of God in communicating blessings to the soul.

Assigning a peculiar value to the writings of St Paul, the followers of Constantine rejected the epistles of St Peter[6], whom they branded as a traitor to the Gospel, and

---

[1] μηδὲ ἐξ αὐτῆς γεννηθῆναι τὸν Κύριον, ἀλλ' οὐρανόθεν τὸ σῶμα κατενεγκεῖν. Pet. Sicul. *ibid.*: cf. Photius, lib. I. c. 7.

[2] ὡς διὰ σωλῆνος. They even spoke of the Virgin as scarcely fit to be numbered with the good and virtuous; adding that she bore sons to Joseph after the birth of our Saviour: Pet. Sicul. p. 18.

[3] It was called κακούργων ὄργανον καὶ ὑπὸ ἀρὰν κείμενον. Photius, lib. I. c. 7: cf. Pet. Sicul. *ibid.* Yet it appears that some at least of the Paulicians made use of a wooden cross with superstitious objects. Phot. lib. I. c. 9.

[4] Photius, *ibid.* Some of them however had their children baptized (Neander, v. 363), perhaps with an idea that the sacrament would benefit the body.

[5] ......λέγοντες, ὅτι οὐκ ἦν ἄρτος καὶ οἶνος, ὃν ὁ Κύριος ἐδίδου τοῖς μαθηταῖς αὐτοῦ ἐπὶ τοῦ δείπνου, ἀλλὰ συμβολικῶς τὰ ῥήματα αὐτοῦ αὐτοῖς ἐδίδου, ὡς ἄρτον καὶ οἶνον. Pet. Sicul. *ibid.*

[6] τὰς δύο καθολικὰς...Πέτρου τοῦ πρωταποστόλου οὐ δέχονται, ἀπεχθῶς πρὸς αὐτὸν διακείμενοι, κ.τ.λ. Pet. Siculus, *ubi sup.* cf. Photius, lib. I. c. 8. They rejected also the writings of the Old Testament (τὴν οἱανοῦν βίβλον παλαιάν), regarding them as the production of a system which was under the dominion of the Demiurgus. Of the writings of the New Testament they seem to have adopted four Gospels (laying stress, however, on that according to St Luke), fourteen Epistles of St Paul (of which one was

as the head of the Judaizing party in the Church. This anti-Jewish feeling, everywhere apparent, made them anxious to revive (as they supposed) an apostolic ministry, to simplify the ritual of the Church, and disentangle the surviving elements of Christianity from numerous aftergrowths of error. Thus they styled themselves the 'Catholics' and 'Christians' proper, as distinguished from the 'Romans,' or professors of the state-religion[1]. They would tolerate no difference of class or order, such as that subsisting in the Church between the clergy and the laity. Their ministers[2] were simply *teachers*, standing in a close relation to the Holy Spirit, and at first peculiarly awakened by His impulse.

THE PAULICIANS.

of the ministry and ritual of the Church.

How far the Paulicians had been guilty of the grosser violations[3] of the moral law imputed to them by opponents, it is difficult to ascertain precisely: but one principle on which they acted in the time of persecution is an argument against their purity of conscience. They were ready to disguise their tenets, under pressure, and resorted even to the worship and communion of the Church in order to escape the eye of the police, and to propagate their system with impunity.

Their moral system.

The founder of it, Constantine (Sylvanus), after labouring to spread it in Armenia for a long term of years, was stoned to death, at the instigation of the emperor, by some of his own disciples (**684**). The officer, who was entrusted with this duty, Symeon (Titus), afterwards passed over to the sect, and occupied the place of Con-

Fate of Constantine, the founder.

---

addressed to the Laodiceans), the Epistles of St James, St John, and St Jude, and the Acts of the Apostles. *Ibid.* and cf. Neander, v. 368 sq.

[1] καθολικὴν δὲ ἐκκλησίαν τὰ ἑαυτῶν καλοῦσι συνέδρια. Photius, lib. I. c. 9: cf. lib. I. c. 6. Another of their titles was that of χριστοπολίται. See the *Anathemas* published in Tollius, *Insignia Itinerarii Italici*, p. 122.

[2] They rejected not only the name ἱερεῖς but πρεσβύτεροι also, as savouring of Judaism. Pet. Sicul. p. 20. At the head of their ministerial system were, (1) apostles or prophets, (2) teachers and pastors (διδάσκαλοι and ποιμένες), (3) itinerant messengers of the truth associated with the prophets (συνέκδημοι), (4) νοτάριοι, perhaps scribes, or copyists of religious records. Neander, v. 365. The same dread of Judaism induced them to relinquish the current title ναοί (temples), and to call their places of assembly 'oratories' (προσευχαί). Photius, lib. I. c. 9.

[3] This feature of their system is dwelt upon by John of Ozun, a contemporary (above, p. 79, note): and he is supported by the other writers. On the other hand, see Neander, v. 366 sq.: Gieseler, *Theol. Studien und Kritiken* for 1829, pp. 120 sq.

*THE PAULI-
CIANS.*

His successors.

stantine until the year **690**; when a further inquisition, prompted by Justinian II., ended in a fresh proscription, and brought Symeon, with a multitude of others, to the stake. He was followed in the second generation by Gegnæsius (Timothy), whose claim to be regarded as the single leader of the party (circ. **715**), on the ground that the influence of the Holy Spirit, who had rested on his father, was exclusively transmitted unto him, provoked a secession from his standard. The dissentients took the side of Theodore, his brother, who affirmed that an equal ministerial gift had come to him directly from on high[1].

Schism among the Paulicians.

Conduct of Gegnæsius.

The growth of the Paulicians now demanding the attention of the government, Gegnæsius, in **717**, was summoned to Constantinople, and interrogated by the patriarch concerning his behaviour and his creed. By means of equivocal expressions[2], intermingled with anathemas on all who varied from the teaching of the Church, he was able to secure the interest of Leo the Isaurian, and took back with him a letter of protection for himself and his adherents. Migrating across the frontier, he established his metropolis within the territories of the Caliph, at the town of Manalis (near Samosata), and died about the year **745**. Another schism arose, dividing the Paulicians into bitter factions, one of whom, preserving their allegiance to the son of Gegnæsius, fell a prey to the armies of the Moslems. The pretender, Joseph (or Epaphroditus), menaced by a like incursion, fixed his chair in Pisidia; and the sect of the Paulicians in his life-time was diffused over many parts of Asia Minor.

Fresh secession at his death.

Decline of Paulicianism.

Joseph was succeeded (circ. **750**) by the cynical or (it may be) the immoral Baanes (ὁ ῥυπαρός), under whom the delusion seems to have been rapidly declining: but it now attracted a more able and exalted leader, Sergius[3]

---

[1] Photius, lib. I. c. 18.

[2] See Neander's remarks on this interview, *ibid.* 344. As it is plain that the Paulicians were strongly opposed to image-worship, and as their abhorrence of this practice was the first point of attraction for their converts, many of whom had been Iconoclasts (John of Ozun, *Oratio*, pp. 76, 89), we may conjecture that the emperor Leo, the antagonist of images, was on that account more lenient to Gegnæsius and his party.

[3] Pet. Siculus, *ibid.* p. 54. The case of Sergius shews that although the reading of the Bible was not positively interdicted, it was usual for the laity to shrink from this personal investigation of the mysteries of the faith, and for the clergy in some cases to encourage the delusion.

(or Tychicus), a native of Galatia, and the second founder of Paulicianism. Assiduous in his study of the writings of St Paul, to whom, as he imagined, Christian truth had been almost exclusively revealed, he clung notwithstanding to the dualistic errors, which had marked the anterior stages of his sect; and while surpassing all his predecessors in the moral duties of religion[1], he indulged an extravagance of speech that bordered upon self-idolatry[2]. His efforts to extend his influence were untiring; in the course of four-and-thirty years, he traversed every part of Asia Minor[3], and enjoying many glimpses of imperial favour in the reign of Nicephorus I.[4], succeeded in imparting to the sect a far more stable frame-work.

But this interval of calm was short. The progress of a noxious error, pictured in the strongest colours to the mind of Leo the Armenian, was sufficient to arouse his vengeance: he despatched inquisitors[5] into the misbelieving districts, with the hope of eradicating all who shewed no symptom of repentance. A number of them fled afresh into the territories of the Caliph; the emir of Melitene granting them a small asylum in the town of Argaum, from which place, in defiance of the wish of Sergius[6], who was himself a refugee, they made incursions into the border provinces of the empire. At the death[7] of

THE PAULICIANS.

Revival un der Sergius.

Persecutions of the Paulicians.

---

[1] The following is the testimony of an implacable opponent: Καὶ ταπεινὸν ἦθος καὶ δεξιώσεως κατεσχηματισμένος τρόπος καὶ ἡμερότης οὐ τοὺς οἰκείους ὑποσαίνουσα μόνον, ἀλλὰ καὶ τοὺς τραχύτερον διακειμένους ὑπολεαίνουσά τε καὶ συλαγωγοῦσα. Photius, lib. I. c. 22: cf. Pet. Sicul. p. 58.

[2] He was understood to argue as if he were the Paraclete, or Holy Ghost (Photius, lib. I. p. 111); but it may be that his object was to represent himself as, in a higher sense, the organ of the Spirit, for the restoration of the Gospel. He spoke of himself, however, as 'the shining light,' 'the light-giving star,' 'the good shepherd,' &c. *Ibid.* p. 98.

[3] Ἀπὸ ἀνατολῶν καὶ μέχρι δυσμῶν, καὶ βορρᾶ καὶ νότου ἔδραμον κηρύσσων τὸ εὐαγγέλιον τοῦ Χριστοῦ, τοῖς ἐμοῖς γόνασι βαρήσας. Extract from one of his letters, in Pet. Sicul. p. 60.

[4] Theophanes, *Chron.* p. 413, ed. Paris. He granted them a plenary toleration in Phrygia and Lycaonia. We learn from the same authority, that in the following reign many persons at Constantinople (though they proved a minority) resisted all attempts to punish heretics with death: p. 419.

[5] The cruelty of these officials roused the spirit of the sufferers, who cut them off at Cynoschora in Armenia. Pet. Sicul. p. 66.

[6] *Ibid.* p. 62.

[7] He was assassinated by a zealot of Nicopolis: cf. Gieseler, in *Studien und Kritiken* for 1829, p. 100.

THE PAULI-
CIANS.

Their suppression in the East.

their leader in 835, the constitution of the system underwent a rapid change: a band of his assistants[1] (συνέκδημοι) were at first exalted to supremacy of power; but as soon as the persecuting spirit[2] was rekindled in the breast of the empress Theodora (circ. 844), the sect was converted into a political association, and soon after grew notorious for its lawlessness and rapine. At the head of it was a soldier, Karbeas, who in alliance with the Saracens and many of the rival schools of Paulicians (drawn by a common misery together), was enabled to sustain himself in a line of fortresses upon the confines of Armenia, and to scourge the adjacent province[3]. His dominion was, however, broken, and well-nigh extinguished under Basil I.[4] (867—886); though some of the phases of Paulicianism were constantly revived among the sects of the following period.

[1] Pet. Sicul. pp. 70 sq.
[2] A hundred thousand men are said to have been hanged, beheaded, or drowned. Constantini Porphyrog. Continuator, lib. IV. c. 16; inter *Scriptores Byzant.* p. 103, ed. Paris.
[3] Ibid. c. 23, 24, 25.
[4] In 969 a remnant of them were transported from the eastern districts to Philippopolis in Thrace by the emperor John Tzimisces. From thence they were able to extend themselves into other parts of Europe; but it is remarkable that some of their posterity are still found in the place to which they were transported. Neander, VI. 341: cf. Gibbon, V. 281—283; ed. Milman; and Spencer's *Travels in European Turkey*, II. 353.

CHAPTER IV.

ON THE STATE OF INTELLIGENCE AND PIETY.

THE standard of intelligence continued, on the whole, to be higher in the East than in the West; and more especially in districts where the Moslems were repulsed, it was subjected to fewer fluctuations. The religious spirit of the people, in like manner, underwent but little change, and, with the sole exception of the controversy on the use of pictures, which had stimulated every class of the community and made them take a side, their piety was generally confined to dreamy contemplation, or expressed in a calm routine of worship[1], tinctured more or less with superstition[2]. In the discipline and ritual of the Church it is easy to remark the same kind of uniformity; the Trullan Council (691), by a series of one hundred and two canons[3], having furnished all the Eastern patriarchates with a code of discipline, which has been constantly in force from that day to our own.

Of the west, as already noticed[4], Ireland was the brightest spot in the beginning of this period. Under Theodore[5],

---

[1] Theodore, himself a Greek of Tarsus, informs us that the Greeks, lay and clerical, were ordered to communicate every Sunday (*Pœnitent.* lib. I. c. 12, Councils &c. III. 186): and Beda (*Epist. ad Ecgberctum*, § 9) implies that in the east at large ('totum Orientem') it was not unusual for the pious to receive the sacrament every day.

[2] Pictures seem to have been perverted by the Oriental, as relics were in the Latin churches. Many of them had the reputation of working miraculous cures; and the 'Legends' of the period are full of instances establishing the almost universal spread of this and of similar delusions.

[3] Concil. Quinisext., Mansi, XI. 935—988: see above, p. 47.

[4] Above, p. 16, n. 2: pp. 19, 22.

[5] Above, pp. 14, 59, n. 4. Beda seems to have gathered into himself all the learning of the Irish, Frank and English churches, and to have transmitted it through the Northumbrian schools to Alcuin, who in turn transplanted it into France just as the northern invasions threatened to extinguish it here.

MEANS OF GRACE AND KNOWLEDGE.

Western Church.

and from his death to the invasions of the Northmen, much of the illumination still proceeding from the sister-island is reflected in the schools of Britain, where 'the ministers of God were earnest both in preaching and in learning;' and which acted as a 'seminary of religion,' whither pupils now resorted 'from foreign countries seeking after wisdom[1].' It was different in the Frankish and Burgundian provinces of Gaul, in which literature had been suffered to degenerate by the barbarous Merovingian kings. The flourishing schools of the Roman municipia had entirely disappeared[2], and their place was but inadequately filled by monastic and cathedral institutions, now set apart almost exclusively for the education of the clerics and the members of religious orders. Charlemagne, aided more especially by Alcuin[3], and other learned foreigners and natives, opened a fresh era in the history of letters; and the whole of his mighty empire underwent a salutary change. He laboured to revive religion by the agency of sounder learning[4], and in order to secure this end established a variety of schools,—the palatine, parochial, monastic, and cathedral[5].

Efforts of Charlemagne in behalf of learning.

But we should remember that the northern tribes, who

[1] The remark of King Alfred (Preface to his translation of Gregory's *Pastoral*), on contrasting the decay of learning after the barbaric inroads of the Danes. Beda (IV. 2) mentions that, after the coming of Theodore, all who wished to be instructed in sacred literature 'haberent in promptu magistros qui docerent.'

[2] See Guizot's *Sixteenth Lecture*, where he shews that from the sixth to the eighth century the surviving literature of France is exclusively religious. 'Ante ipsum enim dominum regem Carolum, in Gallia nullum studium fuerat liberalium artium.' *Annal. Lauriss.* A.D. 787; Pertz, I. 171. The state of learning in Italy itself was little better, owing to the savage spirit of the Lombards. Hallam, *Literature of Europe*, pt. I. ch. I. § 8.

[3] Above, p. 61. Some of the other more distinguished foreigners were Peter Pisanus, Paul Warnefrid, and Paulinus, patriarch of Aquileia, Leidrad, archbishop of Lyons (a native of Noricum), and Theodulph, bishop of Orleans, of Gothic parentage. Angilbert, the prime minister of Pepin and secretary of Charlemagne, was a native Frenchman, and a great promoter of schools and learning.

[4] See above, p. 56, n. 2.

[5] The best account of these institutions may be seen in Keuffel, *Hist. Originis ac Progr. Schol. inter Christianos*, pp. 161 sq. The *trivium* and *quadrivium*, elements of the 'seven liberal arts,' made part of the education given in the schools of Charlemagne. Theodulph, bishop of Orleans (*Capitulare*, c. 20: Mansi, XIII. 993 sq.), established village schools ('per villas et vicos') for all classes of the people.

broke up the empire of the Cæsars and were now planted on its ruins, not unfrequently retained their native dialects as well as a crowd of pagan customs and ideas[1]. Some of them, indeed, the Visigoths, the Franks, the Burgundians, and the Lombards, gradually forgot their mother-tongue, and at the end of the ninth century had thrown it off entirely[2]. But a number of their northern kinsmen did not follow their example. This variety of languages, combining with the remnants of barbaric life, would everywhere impose an arduous task upon the clergy of the west; yet few of them, it must be owned, were equal to their duty[3]: and the ill-advised adoption of the Latin language[4] as the vehicle of public worship (though at first it might have proved convenient here and there) contributed to thwart the influence of the pastor and retarded the improvement of his flock. It is true that considerable good resulted from the energy of individual prelates, who insisted on the need of clergy able to instruct their people in the elements of Christian knowledge[5], and to preach

MEANS OF GRACE AND KNOWLEDGE.

Evil growing out of the variety of language.

Attempts to mitigate these evils.

---

[1] *e. g.* numerous traces of this lingering heathenism have been collected in Kemble's *Saxons*, vol. I. App. F: cf. Gieseler, II. 160—162.

[2] Palgrave, *Hist. of Normandy*, I. 64.

[3] See above, pp. 46, 56. The *Capitulare ad parochiæ suæ Sacerdotes* of Theodulph, bishop of Orleans (786—821), while it displays somewhat elevated views of the pastoral office, indicates a sad deficiency in the knowledge of the general body of ecclesiastics. In like manner it was necessary to make the following decree at the English synod of Clovesho (747): 'That priests who know it not should learn to construe and explain in our own tongue the Creed and Lord's Prayer and the sacred words which are solemnly pronounced at the celebration of the mass, and in the office of baptism,' etc. Johnson, *English Canons*, I. 247; ed. Oxf. 1850. The literary qualifications needed in all ecclesiastics are enumerated in the *Capitular* of 802, apud Pertz, III. 107.

[4] The same feeling of respect for the usages of Rome induced the Frankish and English churches to adopt her psalmody and choral service. See Neander, v. 175, 176. The mission of John, 'the archchanter,' and the establishment of the 'cursus Romanus' in England (679), are described by Beda, *Hist. Eccl.* IV. 18. The Scottish (Irish) rites, however, had not been entirely superseded in the north of England at the close of the eighth century. Maskell's *Ancient Liturgy*, Pref. p. liv. In Ireland they retained their old supremacy until the arrival of the English, when the Anglican ritual was ordered to be observed 'in omnibus partibus ecclesiæ,' by the synod of Cashel (1172), c. 7; Wilkins, I. 473.

[5] Cf. the preceding note 3. Beda (*ep. ad Ecgberctum*, § 3): 'In qua videlicet prædicatione populis exhibenda, hoc præ cæteris omni instantia procurandum arbitror, ut fidem catholicam quæ apostolico symbolo continetur, et Dominicam orationem quam sancti Evangelii nos Scriptura edocet, *omnium* qui ad tuum regimen pertinent, memoriæ radicibus infi-

in the language of the country. Thus, in England it was ordered[1] that the priests shall often invite the people to meet on the Lord's day and other festivals 'to hear the word of God and to be often present at the sacraments of the masses and at preaching of sermons': and the rigorous observance[2] of the Lord's day in particular would give them opportunities of profiting by the injunction. It was urged anew in the reign of Charlemagne; *e.g.* at the Council of Mentz[3] (813), and in the same year at Arles, where the clergy are directed to preach on festivals and Sundays, not only in the cities, but in country parishes[4].

The growing education of the people would enable a far greater number of them to peruse the holy Scripture; nor did any wish exist at present to discourage such a study[5].

gere cures. Et quidem omnes qui Latinam linguam lectionis usu didicerunt, etiam hæc optime didicisse certissimum est: sed idiotas, hoc est, eos qui propriæ tantum linguæ notitiam habent, hæc ipsa *sua lingua* dicere, ac sedulo decantare facito.' The same is frequently enjoined elsewhere, *e. g.* Council of Mentz, 813, can. 45: Mansi, xiv. 74. A short form of abjuration of idolatry and declaration of Christian faith, in the vernacular language, is preserved among the works of Boniface: ii. 16, ed. Giles.

[1] Council of Clovesho, 747, can. 14. Johnson's *English Canons* i. 249. Chrodegang of Metz directed that the Word of salvation should be preached at least twice a month, though expressing a desire that sermons might be still more frequent: *Regula*, c. 44; Mansi, xiv. 337.

[2] The Penitential of Theodore (lib. i. c. 11, lib. ii. c. 8) is most stringent on this head: cf. a law of King Ine against Sunday working (Thorpe, i. 104; Johnson, i. 132), and one of the 'Laws of the Northumbrian Priests' (§ 55) against Sunday traffic and journeying of all kinds (Thorpe, ii. 298, Johnson, i. 379). See Schröckh, xx. 315, 316, for the views entertained by John of Damascus on the nature of the Lord's day. It is plain from the prohibitions of the Councils (*e. g.* of Châlons, 649, c. xix.) that the church-inclosure was at times converted into an arena of Sunday merriment and dissipation.

[3] Can. xxv: 'Juxta quod intelligere vulgus possit.'

[4] Can. x: 'Etiam in omnibus parochiis.' It was added in the Council of Tours (813), c. xvii., that preachers should translate their sermons either into *Romana rustica* or *Theotisca* (Deutsch), 'quo facilius cuncti possint intelligere quæ dicuntur.' Charlemagne had already published a collection of discourses (Homiliarium), which had been compiled by Paul Warnefrid (Diaconus), from the sermons of the Latin Fathers. See Ranke's article in the *Studien und Kritiken*, 1855, 2tes Heft, pp. 382 sq.

[5] See *e.g.* the passages above quoted, p. 56, and a still finer one translated into Anglo-Saxon, and preserved in Soames' *Bampton Lectures*, 92, 93: cf. also the language of Ildefonsus of Saragossa, in Baluze's *Miscellanea*, vi. 59. Alcuin, writing to the emperor (circ. 800), thus alludes to a query put to him by a layman who was conversant with the Scriptures; 'Vere et valde gratum habeo, *laicos quandoque* ad evangelicas effloruisse quæstiones, dum quendam audivi virum prudentem aliquando

It was, however, long restricted by the scarcity of books, and still more by the want of vernacular translations; though the latter had begun to be remedied, at least in some scanty measure, by the English and the German[1] Churches. Ulfilas, the father of this kind of literature, was followed, after a long interval, by the illustrious Beda, who, if he did not render the whole Bible[2] into Anglo-Saxon, certainly completed the Gospel of St John[3]. Aldhelm, who died in 709, is said to have made a version of the Psalms[4]; and we may infer from the treasures of vernacular literature handed down by the scholars of the period next ensuing, that not a few analogous productions were destroyed in the conflict with the Danes.

MEANS OF GRACE AND KNOWLEDGE.

Vernacular translations of the Bible.

But a more fascinating species of instruction was supplied in the 'Lives of Saints[5].' The number of these works, surviving at the present day, is actually prodigious[6]; and the influence they exerted on the mediæval mind was

Lives of Saints:

dicere, clericorum esse evangelium discere, non laicorum,' etc. *Epist.* CXXIV. (al. CLXIII.) *Opp.* I. 180. It has been observed, that in the catalogues of mediæval libraries, copies of the Holy Scriptures constitute the greater number of the volumes. Palgrave, *Hist. of Normandy*, I. 63. The subject has been examined also by Mr Buckingham, in his *Bible in the Middle Ages*, Lond. 1853.

[1] The influence exerted by Christianity on the old-German Language has been recently investigated by Von Raumer, *Einwirkung des Christenthums auf die althochdeutsche Sprache*, Stuttgart, 1845, where translations, glosses, and other fragments of vernacular piety have been discussed. But many of these specimens belong to the following period.

[2] See Lappenberg, *Anglo-Saxon Kings*, I. 203; and Gilly's *Introd.* to the *Romaunt Version of the Gospel according to St John* (Lond. 1848), pp. XI. sq.

[3] 'Evangelium quoque Johannis, quod difficultate sui mentes legentium exercet his diebus, lingua interpretatus Anglica, condescendit minus imbutis Latina.' Wil. Malmesbur. *de Gestis Regum*, lib. I. p. 89, ed. Hardy.

[4] Wright, *Biog. Brit. Lit.* I. 222. There was also a large stock of Anglo-Saxon religious poetry, of which Cædmon's *Metrical Paraphrase of Parts of the Holy Scriptures* (ed. Thorpe, 1832) is a very striking type. Cædmon died about 680. He was desired by the abbess Hilda of Whitby to transfer into verse the whole of the sacred history. Wright's *Biog. Brit. Lit.* I. 195. The interesting *Anglo-Saxon Ritual*, published, in 1839, by the Surtees Society, is one of a large class of interlinear translations, and may be assigned to the commencement of the ninth century: Stevenson's *Preface*, p. x.

[5] Gregory of Tours, who died 593, in a series of publications of this class, gave an impulse to the wonder-loving spirit of the age.

[6] See a calculation in Guizot's *Seventeenth Lecture*, based on the materials still surviving in the *Acta Sanctorum*.

deep and universal. While they fed almost every stream of superstition, and excited an unhealthy craving for the marvellous and the romantic, they were nearly always tending, in their *moral*, to enlist the affections of the reader on the side of gentleness and virtue; more especially by setting forth the necessity of patience, and extolling the heroic energy of faith. One class of these biographies deserves a high amount of credit: they are written by some friend or pupil of their subject; they are natural and life-like pictures of the times, preserving an instructive portrait of the missionary, the recluse, the bishop, or the man of business; yet in many cases the acts and sufferings of the mediæval saint have no claim to a place in the sphere of history, or else they have been so wantonly embellished by the fancy of the author, that we can disentangle very few of the particles of truth from an interminable mass of fiction. As these 'Lives' were circulated freely in the language of the people[1], they would constitute important items in the fire-side readings of the age; and so warm was the response they found in men of every grade, that notwithstanding feeble efforts to reform them[2], or at least to eliminate a few of the more monstrous and absurd, they kept their hold on Christendom at large, and are subsisting even now in the creations of the mediæval artist[3].

Keeping pace with this expansion in the field of

[1] An interesting specimen (*Anglo-Saxon*) has been edited with a translation by C. W. Goodwin (Lond. 1848). The subject of it is St Guthlac. a hermit of Crowland (written about 750, by a monk named Felix). There are many others preserved in our MSS. repositories.

[2] This had been attempted as early as the time of pope Gelasius (496); Mansi, VIII. 149: but the taste for legendary compositions went on increasing. Much of the increase in the number of the 'saints' is due to the liberty which every district seems to have enjoyed of enlarging its own calendar at pleasure. There is no instance of a canonization by the pope until the case of Swibert (about 800); and that has been disputed (Twysden, *Vindication of the Church of England*, p. 219, new ed.). According to Gieseler, II. 421, the earliest was Ulrich, bishop of Augsburg, in 993. Charlemagne, who was anxious to withstand the superstitions of his age (*e. g.* baptizing of bells, the 'sortes sanctorum,' etc.), published a capitulary (789, c. 76), *De pseudographiis et dubiis narrationibus;* and in the capitulary of Frankfort (794, c. 40) is the following injunction: 'ut nulli *novi sancti* colantur, aut invocentur, nec memoriæ eorum per vias [*i. e.* wayside chapels] erigantur; sed ii soli in ecclesia venerandi sint, qui ex auctoritate passionum aut vitæ merito electi sunt.'

[3] Didron's *Christian Iconography*, I. 192.

hagiology, the reverence which had long been cherished for the veritable saints continued to increase in every province of the Church; and even to resemble, here and there, a lower kind of worship. None of the more enlightened, it is true, have failed to distinguish[1] very clearly in their works between the honour of regard and imitation to be offered to the saint, and the supremacy of love and homage which is due to God alone: but in the mind of unreflecting peasants such distinctions were obliterated more and more, and numbers of the saints, apocryphal as well as true, had come to be regarded in the light of tutelar divinities[2]. At the head of a catalogue of saints, on whom a special veneration[3] was bestowed, is the blessed Virgin Mary; the exaggerations of this honour, which peep out in the earlier times, assuming more unchristian phases, in proportion as the worship of the Church was contracting a more sensuous tone. The synod held at Mentz[4], 813, in drawing up a list of feast-days, has included one for the 'Purification of St Mary[5],' handed down from better ages;

CORRUPTIONS AND ABUSES.

Exaggeration of the honour due to saints.

---

[1] *e. g.* Isidor. Hispalens. *De Eccles. Officiis,* lib. I. c. 34. Beda speaks of the transformation of the Pantheon at Rome into the Church of the Virgin and all Martyrs: 'ut, ubi quondam omnium non deorum sed dæmoniorum *cultus* agebatur, ibi deinceps omnium fieret *memoria* sanctorum.' *Chronicon,* A.D. 614; *Monum. Hist. Britan.* p. 97.

[2] Neander, v. 182, 183. But notwithstanding a large number of examples in this country where the saints are spoken of as 'intercessors' with God, they are scarcely ever at this period addressed *directly,* the petition being that '*God would make them* intercessors in our behalf.' Soames, *Bampton Lect.* p. 195, and notes. The passage sometimes quoted from Theodore, which speaks of more objectionable formulæ as then actually existing in the Litany of the Church: '*Christe, audi nos; ac deinde, Sancta Maria, ora pro nobis;* neque dicitur, *Christe, ora pro nobis,* et *Sancta Maria,* vel *Sancte Petre, audi nos;* sed, *Christe, audi nos; Fili Dei, te rogamus, audi nos,*' is spurious. Alcuin's apostrophe to S. Willebrord, if genuine, reads very like a prayer. Opp. II. 195.

[3] See Ildefonsus, *De Illibata Virginitate B. Virginis,* in Biblioth. Patr. VII. 432 sq. ed. Colon. 1618; and, for the Eastern church, John of Damascus, *Sermo in Annunciat. Dominæ nostræ* Θεοτόκου: Opp. II. 835 sq.

[4] Can. 36. Mansi, XIV. 73. At the same council four great fasts are mentioned: the first week in March, the second week in June, the third week in September, and the last full week in December before Christmas-day; at all which seasons public litanies and masses were to be solemnized at nine o'clock, on Wednesdays, Fridays, and Saturdays.

[5] Also called *Festum Symeonis,* and *Festum Symeonis et Hannæ.* In the Greek Church, where the honour is directed chiefly to our Lord, the title of the corresponding feast is ἑορτὴ τῆς ὑπαπαντῆς. Beda has a Homily upon it in the course of the festivals; *Opp.* VII. 327: and Ba-

CORRUPTIONS AND ABUSES.

Festival of the Assumption of the Virgin.

but in that list is also found the festival of the *Assumption of the Virgin* (August 15th), which communicated a far stronger impulse to the creature-worship of the masses. It grew[1] out of a spurious legend methodized by Gregory of Tours, in which it was affirmed that the original Apostles, on assembling at the death-bed of the Virgin, saw her carried by a band of angels into heaven.

Other festivals now generally observed in the Western Church.

The other festivals[2], excluding Sundays, now appointed or continued in the Frankish church, relate to the Nativity, the Circumcision, the Epiphany, and the Ascension of the Lord, the feast (or 'dedication') of St Michael[3], the martyrdoms ('natales') of St Peter and St Paul, of St Remigius, St Martin, St Andrew, and the nativity of St John the Baptist[4]: to which number, ancient festivals of saints and martyrs, who were buried in each diocese, together with the feasts of dedication for the several churches, were appended by the same authority. To this period also it is usual to assign the institution of the festival in honour of 'All Saints,' which, notwithstanding, had been long observed upon the octave of Whitsunday by the Christians of the East. It was ranked as a provincial celebration in the time of Boniface IV., when he was allowed to convert the famous Pantheon to the ser-

ronius, *Annal.* ad an. 544, informs us that Gelasius laid the foundation for its observance when he abolished the *lupercalia*.

[1] The various conjectures of the Fathers on the subject of the Virgin's end, have been stated at length by Gieseler, II. 313, n. 12. The apocryphal writing *Transitus S. Mariæ*, from which Gregory of Tours (*De gloria Martyrum*, lib. I. c. 4) derived the story now in circulation, had been placed by pope Gelasius among the interdicted books: above, p. 90, n. 2. Another festival, the *Birth of the Virgin* (Sept. 8), is dated also from this period.

[2] Concil. Mogunt. as above. The services of Easter and Whitsunday are to be continued for a whole week; and that of Christmas for four days.

[3] Not adopted in the East till the 12th century; Guerike, *Manual of Antiq. of the Church*, p. 195, ed. Morrison.

[4] In a second and an earlier list (*Capitular.* lib. I. c. 158), the feasts of St Stephen, St John the Evangelist, and the Holy Innocents, are also included: while with regard to the Assumption, it is added, 'De adsumptione S. Mariæ *interrogandum relinquimus*.' It is plain that this doubt continued to exist in the Anglo-Saxon Church. See the extract from a vernacular sermon in Soames' *Bampton Lect.* pp. 226, 227. The 13th canon of Clovesho (747) orders, in the case of England, that the 'nativities' of saints should be observed according to the Roman martyrology: Johnson, I. 249.

vice of the Gospel; and the usage thus adopted in the Roman dioceses was extended to the whole of the Western Church by Gregory IV. in 835[1].

Corruptions and abuses.

The state of feeling with regard to relics[2], which grew out of an excessive veneration for the saints, was rapidly assuming the extravagance and folly that have marked its later stages.

Relics.

The deplorable abuse of the imitative arts has been noticed in the rise and progress of the image-controversy. We there saw that the evil was resisted[3] for a time in the Frankish and the English Churches, while it gained a still firmer hold on other parts of Christendom, and threatened to subside into absolute idolatry.

Images.

The disposition to erect and beautify religious houses, which prevailed in the east and west alike, is often to be traced to purely Christian feelings[4]: not unfrequently, however, it proceeded from a mingled and less worthy motive,

Religious foundations.

---

[1] Guerike, p. 181. The following is the language of Alcuin (799) respecting the institution of this festival, and the mode in which it should be kept: 'Quod ut fieri digne possit a nobis, lumen verum, quod illuminat omnem hominem, Christus Jesus, illuminet corda nostra, et pax Dei, quæ exsuperat omnem sensum, per intercessionem omnium Sanctorum Ejus, custodiat ea usque in diem æternitatis. Hanc solemnitatem sanctissimam tribus diebus jejunando, orando, missas canendo, et eleemosynas dando per invicem, sincera devotione præcedamus.' *Ep.* LXXVI. (al. XCI.); *Opp.* I. 113.

[2] *e. g.* Theodor. *Penitential*, lib. II. c. 1: 'Reliquiæ tamen sanctorum venerandæ sunt. Si potest fieri, candela ardeat ibi per singulas noctes. Si autem paupertas loci non sinit, non nocet eis.' It was customary in the Frankish empire for chaplains to carry the relics of St Martin and others at the head of their armies ('patrocinia vel pignora sanctorum'): cf. Schröckh, xx. 127, 131: and the same feeling led the persecuted Spaniard to discover the potent relics of St James (between 791 and 842) in the person afterwards called St James of Compostella: *Acta Sanct.* Jul. tom. VI. p. 37. Even Alcuin (*Homil. de Natali S. Willebrord.*, *Opp.* II. 195) believed that the saintly missionary might continue to work miracles on earth, through the special grace of God.

[3] See above, p. 78. The same kind of exaggerated veneration was bestowed on the real or imaginary fragments of the cross; and in 631 the Emperor Heraclius, on defeating the Persians (above, p. 29), and recovering the precious relic from their hands, established a festival in honour of it, called σταυρώσιμος ἡμέρα (Sept. 14), adopted soon afterwards at Rome, under the designation, *Festum exaltationis crucis:* see *Liber Pontif.* ed. Vignol. I. 310.

[4] *e. g.* Einhard. *Vit. Karoli Magn.* c. 26: Pertz, II. 457. In a capitulary, 811 (Mansi, XIII. 1073), addressed to the prelates of the empire, the emperor tells them that, however good a work is the building of fine churches, the true ornament is to be found in the life of the worshippers ('præferendus est ædificiis bonorum morum ornatus et culmen').

CORRUPTIONS AND ABUSES.

Pilgrimages.

from the impulses of servile fear, and from a wish in the soul of the promoter to disarm the awakened vengeance of his Judge[1]. Another form in which these errors came to light was the habit of performing pilgrimages to some holy spot or country, where men dreamed of a nearer presence of the Lord, or some special intercession of the saints. A multitude of English devotees[2] betook themselves to Rome: and while it may be granted that excursions of this kind were often beneficial to the arts and letters of the country[3], no one has denied that many of the pilgrims, more especially the female portion, fell a prey to the laxity of morals which the custom almost everywhere induced. The less intelligent appear to have expected that a pilgrimage would help them on their way to heaven, apart from any influence it might have in stimulating the devotions of the pious: but this fallacy was strenuously confuted by the leading doctors of the age[4].

Practical results of

It has been shewn already[5] that the notion of a pur-

---

[1] The form of bequest often runs as follows; 'Pro animæ nostræ remedio et salute:' 'ut non inveniat in nobis ultrix flamma quod devoret, sed Domini pietas quod coronet.' See other forms of the same class in Schröckh, xx. 110, 111. However such expressions should not be analyzed too critically: clearly they were not intended as expositions of doctrine or creed, and pious forms in every age are liable to be misused.

[2] See above, p. 41, n. 3. Boniface was constrained to deprecate the frequency of pilgrimages, on the ground that they were often fatal to the virtue of the females: 'Perpaucæ enim sunt civitates in Longobardia, vel in Francia, aut in Gallia, in qua non sit adultera vel meretrix generis Anglorum: quod scandalum est, et turpitudo totius ecclesiæ vestræ:' *Ep.* LXIII; *Opp.* I. 146.

[3] This was certainly the case in men like Benedict Biscop, of whom Beda has remarked, 'Toties mare transiit, numquam, ut est consuetudinis quibusdam, vacuus et inutilis rediit, sed nunc librorum copiam sanctorum, nunc reliquiarum beatorum martyrum Christi munus venerabile detulit, nunc architectos ecclesiæ fabricandæ, nunc vitrifactores ad fenestras ejus decorandas ac muniendas, nunc cantandi et in ecclesia per totum annum ministrandi secum magistros adduxit, etc.' *Homil. in Natal. Benedict.*, *Opp.* VII. 334.

[4] Thus the 45th canon of the Council of Châlons (813) condemns all the pilgrimages undertaken in an irreverent spirit, with the hope of securing a remission of past sins, where no actual reformation was desired: but it is no less ready to commend such journeys when accompanied by true devotion ('orationibus insistendo, eleemosynas largiendo, vitam emendando, mores componendo'): cf. Alcuin, *Epist.* CXLVII. (al. CXCVI.) *Opp.* I. 208.

[5] Above, pp. 58, 59. Stories, like that which is told of Fursey, the Irish monk (Bed. *Hist. Eccl.* III. 19), would deepen the popular belief in a purgatorial fire.

gatorial fire, to expiate the minor sins ('leves culpæ') which still adhered to the departed, had been definitely formed under Gregory the Great, and from him was transmitted to the Christians of the West. This notion, while it threw a deeper gloom upon the spirits of the living, led the way to propitiatory acts intended to relieve the sufferings of the dead. It prompted feelings and ideas widely differing from those which circulated in the earlier Church[1]: for there, when the oblations were presented in the name of a departed worthy, they commemorated one already in a state of rest, though sympathizing with his brethren in the flesh, and expecting the completion of his triumph. The result of those mediæval masses for the dead[2] was to occasion a plurality of altars[3] in the churches, to commence the pernicious rite of celebrating the Eucharist without a congregation ('missæ privatæ,' or 'solitariæ'), and to reduce

Marginalia: CORRUPTIONS AND ABUSES. *the doctrine of purgatory. Masses for the dead. Private masses.*

---

[1] Cf. Bp. Taylor's *Dissuasive*, bk. II. § 2: *Works*, VI. 545 sq., ed. Eden.; Schröckh, xx. 175 sq.—With regard to the doctrine of the Eucharist, considered as a sacrificial act, commemorating the Great Sacrifice, and as the means of feeding upon Christ by faith, more will be observed in the following period, when the views of the Church at large began to be more technically stated. That the dogma of a physical transubstantiation of the elements was not held in the 7th century, is clear from Isidor. Hispalensis, *De Eccles. Officiis*, lib. I. c. 18: Ildefonsus, *De Cognitione Baptismi* (in Baluze's *Miscellanea*, VI. 99). The current doctrine of the Greek Church is to be sought in a work of Anastasius (a learned monk of Mount Sinai, at the close of the seventh century) entitled Ὀδηγός, seu *Dux viæ adversus Acephalos*, c. 23, ed. Ingolstadt, 1606; and in John of Damascus, *De Fide Orthodoxa*, lib. IV. c. 13: *Opp.* I. 267 sq. It was already common for the Easterns to make use of the terms μεταβολή, μεταστοιχείωσις, μεταποίησις, although neither then, nor at the present day, was it intended to express a 'physical' change in the substance of the elements after consecration, but a change which they define as 'sacramental and mystical.' Palmer, *Treatise on the Church*, II. 167, 3rd edit.: cf. L'Arroque, *Hist. of the Eucharist*, c. XI. XII.

[2] The usages and modes of thought in reference to them may be gathered from the following passage: 'Nonnulli solent interrogare, si pro omnibus regeneratis liceat sacrificium Mediatoris offerre, quamvis flagitiosissime viventibus, et in malis operibus perseverantibus? De hac quæstione varia expositio Patrum invenitur.' The point is finally determined thus: 'Illic saltem de minimis nihil quisque purgationis obtinebit, nisi bonis hoc actibus, in hac adhuc vita positus, ut illic obtineat, promereatur.' It occurs in the long Penitential falsely ascribed to Theodore, Thorpe, II. 53. In the East (Council *in Trullo*, can. 83) it was necessary to condemn a custom of administering the communion to the dead.

[3] See *Capitular.* A.D. 805, I. c. 6 (Pertz, III. 132), 'De Altaribus, ut non superflua sint in Ecclesiis.'

CORRUPTIONS AND ABUSES.

General system of church-penance.

in many parts the number of communicants[1]: but scandals of this kind, like many others then emerging to the surface of the Church, were warmly counteracted by the better class of prelates[2].

The establishment of these propitiatory masses for the dead, itself an effect of the novel dogmas which had flowed from the belief in purgatory, had contributed to work still further changes in the system of church-penance. It is true that the writers of this period lay great stress on the renovation of the heart as the index of a genuine contrition[3]; they recoil from the idea that alms, or any outward act, can be accepted as an expiation for man's sin, so long as the disposition of the sinner is unchanged[4]; yet the efforts[5] which were made by a series of active prelates to discriminate minutely between heavier and lighter sins, and to allot in each single case the just amount of penance, in proportion to the magnitude of

---

[1] See above, p. 85, n. 1. In the Western Church, where a neglect of the Eucharist was not followed by excommunication (Theodor. *Pœnit.* lib. I. c. 12), it was necessary to exhort the laity to a more frequent participation: *e. g.* Council of Clovesho (747), can. 23: Johnson, I. 253, 254. The Council of Châlons (813), can. 47, orders all Christians to communicate on Maundy-Thursday: Mansi, XIV. 103.

[2] *e. g.* Solitary masses are condemned by the Council of Mentz (813), can. 43; and by Theodulph, bishop of Orleans, *Capitulare ad Sacerdotes*, c. VII; Johnson, I. 456: cf. *ibid.* 419.

[3] The Council of Châlons, above cited (813), is full of cheering thoughts on this point as on many others. Its language was, 'Neque enim pensanda est pœnitentia quantitate temporis, sed ardore mentis et mortificatione corporis. Cor autem contritum et humiliatum Deus non spernit:' can. 34. In can. 38 it repudiates what was known as 'libelli pœnitentiales' (certificates of penance irregularly acquitting the offender), 'quorum sunt certi errores, incerti auctores.'

[4] *e.g.* The emphatic language of the synod of Clovesho; can. 26, 27; Johnson, I. 255—259. Twelve means and conditions of forgiveness are recited in the so-called Penitential of Cummeanus; Wasserschleben, *Bussordnungen*, p. 304. The fanatical austerity with which conditions of this class were sometimes carried out, resulted in a kind of oriental self-destruction, and induced the Frankish emperor to pass a special law (*Capitul.* 789, c. 77, ed. Baluze, I. 239) forbidding all such penitents to shew themselves in public. A milder form of the same feeling is betrayed in the 10th canon of Toledo (683), where we learn that it was not uncommon for persons (even prelates) in a time of dangerous illness to submit themselves to public penance, for the greater security, although their conscience did not accuse them of any special sin.

[5] See above, p. 59, n. 4. Another contribution to the series was made at the opening of the ninth century by Halitgar, bishop of Cambray (Cameracensis), printed in Canisius, *Lect. Antiq.* ed. Basnage, tom. II. part ii. pp. 87 sq.

the offence[1], are dark and distressing proofs of the corruptions then prevailing in the Church, no less than of the servile spirit that was influencing her teachers. In the case of overt sins, where public satisfaction was required, the form of it was generally determined by the bishop when he came on his visitation-tour[2]; but all offences of a private nature, though not uniformly[3], were most frequently confessed in secret to a priest, who, varying from the ancient practice, instantly conceded absolution[4],—with the tacit understanding, in all cases, that the penance he directed would be afterwards performed.

Confession and satisfaction.

Yet, far as the actual system of the Church, in this and other features, had diverged from apostolic usage; largely as alloy had now been fused into the gold, and thickly as the tares were mingling with the wheat implanted by the heavenly Sower,—there is ample testimony in the canons of reforming synods, and still more in the exalted lives of men like Aidan, Gregory, Eligius, Liudger, Bede, and Alcuin, or of John the Almoner, of Maximus and others in the East, to certify us that reli-

Tokens of vitality within the Church.

---

[1] See especially Halitgar's *Penitential* and the compilation which has been published, wrongly of course, under the name of Egbert, Thorpe, II. 129—239. One of the worst features of this system, as it is here expounded, was the redemption, or commutation, of penances by means of money-payments, e.g. Cummeanus, apud Wasserschleben, p. 464: cf. *Canons enacted under Edgar;* Thorpe, II. 284—288: see the sect. '*Of satisfaction for sin,*' in the *Penitential Canons* (963); Johnson, I. 440. It led to the transferring of the civil 'bots,' or compensations, to the higher province of religion, and could hardly fail to foster the pernicious thought that it was possible in many cases to buy off the displeasure of the Lord; although an inference like this was strongly censured in the 26th canon of Clovesho; and in one 'Enacted under Edgar,' § 19, it is added that the penitent, however wealthy, 'must supplicate for himself, with true love of God.' Cf. Bedæ *Ep. ad Ecgberctum,* § 11 (p. 343, ed. Hussey).

[2] See above, p. 46, n. 1: and *Capitular.* II., A.D. 813, c. 1.

[3] Theodor. *Pænit.* lib. I. cap. 12. § 7. "Confessio autem Deo soli agatur licebit si necesse est;" it is added "et hoc, *necessarium,* in quibusdam codicibus non est;" and so in fact it stands in Cummeanus, XIV. 13. The statements of Theodulph of Orleans (*Capit.* c. 30: Mansi, XIII. 1002), and of the Council of Châlons, above cited, c. 33, are still clearer proofs that confession to a priest was not generally regarded as *essential* to forgiveness of sins.

[4] Thus Boniface in his *Statuta* (*Opp.* II. 22—25) enjoins, c. 31: 'Curet unusquisque presbyter statim post acceptam confessionem pœnitentium, singulos data oratione reconciliari.'

M. A.   H

CORRUPTIONS AND ABUSES.

gion was not mastered by the powers of darkness, but that, on the contrary, the Spirit of her Lord and Saviour was still breathing in the Christian Church, and training men for heaven.

Second Period of the Middle Ages.

THE CHRISTIAN CHURCH FROM THE DEATH OF CHARLEMAGNE TO GREGORY VII.

814—1073.

CHAPTER V.

§ 1. *GROWTH OF THE CHURCH.*

IN THE SCANDINAVIAN KINGDOMS.

Danish and Swedish Church.

First steps in the conversion of the Northern nations.

THE age in which the hardy Northmen were descending on the rest of Europe and preparing to involve their fortunes in the politics of neighbouring countries, was distinguished by the earliest missionary efforts to engraft them on the Christian Church. This project is attributable in some measure to the enterprising Liudger, but his zeal, after reaping a small harvest of conversions[1], was restrained by an order of the Frankish monarch[2].

In the evening of his reign, however, when the Saxons were all conquered, Charlemagne, it is said, was purposing to found an archbishopric at Hamburg, with a view to the further planting of the Gospel in the Scandinavian kingdoms[3]. The completion of this noble scheme had been reserved for his successor, Louis the Pious, who by the

---

[1] See above, p. 25. The Englishman, Willehad, also (p. 26) preached as early as 780 to the Ditmarsi, in the neighbourhood of Hamburg. The best modern account of the propagation of the Gospel in these regions is Münter's *Kirchengeschichte von Dänem. und Norweg.* Leipz. 1823: cf. also Kruse's *S. Anschar*, Altona, 1823.

[2] 'Fuit autem cupiens anxie gratia docendi Northmannos adire, sed rex Karolus nullatenus assensum præbuit.' *Vit. S. Liudger.* apud Pertz, II. 414.

[3] .... 'Unde prædicatio verbi Dei finitimis fieret populis, Sueonum, Danorum, Norweorum, Farriæ, Gronlandan, Islandan, Scridivindan, Slavorum; necnon omnium septentrionalium et orientalium nationum quocumque modo nominatarum, qui paganicis adhuc erroribus involvuntur.' *Vit. S. Rimbert.* c. 1: Ibid. II. 765.

succours he despatched[1] to Harald, king of Jutland, made a way for the introduction of the Christian faith. A mission was at first directed[2] by the earnest and experienced Ebbo, archbishop of Rheims. He carried a commendatory letter[3] from pope Paschal I. (circ. 822), and was attended by the learned Halitgar[4], bishop of Cambray. Their labours were rewarded[5], more especially in Jutland; and in 826 the king himself, together with his consort and a retinue of Danes, was solemnly baptized at Mentz[6] in the presence of the emperor, his patron. Harald now returned to his native country, and was anxious to engage the help of some active prelate, who would give himself entirely to the work of organizing missions for the other parts of Denmark.

These important functions were devolved on Anskar[7] (Ansgar), who was destined to be afterwards called the 'Apostle of the North.' He was born in the diocese of Amiens, 801, and educated at Corbey, an adjoining monastery, under Adalhard[8], the grandson of Charles Martel, and Paschasius Radbert, a professor of theology. In 822 Anskar was removed to a new foundation[9], lately planted by the monks of Corbey, in Westphalia, on the banks of the Weser. He there acted as the head of a thriving school[10] and preached among the natives, until, at the request of Louis, he was added to the suite of the Danish monarch. Like his predecessor, Ebbo, he is said to have

DANISH AND SWEDISH CHURCH.

Successful Mission of Ebbo into Jutland.

The missionary life of Anskar 826—865.

---

[1] *Annales Fuldens.* A.D. 815; Pertz, I. 356.
[2] *Vit. S. Anskarii*, c. 13: *Ibid.* II. 699.
[3] Lappenberg's *Hamburg. Urkundenbuch*, I. 9; ed. 1842.
[4] See p. 96, n. 5.
[5] *Annales Fuldens.* A.D. 822: Pertz, I. 357. The starting-point of their operations was at Welanao, the modern Münsterdorff, near Itzehoe, in Holstein.
[6] *Ibid.* A.D. 826; p. 359; cf. the contemporary *Carmina* of Ermoldus Nigellus, 'in honorem Hludowici,' reprinted in Pertz, II. 467 sq.
[7] The interesting *Life of Anskar* is the work of Rimbert and another of his pupils, and was composed before the year 876. It is reprinted in Pertz, *Monum. Germ.* II. 689—725.
[8] See Palgrave, *Hist. of Normandy*, I. 169, 209.
[9] Called the *new* Corbey or Corvey. The abbot (*Vit. Anskar.* c. 7) for a time was Count Wala, brother of Adalhard, who was separated from his wife and thrust into that position by an order of the jealous Louis. See the rhetorical accounts of Adalhard and Wala, by Paschasius Radbert, in Pertz, II. 524—569; and *Radberti Opp.* 1507, ed. Migne.
[10] *Vit.* c. 6.

been armed with a commendatory letter[1] from pope Eugenius II. He departed from his cloister in **826** or **827**, accompanied by a single coadjutor, Autbert, who assisted him in the foundation of a school in Nordalbingia, on the borders of Schleswig. Here they educated a small band of native youths whom they had ransomed out of slavery[2]. But their proceedings were suspended for a time by a rebellion of the pagan Danes, who, in **828**, were able to expel the king, and all whom they suspected of alliance with the Franks.

A second field, however, was soon opened to the diligence of Anskar. Guided by the will of Louis, and surrendering the Danish mission to another monk named Gislemar[3], he migrated in **831** to Sweden, where, as he had been informed, a multitude of persons were now anxious to embrace the Gospel[4]. His companion was a brother-monk of Corbey, Witmar; and the missionaries, rescued only with their lives from an attack of northern pirates, landed on the coast of Sweden at Biorka[5], near the ancient capital, Sigtuna. Here they gained permission from the king to enter on their labours, and were welcomed more especially by Christian captives[6], whom the Swedes had carried off from the adjoining districts. After making

---

[1] Lappenberg, *Hamburg. Urkundenbuch*, I. 29. Pope Gregory IV. (about 834) is said to have confirmed the appointment of Anskar as 'primum Nordalbingorum archiepiscopum,' and to have commissioned him and his successors as the papal legates 'in omnibus circumquaque gentibus Danorum, Sueonum, Noruehorum, Farrie, etc.;' but this document, if not altogether spurious, is at least interpolated. Jaffé, *Regest. Pontif. Roman.* p. 228: cf. Wiltsch, *Kirchl. Geographie*, § 252, n. 8. Some of the language here employed agrees with expressions in the *Life of S. Rimbert*, cited above, p. 100, n. 3.

[2] 'Ipsi quoque Divino inspirati amore ad promulgandam devotionis suæ religionem cœperunt curiose pueros quærere, quos emerent, et ad Dei servitium educarent,' etc. *Vit. S. Anskar.* c. 8. Autbert died two years after.

[3] 'Patrem [? the prior] devotissimum Gislemarum, fide et operibus bonis probatum, etc.' *Ibid.* c. 10.

[4] *Ibid.* c. 9. They seem to have heard of Christianity by means of the traffic carried on between Dorstede (Wyk te Duerstede) and some of the Swedish ports: cf. c. 27. About 830 they sent envoys to the court of Louis the Pious requesting a supply of regular instructors, c. 9. The chronology adopted in this narrative is that of Dahlmann, the last editor of the *Life of Anskar*. With regard to earlier traces of the Gospel see Schröckh, XXI. 320.

[5] *Vit.* c. 11, and the note in Pertz, II. 697.

[6] *Ibid.*

one important convert, Herigar (or Hergeir), a distinguished Swedish noble, messengers were sent to Louis with the tidings of success; and Anskar, in **832 or 833**, was raised to the archbishopric of Hamburg[1], which had been selected as the centre of the northern missions. He soon afterwards betook himself to Rome, and as the guest of Gregory IV. was bound more closely in allegiance to the pope, and flattered by the present of a pall[2]. With the desire of strengthening the work of Anskar, Ebbo, whom we saw already forwarding the Gospel in the north, deputed his own missionary office to his nephew Gauzbert[3], who henceforward (with the name of Simon) was especially directed to evangelize the Swedes.

DANISH AND SWEDISH CHURCH.

Anskar, archbishop of Hamburg.

For some time very little was effected by the holy zeal of Anskar. An opponent of the Christian faith, the persecuting Horic (Erich), was the single lord of Denmark; and the efforts of the missionary, who was planted on the frontier of the kingdom, were confined to the redemption and religious training of a multitude of youthful slaves. In **837** the see of Hamburg also was invaded by the northern pirates (Vikings), who demolished[4] all the outward fabric of religion. While the bishop with a few necessitous attendants wandered to and fro among the ruins of his diocese, a fresh disaster had occurred in Sweden (**837**), where the heathen population rose in arms against the missionaries, and expelled them from the country[5].

Interruption of his labours.

---

[1] .... 'cui subjaceret universa Nordalbingorum ecclesia, et ad quam pertineret omnium regionum aquilonalium potestas ad constituendos episcopos, sive presbyteros in illas partes pro Christi nomine destinandos.' *Ibid.* c. 12: cf. *Capitular.* ed. Baluze, I. 681. Anskar was consecrated by Drogo, archbishop of Metz, and 'archicapellanus'; Ebbo and others assisting.

[2] *Ibid.* c. 13: but cf. above, p. 102, n. 1.

[3] *Ibid.* c. 14: .... 'ad partes veniens Sueonum, honorifice et a rege et a populo susceptus est, cœpitque cum benevolentia et unanimitate omnium ecclesiam inibi fabricare, et publice evangelium fidei prædicare.' Funds for the mission were provided in this case, and in that of Anskar, by the gift of a monastery from the crown.

[4] 'Ibi ecclesia miro opere magisterio domni episcopi constructa, una cum claustra monasterii mirifice composita, igni succensa est. Ibi biblioteca [*i. e.* the copy of the Bible], quam serenissimus jam memoratus imperator eidem patri nostro contulerat, optime conscripta, una cum pluribus aliis libris igni disperiit.' *Vit. S. Anskar.* c. 16.

[5] *Ibid.* c. 17. Ebbo was now entangled in the political troubles of the

DANISH AND SWEDISH CHURCH.

Farther progress of the mission.

But a brighter epoch was approaching. Anskar, at the end of seven years, was able to regain his hold on the affections of the Swedes. In 844 he persuaded Ardgar[1], an anchoret in holy orders, to direct the movements of the sinking mission; and in 849 his own hands were considerably strengthened by annexing to his archbishopric the larger see of Bremen[2], which was vacant by the death of Leuderic in 847. His elevation is to be ascribed to the interest of Louis the Germanic, but the union of the sees was afterwards confirmed[3] by a rescript of pope Nicholas I. (864). Relieved in this way from the embarrassment occasioned by his want of funds, he gave himself entirely to the wider planting of the faith.

Horic favourable to the Christians.

His progress was facilitated by disarming, if not absolutely winning over[4], the impetuous Horic, king of Jutland; and a number of the Danish Christians, who had long been worshipping in secret, publicly avowed and exercised their faith[5]. The mission now expanded freely on all sides.

It was at this juncture that the Swedes, on the return of the hermit Ardgar, were in want of an authorized instructor; and accordingly the great apostle of the North-men,

empire; but a short time before his death he gave utterance to a firm belief that Christianity would ere long penetrate the furthest corner of the north: .... 'si aliquando propter peccata quodammodo impeditum fuerit, quod nos in illis cœpimus gentibus, non tamen umquam penitus extinguetur, sed fructificabit in Dei gratia et prosperabitur, usque quo perveniat nomen Domini ad fines orbis terræ.' *Ibid.* c. 34.

[1] *Ibid.* c. 19, 20; where an account is given of the zeal and fortitude displayed by Herigar and other Christians while the mission was suspended. Ardgar ultimately returned to his hermitage (? 850).

[2] Anskar hesitated in the first instance (*Vit.* c. 22), but was overpowered by the king and the Council of Mentz (? 847). It appears that the see of Hamburg was now reduced, by the desolations of the Northmen, to four 'baptismal churches.' *Ibid.*: cf. Giesebrecht's *Wendische Geschichte*, I. 161; Berlin, 1843: Pagi, ad an. 858, §§ 3 sq.

[3] Lappenberg, *Hamburg. Urkund.* I. 25. The see of Bremen had been formerly subject to the primate of Cologne, but was by this act transferred to Hamburg.

[4] 'Ille quoque omnia, quæ ei ex Divina intimabat scriptura, benigne audiebat, et bona prorsus ac vere salutaria esse laudabat, seque his plurimum delectari ac libenter Christi gratiam velle promereri.' *Vit. Anskar.*, c. 24.

[5] 'Multi namque ibi antea erant Christiani, qui vel in Dorstado vel in Hammaburg baptizati fuerant, quorum quidam primores ipsius vici habebantur, et gaudebant facultatem sibi datam Christianitatem suam observandi.' *Ibid.*

girding up his loins afresh, and taking with him Erimbert[1], a priest, set out for the court of Olof, king of Sweden[2], where he hoped to secure a footing for the Gospel. He was aided by a timely nomination as ambassador of Louis the Germanic, and had also the protection of an envoy from the friendly court of Jutland. After hesitating for some time, it was decided by the Swedish nobles that the future toleration of the Christian faith should be determined by appealing to the heathen lots[3]; which providentially accorded with the earnest prayers of Anskar[4]. He now left his colleague, Erimbert, in Sweden, and re-visited his diocese[5] (circ. 854). Another storm was blackening the horizon of the Danish Church; the king of Jutland, who had been a patron of the mission, was supplanted by a second Horic, under whom assemblies of the Christian population had been strongly interdicted; but a kindlier spirit was ere long infused into the royal counsels; and when Anskar sank beneath his burdens in 865, he left a flourishing community behind him both in Schleswig and in Jutland.

<small>DANISH AND SWEDISH CHURCH.</small>

<small>*Anskar's fresh visit to Sweden:*</small>

<small>*its happy issue.*</small>

<small>*Fresh reverse in Denmark:*</small>

<small>*soon terminated.*</small>

He was followed in the see of Hamburg-Bremen (865–888) by a prelate of congenial temper. This was Rimbert[6], his biographer and pupil. But the widening irruptions of the pagan Northmen[7] counteracted all the efforts of the missionary, and uprooted many ancient in-

<small>*Renewal of the troubles of the Church.*</small>

---

[1] It was on this person that Gauzbert, who had been expelled from Sweden, now devolved his missionary office. *Ibid.* c. 25, 30.

[2] The interview is recorded at length, *ibid.* c. 26.

[3] For an account of the northern mythology, see the references above, p. 18, n. 3, to which Mallet's *Northern Antiquities* may be added.

[4] 'Exeuntes igitur more ipsorum in campum, miserunt sortes: ceciditque sors, quod Dei voluntate Christiana religio ibi fundaretur.' *Vit. Anskar.*, c. 27.

[5] *Ibid.* c. 28.

[6] See the *Life of Rimbert* (Pertz, II. 765—775), written either by a cleric of the diocese of Bremen, or by a monk of Corbey, soon after his death.

[7] Some of them effected a landing in Belgium as early as 820, but were repelled (Palgrave, *Hist. of Normandy*, I. 255). The Danish invasions of England, and the Norwegian invasions of Ireland and Scotland, began at the close of the preceding century. Alcuin already speaks of the 'populus paganus' in 797; *Epist.* LIX.: al. LXXIV. *Opp.* I. 78: cf. Worsaae's *Danes and Norwegians in England, Scotland, and Ireland*, passim. They ravaged every part of France and won a permanent settlement in Neustria about 911. Palgrave, I. 671 sq.

<small>DANISH AND SWEDISH CHURCH.</small>

stitutions in the other Christian provinces of Europe. Rimbert was succeeded by Adalgar[1], but the sphere of his labours was still more contracted by the inroads of the Slaves and the Hungarians[2]. At the opening of the tenth century the throne of Denmark had been filled by a usurper, Gurm, who shewed a bitter hatred to the Church: but in 934, his violence was checked by Henry I. of Germany, who wrested Schleswig from his grasp, and planted there a colony of Christians[3]. The next king of Denmark, Harald Blaatand, in a long reign of fifty years (941—991) was favourable[4] to the propagation of the Gospel; and Adaldag, the archbishop of Hamburg-Bremen, actively proceeded in the organizing of the Danish Church. This work, however, was again suspended through the violent reaction of the pagans[5], headed by the faithless son of Harald, Sveno (Svend), who, on his accession to the throne, immediately expelled the clergy, and was afterwards the scourge of England[6]. There, indeed, his fury was at length exchanged for something like repentance[7]; and his son, the distinguished Cnut (Canute the Great, 1014—1035), was assiduous in despatching missionaries[8]

<small>*Favourable policy of Harald.*</small>

<small>*Establishment of*</small>

---

[1] Lappenberg, *Hamburg. Urkund.* I. 43.

[2] Adam. Bremensis (who wrote about 1075), *Hist. Eccles.* lib. I. c. 32 sq.

[3] *Ibid.* lib. I. c. 48—50, and Schröckh, XXI. 344 sq. The new archbishop of Hamburg-Bremen, Unni, availed himself of this favourable turn in the fortunes of the Church, and renewed the mission to the heathen. One of the petty kings of South Jutland, Frodo, is said to have been baptized by Unni; and this led to the establishment of bishoprics at Schleswig, Ripen, and Aarhus. See Council of Ingelheim, A.D. 948; and the conflicting account of Adam of Bremen, lib. II. c. 2. Not long after bishoprics were planted at Odensee, in the island of Funen; at Roskild, in Zealand, as well as at Lund and Dalby. Wiltsch, *Kirch. Geograph.* I. 389.

[4] Respecting his conversion, see the story of Wittekind, a monk of Corbey, in the *Scriptores Rerum German.* ed. Meibom. I. 660; and cf. Neander, V. 397, 398.

[5] Adam. Bremensis, *Hist. Eccl.* lib. II. c. 15 sq.

[6] *Ibid.* c. 28, 36: see below, on the 'Limitation of the Church.'

[7] He is even said to have laboured in behalf of the religion he had formerly betrayed and persecuted. Saxo Grammaticus, *Hist. Danorum*, lib. X. pp. 186—188, ed. Stephan.

[8] Bishops and priests are said to have been ordained for this purpose by Æthelnoth, the archbishop of Canterbury. Adam. Bremen. lib. II. c. 36 sq. Münter, *Kirchengesch. von Dänemark*, I. 322. The zeal of Cnut was stimulated at the remembrance of the wrongs inflicted on the Church at large by his persecuting father: and the same motive, mingled with

to evangelize his Scandinavian subjects, until Denmark, as a nation, paid her homage unto Christ[1].

In Sweden, where the elements of strife resembled those of Denmark, little progress had been made in the diffusion of the Gospel[2], since the happier days of Anskar. Many seeds, however, planted by his care and watered by the visits of his scholar, Rimbert, still continued to bear fruit. The mission was resumed[3] in 930 by Unni, archbishop of Hamburg; and some other neighbouring prelates joined him in his work. The reign of Olaf Skötkonung, commencing with the eleventh century, was marked by a more vigorous advancement on all sides. He was baptized about 1008, and afterwards secured the help of English clergymen, as Sigefrith, Rodulf, Sigeward, and others, who expended all their strength in building up the Scandinavian Churches[4]. The first bishopric of Sweden[5] was now placed at Skara, in West-Gothland, where the Christians more especially abounded; and the policy of future kings, excepting Svend, the latest champion of

DANISH AND SWEDISH CHURCH.

religion under Cnut the Great.

Fresh efforts to convert the Swedes: triumphant under Olaf Skötkonung.

---

excessive reverence for the pope, impelled him to set out on a pilgrimage to Rome (in 1027): *Anglo-Sax. Chron.* ad an. 1031: cf. Lappenberg, *Anglo-Saxon Kings*, II. 211 sq.

[1] The nephew of Cnut, Sveno Estrithson, who succeeded to the crown of Denmark in 1047, cooperated with Adalbert, the archbishop of Hamburg-Bremen, in propagating the Gospel in the northern islands and elsewhere (Adam. Bremen. lib. IV. c. 16); but in Friesland, on the coast of Schleswig, as well as in the corners of North Jutland and of Schonen, paganism subsisted for a century or more.

[2] Adam. Bremen. lib. I. c. 51.

[3] *Ibid.* lib. II. c. 2, c. 16. There were still, however, many heathen, or but half-converted Christians, even in the north of Sweden: cf. Schröckh, XXI. 361, 362. Among the upper Swedes the pagan system lingered till the middle of the 12th century.

[4] Adam. Bremen. lib. II. c. 38, 40, 44. Some of these English missionaries (*e. g.* Wulfrith), by their violent attacks on paganism, aroused the vengeance of the Swedes.

[5] It was filled by an Englishman named Turgot, but his orders were derived from the archbishop of Hamburg, Unwan. Other Swedish bishoprics were soon afterwards founded at Lincöping, Wexiö, Upsala, Strengnaes, and Westeråhs. Jealousies appear to have arisen between the later prelates of Hamburg-Bremen and the kings of neighbouring states (Adam. Bremen. lib. III. c. 15—17): but the difference was adjusted for a while in the time of archbishop Adalbert, who was (1068) acknowledged as the primate of twelve dioceses (Wiltsch, *Kirchl. Geograph.* I. 390), and also as a kind of Scandinavian pontiff. In 1104, however, the more northern bishops were subordinated to the metropolitan of Lund. Münter, *Kircheng.* II. 76.

idolatry¹, contributed to swell their numbers. In **1075** the public services of Thor and Odin were all absolutely interdicted by a royal order, and the cause of Christianity henceforth was everywhere triumphant.

The first entrance of the Gospel into Norway was effected also through an English channel. Hacon (Hagen) is said to have been educated² at the court of Æthelstan (**924—941**); and on his return to his native country, where he made himself supreme, he laboured, with the aid of priests from England, to displace the pagan worship³. His endeavours soon aroused the hatred of his subjects, who accordingly compelled him to take part in their sacrificial rites⁴, and murdered the promoters of the Christian religion. On his death, which was embittered by the thought of his criminal compliance with idolatry, the Northmen were subdued by Harald Blaatand, king of Denmark (**962**), who, in order to revive a knowledge of the Gospel, had recourse to oppression and the sword. His measures were reversed soon after by the equal violence of Hacon jarl, an implacable opponent of the truth⁵. It was, however, introduced afresh by Olaf Tryggvasön (**995—1000**), who had been converted while engaged in foreign travel⁶, and was finally baptized in the Scilly Islands⁷. Anxious to diffuse the blessings of the Gospel,

---

¹ The pagan party were exasperated by the efforts of Adelward (a bishop sent from Bremen, 1064) to subvert their ancient temple at Upsala. Adam. Bremen. lib. III. c. 17; lib. IV. c. 44. This attempt was prudently resisted by the Christian monarch, Stenkil; but his son Inge (1067), who yielded to the over-zealous missionaries, was expelled by the heathen under Svend, and restored only by the help of his Danish neighbours.

² This is the account of the Scandinavian Chroniclers: see the evidence on both sides in Lappenberg, *Anglo-Saxon Kings*, II. 105, 106.

³ See Münter, as above; Torfæus, *Hist. Norvegica*, Pars II. pp. 215 sq. ed. Hafniæ, 1711; and, for the most ancient authority, the *Heimskringla* (Hist. of Norwegian Kings), by Snorro Sturleson, who died in 1241.

⁴ He finally consented to eat horse-flesh, after drinking in honour of Odin, Thor, and Bragi [? Fricge]. Torfæus, Pars II. pp. 219 sq.

⁵ *Ibid.* 237 sq. He had been himself a Christian in the previous reign, but had apostatized on his accession to the throne.

⁶ He had travelled in Greece, Russia, England, and the north of Germany. In the last-mentioned country, he fell in with Thangbrand, a soldier-like priest of Bremen, who appears to have turned his thoughts to the consideration of the Gospel.

⁷ He had landed there while engaged in a piratical expedition. Some

he took with him into Norway (**977**) an ecclesiastic of the name of Thangbrand, but their efforts were too often thwarted by the violence with which their teaching was accompanied. The jarls, who governed Norway as the envoys from the courts of Denmark and Sweden, after Olaf was deposed (**1000**), extended toleration to the Christians, and as soon as the foreign yoke was broken by the valour of Olaf the Holy (**1017—1033**), every stronghold[1] of the pagan system was unsparingly demolished, and the Gospel, partly by instruction[2], but still more by dint of arms[3], was planted on the ruins.

Iceland, which was destined to enjoy the highest reputation as a seat of mediæval learning, had been colonized by the Norwegians in **870**. But the tidings of the Gospel did not reach it, or at least made no distinct impression[4], till a Saxon prelate, Friedrich, influenced by the reasons of a native chieftain, who had roved the German seas, attempted to secure a footing in **981**. He was, however, fiercely counteracted by the scalds (or pagan minstrels): and after labouring to little purpose, for a period of five years, he gave up the mission in despair. A fresh attempt

Marginalia: ICELANDIC CHURCH. *finally successful.* — *The conversion of Iceland.*

---

time before, in conjunction with Svend of Denmark, he had ravaged all the southern coasts. Lappenberg, II. 157, 158. He was afterwards confirmed in England, which he promised not to visit for the future as an enemy (*Saxon Chron.* A.D. 994).

[1] See, among other instances, the account of the destruction of a colossal 'Thor' in the province of Dalen: Neander, v. 410, 411.

[2] In this he was assisted by the founding of schools, and by the labours of ecclesiastics out of England (see above, p. 106, n. 8), some of whom passed forward into Sweden. The Norwegian sees of Nidaros (Drontheim), Opslo, Bergen, Hammer, and Stavanger, were not organized until the following period (Wiltsch, *Kirchl. Geogr.* II. 96): but Olaf was the founder of the mother-church of Drontheim. Nominally all the Scandinavian churches were still subject to the archbishopric of Hamburg, but it seems from a rescript of pope Alexander II. (1061), that it was customary for the Norwegian bishops to be consecrated either in England or in France. Lappenberg, *Hamburg. Urkund.* I. 84: Mansi, XIX. 942 sq.

[3] The sufferings of the heathen party predisposed them to assist the English monarch, Cnut, 1028, in dethroning Olaf (Lappenb. II. 215, 216); but the fortunes of the Church were unaffected by this conquest.

[4] We learn from Münter's *Geschichte* (as above), I. 520, that when the Northmen landed, they found some traces of an older Christianity which had been planted in Iceland by the agency of Irish missionaries: cf. Neander, v. 412, note. One of the fullest histories of the Icelandic Church is that by Finnur Joensen (Finus Johannæus), *Hist. Eccles. Islandiæ*, Hafniæ, 1772—1775.

was made by Olaf Tryggvasön, the king of Norway, who persuaded Stefner, a young Christian Icelander (**996**), to carry back the Gospel to his fellow-countrymen. His labours also were resisted, as were those of the royal chaplain and ambassador, the military Thangbrand (**997 —999**). But the progress of religion in the mother-country rapidly abated the objections of the colonists, and as early as **1000** laws were enacted[1] by the native legislatures favourable to the ultimate supremacy of the Gospel. While a number of the ancient practices were suffered to remain in secret, it was now determined that all Icelanders should be baptized, and that the *public* rites of paganism should in future be abolished. A numerous class of natives, as we may suppose, continued to hand down the hereditary rites[2]; but through the teaching of new bands of missionaries[3], chiefly English and Irish, they were gradually converted and confirmed.

A fresh accession to the Churches of the North was the distant Greenland, also partly colonized from Norway, at the end of the tenth century. Its apostle was an Icelander, Leif, who entered on his work in **999**: and in **1055** the community of Christians had been fully organized by the appointment of a bishop[4].

At the same time Christianity was carried to the

---

[1] This step was facilitated by winning over (some say, with the help of a bribe) the chief-priest Thorgeir, who was also supervisor of the legislative acts: Schröckh, XXI. 389.

[2] Some revolting customs, *e. g.* the exposing of infants, lingered for a while, notwithstanding the attempt of Olaf, king of Norway (1019—1033), to suppress them: Neander, V. 419.

[3] One of the most conspicuous was Bernhard, an Englishman, sent into Iceland by Olaf the Holy. In 1056 the first diocesan bishop, Isleif, was placed at Skaalholt (Adam of Bremen, *De Situ Daniæ*, c. 228). He was consecrated by Adalbert of Hamburg-Bremen. Another see was founded in 1105 at Holum. Wiltsch, *Kirchl. Geogr.* II. 96, n. 8.

[4] This was bishop Albert, sent by Adalbert of Hamburg-Bremen. Münter, I. 555 sq.: cf. the bull of Victor II. (1055) confirming the privileges of the archbishop of Hamburg, in Lappenberg, *Hamburg. Urkund.* I. 77, and Adam of Bremen, *De Situ Daniæ*, c. 244. The last glimpse of this ancient Church of Greenland is seen in 1408. Religion seems to have expired soon after with the swarm of Icelandic and Norwegian settlers, who gave place to the present Esquimaux. In 1738, the Moravians made a fresh attempt to introduce the Gospel into Greenland.—There is an interesting tradition (Münter, I. 561) of a Saxon or Irish missionary, who is said to have crossed from Greenland into North-America, in 1059, and there to have died a martyr.

Orkney, Shetland, and the Faroe Islands, which were peopled mainly by Norwegians[1]. In the former cases the success of Olaf Tryggvasön was due in no small measure to the force of arms[2]; and even in the Faroe Islands, where at first he was able to proceed more calmly, through the medium of an earnest native, Sigmund[3], not a few of his efforts were coercive. But the work was afterwards resumed, in a better spirit, by succeeding kings of Norway[4].

MORAVIAN CHURCH.

land, and Faroe Islands.

AMONG THE SLAVIC OR SLAVONIAN RACES.

This large and important family of men[5], extending eastward from the Elbe to the Don, and southward from the Baltic to the Adriatic (with a few exceptions[6] in Croatia and Carinthia), had continued, till the present period, strangers to the Gospel. The exertions made by Arno, the archbishop of Salzburg (800), were repeated in the time of Louis the Pious, by Urolf, the archbishop of Lorch[7] (Laureacum).

It was through this channel that the earliest missions were established in Moravia. But the nation was still generally addicted to the pagan worship, when two learned and experienced brothers, monks of the Greek communion, entered on the same arena. These were Cyril[8] (Constantine) and Methodius[9], who had already

Propagation of Christianity among the Slaves.

Conversion of Moravia.

---

[1] Worsaae, *Danes and Norwegians*, &c. pp. 220, 221.
[2] See Torfæus, *Orcades*, Havniæ, 1697: Münter, I. 548.
[3] Torfæus, *De rebus gestis Færeyensium*, Havn. 1695; Neander, v. 421.
[4] On the conversion of the Northmen who settled in *Christian* countries, see below, § 2, 'Limitation of the Church.'
[5] The origin and antiquities of these races have been thoroughly investigated by Shafarik, *Slawische Alterthümer*, Leipzig, 1843.
[6] See above, p. 26.
[7] Also called the bishop of Passau, the two sees having been united since the year 699 (Wiltsch, I. 376); but the primate of Lorch disappears for a century, and then, after a long struggle with the archbishops of Salzburg, dies out entirely (*Ibid.* 379): cf. Gieseler, II. 452, n. 1.
[8] Cyril, in 848, was sent by the emperor Michael to instruct the Chazari (also a Slavonian tribe), who bordered on the Greek possessions in the Crimea. (Asseman, *Kalendar. Universæ Ecclesiæ*, III. 13 sq. ed. Rom. 1755.) Some of the natives embraced Christianity, but others were perverted by the Jews and Moslems.
[9] It is possible that the Methodius here mentioned is the same

MORAVIAN CHURCH.

Jealousies between the Greek and German missions.

been successful in a different field of labour. They arrived in Moravia, 861 or 862, and by the use of the native tongue in public worship, and the dissemination of the Scriptures[1], were enabled very soon to gather in a harvest of conversions. But the jealousy which had been re-awakened at this time between the Greek and Latin Churches, added to a host of diplomatic reasons on the part of the Moravian princes, made it necessary for the leaders of the mission to secure an understanding with the Western pontiff, who was anxious on his part to cultivate their friendship. Cyril and Methodius went to Rome in 867; and the former either dying on the journey or (as others say) retiring to a convent, his companion was now chosen by the pope, and consecrated metropolitan of Pannonia and Moravia[2]. He immediately resumed his labours (868) in this new capacity. Soon after, the political disturbance, which commenced with the year 870, impelled him to seek refuge in the neighbouring district of Moravia, where the German spirit was supreme, and where a mission had been planted from the see of Salzburg[3]. As Metho-

Labours of Methodius.

person who was instrumental in the conversion of Bulgaria. See below, p. 122: and cf. Schröckh, xxi. 409 sq. There is, however, great diversity in the accounts of these two eminent missionaries. The most critical are the work of Asseman, quoted in the previous note, and two publications of Dobrowsky, *Cyrill und Methodius der Slaven Apostel*, Prag, 1823, and *Mähr. Legende von Cyrill und Method.*, Prag, 1826: cf. also the Russian version in Nestor's *Annales*, ed. Schlözer, c. x.; tom. III. pp. 149 sq.

[1] Whether Cyril actually invented the Slavonic writing, or remodelled some existing alphabet, has been disputed; but there is no doubt as to his translation of the Scriptures into the language of the people: Neander, v. 434, 435. The following is the account given of their missionary labours: 'Cœperunt itaque ad id quod venerant peragendum studiose insistere, et parvulos eorum literas edocere, officia ecclesiastica instruere, et ad correctionem diversorum errorum, quos in populo illo repererant, falcem eloquiorum suorum inducere.' *Vit. Constantini*, § 7: in *Acta Sanctorum*, Mart. tom. II. pp. 19 sq.

[2] This statement is derived from the title of a letter addressed by John VIII. to Methodius (879), in Boczek, *Codex Diplomaticus et Epistolaris Moraviæ* (Olomuc. 1836), I. 29: cf. an earlier letter of the same pontiff (circ. 874) to Louis the Germanic. *Ibid.* I. 34. It appears also from a rescript 'ad Salonitanos clericos' (Mansi, XVII. 129), that Methodius had certain 'episcopi regionarii' under him. His see was Welehrad, the capital of the ancient kingdom of Moravia. Potthast, *Bibl. Hist.* II. 371.

[3] See the anonymous account of a priest of Salzburg (quoted in p. 26, n. 1). As late as 865, the archbishop of Salzburg consecrated several churches in this district.

dius was devoted all his life-time to the creed and ritual of the Greeks, and constantly made use of the Slavonic language, he excited the displeasure[1] of his German fellow-workers, who, as soon as they found their influence on the wane, did not hesitate to brand him as a traitor to the faith. In 879 he responded to a summons of the pope[2], whom he convinced (880) of his orthodoxy[3], as well as of the propriety of using the vernacular language[4] in the public worship of the Church; and in the following year he was reinstated in his sphere of duty, and invested with still larger powers. But meanwhile a serious misunderstanding had grown up between him and the Moravian king, Swatopluk, who succeeded Wratislav, his uncle (870 —894). Other influential persons[5] in like manner threw their strength into the German faction, and Methodius, while proceeding with his missionary work in the same earnest spirit as before, was under the necessity of vindicating himself a second time from the calumnies of his

MORAVIAN CHURCH.

Fresh misunderstanding with the German party.

---

[1] *Ibid.* ......'usquedum quidam Græcus Methodius nomine, noviter inventis Slavinis literis, linguam Latinam *doctrinamque Romanam,* atque literas auctorabiles Latinas philosophice superducens, vilescere fecit cuncto populo ex parte missas et evangelia, ecclesiasticumque officium illorum, qui hoc Latine celebraverunt. Quod ille [*i. e.* Richbald, the head of the Salzburg mission] ferre non valens, sedem repetivit Juvaviensem.'

[2] Above, p. 112, n. 2, and in Mansi, XVII. 133. The drift of the summons was, 'ut veraciter cognoscamus doctrinam tuam :' cf. *Epist. ad Zuventapu de Moravna* (? Morawa, in Pannonia), in Boczek, *ubi sup.* I. 40.

[3] 'Nos autem illum in omnibus ecclesiasticis doctrinis et utilitatibus orthodoxum et proficuum esse reperientes, vobis iterum ad regendam commissam sibi ecclesiam Dei remisimus,' etc. *Ep. ad Sphentopulcum comitem;* Mansi, XVII. 181. Neander (v. 438) infers that the Greek mode of stating the Procession of the Holy Ghost was also conceded by this pope.

[4] 'Literas denique Sclavonicas a Constantino quondam philosopho repertas, quibus Deo laudes debite resonent, jure laudamus, et in eadem lingua Christi Domini nostri præconia et opera ut enarrentur, jubemus... Nec sanæ fidei vel doctrinæ aliquid obstat, sive missas in eadem Sclavonica lingua canere, sive sacrum Evangelium, vel lectiones Divinas novi et veteris Testamenti bene translatas et interpretatas legere, aut alia horarum officia omnia psallere.' *Ibid.* The injunction, therefore, was, that in all the Moravian Churches the Gospel should be first read in Latin and then in Slavonic ('sicut in quibusdam ecclesiis fieri videtur').

[5] *e.g.* The bishop of Neitra, Wiching (a German), whom the papal rescript, above quoted, n. 4, had subordinated to Methodius: see the letter of the same pope (881), Boczek, *ubi sup.* I. 44: Asseman, *Kalend. Univers. Eccl.* III. 159 sq.

BOHEMIAN CHURCH.

Destruction of Moravian independence.

opponents. He set out for Rome in 881; but as there is no certain trace[1] of him after this date, it has been inferred that he did not survive the journey. His Slavonic coadjutors are said to have been subsequently banished from Moravia[2]; and although a strong reaction was produced by the ensuing reign of Moimar, who was able to dissociate the Moravian Church entirely from the intermeddling of the German[3], all his projects were defeated in 908, when the armies of adjacent countries, more especially Bohemians and Hungarians, trampled on his crown. For nearly thirty years the progress of the Gospel in Moravia was retarded by these struggles; and when Moravian Christians reappear on the page of history, they are subject to the bishops of Bohemia. Afterwards a see was established at Olmütz[4].

The Gospel in Bohemia.

The first seeds of religion had been scattered in Bohemia by the same active hand[5]. Its duke, Borziwoi, was converted by Methodius[6] (circ. 871), while on a visit to the court of the Moravian king, Swatopluk, who was at that time his superior lord. On his return to his own dominions, he took with him a Moravian priest, by whom his wife, Ludmilla[7], afterwards conspicuous in devotion, was admitted to the Christian fold. But heathenism[8], in spite

---

[1] See Dobrowsky, *Cyrill und Methodius,* pp. 115 sq.
[2] Ibid.
[3] On the jealousy excited by these controversies, see the remonstrance of Theotmar, archbp. of Salzburg, and of Hatto, archbp. of Mentz, addressed to pope John IX. (900—901): Mansi, XVIII. 203, 205. They view the independence of the Moravians as a violation of the rights of the bishop of Passau, and of the German Church at large, from whom, as it is alleged, the conversion of Moravia had proceeded.
[4] See Wiltsch, I. 361, 363. Some place the foundation of this see at the year 1062.
[5] The following entry in the *Fuldenses Annales,* A.D. 845, will take us back somewhat further: 'Hludowicus 14 ex ducibus Boemanorum cum hominibus suis Christianam religionem desiderantes suscepit, et in octavis Theophaniæ baptizari jussit.' Pertz, I. 364.
[6] This point is not quite established, but the evidence in favour of it is considerable. Dobrowsky, *Cyrill und Method.* p. 106: *Mähr. Legende,* p. 114: cf. Neander, v. 442, note.
[7] See one *Life of Ludmilla,* addressed to bishop Adalbert of Prague, about 985, in *Acta Sanctorum,* Sept. tom. v. 354, and a second in Dobner's contribution to the *Abhandlungen der böhmisch. Gesellschaft der Wissenschaften,* for 1786, pp. 417 sq. But neither of these legends is of much historical value.
[8] At the head of this party was Dragomir or Drahomira, wife of Wratislav, who is charged with the assassination of Ludmilla.

of her untiring efforts and the piety of Wratislav her son, maintained its rule in almost every district of Bohemia; and the struggle was prolonged into the reign of her grandson Wenzeslav[1] (928—936), who seems to have inherited her faith and saintliness of life. He was murdered at the instigation of his pagan brother, Boleslav the Cruel, and for many years the little band of Christians had to brave a most bitter persecution. In 950, Boleslav was conquered by the armies of Germany, under Otho I.; which paved a way to the establishment and wider propagation of the truth. Still more was effected by the sterner policy of Boleslav the Pious (967—999); in whose reign also a more definite organization was imparted to the whole of the Bohemian Church by founding the bishopric of Prague[2]. It was filled in 983 by a learned German, Adalbert (or Wojtĕch). Noted for the warmth of his missionary zeal[3], he laboured, with the aid of Boleslav, to drive out the surviving elements of paganism, by circulating a more stringent code of disciplinary injunctions[4]. The imprudent haste and harshness of his measures, added to the national dislike of everything Germanic, soon compelled him to resign his post, when he retreated to a convent. In 994, he was ordered to resume his duties by the voice of the Roman synod[5], and reluctantly obeying the injunction he returned into Bohemia; but the jealous spirit he had stirred in the Slavonian populace ere long ejected him afresh. His policy however was triumphantly established

BOHEMIAN CHURCH.

Adalbert, archbishop of Prague:

his expulsion.

---

[1] See the *Life of Wenzeslav* (Wenceslaus); *Acta Sanctor.* Sept. VII. 825.
[2] Wiltsch, I. 361, 363, n. 22: but the rescript attributed to John XIII., confirming the foundation of the bishopric, is spurious. Jaffé, *Regesta Pontif.* p. 947. The first prelate was Diethmar, a monk of Magdeburg: see Cosmas Pragensis, who wrote a *Bohemian Chronicle* about 1100: tom. I. pp. 1993 sq. in Mencken. *Script. Rer. Germanic.*
[3] He finally died a martyr in 997, while seeking to convert the Prussians, in the neighbourhood of Dantzig. See a *Life of Adalbert* in Pertz, VI. 574. He had also laboured in a mission to the Hungarians, see below, p. 127. The efforts of Adalbert in behalf of the ferocious Prussians were repeated by Bruno, the court-chaplain of Otho III.: but he too perished in 1008, together with eighteen of his companions. *Act. Sanct. Ord. Benedict.* VIII. 79 sq.
[4] Among other things he combated polygamy, clerical concubinage, arbitrary divorces, the traffic in Christian slaves which was largely carried on by Jews, &c. See the *Life of Adalbert*, as above: and cf. Schröckh, XXI. 440, 441.
[5] See both the *Lives* of him, in Pertz, VI. 589, 602.

POLISH CHURCH.

Triumph of the German spirit.
The Gospel in Poland.

Adoption of coercive measures.

in the time of Severus[1] a later primate (**1030–1067**); for although the Slavo-Latin ritual[2], as imported from Moravia, was still cherished here and there, it gradually retired before the influence of the Roman or Germanic uses.

As the Gospel had passed over from Moravia to Bohemia, so the latter was the instrument of God for planting it among the kindred tribes of Poland. Their dominion at this period was extending northward to the Netze, and embraced all the modern province of Silesia. In **966**, the Polish duke[3], Mjesko or Miecislav, who had married a Bohemian princess (Dambrowka), was converted to the Christian faith; and many of the courtiers following his example were baptized on the same occasion. But his violent suppression of the pagan worship (**967**), as in cases we have seen already, could not fail to produce an obstinate resistance[4] on the part of the uninstructed. In the following reigns, when Poland for a time was freed from the superiority of the empire, this obnoxious policy continued; and the slightest violation of the canons of

---

[1] Schröckh, XXI. 442 sq.

[2] One of the conditions mentioned in the rescript which relates to the founding of the see of Prague is to the effect that Divine service shall in future be performed '*non secundum ritus aut sectam Bulgariæ gentis, vel Ruziæ aut Sclavonicæ linguæ,* sed magis sequens instituta et decreta apostolica,' &c. Boczek, *Codex Diplomaticus Morav.* I. 86. But spurious though this rescript is, a multitude of better proofs assure us that the question here suggested was a source of much dispute. See the account of a struggle between the Latin and Slavonic services at the convent of Sasawa, in Mencken. *Script. Rer. German.* III. 1782 sq. After a vehement letter of Gregory VII. (1080) to Wratislav, duke of Bohemia, prohibiting the use of the Slavonic ritual (Mansi, XX. 296), the monks who adhered to the use of it were (in 1097) expelled, and their service-books destroyed (Mencken. III. 1788). In some parts of Bohemia, the vernacular ritual was revived, or kept its ground; and one convent in the suburbs of Prague retains it at this day. Gieseler, II. 458, n. 17.

[3] See Thietmar (or Ditmar), *Chronicon*, lib. IV. c. 35: in Pertz, V. 783, and the Polish historian, Martinus Gallus (who wrote about 1130), lib. I. c. 5, ed. Bandtke, 1824: cf. Schröckh, XXI. 491 sq., where the traces of a somewhat older Christianity have been collected.

[4] Accordingly we find that the Gospel had made little progress in 980: Schröckh, XXI. 496. For some time there was but one Polish bishopric, that of Posen, founded (it is said) by the Emperor Otho I. in 970, and subordinated to the metropolitan of Magdeburg. When Poland, in the following century, became an independent kingdom, the archbishopric of Gnesen took the lead of other sees (including Colberg, Cracow, and Wratislavia or Breslau) which were founded. Wiltsch, I. 395—397: cf. Schröckh, XXI. 497 sq. A council was held in Poland (1000) by the Emperor Otho III. Mansi, XIX. 267.

the Church was punished by the civil power[1]. A fresh impulse was communicated to the progress of religion by the reign[2] of Casimir I. (1034—1058), who was previously an inmate either of the Benedictine house at Clugny, or of a German convent at Braunweiler. By him all the ritual of the Church, that had hitherto retained a portion of the impress it derived from the Christians of Moravia and Bohemia[3], was brought into more general agreement with the liturgies and customs of the West[4].

WENDISH CHURCH.

In addition to the tribes already folded in the Christian Church, were others also of Slavonic blood, most commonly entitled Wends. They had settled in the districts bordering the Elbe, the Oder, and the Saale, and were already vassals of the German empire. Like the northern Saxons of the former period, they were men of a fierce and indomitable spirit, who regarded the persuasions of the missionary as designed to perpetuate their bondage. This political repugnance to his visits was increased by his imperfect knowledge of the Slavic dialects[5]; and as their nationality was more and more endangered by the heavy yoke[6] of their oppressors, they were constantly attempting to regain their independence, and extinguish the few glimmerings of truth that had been forced into their minds. Accordingly, the progress of religion in these districts had been slow and superficial; but the death of their conqueror, Henry I., in 936, was followed by a different mode of treat-

Attempts to introduce the Gospel among the Wends.

---

[1] *e.g.* 'Quicunque post septuagesimam carnem manducasse invenitur, abscisis dentibus graviter punitur. Lex namque divina in his regionibus noviter exorta *potestate tali*, melius quam jejunio ab episcopis instituto, *corroboratur*.' Thietmar, *Chron.* lib. VIII. c. 2.

[2] The strange circumstances connected with his elevation are related in Martinus Gallus, *Chronicon*, as above; and Cromer, *de Rebus Polonorum*, lib. IV. p. 50, ed. Colon.

[3] See Friese, *Kirchengeschichte des Königreichs Poland*, I. 61 sq., Breslau, 1786.

[4] As early as 1012, the king of Poland, Boleslav, betrays a strong leaning to the Church of Rome (Thietmar, *Chronic.* lib. VI. c. 56), and many of his successors carried this feeling of deference much further.

[5] See a striking exemplification of this in Thietmar's *Chronicon*, lib. II. c. 23 (Pertz, V. 755).

[6] 'Quibus mens pronior est ad pensiones vectigalium quam ad conversionem gentilium,' was the censure passed upon the German conquerors by the then king of Denmark. Neander, V. 446, note. The same is the complaint of the Chronicler Helmold (lib. I. c. 21). 'Semper proniores sunt tributis augmentandis, quam animabus Domino conquirendis.'

WENDISH CHURCH.

Foundation of several bishoprics.

ment, and a somewhat larger measure of success. Desirous of promoting their conversion, Otho I. founded many bishoprics[1] among the Wends, and placed them under the direction of a better class of men,—of missionaries who had been distinguished by their skill in other fields of labour. In 946 a prelate of this kind was sent to Havelberg; another to Aldenburg, in 948; a third to Brandenburg, in 949. Those of Meissen (Misna), Cizi, and Merseburg followed in 968, and in that, or in the previous year, the organization of the Wendish Church was finished by erecting the metropolitical see of Magdeburg, according to a plan propounded by the council of Ravenna[2] (967). The first primate, Adalbert, had been educated in the monastery of Treves, and is said to have been chosen several years before to plant a fruitless mission in a distant tribe of Slaves[3]. His present work also was thwarted by a general insurrection of the heathen Wends, assisted by unstable soldiers of the Cross. Impatient of the German rule, or maddened by some special grievances occurring at the time, they ravaged[4] all the neighbouring districts, more especially the seats of missionary enterprise; and though the leader of the movement, Mistewoi, a Christian, afterwards deplored his furious onslaught, it was long ere the wounds he had inflicted on the Church were altogether healed.

A salutary change is dated from the reign of his holy grandson, Gottschalk, who is famous in the German annals

[1] Wiltsch, I. 394, 395. The bishopric of Cizi (Zeiz) was in 1029 transferred to Naumburg; that of Aldenburg (Oldenburg) was transferred to Lübeck in 1163, and was from the first a suffragan of the archbishopric of Hamburg-Bremen, and not, like the rest, of Magdeburg. It seems to have been afterwards divided, and two other bishoprics established, for a time, at Ratzeburg and Mecklenburg. See the *Chronicon Slavorum* by Helmold, a missionary at Bosov, about 1150, in Leibnitz's *Scriptores Brunsv.* II. 537 sq.

[2] Mansi, XVIII. 501—503; cf. Schröckh, XXI. 482 sq. One object of the Emperor in urging the foundation of this new archbishopric appears to have been a wish to abridge the inordinate power of the see of Mentz. The pall was sent to the new German primate in 968. Mansi, XIX. 5.

[3] It is generally supposed that the Slavonic tribe in question was that of the *Russians;* but Neander (v. 447, 452) argues that the Slavonians in the isle of *Rügen* were intended by the chroniclers.

[4] See Helmold, as above, lib. I. c. 14 sq., Giesebrecht's *Wendische Geschichten* (from 730 to 1182), I. 257; Berlin, 1843. When Mistewoi professed himself a Christian, after his repentance, he was compelled to retire from the scene of his impiety, and died at Bardevik. Helmold, *ibid.* c. 16.

as the founder of the Wendish empire (**1047**). He was trained in a Christian school at Lüneburg, and the military ardour he had shewn at an earlier period was eventually directed to the propagation of the Gospel[1]. Aided by an ample staff of clerics, whom he drew more especially from the archbishopric of Bremen[2], he proceeded with unwavering zeal in the conversion of his people. Yet so strongly were they wedded to their heathen rites, that after labouring among them twenty years he fell a victim to his Christian fervour (**1066**), dying[3], with a number of his chief assistants, in the midst of revolting tortures. From this period the reaction in behalf of paganism went on rapidly increasing, until few[4], if any, traces of the mission were left.

Meanwhile, another family of Slaves, united by a line of Scandinavian[5] princes, were engrafted on the Eastern Church. The Russians had now gradually expanded from the neighbourhood of Moscow, on one side to the Baltic, on the other to the Euxine Sea. Their predatory and commercial habits brought them pointedly before the notice of the emperors and prelates of the East, and efforts seem to

RUSSIAN CHURCH.

The zeal and martyrdom of king Gottschalk.

Extirpation of the Gospel.

Conversion of the Russians;

---

[1] He is even said to have preached, or expounded, the Gospel to his subjects: 'Sane magnæ devotionis vir dicitur tanto religionis Divinæ exarsisse studio, ut sermonem exhortationis ad populum frequenter in ecclesia ipse fecerit, ea scilicet, quæ ab episcopis vel presbyteris mystice dicebantur, cupiens Slavicis verbis reddere planiora.' Helmold, *ibid.* c. 20.

[2] Bremen, as the point of departure for the northern missions, seems to have been a rallying-place for all kinds of unfortunate ecclesiastics: 'Confluebant ergo in curiam ejus [*i.e.* of Adalbert, or Albrecht, the archbishop] multi sacerdotes et religiosi, plerique etiam episcopi, qui sedibus suis exturbati mensæ ejus erant participes, quorum sarcina ipse allevari cupiens *transmisit eos in latitudinem gentium.*' *Ibid.* c. 22: cf. Adam of Bremen, *Hist. Eccl.* c. 142.

[3] The place of his death was Leutzen. The last victim was the aged bishop of Mecklenburg, who, after he had been dragged through the chief cities of the Wendish kingdom, was sacrificed to the war-god, Radegast, whose temple stood at Rethre. Helmold, *ibid.* c. 23.

[4] Religion seems to have been kept alive in some measure among the Sorbi (between the Elbe and the Saale), through the zealous efforts of Benno, bishop of Meissen (1066—1106). See a *Life* of him in Mencken. *Script. Rer. German.* II. 1857 sq. But in other districts what is stated by the Chroniclers will too generally apply: 'Slavi servitutis jugum armata manu submoverunt, tantaque animi obstinantia libertatem defendere nisi sunt, ut prius maluerint mori quam *Christianitatis titulum resumere,* aut tributa solvere Saxonum principibus.' Helmold. *ibid.* c. 25.

[5] Cf. Milman's note on Gibbon, v. 304. Ruric, the father of this dynasty, became the king of Russia in 862.

RUSSIAN CHURCH.

have been made as early as **866** to evangelize[1] the warlike tribes that bordered on the Greek dominions. It is probable that sundry germs of Christianity[2] were carried home already by invaders, who at this and later times had prowled upon the Bosphorus; and in **945** we see distincter traces of the progress of the Gospel, more especially in Kieff[3]. But the baptism[4] of the princess Olga, who is reverenced as the 'Helena' of Russian Christianity, was the commencement of a brighter period in the triumphs of the faith (circ. **955**). Her son, indeed, Sviatoslav I. (**955–972**) resisted all her gentle efforts to embrace him in the Christian fold; but the suggestions she instilled into the heart of Vladimir, her grandson, led the way, after many painful struggles[5], to his public recognition of the Gospel (circ. **980**). On his marriage with the sister of the Byzantine emperor, the Church of Russia was more intimately bound to the orthodox

their dependence on the Church of Constantinople.

---

[1] Photius, the patriarch of Constantinople (*Epist.* II. p. 58, ed. Montague: cf. Pagi, in Baronii *Annales*, A.D. 861), in writing against the pretensions of the Roman see (866) exults in the conversion of the Russians, by the agency of Eastern missionaries: but his statement is extravagant and overcoloured. See Mouravieff's *Hist. of the Church of Russia* p. 8, translated by Blackmore, Oxf. 1842. An attempt has been made by the archimandrite ·Macarius, *Hist. of Christianity in Russia before St Vladimir* (St Petersb. 1846), to establish a tradition of the middle ages that St Andrew preached the Gospel in Russia.

[2] In a catalogue of sees subject to Constantinople, there is mention of a metropolitan of Russia as early as 891 (Mouravieff, as above, p. 9): yet many of these earlier accounts are not trustworthy throughout. The great authority is Nestor, a monk of Kieff, who wrote in the eleventh century. His *Chronicle* has been edited in part, with a valuable commentary, by Schlözer, Göttingen, 1802—1809.

[3] In a treaty between king Igor and the Byzantine court (945), there is an allusion to Russian (Varangian) converts and to a church dedicated in honour of the prophet Elias, at Kieff, the ancient capital of the empire. Nestor, *Annal.* IV. 95 sq. ed. Schlözer. Kieff became an episcopal see in 988. Wiltsch, I. 429.

[4] This took place at Constantinople, whither she repaired in order to obtain a knowledge of the truth. The emperor Constantine Porphyrogenitus was her godfather. Nestor, v. 58 sq. There is some reason for supposing that she made an application to Otho I., in 959 or 960, requesting him to lend assistance in promoting the extension of the faith: see above, p. 118, n. 3; and cf. Schröckh, XXI. 515—517.

[5] At first he was like his father, ardently devoted to the pagan worship: he was solicited in succession by Muhammedan and Jewish missionaries from Bulgaria and adjacent parts (Mouravieff, pp. 10, 11); and then, after oscillating (it is said) between the Greek and Roman rites, determined to accept the former. See a fragment, *De Conversione Russorum*, published by Banduri, in the *Imperium Orientale*, II. 62 sq. and Neander's note, v. 453. He was finally baptized at Cherson (on the

communion of the East¹; and missionaries from Constantinople ardently engaged in softening and evangelizing the remoter districts of the kingdom. Aided by the royal bounty, they erected schools and churches in the leading towns, and making use of the Slavonic Bible and other Service-books, which were translated to their hands by Cyril and Methodius², they obtained a ready entrance to the native population, and the Church, as an effect of their judicious zeal, expanded freely on all sides. In the time³ of Leontius, metropolitan of Kieff, the formation of a number of episcopal sees⁴ presented a substantial basis for the future conquests of the truth; and under two immediate successors of Vladimir (1019—1077), their empire was Christianized completely. But the fierce irruption of the Mongols (1223), resulting as it did in their occupation of the country till 1462, was fatal to the health and progress of the Russian state; although the unity of purpose now imparted to it by religion enabled it to wrestle with the infidels, and finally to drive them out.

BULGARIAN CHURCH.

Another tribe, in part at least if not entirely, of Slavonic origin⁵ was now united to the Eastern Church. It was the tribe of the Bulgarians, who were driven by the onward march of population to the southern borders of the Danube, where they founded a considerable state in Dardania, Macedonia, and Epirus. While a party of their ruder kinsmen on the Volga were embracing the Koran⁶, a wish

The Gospel among the Bulgarians.

Dnieper), where a bishopric was already planted, and on his return to Kieff proceeded to destroy the monuments of heathenism, particularly the images of Peroun, the god of thunder: Mouravieff, pp. 13, 14.

¹ This was still further shewn by the adoption of the Greek canon-law, as well as of the Constantinopolitan service-books, &c. Mouravieff, pp. 17, 357. Greeks, in like manner, were employed in constructing the first Russian churches (*Ibid.* 161), and introducing the choral music of Constantinople (*Ibid.* p. 22).

² See above, p. 112; Mouravieff, p. 8.

³ *Ibid.* p. 16. The next king, Yaroslaf, added greatly to the number of the schools and churches, and even translated many books of devotion, p. 20. He was also the chief founder of the Russian convents, which adopted the Rule of the Studium monastery at Constantinople. *Ibid.* p. 24.

⁴ *e.g.* of Novogorod, of Rostoff, Chernigoff, Vladimir, and Belgorod. During the oppression of the Mongols, which lasted two hundred years, the metropolitical chair was transferred to Vladimir, and finally in 1320 to Moscow.

⁵ Gibbon, v. 290, 291, ed. Milman : Schröckh, xxi. 399.

⁶ The Caliph, Muktedir, sent missionaries among them in 921, at the

BULGARIAN CHURCH.

had been inspired into the others for instruction in the doctrine of the Gospel. In 811 many hordes of the Bulgarians, after vanquishing Nicephorus I., pursued their devastations to the city of Adrianople, and among the other captives carried off its bishop and a multitude of Christians. In this way it is likely that the seeds of truth[1] were scattered in Bulgaria. Somewhat later, Constantine, a captive monk, endeavoured to mature them, and his hands were strengthened by a princess of the country, who was educated as a Christian at Constantinople, whither she had been transported in the wars. By her suggestions, and a spirit-stiring picture of the day of judgment, furnished to her by a Grecian monk and artist, her brother, Bogoris[2], the Bulgarian king, (in 863 or 864) was drawn to listen to her creed; and as the agency by which he had been won proceeded from the Eastern Church, the patriarch of Constantinople, Photius, entered on the task of training him more fully in the rudiments of truth, and of planting it among his subjects[3]. But he seems at first to have been dissatisfied with the ground on which he stood: and either from a wish to obviate the lack of an efficient clergy, and the jangling and uncertainty produced by rival missions[4], or from a lower and political dislike to be involved in more intimate relations with the court of Byzantium, he soon afterwards betook himself for counsel to the Christians of the West. In 866 or 867 an embassy was sent to Ratisbon, invoking the assistance of Louis the Germanic[5], and either then, or a short time earlier, envoys

Quarrel between the Roman and Byzantine patriarchs.

---

request of their own chieftain, to complete their training in the system of Muhammed: cf. a Russian work quoted by Gieseler, II. 486, n. 2.

[1] See the continuation of Theophanes, in the *Scriptores Byzantin.* ed. Venet. p. 100.

[2] *Ibid.* lib. IV. c. 13—15: cf. Neander, v. 433, 434. It seems doubtful whether the present artist, whose name is Methodius, was identical with the missionary of that name, whom we have seen above, p. 112. Bogoris after his baptism was called Michael, the Greek emperor Michael III. standing as his godfather, by proxy.

[3] Photii *Epist.* I.; ed. Lond. 1651.

[4] It seems, from the letter of Nicholas I. (below, p. 123, n. 1), that missionaries of different nations were labouring in Bulgaria, and propounding different doctrines, so that the people hardly knew whom to believe: 'multi ex diversis locis Christiani advenerint, qui prout voluntas eorum existit multa et varia loquuntur, id est, Græci, Armeni, et ex cæteris locis:' c. 106.

[5] *Annales Fuldens.* A.D. 866 (Pertz, I. 379): 'Legati Bulgarum Rades-

were directed to the pope. Accordingly, in the following year, two Italian bishops[1] set out for Bulgaria, bearing with them a long series of directions and decisions from the pen of Nicholas I. As we shall see at large hereafter, this new act of intervention in the bounds of a diocese already occupied by others added fuel to the flames of jealousy and envy, which had long been growing up between the pontiffs of the Greek and Latin Churches. As at an earlier period, they were not slow in exchanging fulminations[2]; during which the capricious author of the storm went over to the side of Photius and immediately[3]

BULGARIAN CHURCH.

ponam ad regem venerunt, dicentes regem illorum cum populo non modico ad Christum esse conversum, simulque petentes, ut rex idoneos prædicatores Christianæ religionis ad eos mittere non differret.' The king appointed a bishop together with a staff of priests and deacons, who might undertake the mission, but on arriving at Rome they found that the pope had already sent auxiliaries enough for the occasion. *Ibid.* A.D. 867: cf. Le Quien, *Oriens Christianus*, I. 99 sq.

[1] *Vit. Nicolai*, in Vignol. *Lib. Pontif.* III. 210, 211. In 867 other missionaries, priests, and bishops, were dispatched to Bulgaria (*Ibid.* pp. 212, 213), 'ut, quia ipsum Formosum [the archbishop-designate of Justiniana Prima in Bulgaria] plebem dimittere sibi creditam non oportebat episcopum, ex his presbyteris ad archiepiscopatum eligatur, et sedi consecrandus apostolicæ mittatur.' The copious answer of Nicholas to the questions of the Bulgarian envoys will be found in Mansi, xv. 401 sq. Among other passages of this memorable document there is an emphatic condemnation of compulsory conversions, such as Bogoris appears to have attempted: c. 41.

[2] See the encyclical epistle of Photius to the Oriental patriarchs, in his *Epist.* ed. Lond. 1651, pp. 47 sq. The following is a specimen of his vehement language: Καὶ γὰρ δή, καὶ ἀπὸ τῶν τῆς Ἰταλίας μερῶν συνοδική τις ἐπιστολὴ πρὸς ἡμᾶς ἀναπεφοίτηκεν, ἀρρήτων ἐγκλημάτων γέμουσα, ἅτινα κατὰ τοῦ οἰκείου αὐτῶν ἐπισκόπου οἱ τὴν Ἰταλίαν οἰκοῦντες μετὰ πολλῆς κατακρίσεως καὶ ὅρκων μυρίων διεπέμψαντο, μὴ παριδεῖν αὐτοὺς οὕτως οἰκτρῶς ὀλλυμένους, καὶ ὑπὸ τηλικαύτης βαρείας πιεζομένους τυραννίδος, καὶ τοὺς ἱερατικοὺς νόμους ὑβριζομένους, καὶ πάντας θεσμοὺς ἐκκλησίας ἀνατρεπομένους, p. 59. The emperors of the East supported Photius, and when their letters were forwarded by Bogoris to Rome, the pope in his turn (867) issued an encyclical epistle to Hincmar archbishop of Rheims and the other archbishops and bishops of France, denouncing the Greek Church on various grounds, (see below on the 'Schism between the Eastern and Western Churches,') and especially the envy of the Byzantine patriarch because the king of Bulgaria had sought 'a sede B. Petri institutores et doctrinam.' Mansi, xv. 355.

[3] 'Magna sub velocitate' is the language of Hadrian II. (869), when he laboured to re-establish his jurisdiction in Bulgaria. Vignol. *Lib. Pontif.* III. 253: but the Roman missionaries were immediately expelled. A fragment of a letter written by the pope to Ignatius, patriarch of Constantinople, on the consecration of the Greek archbishop of Bulgaria is preserved in Mansi, XVI. 414, and in XVII. 62, 67, 68, 129, 131, 136, are letters from John VIII., in which he laboured to convict the Eastern

OTHER SLAVONIC CHURCHES.

Bulgaria finally annexed to the Eastern Church.
Partial conversion of the Chazars.

compelled the Roman mission to withdraw. The Church of Bulgaria was now organized afresh, according to the Eastern model, and continued for a while dependent on the see of Constantinople[1].

The Chazars, who dwelt in the vicinity of the Crimea, on the borders of the Eastern empire, followed the example of Bulgaria; though the preachers of the Gospel had to struggle with a host of proselyting Jews, as well as with the propagandists of Islamism[2]. About 850, some inquiring members of this tribe implored the emperor (Michael III.) to send a well-instructed missionary among them; and the agent chosen for that work was Constantine (or Cyril), afterwards conspicuous for his zeal in building up the Churches of Moravia and Bohemia[3]. Many of the natives, touched by his glowing sermons, were converted to the truth, and permanently associated with the see of Constantinople. Still, as late as 921, their leading chieftain was a Jew, and others were addicted to the system of Muhammed[4].

Conversion of the Croats

The Chrobatians or Croats, who had emigrated in the seventh century from Poland to the region[5] bounded by the Adriatic and the Saave, were Christianized, in part, at the commencement of this period. It is said[6]

emperors and prelates of a breach of duty in withdrawing the Bulgarians from the papal jurisdiction. In the first of this series of remonstrances he warns king Michael (Bogoris) of the errors of the Greeks, and adds: 'Mihi credite, non gloriam ex vobis, vel honorem, aut censum expectantes, non patriæ regimen et reipublicæ moderamen adipisci cupimus; sed diœceseos ejusdem regionis curam et dispositionem resumere volumus.'

[1] Le Quien, *Oriens Christianus*, I. 104.
[2] See the *Life of Constantine* (Cyril) above referred to, p. 112: 'Cazarorum legati venerunt, orantes ac supplicantes, ut dignaretur [addressing the emperor Michael, circ. 850] mittere ad illos aliquem eruditum virum, qui eos fidem catholicam veraciter edoceret, adjicientes inter cætera, quoniam nunc Judæi ad fidem suam, modo Saraceni ad suam, nos convertere e contrario moliuntur.' § 1.
[3] Above, pp. 111—116.
[4] The chief authority for this statement is a Muhammedan ambassador, who travelled in those regions, 921, and reported that he found as many Moslems as Christians, besides Jews and idolaters. See Frähn, in the *Mémoires de l'Académie de St Pétersbourg* (1822), tome VIII. 598 sq.; and Gieseler, II. 486, n. 3.
[5] They were, in part, separated from the Adriatic by the narrow kingdom of Dalmatia, peopled chiefly by the Slaves, and subject at the opening of this period to the Roman patriarch: Wiltsch, I. 399.
[6] Döllinger, III. 22, 23. Croatia was included in the ecclesiastical

that a Roman mission was dispatched among them, at the wish of their chieftain, Porga, which resulted in their subsequent connexion with the pontiffs of the West.

OTHER SLAVONIC CHURCHES.

Here also may be noted the conversion of some kindred tribes who were impelled into the interior of Hellas[1]. They were gradually brought under the Byzantine yoke, and, after the Bulgarians had embraced the offers of the Gospel, they attended to the exhortations of the missionaries sent among them by the emperor Basil (circ. 870).

and other Slavic tribes.

The evangelizing of the larger tribe of Servians, who inhabited the numerous mountain-ridges stretching from the Danube to the shores of the Adriatic, was not equally felicitous and lasting. Through their nominal dependence on Byzantium[2], many of them were already gathered to the Christian Church, but when they were enabled to regain their freedom in 827, they seem to have refused allegiance[3] to the creed of their former masters. Subsequently, however, the victorious arms of Basil (circ. 870) made a way to the re-admission of a band of Christian teachers furnished from Constantinople. Through their efforts, aided by vernacular translations[4], a considerable change was speedily produced; and early in the tenth century we read[5] that an important staff of native clergy were ordained for the Servian Church by the Slavonic bishop of Nona (in Dalmatia). From their geographical position on the border-land between the Eastern and the Western Empire, the inhabitants of Servia could retain a kind of spiritual[6] as well as civil independence; but

The Gospel among the Servians.

Their ecclesiastical position.

---

province of Dioclea, and though subject for a time, at the close of the ninth century, to the see of Constantinople, it was afterwards (1067) embraced anew in the jurisdiction of the pope. Wiltsch, I. 399, 400.

[1] Fallmerayer, *Geschichte der Halbinsel Morea während des Mittelalters*, I. 230 sq. In like manner nearly all the Mainotes, the descendants of the ancient Greeks, who had retreated to the rocky fastnesses in the neighbourhood of mount Taygetus, embraced the Gospel at this period. Ibid. I. 137. Constantine Porphyrogen. *De Administrat. Imper.* § 50 (ed. Bekker, p. 224) speaks of the obstinacy with which they had clung to the pagan worship of the Greeks.

[2] Ranke, *Hist. of Servia*, Lond. 1853, pp. 2, 3.
[3] Döllinger, III. 23.
[4] Ranke, p. 3.
[5] Ibid.
[6] The patriarch of Constantinople granted them the privilege of always electing their archbishop (of Uschize) from their own national clergy.

HUNGARIAN CHURCH.

their leanings on the whole were to the Church of Constantinople.

AMONG THE HUNGARIANS.

Inroads of the Magyars.

The one serious obstacle remaining to the spread and perpetuity of truth in every part of Eastern Europe were the settlements of the Hungarians (Magyars). Descended from a Tatar or a Finnish tribe[1], they fell upon the province of Pannonia at the close of the ninth century (circ. 885), and, after breathing for a while among their permanent possessions, hurried onward like a stream of fire, to desolate the plains of Italy, and terrify the nations westward of the Rhine[2]. The triumphs[3] of the German princes, Henry the Fowler and Otho the Great (934, 955), eventually delivered Christendom, and shut the Magyars within their present boundaries upon the Danube. There they mingled with the early settlers (the Avars[4]), and others whom they carried off as captives from the neighbouring Slavonic tribes[5].

Ibid. p. 7. At other times they seem to have been in communication with the court of Rome, which was continually repeating its claims to jurisdiction over all the Illyrian dioceses (see *e. g.* a letter of John VIII. to the bishop-elect of Nona (879), urging him not to receive consecration from any but the pope himself. Mansi, XVII. 124). Gregory VII. was the first who saluted the Grand Shupane of Servia by the title of 'king:' but the attempts to win him over to the Latin Church were always made in vain: Ranke, p. 5.

[1] Gibbon, v. 294 sq.; ed. Milman. The best modern history of them is Mailáth's *Geschichte der Magyaren*, Wien, 1828. It is not improbable that the religious system of the heathen Magyars was borrowed from the Persians. It was dualistic, and the evil principle was named Armanyos (=Ahriman). Dölling. III. 33.

[2] Gibbon, v. 300. 'Oh! save and deliver us from the arrows of the Hungarians,' was the cry of the persecuted Christians, who were massacred by thousands.

[3] Gibbon, *ibid.* pp. 302, 303.

[4] A mission had been organized for them by Charlemagne, who had nominally ruled the whole of modern Hungary (see above, p. 26); but, as we gather from a rescript of Benedict VII. (974), dividing Pannonia between the archbishops of Salzburg and Lorch (Laureacum), the province of the latter had been heathenized afresh ('ex viciniorum frequenti populatione barbarorum deserta et in solitudinem redacta'); Boczek, *Codex Diplom. Morav.*, I. 93: Mansi, XIX. 52 sq.

[5] This appears from a report afterwards sent to the pope in 974 respecting the extension of the Gospel in Hungary. Mansi, XIX. 49 sq.,

At this propitious moment a few seeds of Christianity were introduced among them by the baptism[1] of two 'Turkish' (or Hungarian) chiefs at Constantinople (**948**). One of these, however, Bulosudes, speedily relapsed into his former superstitions: and the other, Gylas, though assisted by a prelate[2] who accompanied him on his return, was not able to produce any powerful impression. The espousing of his daughter[3] to Geisa, the Hungarian duke (**972–997**), was more conducive to the propagation of the faith. But her husband, though eventually baptized, was still wavering in his convictions, when the German influence, now established by the victory of Otho (**955**), was employed in the conversion of the humbled Magyars. As early as **970** missions had been organized by prelates on the German border, none of whom were more assiduous in the work than Piligrin of Passau[4]. It is not, however, till the reign of Stephen (Waik), the first 'king' of Hungary (**997—1038**), that the evangelizing of his subjects can be shewn to be complete. Distinguished from his childhood[5] by the interest he took in all that concerned the welfare of religion, he attracted a large band of monks and clerics from adjoining dioceses[6], and endeavoured to enlarge the borders of the Christian fold. Religious houses,

HUNGARIAN CHURCH

First seeds of Christianity in Hungary.

Triumph of the Gospel.

---

and as above, n. 4. From the same source we learn that many of these captives were already Christians, which facilitated the conversion of their masters.

[1] Cedrenus, *Hist. Compend.* in the *Scriptores Byzant.*, ed. Paris, 636: cf. Mailáth, as above, I. 23 sq.

[2] A Constantinopolitan monk, named Hierotheos. *Ibid.*

[3] See the somewhat conflicting evidence in Schröckh, XXI. 530. Thietmar (Ditmar), *Chronic.* lib. VIII. c. 3 (Pertz, v. 862), gives the following account of the impiety of Geisa: 'Hic Deo omnipotenti variisque deorum illusionibus immolans, cum ab antistite suo ob hoc accusaretur, divitem se et ad hæc facienda satis potentem affirmavit.'

[4] See p. 126, n. 5. Among other missionaries whom he sent was a Swiss monk of Einsiedeln, who was afterwards bishop of Ratisbon. But his labours were indifferently received (*Life of Wolfgang*, in Mabillon, *Acta Sanct. Ord. Bened.*, Sæc. v. p. 817). The same field attracted Adalbert of Prague, on his expulsion from Bohemia: see above, p. 115, and cf. Mailáth, *Gesch. der Magyaren*, I. 31.

[5] *Life of Stephen* (written about 1100 by an Hungarian bishop), in Schwandtner, *Scriptor. Rer. Hungar.* I. 416 sq.

[6] 'Audita fama boni rectoris, multi ex terris aliis canonici et monachi ad ipsum quasi ad patrem confluebant.' *Life of* (two Polish monks) *Zoerard and Benedict*, by a contemporary bishop, in the *Acta Sanctorum*, Jul., tom. IV. p. 326.

*HUNGA-
RIAN
CHURCH.*

schools, and churches started up on every side¹, and Hungary was now distributed, like other countries, into parishes and sees, and placed under the archbishopric of Gran² (Strigonium). More than once, however, Stephen had recourse to the arm of the civil power in advancing the dominion of the faith, especially in **1003**, when he had made himself supreme in Transylvania and in one portion of Wallachia³. The effect of this unchristian element in his proceedings was a terrible revulsion at his death in favour of paganism⁴.

The Hungarian Church dependent on the Roman.

Instead of cleaving to the Churches of the East, by which the Gospel was at first imparted to them, the Hungarians, under Stephen more especially, were drawn into the closest union with the popes. He married a Bavarian princess, sister of the emperor Henry II., and his policy was always to preserve an amicable bearing in relation to the German empire. By the interest of Otho III.⁵, he was advanced to the dignity of king, that honour being formally conferred upon him in **1000**⁶ by Silvester II. A more lasting symbol of dependence on the West is found in the general use of Latin as the medium for the worship of the Church, and even as the language of the courts of justice⁷.

IN CENTRAL ASIA.

Continuance of the Nestorian missions.

The missionary zeal we have remarked⁸ in the Nestorian body, as distinguished from the other Christians of

---

¹ See the *Life of Stephen*, as above, pp. 417 sq.
² Wiltsch, I. 398, 399.
³ *Life of Stephen, ibid.*; cf. Neander, v. 460.
⁴ He was aided, for some years, by his son Emmerich (Henry), who, however, died before him in 1032; and afterwards on two occasions (1045 and 1060) a desperate attempt was made to re-establish paganism by force. See the Hungarian *Chronicle*, in Schwandtner's *Scriptores Rer. Hungar.* I. 105, 113 sq.
⁵ 'Imperatoris autem gratia et hortatu, gener Heinrici, ducis Bawariorum, Waic [=Stephen] in regno suimet episcopales cathedras faciens, coronam et benedictionem accepit.' Thietmar (Ditmar), *Chr.* lib. IV. c. 38 (Pertz, v. 784).
⁶ Fejér, *Codex Diplomaticus Hungariæ* (Budæ, 1829), I. 274: cf. *Life of Stephen*, as above, p. 417. But considerable doubts have been expressed as to the genuineness of this papal rescript: see Gieseler, II. 463, Schröckh, XXI. 544 sq.
⁷ Döllinger, III. 35, 36.
⁸ See above, pp. 26—28.

the East, continued to the present period, when it gained its highest point. Protected by the favour of the caliphs[1], the disciples of the Nestorian school were able, after strengthening the Churches they had planted in their ancient seats, to propagate a knowledge of the Gospel in the distant hordes of Scythia. A Tatar or a Turkish chieftain[2], bordering on China, with his subjects to the number of two hundred thousand, was converted at the close of the tenth century; and this would naturally conduce to the formation of ulterior projects in behalf of the adjacent tribes of Turkistan[3]. It seems that from the date of the conversion here recorded, Christianity maintained a stable footing in those quarters till it fell beneath the devastating inroads[4] of Timur (or Tamerlane). Its chief promoters were a series of the native khans who had inherited, for many generations, the peculiar name of 'Prester John'[5], or were at least distinguished by that title in the credulous accounts of tourists and crusaders[6].

§ 2. LIMITATION OF THE CHURCH.

The desolating march of the Hungarians[7] into Europe has been noticed on a former page. Yet deeply as those ravages were felt, they did not permanently curtail the area of the Western Church. A heavier blow had been inflicted by the ruthless hordes of Northmen (principally

---

[1] This protection was not, however, uniformly granted: *e.g.* in 849 the Christians of Chaldæa underwent a bitter persecution. Le Quien, *Oriens Christ.* II. 1130.

[2] Asseman. *Biblioth. Orient.*, tom. II. 444 sq: Mosheim, *Hist. Tartar. Eccles.*, pp. 23 sq., ed. Helmstad. 1741. He was baptized by the Nestorian primate of Maru in Chorasan: (cf. Le Quien, *Oriens Christ.* II. 1261 sq.)

[3] On the spread of Nestorianism in these regions, see above, p. 26, and cf. Wiltsch, I. 461.

[4] Mosheim, *ibid.* pp. 27 sq.

[5] Asseman, tom. III. part II. p. 487: cf. the discussion on this point in Schröckh, xxv. 186—194. Some writers have inferred that the original 'Prester John' was a Nestorian priest, who had been raised to the throne of the Tatar princes; but others, it would seem more probably, look upon the form 'Prester' as a western corruption of some Persian, Turkish, or Mongolian word.

[6] *e.g.* Joinville's *Memoirs of St Louis*, pp. 477 sq., in Bohn's *Chronicles of the Crusaders.*

[7] Above, p. 126.

RAVAGES OF THE NORTHMEN.

Danish and Norwegian vikings), who alighted on the fairest field of Christendom to cover it with violence and death[1]. In their unhallowed thirst for gold they pillaged almost every church and abbey on their way, in Germany, in France, in Belgium, in the British Islands; and, success inflaming their cupidity, they ventured even to the coasts of Italy and Spain, and came into collision with the other spoilers of the Church, the Moslems and the Magyars. Their path was uniformly marked by ruined towns and castles, by the ashes of the peaceful village and the bones of its murdered inmates: literature was trampled down and buried, order and religion were expiring on all sides; while the profaneness and brutality of which the Northmen are convicted baffle or forbid description[2].

Their establishment in the British Islands,

Nowhere did the tempest fall with greater violence than on the borders of the British Church[3]. The inroads of the Scandinavian vikings form the darkest passage in her annals. Landing year by year a multiplying swarm of pirates, they continued to enchain and spoil her from 787[4] until the date of the Norman Conquest. After the disastrous war of 833—851, very many of them left their barks and settled in the conquered lands, more especially the Northern and the Eastern districts. It now seemed, indeed, as if the Anglo-Saxon had been destined to succumb in turn before the ruder spirits of the North, as he had formerly expelled the British Christians. But this fear was gradually abated when a number of the Anglo-Danes, abandoning the gods of the Walhalla, were

and gradual conversion.

---

[1] The best modern account of these miscreants is in Palgrave's *Hist. of Normandy*, I. 297 sq.: Lappenberg's *Hist. of England under the Anglo-Saxon Kings*, vol. II., and Worsaae's *Danes and Norwegians in England, Scotland, and Ireland:* on their inroads into Spain and Portugal, see Conde, *Dominacion de los Arabes en España*, I. 276, 284; ed. Barcelona, 1844.

[2] The chronicles of the period give intensity of meaning to the cry of the persecuted Church: 'A furore Normannorum libera nos.' See Palgrave, I. 460.

[3] .... 'per Angliam et circa illam pervagantes monasteria cum monachis et sanctimonialibus, ecclesias cum clericis incendere, civitates, urbes, oppida, villasque cremare, agros devastare, strages hominum multas agere, minime cessabant.' Florent. Wigorn. *ad Chron. Append.* in *Monument. Britan.* p. 640.

[4] *Saxon Chron.* ad. an. A simple picture of the barbarities committed by the Danes has been preserved in the after-portions of this Chronicle.

absorbed into the Church. Anterior to the treaty of **878** between the English, under Alfred, and the Northmen, under Guthrum (Gorm), the latter had been well-affected to the Gospel; and his baptism made a way to the evangelizing of his subjects in East-Anglia, where he governed till his death, 891[1]. After a very short time the religion of the vanquished was generally adopted by the Danish settlers in Northumbria. The peace of the Church and country, consolidated under Edgar, was broken in upon by new hordes of the heathen under his unhappy successor. But in the time of the Scandinavian dynasty, beginning with Cnut the Great[2] (**1016–1035**), the permanent Danish settlers, who now might be distinguished from the lawless viking that was prowling on the seas, were thoroughly blended with the English population. Similar results ensued in Scotland[3], where, at least among the Highlands, the majority of settlers were Norwegian, and united to the crown of Norway: while their brethren, who had won important colonies in Ireland, were not slow in copying their example[4].

RAVAGES OF THE NORTHMEN.

After paralysing all the vigour of the sons of Charlemagne by their desultory inroads, many bands of Northmen settled down in France (circ. **870**), and gradually submitted to the Gospel[5]. In **876** and following years, their mighty chieftain, Rollo, wasted all the north and midland provinces, but, after a most bloody contest, was bought off by the surrender of a large portion of the Frankish territory of Neustria (**911**), and married to a Christian princess. On his baptism[6], in **912**, the Gospel was successively diffused in

Their establishment in Normandy:

---

[1] *Alfred and Guthrum's Peace*, in Thorpe, *Anglo-Saxon Laws*, I. 152. In 942 Odo, whose father was a Dane and fought against the English under Alfred, occupied the see of Canterbury: and a number of the other clerics were of Scandinavian blood. Worsaae, 134, 135.

[2] On his zeal in extirpating heathenism and in restoring the external fabric of religion, see Lappenberg, II. 203 sq. Among other proofs of a better state of things was the institution of a festival in honour of archbishop Ælfheah (Elfeg), who had been deliberately murdered after the general massacre at Canterbury (1011). *Saxon Chron.*, ad. an. 1012.

[3] See above, p. 111. Iona was again a missionary center for the Christianizing of the southern islands, and the Gospel was at times conveyed from it to Norway and Iceland. Worsaae, pp. 275, 276.

[4] *Ibid.* pp. 333 sq. Norwegian kings reigned in Dublin, Waterford, and Limerick, for three centuries. p. 316.

[5] Palgrave, I. 503, 504.

[6] *Ibid.* 690.

every quarter of the dukedom. Missions¹ had been formed already under Hervé, primate of the Gauls, and Guido, archbishop of Rouen; yet, until the final victory of Rollo, many converts had been ill-instructed in the faith, and not unfrequently retained their pagan habits and ideas².

The condition of the Church in the Iberian peninsula was now less hopeful than in Britain, Germany, or France; for though at first the Moslems³ did not practice anything like systematic persecution⁴, they resisted all the missionary efforts of the Christians, and by proselyting in their turn extended the dominion of the caliph⁵. Nothing daunted by the checks they had received from Charles Martel, they sometimes overleapt the Pyrenæan barrier; and in Spain, the mountain-districts, where the Church had taken refuge, or at least in which alone she dwelt secure and independent, were contracted more and more by the encroachments of Islam. She was still more fearfully afflicted in the gloomy period (850—960), when the Moslems, irritated in some cases by the vehemence with which their system was denounced, adopted a more hostile policy, and panted for the blood of their opponents. At this juncture, we are told, multitudes⁶ of Spanish Christians perished by the scourge or in the flames, exhibiting, indeed, the firmness of the earliest martyr, but deficient in his calm forbearance and his holy self-possession. A considerable section of the Church, desirous of restraining what had grown into a kind of passion, drew a difference between these martyrdoms and those of ancient times; and in a

---

¹ See the Pastoral of archbp. Hervé, in the *Concilia Rothomagensis Provin.*, Rouen, 1717. It was based upon instructions given him (900) by pope John IX.; Mansi, XVIII. 189 sq.

² In the document above cited the pope speaks distrustfully of men who had been baptized and re-baptized; 'et post baptismum gentiliter vixerint et paganorum more Christianos interfecerint, sacerdotes trucidaverint, atque simulacris immolantes idolothyta comederint.'

³ See above, p. 32.

⁴ See the *Memoriale Sanctorum* of Eulogius, in Schott's *Hispania Illustrata*, vol. IV., as adduced by Neander, v. 461, 462; and, on the general feeling of the Moslems to the Christians at this period, see Conde, *Dominacion de los Arabes en España*, I. 88, 101, 180; Schröckh, XXI. 293—299; Gieseler, II. 305 sq.

⁵ By intermarriages and other means: see Geddes, *Hist. of the Expulsion of the Moriscoes*, in his *Miscell. Tracts*, I. 104 sq.

⁶ As in the last note, and in the *Indiculus Luminosus* of Alvar of Cordova, *passim*.

council[1], held at Cordova (852), and prompted, some have said, by Abdu-r-Rahmán II., it was ruled that, for the future, Christians, under persecution, should not rush unbidden to the danger, but should wait until the summons of the magistrate compelled them to assert their faith. The ultimate predominance of these, and other like pacific counsels, gradually disarmed the fury of the Moslems; and the bleeding Church of Spain enjoyed an interval of rest.

PERSE-
CUTIONS IN
SPAIN.

[1] Mansi, xiv. 969. Eulogius, however, afterwards (859) the victim of his stern and unflinching hatred of Islamism, has denounced this synod as unlawful: *Memoriale Sanct.* lib. II. c. 15: cf. his *Apologeticus pro Martyribus adversus Calumniatores*, where he vigorously defends the conduct of the most fanatic martyrs. He was followed in this line by Alvar, his biographer.

CHAPTER VI.

CONSTITUTION AND GOVERNMENT OF THE CHRISTIAN CHURCH.

§ 1. *INTERNAL ORGANIZATION.*

Internal Organization.

Monarchical form of the Western Church.

THE form of government prevailing in the Western, as distinguished from the Eastern Church, was threatening to become an absolute autocracy. This change is due entirely to the growth of the papal usurpations, which almost reached a climax under Hildebrand, or Gregory VII. (**1073**). The Romanizing spirit of the west will consequently form a leading item in our sketch of the internal constitution of the Christian body at this period of its progress.

Promoted by the 'Forged Decretals.'

The attention of the reader should especially be drawn to one of the mightiest engines in the triumphs of the papacy, a series of Decretals, known as the *Pseudo-Isidore*[1],

[1] Cf. the allusions to this series above, p. 41, n. 1; p. 59, n. 2. Some of the documents had already appeared in the collection of Dionysius Exiguus (circ. 526), and others in a later one ascribed to Isidore of Seville: but the impostor [Möhler, *Schriften und Aussätze*, I. 309, makes him only a romanticist!] who had assumed the name of Isidore, at the beginning of the 9th century, fabricated many others, and professed to carry back the series of papal rescripts as far as A.D. 93. A large portion of these were afterwards received into the Roman canon-law. See Spittler's *Geschichte des canon. Rechts bis auf die Zeiten des falschen Isidorus:* Werken, I. 220 sq. *Halle*, 1778. It is almost certain that the Pseudo-Isidore decretals were first published, as a body, in Austrasia, and in the interest of the see of Mentz; between the years 829 and 845; though some of them appear to have been circulated separately in the time of Charlemagne. The forgery has been imputed to Riculf, archbishop of Mentz 787—814; but it is more probably due to the deacon Benedict who lived in the time of archbishop Otgar of Mentz, 826—847. See Robertson, *Church History*, II. 268, 269; Gieseler, II. 331, n. 12;

which had been fabricated, in some measure out of the existing canons, at the close of the eighth century or the beginning of the ninth; and in the latter period, after suffering fresh interpolations, were made current in the churches of the west. While tending to exaggerate the power and privileges of the sacerdotal order generally, they strengthened more and more the aspirations of the papal see[1], by representing it, on the authority of ancient usage, as the sole and irresponsible directress of the theocratic system of the Church. As early[2] as 857, the Pseudo-Isidore decretals had been openly enlisted to repress ecclesiastical commotions[3], and to settle questions of the day; and subsequently to the year 864[4], they were adduced in many of the papal rescripts,—it would seem, with no shadow of misgiving.

Prior to this date the claims to supremacy of power, so steadily advanced by the adherents of the Roman church, were seldom carried out to their natural results. Under Stephen V. (816), Paschal I. (817), Eugenius II. (824), Valentine (827), Gregory IV.[5] (827), Sergius II.[6] (844),

---

Guizot, *Lect.* xxvii. The first person who critically impugned the *genuineness* of the collection (as distinguished from its binding force) was Peter Comestor in the 12th century; but the cheat was not generally exposed until the time of the Reformation, when the Magdeburg Centuriators (*cent.* II. c. 7, *cent.* III. c. 7) pointed out the almost incredible anachronisms and other clumsy frauds by which the bulk of the decretals are distinguished. They have since been openly abandoned by Bellarmine, *de Pontif. Roman.* lib. II. c. 14; Baronius, *Annal. Eccl.* ad an. 865, § 8; Fleury, *Hist. Eccl.* tom. XIII. Disc. Prélim. p. 15.

[1] *e.g.* 'Quamobrem sancta Romana Ecclesia ejus [i. e. S. Petri] merito Domini voce consecrata, et sanctorum Patrum auctoritate roborata, primatum tenet omnium ecclesiarum, ad quam tam summa episcoporum negotia et judicia atque querelæ, quam et majores ecclesiarum quæstiones, quasi ad caput, semper referenda sunt.' Vigilii *ep. ad Projuturum,* c. 7; cf. Mansi, IX. 29, *note.*

[2] Cf. above, p. 41, n. 4.

[3] *e.g.* Hincmar, who afterwards questioned their binding force, when cited by the popes against himself, could hold them out notwithstanding as a warning to church-robbers ('raptores et prædones rerum ecclesiasticarum'): *Epist. Synodal.* in Mansi, xv. 127.

[4] Gieseler, II. 333, n. 15.

[5] The important letter (Mabillon, *Vet. Anal.* p. 298) bearing the name of this pope and addressed to bishops everywhere, is at the least of questionable authority: Jaffé, *Regest. Pontif. Rom.* p. 227. One clause of it runs thus: 'Cum nulli dubium sit, quod non solum pontificalis causatio, sed omnis sanctæ religionis relatio ad sedem apostolicam, quasi ad caput, debet referri et inde normam sumere.'

[6] An 'anti-pope' (John), chosen 'satis imperito et agresti populo,'

INTERNAL ORGANIZATION.

Impulse given to the Papal usurpations by Nicholas I.

Leo IV.[1] (847), Benedict III.[2] (855), they had made no measurable progress: but when Nicholas I. (858—867) was seated on the throne, the theory of papal grandeur, which had long been floating in the mind of western Christendom, began to be more clearly urged and more consistently established[3]. In the course of his reign, however, he experienced more than one indignant check[4] from the resistance of a band of prelates who stood forward to uphold the independence of provincial churches, and the ancient honour of the crown. The staunchest of these anti-papal champions was the Frankish primate Hincmar[5]: but they could not

was interpolated after Gregory IV., but soon afterwards expelled, ab 'urbis principibus.' *Liber Pontif.* ed Vignol. III. 39, 40. Sergius (844) appointed a vicar for all the transalpine provinces; cf. his *Epistle* in Mansi, XIV. 806.

[1] On the death of Leo IV. the papal chair is said to have been occupied by a *female* pope, Johanna (Johannes Anglicus): but as the story, in addition to its great improbability on chronological and other grounds, is not found in any writer of the period, or for centuries later, it is now almost universally rejected by the critics. Prior to the Reformation, few, if any, doubted the existence of the *papess*. See the evidence fairly stated in Schröckh, XXII. 75—110; Gieseler, II. 220, n. I. The story may have possibly originated in the soft or dissolute lives of men like John VIII. and his later namesakes.

[2] Another 'anti-pope' Anastasius was elected on the death of Benedict III., but speedily deposed. *Liber Pontif.* III. 154.

[3] One of the earliest indications of this purpose may be found in a rescript (863), where the primacy of Hincmar (of Rheims) is confirmed on the express condition, 'si tam in præsenti quam semper, *in nullo ab apostolicæ sedis præceptionibus quoquomodo discrepaverit*.' Mansi, XV. 875. On the vast influence exercised by Nicholas I. in the establishment of the ultra-papal claims, see Planck, *Geschichte des Pabsthums von der mitte des neunten Jahrhunderts an*, I. 35—147; Milman, *Latin Christianity*, bk. 5, ch. 4; Neander, VI. 10 sq.

[4] e.g. the account in the Appendix to the *Annales Bertiniani* (Pertz, I. 463), when the two Frankish archbishops, Gunthar of Cologne and Thietgaud of Trèves, protested against the sentence which the pope had passed in condemnation of themselves and the synod of Metz (863). But as the Frankish promoters were abetting the illicit union of the king Lothair II. with his mistress, Waldrade, their resistance was deprived of all moral force, and was eventually conducive to the despotism of Nicholas: cf. Milman, II. 301 sq. For the peremptory proceedings of the Roman synod on this question, see Mansi, XV. 651.

[5] He had deposed the bishop of Soissons, Rothad, in 863, notwithstanding his appeal to Rome, and when this prelate in the following year detailed his grievances before a Roman synod, the pope was able in the end to effect his restoration (Jan. 22, 865): *Lib. Pontif.* III. 207; Mansi, XV. 693. It was on this occasion that Nicholas entrenched himself behind the Pseudo-Isidore decretals: 'Absit ut cujuscumque [pontificis Romani], qui in fide catholica perseveravit, vel decretalia constituta vel de ecclesiastica disciplina quælibet exposita non amplectamur opuscula,

keep their ground in opposition to the centralizing spirit of the age; particularly when that spirit had evoked the forged decretals, and consigned them to intrepid pontiffs such as Nicholas I.

A slight reaction, it is true, occurred under Hadrian II. (867), when the zeal of Hincmar stirred him up afresh to counteract[1] the imperious measures of the Roman church, and warn it of the tendency to schism which its frequent intermeddling in the business of the empire could not fail to have excited. Still, on the accession of pope John VIII. (872), it entered into closer union[2] with the reigning house of France, and in spite of the remonstrances of Hincmar and of other prelates like him, it continually enlarged the circle of its power. John VIII. was succeeded by Marinus I.[3]

quæ dumtaxat et antiquitus sancta Romana ecclesia conservans nobis quoque custodienda mandavit, et penes se in suis archivis recondita veneratur...decretales epistolæ Romanorum pontificum sunt recipiendæ, etiamsi non sunt canonum codici compaginatæ.'

[1] See his bold letter to Hadrian II. (870) in Hincmar, *Opp.* II. 689, ed. Sirmond. Hadrian had come forward to defend the cause of the emperor Louis II., and even threatened to place the adherents of Charles the Bald under an anathema: Mansi, xv. 839. Another specimen of Hincmar's independence is the letter written in the name of Charles the Bald to Hadrian II. (Hincmar, *Opp.* II. 701), who had interfered in behalf of Hincmar's nephew (Hincmar, bishop of Laon), after he was deposed by the synod of Douzi (Duziacum) in 871: Mansi, xvI. 569 sq. In this case also the assumptions of the pontiff had been based on the pseudo-Isidore decretals, which led Hincmar (though not critical enough to see their spuriousness) to draw an important difference between merely papal rescripts and the laws of the Christian Church when represented in a General Council: cf. Hincmar's *Opuscul.* LV. *Capitulorum adv. Hincmar. Laud.*: Opp. II. 377 sq.

[2] John VIII., in 876, approved the conduct of Hincmar in deposing his unworthy nephew (Mansi, xvII. 226), and afterwards espoused the cause of Charles the Bald, whom he crowned as emperor. The tone of Charles was altered by this step, and he permitted the appointment of a papal vicar with the right of convoking synods, notwithstanding the remonstrances of Hincmar (*Opp.* II. 719). The prodigious powers of this legate may be gathered from the following statement: 'ut, quoties utilitas ecclesiastica dictaverit, sive in evocanda synodo, sive in aliis negotiis exercendis per Gallias et per Germanias apostolica vice fruatur, et decreta sedis apostolicæ per ipsum episcopis manifesta efficiantur: et rursus quæ gesta fuerint ejus relatione, si necesse fuerit, apostolicæ sedi pandantur, et majora negotia ac difficiliora quæque suggestione ipsius a sede apostolica disponenda et enucleanda quærantur:' cf. Gieseler, II. 348, n. 31.

[3] This was the first pope, who before his elevation to that rank had actually been made a bishop. *Annal. Fuldens.* A.D. 882 (Pertz, I. 397), where the election is spoken of as 'contra statuta canonum.'

(882), Hadrian III. (884), Stephen VI. (885), Formosus[1] (891), Boniface VI. (896), Stephen VII. (896), Romanus (897), Theodore II. (897), John IX. (898), Benedict IV. (900), Leo V. (903), Christopher (903), Sergius III. (904), Anastasius III. (911), Lando (913), John X.[2] (914), Leo VI. (928), Stephen VIII. (929), John XI. (931), Leo VII. (936), Stephen IX. (939), Marinus II. (942), Agapetus II. (946), John XII.[3] (955). They fill what is to be regarded as the vilest and the dreariest passage in the annals of the papacy; yet notwithstanding the decisive language in which the sins and corruptions[4] of the Roman church were censured here and there, it kept its hold on the affections of the masses, and continually made good its claim to a supremacy of power[5].

At the close of a second troublous period, during which the see of Rome was governed, as before, by lax and

---

[1] The corpse of Formosus was exhumed by Stephen VII. and all his official acts annulled. *Chron. S. Benedict.* (Pertz, v. 204: cf. I. 53, 412). But although these proceedings were in turn condemned (898) by John IX. (Mansi, xviii. 221), a long and disgraceful contest was kept up between the advocates and enemies of Formosus.

[2] In the Pontificate of John X. and those of his immediate successors, the Roman Church was at the mercy of a band of unprincipled females. See Schröckh, xxii. 242 sq. Döllinger, iii. 136. When we have made a large abatement for the credulity of the Italian chronicler Luitprand, who was a contemporary (see his *Antapodosis*, in Pertz, v. 273 sq.), enough will be left to prove the horrible degeneracy and the unblushing licence of the Roman see at this period of its history: cf. the treatise of Ratherius, bishop of Verona, *de Contemptu Canonum* (in D'Achery's *Spicilegium*, I. 317 sq.). He speaks of the utter corruption of morals as extending 'a vilissimo utique ecclesiæ usque ad præstantissimum, a laico usque ad pontificem (pro nefas!) summum.'

[3] Iniquity reached a climax in this pontiff, who was raised to the papal throne at the age of eighteen. He was deposed (Dec. 4, 963) by the emperor Otho (Luitprand, *De rebus Gestis Othonis*, in Pertz, v. 342), who secured the appointment of Leo VIII. and maintained him at the helm of the Western church, in spite of the opposition of both John XII. and Benedict V.: Mansi, xviii. 471; Luitprand, *ubi sup.* c. 20; *Contin. Reginon. Chron.* A.D. 964 (Pertz, I. 626).

[4] The centre of this party was Arnulph, archbishop of Orleans: see Neander, vi. 33 sq. His freer spirit was imbibed by Gerbert, who in 999 was himself raised to the papal chair, and took the name of Silvester II., but his brief reign (of four years) prevented him from carrying out his projects of reform. *Ibid.* and Hock's *Gerbert oder papst Sylvester II. und sein Jahrhundert*, ed. Wien, 1837.

[5] The synod of Rheims (991) furnished an almost solitary instance of contempt for the papal jurisdiction. Mansi, xix. 109 sq.; Richer (in Pertz, v. 636 sq.).

worthless rulers,—Leo VIII. (963–965), Benedict V. (964), John XIII. (965), Benedict VI.[1] (972), Benedict VII. (974), John XIV.[2] (983), Boniface VII. (984), John XV. (985), Gregory V.[3] (996), Silvester II. (999), John XVII. (1003), John XVIII. (1003), Sergius IV. (1009), Benedict VIII.[4] (1012), John XIX.[?] (1024), Benedict IX.[5] (1033), Gregory VI. (1045), Clement II. (1046), Damasus II. (1048),—there had grown up in almost every country a desire to promote a reformation of the Church, to counteract the spread of secularity, and put an end to the ravages of discord and corruption. But it chanced that the master-spirit of this healthier movement had been trained from his very cradle in the tenets of the Pseudo-Isidore decretals, and the reader will accordingly perceive, that all the efforts he originated for the extirpation of abuses, were allied with a strong determination to extend the dominions of the papacy, by making it, as far as might be, independent of the German empire. Such was the incessant aim of Hildebrand[6], who, long before his elevation to the papal throne, directed the reforming policy, as well

INTERNAL ORGANIZATION.

Desire of reformation.

The 'reforming' party advocate the ultra-papal claims.

---

[1] He was put to death by the lawless faction, headed by the females above mentioned, p. 138, n. 2. Respecting Donus or Domnus, who is said to have succeeded for a few days, see Jaffé, pp. 331, 332.

[2] John XIV. was starved to death, or executed (984) by Boniface VII. his successor (*Rerum Ital. Script.* ed. Muratori, III. ii. 333—335), who had been consecrated pope as early as 974, but soon afterwards expelled. Heriman. *Chron.* A.D. 974 (Pertz, VII. 116).

[3] After the consecration of Gregory V. his place was seized (997) by an 'antipope' (John XVI., called Calabritanus and Philagathus), but the intruder was in turn defeated and barbarously mutilated. *Vit. S. Nili* (Pertz, VI. 616).

[4] This pope was, in like manner, supplanted for a time (1012) by an 'antipope,' Gregory. Thietmar. *Chron.* lib. VI. c. 61 (Pertz, V. 835).

[5] Benedict IX., one of the most profligate of the pontiffs, owed his elevation to the gold of his father. At the time of his election he did not exceed the age of twelve years. Heriman. *Chron.* (Pertz, VII. 121), Glaber Radulphus, *Hist.* lib. IV. c. 5: lib. V. c. 5 (in Bouquet's *Historiens des Gaules*, etc. x. 50 sq.). In 1045 he sold the popedom (see authorities in Jaffé, pp. 361, 362), but seized it afresh in 1047: so that with an 'antipope' (Silvester III. 1044—1046) and Gregory VI. (who was appointed in 1045, on the retirement of Benedict IX.) there were now three rival popes. All of them were deposed by the Synod of Sutri (1046), at the instance of the emperor Henry III. See the account of Desiderius (afterwards pope Victor III.), *De Miraculis, etc. dialogi* (in *Biblioth. Patr.* ed. Lugdun. XVIII. pp. 853 sq.).

[6] He was seconded throughout by Peter Damiani, cardinal bishop of Ostia, who was equally anxious to abolish simony, to check the immorality of the priesthood, and to widen the dominions of the pope.

INTERNAL ORGANIZATION.

as the encroachments of successive pontiffs,—Leo IX. (**1048**), Victor II. (**1054**), Stephen X. (**1057**), Benedict X. (**1058**), Nicholas II.[1] (**1059**), and Alexander II. (**1061–1073**). A field was thus preparing for that mighty conflict of the secular and sacerdotal powers, which was doomed under Gregory VII. to agitate the Christian Church in every province of the west.

Effect of these claims on the metropolitan constitution.

But while the arm of the papacy grew stronger in proportion to the weakness of the Carolingian monarchs; while it rapidly extended its possessions, in the east as far as Hungary, and up to Greenland in the north, the augmentation of its power was followed, as a natural result, by the curtailment of the privileges of the metropolitan bishops. Hincmar felt these fresh invasions more acutely than his neighbours: he objected to the intermeddling of the pontiff in the case of an appeal to Rome, upon the ground that such an act was fatal to episcopacy[2] in general; and when afterwards a papal vicar, with extraordinary powers, was nominated for the Gallican and German churches, the same class of prelates openly disputed the appointment; they protested that they would not acquiesce in novelties put forward by the delegate of Rome, except in cases where his claims to jurisdiction could be shewn to be compatible with ancient laws and with the dignity of metropolitans[3]. A recent law demanding vows of absolute obedience to the pope[4], on the conferring of the pallium,

---

[1] This pontiff, on the death of the emperor (Henry III.) effected an important change in the relations of the papacy, by which it was determined that the pope should in future be elected by the cardinals (bishops, priests, and deacons), with the concurrence of the rest of the Roman clergy and laity, and subject to an ill-defined acquiescence of the emperor. See the best version of this act in Pertz, *Leges*, II. Append. p. 177: and cf. Hallam, *Middle Ages*, II. 180 (10th ed.).

[2] 'Hanc tenete,' are the words he puts into the mouth of his Romanizing nephew, 'et evindicate mecum compilationem [*i.e.* the Pseudo-Isidore decretals], et nulli nisi Romano pontifici debebitis subjectionem; et *dissipabitis mecum Dei ordinationem in communis episcopalis ordinis discretam sedibus dignitatem*.' Hincmar, *Opp.* II. 559, 560.

[3] Hincmar, *Opp.* II. 719.

[4] Cf. above, p. 136, n. 3. The first case on record is that of Anskar, the apostle of the North. He had received the pallium as archbishop of Hamburg (above, p. 103), without any such condition: but when Nicholas I. (864) confirmed the union of the two sees of Hamburg and Bremen (above, p. 104), he announced to Anskar that it was granted on condition, that himself and his successors not only acknowledge the six

served to deepen this humiliation of the Western primates; and in newly-planted churches, where the metropolitan constitution was adopted, under Roman influence, it was seldom any better than a shadow. Though the primates usually confirmed the bishops of their province, and were still empowered to receive appeals from them and from their synods, they were rigorously watched, and overruled in all their sacred functions, by the agents or superior mandates of the Pope[1]. The notion had diffused itself on every side, that he was the 'universal bishop' of the Church[2], that he was able to impart some higher kind of absolution[3] than the ordinary priest or prelate, and was specially commissioned to redress the wrongs of all the faithful. It may be that his intervention here and there was beneficial, as a counterpoise to the ambition of unworthy metropolitans, protecting many of their suffragans and others from the harshness of domestic rule: but on the contrary we should remember that the pontiffs also had their special failings, and the growth of their appellate jurisdiction only added to the scandals of the age. It

Its virtual supersession.

---

general councils, but profess on oath to observe with all reverence 'decreta omnium Romanæ sedis præsulum et epistolas quæ sibi delatæ fuerint.' Lappenberg, *Hamb. Urkunden-buch*, I. 21. In 866 Nicholas was under the necessity of upbraiding Hincmar, among other acts of disrespect, for not using the pallium 'certis temporibus:' Mansi, XV. 753. On the rapid alteration of the views of prelates with regard to the importance of this badge, see Pertsch (as above, p. 37), p. 145.

[1] Among the latest champions for the metropolitan system in its struggle with the papacy, were the archbishops of Milan: see the contemporary account of Arnulph (a Milanese historian), in Muratori, *Rerum Ital. Script.* IV. 11 sq. When Peter Damiani and Anselm, bishop of Lucca, were sent as papal legates to Milan in 1059, this protesting spirit was peculiarly awakened: 'Factione clericorum repente in populo murmur exoritur, *non debere Ambrosianam ecclesiam Romanis legibus subjacere, nullumque judicandi vel disponendi jus Romano pontifici in illa sede competere.*' Damiani, *Opusc.* V. *Opp.* III. 75: Mansi, XIX. 887 sq.: cf. Neander, on the whole of this movement; VI. 62—70.

[2] 'Summum pontificem et universalem papam, non unius urbis sed totius orbis:' cf. Schröckh, XXII. 417, 418. The condemnation of orders conferred by Scottish teachers, which was issued by the Councils of Châlons (813), c. 43 (Labbe, VII. 1270); and of Cealchythe (816), c. 5 (Councils, &c. III. 581), cannot be understood as indicating any resistance to papal jurisdiction specially maintained by the Scots; but must be regarded as a precaution for securing the purity of the succession and the regular authority of the diocesans. It is really to be viewed as a measure of the same sort as the disuse of *Chorepiscopi*.

[3] See examples in Gieseler, II. 384, 385.

INTERNAL ORGANIZATION.

General character of the bishops.

was not, however, till a period somewhat later that these features of the papal system, traceable to the ideas which gave birth to the 'spurious decretals,' were unfolded in their ultimate and most obnoxious shape.

The organizing of the several dioceses had continued as of old. The bishop[1] was, at least in theory, the father and the monarch of his charge. But the effects of his episcopate were often damaged[2] or destroyed by his utter inexperience, by the secularization of his heart, and his licentious habits. It is clear that not a few of the Western prelates had been wantonly obtruded on their flocks, through private interest and family connexions, or indeed, in many cases, through the open purchase of their sees from the imperial power. By this kind of bishops the disease that had been preying on the Church for centuries was propagated still more widely; and those prelates who were far less criminal allowed themselves to be entangled in the business of the State, to the abandonment of higher duties. Yet, in spite of this unhappy prevalence of episcopal delinquency, occasional exceptions meet us in all branches of the Church: the synodal enactments[3] that

---

[1] The chorepiscopi, whom we saw expiring in the former period (p. 46, n. 2), lingered here and there. The synod of Paris (829) complains of them (lib. I. c. 27) as wishing to intrude into the province of the bishops. Nicholas I. in 864 (Mansi, XV. 390) directs that ordinations made by them should not be rescinded, but that in future they should abstain from every function that was peculiar to the episcopate: cf. a rescript of 865 (*Ibid.* xv. 462), and one of Leo VII., about 937 (*Ibid.* XVIII. 379), in which a like prohibition is repeated. The synod of Metz (888), can. 8, directs that churches consecrated by chorepiscopi only shall be consecrated anew by the bishop: *ibid.* XVIII. 80.

[2] A child of five years old was made archbishop of Rheims (925). The see of Narbonne was purchased for another at the age of ten. Hallam, *Middle Ages*, II. 172. His statement, from Vaissète, that it was almost general in the Western church to have bishops under twenty, is, of course, an exaggeration. The following picture is drawn by Atto, bishop of Vercelli (about 950), in D'Achery's *Spicileg.* I. 421: 'Illorum sane, quos ipsi [*i.e.* principes] eligunt, vitia, quamvis multa et magna sint, velut nulla tamen reputantur. Quorum quidem in examinatione non charitas et fides vel spes inquiruntur, sed *divitiæ, affinitas* et obsequium considerantur.' And again, p. 423: 'Quidam autem adeo mente et corpore obcæcantur ut *ipsos etiam parvulos* ad pastoralem promovere curam non dubitent,' etc.

[3] *e.g.* A synodal letter of the pope to the bishops of Brittany (848), Mansi, XIV. 882, or still earlier, the reforming synod of Paris, 829, at which three books of more stringent canons were drawn up. The Council of Pavia (Papiense or Ticinense), held in 850, among other salutary injunctions prohibiting episcopal extortion and intemperance, directed

acquaint us with the spread of evil testify no less to the existence of a nobler class of bishops, actively engaged in their sacred avocations and deploring the enormities around them.

Degeneracy of the parochial clergy:

As we readily foresee, the mass of the parochial clergy[1] were infected by the ill example of the prelate. They had taken holy orders, in some cases, from unworthy motives, chiefly with a view to qualify themselves for the acceptance of the tempting church-preferment, which had rapidly increased in value since the time of Charlemagne. Others gained possession of their benefices through the help of unhallowed traffic with the patron, or descendant of the founder, of a church. This crime of simony, indeed, was one of the most flagrant characteristics of the age[2]. It urged a multitude of worthless men to seek admission into orders solely as the shortest way to opulence and ease: while some of them, regardless of propriety, are said to have farmed out the very offerings of their flock[3], and pawned the utensils of the church[4].

and of others,

Nor were other seculars more scrupulous, and worthy of their calling. The itinerating priests[5], whom we en-

that bishops should, when possible, celebrate mass every day, should read the Holy Scriptures, explain them to their clergy, and preach on Sundays and holy-days. Can. 2—5. The works of mercy wrought by individual bishops (such as Radbod of Trèves and Ethelwold of Winchester) are recounted by Neander, VI. 88, 89, and note.

[1] Bowden's *Gregory the Seventh*, I. 43 sq. 'Ipsi primates utriusque ordinis in avaritiam versi, cœperunt exercere plurimas, ut olim fecerant, vel etiam eo amplius rapinas cupiditatis: deinde mediocres ac minores exemplo majorum ad immania sunt flagitia devoluti.' Glaber Radulphus, *Hist.* lib. IV. c. 5.

[2] Cf. above, p. 143, n. 2. It began to be prevalent as early as 826 (Pertz, *Leges*, II. App. pp. 11 sq.). It was denounced by Leo IV. (circ. 850) in the letter to the bishops of Brittany (Mansi, XIV. 882). Subsequently it grew up to an enormous pitch (Lambert's *Annales*, A.D. 1063, 1071, in Pertz, VII. 166, 184), and the correction of it was a chief aim of the reforming movement under Hildebrand, who was resolved to cut it off, especially in the collation of the crown-preferment. There was also at this period no lack of pluralists: *e.g.* two of the *archicapellani* of Louis the Pious held three abbeys each. Palgrave, *Normandy*, I. 239, 247.

[3] See Vidaillan, *Vie de Greg. VII.* I. 377, *Paris*, 1837.

[4] Hincmar of Rheims was compelled to issue a decree against these practices. Bowden, as above, p. 49.

[5] See above, p. 45. The 23rd canon of the council of Pavia (850) renews the condemnation of these 'clerici acephali:' cf. Life of Bp. Godehard of Hildesheim, c. IV. § 26 (*Acta Sanct.* Maii, I. 511), where they are said to wander to and fro 'vel monachico vel canonico vel etiam Græco habitu.'

INTERNAL ORGANIZATION.

countered in the former period, still continued to produce disorder on all sides. They were not, however, so degraded as the larger class of chaplains, who are said to have literally swarmed in the houses of the gentry¹. Very frequently of servile origin, they were employed by the feudal lords in humble, and, at times, in menial occupations, which exposed them to the ridicule of the superior clergy, and destroyed their proper influence on society at large. It is not therefore surprising, that so many councils of this age unite in deploring the condition of both morals and intelligence in the majority of the ecclesiastics. This degeneracy was most of all apparent in the church of Italy², and, in the early years of Hildebrand, the clergy of the Roman see are mentioned as preeminent in every species of corruption³. There as elsewhere nearly all the healthier impulse that was given to the sacred orders by the energy of Charlemagne, had been lost in the ensuing troubles which extinguished the dominion of his house (887).

more especially in Italy.

Decay of the order of Canons.

The decline of the cathedral canons⁴ is a further illustration of this change. Materialized by the prevailing lust of wealth, they strove to make themselves completely

---

¹ The following is a picture of them drawn by Agobard, archbp. of Lyons, in his *De privilegio et jure Sacerdotii*, c. XI.: 'Fœditas nostri temporis omni lachrymarum fonte ploranda, quando increbuit consuetudo impia, ut pæne nullus inveniatur quantulumcunque proficiens ad honores et gloriam temporalem, qui non domesticum habeat sacerdotem, non cui obediat, sed a quo incessanter exigat licitam simul atque illicitam obedientiam, ita ut plerique inveniantur qui aut ad mensas ministrent,' etc.

² See the works of Ratherius, a reforming bishop of Verona (who died in 924), in D'Achery's *Spicilegium*, I. 345 sq. The ignorance and immorality of his own clergy, and of the Italians generally, appear to have been almost incredible. Another eye-witness speaks in the same strain of the Milanese ecclesiastics: 'Istis temporibus inter clericos tanta erat dissolutio, ut alii uxores, alii meretrices publice tenerent, alii venationibus, alii aucupio vacabant, partim fœnerabantur in publico, partim in vicis tabernas exercebant cunctaque ecclesiastica beneficia more pecudum vendebant.' *Life of Ariald* (a vehement preacher, who fell a victim to his zeal in 1067), § 2, in Puricelli's *History of the Milanese Church;* Milan, 1657. The same scandals and corruptions were prevailing at this period in the East: *e.g.* Neale, *Church of Alexandria*, II. 190, 211.

³ Hildebrand's uncle would not allow him to complete his education there, 'ne Romanæ urbis corruptissimis tunc moribus (ubi *omnis pæne clerus aut simoniacus erat aut concubinarius,* aut etiam vitio utroque sordebat) inquinaretur ætas tenera,' etc. See Vidaillan, *Vie de Greg.* I. 372.

⁴ Cf. above, p. 44.

independent of the bishop; and as soon as they had gained the power of managing their own estates[1], we see them falling back into the usual mode of life[2], except in the two particulars of dwelling near each other in the precincts of the cathedral, and dining at a common table. As a body, they had lost their ancient strictness, and were idle, haughty, and corrupt. The failure of all attempts to effect a general reform of the existing bodies resulted in the formation, under the influence of Ivo of Chartres, of a new order, the canons regular of St Augustine, very closely resembling Benedictine monachism.

INTERNAL ORGANIZATION.

In this connexion we may touch on a kindred point, the marriage, or in other cases the concubinage, of clerics. At no period did the law of celibacy find a general acceptance[3], notwithstanding the emphatic terms in which it was repeated[4]; and when Hildebrand commenced his task as a reformer, aiming chiefly at ecclesiastical delinquents, numbers of the bishops and the major part of the country-clergy[5] were exposed to his stern reproaches. In some

Continuance of clerical marriages.

---

[1] The earliest instance on record is the chapter of Cologne, whose independence was confirmed by Lothair in 866, and afterwards by a council at Cologne in 873: Mansi, XVII. 275; cf. Gieseler, II. 387 (note).

[2] The following is the language of Ivo, the holy bishop of Chartres, who wrote about 1090: 'Quod vero communis vita in omnibus ecclesiis pæne defecit, tam civilibus quam diocesanis, nec auctoritati sed desuetudini et defectui adscribendum est, refrigescente charitate, quæ omnia vult habere communia, et regnante cupiditate, quæ non quærit ea, quæ Dei sunt et proximi, sed tantum quæ sunt propria.' Epist. 215. Gieseler, II. 388. From the *Annales* of Hirschau, (J. Trithemius) A.D. 973, we learn that the example had been set in that year by the canons of Trèves: I. 116, ed. 1690.

[3] See above, p. 47.

[4] *e.g. Canons at Eanham* (1009), § 2, where it is affirmed that some of the English clerics had more wives than one. Johnson, I. 483.

[5] *e.g.* we are told of the Norman prelates and the other clergy: 'Sacerdotes ac summi pontifices libere conjugati et arma portantes ut laici erant.' *Life of Herluin*, abbot of Bec, in Mabillon, *Act. Sanct. Ord. Bened.*, sæc. VI. part II. p. 344. Ratherius of Verona (above, p. 144, n. 2) found it an established custom for the clergy to live in wedlock, and for their sons to be clergymen in their turn: D'Achery's *Spicilegium*, I. 370, 371. Aventinus (*Annales Boiorum*, lib. v. c. 13, p. 541, ed. Gundling), speaking of this same period, remarks: 'Sacerdotes illa tempestate publice uxores, sicuti cæteri Christiani, habebant, filios procreabant, sicut in instrumentis donationum, quæ illi templis, mystis, monachis fesere, ubi hæ nominatim cum conjugibus testes citantur, et honesto vocabulo *presbyterissæ* nuncupantur, invenio.' According to Mr Hallam (*Middle Ages*, II. 173) the sons of priests were capable of inheriting by

INTERNAL ORGANIZATION.

The struggle to suppress them on the Continent.

quarters, and especially at Milan, where the ordinances against clerical marriage had been rigorously urged, there was a party[1] who contended for the lawfulness of such alliances, deriving their ideas from the Bible and the earlier doctors of the Church. But the great body of the people, blinded by the prejudices of the age[2], and disgusted by the lewdness and corruption which had shewn itself in spite of the marriage of the clerics, took the side of men like Hildebrand, abstaining even from the public services conducted by the married priest[3], and indicating their disapprobation by ridicule and not unfrequently by their assaults on his property or person[4]. A like spirit is betrayed in the still earlier movement that was headed by the English primate, Dunstan[5] (961–988). He was truly anxious for the moral elevation of his clergy; but the measures he adopted to secure it were not able to achieve a permanent success. He hoped to counteract the barbarism and immorality around him by abstracting the ecclesiastics from the world, that is, by prohibiting their marriage: and this object seemed to him most easy of attainment by the substitution of monastic and unmarried clergy in the place of degenerate seculars and canons[6]. By his

Dunstan's measures for the same end.

the laws of France and also of Castile; in the latter country in consequence of the indulgence shewn to concubinage in general.

[1] See the controversy at length in Neander VI. 61 sq.; and Milman, *Latin Christianity*, III. 13 sq., who, with many other instances, mentions the letter of Ulric, bishop of Augsburg (900), to pope Nicholas I. (in Eccard, II. 23). An actual permission to marry was given to his clergy by Cunibert, bishop of Turin, himself unmarried, in the hope of preserving his diocese from the general corruption. *Ibid.* p. 53.

[2] These were so strong that even Ratherius of Verona looked upon the man who was 'contra canones uxorius' in the light of an adulterer. D'Achery, I. 368. On this account it is not easy to distinguish between the lawful and illicit connexions of the clergy. Hildebrand, Damiani, and other zealots spoke of such alliances in general as reproductions of the 'Nicolaitan heresy.' See Damiani *Opuscul.* XVIII., *contra Clericos intemperantes.*

[3] In accordance with the bidding of the Council of Lateran (1059): Mansi, XIX. 907.

[4] Arnulph, *Hist. Mediol.* lib. III. c. 9: cf. Fleury, liv. LXI. s. 26.

[5] See the accounts in Soames, *Anglo-Saxon Church*, pp. 195 sq., ed. 1844: and Lappenberg, *Anglo-Saxons*, II. 126 sq.

[6] '...statuit [969], et statuendo decretum confirmavit, videlicet ut canonici omnes, presbyteri omnes, diaconi et subdiaconi omnes, aut caste viverent aut ecclesias quas tenebant una cum rebus ad eas pertinentibus perderent.' Oswald, bishop of Worcester, was especially active in carrying out this edict, and founded seven monasteries in his own diocese

influence, and the aid of the civil power which he wielded at his pleasure, many of the elder clerics were ejected, and Benedictine monks[1] promoted to the leading sees and richer livings. But soon afterwards, this rash proceeding led the way to a violent reaction: and the following period had to witness many struggles for ascendancy between the monks and seculars of England. When the latter gained a victory, we learn that their wives[2] were partakers of the triumph.

INTERNAL ORGANIZATION.

Degeneracy of the monks.

Contrary to the idea of Dunstan, the corruptions of the age had found admission even to the cloisters. It was customary[3] for the royal patron of an abbey to bestow it, like a common estate, on some favourite chaplain of his court, on parasites or on companions of his pleasures, paying no regard to their moral character and intellectual fitness. Others gained possession of the convents by rapacity and sold them to the highest bidder, not unfrequently to laymen[4], who resided on them with their wives and families, and sometimes with a troop of their retainers[5]. It should also be observed, that in the present

---

alone. '...Post hæc in aliis Angliæ partibus ad parochiam suam nil pertinentibus insignes ecclesias ob præfixam causam clericis evacuavit, et eas...viris monasticæ institutionis sublimavit.' Eadmer, *Vit. S. Oswaldi* (in Wharton's *Anglia Sacra*, II. 200).

[1] Lappenberg, II. 136, 137. It is by no means easy to disentangle the several measures taken in the English church for the reform of monasticism and for the improvement of clerical morality in general; or to determine what was the action of the statesmanlike mind of Dunstan, and what of the narrower and severer piety of his followers. But there is no doubt that Dunstan's personal share in these transactions has been exaggerated, for he did not turn out the secular clerks of his own cathedrals, either at Worcester or Canterbury. A great deal of the evidence for his prohibition of clerical marriages is very questionable. On the whole question of clerical celibacy treated historically, see Lea's *History of Sacerdotal Celibacy*, Philadelphia, 1867.

[2] 'Principes plurimi et optimates abbates cum monachis de monasteriis, in quibus rex Eadgarus eos locaverat, expulerunt, et clericos, ut prius, loco eorum *cum uxoribus* induxerunt.' Matth. Westmonast. *Flor. Hist.* p. 193, ed. Francof. 1601.

[3] Bowden's *Gregory the Seventh*, I. 46. It was complained of Charles the Bald that he gave away religious houses recklessly, 'partim juventute, partim fragilitate, partim aliorum callida suggestione, etiam et minarum necessitate, quia dicebant petitores, nisi eis illa loca sacra donaret, ab eo deficerent.' *Epist. Episcoporum ad Ludovicum Regem*, in Baluze, II. 110.

[4] Known by the name of *abba-comites*: cf. Palgrave, *Normans*, I. 184 sq.

[5] Council of Trosli, as below, p. 143, n. 2.

Attempts to reform them.

Benedict of Aniane.

age, when many of the chief foundations were most anxious to obtain exemptions from the bishops[1], and had no efficient champions in the Roman see, they were deprived of their strongest remedy against the evils which beset them. The appearance of a race of worldly-minded abbots was the signal for the relaxation of monastic discipline[2] in every quarter of the west: and this degeneracy produced in turn the open violation of the rules of St Benedict.

An effort, it is true, was made, as early as **817**, under Louis the Pious, to check these rampant evils in the convents of his kingdom. It was mainly stimulated by the zeal of Benedict[3] of Aniane (**774—821**), who, following at a humble distance in the steps of the elder Benedict and borrowing his name, is honoured as the second founder of monasticism in France[4]. Disorders of the grossest kind, however, had continually prevailed until the time of Berno[5], the first abbot of Clugny (**910**), and Odo[6], his successor (**927—941**), who endeavoured to effect a thorough reformation. In the hands of the latter abbot, not a few of the

---

[1] See above, p. 42. The privileges actually granted to them did not at first exempt them from the ordinary jurisdiction of the bishop; although he had no longer any power to modify the rules of the fraternity. *e.g.* in the Council of Fîmes (Concil. apud S. Macram), 881, his authority is still recognized: for the fourth canon orders that all monasteries, nunneries, and other religious houses shall be visited by the bishop and the king's commissioners, and a report drawn up of their condition. Mansi, xvii. 540. The exemption of the abbey of Clugny was made *absolute* by Alexander II. in 1063, and other instances soon afterwards occurred. Gieseler, ii. 420. In the newly-founded Russian church the common practice of the East obtained; the bishop having the sole right of appointing the archimandrites and also of depriving them. Mouravieff's *Hist. of the Russian Church*, pp. 359, 360.

[2] See the complaints of the council of Trosli (near Soissons) 909, can. 3, which taxes both the monks and nuns with every species of excess: Mansi, xviii. 270. The degeneracy is traced to the influence of the lay-abbots, who were then in possession of nearly all the monasteries of France.

[3] His measures are detailed in a *Capitulary* (*Aquisgranense* (817): Baluze, i. 579) containing eighty articles, which may be viewed as a commentary on the rule of Benedict the elder. See Guizot's remarks upon it, *Lect.* xxvi. Among other things he urges that 'the reformation of the sixth century was at once extensive and sublime: it addressed itself to what was strong in human nature: that of the ninth century was puerile, inferior, and addressed itself to what was weak and servile in man.'

[4] In the Frankish empire at this period there were eighty-three large monasteries. Döllinger, iii. 192.

[5] See his *Life* in Mabillon, *Act. Sanct. Ord. Ben.* sæc. v. pp. 67 sq.

[6] *Ibid.* pp. 150 sq.

ascetic laws were made more stringent and repulsive[1]: yet the fame of the order from this period was extended far and wide[2]. In spite of an extreme austerity in many of its regulations, they presented a refreshing contrast to the general corruption; and their circulation gave a healthier tone to all the churches of the west[3].

Rise of the Cluniac monks.

The impulse which had led to this revival of the Benedictine order, urged a number of congenial spirits to take refuge in the mountains and the forests, with the hope of escaping from the moral inundation, or of arming for a future struggle with the world. Of these we may notice Romuald[4], who in after life became the founder (circ. **1018**) of a large community of hermits, known as the Camaldulenses; John Gualbert[5], in whose cell the order of the Cœnobites of Vallombrosa had its cradle (circ. **1038**); and especially the younger Nilus[6], a recluse of Calabria, who stood forward in the tenth century as an awakening preacher of repentance in his own and in the neighbouring districts.

Some other religious spirits.

§ 2. *RELATIONS OF THE CHURCH TO THE CIVIL POWER.*

The influence of the State preponderated as before in all the Eastern churches. This was shewn especially in

---

[1] Among other changes, the Ordo Cluniacensis observed an almost unbroken silence 'in ecclesia, dormitorio, refectorio, et coquina.' See their *Consuetudines* (circ. 1070) lib. II. cap. III. *De Silentio;* cap. IV. *De signis loquendi;* in D'Achery's *Spicilegium,* I. 670 sq.

[2] In the year of his death, Odo left his successor two hundred and seventy deeds of gift which had been made to the order in thirty-two years. Döllinger, III. 194. The abbots Majolus and Odilo advanced its reputation more and more. See the *Life* of the latter in Mabillon, sæc. VI. part 1, pp. 631 sq.

[3] The greatest difficulty was presented by some of the German monasteries, where the inmates rose into rebellion. See the instances in Gieseler, II. 415, n. 9. The example, however, of Hanno, archbp. of Cologne, in 1068, was followed very generally. Lambert of Hersfeld, *Annales* in Pertz, VII. 238. The 'congregation of Hirschau' also sprang up at this time (1069): it was based on the rule of Clugny. Bernold's *Chronicon,* in Pertz, VII. 451.

[4] See his *Life* in Damiani, *Hist. Sanctorum;* Opp. II. 426; and the *Rule* of the Camaldulensians, in Holstein's *Codex Reg. Monast.* II. 192 sq.

[5] *Life* in Mabillon, sæc. VI. part II. pp. 266 sq.

[6] An interesting sketch of his labours is given by Neander, VI. 105—110.

<small>RELATIONS TO THE CIVIL POWER.</small>

<small>*Difference between the East and West.*</small>

<small>*Causes of a movement in the West against the supremacy of the crown.*</small>

the appointment of their bishops, who, with the exception of the patriarchates which still languished under the dominion of the Saracens, were for the most part chosen absolutely by the crown. In Russia[1] and the other kingdoms where the Gospel had been planted by the agency of Oriental missions, the alliance with the civil power was also intimate and undisturbed. But it was otherwise in nearly all the churches of the west. The daring and aggressive genius of the papacy, which now stood forward on the plea of acting as their champion, had embarrassed the alliance on the one side; while the grasping worldliness of laymen generally, and the venality or violence with which the civil power had tampered with the church-preferment[2], seemed to justify the disaffection that arose in every quarter. Very much of it is traceable to a confusion of ideas relating to the temporalities of the Church. The laity, and more especially the crown, regarded the endowments made by them or by their predecessors for the service of religion, in the light of public loans, which still remained at their disposal; and the practice of conceding to church-founders what is called the *right of patronage*[3], appeared in some degree to favour this construction. An effect of these prolific errors might be seen, most glaringly perhaps, on filling up the vacant sees. In harmony with the prevailing feudalism a bishopric was granted at this period like an ordinary fief[4]; and emperors, in their capacity of

---

[1] The bishops were usually selected by the prince of the district with the consent of the superior clergy and the chief of the citizens, and were then presented to the metropolitan for consecration. Mouravieff's *Hist.* by Blackmore, p. 359. The Hungarian bishops, although chiefly foreigners at first, and in communion with the Western Church, were similarly nominated by the crown. Döllinger, III. 35.

[2] See above, pp. 143 sq.; and other examples in Gieseler, II. 239, n. 10. Under Henry IV., the rival of Hildebrand, simony was practised at the imperial court in the most scandalous manner (*e.g.* Lambert's *Annales*, A.D. 1063, 1071: Pertz, VII. 166, 184).

[3] From the first, however, the privilege of appointing to a church could not lawfully be exercised without the approval of the bishop of the diocese, to whose jurisdiction also the new incumbent was made subject (see *Council* of Rome, in 826, and again in 853, c. 21; Mansi, XIV. 493, 1006, 1016). But this rule, like others of the kind, was continually evaded.

[4] Besides taking the oath of allegiance, like other vassals, prelates were on this ground compelled to render to the king a twofold service, one of following him in time of war, the other of appearing frequently at

suzerain, affected to confer investiture upon the spiritual as well as on the temporal nobility. So blind were many of them to the plain distinction between the property and sacred duties of a see, that their appointment now began to be confirmed by the delivery of a ring and crozier,— symbols of the *spiritual* functions of the bishop. He was thus insensibly becoming a mere feudatory, or a vassal of the crown[1].

We saw that under Charlemagne[2] prelates were again occasionally chosen in obedience to the ancient canons; and the clergy lost no opportunity of pleading this concession in their efforts to retain the freedom it had promised[3]. Still the privilege was scarcely more than verbal at the best[4]: and under Otho I., who laboured to curtail the power of the German and Italian clergy[5], it was formally annulled. He acted on the principle, that popes and

RELATIONS TO THE CIVIL POWER.

Nominations to vacant sees.

---

court. They were also amenable to the judicial sentence of the king, regarded as their liege-lord, and even were at times deposed by him. Hasse, as below. On the state of feeling with regard to the participation of ecclesiastics in the wars, see Neander, vi. 83 sq.

[1] Hasse's *Life of Anselm*, by Turner, p. 53, Lond. 1850: see Church's *Essays* (from the *Christian Remembrancer*), and his *Life of Anselm*. As consecration was subsequent to investiture, the jurisdiction of the prelate *seemed* to be derived from the state. The indignation of the Hildebrandine party at this juncture may be gathered from Humbert's treatise *Adversus Simoniacos*, lib. iii. c. 11 (in Martene's *Thesaurus Anecdot.* tom. v. p. 787).

[2] Above, p. 53.

[3] Thus, at the Council of Valence (855), c. 7 (Mansi, xv. 7), it was decreed that 'on the death of a bishop, the monarch should be requested to allow the clergy and the community of the place to make an election according to the canons.' But the synod goes on to intimate that monarchs not unfrequently sent a nominee of their own, and that their permission was in all cases needed before an election could take place. See the energetic letter of Hincmar to Louis III. of France, on the subject of royal interference in elections: *Opp.* tom. ii. p. 190.

[4] Bowden, *Life of Gregory*, i. 45: cf. Guizot, ii. 320.

[5] Vidaillan, *Vie de Greg. VII.* i. 365, 366. After deposing pope Benedict V. (964) and restoring Leo VIII., Otho held a council at Rome, which, in his presence, granted him and his descendants the right of choosing the popes in future, and of giving investiture to the bishops of the empire. See the acts of this council in Luitprand, *de Rebus Gestis Ottonis*, c. 10 sq. (Pertz, v. 342): and De Marca, *De Concordia*, lib. viii. c. 12, § 10. This decree was prompted by the growth and bitterness of the political factions which at that time were convulsing every part of Italy. But acts of violence among the populace were not uncommon, at an earlier period, in the filling up of vacant sees: *e.g.* the decree of Stephen V. (816), in Mansi, xiv. 147.

RELATIONS TO THE CIVIL POWER.

bishops were like other functionaries of the empire, and as such were subject to his beck. These fresh assumptions were indeed renounced by Henry II., but soon afterwards repeated: and it was on the absolute appointment of pope Leo IX. (1049) by Henry III. of Germany, that Hildebrand at length emerged from private life, to bring the struggle to a crisis. He was able in 1059, while engaged as the subdeacon of the Roman church, to wrest the nomination of the popes entirely from the civil power[1], although reserving to it for the present a precarious right of confirmation. But this partial victory incited him the more to persevere in his original design of compassing what he esteemed the ancient freedom of the Church. Accordingly, as soon as he was elevated to the papal throne, he hastened to prohibit every form of 'lay-investiture:' and the dispute which he had thus embittered was not closed for half a century[2].

Encroachments on the side of the Church:

While it is plain that the civil power exceeded its own province in suppressing the episcopal elections and in arbitrary misappropriation of the other church-preferment, there was also an aggressive movement on the side of the ecclesiastics. This, indeed, is the most prominent and startling feature of the times. It was of course developed to the greatest height among the popes, who had already shewn themselves peculiarly impatient of the secular authority. We saw that under Charlemagne they were able to effect but little in curtailing his imperial powers; and in 823 Paschal I. even felt obliged to clear himself by oath before the *missi* (or commissioners) of Louis the Pious[3]; yet from this period onwards the pretensions of the Roman court were less and less disputed by the Carolingian princes[4]. Its ascendancy increased

---

[1] See above, p. 140, n. 1.
[2] By the Concordat of Worms, 1122; see below, 'Relations of the Church to the Civil Power,' *Period* III.
[3] *Life of Louis*, by Theganus, in Pertz, II. 597. Other examples of this supremacy of the civil power at Rome itself may be seen in Gieseler, II. 231, 232.
[4] The following fragment (circ. 850) of a letter from Leo IV. to the emperor Louis II., which has been preserved in Gratian (*Decret.* Pars II. Caus. II. Qu. VII. c. 41), is one of the latest recognitions of the imperial rights: 'Nos, si incompetenter aliquid egimus, et in subditis justae legis tramitem non conservavimus, *vestro ac missorum vestrorum cuncta volu-*

on the dismemberment of the Frankish empire, and still further when all central government was enervated by the progress of the feudal system. Aided by the 'Forged Decretals,' which endeavoured among other kindred objects to exalt the Church above the influence of the temporal princes, Nicholas I.[1] was able to achieve a number of important triumphs. He came forward, it is true, on two occasions, as a champion of the wronged, a bold avenger of morality[2], and therefore carried with him all the weight of popular opinion. His success emboldened John VIII. in 876 to arrogate in plainer terms, and as a privilege imparted from on high, the right of granting the imperial crown[3] to whomsoever he might choose: and since this claim was actually established in his patronage and coronation of the emperor Charles the Bald[4], the intermeddling of the pope in future quarrels of the Carolingians, and indeed of other princes, was facilitated more and more. The claim grew up, as we shall see in Hildebrand, to nothing less than a theocratic power extending over all the earth.

RELATIONS TO THE CIVIL POWER.

especially of the popes:

Nor was the spirit of aggression at this time restricted to the Roman pontiffs. It had also been imbibed by other prelates of the west. In England[5], it is true, if we except collisions in the time of Odo and Dunstan, there is little or no proof that the ecclesiastics were forgetting their vocation. While the Church continued, as before, in close alliance with the civil power, she exhibited no tendency to cripple or dispute the independence of the crown. But

but also of the prelates generally.

---

mus emendare judicio,' etc. 'But every thing soon changes, and the Church in her turn governs the emperor.' Guizot, II. 326.
[1] A contemporaneous admirer says of him, 'regibus ac tyrannis imperavit, eisque, ac si dominus orbis terrarum, auctoritate præfuit.' Regino's *Chron.* ad an. 868.
[2] See above, p. 136, n. 4: and cf. Guizot, II. 341 sq.
[3] *Epist.* cccxv. cccxvi. : Mansi, xvii. 227, 230.
[4] It should be remarked, however, that Charles the Bald, in earlier life a warm defender of the liberties of the Frankish Church (see above, p. 137), was not, in 876, entirely made a vassal of the pope's. See Goldast's *Collectio Constitut. Imperial.* II. 34.
[5] As before noticed (p. 49), the civil and spiritual tribunals had been acting most harmoniously together till the Norman Conquest. Some ecclesiastical causes were referred to the decision of a synod of the prelates; but many which at a later period were reputed ecclesiastical were subjected, like the ordinary causes of the laity, to the judgment of the shiremoot or county-court. This extended even to the probate of wills. Kemble, *Saxons*, II. 385.

<small>RELATIONS TO THE CIVIL POWER.</small>

it was otherwise in continental nations. There we see the monarch struggling on one side with his disaffected nobles, on the other with the prelates of his realm; and not unfrequently succumbing to the usurpations of the latter. Before the death of Charlemagne, for example, his authority in matters even of religion was so great, that councils[1] deemed it proper to address him in a tone which bordered almost on servility: yet more than one of his successors formally acknowledged their dependence on the members of the hierarchy, and submitted to its most humiliating censures[2]. The extent of this vast but ill-defined preponderance may be gathered from the transfer that was made of the *regalia* (royal privileges) to the hands of the superior clergy[3].

Exceptions to this rule.

Some, indeed, of the better class of prelates, while they rendered due obedience to the civil ruler, kept aloof from all secular affairs[4]: the rest however, more especially throughout the tenth century, yielded to the worldly spirit of the age; they could too seldom be distinguished from the other vassals. But this close connexion with the crown was operating as a check on hierarchical ambition:

---

[1] *e.g.* the councils of Arles and Mentz, both held in 813, on making a report to him of ecclesiastical matters that were crying for a reformation, beg him to supply what he might deem corrections, and confirm their work by his authority. Mansi, XIV. 62, 65.

[2] *e.g.* Louis the Pious (835) was deposed and afterwards absolved by a party of bishops: Mansi, XIV. 657. See Palgrave, *Hist. of Normandy*, I. 295, 296. Louis the Germanic was treated in like manner by a synod at Metz (859): Baluze, *Capitular.* II. 121. In the synod of Savonières (Tullensis, apud Saponarias) held in the same year, Charles the Bald acknowledged his dependence on the bishops in the most abject terms: Baluze, II. 129: cf. Guizot, II. 326, 327. The general principle on which the bishops claimed to exercise these powers was frequently avowed in the synods: *e.g.* Fîmes, *apud S. Macram* (881), c. 1; Mansi, XVII. 538: Trosli (909), c. 1; Mansi, XVIII. 267.

[3] Among these *regalia* may be mentioned the right of tolls, markets, and coinage which was granted among other privileges by Louis the Pious, on the principle 'ut episcopos, qui propter animarum regimen principes sunt cœli, ipse eosdem nihilominus principes efficeret regni.' Gieseler, II. 255, 374. These grants, however, were made not unfrequently by the sovereigns with a political object, to secure the allegiance of the bishops, to balance them against the inordinate power of the feudal lords; to retain a certain amount of patronage that could not be made hereditary, and to interpose tracts of sacred estates between the territories of princes devoted to private war. Hasse's *Life of Anselm*, p. 51.

[4] Thus, for example, reasoned Radbod, archbp. of Utrecht. See his *Life*, in Mabillon, *Act. Sanct. Bened.* sæc. v. p. 30.

it eventually gave birth to an important school of royalists, who vindicated the imperial interest[1] from the attacks of an extreme or Romanizing party.

Of the minor and less obvious benefits accruing to society at large from the exalted power of the ecclesiastics, one is to be found in the exertions which they made to mitigate the ravages of private or intestine wars, now common in all quarters. They were able in the end (circ. **1032**) to establish certain intervals of peace[2] ('Treugæ Dei'), extending from the Thursday to the Monday morning of each week: for which space it was ordered, under pain of excommunication, that all acts of violence as well as law-proceedings should be everywhere suspended. The same influence was directed also, though more feebly, to the abolition of the ordeal-trials, or as they were commonly entitled, 'judgments of God.' The zealous Agobard of Lyons was conspicuous in this movement[3]: but the custom, deeply rooted in antiquity, was not to be subverted at a blow. It kept its hold on the Germanic races till a far later period, notwithstanding constant efforts, made in councils, for its suppression, partly no doubt through the sanction or connivance of the ill-instructed teachers of the Church.

RELATIONS TO THE CIVIL POWER.

Beneficial result of clerical ascendancy.

---

[1] How large this party grew may be inferred from the case of England, where the bishops almost to a man united with the crown in opposition to archbp. Anselm and his view of the investiture-controversy. On one occasion he complained of this most bitterly, adding, 'et me de regno, potius quam hoc servarent, expulsuros, et a Romana ecclesia se discessuros.' *Epist.* lib. IV. ep. 4.

[2] See Ducange, under *Treva, Treuga,* seu *Trevia Dei:* cf. Neander's remarks, VI. 87, 88; and Balmez, *Protestantism and Catholicity compared,* c. XXXII. pp. 139 sq. The provincial synod of Limoges (1031) placed a number of refractory barons, who refused to join in the 'Treuga Dei,' under an interdict: Mansi, XIX. 530, 542.

[3] *e. g.* in his treatise *Contra Judicium Dei.* Pope Stephen VI. (circ. 886) condemns both fire and water-ordeals. He adds, 'Spontanea enim confessione vel testium approbatione publicata delicta ... commissa sunt regimini nostro judicare: occulta vero et incognita Illi sunt relinquenda, Qui solus novit corda filiorum hominum.' Mansi, XVIII. 25. On the other hand, the 'judicium aquæ frigidæ et callidæ' was defended even by Hincmar of Rheims: *Opp.* tom. II. 676. "Wager of Battle" was strongly denounced by the Council of Valence (855), c. 12, under pain of excommunication, which incapacitated the subject of it for performing any civil function: Mansi, XV. 9. On the whole subject of ordeal and wager of battle, see Lea's *Superstition and force,* Philadelphia, 1870.

CHAPTER VII.

ON THE STATE OF RELIGIOUS DOCTRINE AND CONTROVERSIES.

WESTERN CHURCH.

WESTERN CHURCH.

The mighty influence of St Augustine,

THE works of St Augustine had continued to direct the mind of Western Christendom. He was the standard author of the age, and to his writings it was commonly indebted for the traces it retained of earnestness and evangelic truth. Inferior only to the sacred penmen, whom his ample expositions of the Scriptures were believed to represent with a peculiar fidelity, he was consulted as the ablest guide in all the speculative provinces of thought: and we shall see in the review of a discussion, which affected many branches of his system of theology, that all the combatants professed a high respect for him, and that the vanquished fled for shelter to his works. In cases even where the Augustinian spirit did not find its way directly, it was circulated, in a somewhat milder form[1], by influential writers of his school, especially by Gregory the Great and Alcuin.

and his school.

The majority of authors whom this period has produced will take their place at the beginning of it. They were nearly all of them brought up in the scholastic institutions of the Frankish empire[2]. One of Alcuin's many pupils,

---

[1] *e. g.* Alcuin, *de Fide S. Trinitatis,* lib. II. c. 8 (*Opp.* I. 717), uses language inconsistent with a belief in the extreme position of a 'prædestinatio duplex,' and his view was shared by Rabanus Maurus. Cf. S. Augustine *Epist.* 214 (al. 46) *ad Valentin.* § 2; *Opp.* II. 790.

[2] Some of the principal were the *Schola Palatina* (patronized by Louis the Pious, Lothair, and Charles the Bald), and those of Orleans, Fulda, Corbey (old and new), Rheims, Tours, Hirschau, Reichenau, and St Gall.

and, like him, an indefatigable friend of education, occupied the foremost rank of theologians in the west. This was Rabanus Maurus, who had been the master of the school, and afterwards the abbot, of Fulda (822), before his elevation to the archbishopric of Mentz (847). His numerous *Commentaries*[1] on the writings of the Sacred Canon, and on some of the Apocrypha, evince a familiarity with older Christian literature; and the devotional feeling which pervades them may convince us that the piety of better ages, though too frequently declining, was not dead. Another of his works, *De Institutione Clericorum*, while important in a liturgical point of view, contributed to the more careful training of the candidates for holy orders, and inspired them with a deeper sense of the importance of their work. Rabanus was a favourite author in the west for many centuries after his death[2].

WESTERN CHURCH.

Rabanus Maurus (776—856).

Another of the Carolingian literati was Agobard[3], archbishop of Lyons (813—841), equally conspicuous for his scholarship and his activity in the affairs of state[4]. But he is better known as a reformer of religion. Many of his treatises were aimed at the ignorance and superstitions of the times, especially at those connected with the growing use of images[5].

Agobard of Lyons (d. 841).

See Bähr's *Geschichte der römisch. Literatur in karoling. Zeitalter*, Carlsruhe, 1840. Its character in this, even more than in the former period, was exclusively *religious;* science (mathematics, astronomy, and medicine) being for the most part abandoned to the Arabs, who patronized such studies, more especially in Spain. Their great college of Cordova, which became for Europe what Bagdad was for Asia, was founded in 980. See Middeldorpf, *Comment. de Institutis Literariis in Hispania, quæ Arabes auctores habuerunt*, Göttingæ, 1810.

[1] Very many of his works (including *Homilies*, as well as ethical and ecclesiological treatises) were published, in 6 vols. folio, at Cologne, 1627: see also a sketch of Rabanus, by Kunstmann, Mainz, 1841.

[2] Mabillon, *Act. Sanct. Ord. Bened.* Sæc. vi. *Præfatio*, § 1.

[3] The best edition of his works is that of Baluze, Paris, 1666, 2 vols. 8vo: cf. Hundeshagen, *de Agobardi Vita et Scriptis*, Giessæ, 1831.

[4] His fame in this capacity is stained by the countenance he gave to the rebellious sons of Louis the Pious, contrasting ill with Rabanus Maurus. Neander, vi. 157.

[5] *e. g.* He condemned the 'battle-trial,' and the 'water-ordeal' (see above, p. 155): and his treatise, *De Picturis et Imaginibus*, is a resolute attack on all forms of image-worship, and a protest against the sensuous bias of the Church. He also laboured to reform the liturgy of his province; and the two works, *De Divina Psalmodia* and *De Correctione Antiphonarii*, are a defence of his proceedings. The great number of

Claudius of Turin (d. 839).

In this and other points he may be linked with Claudius, bishop of Turin, who died in 839, after an episcopate of eighteen years. Excited, as it seems, by principles which he had learned from holy Scripture and the works of St Augustine[1], he stood forward to revive, as far as he was able, a more truly Christian spirit in the members of the Church. He ardently declaimed against all forms of creature-worship, not excluding invocation of the saints; and, on his arrival in his diocese, all symbols, whether pictures, images, or crosses, which could possibly give rise to adoration, were ejected from the churches[2]. In addition to his writings on these subjects, of which fragments only are preserved, he was a fertile commentator on the Bible; yet, with one or two exceptions[3], all his labours in this field of thought are still inedited.

A list of other kindred works, though varying much in character and worth, was added to the hermeneutical productions of the age. The chief were, (1) *Commentaries*

Jews who had settled in the Frankish empire at that period urged him to take up his pen against them: *e. g. De Insolentia Judæorum*, and *De Judaicis Superstitionibus*.

[1] The adversaries of Claudius have endeavoured to convict him of Adoptionism, on the ground that he was educated in Spain (see above, p. 61); but his Augustinianism is proved by Neander, VI. 120 sq.

[2] In this measure he was strongly resisted by his former friend the abbot Theodemir, by Dungal, an Irishman, by Jonas bishop of Orleans, and others: but he kept his ground until his death, apparently through the support of the Frankish emperor. See Schröckh, XXIII. 407—421: Döllinger, III. 57, 58. It is remarkable that Jonas of Orleans admitted the flagrant abuse of images prevailing in the Church of Italy, and only found fault with Claudius for supposing that the same abuse existed in the French and German churches. He defends the 'adoration' of the *cross* ('ob recordationem passionis Dominicæ'), but explains the act to mean no more than 'salutare.' See his treatise *De Cultu Imaginum*, in *Bibl. Patrum*, ed. Lugdun. XIV. fol. 183. This prelate was a stern and faithful censor of all forms of immorality. See his *De Institutione Laicali*, in D'Achery's *Spicilegium*, I. 258—323. Leger and other writers on the Waldenses have endeavoured to connect Claudius of Turin with that body, representing him as the leader of a secession which is thought to have taken place as early as the 9th century; but on no better grounds than conjecture.

[3] His *Commentary on the Epistle to the Galatians* will be found in *Biblioth. Patr.*, ed. Lugdun. XIV. 139 sq., and that *on the Epistle to Philemon* in the *Spicilegium Romanum*, IX. 109 sq. Introductions to other books have also been published (Gieseler, II. 262, n. 19): see, especially, *Specimens* of his inedited works, with dissertations by Rudelbach, Havniæ, 1824.

of Haimo[1], bishop of Halberstadt (**841—853**), and formerly a fellow-student of Rabanus Maurus: (2) the popular and widely-circulated *Glossa Ordinaria* (or an exposition of the difficult texts of Scripture), compiled by Walafrid Strabo[2], abbot of Reichenau (**842—849**): but (3) worthy of especial mention is the sober and elaborate *Commentary on St Matthew*, by Christian Druthmar[3], a monk of Corbey, and divinity-lecturer in the diocese of Liège, who died about **840**.

These all, together with the great majority of writers who come forward at the present period, yield a simple and unreasoning assent to the traditions of the past: but in a work of the deacon Fredegis, who had been trained in Alcuin's school at York, we may discover symptoms of a more philosophizing tendency[4]. That tendency, however, was betrayed far more distinctly in the Irishman[5] John Scotus (Erigena), who was regarded as an oracle of wisdom by the court of Charles the Bald. He was the earliest of the mediæval writers in the west, who ventured to establish Christian dogmas by a dialectic process; who, in other words, attempted to evince the union, or consistency at least, of human reason and theology. In this respect he must be viewed as a precursor of the schoolmen[6] who, in close alliance with the Aristotelian

marginalia: WESTERN CHURCH. Haimo of Halberstadt (d. 853). Walafrid Strabo (d. 849.) Druthmar (d. 840). Fredegis. John Scotus Erigena (d. 875?): a precursor of the Western schoolmen:

---

[1] There is some difficulty in ascertaining what works are really his. See Oudinus, *De Scriptoribus Eccl.* II. 330: Schröckh, XXIII. 282 sq.: Mabillon, *Acta Benedict.* v. 585 sq.

[2] The *Glossa Ordinaria* was published at Antwerp in 6 vols. folio, 1634. Another important work of Walafrid Strabo is of a liturgical character, *De Exordiis et Incrementis Rerum Ecclesiasticarum*, published in Hittorp's collection *De Divinis Officiis*, Colon. 1568.

[3] In the *Biblioth. Patrum*, ed. Lugdun. xv. 86 sq. The preface to this commentary shews that Druthmar was averse to mystical interpretations of the Bible, except when they are subordinated to the literal or historic sense. Neander, VI. 159.

[4] See his *Epistola de Nihilo et Tenebris ad proceres Palatii*, in Baluz. et Mansi, *Miscell.* II. 56.

[5] Neander has pointed out several circumstances which indicate that the Irish monasteries still continued to influence literature in the West; VI. 161, 162 (note): see also Lanigan, *Hist. of Irish Church*, III. 260 sq. John Scotus Erigena is to be carefully distinguished from a monk, named John, whom king Alfred invited from France to the English court. See Mabillon's *Annales Benedict.* III. 243.

[6] For the rise of scholasticism in the East, see above, pp. 57, 70, 71. Its cradle, or at least the earliest school in which it was cultivated by the Westerns, was the monastery of Bec in Normandy. Lanfranc and Anselm (afterwards archbishops of Canterbury) took the lead in its diffusion (see

WESTERN CHURCH.

but his philosophic system that of Neo-Platonism.

philosophy[1], were bent on systematizing the traditions of the Church, and proving that the Christian faith is truly rational[2]. But Scotus, while agreeing with the schoolmen in his point of departure, differed widely from them all in his results. He was a Neo-Platonist; and, like the Alexandrian doctors of an earlier age, could see in Christianity no more than a philosophy,—an earthly manifestation of the Absolute, intended to direct and elevate the human spirit and prepare it for eventual absorption into God[3]. It is a startling feature of the times that one, whose theories were so divergent from the teaching of the Church, was called to speak as an authority on two of the most awful topics of the faith. These were the doctrines of Predestination and the Eucharist; which, owing to the great activity of thought engendered in the Carolingian schools, were now discussed with unwonted vehemence.

Gottschalk (d. 868?) and the predestinarian controversy.

The former of these controversies[4] took its rise from Gottschalk, who in earlier life had been a monk of Fulda, under the eye of Rabanus Maurus; but had left it for the cloister of Orbais in the diocese of Soissons. Going

Möhler's *Schriften und Aufsätze*, I. 32 sq.); Lanfranc having first tried the temper of his new weapon in the Eucharistic controversy with Berengarius: see below.

[1] The logical writings of Aristotle (the first two treatises of the *Organon*) were known in the West from the ninth century, but only, till the thirteenth, by the Latin translation of Boetius. Cousin's *Ouvrages inédites d'Abélard*, Introd. p. li.: Smith's *Biog. Dict.* I. 325.

[2] 'Auctoritas ex vera ratione processit, ratio vero nequaquam ex auctoritate .... Nil enim aliud videtur mihi esse vera auctoritas, nisi rationis virtute cooperta veritas, et a sacris patribus ad posteritatis utilitatem literis commendata.' Scotus, *De Divisione Naturæ*, p. 39, ed. Oxon. 1681. The entire works of Scotus have been recently collected and edited by Floss, in Migne's *Patrologia*, Paris, 1853: cf. a review of that publication in the *Theol. Quartalschrift*, Tübing. 1854, I. 127 sq.

[3] On the whole of his philosophico-religious system, see Ritter, *Gesch. der Christ. Philosophie*, III. 206 sq.; Neander, VI. 163 sq.; Guizot, *Lect.* XXVIII.; Dorner, II. 344—358. His pantheism is clearly established by the treatise *De Divisione Naturæ*: but very much of his philosophizing was unintelligible to the age. He seems to have imbibed that tendency from his familiarity with Greek writers, and especially with Dionysius the Areopagite, whom he translated into Latin. This translation excited the suspicions of pope Nicholas I. (Mansi, XV. 401). His great work was condemned by the University of Paris in 1209: Dorner, p. 358.

[4] The great authority is Mauguin's collection of ancient authors, *De Prædestinatione et Gratia*, Paris, 1650: cf. Ussher's *Gotteschalci et Prædest. Controv. Hist.* Dublin, 1631; Cellot's *Hist. Gotteschalci Prædestinatiani*, Paris, 1655.

far beyond his favourite author, St Augustine[1], he maintained the most rigorous opinions on the subject of Divine predestination, stating it in such a way as to imperil human freedom. He contended for a twofold system of decrees ('prædestinatio duplex'), which consigned the good and bad, elect and reprobate alike, to portions from eternity allotted to them, irrespectively of their own conduct in the present life. In other words, Divine foreknowledge in his system was identified completely with predestination; and the latter was as arbitrary in relation to the lost as to the saved,—the one infallibly attaining to eternal life, the other being so necessitated to continue in his sins, that he can only be in *name* a subject of God's grace, and only in *appearance* a partaker of the sacraments. *WESTERN CHURCH. His extreme positions:*

The Church had hitherto been occupying, on the present as on other kindred points, an intermediate place, affirming, but with no attempt to reconcile, the absolute necessity of superhuman powers, while she insisted on the salvability of all men. Notwithstanding her profound respect for St Augustine and her hatred of Pelagianism, she did not countenance the fatalistic theory of grace, which threatens, and constructively subverts, the principle of our responsibility to God. Accordingly, as soon as Gottschalk published his opinions[2], he encountered a decisive opposition from the leading doctors of the age. His old superior, Rabanus Maurus, now archbishop of Mentz, influenced (it may be) to some extent by personal dislike, put forth a vehement reply to what he deemed an utter violation of the faith. Although himself a warm believer in the doctrine of Divine decrees[3], Rabanus shrank from *how different from those of the Church. Rabanus Maurus his opponent.*

---

[1] See a fair statement of this vexed question in Guizot's *Civilization in France*, Lect. v. It is plain, however, that St Augustine in some passages made use of language bordering on the positions of Gottschalk; and the 'gemina prædestinatio sive electorum ad requiem, sive reproborum ad mortem' is at least as old as Isidore of Seville, *Sentent.* lib. II. c. 6.

[2] He appears to have had an earlier controversy with Rabanus, while he was a monk at Fulda (Kunstmann's *Hrabanus Maurus*, p. 69); but he did not develope his opinions fully till some years later, when he was returning from a tour in Italy. He then disclosed them to Notting, bishop of Verona (847), who brought the question under the notice of Rabanus Maurus.

[3] Nearly all the statements in his *Epist. ad Notingum* (apud Mauguin, I. 3) are borrowed from the works of St Augustine and Prosper. Neander, VI. 185.

all approximation to the thought that the causality of sin is traceable to God. In his view the Divine foreknowledge is distinguishable from Divine predestination; and those only whom the Lord foreknows as the incorrigibly wicked, are abandoned to eternal death ('præsciti'). Gottschalk, in the following year (848), defended his positions[1] at the council of Mentz, stating (it is said) emphatically that the scriptural phrases which record our Saviour's death for *all* men should be limited to the 'elect;' and that the rest of the human family, as the result of a constraining act of God, have been irrevocably destined to perdition[2]. As the voice of the synod was against him, Gottschalk was now handed over to his metropolitan, the proud and energetic Hincmar, who soon afterwards (849) procured his condemnation[3] at Kiersy-sur-Oise (Carisiacum), and shut him up in a monastic prison, where he lingered under the ban of the archbishop till 868, refusing to abjure or modify his errors.

But the controversy kindled by him in the Frankish Church was not so easily extinguished. Many influential writers, moved either by pity for his barbarous fate[4] or by

---

[1] See fragments of his defence in Hincmar, *de Prædestinatione*, c. 5, c. 21, c. 27: cf. *Annales Fuldenses*, A.D. 848, in Pertz, I. 365.

[2] Rabani *Epistola Synodalis ad Hincmarum* (Mansi, XIV. 914): ... 'quod prædestinatio Dei, sicut in bono, sit ita et in malo: et tales sint in hoc mundo quidam, qui propter prædestinationem Dei, quæ eos cogat in mortem ire, non possint ab errore et peccato se corrigere; quasi Deus eos fecisset ab initio incorrigibiles esse et pœnæ obnoxios in interitum ire.' But it must be borne in mind, that this statement of the views of Gottschalk is the work of an adversary, and as such may have been overcoloured.

[3] Mansi, XIV. 919. By this synod, the unfortunate monk was ordered to be flogged, according to a rule of St Benedict, for troubling the deliberations on ecclesiastical affairs, and intermeddling with politics. While he lay in prison at the monastery of Hautvilliers, he wrote two more confessions of his faith, adhering to his former tenets: Mauguin, I. 7. The importance he attached to the controversy may be estimated from the violent language of his prayer, 'Te precor, Domine Deus, gratis Ecclesiam Tuam custodias, ne sua diutius eam falsitate pervertant [alluding to his opponents], *hæreseosque suæ pestifera de reliquo pravitate subvertant*, licet se suosque secum lugubriter evertant,' etc. He also offered to prove the truth of his tenets by submitting to the ordeal of fire, :......... 'ut videlicet, quatuor doliis uno post unum positis atque ferventi sigillatim repletis aqua, oleo pingui, et pice, et ad ultimum accenso copiosissimo igne, liceret mihi, invocato gloriosissimo nomine Tuo, ad approbandam hanc fidem meam, imo fidem Catholicam, in singula introire et ita per singula transire,' etc.

[4] This feeling seems to have been shared by pope Nicholas I. to

their predilection for his theological opinions, had immediately appeared in his behalf. Of these the chief were Prudentius[1], bishop of Troyes; Servatus Lupus[2], the accomplished abbot of Ferrières; and Ratramnus[3], a learned monk of Corbey; none of whom, however, would commit himself to the extreme positions of his client. They affirmed that the predestination of the *wicked* is not absolute, but is conditioned on Divine foreknowledge of all sins that would result from the voluntary act of Adam,—holding fast, on this and other points, to the more sober views of St Augustine.

Hincmar and his party were now driven to defend their harsh proceedings, and as they could no longer count upon the help of Rabanus Maurus, who withdrew entirely from the conflict[4], they put forward as the champion of their cause the learned and free-thinking guest of Charles the Bald—Erigena. His famous treatise, *De Prædestinatione*[5], appeared in 851: but arguing, as he did, on purely philosophic grounds, for the unbiassed freedom of the will, and contradicting all established doctrines of the nature both of good and evil, he gave equal umbrage to his enemies and friends. The former instantly assailed him (852) by the hands of Prudentius of Troyes[6] and Florus[7] a deacon of Lyons; while the primate Hincmar, compromised by his ill-chosen coadjutor, went in search of other means for quieting the storm.

A work of Amulo, archbishop of Lyons, now lost,

whom Gottschalk had eventually appealed. Hincmar, *Opp.* II. 290, ed. Sirmond.
[1] See his *Letter to Hincmar* (circ. 849) in Cellot's *Hist. Gotteschal. Prædest.* pp. 425 sq. But he also, like others of the period, would interpret passages like 1 Tim. ii. 4, exclusively of the 'elect.'
[2] His work, *De Tribus Quæstionibus*, is printed in Mauguin, I. pt. II. 9: see also the *Works* of Servatus Lupus, ed. Baluze, Antv. 1710.
[3] *De Prædestinatione Dei* (circ. 850), in Mauguin, I. pt. I. 27 sq. His name was frequently mis-read into *Bertram*, perhaps Be. (=Beatus) Ratramn.
[4] See his letters to Hincmar, in Kunstmann's *Hrabanus*, pp. 215 sq.
[5] In Mauguin, I. pt. I. 103 sq.
[6] *De Prædestinatione contra Joh. Scotum*, in Mauguin, I. pt. I. 191 sq.
[7] He wrote, in the name of the Church of Lyons, *De Prædestinatione contra Joh. Scoti erroneas Definitiones;* ibid. 575 sq.: see Neander, VI. 202, 203, on the character of this reply. The council of Valence (855) repeated the condemnation of Scotus (c. IV. c. VI.) in the most contemptuous terms.

Remigius of Lyons vindicates the general theory of Gottschalk.

was written with this object: but Remigius, his successor and the leading prelate of the south of Gaul, did not inherit his opinions[1]. He condemned the cruelty by which the author of the movement was repressed, and strove in a less ruffled tone to vindicate his orthodoxy from the imputations of the northern province. He contended that in Gottschalk's system of theology the absolute predestination of the wicked had been neither stated nor implied; and while confessing his own predilection for the view that God does not wish the salvation of *all* men, he declared his willingness to leave that question open till it was authoritatively settled by the Church. His manifesto roused

Hincmar's reply at the synod of Kiersy, 853.

the zeal of Hincmar to the very highest pitch, and in another synod[2] held at Kiersy (853), his party reasserted nearly all the views which Gottschalk had continued to reject. In a short series of propositions, based entirely on the works of St Augustine, they affirmed, with other truths admitted by their adversaries, that no human being whom the Lord foreknew as wicked had been foreordained to perish, and that Christ had died a sacrifice for all men, willing all men to be saved[3]. The counter-movement in

The rival synod of Valence, 855.

the southern province ultimately issued in a rival synod, which assembled at Valence[4] in 855. Its effect, however, was to bring the disputants more closely to each other. It declared expressly that the sin of man, although an object of Divine foreknowledge, was in no degree necessitated by an act of predetermination: and while all the prelates were agreed that Christ did not redeem habitual unbelievers[5], they confessed that many are in truth re-

---

[1] Hincmar, and Pardulus bishop of Laon, had already written two letters to Amulo; sending him at the same time a copy of the letter from Rabanus Maurus to Notting of Verona. These three documents Remigius now proceeded to examine in his *Liber de Tribus Epistolis*, in Mauguin, I. pt. II. 61 sq. The notion that the wicked are necessitated to commit impiety he spurns as 'immanis et detestabilis blasphemia' (c. XLI.), and denies that it was held by any one; reflecting strongly on Rabanus Maurus, who imputed it to Gottschalk. See Neander, VI. 203 sq.; and Milman, *Latin Christianity*, III. 241 sq.

[2] Mansi, XIV. 995; cf. 920.

[3] 'Christi sanguinem pro omnibus fusum, licet non omnes passionis mysterio redimantur:' c. 4.

[4] Mansi, XV. 1 sq. Remigius had already censured the 'four chapters' of Kiersy: Mauguin, I. pt. 2. 178.

[5] They even spoke of universal redemption as a 'nimius error:' c. 4.

generated at their baptism, who in after-life may forfeit the initial grace of God by their unholy conduct[1].

WESTERN CHURCH.

Hincmar now took up his pen and laboured to confirm the views he had espoused, in two elaborate productions[2], one of which is lost; and in 859, he was able to effect a better understanding with the prelates of the south at the council of Savonières in the diocese of Toul[3]. There, eight metropolitans, with more than thirty bishops, received some general statements of the Augustinian dogmas; and the combatants on either side, exhausted by the struggle, were now willing to lay down their arms, without coming to any more definite conclusion, yet without granting to Gottschalk any alleviation of his wretched imprisonment[4].

Termination of the struggle, at Savonières, 859.

The second controversy that sprang up in the Carolingian era of the Church related to the mode in which the Body and Blood of Christ are taken and received in

The Eucharistic controversy.

---

[1] ... 'ex ipsa tamen multitudine fidelium et redemptorum, alios salvari æterna salute, quia per gratiam Dei in redemptione sua fideliter permanent, alios quia *noluerunt permanere in salute fidei*......ad plenitudinem salutis et ad perceptionem æternæ beatitudinis nullo modo pervenire.' c. 5. The following passage from the *Annales Bertiniani* (by Prudentius of Troyes), A.D. 859 (Pertz. I. 453), appears to intimate that pope Nicholas I. approved of the canons of Valence: 'Nicolaus, pontifex Romanus, de gratia Dei et libero arbitrio, de veritate geminæ prædestinationis et sanguine Christi, ut pro *credentibus* omnibus fusus sit, fideliter confirmat.' The Jesuits, who are strongly opposed to Gottschalk, labour hard to set aside this passage.

[2] The extant work, written between 859 and 863, is entitled *De Prædestinatione Dei et Libero Arbitrio adversus Gotteschalkum et cæteros Prædestinatianos*: see his *Works* by Sirmond, tom. I.

[3] Conc. Tullense I. (*apud Saponarias;* Mansi, xv. 527) read over six doctrinal canons, which had been agreed upon at a smaller synod, held about a fortnight before at Langres (Lingonense; *ibid*. xv. 525), apparently in preparation for this meeting with Hincmar; and which had been framed at Valence in 855 (*ibid*. xv. 3). The prelates, however, for the sake of peace, now omitted the reference to the four Kiersy propositions, which had been pointedly condemned at Valence, 'propter inutilitatem, vel etiam noxietatem, et errorem contrarium veritati;' c. 4. Cf. Gieseler, II. 297 sq.; Neander, VI. 208.

[4] He died in prison, 868. Neander (p. 204) cites from Mauguin the terms of well-deserved rebuke, in which Remigius condemned Hincmar's cruel treatment of Gottschalk. This unhappy monk had been involved (circ. 850) in another dispute with Hincmar, touching the expression, 'Te, *trina Deitas* unaque, poscimus,' which occurs in an ancient hymn. The primate had forbidden the use of it on the ground that it savoured of Tritheism: but Gottschalk and the other Frankish Benedictines, represented by Ratramnus, justified the phrase (Hincmar's *Works*, I. 413 sq.), and Hincmar was compelled to let the matter rest. On Hincmar's career generally see his Life by J. C. Prichard, Oxford, 1849.

WESTERN CHURCH.

The work of Paschasius Radbert, 831.

the Lord's Supper. It employed the leading theologians of the west for several years: and when religion had emerged from the benumbing darkness of the tenth century, it furnished a perplexing theme for the most able of the schoolmen. As the spirit of the Western Church contracted a more sensuous tone, there was a greater disposition to confound the sacramental symbols with the grace they were intended to convey, or, in a word, to *corporealize* the mysteries of faith. Examples of this spirit may be found in earlier writers who had handled the great question of the Eucharist: but it was first distinctly manifested by Paschasius Radbert in 831. He was a monk, and afterwards (844—851) the abbot, of Corbey; and in a treatise[1], *On the Sacrament of the Body and Blood of Christ*, appears to have maintained that, by the act of consecration, the material elements are so transformed as to retain no more than the appearance ('figura') of their natural substance, being truly, though invisibly, replaced by Christ Himself in every way the same as He was born and crucified[2]. The work of Radbert was composed in the first instance for a pupil, but when he presented a new edition of it (844) to Charles the Bald, it startled nearly all the scholars of the age. Rabanus Maurus[3] wrote against it;

---

[1] The best edition is in Martène and Durand's *Veter. Script. Collect.* IX. 367 sq.; or Radberti *Opp. omnia*, ed. Migne, 1852.

[2] *e. g.* 'Quia Christum vorari fas dentibus non est, voluit in mysterio hunc panem et vinum vere carnem Suam et sanguinem, consecratione Spiritus Sancti, potentialiter creari, creando vero quotidie pro mundi vita mystice immolari, ut sicut de Virgine per Spiritum vera caro sine coitu creatur ita per eundem ex substantia panis ac vini mystice idem Christi corpus et sanguis consecretur,' *etc.* c. IV.: 'Substantia panis et vini in Christi carnem et sanguinem efficaciter interius commutatur,' c. VIII. It may be noted, as an index to the principles of Radbert, that he also argued for the miraculous delivery of the Virgin in giving birth to our blessed Lord ('absque vexatione matris ingressus est mundum...... sine dolore et sine gemitu et sine ulla corruptione carnis'): Pasch. Radbert. *de Partu Virginis*, in D'Achery's *Spicilegium*, I. 44. He was again opposed in this view by Ratramnus: *Ibid.* I. 52.

[3] 'Quidam nuper de ipso sacramento corporis et sanguinis Domini non rite sentientes dixerunt, hoc ipsum esse corpus et sanguinem Domini, quod de Maria Virgine natum est, et in quo ipse Dominus passus est in cruce et resurrexit de sepulcro. *Cui errori quantum potuimus*, ad Egilonem abbatem [*i.e.* of Prüm] scribentes, de corpore ipso quid vere credendum sit aperuimus.' *Epist. ad Heribaldum Autissiodorensem epis.* (bp. of Auxerre). The passage is given, in its fullest form, in Mabillon's *Iter Germanicum*, p. 17. The letter to Egilo has perished, unless it be

but unhappily no full account of his objections is preserved. Another monk of Corbey, Ratramnus, whom we saw engaging in a former controversy, was the main antagonist of Radbert. He put forth, at the request of the emperor, a treatise[1] *On the Body and Blood of the Lord*. It is divided into two parts, the first entering on the question, whether the body and blood of Christ are taken by the faithful communicant in mystery or in truth ('in mysterio an in veritate"); the second, whether it is the same body as that in which Christ was born, suffered, and rose from the dead. In answering the former question he declared, with St Augustine, that the Eucharistic elements possess a twofold meaning. Viewed externally they are not the thing itself (the 'res sacramenti'); they are simply bread and wine: but in their better aspect, and as seen by faith, the visual organ of the soul, they are the Body and Blood of Christ. The latter question was determined in the same spirit, though the language of Ratramnus is not equally distinct. While he admitted a 'conversion' of the elements into the body of the Lord, in such a manner that the terms were interchangeable, he argued that the body was not Christ's in any carnal sense, but that the Word of God, the Bread Invisible, which is invisibly associated with the Sacrament, communicates nutrition to the soul, and quickens all the faithful who receive Him[3]. Or, in other words, Ratramnus

Refuted by Ratramnus.

The nature of his reply.

---

identical with a document edited by Mabillon in *Act. Sanct. Ord. Bened.* sæc. IV. pt. II. 591. Other traces of the doctrine of Rabanus on the Eucharist are left in his *De Instit. Clericorum*, lib. I. c. 31: cf. Soames's *Bampton Lect.* pp. 412, 413. Radbert himself was forced to allow, in writing to a monk Frudegard (*Opp.* p. 1351, ed. Migne) that 'many' doubted the truth of his teaching: and the Romanists admit that he was the first writer who explained their views of the Lord's Supper with precision. See L'Arroque's *Hist. of the Eucharist*, p. 387, Lond. 1684.

[1] The best edition is by Boileau, Paris, 1712. Respecting the genuineness of the work, see Fabricius, *Bibl. Latinitatis Med. Ætat.* I. 661 sq.

[2] Adding, by way of explanation, 'utrum aliquid secreti contineat, quod oculis fidei solummodo pateat,' § 1. He afterwards illustrates the efficacy of the Lord's Supper by the analogous application of the element of water in the sacrament of Baptism.

[3] 'Verbum Dei, qui est Panis Invisibilis, invisibiliter in illo existens sacramento, invisibiliter participatione Sui fidelium mentes vivificando pascit.' See Neander, VI. 214 sq.; Döllinger, III. 73. The work of Ratramnus was placed in the *Index Librorum Prohibitorum* of 1559; but some Roman Catholic writers (*e.g.* Mabillon, *Act. Sanct. Bened.* sæc. IV. pt. II. præf. p. xliv) try to vindicate him from the charge of 'heresy.'

WESTERN CHURCH.

His views accordant with the general teaching of the age.

John Scotus takes the opposite extreme.

was in favour of a real, while he disbelieved a corporal, or material presence in the Eucharist.

His views were shared, to some extent at least, by Florus, Walafrid Strabo, Christian Druthmar, and others[1] on the continent, and were identical with those professed in England till the period of the Norman conquest[2]. The extreme position on the other side appears to have been taken by Erigena, who was invited, as before, to write a treatise on the subject of dispute. Although his work[3] has perished, we have reason to infer from other records of his views, that he saw little more in the Eucharist than a memorial of the absent body of the Lord,—or a remembrancer of Christian truths, by which the spirit of the faithful is revived, instructed, and sustained[4].

Paschasius, unconvinced by opposition, stedfastly adhered to his former ground[5]; and as the theory which he

---

[1] See extracts from their works in Gieseler, II. 289, n. 8. Amalarius, a priest and abbot in the diocese of Metz, took part in the Eucharistic controversy, arguing for a triplicity of the body of Christ (de tripartito Christi Corpore), *i. e.* a distinction between the natural body of Christ and the Eucharistic, first, as it exists in the living Christian, and secondly, as it abides in the Christian after death. He opened the revolting question of *Stercoranism* (the liability of the Eucharistic elements to the same kind of decomposition in the human system as that which is undergone by ordinary food): see Mabillon, *Act. Sanct. Bened.* præf. ad sæc. IV. pt. II. p. xxi. The views of Amalarius on the symbolic nature of the Eucharist may be seen in his answer to Rantgar, bp. of Noyon, in D'Achery's *Spicileg.* III. 330.

[2] This point has been triumphantly established by many writers; *e. g.* Soames's *Bampton Lect.* Serm. VII. and notes. Ælfric, the great Anglo-Saxon doctor, was familiar with the work of Ratramnus: *Ibid.* p. 421.

[3] The work of Ratramnus has been attributed to him, and many writers have maintained that only one book was written (see Lauf's essay on this point in the *Theolog. Studien und Kritiken* for 1828, I. 755 sq.): but the other view that there were originally two treatises, composed under royal patronage, appears to be the more probable. Neander, VI. 217.

[4] Hincmar (*Opp.* I. 232) condemns as one of the opinions of Scotus, that the Eucharist was '*tantum* memoria veri corporis et sanguinis Ejus.' Adrevald has also written an *Opusculum de Corpore et Sanguine Domini contra Joannem Scotum*, in D'Achery's *Spicileg.* I. 150: and in a MS. lately found at Rome, containing a commentary of Scotus on the *Hierarchia Cœlestis*, the Eucharist is said to be 'typicam similitudinem spiritualis participationis Jesu, quam fideliter solo intellectu gustamus.' Note to the English edition of Döllinger's *Ch. Hist.* III. 73. Cf. Scoti *Opp.* ed. Floss, p. 41.

[5] See his *Expositio in Matth.* lib. XII. c. XXVI. *Opp.* p. 891, ed. Migne. His view appears to be supported in Haimo's *Tractatus de Corp. et Sang. Domini* (D'Achery, I. 42).

defended was in unison with the materializing spirit of the age, it was gradually espoused in almost every province of the Western Church. The controversy slumbered[1], with a few exceptions, for the whole of the tenth century, when it broke out with reinvigorated force. The author of the second movement, Berengarius, was archdeacon of Angers (1040), and formerly the head of the thriving schools attached to the cathedral of Tours. Embracing the more spiritual view of the Eucharist, as it had been expounded by Ratramnus[2], he was forced at length into collision with a former school-fellow, Adelmann[3], who warned him in 1045 and 1047 of scandals he was causing in the Church at large by his opinions on this subject. Like the rest of the mediæval reformers, Berengarius had inherited a strong affection for the works of St Augustine[4]; and his confidence in the antiquity and truth of his position is expressed, with a becoming modesty, in his appeal to the celebrated Lanfranc[5], prior of Bec, in Normandy. This letter had been forwarded to Rome, where Lanfranc was in 1050, and on being laid before a council[6], which was sitting at the time, its

WESTERN CHURCH.

Lull in the controversy.

Revived by Berengarius (d. 1088).

His view condemned at Rome, 1050.

---

[1] Cf. L'Arroque, *History of the Eucharist*, part II. ch. XVI. Herigar, abbot of Lobes, in the diocese of Liège (circ. 1000), compiled 'contra Ratbertum multa catholicorum patrum scripta de corpore et sanguine Domini' (D'Achery, II. 744): and Gerbert (afterwards, in 999, Silvester II.) put forth a modified version of the theory of Radbert (in Pez, *Thesaurus Anecdot.* tom. I. pt. II. 133—149) especially denouncing the 'Stercoranists.' On the other hand, that theory was advocated in its fulness by Gezo, abbot of Tortona (circ. 950; in Muratori's *Anecdota*, III. 237), and confirmed in the eyes of the vulgar by miraculous stories, which asserted nothing less than a physical change in the Eucharistic elements.

[2] Owing to the early confusion between the works of Scotus and Ratramnus (see above, p. 168, n. 3), Berengarius is continually charged with drawing his opinions on the Eucharist from the erratic Scotus; but there is no question, after his own constant reference to the treatise of Ratramnus, that *it* was the work intended by his adversaries.

[3] Then residing at Liège, afterwards (1048) bishop of Brescia. See Adelmann, *De Veritate Corporis et Sanguinis Domini*, ed. Schmidt, Brunsv. 1770, in which edition other documents are printed. The rumour which had reached Liège was, that Berengarius denied 'verum corpus Christi,' and argued for 'figuram quandam et similitudinem.'

[4] See Neander, VI. 223.

[5] Lanfranc. *Opp.* ed. D'Achery, p. 22. One of the best modern accounts of this controversy is in Ebrard's *Doctrine and History of the Lord's Supper* (in German), I. 439 sq. Francof. 1845.

[6] Mansi, XIX. 757: Lanfranc. *Opp.* p. 234: Berengar. *de Sacra Cœna*, p. 35; ed. Berolin. 1834. The sentence was confirmed in the following

WESTERN CHURCH.

He is acquitted at Tours, 1054:

condemned afresh, 1059.

author was condemned unheard. His friends, however, more particularly Bruno[1], bishop of Angers, did not abandon him in this extremity; and after a short interval of silence and suspense[2], he was relieved from the charge of heresy in a provincial synod held at Tours[3] in **1054**. The papal representative was Hildebrand, who listened calmly to the arguments of the accused, and when he had most cordially admitted that the bread and wine are (in one sense) the Body and Blood of Christ[4], the legate took his side, or was at least completely satisfied with the account he gave of his belief. Confiding in the powerful aid of Hildebrand, he afterwards obeyed a summons to appear in Rome[5] **(1059)**, but his compliance ended in a bitter disappointment of his hopes. The sensuous multitude, who had become impatient of all phrases that ex-

September, at Vercelli, where the book of Scotus (? Ratramnus) is connected with the doctrine of Berengarius: Mansi, XIX. 773; Berengar. *de Sacr. Cœna*, pp. 42, 43. He was anxious to appear at this later synod, but was prevented by the king of France (Henry I.), the patron of the abbey of Tours, in which Berengarius was an inmate.

[1] See his friendly but guarded *Letter to Berengarius*, printed in De Roye, *De Vita Berengarii*, p. 48, ed. Andegav. 1657.

[2] In this interval is to be placed the council of Paris, if such a council was actually held. See Neander, VI. 231, 232. In any case, it is plain that popular opinion was strongly against Berengarius. The Bishop of Liège (Deoduin), in an *Epistle* to the king (*Bibl. Patr.* ed. Lugdun. XVIII. 531), alludes to this excited state of public feeling in violent terms, and even charges Berengarius and Bruno of Angers with denying other articles of faith ('qualiter...antiquas hæreses modernis temporibus introducendo adstruant, corpus Domini non tam corpus esse quam umbram et figuram corporis Domini, legitima conjugia destruant, et, quantum in ipsis est, baptismum parvulorum evertant').

[3] See Berengarius, *ubi sup.* pp. 50 sq., and the varying account of Lanfranc, *de Eucharist.* c. IV.

[4] 'Panis atque vinum altaris post consecrationem sunt corpus Christi et sanguis.' From this and other passages it is plain that Berengarius did not view the Eucharist as a bare symbol. What he controverted was the theory of men like archbishop Guitmund, circ. 1075 (*de Corpore et Sanguine Christi*, in *Bibl. Patr.* ed. Lugd. XVIII. 440), who maintained that the bread and wine were changed 'essentialiter.' The same writer mentions that, while some of the 'Berengariani' admitted 'tantummodo umbras et figuras,' Berengarius himself and others ('rectis Ecclesiæ rationibus cedentes') affirmed a real though uncorporeal presence: 'dicunt ibi corpus et sanguinem Domini revera, sed latenter contineri, et, ut sumi possint, quodammodo (ut ita dixerim) impanari.' This view was certainly shared by Bruno, above, n. 1; and, in so far as we can judge, by Hildebrand himself. Neander, VI. 233 (note).

[5] Mansi, XIX. 758.

pressed a spiritual participation in the Eucharist[1], now clamoured for his death, and through the menaces of bishop Humbert, who was then the leading cardinal, he was eventually compelled to sign a formula of faith, in which the *physical* conversion of the elements was stated in the most revolting terms[2]. The insincerity of this confession was indeed soon afterwards apparent: for on his return to France he spoke with bitterness, if not contempt, of his opponents[3], and at length proceeded to develope and defend his earlier teaching. His chief antagonist[4] was Lanfranc, who, while shrinking from expressions such as those which emanated from the Roman synod, argued strongly for a change of substance in the bread and wine[5]. The controversy, in their hands, became a battle-field for putting the new dialectic weapons to the proof; and in a long dispute, conducted with no common skill, they both were able to arrive at clearer definitions than had hitherto been current in the Church. The feverish populace, however, with the great majority of learned men, declared for Lanfranc from the first; and more than once his rival only just escaped the ebullition of their rage[6]. The lenient tone[7] of Alexander II. in dealing with reputed misbelief, was due perhaps to the pacification of his favourite, Hildebrand; and when the latter was exalted to the papal throne as Gregory VII. (1073), the course of Berengarius promised to grow smoother. But that interval of peace was short. His adversaries, some of whom had private grounds of disaffection to the reigning pontiff, made common cause

Contro-versy re-opened.

Lanfranc, his opponent.

---

[1] Berengarius, *de Sacra Cœna*, p. 72.
[2] ... 'verum corpus et sanguinem Domini nostri Jesu Christi esse, et *sensualiter* non solum sacramento, sed in veritate, manibus sacerdotum tractari, *frangi et fidelium dentibus* atteri;' Lanfranc. *Opp.* p. 232.
[3] See a contemporary writing (? by Bernaldus), in *Bibl. Patr.* ed. Lugd. XVIII. 835.
[4] Another was Guitmund (see p. 170, n. 4), and a third Durandus, abbot of Troarn (Lanfranc. *Opp.* ed. D'Achery, Append. pp. 71 sq.).
[5] 'Credimus terrenas substantias, quæ in mensa Dominica per sacerdotale mysterium Divinitus sanctificantur, ineffabiliter, incomprehensibiliter, mirabiliter, operante superna potentia, converti in essentiam Dominici corporis, reservatis ipsarum rerum speciebus, et quibusdam aliis qualitatibus,' etc. *De Eucharist.* c. XVIII. p. 244.
[6] *e.g.* at the synod of Poitiers (1076): *Chronicon. S. Maxentii*, in Labbe's *Biblioth. MSS.* II. 212.
[7] See the statement of the writer quoted above, n. 3.

WESTERN CHURCH.

Cited to appear again at Rome, 1078.

with the more stringent cardinals; and in **1078**, the author of the movement, which continued to distract the Western Church, was cited to appear a second time at Rome[1]. The pope himself, adducing the authority of Peter Damiani as an equipoise to that of Lanfranc, was at first content with an untechnical confession that 'the bread and wine are, after consecration, the true Body and Blood of Christ;' which the accused was ready to accept[2]. But other members of the Roman church, incited by the cardinal Benno[3], Gregory's implacable opponent, now protested that, as formulæ like these did not run counter to the faith of Berengarius, he should be subjected to a stricter test. To this demand the pope was driven to accede[4], and in a numerous council[5], held at Rome in the following February (**1079**), the faith of the accused again forsook him.

His second recantation, **1079.**

He subscribed a new confession teaching the most rigorous form of transubstantiation[6], and retired soon afterwards from Rome with testimonials of his orthodoxy granted by the pope[7]. As in the former case, his liberation was accompanied by bitter self-reproach; but though he seems to have maintained his old opinions[8] till his death, in **1088**, no further measures of repression were adopted by his foes.

---

[1] See the account of Berengarius himself in Martène and Durand's *Thesaur. Anecdot.* IV. 103; Mansi, XIX. 761.

[2] 'Profiteor panem altaris post consecrationem esse verum corpus Christi, quod natum est de Virgine, quod passum est in cruce, quod sedet ad dexteram Patris; et vinum altaris, postquam consecratum est, esse verum sanguinem, qui manavit de latere Christi.'

[3] He calls in question the 'orthodoxy' of Gregory himself, as well he might, for fraternizing with Berengarius. See his work *De Vita Hildebrandi* (in Goldast's *Apolog. pro Henrico IV.* p. 3.)

[4] Cf. Neander, VI. 244, 245.

[5] Mansi, XX. 523.

[6] 'Corde credo et ore confiteor, panem et vinum, quæ ponuntur in altari, per mysterium sacræ orationis et verba nostri Redemptoris *substantialiter* converti in veram et propriam et vivificatricem carnem et sanguinem Jesu Christi Domini nostri, et post consecrationem esse verum Christi corpus, quod natum est de Virgine, et quod pro salute mundi oblatum in cruce pependit, et quod sedet ad dexteram Patris; et verum sanguinem Christi, qui de latere Ejus effusus est, non tantum per signum et virtutem Sacramenti, *sed in proprietate naturæ et veritate substantiæ.*'

[7] D'Achery's *Spicileg.* III. 413. All who call Berengarius a heretic are anathematized.

[8] See Gieseler, II. 411, and Neander, VI. 247, on the one side; and Döllinger, III. 79, 80, on the other.

In him expired an able but inconstant champion[1] of the primitive belief respecting the true Presence in the Supper of the Lord. While he contended that the substance of the elements is not destroyed at consecration, he regarded them as *media* instituted by the Lord Himself for the communication, in a supernatural manner, of His Body and His Blood to every faithful soul. He argued even for the fitness of the term 'conversion' as equivalent to 'consecration,' and in this respect allowed *a* change in the bread and wine; a change, however, which, according to his view, was nothing like a physical transubstantiation, but was rather a transfiguration, which the elements appeared to undergo, when contemplated by a living faith in Christ, who had appointed them as representatives and as conductors of Himself.

_{WESTERN CHURCH.}

_{*Summary of his belief.*}

The great bulk of the church-writers who had been produced in the period under our review, are far less worthy of enumeration. We must not, however, pass in silence men[2] like Alfred the Great, the Charlemagne of England (871—901) who, after struggling with the barbarous Northmen, and at length subduing them, stood forward as the ardent patron of the Church and a restorer of religion. Almost every trace of native scholarship[3] had been obliterated in the conflict with the Danes, but through the holy efforts of the king himself[4], assisted by a band

_{*Alfred the Great* (d. 901).}

_{*His influence as a patron of learning and religion.*}

---

[1] The later Roman Catholic writers, Mabillon, Martène, and Durand, admit, after the discovery of some original documents, that he only denied transubstantiation, but conceded a 'real presence.' Gieseler, *ibid.* It is plain, however, that the movement which he headed, numbered others who denied the presence of the Lord in any sense whatever: see above, p. 170, n. 4.

[2] Cf. *The Laws of Howel the Good*, the Cambrian prince and legislator of the 10th century.

[3] See above, p. 86, n. 1.

[4] A *Jubilee edition* of his *Complete Works* has been published. His most valuable treatises (ecclesiastically speaking) are the Anglo-Saxon editions of the *Pastoral of Gregory the Great*, and Bede's *Church History*: to which we may add the freer version of Boetius *de Consolatione* and the *Soliloquies* of St Augustine. The *Laws of King Alfred* are re-published in Thorpe's *Ancient Laws*, &c. I. 44—101. It was mainly through the influence of king Alfred that so many vernacular glosses on the Scriptures and the Service-books were undertaken at this period. See Wright's *Biograph. Britan.* (Anglo-Saxon Period) pp. 426, 427. The *Rule of St Benedict* was afterwards translated into Anglo-Saxon by Ethelwold. *Ibid.* 440.

WESTERN CHURCH.

of literati[1], a new impulse was communicated to the spiritual and intellectual progress of the Anglo-Saxon race. The English, it is true, like other churches of the west[2], was not exempted from the corruptions which prevailed so widely in the tenth century: but from the age of Alfred, a more general diffusion of religious truth, in the vernacular language, raised the standard of intelligence. His policy was carried out[3] by Ælfric, the Canonist, Homilist, Grammarian, Monastic Reformer, and Hagiographer, to whom we are indebted for a large proportion of the vernacular literature of his age, but whose identification is one of the most obscure problems of English History[4]. Ælfric left behind him a set of eighty Anglo-Saxon Homilies for Sundays and great festivals, compiled in almost every case from the earlier doctors of the west; and a second set for Anglo-Saxon Saints' days. There is extant also a collection of contemporary Homilies ascribed to a Bishop Lupus, who has been conjecturally identified with Archbishop Wulfstan of York[5].

Ælfric.

Wulfstan, or Lupus.

[1] Some of these were Plegmund, archbp. of Canterbury, who died 923; Werefrith, bp. of Worcester (d. 915), Grimbald, John of Corbey (confounded with John Scotus Erigena), and Asser, the biographer of Alfred, and a native of Wales. See Wright, *ubi sup.* pp. 405—418.

[2] The almost solitary exceptions on the continent, at least till the *close* of the tenth century, are Ratherius of Verona, and Atto of Vercelli; see above, p. 144, n. 2; p. 142, n. 2. The latter, it may be added, wrote a *Commentary* of some value on the Epistles of St Paul: ed. Vercelli, 1768.

[3] See his *Preface* to the *Homilies*, where, in declaring that his aim was to edify unlettered people, who knew nothing but 'simple English,' he alludes to the 'prudent' labours of king Alfred.

[4] The difficulty of distinguishing between the many owners of the name of Ælfric is confessed on every hand. See Wharton's *Dissertatio utrum Elfricus Grammaticus?* (who makes the most distinguished Ælfric an archbishop of York:) and, on the other side, Mores' *De Ælfrico Dorobernensi Archiepiscopo*, ed. Thorkelin, Lond. 1789, who identifies him with the archbishop Ælfric of Canterbury. The editor of the Ælfric *Homilies* (Mr Thorpe) assigns them to the archbishop of *York*. But all that can be certainly advanced is that the homilist was a West-Saxon monk, a pupil of Ethelwold bishop of Winchester; and that there are almost insuperable objections to identifying him with either prelate. See an elaborate article in Niedner's *Zeitschrift für die historische Theologie*, 1855. Heft IV. pp. 487 sq. Wright, *ubi sup.* 485, 486.

[5] See Wanley's *Catalogue of Anglo-Saxon MSS.* (in Hickes' *Thesaurus*), II. 140—143. There was another Wolstan (or Wulfstan) at the close of the tenth century. He was a monk of Winchester and a respectable Latin poet. Wright, pp. 471—474. Contemporary with him was the

—1073] *State of Religious Doctrine and Controversies.*

WESTERN CHURCH.

On the continent of Europe very few of the scholars had attained to greater celebrity than Gerbert, a monk of Aurillac, and subsequently pope Silvester II. (999–1003). His fund of scientific knowledge[1] was derived from the Muhammedans; and, as the fruit of an awakened intellect, he was at first a strenuous adversary of the ultra-papal claims[2]. His influence was extended far and near, especially by a distinguished pupil, Fulbert, in whose hands the school of Chartres grew into a mighty agent for diminishing the darkness of the age.

Gerbert, or Silvester II. (d. 1003).

Fulbert, bishop of Chartres. (d. 1028).

By this and other kindred institutions[3] it was shewn that a fresh era of comparative illumination had now opened in the west. The seeds of knowledge and of moral culture, planted in the time of Charlemagne, were beginning to produce more salutary fruits; for though the systems of the schoolmen were in many points imperfect, they may justly be regarded as a great advance upon the barbarism which marked the seventh century, and the materializing spirit of the tenth.

EASTERN CHURCH.

The Eastern Church, while it continued to preserve its former intellectual level[4], manifested a deplorable defect

---

Latin poetess Roswitha, a nun of Gandersheim. See her *Carmina*, ed. Witemb. 1707.

[1] His mathematical and astronomical learning was suspected; and the vulgar thought him guilty of alliance with the devil. Only a few of his works have been published. See especially his *Epistles*, in the *Scriptores Franc.*, ed. Duchesne, II. 787 sq. His treatise on the Eucharist is mentioned above, p. 169, n. 1.

[2] See above, p. 138, n. 4.

[3] Those more especially influenced by Gerbert were Bobbio, Rheims, Aurillac, Tours, and Sens.

[4] Above, p. 64. Of the Eastern dissenting bodies the Armenians, who are like the Jacobites in nearly every feature, were most flourishing throughout the present period. See Neumann's *Gesch. der Armenischen Literatur*, pp. 114 sq. Leipzig, 1836; Stanley, *Lectures on the Eastern Church*, pp. 7 sq. Their separation is said to have arisen from the accidental absence of the Armenian bishops from the Council of Chalcedon (451); hence they never received its decrees, and, in 596, they repudiated it, under their patriarch Abraham I., at the synod of Tovin. The chief patriarch was henceforth called 'Catholicos,' and resided in the convent of Echmiadzin, now belonging to Russia: Golovin's *Caucasus*, p. 168, Lond. 1854. An attempt was made about 866 to win them over to the Eastern Church, but it was fruitless. See *Spicileg. Rom.* tom. x. pt. II. 449.

176　　　　*State of Religious Doctrine and Controversies.* [A.D. **814**

EASTERN
CHURCH.

The revival of the Iconoclastic controversy.

of earnestness and moral health. We gather this especially from records of the image-controversy, which, although it had rapidly subsided after the council of Nicæa (**787**), started into life again at the commencement of the present period. It had been revived, indeed, by some of the Frankish prelates[1] (such as Agobard and Claudius of Turin); but there, as images were not so grievously abused, the agitation they excited was not permanent. In the Byzantine capital, however, the Iconoclasts grew up into a powerful body, and were able, for a time at least, to sway the fortunes of the Eastern Church.

Leo the Armenian (d. 820).

The germs of a reaction seem to have been always cherished in the army, who, as we observed, had been the main support of an Iconoclastic monarch[2]; and when Leo the Armenian (**813—820**) was invested with the purple, they rejoiced to see him take the lead in the suppression of all images (the symbol of the cross excepted). Leo strove at first to bring about his reformation by conciliatory means[3]; but as Nicephorus, the patriarch of Constantinople, was inflexibly devoted to the present ritual of the church, he fell under the severe displeasure of the court. As in the former time, the spirit of resistance still continued to be strongest in the monks[4]. They were now headed by the abbot of the Studion (a great monastery of Con-

The resistance of Nicephorus: and the Constanti-

---

[1] Above, pp. 157, 158. In 825 a synod had been held at Paris under Louis the Pious, for the purpose of ascertaining what the Fathers thought of the use of images in Divine worship. The prelates there assembled did not hesitate to censure the prevailing superstitions on this subject, more especially in Italy (Mansi, XIV. 424), and also animadverted on the language of the pope in his attempt to answer the *Libri Carolini* (above, p. 77). At the same time they were opposed to the violent proceedings of the Iconoclasts. Some of the Frankish prelates even went on a mission, first to Rome, and then to Constantinople, in the capacity of mediators between the pope and the emperor Michael II. See Life of Louis the Pious, in Pertz, II. 631.

[2] Above, p. 75.

[3] He represented, among other things, that the 'people' were opposed to image-worship (ὁ λαὸς σκανδαλίζεται διὰ τὰς εἰκόνας, λέγοντες ὅτι κακῶς αὐτὰς προσκυνοῦμεν, καὶ ὅτι διὰ τοῦτο τὰ ἔθνη κυριεύουσιν ἡμῶν): but this antipathy (as will appear in the sequel) was far from general. He urged also the importance of scriptural proof for the practice (πεῖσον ἡμᾶς δι' οὗ ἐκεῖνα προσκυνεῖτε, τῆς γραφῆς μὴ ἐχούσης ῥητῶς πώποτε). For an account of the whole interview between Leo and the patriarch, see the *Chronograph.* (in Continuation of *Theophanes*), p. 437, and the *Life of Nicephorus*, by his pupil, Ignatius, in the *Acta Sanct.* Mart. II. 296, 704.

[4] Above, p. 74, n. 1.

stantinople), Theodore Studita (759—826), who maintained that an inferior worship (προσκύνησις) of the sacred images was to be recognized as an essential article of faith[1]. His violence, united with the firmness of Nicephorus, impelled the emperor to enter on a strenuous course of action. He forbade the public meetings of the monks, and bound them to maintain a total silence on the subject of dispute[2]; himself avowing no desire at present to expel the images entirely. But as soon as he could count upon the help of many of the bishops, he convened a synod[3] at Constantinople (815) for this purpose; and, on finding that the patriarch was still immoveable, proceeded to eject him from his throne. It was bestowed on a severe Iconoclast, Theodotus, but all the ardent image-worshippers immediately renounced communion with him[4]. Their resistance now brought down upon their heads the most inhuman persecutions, and a number of the monks (their leader, Theodore, included) felt the lashes of the vigilant police, and died in prison or in exile[5].

EASTERN CHURCH.

nopolitan monks under Theodore the Studite.

Iconoclastic synod (815):

persecution of the image-worshippers.

---

[1] He argued, that the hostility to images arose from disbelief in the reality of Christ's human nature. See his Βίβλος δογματική (three discourses against Iconoclasm), *passim*. Most of his numerous works relate to the same question, and are written in the same vehement tone. See a portion of them in Sirmond's *Opp.* tom. v. (Paris, 1696), where a Greek *Life of Theodorus* (? by a monk named Michael) will also be found. Other works are enumerated in Smith's *Biograph. Dict.* III. 1057.

[2] Theodore, the Studite, in a vehement circular, denounced all those who yielded to the edict. *Epist.* lib. II. ep. 2.

[3] Mansi, XIV. 135. This synod (never recognized in the Western Church) condemned the Acts of the Council of Nicæa (787), and decreed that all paintings in the churches should be destroyed, as well as the ecclesiastical vestments and vessels which were marked by any sacred image. Neander (VI. 272), relying perhaps on a letter of the next emperor, Michael (Mansi, XIV. 417), supposes that a council ('locale concilium') had been held anterior to the deposition of Nicephorus, in order to effect a compromise between the opposite extremes. The images or pictures were to be raised into a higher part of the churches, 'ne ab indoctioribus et infirmioribus adorarentur.'

[4] The conforming party, who resorted to a kind of mental reservation (οἰκονομία, as they called it), were regarded by the rest as traitors. See the letter of Theodore to Nicephorus, the banished patriarch, lib. II. ep. 18. We learn from another of these letters (lib. II. ep. 215) that men of his way of thinking travelled into Italy for ordination, shunning the Iconoclasts as nothing less than heretics. They did not, however, yield to the exclusive theory of Rome, but viewed the pope as one of the patriarchs (τὸ πεντακόρυφον κράτος τῆς ἐκκλησίας), though granting him the first place in general councils (lib. II. ep. 129).

[5] See besides the *Life of Theodore*, the touching story of his pupil, Nicetas, another Studite monk, in the *Act. Sanct.* Febr. tom. I. 538 sq.

EASTERN CHURCH.

Gentle policy of Michael II.

The accession of the new emperor, Michael II. (820—829), filled the image-worshippers with hope. He *tolerated* them on principle, and laboured even to effect a general understanding in the disputants on either side[1]. But men like Theodore the Studite could not listen to a proposition, which in their eyes would involve a compromise of truth[2]. The schism was, accordingly, continued to the end of the reign.

Persecutions under Theophilus (d. 842).

Images finally restored under Theodora, 843.

Theophilus, the heir of Michael II., succeeded to the throne in 829, and for thirteen years directed all his energies to silence and convert the monks, who clung as formerly to image-worship. Very many of his acts are stained by cruelty, although his enemies have been unable to deny that he was zealous in promoting what he deemed the cause of God, and upright in discharging his imperial duties[3]. But it happened now, as at the death of Leo IV.; his able and intriguing relict, Theodora, who administered affairs in the minority of her son (Michael III.), restored the interdicted worship[4], banished John the Grammarian, patriarch of Constantinople, who was true to his opinions, and established in his place a zealot named Methodius. On the first Sunday of Lent (Feb. 18, 843), the use of images was introduced afresh into the churches of the Eastern metropolis, where the event has been commemorated ever since by an annual feast, entitled 'Feast of Orthodoxy.' With some brief exceptions, the Iconoclastic troubles vanish at this stage. The subsequent decrees of

---

[1] See the *Life of Theodore the Studite*, as above, c. 102—122. This emperor, in writing to the Western Church, has left a most melancholy picture of the extravagances of the image-party. 'Psallebant et adorabant, atque ab eisdem imaginibus auxilium petebant. Plerique autem linteaminibus easdem imagines circumdabant, et filiorum suorum de baptismatis fontibus susceptrices [*i. e.* sponsors] faciebant.................. Quidam vero sacerdotum et clericorum colores de imaginibus radentes, immiscuerunt oblationibus et vino,' *etc.* Mansi, XIV. 420. Even Theodore himself, while arguing for the absolute necessity of images for fixing in our minds the truth of the Incarnation, was compelled to acknowledge that, in some cases, reverence for them had issued in idolatry. See for instance, his *Epist.* lib. II. ep. 151: and Neander, VI. 281, 282.

[2] *Epist.* lib. II. ep. 171.

[3] See the evidence respecting him fairly stated in Schlosser's *Geschichte der bilder-stürm. Kaiser*, pp. 469 sq.

[4] *Ibid.* 544 sq. For the strange way in which her scruples, as to the salvation of her husband, were removed, see the *Continuation of Theophanes*, lib. IV. c. 4.

councils at Constantinople[1], in 869 and 879, may be regarded as the formal winding-up of the discussion,—till it was at length reopened by the Western Churches in the sixteenth century. EASTERN CHURCH.

The master-spirit of the image-worshippers, as we have seen already, was the abbot Theodore, the Studite. Nearly all his published writings bear upon this point: but he has left a multitude of other works behind him[2]. He was held in very high repute, and thus transmitted the impression which was made upon the Eastern Church by John of Damascus, whom in many features he resembled. In the latter half of the ninth century and the commencement of the tenth, there was no lack of scholars at Constantinople, owing to the special patronage afforded to them by the emperors Basil the Macedonian (867–886) and Constantine Porphyrogennetus (913–959). Indeed the whole of the present period witnessed a variety of literary labours in the East, although they are too often compilations[3] (or *Catenæ*) from the older stores of knowledge. *The literary labours of Theodore the Studite.* *Age of Catenæ.*

Simeon[4] (ὁ Μεταφραστής), who appears to have flourished about 900, was not destitute of originality, but it is manifested chiefly in his numerous Lives of Saints[5]; the greater part of which, however, may have been recastings from the earlier Legends. None of the expositors of Holy Scripture is more worthy of a passing notice than the Thracian bishop, Œcumenius (circ. 950). Though he *Simeon Metaphrastes.*

---

[1] Here, as in the earlier synod (843), the language of the second council of Nicæa was confirmed. In 869, the third canon puts the worship of the sacred image of our Lord upon a level with the worship of the Gospels: Mansi, xvi. 400. Traces of a short reaction of Iconoclasm, about 860, are found in an epistle of pope Nicholas I.; Mansi, xv. 161.

[2] See above, p. 177, n. 1.

[3] *e.g.* Constantine Porphyrogennetus suggested the formation of compendious works from all the earlier writers. They were arranged under fifty-three heads, embracing history, politics, and morals. Schröckh, xxi. 130 sq.

[4] See Leo Allatius, *De Simeonum Scriptis Diatriba*.

[5] The number of these is reckoned at six or seven hundred: but many seem to have been compiled by other writers. *Ibid.* and Fabricius, *Biblioth. Græca*, ed. Harles, x. 186 sq. The rest of his works are *Annals, Sermons, Poems*, &c. See the list in Smith's *Biogr. Dict.* iii. 953, 954. His credulity was quite prodigious, for expressions like the following seem to indicate that he believed his own stories. He is speaking of his namesake Symeon Stylites, the elder: 'Ἀλλὰ δέδοικα μὴ τοῖς μετὰ ταῦτα μῦθος εἶναι δόξῃ τῆς ἀληθείας γεγυμνωμένος.

borrowed largely from St Chrysostom, his Commentaries[1] on the *Acts*, the *Canonical Epistles*, and the *Apocalypse*, betoken a sound judgment in the choice of his materials, and are always neatly, if not elegantly written. As a general scholar, tinctured also with the love of science, we may notice an Egyptian prelate, Eutychius[2] (Said Ebn-Batrich), patriarch of Alexandria (933–940).

But the ripest and most highly gifted of the Eastern scholars, in the period under our review, was Photius[3], an exalted servant of the court of Byzantium in the middle of the ninth century. His character, indeed, is sullied by ambition, and too oft by his forgetfulness of higher duties and unprincipled devotion to the world; yet as a writer no one will deny that he conferred a lasting boon on that and succeeding ages. In addition to his *Bibliotheca* (criticisms in almost every field of ancient literature), his *Nomocanon* (or a digest of ecclesiastical laws), his interesting *Letters*, and a string of minor works, he published treatises directly bearing on theology and sacred exegesis. Some of these are in the form of *Homilies* and *Commentaries*[4], and in one (the *Amphilochia*) he attempts to solve a number of perplexing questions in divinity. The rest are chiefly aimed at misbelievers (such as the Paulicians), or impeach the orthodoxy of the rival Church of Rome.

From Photius, therefore, we may pass to a dispute in which he played a leading part, the controversy which resulted in the

---

[1] The Exposition of the *Gospels* frequently attributed to him appears to be the work of a later writer, Euthymius Zigabenus (or Zygadenus), a monk of Constantinople (published in 3 vols. 8vo. Leipzig, 1792). The Commentaries of Œcumenius have been often printed (*e.g.* Paris, 2 vols. folio, 1631). For that on the Apocalypse, see Cramer's *Catenæ*, Oxf. 1840.

[2] His *Annales* (reaching to the year 940) were edited by Pocock, Oxon. 1659: besides which he wrote a treatise on Medicine, and a *Disputation between a Christian and a Heretic*. See Neale's *East. Church*, 'Alexandria,' II. 181—183.

[3] See the ample article in Smith's *Biograph. Dict.* III. 347—355.

[4] A copy of the Commentary of Photius on the Pauline Epistles, mentioned by the writer of the article above, is among the Cambridge University MSS. (Ff. I. 30).

SCHISM BETWEEN THE EASTERN AND THE WESTERN CHURCHES.

Separation of East and West.

The materials of dissension had been long accumulating, and there needed only a direct collision of the Roman and Byzantine patriarchs to tear asunder the surviving fibres which composed the bond of peace. Apart from the divergencies of temperament and intellectual bias, which in periods like the present were not easily adjusted, the old leaven[1] of ambition, jealousy, and envy had fermented more and more. One subject of dispute assumed the gravest character, relating as it did to the Procession of the Holy Ghost. It had already occupied the leading theologians of the East and West (for instance, Alcuin and John of Damascus), and was now put forward still more prominently on both sides[2]. The Greeks, while they admitted fully[3] that the Holy Spirit is communicated by, and through, the Son, and therefore may be called "the Spirit of the Son," denied as fully that the Godhead of the Holy Ghost proceeded *equally* from Both the other Persons of the blessed Trinity. To argue thus appeared to them a violation of the truth, that God the Father is to be regarded as the single Root or underived Principle of Godhead (as the ἀρχή of all being). Other grounds of discord came to light later, but from the importance of the doctrine, the Procession of the Holy Ghost has ever been the

The Greek doctrine of the Procession of the Holy Ghost.

---

[1] Above, pp. 37, 38, 47; p. 54, n. 1; p. 57, n. 1; p. 122. Döllinger traces the origin of the schism directly to the Council *in Trullo* (691), when the Greek bishops shewed what he thinks an unjustifiable 'fastidiousness on the subject of the superiority of the Church of Rome,' III. 83: cf. Neander, VI. 298, 299; Stanley's *Eastern Church*, pp. 23 sq.

[2] The following is the title of a tract by Photius: Κατὰ τῶν τῆς παλαιᾶς 'Ρώμης ὅτι ἐκ Πατρὸς μόνου ἐκπορεύεται τὸ Πνεῦμα τὸ Ἅγιον ἀλλ' οὐχὶ καὶ ἐκ τοῦ Υἱοῦ. It is printed in the *Panoplia* of Euthymius Zigabenus (pp. 112, 113, ed. Tergovist. 1710). On the introduction of the clause *Filioque* into the western creeds, see above, p. 57, n. 1, and the references there.

[3] Neale's *Eastern Church*, Introd. Dissert. III. The language of John of Damascus (quoted by Neander, VI. 295) is as follows: Υἱοῦ δὲ Πνεῦμα, οὐχ ὡς ἐξ αὐτοῦ, ἀλλ' ὡς δι' αὐτοῦ ἐκ τοῦ Πατρὸς ἐκπορευόμενον· μόνος γὰρ αἴτιος ὁ Πατήρ. 'Juxta vero Latinos, *a Patre et Filio*: quamvis in quibusdam Græcorum expositionibus eundem Spiritum *a Patre per Filium* procedere reperiamus.' Scotus Erigena, *De Divisione Naturæ*, p. 85, ed. Oxon. 1681. Cf. Laud, *Conf. with Fisher*, pp. 17—20, Oxf. 1839.

SEPARATION OF EAST AND WEST.

Deposition of the patriarch Ignatius, 858.

The conduct of his rival Photius.

His claims recognized by papal legates: but denied at Rome, 863.

most conspicuous topic in the quarrels of the East and West.

The deposition of Ignatius[1] by the worthless Cæsar Bardas, uncle of Michael III., was followed by the elevation of Photius to the patriarchal throne of Constantinople (858). He was before a courtier and a layman, but, as happened not unfrequently in such an age, he passed at once through the subordinate gradations of the ministry, and in a week had reached the highest honours of the Church[2]. Ignatius was, however, far too conscious of integrity to sign his own disgrace, and sentence was accordingly pronounced against him at a council[3] drawn together by his rival in the following year (859). But as the friends of the deposed were still a formidable body[4], Photius ventured to invoke the mediation of the Church of Rome[5], and for that purpose put himself into communication with the equally ambitious pontiff, Nicholas I. The latter, bent as we have seen on carrying out the Pseudo-Isidore Decretals[6], now came forward as an autocratic judge[7]. In this capacity he sent two legates to Constantinople (860), but they were not proof against the threats and bribery of the court[8]. They recognized the claims of the intruder, Photius (861); yet their sentence was ere long repudiated[9] by a Roman Synod (863), which, after weighing all the merits of Ignatius, did not hesitate to launch anathemas upon his rival. This event was fol-

---

[1] See the contemporary *Life of Ignatius*, by Nicetas Paphlago, a warm admirer of him, in Mansi, xvi. 209 sq. According to this authority, Bardas had been excommunicated by Ignatius on the charge of incest with the wife of his own son.

[2] *Ibid.* 229, 232. Photius urged on his own behalf that the appointment was pressed upon him by the clergy as well as by the court.

[3] The report of its proceedings was destroyed at the eighth session of the following council in 869.

[4] See Photii *Epist.* III. VI. VIII.; ed. Montague, Lond. 1651.

[5] See the reply of Nicholas I. (Sept. 25, 860) to a letter of the emperor (now lost), in Mansi, xv. 162: and the somewhat fulsome letter of Photius himself in Baronius, *Annales*, ad an. 859, § 61.

[6] Above, pp. 134 sq. He actually rebuked Photius in 862 for his slowness in perceiving the weight of such Decretals. Mansi, xv. 174.

[7] In the *Letter* to the emperor above cited, and another of the same date to Photius. Mansi, xv. 168.

[8] *Ibid.* xv. 216, where Nicholas informs the emperor that the unworthy legates have been excommunicated.

[9] *Ibid.* xv. 178 sq., 245 sq.

lowed by an angry correspondence between the emperor Michael and the pope¹; while Photius², throwing off the mask and waiving all his former courtesy, proceeded in a council held at Constantinople to denounce the Latin Church in general, and even to anathematize the pope (867). The quarrel was embittered by occurrences already noted in the missions of Bulgaria³. The diffusion of the Gospel in that country had been due at first to the Byzantine Church, but on the introduction of a staff of Latin clergy in 866, the province had been wrested from the hands of Photius. He alluded to this point in the 'Encyclica,' which he put forth on summoning the council of 867, and even went so far as to charge the Western missionaries with departures from the faith⁴.

But at this crisis, a new emperor, Basil I. (the Macedonian), whom Photius estranged by rejecting him from the Communion⁵, on the ground of his complicity in the assassination of his predecessor, took the side of the opponents and proceeded to restore Ignatius to his see. The pope was now invited to acknowledge him afresh⁶, and at the numerous council of Constantinople⁷ (Oct. 5, 869—March

SEPARATION OF EAST AND WEST.

His quarrel with pope Nicholas I.

and the Latin Church.

Restoration of Ignatius,

---

¹ The emperor's letter is lost, but its contemptuous character may be inferred from the more dignified reply of Nicholas (865). *Ibid.* xv. 187 sq. He despises the imperial threats ('Nolite nobis minas praetendere, quoniam nec illas metuimus, nec per has praecepta vestra faciemus;' *ib.* 213), being no longer subject to the Eastern court: cf. the equally characteristic letter to the emperor (866): *Ibid.* 216 sq.

² See *Epist.* II. pp. 47 sq. This was an encyclical letter addressed to the leading bishops of the East, inviting them to take part in a synod. For a brief notice of its acts, see Anastasius, *Præf. ad Concil. Œcumen.* VIII. [*i. e.* the so-called œcumenical council of Constantinople, 869]: Mansi, XVI. 1 sq.

³ Above, pp. 121, 122.

⁴ He dwelt especially on the Western doctrine of the Procession of the Holy Ghost, the celibacy of the clergy, and fasting on the Sabbath (Saturday). The cause of the Latins was defended, among others, by the learned Ratramnus of Corbey, whose reply (in D'Achery's *Spicilegium*, I. 63—112) is characterized by great moderation.

⁵ See on this point the annotations of Neander, VI. 314. The same view is taken by the writer in Smith's *Biogr. Dict.* III. 349.

⁶ Mansi, XVI. 46.

⁷ *Ibid.* XVI. 1 sq. This council was preceded by a kindred one at Rome (June, 869: see Jaffé, pp. 256, 257), and Roman influence, telling as it did in favour of Ignatius, was predominant throughout. Some of the Greek prelates, it is true, protested, 'non bene factum fuisse, quod ecclesiam Constantinopolitanam tanta subjectione Romanæ subdi ecclesiæ permiserint' (Mansi. XVI. 29); and the following entry of a Frankish

SEPARATION OF EAST AND WEST.

at the Council of Constantinople, 869.

Reappointment of Photius, 878,

approved by the Council of Constantinople, 879.

13, 870), where Photius was again condemned, the schism between the rival patriarchs, as well as that between the Christians of the East and West, appeared[1] to have been healed.

In 878, when Ignatius was no more, the choice of the emperor fell upon their ancient adversary, Photius, whom he had already called from banishment. It seems, however, that there was a numerous party in the East, who were all bitterly opposed to the imperial nomination, on the ground that Photius still lay under sentence of a council headed by the pope. To satisfy the scruples of this school[2] an effort was next made to win his approbation of their recent conduct, such appearing the most likely way to bring the quarrel to a close. Accordingly the pontiff, John VIII., more pliant than his predecessors, and affecting to undo the late decisions at Constantinople by a special act of grace[3], despatched his legates to the scene of the dispute (Aug. 16, 879): but in the following council, while the Easterns seemed to recognize his right of interference, they most artfully evaded all the ultra-papal claims, to the annoyance of the Roman Church[4]. The

---

chronicler (quoted by Gieseler, II. 471) is most significant: 'In qua synodo de imaginibus adorandis aliter quam orthodoxi doctores ante definierant, statuerunt; quædam etiam *pro favore Romani pontificis*, qui eorum votis de imaginibus adorandis annuit, et quædam contra antiquos canones,' etc. The claim of the council to be called *œcumenical* (cf. above, p. 76, n. 2) is entirely set aside by the fact that the other three patriarchs were not represented; the pretended envoys of those sees being in truth agents from the Saracens, who had come to Constantinople on matters of business (Photii, *Epist.* CXVIII.: cf. Palmer, *Treatise on the Church*, II. 161, 162; 3rd edit.).

[1] The old controversy about Bulgaria was, however, still unsettled, and we find John VIII. (878) repeatedly holding out the threat of excommunication against Ignatius on account of an assertion of patriarchal rights in ordaining clergy for that district: Mansi, XVII. 67. The Eastern influence finally triumphed; the province of Achrida or Justinianopolis adhering to the see of Constantinople. Wiltsch, I. 405. But the struggle has been renewed in our own days, in 1860 and 1861.

[2] Neander, VI. 321, 322.

[3] See his *Letters* in Mansi, XVI. 479 sq. The policy of John VIII. was chiefly aimed at securing for himself the province of Bulgaria; and at least, according to the *Roman* version of the matter, Photius had accepted this condition, but had afterwards falsified the papal rescript, so that before it was submitted to the council it appeared more favourable to the independence of the Eastern Church.

[4] The *Acts* of the council are in Mansi. XVII. 373 sq. In the fifth

sanction of that church, indeed, was for a time conceded to their Acts[1]; but when she saw that the Byzantine patriarch determined to retain his jurisdiction in Bulgaria, notwithstanding her reiterated threats, she had recourse to another fulmination[2] (circ. 881), and thus the intercommunion of the two rival churches was again suspended.

For a century and a half at least the marks of intercourse are slight and discontinuous. In 1024 (or thereabouts) the emperor Basil II., struck by the degraded state of Western Christendom, proposed to reestablish a concordat, on the understanding that the patriarchs of Rome and of Byzantium should hereafter act upon a level; and it seems that John XIX. was only frightened from considering the suggestion by the ferment it excited in the West[3]. Indeed a kindlier feeling had been now more generally diffused, as we may gather from the fact that public worship, in accordance with the ritual of the Greeks, was tolerated at Rome, and the converse at Byzantium. But this very circumstance eventually became the ground of fresh disputes, and led the way to the final schism. The patriarch of Constantinople, Michael Cerularius, in 1053, peremptorily forbade the celebration of the Latin

SEPARATION OF EAST AND WEST.

Fresh quarrel with the pope.
Attempt to restore communion (circ. 1024).

Final rupture, 1054.

---

session (Jan. 26, 880), the Roman legates declared that they recognized Photius as the lawful patriarch, and rejected the council of 869, at which he was condemned. In the second session (Nov. 16, 879), the claims of the papal legates with regard to Bulgaria were mildly repelled. But the most remarkable feature of the synod was its reaffirmation of the Niceno-Constantinopolitan Creed, without the clause 'Filioque.' *Ib.* p. 515.

[1] Thus the pope writes to Photius (Aug. 13, 880): 'Ea, quæ pro causa tuæ restitutionis synodali decreto Constantinopoli *misericorditer* acta sunt, recipimus.' He rejects, however, any of the Acts to which his legates may have assented 'contra apostolicam præceptionem.' Mansi, xvii. 185. The synod was afterwards called by the Latins 'Pseudosynodus Photiana.' The Greeks regard it as 'œcumenical.'

[2] Mansi, xvi. 449; xvii. 537. For the later measures of the popes against Photius, see *ibid.* xviii. 11. He was again displaced in 886, from political motives, by Leo VI., and died an exile in Armenia (circ. 891).

[3] Glaber Radulph. *Hist.* lib. iv. c. i. After stating the proposal as above, he continues: 'Dum ergo adhuc leni sub murmure hujusce machinatores in conclavi sese putarent talia tractavisse, velox fama de ipsis per universam Italiam decucurrit. Sed qualis tunc tumultus, quam vehemens commotio per cunctos exstitit, qui audierunt, dici non valet.' A remonstrance on the subject was addressed to the pope by William of Dijon.

SEPARA-
TION OF
EAST AND
WEST.

ritual in his province[1]; and, assisted by Leo, metropolitan of Bulgaria, published an intemperate attack[2] on all the members of the Western Church. This angry missive roused the indignation of the Latins, more especially of the polemic cardinal Humbert[3], whose reply, though very bitter in its tone, is marked in some respects by larger views of evangelic freedom. All attempts to calm the passion of the disputants were vain: and when the papal legates, at the instance of a Romanizing emperor[4], arrived at Constantinople in 1054, they found the patriarch immoveably opposed to their pretensions. They departed, therefore, after placing on the altar of the church of St Sophia (July 16) an imperious writ of excommunication[5], which was followed in its turn by an anathema from Cerularius and his clergy[6]. The disunion of the Roman and Byzantine sees was consummated by these acts; and as the patriarchs of Alexandria, Antioch[7], and Jerusalem

---

[1] See the letter of Leo IX. (1054) to Cerularius of Constantinople and Leo of Achrida: Mansi, xix. 635.

[2] It is only extant in the Latin version of cardinal Humbert, in Baronius, *Annal*, ad an. 1053, §§ 22 sq. It was addressed to John, bishop of Trani (in Apulia), but through him 'ad universos principes sacerdotum et sacerdotes Francorum et monachos et populos et ad ipsum reverendissimum papam.' He insists, among other trivial things, on the importance of using common or leavened bread in the celebration of the Eucharist, instead of the paschal or unleavened bread, which after the eighth century had been common among the Latins: see the *Dissertation concerning Azymes*, in Neale's *Eastern Church*, Introd. II. 1051 sq. The ground of the objection to the Latin custom was alleged to be its Judaizing tendency. See another angry work in opposition to the Latin Church by Nicetas, a Studite monk, in Canisius, *Lect. Antiq.* III. pt. I. pp. 308 sq., where Humbert's *Responsio* is also printed. Nicetas afterwards recanted.

[3] See above, p. 171. His refutation is printed at length in Canisius, *Lect. Antiq.* III. pt. I. pp. 283 sq.

[4] This tenderness for Rome is indicated in the letter addressed to him by Leo IX. (1054): Mansi, xix. 667.

[5] See the *Brevis Commemoratio* of Humbert in Canisius, *Ibid.* pp. 325 sq. Among other charges levelled at the Orientals in this document the following are remarkable: 'Sicut Arriani rebaptizant in nomine sanctæ Trinitatis baptizatos, *et maxime Latinos;* sicut Donatistæ affirmant, excepta Græcorum Ecclesia, Ecclesiam Christi et verum sacrificium atque baptismum ex toto mundo periisse; sicut Nicolaitæ *carnales nuptias* concedunt et defendunt sacri altaris ministris; sicut Severiani maledictam dicunt legem Mosis; sicut Pneumatomachi vel Theomachi absciderunt a symbolo Spiritus Sancti processionem a Filio,' etc.

[6] In a synod held at Constantinople (1054); see Leo Allatius, *De Libris Ecclesiasticis Græcorum*, ed. Paris. 1645, pp. 161 sq.

[7] Peter of Antioch acted at first the part of a mediator: see *Monu-*

adhered to the more powerful see of Constantinople, the estrangement was transmitted almost universally to other countries of the East[1].

SECTS.

THE EASTERN AND WESTERN SECTS.

The rise and growth of the Paulicians[2] have been fully traced already, though their influence gave a colour to the present period of the Church. They flourished chiefly in Armenia, on the borders of the Zendic or Parsee religion; and a mixture of their creed with it appears to have produced the sect of the Thontrakians, founded by one Sembat, a Paulician (between 833 and 854) in the province of Ararat[3]. In spite of persecution[4] it made numerous converts, more especially when it was joined by an Armenian bishop, Jacob, in 1002.

The sect of the Thontrakians.

This century also witnessed a revival[5] of the mystic sect of Euchites (or Enthusiasts), who afterwards were known by an equivalent Slavonic name, the Bogomiles. Proceeding from the Eastern Church they seem to have maintained substantially the Zendic doctrine of two principles, and also to have held with it exaggerated views of the importance of monastic life, which they regarded as the one effective agent for the subjugation of the flesh and for disarming all the powers of darkness.

Revival of the Euchites.

menta Eccl. Græc. ed. Coteler. II. 123 sq. In the same collection (pp. 138 sq.) are letters addressed to Peter by Cerularius, in which he complains of the pride and insolent demands of the legates, and points out what he considers fresh scandals in the Latin Church.

[1] At the period of the separation it seems probable that the number of episcopal sees was nearly equal on both sides. Palmer's *Treatise on the Church*, I. 164, 165, 3rd edit.

[2] Above, pp. 78—84.

[3] See Chamchean's (or, as the Germans write it, Tschamtschean's *Geschichte von Armenien*, II. 884 sq.; Neander, VI. 342 sq.

[4] The Armenian Church (cf. above, p. 175, n. 4) had retained a large amount of Judaizing elements (even animal sacrifices in memory of the dead), and accordingly the antagonism between it and the Paulicians was complete. *Ibid.* Akin to the Armenians in their tenderness for Judaism, were the new sect of *Athinganians*, who appeared in Phrygia. Neander (VI. 347 sq.) conjectures that they were a remnant of the Judaizing misbelievers whom St Paul rebukes in the Epistle to the Colossians (ii. 21 sq.).

[5] Several traces of them in the interval between the fourth and eleventh centuries, have been pointed out by Gieseler, II. 489 (note). They seem to have had a regular church constitution, and to have named

SECTS.

Transmission of many of their principles to the West

Many of these oriental sects, desirous of securing proselytes or driven from their early haunts by dint of persecution, migrated, as it would seem, most frequently along the course of the Danube, into several countries of the West. The progress of the Bogomiles and the related school of Cathari belongs to the following period: but the seeds of lasting controversies were now scattered far and wide, in Italy, in France, and even in the Netherlands and some parts of Germany. The name with which the sectaries are branded in the works of a host of undiscriminating adversaries, is the odious name of Manichæans[1],—misbelievers who had formerly aroused the zeal of St Augustine. They had gained a stable footing in the church of Orleans (circ. 1020), and attracted notice almost simultaneously in other distant spots.

The so-called Manichæans in Europe. Their distinctive tenets.

So far as we can gather from the extant traces of the movement[2], all its chief adherents were distinguished by a tendency to rationalism, while they preserved the mystic and ascetic elements of thought we have just noted in the Euchite. Questioning the possibility of supernatural birth,

the chief teachers 'apostles.' The fullest source of information respecting them at the latter date is the Περὶ ἐνεργείας δαιμόνων Διάλογος of the very learned Michael Psellus (circ. 1050), ed. Norimberg. 1838. Among other startling practices he mentions that the Euchites were 'devil-worshippers:' perhaps connected in some measure with the 'Yezeedees,' on whom see Badger's *Nestorians*, I. 111—134: Lond. 1852.

[1] The other view (advocated, for instance, by Gieseler, II. 491) is, that the western sects, now stigmatized as *Manichæans*, were really descended from the ancient Manes, whose disciples had not been extinguished in some parts of Italy. This class of writers grant, however, that after the crusades there was a kind of fusion of the eastern and western sects, and that the Bogomiles (or Euchites) were then exactly like the French and Italian 'Manichæans.' The view adopted in the text is that of Muratori, *Antiq. Italiæ medii Ævi*, v. 81—152; Gibbon, v. 283 sq., ed. Milman; and Neander, VI. 348. See Robertson, *Church History*, II. 423.

[2] See especially the *Acts* of the synods of Orleans (1022) and of Arras (1025) in Mansi, XIX. 373, 423; Glaber Radulph. *Hist*. lib. iii. c. 8; and the *Chronicle* of Ademar, a contemporary monk of Angoulême, in Bouquet, x. 154. Besides the tenets mentioned above, these sectaries made light of all the mediæval saints, and reverenced none except apostles and martyrs: they opposed the veneration of the cross; they ridiculed the consecration of churches; they insisted on the greater dignity of the unmarried state, and even spoke of sexual intercourse when sanctified by matrimony as a thing accursed. Like the Euchites, they are said to have worshipped the devil (above, n. 5), and to have religiously abstained from every kind of animal food.

they represented the humanity of Christ as the mere semblance of a body, and accordingly concluded that His death and resurrection also were unreal: while the same Docetic theory resulted in contempt of all material *media* instituted to promote the culture of the soul. They undervalued, if they did not openly abjure, the holy sacraments, professing to administer a spiritual baptism and a spiritual Eucharist instead of corresponding ordinances in the system of the Church[1].

On the detection of this band of heretics in Aquitaine and other parts of France, a synod was convened at Orleans in **1022**, where thirteen of the 'Manichæans,' who were true to their convictions, suffered at the stake[2]. Soon afterwards a kindred faction was impeached in the dioceses of Liège and Arras by a synod held at the latter place[3] (**1025**). But notwithstanding the extreme severity[4] with which the leading misbelievers were repressed, the sect went on fermenting, more especially among the working class[5]. Besides a host of other 'Manichæans' who were executed in these parts and even in the north of Germany[6], the neighbourhoods of Milan and Turin supplied fresh victims to the sanguinary spirit of the age (**1030**). The heretics abounded most at Monteforte[7]; and their creed, so far

Sects.

Persecution of the sectaries.

---

[1] See the remarks of Neander on this point, VI. 352. The sect administered a rite resembling confirmation. They termed it the 'consolamentum,' or communication of the Comforter. *Ibid.* At the synod of Arras they brought three reasons against the efficacy of baptism as administered by the Church—'(1) quia vita reproba ministrorum baptizandis nullum potest præbere salutis remedium: (2) quia quidquid vitiorum in fonte renunciatur postmodum in vita repetitur: (3) quia ad parvulum non volentem neque currentem, fidei nescium, suæque salutis atque utilitatis ignarum, in quem nulla regenerationis petitio, nulla fidei potest inesse confessio, *aliena* voluntas, aliena fides, aliena confessio nequaquam pertinere videtur.' Mansi, XIX. 425.

[2] Authorities above, p. 188, n. 2.

[3] Mansi XIX. 423 sq. The abp. Gerhard II. refuted the objections of the sectaries at length. *Ibid.*

[4] Almost the only prelate who denounced the persecuting spirit of the times was Wazo, bishop of Liège (d. 1047); see his noble language in the *Gesta Episcoporum Leodiensium,* in Martène and Durand's *Collectio,* IV. 898 sq.

[5] They were particularly stimulated, first by Gundulf, an Italian, and then by a teacher of the name of Ramihed, who was at last hunted down and burned.

[6] Herimanni *Chron.* an. 1052 (Pertz, VII. 130).

[7] Glaber Radulph. *Hist.* lib. IV. c. 2. A new name began to be

SECTS.

as we can judge, had even fewer elements of truth[1] than were surviving in the other branches of the sect.

applied in Italy at this period to all kinds of sects. It was that of *Patareni*, or *Paterini*, which appears to be derived from 'pataria,' a Milanese word = 'popular faction.' It was originally the nickname given by the clergy to the popular party of Milan during the agitations against the marriage of the priests: Schröckh, XXIII. 349, 350; Neander, VI. 67, 68.

[1] See Landulphi *Hist. Mediolan.* lib. II. c. 27 (in Muratori, *Script. Ital.* IV. 88. sq.), where an account is given of the sect by one of its functionaries, Gerhard, who was summoned by archbp. Heribert of Milan. According to him, the doctrines of the Gospel, though in words accepted as the truth, were robbed of all their meaning by an ultra-spiritualistic style of exposition. Thus the Son of God is made to signify a soul that has become the object of God's love; the birth of Christ from the Virgin is the new birth of a soul out of the sacred Scriptures; while the 'Holy Ghost' is the true understanding of these Scriptures.

CHAPTER VIII.

ON THE STATE OF INTELLIGENCE AND PIETY.

IN sketching the religious life of Western Christendom at this period, a distinction must be drawn between the tenth century and the remaining portions of the ninth and the eleventh. The influence of the Carlovingian schools, supported as they were by Louis the Pious and Charles the Bald[1], was very widely felt: it ended only when domestic troubles, the partition of the empire, and the savage inroads of the Northmen checked all further growth. The same is, speaking generally, true of England; but the noble efforts of king Alfred[2] to revive the ancient taste for learning rescued his dominions, in some way at least, from the barbaric darkness which continued to oppress the continent of Europe, till the dawn of the Hildebrandine reformation. Nearly all the intermediate time is desert, one expanse of moral barrenness and intellectual gloom[3].

As in the former period[4], the instruction of the masses was retarded by the multiplicity and breaking up of languages, and most of all, by the adherence of the Western Church to Latin only as the vehicle of worship. It was

MEANS OF GRACE AND KNOWLEDGE.

The variations in the degree of intelligence.

Tenth century peculiarly dark.

Decay of the Latin language.

---

[1] In the former reign the literature was almost exclusively religious, owing to the predilections of the monarch, but the court and schools of Charles the Bald displayed a stronger relish for more general learning ('utriusque eruditionis Divinæ scilicet et humanæ' is the language of the Council of Savonières in 859): cf. Guizot, II. 371.

[2] Above, pp. 173, 174.

[3] See, for instance, Mabillon, *Act. Sanct. Ord. Bened.*, sæc. v. Præf. Other writers (*e. g.* Hallam, *Lit. of Middle Ages*, pt. I. ch. I. § 10) consider the tenth an advance upon the seventh century, more particularly in France.

[4] See above, p. 87.

MEANS OF GRACE AND KNOWLEDGE.

Injunctions on preaching.

now, in fact, disused[1] by nearly all excepting clerics. Many of the councils have, however, laid especial stress on the necessity of preaching in the native dialects[2]. They urge that opportunity should be afforded, both in town and country parishes[3], of gaining a complete acquaintance with the precious Word of God. The doctrines of the Saviour's incarnation, death, and final triumph in behalf of man, the gift of the Holy Ghost, the value of the sacraments, the blessedness of joining in the act of public prayer, the need of pure and upright living, and the certainty of future judgment in accordance with men's works, are recommended as the leading topics for the expositions of the priest[4]. But insufficient training[5], even where he was alive

---

[1] Bähr, *Geschichte der römisch. Lit. in karol. Zeit.* p. 59.

[2] *e.g.* The council of Mentz, in 847, orders (c. 2) that bishops should not only be assiduous in preaching, but that they should be able to translate their homilies into *Romana rustica* or *Theotisca* (Deutsch), 'quo facilius cuncti possint intelligere quæ dicuntur.' The practice of the English in this respect is illustrated by Ælfric and Wulfstan (see above, p. 174): and in Ælfric's *Canons*, c. 28 (Johnson, I. 397), the priest is distinctly reminded of his duty to expound the Gospel in English every Sunday and mass-day.

[3] *e.g.* The council of Valence (855), c. 16. Pope Nicholas I. soon afterwards (between 858 and 867) urges the importance of erecting '*plebes*, vel baptismales ecclesiæ' (parish churches), 'ut ibi conventus celebrior populorum fiat et *doctrina fidei prædicetur*.' Mansi, xv. 452.

[4] See, for instance, the *Capitula* of Herard, archbp. of Tours (858), c. 9 (in Baluze, I. 1285): and council of Mentz, as above, n. 2.

[5] The requisite amount of knowledge is laid down by Hincmar in his *Capitula* (852); Mansi, xv. 475. Besides committing several offices and formulæ to memory, the priest is to be able to expound the Apostles' Creed, the Lord's Prayer, the Creed of St Athanasius ('Quicunque Vult'), and understand forty homilies of Gregory the Great. Several councils complained bitterly of unlearned priests: *e.g.* that of *Rome* (826), which also insists on the importance of securing school-masters, 'qui studia litterarum liberaliumque artium dogmata assidue doceant:' c. 34; Mansi, xiv. 1008: cf. *ib.* 493. So grossly ignorant were the clerics of Verona, that Ratherius (d. 974) found many (plurimos) unable to repeat even the Apostles' Creed: D'Achery, I. 381. See *Ratherius von Verona und das zehnte Jahrhundert*, von Albrecht Vogel, Jena, 1854. He had also to contend with others (of Vicenza) who had sunk into anthropomorphism, resolutely maintaining (like the present Mormons) 'corporeum Deum esse:' *Ibid.* 388 sq. This part of Christendom, indeed, would seem to have been very prone to such unworthy speculations. Here sprang up the 'Theopaschites' condemned at Rome (862), when the decision was that the Godhead of our Saviour was impassible, that He 'passionem crucis tantummodo secundum carnem sustinuisse' (Mansi, xv. 658). The same council was under the necessity of condemning an opinion that in baptism 'originale non ablui delictum.'

to his vocation, rendered him unable to imprint those verities effectually upon his semi-barbarous flock. As children they were taught indeed by him and by their sponsors[1] several elements of Christian faith (*e.g.* the Lord's Prayer and the Apostles' Creed): yet there is reason to infer that in the many, more especially of tribes which were now added to the Church, the roots of heathenism were still insuperably strong[2].

Crudeness of the popular instruction.

How far the masses learned to read is not so easily determined. The amount of education must have differed with the circumstances of the country, diocese, or parish: still we are assured that efforts were continually made to organize both town and village schools[3].

Schools,

The richest institutions of this class were the conventual seminaries of the French and German Benedictines; and although they often shared in the deterioration of the order, and were broken up by the invasions of the Magyars and Northmen, we must view them as the greatest boon to all succeeding ages; since in them[4] especially the copies of the Sacred Volume, of the fathers, and of other books were hoarded and transcribed[5].

especially the Benedictine.

The reverence for the Holy Scriptures on the ground of their superhuman character was universally retained[6].

---

[1] Gieseler (II. 265, n. 29) mentions a German-Latin exhortation on this subject belonging to the present period. Still, as we may judge from the council of Trosli (909), c. 15, multitudes of either sex were unable to repeat even the Lord's Prayer and the Creed.

[2] Cf. above, p. 87, n. 1; p. 110; p. 116; p. 132, n. 2.

[3] *e.g.* Council of *Valence* (855), c. 18; council of *Savonières* (859), c. 10. Herard of Tours, in like manner, enjoins (c. 17) 'ut scholas presbyteri pro posse habeant et libros emendatos.' It seems, however, that there was a constant jealousy of the lay or secular schools on the part of the monks, who succeeded in getting several of them closed. Vidaillan, *Vie de Greg. VII.*, I. 290.

[4] Some idea of the contents of a monastic library at this period may be formed from the catalogue belonging to the French convent of St Riquier, in *Chronicon Monast. S. Richarii Centulensis* (D'Achery's *Spicil.* II. 310 sq.).

[5] The founder of a reformed branch of the Benedictines, the *Congregation of Hirschau*, did great service in this way: 'Duodecim monachis suis scriptores optimos instituit, quibus ut *Divinæ auctoritatis libros*, et *sanctorum Patrum tractatus* rescriberent, demandavit. Erant præter hos et alii scriptores sine certo numero, qui pari diligentia scribendis voluminibus operam impendebant.' J. Trithemius [John of Trittenheim], *Annales Hirsaugienses*, I. 227: ed. St Gall, 1690.

[6] See the Benedictine *Hist. Lit. de la France*, IV. 252 sq., V. 291 sq.,

MEANS OF GRACE AND KNOWLEDGE.

Scarcity of entire copies of the Bible.

Vernacular translations.

Too often, however, the supply of biblical as well as other manuscripts appears to have been extremely small[1]; and very few even of the well-affected clergy had sufficient means to purchase more than two or three separate works[2] of the inspired Authors. Copies of the Psalms and Gospels were most frequently possessed.

The laity, when they could read, had also opportunities of gathering crumbs of sacred knowledge, here and there at least, from versions now in circulation[3] of some parts of holy Writ, from interlinear glosses of the Service-books[4], or from poetic paraphrases, harmonies, and hymns in the vernacular,—productions which indeed grow very numerous at this period[5].

and, for England, Ælfric, *On the Old and New Testaments*, translated by L'Isle, Lond. 1638. At the consecration of a bishop the following question was asked: 'Vis ea quæ *ex Divinis Scripturis intelligis* plebem cui ordinandus es et verbis docere et exemplis.' MS. quoted in Soames, *Bampt. Lect.* p. 95. See Maskell's *Monumenta Ritualia*, III. 246. Dunstan urges the advantage of a familiar acquaintance with the Holy Scriptures in his 'Exposition of the Rule of St Benedict:' Cambr. Univ. MSS., Ee. II. 4, fol. 26, b.

[1] Mr Kemble (*Saxons*, II. 434) quotes a letter from Freculf bishop of Lisieux to Rabanus Maurus, in which he says 'in episcopio nostræ parvitati commisso, nec ipsos Novi et Veteris Testamenti repperi libros, multo minus horum expositiones.'

[2] This was implied in the advice of Riculf, bishop of Soissons (889), who urged his country clergy to bestow especial pains upon their schools, and to provide themselves with as many books as possible. If they could not procure all the Old Testament, they were at least to have the Book of Genesis: Fleury, liv. LIV. § 4. In the conventual catalogue above cited, p. 193, n. 4, the 'Bibliotheca,' or entire Bible, was in one copy 'dispersa in voluminibus XIV.'

[3] Above, p. 89. King Alfred is said to have commenced a version of the Psalms into English (W. Malmsbur. *De Gest. Regum.* p. 43, ed. Francof. 1601). The fragments of Ælfric's *Heptateuchus*, a translation of portions of the Pentateuch, Joshua, Judges, &c., have been printed, ed. Thwaites, Oxon. 1698. The *Anglo-Saxon Gospels* (best edited by Thorpe, Lond. 1842) are also traceable to this period. The Slavonic churches of Moravia, Russia, Servia, and probably others, possessed the Bible and Service-books in the vernacular. See above, p. 113, p. 121, p. 125: but it is worthy of remark, that in the cognate church of Dalmatia, subject to the popes, attempts were ultimately made (*e. g.* council of Spalato, 1069) to banish the Slavonic ritual and to substitute the Latin.

[4] Above, p. 89, n. 4: and Wright's *Biogr. Brit.* I. 427. The 'Durham Book' (Cotton MS. Nero, D. IV.), of which the Latin portion was written between 687 and 721, received the interlinear gloss about 950.

[5] Louis the Pious had a metrical version of the Scriptures made under his direction (Palgrave's *Normandy*, I. 188), which most probably

Still, as writers of the age itself complain, a careful study of the Bible was comparatively rare, especially throughout the tenth century; the clerics even giving a decided preference to some lower fields of thought, for instance, to the elements of logic and of grammar[1]. The chief source of general reading was the swarming 'Lives of Saints,' which had retained the universal influence we have noticed on a former page[2]. The Eastern Church was furnished with them even to satiety by Simeon Metaphrastes[3]; and a number of his wildest Legends were transmitted to the West. The general craving for such kinds of food is well attested by the fact that Ælfric had himself translated two large volumes at the wish of the English people, and had subsequently been induced to undertake a third for the gratification of the monks[4].

CORRUPTIONS AND ABUSES.

Popularity of the Lives of Saints.

The counteraction to this growing worship of the saints was now less frequent and emphatic than before. The voice of a reforming prelate, such as Agobard[5] or Claudius of Turin[6], did little to abate the ruling spirit of the age.

Saint-worship.

---

is the *Heliand* (circ. 830), an Old-Saxon Gospel Harmony (ed. Schmeller), alliterative in form. Another Harmony, or *Paraphrase of the Gospels*, is by Ottfried (circ. 868), a monk of Weissenburg. See this and other vernacular pieces in Schilter's *Thesaurus Antiq. Teutonicarum*. The Psalms also were translated into the Low-German dialect (ed. Hagen). Von Raumer (as referred to above, p. 89, n. 1) will point out many other fragments of this class. In the eleventh century, Notker Labeo, a monk of St Gall, and Williram, master of the cathedral-school at Bamberg, added to the stock of vernacular theology; the former having published a German paraphrase of the Psalms, and the latter a German translation and exposition of Solomon's Song.

[1] See the complaint of Notker in Neander, VI. 177. Agobard of Lyons, at an earlier date, in his endeavours to reform the Liturgy, and raise the spiritual character of the priesthood, bears the following witness to the evils of his time: 'Quam plurimi ab ineunte pueritia usque ad senectutis canitiem omnes dies vitæ suæ in parando et confirmando expendunt, et totum tempus utilium et spiritalium studiorum, legendi, videlicet, et *Divina eloquia perscrutandi*, in istiusmodi occupatione consumunt.' *De Correctione Antiphon*. c. 18. Opp. II. 99, ed. Baluze.

[2] p. 90.
[3] Above, p. 179.
[4] See the Preface to an *Anglo-Saxon Passion of St George*, edited by the present writer, for the late *Percy Society*, No. LXXXVIII. Time for reading would be found on Sundays, which were still most rigorously observed: *e.g.* Council of Eanham (1009), c. 15, c. 30 (Johnson, I. 486, 490); Council of Coyaco, in Spain (1050), c. 3.
[5] *De Imaginibus*, c. XXXV: *Opp*. I. 267.
[6] See Neander, VI. 129.

CORRUPTIONS AND ABUSES.

Increase in the number of Saints.

The calendar was crowded more and more with names, occasionally, it is true, the names of genuine saints[1], or those of missionaries who expired in the evangelizing of the heathen; but frequently they represent a host of mythic beings, coloured, if not altogether forged, to satisfy the wants of an uncritical and marvel-hunting generation[2]. In some cases, it is probable, the authors of the Legends put them out as nothing more than historical *romances*, but the ordinary reader did not view them in this light; and therefore the results to which they naturally led, in moulding the religious habits and ideas of the Middle Ages, were extensive and profound[3].

The excessive veneration of the Virgin.

Of all the saints whom Christians venerated more and more, the blessed Virgin was the chief. The story of her exaltation into heaven obtained a general credence, and as men were often vying with each other in attempts to elevate her far above the common sphere of humanity[4], they now devised a public service for this end,—the *Hours* or *Office of St Mary*[5]. It was gradually accepted in the

---

[1] *e.g.* Count Gerald of Aurillac, whose life was written by Odo, the abbot of Clugny, in the *Biblioth. Cluniacensis*, ed. Paris, 1614. He is said to have left many clerics far behind in his knowledge of the Scriptures.

[2] *e.g.* Bellarmine even thinks that the productions of Simeon Metaphrastes were indebted largely to his own inventive powers (they were narrations 'non ut res gestæ fuerant, sed ut geri *potuerant*'): but this idea is rejected by another of the Roman controversialists, Leo Allatius, in his *De Simeonum Scriptis*, pp. 43—47. Many legends also were repeated of different saints merely with a change of names: Gieseler, II. 424, 425. The Church besides was deluged at this period by 'heretical' or 'apocryphal' hymns and martyrologies: see, for instance, the *Pref.* quoted in p. 195, n. 4. Agobard informs us in like manner that it was usual for some persons to sing the most heterodox effusions even in the churches: 'non solum inepta et superflua sed etiam profana et hæretica in ecclesiis decantare.' *De Correct. Antiphon.* c. 18. He proposes instead of these to have a reformed Antiphonary, 'ex purissimis Sanctæ Scripturæ verbis sufficientissime ordinatum.' *Ibid.* c. 19.

[3] We may conceive of this effect more clearly by remembering that Ignatius Loyola was fired to institute the Order of the Jesuits by reading the *Legenda* in a time of sickness. An account of the *Martyrologies* produced by the present period may be seen in Schröckh, XXIII. 209 sq.

[4] *e.g.* Peter Damiani (Hildebrand's coadjutor) has the following: 'Numquid quia ita deificata, ideo nostræ humanitatis oblita es? Nequaquam, domina....Data est tibi omnis potestas in cœlo et in terra.' Sermo XLIV. *Opp.* II. 107. His sermons on the Virgin are always in this strain: cf. Soames' *Bampton Lect.* pp. 232 sq.

[5] Hymns in honour of the Virgin are somewhat older, but Damiani seems to have been among the first who engrafted them on the public

monasteries, where the custom of performing mass on Saturdays[1] to the especial honour of the Virgin also took its rise.

The saints indeed were worshipped by the more enlightened on the ground that every act of veneration paid to them was ultimately paid to Christ Himself, and would redound to the glory of His grace[2]: but in the many it was very different. Owing to their want of spiritual and intellectual culture, a distinction of this kind was for the most part altogether unintelligible. They would naturally confound the courtiers and the king; in other words, the worship of the holy dead, as understood by them, was bordering close upon polytheism. The formal recognition ('canonization') of a saint, not only in one single district but in every province of the Church (a usage dating from the present period[3]), added greatly to the downward impulse.

We have glanced already at the storm excited by the images and pictures of the saints. It seems that on the close of the Iconoclastic troubles they were now employed in East and West alike, although the more intelligent continued to regard them in the light of historical re-

CORRUPTIONS AND ABUSES.

Prevailing ideas of the nature of Saint-worship.

Images.

---

worship of the Church: see his *Opuscul.* XXXIII. c. 3. It was now not unusual to call her 'mater misericordiæ,' 'beata regina mundi,' 'sœsteorra,' etc. Mabillon (*Annal. Benedict.* IV. 462 sq.) traces the *Rosary*, or *Psalter of the Virgin*, to the eleventh century, when it existed in England and the Netherlands.

[1] Damiani, *ubi sup.* c. 4. He met with opposition when he urged this observance on some of the Italian convents. A monk, Gozo, resisted it on the ground that it was an innovation: see Gieseler, II. 428, n. 18.

[2] *e.g.* Such is the language of John XV. in 993 (Mansi, XIX. 170)...... 'quoniam sic adoramus et colimus reliquias martyrum et confessorum, ut Eum Cujus martyres et confessores sunt adoremus, honoramus servos, ut honor redundet in Dominum,' etc. Even Ratherius of Verona was an advocate of saint-worship in this sense: *Præloquia*, lib. IV. p. 892, ed. Ballerini. On the other hand, Claudius of Turin (above, p. 158) condemned the practice. The ideas of king Alfred may be gathered from expressions like the following: 'I Alfred king, in honour of God and of the Blessed Virgin Mary and of all the Saints,' etc....'Whosoever shall misappropriate this gift, may he be by God and the Holy Virgin Mary and all the saints accursed for ever.' *Codex Diplomaticus*, ed. Kemble, II. 106.

[3] See above, p. 90, n. 2. The earliest well-authenticated instance of a canonization by the pope is that of Ulrich, bishop of Augsburg, which took place in 993: Mansi, XIX. 169. The metropolitans, however, in some districts exercised their ancient right till 1153: Pagi, *Breviar. Pontif.* III. 115.

CORRUPTIONS AND ABUSES.

Relics:

the gross abuses respecting them.

membrancers, and not as in themselves the end, or even the especial channels of devotion[1].

A perpetual source of mischief and profaneness was the feverish passion to become possessed of relics of the saints. The gross credulity of some, and the unpardonable fraud of others, multiplied the number of these objects of research to a prodigious and most scandalous extent. They grew at length into a common article of traffic[2]. Monasteries in particular, where many of them were enshrined from motives either of cupidity or superstition, reaped a harvest by exhibiting their treasures to the simple-hearted crowd. A few indeed of the disinterested or less credulous abbots interposed occasionally, and shut up some wonder-working relic from the gaze of the tumultuary assemblage whom it had attracted to the spot[3]. Too often, however, 'the religious,' running with the stream of popular opinion, acquiesced in the circulation of the vilest cheats[4]. The masses were thus more and more confirmed in semi-pagan notions with respect to amulets and charms; believing everywhere, to some extent at least, in the protective and the therapeutic virtues of the relics.

In connexion with this point we may remark, that

---

[1] See above, pp. 158, 175. A remarkable specimen of the reigning modes of thought on this subject is supplied by the *Laws of king Alfred* (Thorpe, I. 44), where the second precept of the Decalogue is omitted, but in order to complete the number ten, we have the following addition, 'Make not thou for thyself golden or silver gods.'

[2] *e.g. Life of Rabanus Maurus*, in *Act. Sanct.* Febr. I. 513. Glaber Radulphus (*Hist.* lib. IV. c. 3) tells a story of an impostor who wandered (circ. 1020) from place to place, under different names, as a vendor of dead men's bones, which he dug up almost indiscriminately. Numbers of relics now began to be imported by the pilgrims on their visits to the East. Thus Simeon of Trèves (circ. 1030) introduced relics of St Catharine to the Western Church, where she was hitherto unknown; Fleury, *Hist. Eccles.*, lib. LIX. s. 27. Perhaps no more striking characteristic of the spirit of the times has been recorded than the contest respecting a St Martial (one of the companions of St Denis the Areopagite?) whom the monks of Limoges endeavoured to exalt into the rank of an apostle. See an account of the controversy in Schröckh, XXIII. 145 sq.

[3] *e.g. Gesta Abbatum Trudonensium* (St Trond), in D'Achery's *Spicileg.* II. 664. Cf. Guérard, *Cartulaire de l'Eglise de Notre-Dame*, p. xxv.

[4] The number of these finally suggested the application of the fire-ordeal (cf. above, p. 155, n. 3) to test the genuineness of relics. See Mabillon's *Vet. Analecta*, p. 568. Schröckh (XXIII. 180 sq.) enumerates some of the most cherished of the relics now discovered or transmitted to the West; *e.g.* a Tear of Christ, Blood of Christ, &c.

a more ancient practice of the Church in seeking to ward off the ravages of sickness, now obtained an almost universal currency. This was the rite which subsequently bore the name of 'extreme unction.' It was at the first applied by private Christians[1], and was not restricted, any more than the anterior custom noticed by St James (v. 14), to *mortal* sickness only. The administration was however, in the eighth century, confined to members of the sacerdotal class[2], the rite itself attaining to the rank of special ordinances, which, in laxer phrase, were not unfrequently entitled 'sacraments[3].'

*CORRUP-
TIONS AND
ABUSES.*

*Extreme
unction.*

As might be augured from the cheerless aspect of the age, a number of the more devout of either sex had been impelled into seclusion, where they lived amid inhospitable woods and wilds. These hermits, it would seem, abounded most in the tenth century[4]. Disgusted with their former selves, or with the desperate state of morals and religion in the town, they hoped to find in solitude an interval of holy calm which they might dedicate to prayer and closer self-inspection.

Solitaries.

A more earthly spirit breathed in the prevailing rage for pilgrimages. Many doubtless undertook them with a mingled class of feelings, differing little, if at all, from those of modern tourists: while the rest would view such journeys, as the Church herself did for the most part, in relation to the penitential system of the age. As the more hopeful doctrines of the cross had been forgotten

*Pilgrim-
ages,*

---

[1] Cf. Neander VI. 145: Klee (Roman-catholic), *Hist. of Christ. Doct.* (in German), Part II. ch. VI. § 5.

[2] 'Omnes presbyteri oleum infirmorum ab episcopo expetant secumque habeant; et admoneant fideles infirmos illud exquirere ut eodem oleo *peruncti a presbyteris* sanentur,' etc. Bonifacii *Opp.* II. 24, ed. Giles. The usage is again sanctioned, more especially in case of mortal sickness, by the council of Pavia (850), c. 8. In the *Canons enacted under Edgar* (Thorpe, II. 258) it is enjoined that "the priest shall give 'husel' (the Eucharist) to the sick, and unction also, *if they desire it.*"

[3] *e.g.* Damiani speaks of *twelve* rites to which this name is applicable, unction in the number: Sermo LXIX; *Opp.* II. 167. It may be noted here that although communion in both kinds was still the rule of the Church, the consecrated wine was often administered, for prudential reasons, through a tube ('calamus,' 'canna,' 'fistula'): see Spittler, *Gesch. des Kelches im Abendmahl.* The practice of receiving the consecrated elements into the *hand* of the communicant began to be discontinued after the Council of Rouen (880): Grancolas, *Les Anc. Liturg.* II. 323.

[4] Capefigue, *L'Eglise au Moyen Age,* I. 251.

marginalia: CORRUPTIONS AND ABUSES. *to Rome,* *and to the Holy Sepulchre.* *The penitential system of the Church.*

or displaced, men felt that the Almighty could no longer be propitious to them while resorting to the common means of grace. Accordingly they acquiesced in the most rigid precepts of their spiritual director and the heaviest censures of the Church. The pilgrimage to Rome stood highest in their favour during all the earlier half of the present period; the extravagant ideas of papal grandeur, and the hope of finding a more copious absolution at the hands of the alleged successor of St Peter, operating very powerfully in all districts of the West[1]. But subsequently the great point of confluence was the Holy Sepulchre, which from the year **1030** seems to have attracted multitudes of every grade[2].

It must, however, be remembered, that the better class of prelates, even where they yielded more or less to the externalizing spirit of the times, have never failed to censure all reliance on these works as grounds of human merit, or as relieving men from the necessity of inward transformation to the holy image of the Lord[3]. A number also, it must be allowed, of the ascetics, both in east and west, exhibited the genuine spirit of humility and self-

---

[1] See above, pp. 141, 142. Such pilgrims were called *Romei, Homines peregrini et Romei, Romipetæ*. Nicholas I. (862) declares, 'Ad hanc sanctam Romanam ecclesiam, de diversis mundi partibus quotidie multi sceleris mole oppressi confugiunt, remissionem scilicet, et venialem sibi gratiam tribui supplici et ingenti cordis mœrore poscentes:' Mansi, xv. 280. Individual bishops protested against this custom; and the council of Seligenstadt (1022) commanded that the German Christians should first perform the penance prescribed by their own clergy, and then, if they pleased to obtain the permission of their bishop, it allowed them to go to Rome: c. 18; Mansi, xix. 398. A similar proof of independence is supplied by archbishop Dunstan: Soames, *Anglo-Saxon Church*, p. 207, ed. 1844.

[2] 'Per idem tempus (circ. 1030) ex universo orbe tam innumerabilis multitudo cœpit confluere ad sepulchrum Salvatoris Hierosolymis, quantam nullus hominum prius sperare poterat. Primitus enim ordo inferioris plebis, deinde vero mediocres, posthæc permaximi quique reges et comites, marchiones ac præsules: ad ultimum vero, quod nunquam contigerat, mulieres multæ nobiles cum pauperioribus illuc perrexere.' Glaber Radulph. *Hist.* lib. iv. c. 6. For earlier instances of these visits, see Schröckh, xxiii. 203 sq., and the treatise of Adamnan *De Situ Terræ Sanctæ*, ed. Ingolstadt, 1619. The fame of St James (San Jago) of Compostella (above, p. 93, n. 2) was now increasing in the West. See Heidegger, *Dissert. de Peregrinat. Religiosis*, pp. 18 sq. Tiguri, 1670.

[3] See *e.g.* the *Libri Tres de Institutione Laicali* of Jonas, bishop of Orleans, *passim*, in D'Achery's *Spicileg.* I. 258—323.

renunciation[1]. Yet, upon the other hand, it is apparent that the penitential discipline of the Church was undermining the foundations of the truth. The theory most commonly adopted was, that penances are satisfactions paid by the offender, with the hope of averting the displeasure of Almighty God. Its operation, therefore, would be twofold, varying with the temperament or the convictions of the guilty. The more earnest felt that the effects of sin could only be removed by voluntary suffering, by an actual and incessant mortification of the flesh. Accordingly they had recourse to measures the most violent, for instance, to a series of extraordinary fasts and self-inflicted scourgings[2], not unlike the almost suicidal discipline which had for ages been adopted by the Yogis of the east. The other and the larger class who shrank from all ascetic practices could find relief in commutations, or remissions, of the penances[3] prescribed by canons of the ancient Church. A relaxation of this kind, now legalized in all the *Libri Pœnitentiales*, was entitled an 'indulgence.' Grants of money for ecclesiastical purposes, a pilgrimage, the repetition of religious formulæ, and other acts like these, were often substituted for a long term of rigorous self-denial[4], and too often also (we must apprehend) for genuine change of heart and life. The magnitude of penances was greater in the case of clerics

marginalia: CORRUPTIONS AND ABUSES. False views of penitence. Self-scourging and extreme asceticism. Indulgences, or commutations of penance.

[1] Thus Anskar, the Apostle of the North, who carried the practice of self-mortification to a high pitch, could pray notwithstanding that he might be kept from spiritual pride which threatened him at times: 'Qua de re tristis factus, et ad Domini pietatem totis viribus in oratione conversus, postulabat ut Sua eum gratia ab hac perniciosissima impietate liberaret.' *Vit. S. Anskar.* c. 35: Pertz, II. 717. In the same spirit, Theodore the Studite could attribute all he had and all he was to God: Διὰ σπλάγχνα οἰκτιρμῶν, οὐκ ἐξ ἔργων μού τινων· οὐ γὰρ ἐποίησά τι ἀγαθὸν ἐπὶ τῆς γῆς ἀλλὰ τοὐναντίον. *Epist.* lib. II. ep. 34.

[2] The great advocate of this extreme asceticism was Damiani, who regarded it as a 'purgatory' on earth. He had to defend his views, however, from the censure of opponents. See his Opuscul. XLIII. *De Laude Flagellorum et Disciplinæ*, and cf. Gieseler, II. 444, n. 10.

[3] This practice of the Church had been condemned (*e. g.* in the reforming synod of Clovesho 747, c. 26; and afterwards in that of Mentz, 847, c. 31), but it had gained an almost universal currency in the present period.

[4] See Muratori, *Antiq. Ital.* v. 710 sq. 'De redemptione Peccatorum.' The custom of granting indulgences to certain 'privileged' churches dates from the profligate pontiff, Benedict IX. (above, p. 139, n. 5): see Mabillon, *Act. Sanct. Ord. Bened.* sæc. v. præf. § 109.

CORRUPTIONS AND ABUSES.

Vicarious fasting.

than in that of laymen; it was greater also in the highborn than the low: but through a sad confusion of ideas it was possible for the more wealthy sinner to compress a seven years' fast, for instance, into one of three days, by summoning his numerous dependents, and enjoining them to fast with him and in his stead[1].

Confession:

Beside the discipline allotted to the individual, on confessing voluntarily to the priest, more overt acts of sin[2] had to be publicly acknowledged on the pain of excommunication. When offenders proved refractory, the issuing of this sentence, backed as it now was by the civil power, incapacitated them for holding offices or reaping honours of the state. Another engine of the spirituality was the more dreadful sentence of *anathema*, by which the subjects of it were excluded altogether from the fellowship of Christians[3]. But the heaviest of those censures, which we find developed in its greatest vigour at the opening of the eleventh century, was termed the *interdict*[4], or utter excommunication, not of individuals merely, but of all the province where a crime had been committed.

Excommunication.

Anathema:

Interdict.

The morose and servile feelings which the penitential system of the Church engendered or expressed, were deepened by the further systematizing of her old presentiments respecting purgatory[5]. The distinction, to be afterwards

---

[1] A case of this very kind occurs in the *Canons enacted under Edgar* (Thorpe, II. 286). It is presumed, of course, that the offending lord who profits by the regulation is penitent himself, but from the whole passage one is bound to draw the inference that a sin was to be liquidated exactly like some ordinary debt. 'The man not possessing means may not so proceed, but must seek it for himself the more diligently; and that [the canon is compelled to add] is also justest, that every one wreak his own misdeeds on himself, with diligent bót (satisfaction). Scriptum est enim: Quia unusquisque onus suum portabit,' p. 289. Damiani (Opuscul. v.: Mansi, XIX. 893) makes use of the following language: 'Centum itaque annorum sibi pœnitentiam indidi, redemptionemque ejus *taxatam per unumquemque annum pecuniæ quantitate* præfixi.'

[2] The bishop inquired into such flagrant cases on his visitation-tour. See Regino, *De Disciplinis Eccl.* lib. II. c. 1 sq., ed. Baluze, 1671.

[3] See Neander, VI. 153.

[4] Earlier instances occur, but till the present period they had been condemned by the more sober class of prelates; *e.g.* Hincmar's *Opusc.* XXXIII. (against his nephew Hincmar of Laon, who had placed his diocese under an interdict). The first example of the mediæval practice which drew down no condemnation, happened in 994: see Bouquet's *Historiens des Gaules*, etc. x. 147. The penalty was legalized in 1031 by the provincial synod of Limoges (Limovicense II.); Mansi, XIX. 541.

[5] See above, p. 95.

evolved, between the temporal and eternal consequences of sin, was still indeed unknown: but in defining that a numerous class of frailties, unforgiven in the present life, are nevertheless remissible hereafter, the dominion of the sacerdotal order and the efficacy of prayers and offerings on the part of the survivors were indefinitely extended to the regions of the dead[1]. From this idea[2], when embodied ultimately in a startling legend[3], sprang the 'Feast of All Souls' (Nov. 2), which seems to have been instituted soon after 1024, at Clugny, and ere long accepted in the Western Church at large.

Perhaps the incident which of all others proved the aptest illustration of the spirit of the age, is found in a prevailing expectation that the winding-up of all things would occur at the close of the tenth century. At first arising, it may be, from misconceptions of the words of the Apocalypse[4] (xx. 1—6), the notion was apparently confirmed by the terrific outbreak of the powers of evil; while a vivid consciousness of their demerit filled all orders of society with a foreboding that the Judge was standing at the door. As soon as the dreaded year 1000 had gone over, men appeared to breathe more freely on all sides. A burst of gratitude for their deliverance[5] found expression in rebuilding or in decorating sanctuaries of

CORRUPTIONS AND ABUSES.

The effects of the belief in purgatory.

Feast of All Souls.

General expectation of the final judgment.

---

[1] Thus John VIII. (circ. 878) declares that absolution is to be granted to those Christians who have died while fighting 'pro defensione sanctæ Dei ecclesiæ et pro statu Christianæ religionis ac reipublicæ,' against pagans and infidels. Mansi, XVII. 104.

[2] Cf. Palgrave, *History of Normandy*, I. 164.

[3] *Vit. S. Odilonis*, c. 14; in Mabillon, *Act. Sanct. Ord. Bened.* sæc. VI. pt. I. p. 701: cf. Schröckh, XXIII. 223.

[4] Hengstenberg, *Die Offenbarung des h. Johannes*, II. 369, Berlin, 1850; Mosheim, *Cent.* X. part II. c. III. § 3: Capefigue, *L'Eglise au Moyen Age*, I. 259 sq. Deeds of gift in the tenth century often commence with the phrase, 'Appropinquante mundi termino.'

[5] Capefigue, pp. 269, 270. Gratitude might enter very largely into men's feelings at this crisis; but more frequently it was the wish to make compensation for sin ('synna *gebétan*' is the Anglo-Saxon phrase) which stimulated men to acts of piety and benevolence. 'Pro redemptione animæ meæ et prædecessorum meorum' may be taken as a fair specimen of the motives which were then in the ascendant: cf. Schröckh, XXIII. 139 sq. and Kemble's *Codex Diplomaticus*, passim. The excitement in connexion with the year 1000 was renewed in 1033, at the beginning of the second thousand years after the Crucifixion. Many were then stimulated to set out for Palestine, where Christ was expected to appear: see above, p. 200.

CORRUPTIONS AND ABUSES.

Impulse given to church-building.
Reformation of religion still deferred.

God and other spots connected with religion. To this circumstance we owe a number of the stateliest minsters and cathedrals which adorn the west of Europe[1].

Much, however, as the terrors of the Lord had stimulated zeal and piety, it is too obvious that the many soon relapsed into their ancient unconcern. The genuine reformation of the Church 'in head and members,' though the want of it is not unfrequently confessed, was still to human eye impossible. She had to pass through further stages of probation and decline. It almost seems as if the consciousness of *individual* fellowship with Christ, long palsied or suppressed, could not be stirred into a healthy action till the culture of the human intellect had been more generally advanced. Accordingly the dialectic studies of the schools, however mischievous in other ways, were needed for the training of those master-minds, who should at length eliminate the pagan customs and unchristian modes of thought which had been blended in the lapse of ages with the apostolic faith. It was required especially that Hildebrandine principles, which some had taken as the basis of a pseudo-reformation, should be pressed into their most offensive consequences, ere the local or provincial Churches could be roused to vindicate their freedom and cast off the papal yoke[2].

[1] 'Infra millesimum tertio jam fere imminente anno contigit in universo pœne terrarum orbe, præcipue tamen in Italia et in Galliis, innovari ecclesiarum basilicas, licet pleræque decenter locatæ minime indiguissent, *etc*...Erat enim instar ac si mundus ipse excutiendo semet, rejecta vetustate, passim candidam ecclesiarum vestem indueret.' Glaber Radulph. *Hist.* lib. III. c. 4.

[2] Schaff (*Ch. Hist.* 'Introd.' p. 51) remarks on the character of this period:—'This may be termed the age of *Christian legalism*, of Church authority. Personal freedom is here, to great extent, lost in slavish subjection to fixed, traditional rules and forms. The individual subject is of account, only as the organ and medium of the general spirit of the Church. All secular powers, the state, science, art, are under the guardianship of the hierarchy, and must everywhere serve its ends. This is emphatically the era of grand universal enterprises, of colossal works, whose completion required the cooperation of nations and centuries; the age of the supreme outward sovereignty of the visible Church. Such a well-ordered and imposing system of authority was necessary for the training of the Romanic and Germanic nations, to raise them from barbarism to the consciousness and rational use of freedom. Parental discipline must precede independence: children must first be governed, before they can govern themselves: the law is still, as in the days of Moses, a schoolmaster to bring men to Christ.'

Third Period of the Middle Ages.

THE CHRISTIAN CHURCH FROM GREGORY VII.
UNTIL THE TRANSFER OF THE PAPAL SEE
TO AVIGNON.

1073—1305.

CHAPTER IX.

§ 1. *GROWTH OF THE CHURCH.*

NORTHERN MISSIONS.

THE districts in the north of Europe, which had hitherto continued strangers to the Christian faith, were for the most part now 'converted;' though the agency employed was far too frequently the civil sword, and not the genuine weapons of the first Apostle.

AMONG THE FINNS.

Military conversion of the Finns.

These tribes, addicted still to a peculiar form of nature-worship[1], were subdued (circ. **1150**) by Eric IX., king of Sweden, whose exertions in diffusing Christianity[2] have won for him the name of saint[3]. Impelled by a misgoverned zeal, he laboured to coerce the Finns into a knowledge of the Gospel. His ally in this crusade was Henry, bishop of Upsala[4], an Englishman, who ultimately perished while attempting to excommunicate a murderer (**1158**). Some real progress was effected[5] in the reign of Eric;

---

[1] Mone, *Gesch. des Heidenthums*, I. 43 sq.

[2] Sweden was itself imperfectly Christianized in the former period (p. 107, n. 3). In 1123 a crusade was formed against the heathen of Scania, where several Englishmen, David, Askil, Stephen and others were distinguished missionaries (Laing's *Sweden*, p. 239, Lond. 1839); and in some of the other districts Eric carried on the work of conversion (Schröckh, xxv. 279).

[3] See his *Life* in the *Acta Sanct.* Maii, IV. 187.

[4] He also was canonized: see his *Life* in the *Acta Sanct.* Januar. II. 249.

[5] A bishopric was founded at Rendamecki, afterwards (? 1228) transferred to Abo. Wiltsch, *Kirchl. Geogr.* II. 259, n. 14. It was included in the Swedish province of Upsala.

but in **1240** we find the natives generally adhering to their ancient superstitions, and most eager to annihilate the little Christian flock. A Swedish jarl, accordingly (**1249**), began a fresh crusade against them, and his violence was copied on a further provocation by the Swedish monarch, Thorkel, who reduced a tribe of Finns beyond the Tawastlanders. It is said that, prior to the date of his incursion, tidings of the faith had reached them through a Russian channel[1].

POMERA-
NIAN
CHURCH.

AMONG THE SCLAVONIC TRIBES.

The rapid progress of the truth among this section of the human family has been already traced[2]. The present period witnessed an extension of the missionary work. The earliest converts were the Pomeranians, then possessing Pomerania Proper, Wartha, and Lusatia. From the date of their succumbing to the Poles (circ. **997**) attempts were made, especially in Eastern Pomerania, to annex the heathen natives to the Church by founding a bishopric at Colberg[3] (**1000**). But their fierce resistance[4] to the missionary long impeded his success; and only when the Polish sway was extended over all the western district by the arms of Boleslav III. in **1121**, could any stable groundwork be procured for the ulterior planting of the Church.

The missionary efforts of the Poles.

A Spanish priest named Bernard[5], who embarked upon the mission in the following year, was found obnoxious, from his poverty, asceticism, and other causes, to the bulk

---

[1] Döllinger, III. 277, 278.
[2] Above, pp. 111 sq.
[3] Wiltsch, I. 397, n. 2. The bishop Reinbern, however, had no successor (see Kanngiesser's *Bekehrungs-Gesch. der Pommern zum Christenthume*, pp. 295 sq., Greifswald, 1824); the diocese being united with that of Gnesen.
[4] 'Sed nec gladio prædicationis cor eorum a perfidia potuit revocari, nec gladio jugulationis eorum penitus viperalis progenies aboleri. Sæpe tamen principes eorum a Duce Poloniæ prælio superati ad baptismum confugerunt, itemque collectis viribus fidem Christianam abnegantes contra Christianos bellum denuo paraverunt.' Martinus Gallus (as above, p. 116, n. 3).
[5] *Vit. S. Ottonis*, in Ludewig's *Script. Rer. Episcop. Bamberg.* I. 460 sq. A more nearly contemporary account of the mission is the *Vit. B. Ottonis*, in Canisii *Lect. Antiq.* ed. Basnage, III. pt. ii. pp. 35 sq.

Pomeranian Church.

Labours of Otho, bishop of Bamberg (d. 1139).

of the heathen natives. He was therefore superseded at his own desire by one more fitted for the task, the cheerful and judicious Otho, bishop of Bamberg, who set out (April 24, **1124**) with an imposing retinue and many tempting presents. He commenced the missionary work at Pyritz (near the Polish frontier), where a large assemblage was collected for the celebration of a pagan feast; and after twenty days no less than seven thousand of them were admitted to the sacrament of baptism. Wartislav, the duke of Pomerania, was a warm supporter of the mission, exercising a most salutary influence by his own renunciation of polygamy, and his endeavours to repress the other heathen customs[1]. Fear of Poland, blended with increasing admiration of the earnestness of bishop Otho, gradually disposed the natives of all ranks to seek for shelter in the Church. From Cammin, where the ducal family resided, Otho bent his course to the important isle of Wollin, whence however he was soon obliged to fly from the assault of an infuriated mob.

Successful at Stettin.

He next addressed his offers to the leading town of Pomerania, Stettin, and succeeded after fresh resistance in demolishing the temple of its chief divinity[2] (Triglav), and in winning over a large band of converts[3]. Having lingered here five months, he crossed again to Wollin, the remaining stronghold of the pagan party, and was now enabled to adopt the town of Julin as the see[4] of the first bishop (Adalbert).

He then took his leave of Pomerania and returned to Bamberg in the spring of **1125**: but learning subsequently

---

[1] From Otho's addresses (in Canisius, as above, pp. 61—63) to the recently-baptized converts we learn, among other things, that the unnatural custom of destroying female children at their birth prevailed to a great extent.

[2] The interesting circumstances connected with this and similar acts are given at length in Neander, VII. 16—21: cf. Mone, I. 178.

[3] Numbers seem to have been influenced by a promise now elicited by Otho from the duke of Poland, to remit the annual tribute of the Christian Pomeranians (*Vit. B. Ottonis*, in Canisius, p. 69).

[4] Owing to quarrels with the Danes, the bishopric was afterwards (1175) transferred to Cammin. Wiltsch, II. 85. It was exempted from all archiepiscopal jurisdiction and placed in immediate dependence on the see of Rome by Innocent II. (1140): Hasselbach, *Codex Pomeraniæ Diplom.* I. 36; ed. Greifswald, 1843. Clement III. sanctioned the transfer of the see in 1188, on the understanding that the bishops should pay annually to the pope 'fertonem (=farthing) auri.' *Ibid.* p. 152.

that a strong reaction had commenced in favour of the ancient religion, he was constrained to enter on a second journey in **1128**. Deflecting from his earlier route[1] he came into the dukedom at the town of Demmin (Timiana), where the Gospel was unknown. A diet held at Usedom (Uznam), soon after his arrival, sanctioned its diffusion in these parts, and Otho lost no time in sending out his staff of missionaries, two and two, among the neighbouring heathen. As before, he frequently encountered opposition from the populace, especially at Wolgast (Hologasta), which he visited in person. A large band of soldiers headed by the duke himself, could hardly keep the multitude in check. At length, however, they consented to behold the demolition of the pagan temples, and promoted the erection of a Church.

On leaving Wolgast Otho steadily declined the services of Albert the Bear, who would have fain employed his sword against the pagans. Gützkow (Gozgangia) was the place at which the missionaries halted next, and where they reaped a larger harvest of conversions[2]. An attempt to gain the Slavic isle of Rügen having failed, they bent their course to Stettin with the hope of counteracting the revival of the pagan rites. The bishop found an ardent coadjutor in a former convert Witstack[3], and their courage, tempered with affection, finally disarmed the frenzy of the zealots, who passed over in great numbers to the Church (**1128**). Henceforward it was everywhere triumphant. Christian, more particularly Saxon, colonists supplied the waste of population which had been occasioned by incessant wars; and as the clergy for the most part were Teutonic also, Pomerania both in language and in creed was Germanized[4].

The Wendish tribes, especially the northernmost (the Obotrites), who had relapsed into polytheism upon the martyrdom of Gottschalk[5] (**1066**), continued for the most

Marginal notes: POMERANIAN CHURCH. Otho's second missionary tour. Bitterly opposed at Wolgast: but finally successful. Vicissitudes of religion:

---

[1] *Vit. B. Ottonis*, as above, pp. 75 sq.
[2] *Ibid.* pp. 77 sq. On the consecration of a stately church, the bishop dwelt at large upon the truth that the one genuine temple of the Lord is in the human heart. His sermon wrought a deep effect, especially in Mizlaf, the governor of the district.
[3] *Ibid.* pp. 83 sq.
[4] Neander, VII. 41.
[5] See above, pp. 118, 119.

part the implacable opponents of the Gospel till the middle of the twelfth century. His son, indeed, assisted by the neighbouring Christian states, restored the Wendish kingdom in 1105, and made some brief and feeble efforts to restore the truth[1]. The dissolution of the empire on the death of Cnut (1131) facilitated the political designs of German princes and the spread of Christianity. The arms of Albert the Bear (1133 sq.) in Brandenburg (Leuticia) and of Henry the Lion, duke of Saxony (1142 sq.), replaced the Wendish Church upon its early footing, and soon after it was able to reorganize a number of the sees[2] that had been ruined in the former period.

Many of the northern Wends[3], however, stubbornly adhered to the ancestral religion until the utter subjugation of the Obotrites in 1162. Their chief apostle was the saintly Vicelin[4], a man of learning and of indefatigable zeal. Attracted to this field of missionary enterprise (1125), he preached at first in the border-town of Neumünster (Faldera), selecting it as a kind of outpost in his plan for the evangelizing of the northern districts of the Elbe. He drew around him a fraternity[5] of laymen and ecclesiastics, and in 1134, when the emperor Lothair II. paid a visit to the north, the earnest labours of the mission had been very largely blessed.

A church in Lübeck, with authority to organize religion in those parts, was now committed to the hands of Vicelin; but the Slavonians, on the death of the emperor (1137), suspecting him of a design against their liberties, rose up

---

[1] The best general accounts are Helmold, *Chron. Slavorum*, lib. I. c. 24 sq. (as above, p. 118, n. 1), and Gebhardi, *Geschichte aller Wendisch-Slavischen Staaten*, I. 143 sq.

[2] Cf. above, p. 118, n. 1. The see of Oldenburg, after being occupied by Vicelin and Gerold, was transferred to Lübeck by Henry the Lion; that of Mecklenburg to Schwerin (1197), 'propter tyrannidem Sclavorum.' Wiltsch, II. 79. The see of Ratzeburg was also revived. *Ibid.* pp. 79, 238.

[3] Helmold, *Chron. Ibid.*

[4] See De Westphalen's *Origines Neomonaster.* in the *Monument. Cimbrica*, II. 234 sq. and *Præf.* pp. 33 sq.: cf. *St Vicelin*, von F. C. Kruse, ed. Altona, 1826. Vicelin studied Biblical and other literature for three years at the university of Paris under Rudolf and Anselm. He was born at Quernheim, a village on the banks of the Weser.

[5] According to Schröckh (xxv. 261), the Rule adopted was that of the 'Præmonstratensians.'

in arms and banished every herald of the faith[1]. Retiring only when the storm was loudest, Vicelin continued to watch over the affairs of his disheartened flock. At length the partial subjugation of the Slaves by Adolph, count of Holstein, opened a more prosperous era; and in **1149**, the toil-worn missionary was promoted to the see of Oldenburg by Hartwig, the archbishop of Bremen. A prolonged misunderstanding now ensued between that primate and the duke, upon the subject of investiture[2]; but though embarrassed by it, Vicelin continued[3] to the last (**1154**) a pattern of devotion and of evangelic zeal. By dint of arms, by missionary labour, and a large infusion of Germanic settlers, gradually displacing the more ancient population, Christianity was now triumphantly diffused in all the broken empire of the Wends.

The latest fortress and asylum of Slavonic heathenism[4] was the extensive isle of Rügen. It had shewn a bitter and imperious zeal in favour of paganism when Pomerania was converted[5]. Otho had, indeed, on more than one occasion, purposed to extend his visits thither, but the warlike bearing of the people, and the fears of his companions had constrained him to desist[6]. It was reduced, however, in **1168**, by an invasion of the Danes[7], who broke in pieces the chief shrine (of Swantewit) at Arcona, and reared a Christian sanctuary upon the site. The natives generally, convinced by the successes of the adversary that their own divinities were powerless, now assented to the Gospel. The ecclesiastical supervision of the island was entrusted to a luminary of the Danish Church, the bishop Absalom of Roskild[8].

WENDISH CHURCH.

elevation to the see of Oldenburg.

Final triumph of the Gospel. Military conversion of Rügen.

---

[1] Helmold, *Chron.* c. 48—c. 55.

[2] It appears that this and other sees were re-erected contrary to the wishes of the duke (Schröckh, xxv. 263). He therefore claimed at least the right of granting investiture to the newly-chosen bishops, as was done by the German kings. To this Hartwig, proud of his primatial dignity, objected as disgraceful to the Church: but Vicelin at length consented.

[3] Helmold, *Ibid.* c. 71 sq.

[4] Mone, *Gesch. des Heidenthums*, I. 173 sq.

[5] Menacing their recently converted neighbours of Stettin and Julin 'quod sine respectu et consilio eorum idolis renunciassent.' *Ibid.* p. 184.

[6] See the account at length in Neander, VII. 32, 33.

[7] Helmold, *Ibid.* lib. II. c. 12, c. 13: Gebhardi, II. 9 sq.

[8] Rügen was thus annexed to his own diocese: Wiltsch, II. 95.

AMONG THE LIEFLANDERS AND OTHER NORTHERN TRIBES.

Livonian Church.

These tribes[1], who bordered mainly on the Baltic and extended northward to the Gulf of Finland, were most probably a branch of the Slavonic family, though largely intermingled, it is said, with others of the Indo-European stock, and also with the Ugrian race of Finns.

Labours of Canon Meinhard.

Livonia had been for some time visited by its northern neighbours, when an aged canon of the name of Meinhard[2] joined himself to certain merchants from the port of Lübeck, or Bremen, who were trading thither in 1186. He had been reared in one of Vicelin's foundations (Segeberg), and was truly anxious to extend a knowledge of the Christian faith. As soon as he had made some progress in the work, he was appointed to the see of Yxkull[3] (Ykeshola, on the Duna) by the German prelate Hartwig, the archbishop of Hamburg-Bremen, who had signalized himself in other missionary fields.

Relapse of his converts.

The hopes, however, which this step excited in the breast of Meinhard, were all blasted when he came into his diocese. The fickle multitude had speedily relapsed, and though he spared no pains to rescue them afresh from the seductions of polytheism, he died without attaining any permanent success (1196).

Succeeded by Berthold.

His post was filled by a Cistercian abbot, Berthold[4], out of Lower Saxony, who after trying more pacific measures, carried on the mission in a very different spirit. Aided by pope Innocent III.[5] he summoned a large army of crusaders from the neighbouring regions; and the terrified Livonians were at length compelled to acquiesce in his demands. He fell in battle: but as soon as the victorious army was withdrawn, the pagans rose afresh to wreak their ven-

---

[1] Respecting their mythology, see Mone, I. 66 sq.

[2] See the *Origines Livoniæ sacræ et civiles* (a *Chronicle* by Henry, a Livonian priest, written about 1226), ed. Francof. 1740, pp. 1—5: Gebhardi, *Gesch. von Liefland*, etc. pp. 314 sq.

[3] It was secured to the province of Hamburg by the grant of pope Clement III. (1188): Lappenberg, *Hamburg Urkundenbuch*, I. 248.

[4] *Origines Livoniæ* (as above, n. 2), pp. 10 sq.

[5] See his three *Letters* on this subject in Raynaldus, *Annal. Eccl.* ad an. 1199, § 38. He directs those who had vowed a pilgrimage to Rome, to substitute for it a crusade against the Livonians.

geance on the Christian body. Berthold was succeeded by a priest of Bremen, Albert (1198–1229), who also came into the diocese attended by a numerous army. He established[1] in 1201 the knightly *Order of the Sword* ('Ordo Fratrum militiæ Christi'), by whose chivalry the elements of paganism were gradually repressed. The centre of his operations was at Riga (built in 1200), to which place the see of Yxkull was transferred[2].

The zeal of Albert now impelled him to extend the Church in the adjoining countries. Esthland (or Esthonia) seems to have been visited already at the instance of pope Alexander III.[3] (1171), but the attempt, as far as we can judge, was fruitless. A fanatical campaign[4] of the Knights of the Sword, aided by the king of Denmark, Waldemar II., had a different issue (1211—1218). The province now succumbed and was evangelized at least in name[5]. The twofold nature of the influences exerted in this work gave rise to a vexatious feud between the Germans and the Danes, which terminated after many years in the ascendancy of the former. Similar disputes had previously grown up between the military Order and the bishops[6].

The conversion of Semgallen[7] followed in 1218, and that of Courland[8] in 1230, though in neither case are we at liberty to argue that the truth was planted very deeply[9].

ESTHONIAN CHURCH.

Suppression of the pagans by force.

Military conversion of Esthland:

Semgallen and Courland.

---

[1] Helyot, *Hist. des Ordres Relig. et Militaires*, III. 150 sq. Better influences were at work in Riga. Thus, archbishop Andreas of Lund, who had come over with the allied Danes in 1205, lectured during the whole winter on the Book of Psalms. Neander, VII. 53.

[2] Wiltsch, II. 82, n. 13. The church of Riga was soon raised to archiepiscopal rank, and a large province assigned it, by pope Alexander IV. Raynaldus, *Annal. Eccl.* ad an. 1255, § 64.

[3] Mansi, XXI. 936. A certain Fulco is there mentioned as the bishop of the Esthlanders.

[4] *Origines Livoniæ* (as above, p. 212, n. 2), pp. 122 sq.

[5] One bishopric was planted at Reval, a second (1224) at Dorpat, and a third at Pernau, finally transferred to the isle of Oesel. Wiltsch, II. 268. The see of Reval was of Danish origin; the German party planting theirs in the first instance at Leal, afterwards at Dorpat: cf. Schröckh, XXV. 304.

[6] *Origines Livoniæ*, pp. 47 sq. The pope at last decided in favour of the Knights. *Ibid.* p. 74.

[7] A bishopric was placed at Seelburg: Wiltsch, II. 268. The natives, however, soon relapsed into heathenism.

[8] Bishopric at Pilten. *Ibid.*

[9] The visit of William of Modena, as papal legate, in 1225, was salutary in appeasing strife and urging the necessity of Christian education.

AMONG THE PRUSSIANS.

Prussian Church.

Prussia, whose inhabitants were chiefly Slaves, with an admixture of the Lithuanian and Germanic blood, was now divided into several independent states, all marked, however, by inveterate hatred of the Gospel. In the time of Adalbert of Prague and Bruno, chaplain of Otho III., this fierce antipathy, embittered, we may judge, by their incessant struggle with the Christian Poles, had shewn itself in the assassination of the missionaries[1]; and as late as the opening of the thirteenth century, the fascinations of a simple and voluptuous paganism[2] retained their ancient power.

Labours of the monk Christian (d. 1241).

The first successful[3] preacher was a monk, named Christian, from a Pomeranian convent (Oliva) near Dantzic (circ. 1210). He was supported warmly by pope Innocent III.[4], and on a visit to the see of Rome (circ. 1214), in which he was attended by two Prussian chiefs, the first-fruits of his zeal, the pontiff made him bishop of the new community.

Reaction.

Ere long, however, the suspicions of the heathen (anti-Polish) party woke afresh, and drove them in their rage to take a signal vengeance on the Christians[5], and to scourge the neighbouring districts

---

Among other things he warned the German clergy, 'ne Teutonici gravaminis aliquod jugum importabile neophytorum humeris imponerent, sed jugum Domini leve ac suave, fideique semper docerent sacramenta.' See the account of his proceedings at length, in Gebhardi (as above), pp. 361 sq.

[1] See above, p. 115, n. 3.

[2] Mone, *Gesch. des Heiden.* I. 79 sq. Among other barbarous and bloody rites, it was the custom to destroy, or sell, the daughters of a family excepting one. On the antiquities of Prussia, see Hartknoch, *Alt und Neues Preussen*, Königsberg, 1684.

[3] He was preceded (in 1207) by a Polish abbot, Gottfried, and a monk, Philip, but the work appears to have been interrupted by the murder of the latter. There is, however, some confusion in the history at this point. See Schröckh, xxv. 314 sq. The original authority is Peter of Dusburg, who wrote his *Chronicon Prussiæ* about 1326. It is edited, with dissertations, by Hartknoch, Jenæ, 1679.

[4] He committed the supervision of the converts in the first place to the archbishop of Gnesen: Innocent III. *Epist.* lib. XIII. ep. 128. But the missionaries had another form of opposition to endure, arising from the jealousy of their own abbots. See Innocent's letter (1213) in their behalf. *Epist.* lib. xv. ep. 147.

[5] Pet. de Dusburg, *Chron. Pruss.* Pars II. c. 1 sq. Nearly three hun-

which belonged to Conrad, duke of Masovia[1]. Through his efforts, aided by the sanction of the pope, a body of Crusaders were attracted to the theatre of strife (**1219**). The 'Order of Knights-Brethren of Dobrin'[2], allied to those whom we have met already in Livonia, was now formed upon the model of the Templars; but as soon as they had proved unequal to the work of subjugating Prussia, the more powerful 'Order of Teutonic Knights' was introduced[3], upon the understanding that the conquered district should remain in their possession. Step by step, though frequently repelled, they won their way into the very heart of Prussia. In the course of these revolting wars, extending over fifty years (**1230—1283**), and waged in part with native pagans, and in part with Russians, Pomeranians[4], and other jealous states, the land was well-nigh spoiled of its inhabitants. A broken remnant[5], shielded in some measure by the intervention of the popes, were now induced to discontinue all the heathen rites, to recognize the claims of the Teutonic Order, and to welcome the instruction of the German priests. The dioceses[6] of Culm, Ermeland, Pomerania, and Samland, organized before the final conquest by Innocent IV.[7] (**1243**), were subdivided into three parts, of which two rendered homage to the Knights, and the remainder to the bishop,

PRUSSIAN CHURCH.

Crusades of the Knights-Brethren; and the Teutonic Knights.

The heathen finally subdued, 1283.

Ecclesiastical organization.

dred churches and chapels were destroyed, and many Christians put to death.

[1] It is clear from a spirited epistle of Innocent III. (lib. xv. ep. 148), that the authorities of Poland and Pomerania pressed hard upon the converts, and employed the Gospel chiefly as an organ for effecting the subjugation of the Prussians. Hence the reaction.

[2] *Chron. Pruss.* ibid. c. 4: Döllinger, III. 281, 282.

[3] *Ibid.* On the following events, see Hartknoch's *Fourteenth Dissertation* (as above, p. 214, n. 3,) and the various documents appended to his work; I. pp. 476 sq.

[4] The chief opposition came from this quarter; Svantepolk, the duke of Pomerania, being jealous of the military Order. He complained of their despotic conduct to the pope, who laboured to secure more favourable terms for the oppressed: see *Privilegium Pruthenis*, A.D. 1249 concessum, in Hartknoch, pp. 463 sq. Eventually, however, the Teutonic Knights were almost absolute in the ecclesiastical affairs. Döllinger, p. 284.

[5] Some few, however, would not yield, but found a sanctuary among their heathen neighbours of Lithuania. *Chron. Pruss.* Pars III. c. 81.

[6] Wiltsch, II. 270 sq., where an inquiry is made as to the subsequent distribution of the Prussian dioceses.

[7] Hartknoch, pp. 477, 478.

as their feudal lord. A multitude of churches and religious houses now sprang up on every side. The Prussian youths were sent for education to the German schools, especially to Magdeburg, and at the close of the present period the Teutonic influence was supreme.

§ 2. VICISSITUDES OF THE CHURCH IN OTHER REGIONS.

Nestorianism in Eastern Asia:

The Nestorian body, though its power was on the wane, continued[1] to unfurl the sacred banner of the cross, almost without a rival, among the tribes of Eastern Asia. We are told, indeed, that one of the Khans of Kerait, who bore the name of 'Prester-John,' despatched an embassy to Rome[2] in 1177, and that a leading member of it was there consecrated bishop. But in 1202[3] the kingdom of Kerait sank before the revolutionary arms of Chinghis-Khan, the founder of the great Mongolian dynasty; although a remnant of the tribe appears to have survived and to have cherished Christianity as late as 1246[4].

tolerated by the Mongols.

While hosts of Mongols poured into the steppes of Russia (1223), threatening to eradicate the growing Church, in north and south alike[5], and even to contract the limits of the German empire (1240), the Nestorian

[1] See above, pp. 128, 129. The residence of their patriarch was still Bagdad.
[2] The authorities for this account are exclusively English. The letter of pope Alexander III. (dated Sept. 27, 1177) is preserved in Benedict of Peterborough, I. 210, and Roger of Hoveden, II. 168; the address is 'Ad Johannem regem Indorum.'
[3] D'Herbelot, *Bibliothèque Orientale*, 'Carit ou Kerit,' p. 235.
[4] Döllinger, III. 287. It is even said (cf. Neander, VII. 65, 66) that Chinghis-Khan espoused the Christian daughter of Ung-Khan, the priest-king of the period.
[5] See the touching narrative of these incursions in Mouravieff, *Hist. of the Russ. Church*, pp. 42 sq. The centre of Russian Christianity, Kieff, after a bloody siege, was given up to fire and pillage; and the metropolitans transferred their residence first to Vladimir and then to Moscow, where they groaned for two centuries under the yoke of the Mongols. Cf. Neale's *Hist. of the Eastern Church*, Int. i. 56. One of the native princes, Daniel ('dux Russiæ'), supplicated the assistance of Pope Innocent IV., who sent a legate into Russia for the sake of negociating the admission of that country into the Latin Church; but Oriental influence baffled the attempt. Capefigue, II. 106.

missionary, as it seems, was still at liberty to propagate his creed, and sometimes very high in the favour of the Khan, whose sceptre quickly stretched across the whole of Persia, and the greater part of Central and of Eastern Asia.

EASTERN ASIA.

The incursions of the Mongols into Europe, joined with a report that some of them had shewn an interest in the Christian faith, excited Innocent IV. to send an embassy[1] among them in 1245. Soon after three Franciscan monks embarked upon a kindred mission into Tartary itself[2]. They found the Khan apparently disposed to tolerate the Gospel, and a number of Nestorian clergy at his court. But this and other hopes[3] of his conversion proved illusive. Actuated, as it seems, by a belief that it was necessary to propitiate the gods of foreign lands before he was allowed to conquer them, the Khan attended with an equal affability to the discourses of the Catholics, Nestorians, Buddhists, and Muhammedans, by all of whom he was solicited to cast his lot among them. In the end, when the posterity of Chinghis saw their arms victorious everywhere, they set on foot a composite religion[4],—the still thriving Lamaism,—as the religion of the state. The first Grand Lama was appointed under Kublai-Khan in 1260, for the eastern (or Chinese) division of the empire[5]. Chris-

Their incursions into Europe.

Negociations with a view to their conversion.

Their adoption of Lamaism.

---

[1] A report of their journey and negociation with the Mongolian general in Persia is given by Vincent of Beauvais (Bellovacensis), in his *Speculum Historiale*, lib. XXXI. c. 33 sq. The arrogance of the pope and the unskilfulness of his Dominican envoys only irritated the Mongolian.

[2] They were accompanied by an Italian, John de Plano Carpini, whose report is given as above. The fullest form of it appears in the Paris edition of 1838.

[3] An embassy of Louis IX. of France (in 1253) grew out of the report that Mangu-Khan, as well as some inferior princes, were disposed to join the Church. The leading envoy was a Franciscan, William de Rubruquis, whose report is in the *Relation des Voyages en Tartarie*, edited by Bergeron, Paris, 1634. He disparages the missionary labours of the Nestorians, and draws a gloomy picture of their own condition. This, however, should be taken 'cum grano salis.' His discussions with the various teachers of religion are most interesting. Neander (VII. 71 sq.) gives a sketch of them. See also Wuttke, *Gesch. des Heidenthums*, I. 215—218, Breslau, 1852.

[4] It was largely intermixed with Buddhism, or rather Buddhism formed the essence and substratum of it. See Schlosser's *Weltgeschichte*, Band. III. Th. II. Abth. I. p. 269: cf. M. Huc's *Voyages dans la Tartarie*, etc., in which its numerous points of resemblance to the mediæval Christianity may be at once discerned.

[5] In Persia (circ. 1258) Hulagu-Khan, whose queen was a Nestorian, favoured Christianity (Asseman, *Bibl. Orien.* tom. III. pt. II. pp. 103 sq.),

EASTERN ASIA.

tianity, however, even there was tolerated, and at times respected by the Khans.

Mission of John de Monte Corvino (d. 1330).

This feeling is apparent in the history of Marco Polo[1], a Venetian, who resided many years at the court of Kublai-Khan (1275—1293); and still more obviously in the reception given to a genuine missionary of the Latin Church, John de Monte Corvino[2], a Franciscan. After sojourning a while in Persia and India, he proceeded quite alone, in 1292, to China, where he preached, with some obstructions, in the city of the Khan, Cambalu (Pekin). He was joined in 1303 by Arnold, a Franciscan of Cologne. His chief opponents were Nestorians, who eventually secured a fresh ascendancy in China, counteracting all his labours. On the death of John (1330), aided though he was at length by other missionaries, every trace of the Latin influence rapidly decayed[3].

Extinction of the Latin influence in China. The Eastern Crusades.

A notice of the mighty movements, known as the Crusades, belongs more aptly to a future page: for much as they subserved the interest of the papacy, entangled the relations of the Greek and Latin Church, united nations and the parts of nations by one great idea, and modified in many ways the general spirit of the times, they wrought no lasting changes in the area of the Christian fold.

and so did many of his successors: but this circumstance aroused the hatred of the Muhammedans (who formed the great majority of the population), till at last the Christian Church was almost driven out of Persia. Neander, VII. 75, 76.

[1] His curious work, *De Regionibus Orientalibus*, written after his return to Europe, has been frequently printed.

[2] The original account of his missionary travels is in Wadding's *Annales Fratr. Minor.* tom. VI.: cf. the sketch in Neander, VII. 77 sq. He instituted schools: he translated the New Testament and Book of Psalms into the Tatar language: and one of his converts (formerly a Nestorian), who appears to have been descended from the 'priest-kings,' began to translate the whole Roman liturgy into the vernacular, but died prematurely (1299). In 1303, Clement V. elevated the Church of Pekin to the rank of an archbishopric. Wiltsch, II. 325. The Nestorians had already occupied the see (circ. 1282), and kept their hold till the beginning of the 16th century. *Ibid.* 366. Some interesting illustrations of the part taken by English sovereigns in promoting these missions may be found in Rymer's *Fœdera*, II. 17, 18, 37, &c.

[3] The next prelate, nominated by John XXII., never took possession of his diocese, probably on account of the change of dynasty by which the Catholics appear to have been expelled (1369). Asseman, *Bibl. Orient.* tom. III. pt. II. 516, 535.

The impulse they communicated to the nations of the west is further shewn by the attempts, in part abortive and in part successful, to eject the Moors from Africa and Spain[1]. Too often, however, the conversion of the unbeliever, in the proper meaning of the phrase, was but a secondary object. The enthusiastic Francis of Assisi[2] is one instance of the better class of preachers; a second is supplied in the eventful life of a distinguished scholar, Raymond Lull[3] (1236—1315). When he perceived how the Crusaders had in vain attempted to put down the Saracens by force of arms[4], he tried the temper of the apostolic weapons, and endeavoured to establish truth by means of argument and moral suasion. In the intervals between his missionary tours, directed chiefly to the Saracens and Jews of his native isle, Majorca, and the north of Africa[5], he hoped to elaborate an argumentative system ('Ars Generalis') by the help of which the claims of Christianity might be established in so cogent and complete a way, that every reasonable mind would yield its willing homage to the Lord[6]. He acted on these principles, and after eight-and-twenty years of unremitting toil, was stoned to death in the metropolis of the Muhammedans, at Bugia (Bejyah).

SPAIN AND NORTHERN AFRICA.

Others in Spain and Africa.

Better spirit manifested in Raymond Lull (d. 1315).

The fanaticism, which found expression in the violence of the Crusaders, still continued to abhor and persecute

Attempts to Christianize the Jews.

---

[1] Capefigue, II. 82, 83. The chief agents in this work were the Franciscans and Dominicans.

[2] See the account of his preaching to the Sultan of Egypt in 1219, in Jac. de Vitry's *Hist. Occid.* c. 32, and Neale's *East. Church*, II. 286.

[3] See Wadding's *Annal. Fratr. Minor.*, ad an. 1275, 1287, 1290, 1293, 1295, and (especially) 1315: cf. also a *Life* of him in the *Act. Sanct.* Jun. v. 661 sq. An edition of his very numerous works was published at Mentz in 1722.

[4] At first indeed he thought that arms might be of service in supporting his appeal (Neander, VII. 263): but subsequently he confessed that such a method was unworthy of the cause (*Ibid.* pp. 265, 266). One of his projects was to found missionary colleges, in which the students might be taught the languages of heathen countries, and at length (1311) the plan received the approbation of pope Clement V. and the Council of Vienne. Professors of Hebrew, Chaldee, and Arabic were in future to be supported at Rome, Paris, Oxford and Salamanca (*Ibid.* pp. 85, 95, 96).

[5] He travelled, on one occasion, into Armenia, with the hope of winning the natives over to the Latin Church.

[6] See his *Necessaria Demonstratio Articulorum Fidei*.

JEWS.

Their occasional success.

the Jews[1]. That wondrous people in the present period manifested a fresh stock of intellectual vigour, and so far as learning[2] reached were quite a match for their calumniators and oppressors. It is true that men existed here and there to raise a hand in their behalf[3]: and of this number few were more conspicuous than the better class of popes[4]. Whenever reasoning[5] was employed to draw them over to the Christian faith, their deep repugnance to the Godhead and the Incarnation of our blessed Lord, as well as to the many forms of creature-worship then prevailing in the Church, is strongly brought to light. Occasionally the attempt would prove successful, as we gather from the very interesting case of Hermann[6] of Cologne, who was converted at the middle of the twelfth century: but issues of this happy kind were most unquestionably rare.

[1] A full account of their condition at this period may be seen in Schröckh, xxv. 329 sq.

[2] Joseph Kimchi (circ. 1160), with his sons David and Moses, were distinguished as Biblical scholars (see list of their works in Fürst's *Biblioth. Judaica*, Leipzig, 1851). Rabbi Solomon Isaac (Rashi) also flourished at the close of the twelfth century. But the greatest genius whom their nation has produced, at least in Christian times, both as a free expositor of Holy Scripture and a speculative theologian, was Maimonides (Moses Ebn-Maimun), born at Cordova in 1131: see Fürst, *Ibid.* Th. II. pp. 290—313.

[3] *e.g.* St Bernard defended them from the onslaught of a savage monk, Rudolph, who, together with the cross, was preaching death to the Jews: Neander, VII. 101, and the Jewish *Chronicle* there cited.

[4] *Ibid.* pp. 102 sq., where many papal briefs are noticed, all protecting Jews and urging gentle measures in promoting their conversion. But Neander overlooks a multitude of other documents in which the popes and councils of the 13th century have handled the Jews more roughly: see Schröckh, xxv. 353 sq.

[5] *e.g.* Abbot Gislebert (of Westminster), *Disputatio Judæi cum Christiano de Fide Christiana*, in Anselm's *Works*, pp. 512—523, ed. Paris, 1721: Richard of St Victor, *De Emmanuele*, *Opp.* pp. 280—312, ed. Rothomagi, 1650. A more elaborate work is by a Spanish Dominican, Raymond Martini, of the 13th century. It is entitled *Pugio Fidei*, and directed first against Muhammedans, and next against Jews; edited by Carpzov, Leipzig, 1687.

[6] See his own narration of the process, appended to the *Pugio Fidei*, as above. He finally entered a convent of the Præmonstratensians at Kappenberg in Westphalia.

CHAPTER X.

CONSTITUTION AND GOVERNMENT OF THE CHRISTIAN CHURCH.

§ 1. *INTERNAL ORGANIZATION.*

REFERRING to a later page for some account of the encroachments now effected by the hierarchy in the province of the civil power, as well as for a sketch of the reactions they produced in England, Germany, and France, we shall at present notice only the internal constitution of the Church regarded as a spiritual and independent corporation.

In the western half of Christendom the pope, who formed its centre, was no more a simple president or primus, charged with the administration of ecclesiastical affairs according to the canons[1]. He had gradually possessed himself of the supreme authority: he was the irresponsible dictator of the Church, the only source of lawful jurisdiction, and *the* representative of Christ[2]. The claim which he put forward in the half-century from Innocent III. to Innocent IV. (1198—1243), though reach-

INTERNAL ORGANIZATION.

The culmination of the papal power.

---

[1] Cf. the language even of Boniface, p. 19, n. 8; and of Dunstan, p. 200, n. 1. In the present period individuals were not wanting to dispute the claim of popes, who promulgated *new* enactments of their own (*e.g.* Placidus of Nonantula, *De Honore Ecclesiæ*, in Pezii Thesaur. Anecdot. II. pt. II. pp. 75 sq., and especially Grosseteste of Lincoln, see below, p. 228): but their power of dispensing with the canons of the Church was almost everywhere allowed, in many cases 'ante factum.' See authorities at length in Gieseler, III. 162 sq. Among the few limitations to which this power was subjected is the case when any dispensation would be 'contra quatuor evangelia,' or 'contra præceptum Apostoli,' *i.e.* 'in iis quæ spectant ad articulos fidei.' John of Salisbury (ep. 198, ed. Giles) limits the papal power in the same manner.

[2] *e.g.* Innocent III. *Epist.* lib. I. ep. CCCXXVI.

INTERNAL ORGANIZATION.

ing to an almost præterhuman height[1], was very generally allowed. The metropolitans and other bishops, having lost their independence, were content to be esteemed his vassals, instruments, or vicars[2]. They were said to be appointed 'by the grace of God and of the apostolic see.' In other words, the scheme which had been advocated by the Pseudo-Isidore 'Decretals' was at length in active operation.

The influence of Gregory VII.

No one clung to this idea so intelligently or promoted its development so much as the indomitable Hildebrand[3], or Gregory VII. (**1073**). His leading principles are stated, both in reference to the Church and civil power, in certain propositions known as the *Dictatus Hildebrandini*[4]. Trained, while serving former pontiffs, in the art of government, he turned his wondrous energy and diplomatic skill to the immediate execution of the projects he had cherished from his youth. These were (1) the absolute ascendancy of papal power, and (2) the reformation of abuses, more especially of those which had been generated by the bishops and the clerics[5]. Hildebrand was seconded from first to

---

[1] The former pontiff, in a passage quoted with approbation by Capefigue (II. 61), styles himself 'citra Deum, *ultra hominem*,' and again, 'minor Deo, *major homine*.' Yet in cases where the popes surrendered any of these claims, their partisans contended (*e.g.* Döllinger, III. 339) that an unpalatable edict of the Roman see could not invalidate the acts of former synods. At the crisis here alluded to, the French bishops almost to a man ('universi pæne Franciæ episcopi') determined on the excommunication of the pope himself, if he abandoned any more of the hierarchical pretensions. See Gerhoh of Reichersberg, *De Corrupto Ecclesiæ Statu*, c. 22.

[2] See Innocent III. *Epist.* lib. I. epp. CCCCXCV, CCCCXCVI. The office of a bishop was regarded as a cession made by him of part of his own universal pastorship. In the *Canon Law* (Sexti Decret. lib. I. tit. II. c. i.) it is affirmed of the Roman pontiff; 'jura omnia in scrinio pectoris sui consetur habere.' The same spirit is betrayed in the absolute limitation of the name 'apostolic see' to the Church of Rome; thereby swallowing up the *other* 'sedes apostolicæ.'

[3] Above, pp. 140 sq.

[4] Bowden's *Life of Greg. VII.* II. 394. Mr Bowden (*Ibid.* II. 50, 51) argues that this series, consisting of twenty-seven propositions, ought not to be ascribed to Hildebrand himself; yet it is obvious that they have preserved, in a laconic shape, the principles on which his policy was uniformly based: cf. Neander, VII. 165.

[5] Above, p. 140. Gregory's earnestness on this point can hardly be questioned. Wedded as he doubtless was to the idea of carrying out the papal claims at any cost, and wanting therefore, as he showed himself, in truthfulness on more than one occasion, he was, notwithstanding, actuated by a firm belief that God had raised him up for moral ends, espe-

last by very many of the nobler spirits of the age[1], who trusted that a sovereign power, if wielded by the Roman pontiffs, might be turned into an agent for the moral exaltation of the Church. But in the Hildebrandine (or 'reforming') party there were many others who had been attracted chiefly by the democratic (or in some, it may be, the fanatic) spirit of the movement[2]. They were glad of an occasion for expressing their contempt of married clergymen, or for escaping altogether from domestic rule.

INTERNAL ORGANIZATION.

The policy of Hildebrand, on this and other questions, was adopted in the main by his successors, Victor III. (1086), Urban II. (1088), Paschal II. (1099), Gelasius II. (1118); but owing to the bitter conflicts with the German emperor as well as to the coexistence of an influential anti-pope, Clement III.[3] (1080—1100), their usurpations in the Church at large were somewhat counteracted. The two following pontiffs, Calixtus II. (1119) and Honorius II. (1124), maintained the Hildebrandine principles with almost uniform success, and in the reigns of Innocent II.[4] (1130), Cœlestine II. (1143), Lucius II. (1144), Eugenius III. (1145), Anastasius IV. (1153), Hadrian IV. (1154), Alexander III.[5] (1159), Lucius III. (1181), Urban III. (1185),

The series of popes.

cially for the repression of the worldly spirit which possessed the mass of the ecclesiastics (*e.g. Epist.* lib. I. ep. 9; Mansi, xx. 66); cf. Neander, VII. 116 sq.

[1] Neander, *Ibid.* 125 (note), 153.

[2] It is plain that Hildebrand always counted on the succour of the populace (cf. above, p. 146), and in his efforts to put down clerical marriages, as well as customs really exceptionable, he relied on what is called the force of 'public opinion,' which he lost no time in seeking to exasperate: see Neander, VII. 128, 135, 147: Döllinger, III. 318. This movement afterwards became unmanageable (Neander, *Ibid.* 202), and it seems that not a few of the later forms of misbelief (*e.g.* the invalidity of sacraments administered by unworthy clergymen) are traceable to the workings of the spirit which the Hildebrandine principles called up.

[3] On his death Theoderic was elected by the rival party, but soon afterwards shut up in a monastery. Albert (also called 'antipapa') followed in 1102, and Silvester IV. (or Maginulfus) in 1105. The last was deposed by Henry V. in 1111, when his dispute with Paschal II. had been adjusted for a time. See Jaffé, pp. 519—521. The antipope to Calixtus II. was Burdinus (Gregory VIII.), 1118—1121.

[4] He was opposed, however, first by Anacletus II. (1130—1138), and next by Victor IV. (1138); but as the schism did not grow out of political considerations, the dominion of the papacy was not much weakened by it. Innocent II. was supported by the almost papal influence of St Bernard, and the peace which he effected was consolidated at the council of Lateran (1139).

[5] Under this pontiff an important decree was made for obviating the

INTERNAL ORGANIZATION.

Decay of the papal grandeur.

Gregory VIII. (**1187**), Clement III. (**1187**), Cœlestine III. (**1191**), the papal claims, though not unfrequently contested at those points in which they trenched upon the civil jurisdiction, were, in sacred matters, still more generally allowed. With Innocent III.[1] (**1198**), the idea of the Roman pontiff as the organ and the representative of God in the administration of all sublunary things was carried, step by step, into the most extravagant results. He was, indeed, the second Hildebrand; but, owing to the circumstances of the age, he far exceeded every other pontiff in the grandeur of his conquests and the vigour of the grasp by which they were retained. Honorius III. (**1216**), Gregory IX. (**1227**), Cœlestine IV.[2] (**1241**), and Innocent IV. (**1243**), inherited his domineering spirit and perpetuated the efforts he had made in carrying out his theory of papal absolutism: but the tide (as we shall see hereafter) now began to turn, and at the close of the present period many of their worst pretensions, after calling up a spirited reaction, had been tacitly withdrawn. The following are the other members of the series, dating from the time of Innocent IV. to the important epoch, when their honours had begun to droop,

divisions which arose at the papal elections: Mansi, XXII. 217. Further regulations were introduced with the same object by Gregory X.: cf. Neander VII. 266. Alexander III. had to encounter a series of formidable rivals, Victor IV. (1159—1164), Paschal III. (1164—1168), Calixtus III. (1168—1178), Innocent III. or Landus Sitinus (1178—1180), backed by the imperial interest; but his triumph was secured by the exertions of men like our English primate, Becket, who appear to have carried with them the general feeling of the age.

[1] See Neander's remarks on his character and conduct, VII. 239 sq. Some of his very numerous *Letters* were edited by Baluze, in 2 vols. folio; and his *Works* are now printed in 4 vols. of Migne's *Patrologia*, Paris, 1855: cf. the able, but Romanizing work of Hurter, *Gesch. Papst Innocenz des Dritten*, Hamburg, 1834. The towering claims of Innocent and his successors were supported by the new school of canonists ('decretists,' afterwards 'decretalists,') which had sprung up especially at Bologna. About 1151, Gratian published his *Concordia Discordantium Canonum* [the *Decretum Gratiani*], in which he forced the older canons into harmony with the Pseudo-Isidore Decretals. As the papal edicts multiplied and superseded more and more the ancient regulations of the Church, a further compilation was required. It made its appearance in 1234, under the sanction of Gregory IX., in five books. A sixth ('Liber Sextus') was added by Boniface VIII. in 1298. See Böhmer's *Dissert.* in his edition of the *Corpus Juris Canonici*, Halæ, 1747.

[2] The papal chair, which he filled only a few days, continued vacant until June, 1243.

and when the papal chair itself was planted at Avignon¹—Alexander IV. (**1254**), Urban IV. (**1261**), Clement IV. (**1265**), Gregory X. (**1271**), Innocent V. (**1276**), Hadrian V. (**1276**), John XX. or XXI.² (**1276**), Nicholas III. (**1277**), Martin IV. (**1281**), Honorius IV. (**1285**), Nicholas IV.³ (**1288**), Cœlestine V.⁴ (**1294**), Boniface VIII. (**1294**), Benedict XI. (**1303**), Clement V. (**1305**).

INTERNAL ORGANIZATION.

The leading agents, or proconsuls, of the pope in the administration of his ever-widening empire, were the legates (or 'legati a latere'), whom he sent, invested with the fullest jurisdiction, into every quarter of the world. Officials of this class appeared occasionally in the time of Hincmar⁵: but their mission was regarded as intrusive, and excited many hostile feelings in the country whither they were bound⁶. The institution was how-

The vast influence of the papal legates.

---

¹ Another vacancy, of two years and nine months, occurred at his death.

² This was the title which the pope himself assumed (thereby, as it has been argued, counting Joan as a pope), although he was really the *twentieth* of the name.

³ The Roman see was vacant at his death for two years and three months.

⁴ Known as the 'hermit-pope:' see Döllinger, IV. 79, 80. He abdicated after a brief reign of three months.

⁵ Above, p. 137, n. 2.

⁶ Thus Chicheley, archbishop of Canterbury, writes at a still later period: 'Be inspection of lawes and cronicles was there never no legat a latere sent into no lond, and specially in to your rengme of Yngland, withowte grete and notable cause......And yit over that, he was tretyd with or he cam in to the lond, when he shold have exercise of his power, and how myche schold bee put in execution,' &c. *Vit. H. Chichele*, p. 129, Lond. 1699. In the year 1100, when the archbishop of Vienne came into England in this capacity he made no impression on the people, but departed 'a nemine pro legato susceptus, nec in aliquo legati officio functus.' Eadmer, ed. Selden, 1623, p. 58. William of Corbeuil, however, the archbishop of Canterbury, who had been sent to Rome, to complain of the intrusion of a legate into England, returned in 1126, the bearer of the very office against which the nation had protested (Gervas. Dorobern., in Twysden's *Script. X.*, col. 1663); being elevated to that office by Honorius II. (Wharton, *Ang. Sac.* I. 792.) The archbishop by accepting the office was enabled to exclude the interference of any other legate from Rome, whilst the pope, by commissioning the archbishop as legate, was enabled to regard all the proper jurisdiction of the metropolitanate as exercised under his own authorization. From the year 1195 to the reformation the archbishops of Canterbury were with scarcely an exception legates, legati nati, commissioned by the popes as a matter of course. The dislike of the English seems to have been directed rather against the Italian extortioners who as Cardinals appeared for a short time with special commission *a latere*.

M. A. Q

INTERNAL ORGANIZATION.

Appeals to Rome.

ever, an essential element of Hildebrandine despotism[1]: and while its operation here and there was salutary, or was tending to correct abuses[2] in some ill-conditioned province, it more frequently became an engine of extortion, and thus added to the scandals of the age. The constant intermeddling of the popes in other churches, by the agency of roving legates, indicated more and more the worldly spirit which possessed them, notwithstanding all their affectation of peculiar purity and all their projects of reform. The 'curia' (or the court) of Rome[3] was now the recognized expression; and no object lay so near the heart of him who bore the legatine authority[4], as the advancement of its temporal interests in opposition to the crown and every species of domestic rule.

The same desire to elevate and to enrich the papacy,

---

[1] *e.g.* see Gregory's *Epist.* to the duke of Bohemia: Mansi, xx. 73. He exhorted the civil authorities to compel the acquiescence of Jaromir, the contumacious bishop of Prague, 'usque ad interniciem.' According to the *Dictatus Hildebrand.*, § 4, the legate was to take precedence of all bishops.

[2] St Bernard's ideal of a legate will be found in the *De Consideratione ad Eugenium*, lib. iv. c. 4. His picture was, however, realized too seldom: 'Nonne alterius sæculi res est, redisse legatum de terra auri sine auro? transisse per terram argenti et argentum nescisse?' c. 5. On the general duties of the legate and his influence in promoting the consolidation of the papacy, see Planck, iv. pt. ii. 639 sq.

[3] 'Neque enim vel hoc ipsum carere macula videtur, quod nunc dicitur *curia Romana* quæ antehac dicebatur *ecclesia Romana.*' Gerhoh of Reichersberg, *De Corrupto Ecclesiæ Statu*, Præfat. (seu *Epist. ad Henricum Card.*) § 1, *Opp.* II. 9, ed. Migne.

[4] The legates constantly urged the right of the pope to dispose of vacant benefices, and even bishoprics. Planck, *ubi sup.* pp. 713 sq. At first he *recommended* individuals, by way of 'petition;' but in the 13th century the 'preces' were changed into 'mandata;' and he finally insisted on the promotion of his favourites (sometimes boys, and chiefly absentees) in the most peremptory manner, by an edict 'non obstante.' It was a case of this kind (1252) which stirred the indignation of Grosseteste, bishop of Lincoln: see the account in Matthew Paris (ed. 1684), p. 740; cf. pp. 749 sq. A former pope (Honorius III.) in 1226 (Matthew Paris, p. 276) had been constrained to make the most humiliating confession by his legate, Otho: 'Idem papa allegavit scandalum sanctæ Romanæ ecclesiæ et opprobrium vetustissimum, notam scilicet concupiscentiæ, quæ radix dicitur omnium malorum: et in hoc præcipue, quod nullus potest aliquod negotium in Romana curia expedire nisi cum magna effusione pecuniæ et donorum exhibitione,' etc.: cf. John of Salisbury's *Policraticus*, lib. v. c. 16. An exact account of the steps by which papal influence was introduced into English church patronage will be found in Bishop Forbes's *Explanation of the 39 Articles*, II. 749, Oxford, 1868.

though blended in some cases with a wish to patronize the feeble and to shelter the oppressed, is seen in a requirement now extended in all quarters, that appeals, instead of being settled in the courts at home, should pass, almost indiscriminately¹, to the Roman court, as the ultimate tribunal of the West. Attempts², indeed, were made (occasionally by the popes³ themselves) to limit this unprincipled recourse to foreign jurisdiction: but the practice, notwithstanding such impulsive acts of opposition, kept its hold on every side, especially in all the newly-planted churches.

Effect of papal absolutism on episcopacy.

The development of papal absolutism, though it tended to protect the bishops from the violence of feudal lords, and even to exempt them altogether from the civil jurisdiction, swallowed up the most important of their rights. The metropolitans, in cases where they did not also fill the post of legate, were compelled to yield obedience to the papal nominee⁴, though he might often be a priest and nothing more. The vows of servitude imposed on them at the reception of the pallium⁵ were exacted also

---

¹ See St Bernard's remarks, *Ad Eugenium*, lib. III. c. 2. Innocent III., a shrewd administrator, checked the excessive frequency of appeals, on the ground that numbers would avail themselves of this privilege merely to buy off the execution of the laws: *e.g.* Concil. Lateran. (1215) c. 7. He enjoined that the sentence of provincial councils should take immediate effect, and that no appeal should lie to Rome unless the forms of law had been exceeded.

² In England there was always a peculiar jealousy on the subject of appeals and when this feeling was aroused in 1164, provision was distinctly made in the 'Constitutions of Clarendon,' that all controversies whatever should be settled in the home-courts: Matthew Paris, p. 84 (from Roger of Wendover, *Flores Histor.* II. 300: ed. E. H. S. 1841). The prelates and others in like manner had required a pledge from Anselm, ' quod nunquam amplius sedem Sancti Petri, vel ejus vicarium, pro quavis quæ tibi queat ingeri causa appelles.' Eadmer, p. 39.

³ See n. 1.

⁴ See above, p. 225, n. 6. The English were extremely scandalised when John of Crema (1125), a cardinal *priest*, assumed these novel powers: Gervase of Canterbury (Dorobern.), ed. Twysden, col. 1663. And we may gather from the following passage of a letter addressed to Gregory VII., that many bishops viewed him as the enemy of all authority except the papal: '*Sublata*, quantum in te fuit, *omni potestate ab episcopis*, quæ eis Divinitus per gratiam Spiritus Sancti collata esse dinoscitur, dum nemo jam alicui episcopus aut presbyter est, nisi qui hoc indignissima assentatione a fastu tuo emendicavit;' in Eccard's *Script. Rer. Germanic.* II. 172.

⁵ Above, p. 141.

INTERNAL ORGANIZATION.

from the other bishops[1], who, in order to secure the friendship of the pope, betook themselves to Rome, and sued for confirmation at his hands. The pride, extortion, and untruthfulness of many of the pontiffs stirred them, it is true, at times into the posture of resistance, and a man like Robert Grosseteste[2] did not hesitate to warn the pope himself, that by persisting in extravagant demands, the Roman Church was likely to become the author of apostasy and open schism. Yet, generally, we find that a belief in the transcendant honours of the Roman see retained the western bishops in their old connexion with it. Galling as they felt the bondage, they had not the heart to shake it off.

Romanizing spirit of the monks.

The stoutest advocates of papal usurpation were the members of religious orders. Gifted with a very large amount of the intelligence, the property[3], the earnestness, and the enthusiasm of the age, they acted as the pope's militia[4], and became in troublous times the pillars of his throne. On this account he loaded them with favours[5].

---

[1] See Neander, VII. 276, 277: Döllinger, III. 332. The protestantism of Matthew Paris breaks out afresh at this indignity, when it was urged more pointedly in 1257. He calls the papal edict 'Statutum Romæ cruentissimum, quo oportet quemlibet electum personaliter transalpinare, et in suam læsionem, imo eversionem, Romanorum loculos imprægnare:' p. 820.

[2] 'Absit, autem, absit, quod hæc sacratissima sedes, et in ea præsidentes, quibus communiter et in omnibus mandatis suis et præceptis obtemperatur, præcipiendo quicquam Christi præceptis et voluntati contrarium, sint causa veræ discessionis.' See the whole of this startling and prophetic Sermon in the *Opuscula R. Grosseteste*, in Brown's *Fasciculus*, II. 255. There is a copious *Life of Grosseteste*, by Pegge; his letters have been published in the *Chronicles and Memorials*, edited by Mr Luard, 1861.

[3] Their property was very much augmented at the time of the Crusades by mortgages and easy purchase from the owners, who were bent on visiting the Holy Land. Planck, IV. pt. II, 345 sq. Others also, to escape oppression, held their lands feudally from the religious houses and the clergy.

[4] For this reason they incurred the bitter hatred of the anti-Hildebrandine school, who called them 'Pharisees' and 'Obscurantes' (Neander, VII. 133, 134). When the Church was oscillating between Alexander III. and the anti-pope (Victor), the Carthusians and Cistercians warmly took the side of the former, and secured his triumph. See *Life of Bishop Anthelm* in the *Act. Sanct.* Jun. v. c. 3.

[5] *e.g.* the abbot was allowed to wear the insignia of the bishop, sandals, mitre, and crosier; and exemptions (see above, p. 148, n. 1) were now multiplied in every province, as a glance at Jaffé's *Regesta Pontific. Roman.* will abundantly shew. The nature of these privileges

Many of the elder Benedictines had departed from the strictness of their rule, and in this downward course they were now followed by the kindred monks of Clugny: but a number of fresh orders started up amid the animation of the Hildebrandine period, anxious to redeem the honour of monasticism, and even to surpass the ancient discipline. Of these the order of Carthusians, founded by Bruno[1] of Cologne (**1084**), at the Chartreuse, near Grenoble, proved themselves the most unworldly and austere. They fall into the class of anchorets, but like the Benedictines they devoted many of their leisure hours to literary occupations[2]. Other confraternities[3] appeared; but none of them were so successful as the order of the Cistercians (monks of Cîteaux near Dijon), who endeavoured to revert in every feature of their system to the model of St Benedict. The founder[4], Robert, having vainly sought for peace and satisfaction in the life of a recluse, established his new convent in **1098**. Its greatest

Rise of the Carthusians, **1084.**

Rise of the Cistercians, **1098.**

---

may be gathered from an epistle of Urban II. (1092) in Mansi, xx. 652. Complaints respecting them were constantly addressed to the succeeding popes: *e.g.* that of the archbishop of Canterbury among the *Epist.* of Peter of Blois (Blesensis), ep. 68; and St Bernard, *Ad Eugenium*, lib. III. c. 4.

[1] See Mabillon, *Act. Sanct. Ord. Bened.* VI. pt. II. 52 sq.: *Annales*, v. 202 sq. Many of the later legends respecting Bruno are purely mythical. The order of the Carmelites founded in Palestine about 1156 was transplanted into the West during the following century and assimilated to the other orders of Friars. They grew up into a somewhat numerous body. See Holstein's *Codex Regular.* III. 18 sq., and Fleury, *Hist. Eccl.* liv. LXXVI. § 55.

[2] Labbe has published their *Institutiones* in his *Bibliotheca*, I. 638. sq.: cf. Neander, VII. 368.

[3] *e.g.* The *Ordo Grandimontensis* (of Grammont) founded about 1070 (see Life of the founder, Stephen, in Martène and Durand's *Ampliss. Collectio*, VI. 1050 sq.; Mabillon's *Annales*, v. 65 sq.): the *Ordo Fontis-Ebraldi* (of Fontevraud), founded in 1094 (Mabillon's *Annal.* v. 314 sq.). The *Order of St Anthony*, founded by Gaston in 1095, attended on the sick, especially the leprous (*Act. Sanct.* Jan. II. 160 sq.): the *Trinitarians* ('Fratres Domus Sanctæ Trinitatis'), founded by John de Matha and Felix de Valois (1198), endeavoured to procure the redemption of Christians who had fallen into the hands of the infidels. See Fleury, liv. LXXV. § 9.

[4] See Mabillon, as above, v. 219, 393 sq.; Manrique, *Annales Cistercienses*, Lugd. 1642; and Holstein, *Codex*, II. 386 sq. Among the other features of the institute we notice a peculiar reverence for episcopal authority: see the papal confirmation of their rules (1119) in Manrique, I. 115.

INTERNAL ORGANIZATION.

Influence of St Bernard.

luminary was St Bernard¹ (1113—1153), who, after spending a short time in the parent institution, planted the more famous monastery of Clairvaux (Clara Vallis), in the diocese of Langres. Aided by the influence of his name and writings, the Cistercian order rapidly diffused itself in every part of Europe², and became ere long the special favourite of the popes³. It formed, indeed, a healthy contrast to the general licence of the age, as well as to the self-indulgence and hypocrisy of many of its cœnobitic rivals⁴.

Monastic orders ill adapted to the times.

But however active and consistent they might be, these orders were imperfectly adapted to the wants of the thirteenth century. As men who had renounced the business of this world, to make themselves another in the cloisters where they lived and died, they kept too far aloof from secular concerns, and even where they had been most assiduous in the duties of their convent, their attachment to it often indisposed them to stand forward and do battle with the numerous sects that threatened to subvert the empire of their patron. Something ruder and more practical, less wedded to peculiar spots and less entangled by superfluous property, was needed if the Church were to retain its rigid and monarchic form⁵. The want was made peculiarly apparent when the Albigenses had begun to lay unwonted stress on their own poverty, and to decry the self-indulgence of the monks.

The rise of the Franciscans, 1207.

At this conjuncture rose the two illustrious orders known as mendicant, (1) the Minors or Franciscans,

---

¹ See Neander's *Life* of him. There is an English Life of Bernard by J. C. Morison. London, 1864.

² At the death of Bernard (1153) he left behind him one hundred and sixty monasteries, which had been formed by monks from Clairvaux.

³ *e.g.* Innocent III. and the council of Lateran (1215), c. 12, held it up as a model for all others.

⁴ One of these was the order of Clugny, presided over (1122—1156) by Peter the Venerable, who, though anxious to promote the reformation of his house, resented the attack which had been made on it by some of the Cistercians. For an account of his friendly controversy with Bernard, see Maitland's *Dark Ages*, pp. 423 sq. There are traces of the controversy in the poem *De Clarevallensibus et Cluniacensibus*, among those attributed to Walter Mapes, ed. Wright, pp. 237 sq.

⁵ Innocent III. seems to have felt this: for, notwithstanding his desire to check the multiplication of fresh orders of monks (*Concil. Lateran.* 1215, c. 13, 'ne quis de cætero novam religionem inveniat'), he could not resist the offers now held out by such an army of auxiliaries.

(2) the Preachers or Dominicans, both destined for two centuries to play a leading part in all the fortunes of the Church. The former sprang from the enthusiasm of Francis of Assisi[1] (1182—1226). Desirous of reverting to a holier state of things (1207), he taught the duty of renouncing every kind of worldly goods[2], and by a strain of spirit-searching, though untutored, eloquence attracted many thousands to his side. The pope[3] at first looked down upon this novel movement, but soon afterwards confirmed the rule of the Franciscans, and indeed became their warmest friend. By founding what was termed an 'order of penitence[4]' (the third estate of Friars), they were able to embrace in their fraternity a number of the working classes, who, while pledged to do the bidding of the pope and to observe the general regulations of the institute, were not restricted by the vow of celibacy nor compelled to take their leave entirely of the world.

INTERNAL ORGANIZATION.

Their alliance with the Pope.

The stricter spirits of this school could not, however, be so easily confined within the limits which their chief was anxious to prescribe. They followed out their principle of sacred communism, or evangelical perfection, to its

The aberrations of an extreme party.

---

[1] See the *Life* of him by Thomas of Celano, his companion (in *Act. Sanct.* Octob. II. 683 sq.); another, by Bonaventura, a Franciscan (*Ibid.* 742 sq.): cf. Chavin de Malan, *L'Histoire de S. François d'Assise*, Paris, 1845; Helyot, *Hist. des Ordres*, etc., tom. VII. The great authority on the Franciscan Order generally is Wadding's *Annales Minorum*, Romæ, 1731—1741. Cf. Pref. to *Monumenta Franciscana*, ed. Brewer, 1858, in the *Chronicles, &c. of Great Britain*. We find the germs of it in an early sect of Euchites, who, from a desire to reach the summit of ascetic holiness, renounced all kinds of property and common modes of life. Neander, III. 342.

[2] In the fashion of the age he spoke of Poverty as his bride and the Franciscan order as their offspring. Before ten years had elapsed, five thousand mendicants assembled at Assisi to hold the second general chapter of their order. Sir J. Stephen's *Essays*, I. 121, 122. The *Order of St Clara* ('Ordo dominarum pauperum') was animated by the same spirit, and adopted the Franciscan rules: Holstein's *Codex*, III. 34 sq.: Helyot, VII. 182 sq. On the stigmatization of St Francis, and the impious extravagances to which it led, see a temperate article in the *Revue des deux Mondes*, Tome VIII. pp. 459 sq.

[3] Innocent III., after hesitating a while, extended to them a cordial, but unwritten, approbation (1209). In 1223, the order was formally adopted by Honorius III.: see Holstein, III. 30 sq. A pledge of absolute obedience to the pope is contained in the first chapter. Nicholas IV. was so ardently attached to them that he enjoined the use of their service-books on the whole Church. Capefigue, II. 180.

[4] Holstein, III. 39 sq.: Helyot, VII. 216 sq.: cf. Sir J. Stephen's remarks on this supplemental institute, I. 127, 128.

INTERNAL ORGANIZATION.

most obnoxious length, and even ventured to affirm that Christ and the original Apostles had nothing of their own. A quarrel was now opened, in the course of which the rigorous faction[1] ('Spirituales' they were called), deriving their ideas[2] very mainly from one-sided views of the Apocalypse, commenced a series of attacks upon the members of the hierarchy and the secularizing spirit of the age. A party of these malcontents were drafted off at length into a fresh community, entitled the Cœlestine-Hermits[3] (**1294**), but in the end they seem to have entirely separated from the Church, and to have been absorbed into the sect of the 'Fratricelli[4],' where, indeed, they underwent a bitter persecution.

The rise of the Dominicans, **1215**.

The twin-order, that of the Dominicans or 'Preachers,' took its rise in **1215** at Toulouse. Its founder was the canon Dominic[5] (b. **1170**), a native of Castile, although the plan was due rather to his bishop Diego (Didacus)

---

[1] They professed to be adhering literally to the will of their founder; but the popes, especially Greg. IX. (1231) and Innocent IV. (1245), took the other (or the laxer) side: see their bulls in Roderic's *Nova Collectio Privilegiorum*, etc., ed. Antverp. 1623, pp. 7, 13.

[2] These may be gathered from a production called the *Introductorius in Evangelium Æternum*, which appeared at Paris in 1254. The subject is exhausted by Gieseler, III. 251 sq.; and Neander, VIII. 369 sq. When Nicholas III. (1279) explained the rule of St Francis still more laxly, the 'spirituales' grew still more indignant. They were headed by the friar John Peter de Oliva, of whose *Postilla super Apocalypsi*, extracts are preserved in Baluze and Mansi, *Miscell.* II. 258 sq. In commenting on Apoc. xvii., he has the following passage: 'Nota quod hæc mulier stat hic pro Romana gente et imperio, tam prout fuit quondam in statu paganismi, quam prout *postmodum fuit in fide Christi, multis tamen criminibus cum hoc mundo fornicata*,' etc.

[3] So called from pope Cœlestine V., their patron: Helyot, VII. 45. They were, however, persecuted by the rest of the Franciscans (*e. g.* Wadding, ad an. 1302, §§ 7, 8).

[4] See Capefigue, II. 147, 148. Among their supporters may be ranked Ubertinus de Casali, a pupil of the Franciscan Oliva above mentioned, n. 2: see the *Articuli Probationum contra fratrem Ubertinum de Casali inductarum*, and his reply before John XXII., in Baluze and Mansi, *Miscell.* II. 276 sq. One charge brought against him is for saying 'quod a tempore Cœlestini papæ non fuit in Ecclesia *papa verus*.'

[5] The oldest *Life* of Dominic is by his successor Jordanus, printed, with others, in the *Act. Sanct.* August. I. 545 sq. For the *Constitutions* of the Order, see Holstein's *Codex*, IV. 10 sq. At the suggestion of Innocent III., the basis of the rule of Dominic was borrowed from the Augustinian: and soon after, at a general chapter-meeting (1220), the principles of Francis of Assisi were adopted, in so far as they abjured all property and income. *Vit. S. Dominici* (by Jordanus), c. 4.

of Osma, who, while journeying in the south of France, had noticed with concern that anti-papal and heretical opinions were most rife, and threatened to disturb all orders of society. His object, therefore, was, in concert with the prelates of the district, to refute the arguments adduced by the heresiarchs, to emulate their poverty, and to win their followers back to the communion of the Church. In carrying out this undertaking, Dominic had been distinguished from the first, and when its author died (circ. 1207) he still continued, with a few of his companions, in the same sphere of duty. In 1209 the misbelieving province of Languedoc was desolated by the earliest of the Albigensian crusades[1]. The leaders of that savage movement found a spy and coadjutor in the overzealous missionary; and soon after he began to organize and head the larger confraternity, whose foremost object was the spiritual benefit[2] of others and the vindication of the Church. Accompanied by the notorious Foulques[3] (or Fulco), bishop of Toulouse, he laid his project at the feet of the sovereign pontiff in an hour when Rome might well have trembled for its empire in the south of France (1215), and readily procured the papal sanction. In the following year the institute was solemnly confirmed[4] by Honorius III. It soon attracted many able and devoted members, and diffused itself on every side.

Though parted from each other now and then by mutual jealousies[5], the Minorites and Preachers commonly proceeded hand in hand[6], particularly in resisting the attacks which they provoked, not only from the clergy and

INTERNAL ORGANIZATION.

Its connexion with the Albigensian crusades.

Controversy between the Mendicants and the Universities.

---

[1] See below, 'State of Religious Doctrine,' § *Sects*.

[2] ...'studium nostrum ad hoc debet principaliter intendere ut proximorum animabus possimus utiles esse.' *Constit.* Prol. c. 3.

[3] Cf. Sir J. Stephen's *Lect. on the Hist. of France*, I. 221, ed. 1851.

[4] The bull of confirmation is prefixed to the *Constitutions* of the order, as above, p. 232, n. 5. According to the pope's idea the Dominicans were to become 'pugiles fidei et vera mundi lumina.'

[5] See the graphic picture of Matthew Paris, *Hist. Major*, A.D. 1243, p. 540. They afterwards contended still more sharply touching the immaculate conception of the Virgin, the Franciscans taking the positive, the Dominicans the negative. Klee, *Hist. of Christ. Dogmas* (German), pt. II. c. iii. § 25.

[6] *e.g.* the generals of the two orders issued a number of caveats in 1255, with a view to cement or re-establish friendly relations. Wadding's *Annal. Minor.* ad an. 1255, § 12.

INTERNAL ORGANIZATION.

monastic orders[1], but from nearly all the Universities. Presuming on their popularity, their merits[2], and the strong protection of the Roman court[3], they thrust themselves into the professorial chairs, and not unfrequently eclipsed all other doctors[4]. Paris was at present the chief seat of European learning, and in it especially (1251), the Mendicants, although in favour with the king, had to encounter a determined opposition[5]. For a while they were discouraged by a bull of Innocent IV.[6], who saw the inroads they were making on the constitution of the Church, and was accordingly induced at length to take the part of the University; but on his death (1254) they found an ardent champion in pope Alexander IV.[7] His influence and the writings of the more distinguished members of their body (such as Bonaventura[8] and Aquinas*) aided

[1] *e.g.* Matthew Paris, A.D. 1243, p. 541; A.D. 1247, p. 630. He was himself a Benedictine, and implacable in his hostility to the new race of teachers.

[2] These must originally have been very considerable, for besides their zeal in missionary labour, they conciliated the good opinion of a class of men like Grosseteste, bishop of Lincoln, who employed them in his diocese. He defended them against the opposition of his clergy, and even charged the latter through the archdeacon 'ad inducendum efficaciter populum ut Fratrum utriusque Ordinis prædicationes devote et attente audiat,' etc.: Brown's *Fascic.* II. 382. He afterwards bequeathed his library to the Franciscans at Oxford, among whom the famous Roger Bacon was educated (Warton, *Eng. Poetry*, II. 89, ed. 1840): though Matthew Paris writes that on his death-bed he complained that they had disappointed his expectations, and had begun to degenerate most grievously: *Hist. Maj.*, A.D. 1253, p. 752.

[3] *e. g.* Gregory IX. (1237) begins a grant of privileges in the following terms: 'Quoniam abundavit iniquitas, et refriguit charitas plurimorum, ecce ordinem dilectorum filiorum fratrum Prædicatorum Dominus suscitavit,' etc., in Matth. Paris, A.D. 1246, p. 607. The popes claimed the right of sending Friars anywhere without the acquiescence of the bishops or the clergy.

[4] Most of the theological professors in the University of Naples, founded 1220, were chosen from the Mendicants. Their first establishment in England was at Oxford, 1221, when, for some time, they produced the leading scholars of the age. Warton, as above, pp. 88, 89.

[5] See Bulæus (Du Boulay), *Hist. Univers. Paris.* III. 240 sq.; Capefigue, II. 167 sq. The latter is a warm apologist of the Friars. Their most vigorous opponent at the time was William de Sancto Amore, a Parisian doctor of divinity, who composed his treatise *De Periculis Novissimorum Temporum*, in 1255. It is printed (as two Sermons) in Brown's *Fasciculus*, II. 43—54. The author was condemned by Alexander IV., but reconciled to Clement IV.

[6] Bulæus, *Ibid.* 270 sq.: cf. Neander, VII. 392.

[7] Bulæus, 273. In this bull he exempts them from the jurisdiction of the bishops and parish priests.

[8] He was general of the Minorites, and often argued for them on the

them in bearing down resistance, and in virtually supplanting for a time the ordinary teachers of the Church.

The Mendicants, as we have seen already, fostered in their bosom many germs of misbelief. In this particular they seem to have resembled the still older groups of Beguins or Beghards[1], who finally took refuge (**1290**) in the third order of the Franciscans[2]. They were chiefly females ('Beguinæ') in the earlier stages of their history, but, subsequently, when the number of them had prodigiously increased[3], the principle on which they had associated was borrowed (circ. **1220**) by the other sex[4] ('Beguini'). They were ridiculed[5] as 'pietists' (boni homines), and in the end appear to have adopted most of the opinions held by the extreme or Apocalyptic school of the Franciscans, so that 'Beguin' often was synonymous with heretic.

Another wing of the great army which the Christians of the Middle Age employed for their defence and the consolidation of the papal empire were the Military Orders. Their triumphant struggle with the heathen of the north of Europe has been mentioned on a former page[6]. It was their leading object to combine the rules of chivalry and knighthood with monastic discipline, which they derived, to some extent, from the Cistercian institutions.

The *Knights Templars*[7] ('Fratres Militiæ Templi') were

---

plea of necessity, alleging that the ordinary ecclesiastics were so corrupt as to neglect all their sacred duties: see *e. g.* his *Liber de Paupertate Christi contra Magist. Gulielmum*, etc.

* See his *Opuscul.* XIX., *contra Impugnantes Dei cultum et religionem.*

[1] See Mosheim, *De Beghardis et Beguinabus Commentarius*, passim. They seem to have existed as early as the eleventh century in Flanders. The name (see Ducange, *sub voc.*) appears to have been extended to all kinds of female associations ('collegia') where the secular and monastic life were partially combined. The inmates ('canonissæ') could leave the establishment and marry.

[2] Helyot, VII. 251.

[3] Matthew Paris (A.D. 1250, p. 696) speaks of the German 'Beguinæ' as an 'innumerabilis multitudo.'

[4] Mosheim, as above, p. 168.

[5] See Ducange, under 'Papelardus.'

[6] pp. 213, 215.

[7] See, on their general history, *L'Art de vérifier les Dates*, I. 512 sq., and the *Hist. Crit. et Apologet. des Chevaliers du Temple*, Paris, 1789. Their *Regula* is printed in Holstein, II. 429 sq.; and in Mansi, XXI. 359 sq.

INTERNAL ORGANIZATION.

founded at Jerusalem (**1119**), and through the powerful advocacy of St Bernard[1] the idea which they attempted to embody won the sanction of the western prelates in the synod of Troyes[2] (Jan. **13, 1128**). The order soon extended into every part of Europe, where it was most liberally endowed. Amid the stirring incidents of the crusades, the Templars had abundant opportunity for justifying the discernment of their patrons. On the fall of Acre in **1291**, they could maintain the Christian cause no longer, and retreated to their rich domains in Cyprus: but suspicions[3] of their orthodoxy which had once been irreproachable were now quite current in the west. A long and shameful controversy ended in the dissolution of the order[4] at Vienne (March **22, 1312**).

The dissolution of the Order.

Their property was all sequestrated and in part transferred[5] to what are known as the *Knights Hospitallers*[6], organized as early as **1048**, to wait on the sick pilgrims in the hospital of St John, at Jerusalem, but not converted into a military order till the twelfth century[7]. They also were ejected from the Holy Land with the last army of

The Knights Hospitallers.

---

[1] He wrote his *Exhortatio ad Milites Templi* at the request of the Grand-master, Hugh des Payens. See also his *Tract. de Nova Militia*.

[2] Concil. Trecense: Mansi, xxi. 357.

[3] The charges brought against them may be classed as follows: (1) Systematic denial of Christ on their admission into the order, accompanied with spitting or trampling on the cross. (2) Heretical opinions concerning the sacraments. (3) Reception of absolution from masters and preceptors, although laymen. (4) Debauchery. (5) Idolatry. (6) General secrecy of practice. See *English Review*, Vol. I. p. 13.

[4] The Templars were not allowed to speak in their own defence, and all the English, Spanish, German and some other prelates were accordingly resolved to take no part in their condemnation. This was the work of the French king Philip the Fair and his creature, pope Clement V., who also carried off a portion of the spoil, by levying fines on the transfer of the property. The Grand-master and others were burnt by the arbitrary act of Philip.

[5] See the remarkable statute *De Terris Templariorum*, 17 Edw. II. st. III. The 'Temple' of London was given, by some private arrangement, to the earl of Pembroke (whose widow founded Pembroke College, Cambridge), but afterwards passed into the hands of the Hospitallers, who leased it to the students of the laws of England.

[6] Helyot, III. 74 sq.; Vertot's *Hist. des Chevaliers Hospitaliers*, etc., Paris, 1726.

[7] The Rule given to the order by Raymond du Puy (1118), in Holstein, II. 445 sq., is silent as to their military duties: but in the same year they performed a prodigy of valour. Helyot, p. 78. They were taken under the special protection of Pope Innocent II., in 1187: Bréquigny, *Table Chronol. des Diplomes*, etc., III. 4, Paris, 1769.

Crusaders, but continued to exist for many centuries. Their chief asylum was at Rhodes (1309), and finally at Malta (1530). *[INTERNAL ORGANIZATION.]*

A connecting link between the rest of the religious orders and the seculars, or 'working clergy,' is supplied by the canons regular of St Augustine whose institution, the result of the failure of all attempts to reform the old secular canons, coincides in date with the opening of this period[1]. Another order of a similar kind was that of the Præmonstratensians (canons of Prémonstré), who sprang up in the diocese of Laon, in **1119**. Their founder, Norbert[2], was himself a secular, but on awakening to a deeper sense of his vocation, he resolved to organize an institution for the better training of ecclesiastics[3]. With this object he endeavoured to unite the cure of souls and a conventual mode of life. *[The order of Præmonstratensian canons.]*

The canons secular, in pursuance of their ancient policy[4], withdrew still further from the reach of their diocesan. At the conclusion of the struggle which the Church maintained against the civil power respecting the episcopal appointments, nearly all the bishops were elected absolutely by the canons of the cathedrals[5], which could not fail to add fresh weight to their pretensions. They exceeded all the *[Power and degeneracy of the canons.]*

---

[1] See above, p. 144.
[2] See his *Life* by a Præmonstratensian in the *Act. Sanct.* Jun. 1. 804 sq., and Hugo's *Ord. Præmonst. Annal.*, Nanceii, 1734. He died archbishop of Magdeburg, in 1134.
[3] It was commended in 1129 by pope Innocent II. (Hugo, II. 109), who afterwards granted to it many privileges. Le-Paige, *Biblioth. Præmonst.*, p. 622, Paris, 1633.
[4] See above, pp. 144, 145.
[5] Thus Innocent III. (1215) enjoins respecting the election of a bishop, 'ut is collatione adhibita eligatur, in quem omnes vel major vel sanior pars capituli consentit:' *Decret. Gregor.* lib. I. tit. VI. c. 42 (in Corpus Juris Canon.). Before this time a certain right of assent had been reserved for 'spiritales et religiosi viri' (including, perhaps, the laity): but by an edict of Gregory IX. (*ibid.* c. 56) it is forbidden, notwithstanding any usage to the contrary, 'ne per *laicos*, cum canonicis, pontificis [*i.e.* of a bishop] electio præsumatur.' This right of election had long been possessed by the Scotch Culdees (Keledei = 'servants of God'), who were an order of canonical clergy, some, if not all, of them being attached to the cathedral churches. Döllinger, III. 270, 271. They were at length superseded in many places by canons regular, and on appealing to Boniface VIII. in 1297, with the hope of recovering their ancient right of electing their bishop, they were unsuccessful. Cf. Spotswood, *Hist. of Church and State of Scotland*, p. 51.

<small>INTERNAL ORGANIZATION.</small>

<small>*Attempts to reform them.*</small>

other clergy both in rank and in worldliness, regarding the cathedral prebend as a piece of private income, suited more especially for men of noble birth[1], and not unfrequently employing substitutes[2] (or 'conduct-clerics') to discharge their sacred duties. Many an effort, it is true, was made to bring about a reformation[3] of the canons, and in some of the western churches the new impulse which accompanied the Hildebrandine movement may have been considerably felt: but, judging from the number of complaints that meet us in the writings of a later period, those reforming efforts were too commonly abortive[4].

<small>*Titular and suffragan bishops.*</small>

We have seen[5] that many of the functions of the chorepiscopi devolved on the archdeacons. After the thirteenth century the supervision of a diocese was often shared by titular or suffragan bishops[6], whom the pope continued to

---

[1] This plea was urged by the chapter of Strasburg in 1232; but the pope (*Decret. Greg. IX.* lib. III. tit. v. c. 37) replied that the true nobility was 'non generis sed virtutum:' cf. Neander, VII. 286.

[2] 'Clerici conductitii:' see Ducange, under 'conductitius.' This point is dwelt upon by a most rigorous censor of the canons, although one of their own order, Gerhoh of Reichersberg. See his *Dialogus de differentia clerici regularis et sæcularis.* 'Nos autem' (says the Secular Canon) 'pœne omnes genere, nobilitate, divitiis excellimus:' Gerhohi *Opp.* II. 1419, ed. Migne.

[3] As early as 1059, Nicholas II. and a Roman synod had enjoined (c. 3) the strict observance of their rule (Mansi, XIX. 897). In very many cases canons were allowed to have private property: but when attempts were made to reform the order, the new canons ('canonici regulares') as distinguished from the old ('canonici sæculares') boasted of their 'apostolical' community of goods. Schröckh, XXVII. 223—226. The name of 'canons' however was everywhere given to the cathedral clergy, whether or no they had ever accepted a rule; and after the foundation of the Augustinian canons or canons regular, the pretence of a rule was scarcely maintained by the canons secular at all. The Augustinian canons occupied most of the Scottish cathedrals and that of Carlisle. The other English cathedrals remained until the Reformation divided nearly equally between the Benedictines and the secular canons; the latter possessed the cathedrals of the Continent with very few exceptions.

[4] Planck, IV. pt. II. 570 sq.

[5] Above, p. 46, n. 2.

[6] 'Episcopi in partibus infidelium.' The number of these increased very much when Palestine became a Turkish province. Councils were then under the necessity of checking their unlicensed ministrations: *e.g.* that of Ravenna (1311) speaks in no gentle terms of 'ignoti et vagabundi episcopi, et maxime lingua et ritu dissoni:' see Planck, II. pt. II. 604 sq.; Neander, VII. 297, 298. These bishops under the title of suffragans were very largely employed in those countries in which, as in England and Germany, the dioceses were large, and the diocesan bishops employed in secular business; a list of the English suffragans may be found in the *Registrum Sacrum Anglicanum* (Oxford, 1858), pp. 142—148.

ordain for countries which the Saracens had wrested from his hands. These bishops found employment more especially in Germany. Where they did not exist, archdeacons were unrivalled in the vast extent of their authority[1], which numbers of them seem indeed to have abused by goading the inferior clerics[2] and encroaching on the province of the bishop[3]. In the hope of checking this presumption, other functionaries, such as 'vicars-general' and 'officials'[4], were appointed to assist in the administration of the churches of the west. But these in turn appear to have excited the distrust and hatred of the people by their pride, extortion, and irreverence[5].

Exorbitance of archdeacons.

Vicars-general and officials.

The more solemn visitations[6] of the bishop were continued; and he still availed himself of the diocesan synod for conferring with the clergy and adjusting purely local questions. Other councils also[7], chiefly what are termed

Synods.

---

[1] This may be ascertained from the *Decret. Gregor. IX.* lib. I. tit. XXIII., which contains ten chapters 'De officio Archidiaconi.'

[2] *e. g.* John of Salisbury (ep. LXXX.) complains at length of the 'rabies archidiaconorum.' Some of them, however, were most exemplary, travelling, staff in hand, through their archdeaconries and preaching in every village. Neander, (VII. 293) quotes such an instance.

[3] Thomassinus, *Vetus et Nova Ecclesiæ Discipl.* pt. I. lib. II. c. 18—20. Alexander III. found it necessary to inhibit the archdeacon of Ely, among others, from committing the cure of souls to persons 'sine mandato et licentia episcopi.' Mansi, XXII. 364.

[4] Thomassinus, *ibid.* c. 8, 9: Schröckh, XXVII. 150 sq. Other duties of the archdeacon were transferred to the 'penitentiary' of the diocese, an officer appointed at the council of Lateran (*Decret. Gregor.* lib. I. tit. XXXI. c. 15) to assist the bishop 'non solum in prædicationis officio, verum etiam in audiendis confessionibus et pœnitentiis injungendis, ac cæteris, quæ ad salutem pertinent animarum.' However, as the archdeacons were generally in deacon's orders, they could not have discharged the duties imposed on the penitentiaries. They should be regarded as ecclesiastical lawyers, not as persons in charge of souls.

[5] See an epistle of Peter Blesensis (of Blois), where at the close of the twelfth century he calls the officials 'episcoporum sanguisugæ:' ep. xxv. Other instances are given by Neander, VII. 294.

[6] See above, p. 46. The council of Lateran (1179), c. 4, passed some curious regulations limiting the equipages of the prelates and archdeacons while engaged on these visitation-tours.

[7] Their number may be estimated from the list in Nicolas' *Chronol.* pp. 239—259. What are called by the Church of Rome 'general' or 'œcumenical' councils, those of Lateran (1123), of Lateran (1139), of Lateran (1179), of Lateran (1215), of Lyons (1245), of Lyons (1274), were such neither in their mode of convocation (having no true representatives from other patriarchates), nor in their reception by the Church at large. See Palmer's *Treatise on the Church*, II. 162 sq., 3rd ed. Provincial synods were commanded to be held every year by the council of Lateran (1215), c. 7.

INTERNAL ORGANIZATION.

Corruptions of the clergy generally.

'provincial' (or, in England, 'convocations'[1]) were assembled through the whole of the present period. Their effect, however, was diminished by the intermeddling of the papal legates and the growth of Romish absolutism[2].

From these councils, much as they evince of the genuine spirit of reform, we are constrained to argue, that the general system of the Church was now most grievously disjointed and the morals of the clergy fearfully relaxed. Abuses of ecclesiastical patronage[3] which Hildebrand and others of his school attempted to eradicate had come to light afresh. A race of perfunctory and corrupted priests, non-residents and pluralists, are said to have abounded in all quarters[4]; and too often the emphatic voice of

[1] See above, pp. 50, 53; p. 153, n. 5. From the foundation of the Anglo-Saxon church, the bishops and abbots had been accustomed to meet in ecclesiastical councils; sometimes in national (Bede, *H. E.* IV. 17), sometimes in provincial assemblies (Sim. Dun. *Mon. Hist. Brit.* p. 670), and this independently of the witenagemots, and before the assembling of a general witenagemot for England was possible. After the Conquest for a long period the ecclesiastical councils were national, and attended by the prelates of both provinces, as, for example, that of London in 1075; (Will. Malmesb. *Gesta Pontificum*, pp. 66—68, ed. Hamilton.) In 1127, the king held a council at London, and the archbishop another at Westminster (H. Hunt. fo. 219, ed. Savile), in a way which has been compared with the modern custom of holding parliament and convocation at the same time. See Wake, *State of the Church*, p. 171, London, 1703. Records of provincial councils are very rare, until the custom of voting money in them arose. That of 1175 however, at Westminster, was clearly a provincial council of Canterbury (Hoveden II. 72), and that of 1195 held by Hubert Walter as legate, at York, was a provincial Council of the Northern province (Hoveden, III. 293—297). Provincial councils become more frequent after the beginning of John's reign; and diocesan ones also in which the money-grants of the clergy were arranged. During the thirteenth century it is difficult to distinguish in every case the ecclesiastical and secular character of these meetings; and towards the end of it, Convocation in two provincial representative assemblies was established on its present basis. The representative principle was introduced rather earlier into the ecclesiastical than into the lay councils; proctors for the cathedral clergy being summoned as early at least as 1225. In 1258 the archdeacons act as proctors or proxies for the clergy of their archdeaconries; in 1273 the bishops are directed to name the representatives; in 1277 the diocesan clergy are represented by proctors, and from 1283 each diocese is represented as at the present day. These Convocations must be carefully distinguished from the Parliamentary assemblies of the clergy which were not provincial. See *Select Charters* (Oxford, 1870), pp. 38, 442—446, 456, &c.

[2] Capefigue, II. 65, 66.
[3] Above, pp. 143 sq.
[4] On this subject, see the *Verbum Abbreviatum* of Peter Cantor (a Paris theologian, who died 1197), c. 34, ed. Montibus, 1639, and Gerhoh of

councils, stipulating as to the precise conditions on which sacred offices were to be held, produced no visible or permanent effect.

One source of the more glaring immoralities[1], which synod vied with synod in denouncing, was the celibacy of the clergy. This had been at length established as the practice of the Western Church through the astute and unremitting efforts of the Roman pontiff. It is true that even Gregory VII. had been constrained to shew indulgence[2] in some cases where the married priest appeared incorrigible; and in England, at the council of Winchester (**1076**), the rigours of the Hildebrandine legislation were considerably abated[3]: but the marriage of the clergy, discredited on every hand, was gradually disused, and died away entirely at the middle of the thirteenth century. The prohibition was at length extended also, after a protracted contest, to sub-deacons and inferior orders[4] of the

INTERNAL ORGANIZATION.

Constrained celibacy:

its extension,

Reichersberg, *De Corrupto Ecclesiæ Statu; Opp.* II. 10 sq. ed. Migne. The language of men like Bonaventura (*Opp.* VII. 330, ed. Lugduni), where, in his defence of the Mendicants, he draws a most gloomy picture of the clergy, should be taken 'cum grano salis;' but his colouring is not very much deeper than that of bishop Grosseteste (*ep.* CVII.), in Brown's *Fascic.* II. 382: cf. his *Sermo ad clerum, contra pastores et prælatos malos;* Ibid. 263. Schröckh (XXVII. 175 sq.) has proved at large from the decrees of councils, that simony, which Hildebrand and others after him denounced, was rife in nearly every country, often in its most obnoxious forms.

[1] *e. g.* Schröckh, XXVII. 205, 206. Men like Aquinas saw clearly 'minus esse peccatum uxore uti quam cum alia fornicari' (*Ibid.* p. 211); but they all felt that the canons of the Church were absolutely binding, and therefore that clerical marriages were sinful.

[2] The imperial party, now in the ascendant, won the sympathy of many of the married priests, and Hildebrand accordingly advised his legates for the present (1081) to dispense with some of the more rigorous canons on this subject: Mansi, XX. 342. As late as 1114, the council of Gran (Strigoniense) decreed as follows, c. 31: 'Presbyteris uxores, quas legitimis ordinibus acceperint, moderatius habendas, prævisa fragilitate, *indulsimus*:' Péterffy's *Concil. Hungar.* I. 57, ed. Viennæ Austr. 1742: Mansi, XXI. 106.

[3] 'Decretum est, ut nullus canonicus uxorem habeat. Sacerdotes vero in castellis vel in vicis habitantes habentes uxores non cogantur ut dimittant; non habentes interdicantur ut habeant,' etc.; Wilkins, I. 367. For the later aspects of the struggle in England and other countries, see the references in Gieseler, III. 205—207, n. 4. Zealots like Roscelin contended that the sons of clergymen were not eligible to any ecclesiastical office. Neander, VIII. 9.

[4] Thomassinus, *Eccl. Discip.* pt. I. lib. II. c. 65. According to the *Decret. Greg.* lib. III. tit. III. c. I, a cleric under the rank of subdeacon

clerical estate. A darker train of evils was the consequence of this unnatural severity. Incontinence, already general[1] among the higher clergy, now infected very many of the rest. Nor was that form of vice the only one which tended to debase the spirit of the seculars and counteract the influence which they ought to have exerted on their flocks. Their levity, intemperance, and extortion[2] had too frequently excited the disgust and hatred of the masses, and so far from meeting with the reverence which their sacred office claimed, they were the common butt of raillery and coarse vituperation[3]. The more earnest of their charge

might retain his wife by relinquishing his office, but subdeacons and all higher orders are compelled to dismiss their wives and do penance: cf. Synod of London (1108): Wilkins, I. 387.

[1] Thus the Gloss. on Distinct. LXXXI. c. 6 (in *Corpus Jur. Canon.*) adds that deprivation is not meant to be enforced 'pro simplici fornicatione;' urging, as the reason, 'cum *pauci* sine illo vitio inveniantur.'

[2] The prevalence of these vices may be inferred from the numerous complaints of men like St Bernard (see passages at length, in Gieseler, III. 208—210, n. 10), and the decrees of councils (*e. g.* Lateran, 1215, cc. 14, 15, 16). The same is strongly brought to light in the reforming (anti-secularizing) movement headed by Arnold of Brescia: see Neander, VII. 205 sq.

[3] See, for instance, the *Collection of Political Songs*, &c., edited by Mr Wright for the Camden Society, and '*Latin Poems commonly attributed to Walter Mapes*' (appointed archdeacon of Oxford in 1196), edited by the same. These specimens, together with the whole cycle of Provençal poetry (the *sirventes* of the Troubadours and the *fabliaux* of the Trouvères), contain the most virulent attacks on the clerical, and sometimes the monastic, order. Much as satire of this kind was overcoloured by licentious or distempered critics, it had, doubtless, some foundation. The champion and biographer of Becket, Herbert of Boseham, did not hesitate to employ the following language in speaking of the clergy: 'Sacerdos quippe nisi sensum Scripturarum præhabuerit, tanquam omni carens sensu, idolum potius quam sacerdos judicatur... Utinam et juxta prophetæ votum illis fiant similes qui ea faciunt, qui tales in Dei ecclesia ordinant. Simia quippe in aula, talis sacerdos in ecclesia.' *Supplementa* Herb. de Boseham, pp. 102 sq., ed. Caxton Soc. 1851. It should, however, be borne in mind that the very evidence on which this account of the clergy is received proves the existence of a better and higher idea, and that the ruling one. The enactments of councils are necessitated by a single case as well as by many, and the fact that such enactments were possible proves that the majority of at least the influential clergy were on the right side. No institution could stand if it were to be judged by vulgar caricatures such as the popular songs are; nor could the history of public morality at the present day be drawn from the police reports. The abuses of certain sorts were through the medieval period great and notorious, but if they had been the rule generally the Church must have long ago ceased to exist. It is observable also that the worst charges are all in general language. No accurate

preferred the ministrations first of monks, and then of mendicants, whose popularity must have been chiefly due to their superior teaching and more evangelic lives. Exceptions there would doubtless be in which the humble parish-priest approved himself the minister of God and was the light and blessing of his sphere of duty: but the acts of such are seldom registered among the gloomy annals of the age.

RELATIONS TO THE CIVIL POWER.

Their general unpopularity.

§ 2. *RELATIONS OF THE CHURCH TO THE CIVIL POWER.*

The Western Church was now exalted by the papacy as the supreme and heaven-appointed mistress of the State; or looking at the change produced by this conjuncture from a different point of view, she ran the risk of falling, under Gregory VII., into a secular and merely civil institution. Having generally succeeded in his effort to repress the marriage of the clergy, he began to realize the other objects that had long been nearest to his heart, the abolition of all 'lay-investitures,' the freedom of episcopal elections, and his own ascendancy above the jurisdiction of the crown[1]. In carrying out his wishes he advanced a claim to what was nothing short of feudal sovereignty in all the kingdoms of the west[2], in some upon the ground that they were the possessions (fiefs) of St Peter[3], and in others as made tributary to the popes by a specific grant[4].

The main features of the Hildebrandine policy.

judgment can be drawn from the generalities of fanatical reformers or from the sneers of professed enemies.

[1] His own election, it is true, had been *confirmed* by the emperor according to the decree of Nicholas II. (above, p. 140, n. 1): but that is the last case on record of a like confirmation. Bowden's *Life of Gregory VII.* I. 323.

[2] In his more sober moments he allowed that the royal power was also of Divine institution, but subordinate to the papal. The two dignities ('apostolica et regia') are like the sun and moon: *Epist.* lib. VII. ep. 25 (Mansi, xx. 308). An apology for Gregory VII. on claiming oaths of knightly service from the kings and emperors, is made by Döllinger, III. 314—316.

[3] Spain was so regarded ('ab antiquo proprii juris S. Petri fuisse'): *Epist.* lib. I. ep. 7.

[4] Thus Gregory VII. (1074) reproaches the king of Hungary for accepting the emperor as lord paramount of his dominions. That

RELATIONS TO THE CIVIL POWER.

Struggle of the pope with Henry IV.

The chief opponent of these ultra-papal claims was Henry IV. of Germany[1]: but his abandoned character, his tampering with the church-preferment, and his unpopularity in many districts of the empire, made it easier for the pope to humble and subdue him. The dispute was opened by a Roman synod in 1075, where every form of lay-investiture was strenuously resisted[2]. After some pacific correspondence, in which Henry shewed himself disposed to beg the papal absolution[3] for the gross excesses of his youth, he was at length commanded to appear in Rome for judgment[4], on the ground that Hildebrand had been entrusted with the moral superintendence of the world. Henry now hastened to repel this outrage: he deposed his rival[5], and was speedily deposed himself and stricken with the papal ban[6] (1076). Supported by a

kingdom is said to be 'Romanæ ecclesiæ proprium......a rege Stephano olim B. Petro oblatum.' The letter goes on to say: 'Præterea Heinricus piæ memoriæ imperator ad honorem S. Petri regnum illud expugnans, victo rege et facta victoria, ad corpus B. Petri lanceam coronamque transmisit et pro gloria triumphi sui illuc regni direxit insignia, quo *principatum dignitatis* ejus attinere cognovit.' Lib. II. ep. 13: cf. above, p. 128, n. 5. On the sturdy language of William the Conqueror, when asked to do homage to Gregory, see Turner, *Hist. of England*, 'Middle Ages,' I. 131, ed. 1830.

[1] See Stanzel, *Gesch. Deutschlands unter den fränk. Kaisern*, I. 248 sq.

[2] On the historical connexion of this law, see Jaffé, p. 417. It runs as follows: 'Si quis deinceps episcopatum vel abbatiam de manu alicujus laicæ personæ susceperit, nullatenus inter episcopos habeatur,' etc.......adding, 'Si quis imperatorum, regum, ducum, marchionum, comitum, vel quilibet sæcularium potestatum aut personarum investituram episcopatuum vel alicujus ecclesiasticæ dignitatis dare præsumpserit, ejusdem sententiæ [*i.e.* of excommunication] vinculo se adstrictum esse sciat:' Mansi, xx. 517. Gregory had already (1073) threatened Philip of France with excommunication and anathema for simoniacal proceedings: *Epist.* lib. I. ep. 85.

[3] His letter (1073) is given at length in Bowden, I. 840 sq. The hopes which it inspired in Gregory are expressed by his *Epist.* lib. I. epp. 25, 26.

[4] See Bruno, *De Bello Saxon.* c. 64 (in Pertz, VII. 351); and Lambert's *Annales*, A.D. 1076. According to the latter writer Henry was summoned, on pain of anathema, to appear in Rome by Feb. 22: but cf. Neander, VII. 144, 145.

[5] The stronghold of the imperialists was the collegiate chapter of Goslar. They were backed on this occasion by the synod of Worms (Jan. 24, 1076), which, not content with a repudiation of the pope, assailed his character with the most groundless calumnies: Lambert, as above; Bowden, II. 92 sq.

[6] Mansi, xx. 469. 'Henrico regi, filio Henrici Imperatoris, qui contra

number of disloyal princes who assembled at Tribur, the terrible denunciation took effect; they formed the resolution of proceeding to appoint another king, and Henry's wrath was, for a time at least, converted into fear[1]. An abject visit to the pope, whom he propitiated by doing penance at Canossa[2], ended in the reconstruction of his party, and the gradual recognition of his rights[3]. The papal ban, indeed, was reimposed in 1080; but Henry had strength enough to institute a rival pontiff[4] (Clement III.): and although his arms were partially resisted by the countess of Tuscany[5] (Matilda) and the Normans under Robert Guiscard[6] who came forward in behalf of Gregory, the subjects of the pope himself were now in turn estranged from him[7]. He therefore breathed his last (1085) an exile from the seat of his ambitious projects[8].

RELATIONS TO THE CIVIL POWER.

It was made apparent in the course of this dispute that numbers were unwilling to concede the pope a right of excommunicating monarchs, even in extreme cases; and

'Reforming' principles developed by it.

tuam ecclesiam inaudita superbia insurrexit, totius regni Teutonicorum et Italiæ gubernacula contradico, et omnes Christianos a vinculo juramenti, quod sibi fecere vel facient, absolvo, et ut nullus ei sicut regi serviat interdico...vinculo eum anathematis vice tua alligo '.... Cf. Paul. Bernried, *Vit. Gregor.* c. 68 sq. This and other works in defence of Gregory will be found in Gretser, *Opp.* tom. VI. Those which take the opposite (or imperial) side have been collected in Goldast's *Apolog. pro Imper. Henrico IV.*, Hanov. 1611.

[1] Neander, VII. 153.
[2] See the humiliating circumstances detailed by Gregory himself (Jan. 28, 1077) in a letter written to the German princes: lib. IV. ep. 12. The tone of this letter is most unapostolic.
[3] The enemies of Henry, it is true, proceeded to elect Rudolph of Swabia for emperor, the pope remaining neutral at first, and afterwards (1080) espousing (Mansi, xx. 531) what he thought the stronger side: but Rudolph's death soon after left his rival in possession of the crown, and ruined the designs of Gregory.
[4] Jaffé, p. 443.
[5] On the relations of Gregory with this princess, see Neander, VII. 155 (note), and Sir J. Stephen's *Essays*, I. 45 sq.
[6] This rude soldier had been excommunicated by Gregory in 1074 (Mansi, xx. 402), but in 1080 (June 29) the services of the Norman army were secured at all hazards. See Gregory's investiture of their leader in Mansi, xx. 314.
[7] See Bowden, II. 318.
[8] One of his last public acts was a renewal of the anathema against Henry and the anti-pope: see Bernold's *Chron.* A.D. 1084 (Pertz, VII. 441). The letters of Gregory VII. bearing on German and imperial topics have been published in a very convenient form by Jaffé, *Monumenta Gregoriana*, Berlin, 1865.

RELATIONS TO THE CIVIL POWER.

that others who admitted this denied the further claim to dispossess an emperor of all his jurisdiction and absolve his subjects from their oath of allegiance[1].

Further papal encroachments.

The relations of the spiritual and temporal authorities were now embarrassed more and more by popes who followed in the steps of Gregory. The second Urban, after placing Philip I. of France[2] under the papal ban (**1094**), forbade a priest or bishop to swear any kind of feudal homage[3] to the sovereign or to other laymen,—an injunction which, if carried out, would have been absolutely fatal to the union of the Church and civil power. This pontiff also headed the new movement[4] of the age for rescuing Palestine from the dominion of the Saracens.

Strengthened by the Crusades.

The project had been entertained before by Gregory VII.[5], who seems to have expected that Crusades, while strengthening his throne, would tend to reunite the Eastern and the Western Christians; but no step was taken for the realizing of his wish until it found a mighty echo in the heart of Urban II.[6] Of the many consequences which resulted from that wondrous impulse, none is more apparent than the exaltation of the papal dignity[7] at the expense of every other. Rome had thus identified her-

---

[1] Cf. on the one side Neander, VII. 149 sq., Gieseler, III. 16, n. 25, with Döllinger, III. 323 sq. Gregory's own defence of his conduct may be seen in his *Epist.* lib. IV. ep. 2. According to Capefigue (I. 294 sq.), the excommunicated emperor was to be avoided like a leper, and therefore his deposition followed as a matter of course.

[2] In this case as in others (cf. p. 136, n. 4) the papal fulmination was a popular act, Philip having repudiated his lawful wife. He was resisted by Ivo, the bishop of Chartres, who begged the pope (*Epist.* 46) to adhere to the sentence he had pronounced through his legate at the council of Autun. The ban was accordingly pronounced afresh at the council of Clermont (1095) in Philip's own territories. Bernold's *Chron.* A.D. 1095 (Pertz, VII. 464).

[3] See Döllinger's remarks on what he calls 'the new and severe addition,' III. 330.

[4] On the Crusades generally, see Wilken, *Gesch. der Kreuzzüge*, Michaud, *Hist. des Croisades*, and Gibbon, ch. LVIII.

[5] *Epist.* lib. II. ep. 31. In lib. II. ep. 49, he begs that men who love St Peter will not prefer the cause of secular potentates to that of the Apostle, and complains of the sad depression of the Eastern Church.

[6] See the acts of the council of Clermont (Nov. 18—28, 1095), in Mansi, XX. 815 sq.

[7] Neander, VII. 176. On the establishment of the kingdom of Jerusalem (1099) the power of the pope was fully recognized in temporal as in spiritual things.

self with the fanaticism of princes and of people, to secure an easy triumph over both.

<small>RELATIONS TO THE CIVIL POWER.</small>

Paschal II., known in English history as the supporter of archbishop Anselm[1] in his opposition to the crown, had sided with Henry V. in his unnatural effort to dethrone his father (1104): but soon afterwards he drove the pope himself into concessions which were deemed an ignominious compromise. Paschal[2] openly surrendered into the hands of the civil power all the secular fiefs which had been bestowed on the clergy, on condition that the king should in his turn resign the privileges of investiture; but subsequently even this condition was abandoned, and the overpliant pontiff went so far as to concede that Henry should invest the prelates, in the usual way, before their consecration. But the pledge was speedily revoked.

<small>Humiliation of Paschal II.</small>

Amid the crowd of conflicting theories as to the limits of the sovereign power in matters ecclesiastical, there grew up in the popedom of Calixtus II. a more tractable and intermediate party[3]; and since all the combatants were now exhausted by the struggle[4], a concordat was agreed

<small>Concordat of Worms, 1122.</small>

---

[1] See Hasse's *Life of Anselm*, Lond. 1850; and Turner's *Middle Ages*, I. 155 sq. The investiture-controversy (cf. above, p. 155, n. 1) was settled in England as early as 1107; the pope and Anselm having conceded that all prelates should, on their election, do homage to the king. This concordat was accepted in the synod of London, 1107: Wilkins, I. 386.

[2] He had already (1106) prohibited every kind of lay investiture like his predecessors (Mansi, xx. 1211): but in 1111, on the advance of an imperial army, he proposed (1) to resign the regalia held by bishops and abbots, '*i.e.* civitates, ducatus, marchias, comitatus, monetas, teloneum, mercatum, advocatias regni, jura centurionum, et curtes, quæ manifeste regni sunt, cum pertinentiis suis, militia et castra regni' (in Pertz, IV. 67); and (2) to grant the king, 'ut regni tui episcopis vel abbatibus libere præter symoniam et violentiam electis, investituram virgæ et annuli conferas,' etc.; *Ibid.* p. 72. The pope, however (see above, p. 222, n. 1), was soon compelled by his party to revoke these concessions: *Ibid.* Append. pp. 181 sq.: cf. Cardinal. de Aragon. *Vit. Paschalis II.*, in Muratori, *Rer. Ital. Script.* III. part I. 363, and Neander, VII. 186—194. A very bold and bitter protest was put forth (circ. 1102) against the temporal assumptions of Paschal, by the church of Liège. Their organ was Sigebert, a monk of Gemblours (Gemblacensis). The letter is printed, among other places, in Mansi, xx. 987.

[3] This school was represented by Hugo, a monk of Fleury, whose *Tractatus de Regia Potestate et Sacerdotali Dignitate* is preserved in Baluze and Mansi's *Miscellan.* IV. 184 sq.

[4] The following language of Calixtus to the emperor (Feb. 19, 1122) deserves attention: 'Nihil, Henrice, de tuo jure vendicare sibi quærit

RELATIONS TO THE CIVIL POWER.

upon at Worms[1] (in September **1122**), and solemnly confirmed by the council of Lateran[2] in the following year (March **27**). It was there determined that the emperor should cease to claim the right of investiture by ring and crosier and should grant to every church the free election of the bishop, while the pope conceded that on their election prelates should receive the 'regalia' from the king by means of the sceptre, and should thus avow their willingness to render unto Cæsar the things that are truly his.

The Ghibellines and the popes.

But though one topic of dispute was now adjusted, fresh ones could not fail to be evoked by the aspiring projects of the papacy: while on the other hand, the opposition offered by the house of Franconia, under Henry IV. and Henry V., was stubbornly continued for a hundred years (**1137—1236**) by the new line of emperors[3] (the Hohenstaufen, Waiblingen or Ghibellines). The pontiff could, however, keep his ground, supported as he was by the political assailants of the empire[4].

His throne, indeed, was shaken for a time in the impetuous movement headed by a minor cleric, Arnold of Brescia[5], who came forward as the champion of the volun-

ecclesia; nec regni nec imperii gloriam affectamus: obtineat ecclesia quod Christi est, habeat imperator quod suum est,' *etc.*; in Neugart's *Codex Diplom. Alemanniæ,* II. 50, ed. 1791.

[1] See Ekkehard, ad an. 1122 (Pertz, VIII. 260); *Vit. Calixti,* in Muratori, *Rer. Ital. Script.* III. pt. I. p. 420: Planck, IV. pt. I. 297 sq.

[2] Döllinger (III. 345, 346) remarks that on the subject of the act of 'homage' as distinguished from the oath of fealty, the concordat was entirely silent, indicating that Calixtus 'tolerated' it. In a letter dated Dec. 13, 1122, he congratulates the emperor on his return 'nunc tandem ad ecclesiæ gremium:' Mansi, XXI. 280.

[3] See Von Raumer's *Gesch. der Hohenstaufen und ihrer Zeit*, Leipzig, 1840.

[4] The Guelphs (Welfs) and Ghibellines became the 'Whigs' and 'Tories' of this period, the pope allying himself with the former: cf. F. von Schlegel, *Philos. of History,* p. 369 (Bohn's ed.), who views the matter differently. The Welfs took their name from the line of princes which gave dukes to Bavaria and Saxony. Under Frederick I. this line was represented by Henry the Lion; and later on by his son Otho IV; both of whom represented the ancient dislike of the Saxons of North Germany to the imperial rule, and so were united in a common antipathy with the popes. The use of the party names however is later than the struggle itself; the power of both Hohenstaufen and Welf was extinct by the middle of the 13th century, and they represent merely imperial and papal partizanship in Italy of a later date.

[5] See Schröckh, XX. 112 sq., and 155, 156, on the different views

tary system, and impugned the right of bishops and of popes themselves to any temporal possession. A republic was proclaimed at Rome (1143); the principles of Arnold spread in every part of Lombardy, and though repressed at length by the imperial arms[1], the fermentation they excited did not cease for twenty years, after which the misguided author of it fell into the hands of the police[2] (1155).

The German empire was now administered by one of the sturdiest of the anti-papal monarchs, Frederic I. or Barbarossa (1152—1190). But after he had proved himself a match for Hadrian IV.[3], he was compelled (1176) to recognize the claims of Alexander III.[4], who, counting on the disaffection of the Lombards, carried out the Hildebrandine principles in all their breadth and rigour. He was seconded in England by the primate Becket[5], who, although he rose to eminence as a minister of the king[6],

The anti-hierarchical movement under Arnold.

Early struggle of Frederic Barbarossa with the popes.

The influence of Becket.

respecting him. Neander's estimate is favourable (VII. 203—209). It appears to be established that Arnold was a pupil of Abélard: *Ibid.* p. 204 (note). Francke, *Arnold von Brescia*, Zurich, 1825, tries to connect him with the Waldenses and Cathari. He was condemned as early as 1139, at the council of Lateran, in company with the anti-pope: cf. S. Bernard. *Epist.* 195, written in the following year to caution the bishop of Constance against Arnold and his principles.

[1] The Romans in this extremity invited Conrad to resume the ancient imperial rights: see *e.g.* the two *Letters* in Martène and Durand's *Collect.* II. 398.

[2] Hadrian IV. desired the emperor to give up 'Arnaldum hæreticum, quem vicecomites de Campania abstulerant... quem tanquam prophetam in terra sua cum honore habebant.' Card. de Aragon. *Vit. Hadriani*, in Muratori, as above, p. 442. He was immediately hanged: cf. Neander, VII. 223.

[3] He had reminded Frederic (1157) that the imperial crown was conferred ('collatam') by the pope, with the addition, 'Neque tamen pœnitet nos desideria tuæ voluntatis in omnibus implevisse, sed si majora *beneficia* excellentia tua de manu nostra suscepisset, si fieri posset, non immerito gauderemus:' see Radevicus *Gest. Frid.* lib. I. c. 9; in Muratori, *Rer. Ital. Script.* VI. 746 sq. The pope, in 1158, was forced to explain away the obnoxious terms: *Ibid.* c. 22; Pertz, IV. 106.

[4] See Von Raumer (as above), pp. 244 sq.; Döllinger, IV. 19, 20; Gieseler, III. § 52, n. 22.

[5] A copious stock of authorities for the *Life* of Becket is contained in the *S. Thomas Cantuariensis*, edited by Giles, 8 vols. Oxf. 1845: see also J. C. Robertson's *Becket, a Biography*, London, 1859.

[6] Sharon Turner has tried to shew that several limitations of the clerical encroachments had been made under his own auspices: *Middle Ages*, I. 233, and note 55, ed. 1830. The instances, however, are not very convincing; and all that can be proved is that whilst Becket was minister, the bishops and abbots were brought under contribution for the scutage. The same writer has shewn (p. 259, n. 112) that at one period

RELATIONS TO THE CIVIL POWER.

threw himself, on his promotion to Canterbury, on the side of clerical immunities and ultimately perished in the cause. The point on which he took his stand was the exemption of all clerical offenders from the civil jurisdiction, urging that, whatever was the nature of their crime[1], they should be tried in the spiritual courts, and punished only as the canon law prescribed. The king insisted, on the contrary, that clerics, when convicted in his courts, should be degraded by the Church and then remanded to the civil power for execution of the sentence. In a meeting[2] called the 'Council of Clarendon' (Jan. 25, 1164), Becket had allowed himself to acquiesce in regulations which he deemed entirely hostile to the Church and fatal to his theory of hierarchical exemption: but the pope immediately absolved him from the oath[3], and afterwards, until his murder (Dec. 29, 1170), countenanced his unremitting opposition to the crown[4]. His canonization, and the miracles[5] alleged to have been wrought on pilgrims who had worshipped at his tomb, conspired to fix the

the clergy were apprehensive lest Henry should have broken altogether with the pope.

[1] The number of crimes charged against clerics (major and minor) in the early years of this reign was very great. *Engl. Review*, vi. 61, 62.

[2] It consisted of the king, the two archbishops, twelve bishops, and thirty-nine lay barons. Though purporting to re-enact the 'customs of England,' the Constitutions of Clarendon infringe at many points on the existing privileges of the Church: *e.g.* the twelfth reduced the patronage of the bishoprics and abbeys almost entirely under the king's control. Wilkins, i. 435.

[3] *Epist. S. Thomæ*, ii. 5, ed. Giles.

[4] Alexander durst not bring the matter to an open rupture, on account of his own misunderstanding with the emperor Frederic: but (June 8, 1165) he reprimanded Henry (*Ibid.* ii. 115) and incited some of the bishops to exert their influence in behalf of Becket. Among other things they were to admonish the king, 'ut in eo quod excesserit satisfaciat, a pravis actibus omnino desistat, Romanam ecclesiam solita veneratione respiciat,' etc.; *Ibid.* ii. 96: cf. ii. 53. Even where he is urging Becket to proceed against his enemies (April, 1166) he adds: 'Verum de persona regis speciale tibi mandatum non damus, nec tamen jus tibi pontificale quod in ordinatione et consecratione tua suscepisti adimimus.' *Ibid.* ii. 12. In a subsequent endeavour to effect a compromise, Henry insisted on the reservation 'salva dignitate regni,' and Becket on 'salva ecclesiæ dignitate,' so that nothing was accomplished. (Robertson, *Becket*, p. 224.) But the king afterwards relented (Jan. 1170) when he found it likely that his kingdom would be placed under an interdict (*Epist. S. Thomæ*, ii. 55).

[5] John of Salisbury, *Vita S. Thomæ*, *Opp.* v. 380, ed. Giles.

triumph[1] of those ultramontane principles which he had laboured more than others to diffuse.

Meanwhile the conflict with the emperor had been reopened. Lucius III. and his immediate successors (1181—1187) were ejected from the papal city by domestic troubles[2]; and the restless Barbarossa threatened to reduce them into bondage, when he was at length diverted from the theatre of strife to lead an army of Crusaders (1189). He did not survive the expedition[3]. The reign of Henry VI. and the minority of Frederic II. favoured the encroachments of the Roman pontiff. Innocent III. (as we have seen[4]) advanced the most exorbitant pretensions, and by force of character as well as circumstances humbled nearly all the European courts. His foremost wishes were the conquest of Palestine and an extensive 'reformation of the Church[5],' but neither of these ends could be achieved, according to his theory, except by the obliteration of all nationalities and the entire ascendancy of Rome above the temporal power. He gave away the crown of Sicily[6] and governed there as guardian of the king: he elevated, and in turn deposed, a candidate for the imperial throne[7]:

RELATIONS TO THE CIVIL POWER.

Frederic Barbarossa renews the contest.

His influence counteracted under Innocent III.

---

[1] See the *Purgatio Henrici Regis pro morte beati Thomæ*, and the *Charta Absolutionis Domini Regis* in Roger de Hoveden, *Chron.* II. 85—37; ed. London, 1869. The vantage-ground secured to Alexander by these acts is shewn in language like the following (Sept. 20, 1172), where he had congratulated Henry on the conquest of Ireland: 'Et quia Romana ecclesia aliud jus habet in insula quam in terra magna et continua, nos eam spem tenentes, quod jura ipsius ecclesiæ non solum conservare velis, sed etiam *ampliare*, et ubi nullum jus habet, id debeas sibi conferre, rogamus,' etc. Rymer's *Fœdera*, I. 45, ed. 1816: Jaffé, p. 751.

[2] Döllinger, IV. 21 sq.

[3] Von Raumer, as above, II. 411 sq.

[4] Above, pp. 224, 225.

[5] Thus he writes (1215): 'Illius ergo testimonium invocamus, Qui Testis est in cœlo fidelis, quod inter omnia desiderabilia cordis nostri duo in hoc sæculo principaliter affectamus, ut ad recuperationem videlicet Terræ Sanctæ ac reformationem universalis Ecclesiæ valeamus intendere cum effectu.' Mansi, XXII. 960. The foundation of the Latin empire at Constantinople (1204) added largely to the papal empire and excited larger expectations. It was destroyed, however, in 1261.

[6] Securing from the crown a surrender of the following points: the royal nomination of bishops, the power of excluding legates, and prohibiting appeals to Rome, and the arbitrary grant or refusal of permission to the bishops to be present at councils: see Planck, IV. pt. I. 452 sq.; Döllinger, IV. 27.

[7] This was Otho IV., who had renounced all participation in ec-

RELATIONS TO THE CIVIL POWER.

he freed the subjects of count Raymond of Toulouse, who was infected with the Albigensian tenets, from their allegiance[1]: he made Philip Augustus of France take back his rightful queen[2]: and, passing over similar achievements, it was he who forced a sovereign of this country (John) to hold his royal dignity as one of the most abject vassals of the pope[3] (1213). The 'Magna Carta' was, however, gained in spite of Innocent's emphatic reprobation[4], and his death in 1216 allowed the imperialists to breathe afresh and make an effort for diminishing the range of papal absolutism. Fretted by their opposition, Gregory IX. betrayed the fiery spirit of his predecessors and pronounced his ban against the emperor Frederic II.[5] (1227). A compromise ensued, in which the quarrel seemed to have been amicably settled: but the interval of calm was short; and on the recommencement of hostilities, the fearless monarch was at length proscribed as an incorrigible misbeliever, who had justly forfeited his crown (March 24, 1239)[6]. The contest thus exasperated

clesiastical elections and the 'jus spolii,' or title to the property of deceased bishops and other clergymen: but afterwards withdrawing from this engagement and seizing some of the temporalities of the Roman see, he was excommunicated by Innocent (1211) and his crown transferred to Frederic II.: Matthew Paris, from Roger of Wendover, A.D. 1210; Döllinger, IV. 31, 32.

[1] See Sir J. Stephen's *Lectures*, I. 219, 220; ed. 1851.

[2] Innocent. *Epist.* lib. III. ep. 11 sq.: Will. Armor. apud Bouquet, XVII. 88.

[3] The pope 'sententialiter definivit ut rex Anglorum Johannes a solio regni deponeretur, et alius, papa procurante, succederet, qui dignior haberetur,' etc. M. Paris, A.D. 1212, p. 195; from Roger of Wendover, III. 241, ed. Coxe. He had before (1208) laid the whole kingdom under interdict. In John's deed of cession he speaks of it as made 'Deo et sanctis Apostolis ejus Petro et Paulo, et Sanctæ Romanæ ecclesiæ matri nostræ, ac domino papæ Innocentio ejusque catholicis successoribus...pro remissione omnium peccatorum nostrorum et totius generis nostri tam pro vivis quam pro defunctis.' M. Paris, A.D. 1213, p. 199; R. Wendover, III. 253. The tribute-money was to be 'mille marcas esterlingorum annuatim.'

[4] Wendover, A.D. 1215, III. 323.

[5] Wendover (1228), IV. 157; M. Paris, p. 291. While under this ban Frederic actually set out on a crusade in spite of the Roman pontiff, issuing his orders 'in the name of God and of Christendom.'

[6] The grounds on which the papal fulmination rested are given at length in the bull of deposition: M. Paris (1239), p. 412: cf. Frederic's own letters, *Ibid.* pp. 415 sq. How far he merited the charge of blasphemy, infidelity, or free-thinking, is discussed by Neander, VII. 248 sq. The recent work, *Historia Diplomatica Friderici Secundi*, ed. Huillard-

did not cease until his death in **1250**, after having more and more developed the conviction in his subjects, that some check must be imposed on the ambition of the Roman see[1].

RELATIONS TO THE CIVIL POWER.

The papacy, indeed, appeared to have come forth triumphant when the last of the Hohenstaufen, Conradin[2], perished on the scaffold (Oct. **29, 1268**): but, in spite of the prodigious energy which it continued to evince, its hold on all the European nations was relaxing, while the hope of Eastern conquest faded more and more[3]. It is alike remarkable that one of the premonitory blows which Roman despotism provoked had been inflicted, half unconsciously, by Louis IX. (St Louis) of France, and at this very juncture. What are known as the 'Gallican Liberties' are clearly traceable to him. In his ordinance of **1268**[4] he proceeds on the idea of building up a 'national church' in strict alliance with the civil power. But a more sensible advance was made in this direction under Philip the Fair[5], whose conduct in ecclesiastical affairs, however selfish, arbitrary and unjust, was tending

Beginning of reaction against the papacy.

Bréholles (Paris, 1853), contains the most accurate information respecting him.

[1] A saying rose in Germany that Frederic would return, or that an eagle would spring from his ashes and destroy the papacy.

[2] Von Raumer, *Gesch. der Hohenstaufen*, IV. 594.

[3] Cf. the remarks of Neander on the dying-out of the Crusades: VII. 260 sq.

[4] Commonly called a 'Pragmatic Sanction;' printed in Capefigue, II. 352 sq. See the critique of this author (II. 171, 172). Another instrument, bearing the title 'Pragmatic Sanction' and more plainly 'Gallican,' was issued by Charles VII. in 1438. Louis IX. also contributed to the foundation of the college of Sorbonne (1259), which afterwards produced a number of intrepid champions in the cause of 'nationality' as it diverges from the Roman theory of universalism.

[5] On his important struggle with Boniface VIII. see Gieseler, III. 133—156, on one side, and Döllinger, IV. 80 sq. or Capefigue, II, 181 sq. on the other. After some preliminary skirmishing, Philip, backed by the States-General (Ap. 10, 1302), wrote a warning letter to the pope, whose indignation knew no bounds. In the famous decretal 'Unam Sanctam,' which appeared in the following November, and is printed in Capefigue, II. 355 (cf. Neander, IX. 11), Boniface asserted the absolute supremacy of papal power ('Porro subesse Romano pontifici omnem humanam creaturam declaramus, dicimus, diffinimus et pronuntiamus omnino esse de necessitate salutis'). He published the ban against his rival (April 13, 1303), but it was powerless. Philip summoned the States-General afresh (June 13), where he preferred a charge of heresy against the pope and stated his intention of appealing to a general council and a future pontiff. Boniface, however, died in October, and the next pope (Benedict XI.)

RELATIONS TO THE CIVIL POWER.

to reverse the whole of the Hildebrandine policy, and threatened more than once to rend the kingdom from its old connexion with the Roman see. The humbled pontiff, watched and crippled at Avignon, was for many years the creature and tool of the kings of France[1].

The grounds of this reaction.

There was, indeed, no general wish to question the supremacy of Rome, so long as she confined herself within the sacerdotal province; but her worldliness, venality, and constant intermeddling in the affairs of state, could hardly fail to lessen the respect with which her claims had been regarded: and as soon as the idea of an appeal from her decisions to a General Council[2] was distinctly mastered, it is clear that the prestige by which her usurpations were supported was already vanishing away. The true relations of the regal and ecclesiastical authority[3] were now discussed with greater freedom. A reaction had commenced. Mankind were growing more and more persuaded that prerogatives like those of Hildebrand or Innocent III. were far from Apostolic, and could not be safely lodged in sacerdotal hands[4]. Prophetic warnings on the fall and secularization of the Church, poured forth by

revoked all the edicts which Boniface had promulgated against the French king.

[1] This period of about seventy years (1305—1309 at Lyons, 1309 to 1376 at Avignon) is known as 'the Captivity,' and was such when regarded from the ultramontane point of view: see *Vitæ Paparum Avenionensium*, ed. Baluze, Paris, 1693.

[2] Frederic II. had done this in his circular *Letters* to the Christian princes and the cardinals: Matthew Paris, p. 416: Neander, VII. 248. The example was followed by Philip the Fair: see above, p. 253, n. 5. A remarkable symptom of the state of feeling on this point is furnished by a poem of the 13th century (Cambr. Univ. MSS. Dd. XI. 78, § 18), where the Romans, after arguing with pope Innocent III., and charging him with becoming 'apostaticus' (fol. 114, a), are made to carry their appeal to a general council, which pronounces in their favour.

[3] *e.g.* by the Dominican, John of Paris, in his *Tractatus de Potestate Regali et Papali*, published in Goldast's *Monarchia sancti Romani Imperatoris*, II. 108 sq. An analysis of it is made in the posthumous volume of Neander, IX. pp. 22 sq. See also the *Quæstio disputata in utramque partem pro et contra pontificiam potestatem*, by Ægidius Romanus (afterwards archbishop of Bourges), in Goldast, II. 95 sq.; Neander, IX. 19. The worst evils of the age were traced to the temporal possessions of the pope and to the spurious 'Donatio Constantini,' on which those possessions were believed to rest: cf. above, p. 40, n. 6.

[4] See especially the '*Supplication du Pueuble de France au Roi contre le Pape Boniface le VIII.*,' in the Appendix to Du Puy's *Hist. du Différend entre le Pape et Philippes le Bel*, Paris, 1655.

earnest souls like Hildegard and Joachim[1], united with the sneers of chroniclers like Matthew Paris and a host of anti-papal songs[2] in waking the intelligence and passions of the many: while the spreading influence of the Universities and Parliaments[3] was tending, by a different course, to similar results. The vices of the sacred curia, uncorrected by the most despotic of its tenants, had excited general grief and indignation, even in the very staunchest advocates of Rome. St Bernard[4], for example, in admonishing Eugenius III. to extirpate abuses, could not help reverting with a sigh to earlier ages of the faith, when 'the Apostles did not cast their nets for gold and silver but for souls.' And both in Germany and in England, the impression had grown current that the Church of Rome, which had been reverenced there as a benignant mother, was now forfeiting her claim to such a title by imperious and novercal acts[5].

RELATIONS TO THE CIVIL POWER.

Premonitory symptoms of the Reformation.

---

[1] The 'abbot Joachim, in his exposition of Jeremy, and the maiden Hildegare in the book of her prophecy,' are frequently cited in these times by writers on the corruptions of the Church (*e.g.* in a Sermon preached by R. Wimbledon at St Paul's Cross, A.D. 1389, and printed in London, 1745). Respecting them and their influence, see Neander, VII. 298—322; Robertson, III. 206—212.

[2] Extracts from German ballads of this class have been collected in Stäudlin's *Archiv für alte und neu Kirchengesch.* IV. pt. iii. pp. 549 sq.: cf. above, p. 242, n. 3. The unmeasured fulminations of the Albigenses and other sectaries will be noticed on a future page. Dante (it is well known) associated a Roman bishop with the apocalyptic woman riding on the beast 'con le sette teste.'

[3] Cf. Capefigue's observations on this point, II. 163. ('On commençait une époque de curiosité et d'innovation.') Comte (*Philos. Posit.* lib. VI. c. 10) fixes on the opening of the 14th century as the origin of the revolutionary process, which has from that date been participated in by every social class, each in its own way.

[4] See his *De Consideratione ad Eugenium*, passim. In *epist.* 238, 'Amantissimo Patri et domino Dei gratia summo Pontifici Eugenio,' he asks: 'Quis mihi det antequam moriar videre ecclesiam Dei sicut in diebus antiquis, quando Apostoli laxabant retia in capturam, non in capturam argenti vel auri, sed in capturam animarum?'

[5] Thus Frederic II., in writing to the king of England (Matthew Paris, A.D. 1228, p. 293), complains that the 'Curia Romana,' which ought to be a nurse and mother-church, is 'omnium malorum radix et origo, non maternos sed *actus exercens novercales*, ex cognitis fructibus suis certum faciens argumentum.' And John of Salisbury, the bosom friend of Hadrian IV., assured that pontiff how the public feeling was now set against the Roman church; 'Sicut enim dicebatur a multis, Romana ecclesia, quæ mater omnium ecclesiarum est, *se non tam matrem exhibet aliis quam novercam.*' Policraticus, lib. VI. c. 24.

RELATIONS TO THE CIVIL POWER.

In other words, the struggle with the civil power had been maturing the predispositions that eventually attained their object in redressing ancient wrongs and in a general re-awakening of the Church.

CHAPTER XI.

ON THE STATE OF RELIGIOUS DOCTRINE AND CONTROVERSIES.

WESTERN CHURCH.

THE man who at this time surpassed all others in religious earnestness, and who has therefore been revered especially by all succeeding ages of the Church, was the illustrious Bernard, abbot of Clairvaux[1]. In reference to his system of theology he bears the title 'last of the Fathers,' representing what is called the 'positive,' patristic or traditionary school, which in the twelfth century was giving place to philosophical inquiries and to freer modes of thought. St Bernard, in his numerous *Letters, Tracts*, and *Sermons* (of which eighty-six are on the 'Book of Canticles' alone), exhibits a decided opposition[2] to the speculative, and as deep a love for the contemplative, or mystical, theology. His general object was to elevate and warm the spirit of the age in which he lived, and all his writings of this class are emanations from a truly Christian heart that, after communing profoundly with itself, appears to have obtained a satisfactory response

St Bernard (d. 1153). *The peculiar tone of his theology.*

---

[1] See above, p. 230, Neander's *Life* of him, translated by Wrench: and *Hist. Littér. de S. Bernard et de Pierre-le-Vénérable* by Dom Clémencet, ed. 1773.

[2] This antagonism is seen especially in his controversy with Abelard (see below). Thus, for instance, he writes in *Epist.* 192: 'Magister Petrus [*i.e.* Abelard] in libris suis profanas vocum novitates inducit et sensum, disputans de fide contra fidem, verbis legis legem impugnat. Nihil videt per speculum et in ænigmate, sed facie ad faciem omnia intuetur, ambulans in magnis et in mirabilibus super se.' The school of the Victorines (inmates of the abbey of St Victor at Paris) came back, as we shall see, in part to the standing ground of St Bernard.

WESTERN CHURCH.

The rise of the Schoolmen.

to its most ardent aspirations in that view of Holy Scripture which had been transmitted by the ancient doctors of the Church.

But meanwhile other principles, allied in some degree to those which characterize the Syrian school of theologians in the fifth century and John of Damascus in the eighth[1], were spreading in all parts of Europe. The *scholastic* era had begun. We saw the earliest trace of it, according to its proper definition, in the monastery of Bec[2], and Anselm, who became the abbot in 1078 and archbishop in 1093, may be regarded as the purest and most able type of schoolmen in the west[3]. He occupied the place of St Augustine in relation to the Middle Age. The basis of his principles indeed was also Augustinian[4]: but the form and colour which they took from the alliance now cemented between them and Aristotelian dialectics, gave to Anselm a peculiar mission, and, compared with his great master, a one-sided character.

Anselm, archbp. of Canterbury (d. 1109).

General drift of Scholasticism.

The leading object of the Schoolmen in the earlier stages of their course was not so much to stimulate a spirit of inquiry, as to write in the defence and illustration of the ancient dogmas of the Church[5]. In this

---

[1] See above, pp. 71, 72.
[2] Above, p. 159, n. 6.
[3] Cf. Möhler's *Essay* entitled *Die Scholastik des Anselmus* in his *Schriften* etc. (Regensburg, 1839), I. 129—176: Bornemann's *Anselmus et Abælardus*, Havniæ, 1840.
[4] Thus, according to his own account (*Epist.* lib. I. ep. 68), it had been his desire in controversy, 'ut omnino nihil ibi assererem, nisi quod aut canonicis aut *B. Augustini* dictis incunctanter posse defendi viderem.' The work here referred to is the *Monologium sive exemplum meditandi de ratione Fidei*, which, together with his *Proslogium* (or *Fides quærens Intellectum*), gives the best insight into his theologico-metaphysical system. Some parts of it were attacked by a monk named Gaunilo, and Anselm replied in the *Apologeticus*. His *Works*, containing a Life by his English pupil, Eadmer, were edited by Gerberon, Paris, 1675, and have been reprinted in Migne's *Patrologiæ cursus*, Paris, 1854. A contemporary, and in some respects an equal, of Anselm, was Hildebert of Lavardin, bishop of le Mans, and afterwards archbp. of Tours, who died about 1135. His works were published at Paris, in folio, 1708.
[5] The principle on which the true scholastic wrote is forcibly stated by Anselm in the following passage: 'Nullus quippe Christianus debet disputare, *quomodo* quod ecclesia catholica corde credit et ore confitetur, *non sit:* sed semper eandem fidem indubitanter tenendo, amando, et secundum illam vivendo humiliter quantum potest, quærere rationem quomodo sit.' *De Fide Trinitat. contra Roscellinum*, c. 2: or still more

capacity, they undertook to shew, (1) that faith and reason are not inconsistent; or, in other words, that all the supernatural elements of revelation are most truly rational: they laboured (2) to draw together all the several points of Christian doctrine, and construct them into one consistent scheme; and (3) they attempted the more rigorous definition of each single dogma, pointed out the rationale of it, and investigated its relation to the rest.

This method of discussion was extended even to the most inscrutable of all the mysteries of faith, the doctrine of the Blessed Trinity in Unity: and some of the scholastics did not hesitate to argue that the truth of it is capable of rigorous demonstration[1]. A dispute as to the proper terms in stating that and other doctrines opened out the controversy of the Nominalists and Realists, a question which employed the subtle spirit of the Schools at intervals for three or more centuries. The author of the former system[2] was the canon Rousellin, or Roscellinus[3], of Compiègne, who, holding that all general conceptions are no more than empty names ('flatus vocis'), or, in other words, are mere grammatical abstractions, chosen to facilitate our intellectual processes, but with no real and objective import, argued boldly from these principles that if, according to the current language of the Church, the essence of the Godhead might be spoken of as One reality ('una res'), the personal distinctness of the three Divine hypostases would be constructively denied. To view the Godhead thus was (in his eye) to violate the Christian faith: it was equivalent to saying that the Persons of the Holy Trinity were not Three distinct

Dispute between the Nominalists and Realists.

Opinions of Roscellinus:

touchingly in the *Proslogium*, c. 1; 'Non tento, Domine, penetrare altitudinem Tuam, quia nullatenus comparo illi intellectum meum; sed desidero aliquatenus intelligere veritatem Tuam, quam credit et amat cor meum. Neque enim quæro intelligere ut credam, sed credo ut intelligam.'

[1] Klee, *Hist. of Christian Dogmas* (German), part II. ch. ii. § 11.
[2] The problem, had, however, been suggested at an earlier date by Porphyry: see Cousin's *Ouvrages inédits d'Abélard*, pp. lx. sq. Paris. 1836: Gieseler, III. 278, n. 5.
[3] The historical notices of Roscellinus are very few: see *Epistola Johannis ad Anselmum*, in Baluze and Mansi, *Miscell.* II. 174: Anselm's *Liber de Fide Trinitatis et de Incarnatione Verbi contra blasphemias Ruzelini*. Gieseler, III. 281, n. 12, has also drawn attention to a letter of Roscellinus, *Ad Petr. Abælardum*, lately found in Munich.

_{WESTERN CHURCH.}

subsistencies ('non tres res'), but names and nothing more, without a counterpart in fact. He urged, accordingly, that to avoid Sabellianism the doctors of the Church were bound to call the Father, Son, and Holy Ghost three real Beings ('tres res') of equal majesty and will. A council held (1092) at Soissons[1] instantly denounced the author of these speculations on the ground that they were nothing short of tritheism: and Anselm, as the champion of the other system (or the school of Realists), took up his pen to write in its behalf[2]. According to his view the genus has a true subsistence prior to, and independent of the individuals numbered in the class it represents: particulars arise from universals, being fashioned after these (the 'universalia ante rem') or modelled on a general archetype that comprehends the properties of all[3].

condemned at the Council of Soissons, 1092; and refuted by Anselm.

But though the Nominalists were now suppressed, they afterwards returned to the encounter, headed by a man of most extraordinary powers. Abelard, born in Brittany (1079), was educated under William of Champeaux[4] (Campellensis), a renowned logician of the Realistic school. The boldness of his speculations and his brilliant talents soon attracted crowds of auditors to Paris, where he opened his

Abelard and his tendencies (d. 1142).

---

[1] See Pagi *Critic. in Baronii Annal.* ad an. 1094. Roscellinus abjured the heresy imputed to him, but afterwards withdrew his recantation. He died at last in retirement.

[2] The treatise above mentioned, p. 259, n. 3. He maintained that God, though Triune, is one 'Ipsum:' Dorner, p. 360. As the title indicates, Anselm looked upon the nominalistic theory of his opponent as subversive also of the doctrine of the Incarnation. He could not understand how Christ assumed humanity in all its fulness, if humanity be not a something real and objective, different from the nature of an individual man: cf. archd. Wilberforce, *On the Incarnation*, pp. 40 sq. The thoughts of Anselm on this doctrine are preserved at length in his remarkable treatise, *Cur Deus Homo*, analysed in part by Schröckh, xxviii. 376—384.

[3] The Nominalists regarded all general ideas (*universalia*) as nothing but abstractions of the human understanding, and derived from the objects presented to its observation (*post rem*). The Realists viewed such general ideas as having their origin entirely in the mind itself (*ante rem*), or as that which is essential in every thing actual (*in re*). Cf. Milman, *Latin Christianity*, iii. 247; Neander, viii. 3; and references in Gieseler, iii. 278, 279, n. 6.

[4] See a *Life* of him in the *Hist. Littér. de la France*, x. 307: cf. Cousin, as above, p. cx. A short Treatise of William de Champeaux, *De Origine Animæ*, is printed in Martène and Durand, *Thesaur. Anecd.* v. 877 sq.

career[1]. Success, however, threw him off his guard; and to the evil habits there contracted[2] many of his future griefs as well as many of his intellectual aberrations may be traced. His earliest publication was an *Introduction to Theology*[3], in which he has confined himself to an investigation of the mysteries connected with the Holy Trinity. It claims for men the right of free inquiry into all the subjects of belief, asserting that the highest form of faith is one which has resulted from a personal acquaintance with the ground on which it rests[4]. The indiscriminate avowal of this principle, united in his pupils with the boast, that nothing really exceeds the comprehension of a well-instructed mind, provoked the opposition of the older school of teachers[5]. The council of Soissons (1121) compelled him to withdraw his more extreme positions, and consign his volume to the flames[6]. But the enthusiasm awakened by his lectures did not die, and as

WESTERN CHURCH.

Condemnation of him at Soissons, 1121:

---

[1] He had indeed lectured for a while already at Laon in opposition to Anselm of that place, whose works are sometimes confounded with those of Anselm of Canterbury: see Cave, ad an. 1103.

[2] See his own epistle *De historia Calamitatum suarum*, in P. Abælardi et Heloisæ Opp. Paris, 1616: cf. *Hist. Littér. de la France* XII. 86 sq., 629 sq.; *Abélard*, par C. de Remusat, Paris, 1845; Milman, *Latin Christianity*, III. 251 sq.

[3] *Introductio ad Theolog. Christ., seu de Fide Trinitatis; Opp.* 973 sq. He tries to shew that the doctrine of the Trinity is a necessary conception of right reason, and as such was not unknown even to the Gentile sages: cf. the larger and revised edition of the treatise entitled *Theologia Christiana*, in Martène and Durand's *Thesaur. Anecd.* v. 1139 sq. Gieseler (III. 282, n. 16) supposes that another work, *Sententiæ Abælardi*, was derived also from this source.

[4] See Neander's remark on the difference between Anselm and Abelard, VIII. 35, 36. The strong feelings of the latter on this point may be estimated from a single passage: 'Asserunt [*i.e.* the anti-philosophic school] nil ad catholicæ fidei mysteria pertinens ratione investigandum esse, sed *de omnibus auctoritati statim credendum esse*, quantumcunque hæc ab humana ratione remota esse videatur. Quod quidem si recipiatur ...cujusque populi fides, quantamcunque adstruat falsitatem, refelli non poterit, etsi in tantam devoluta sit cæcitatem, ut idolum quodlibet Deum esse ac cœli ac terræ Creatorem fateatur.' *Introd. ad Theolog.* lib. II. c. 3, p. 1059.

[5] Walter de Mauretania (Mortagne) was one of these: see his *Epist. ad Petrum Abælard.*, in D'Achery, III. 525.

[6] Cf. his own account, *Hist. Calamit. suar.* c. 9, with Otto Frising. *De Gestis Frider.* lib. I. c. 47 (in Muratori, *Rer. Ital. Script.* tom. VI.). He now retired first to the abbey of St Denis, and afterwards to an oratory in the diocese of Troyes ('the Paraclete'). This he transferred to Heloise when he himself became abbot of Ruys in Brittany (1126—1136).

WESTERN CHURCH.

and at Sens, 1140.

Gilbert de la Porée (d. 1154).

he still adhered to his opinions[1], many charges of heretical teaching were brought against him. Bernard of Clairvaux, whose tone of mind was so completely different from his, had been induced[2] to take the lead in checking the dissemination of his views. The two great doctors were confronted in the council of Sens (June 22, **1140**); where it was decided that the teaching of Abelard was unsound[3], but that the mode of dealing with his person should, on his appeal, be left to the superior judgment of the pope. The latter instantly (July 16) approved their verdict and condemned the misbeliever to perpetual silence[4]. He now published a *Confession* and *Apology*[5] and died soon afterwards, the guest of Peter the Venerable[6] and the monks of Clugny (**1142**).

The zeal of Bernard was now turned against a kindred writer, Gilbert de la Porée (Porretanus), bishop of Poitiers (**1141**), who, in criticizing the established language of the Church, had been apparently betrayed into a class of

---

[1] Another startling work, his *Sic et Non*, had probably appeared in the mean time. Some portions of it are printed in Cousin's *Ouvrages inédits*. It exhibits the multiformity of Christian truth by placing side by side a number of divergent extracts from the Fathers, forming a manual for scholastic disputation: cf. Milman, III. 271. If Bernard saw this treatise, it explains his implacable hostility. Other causes of offence were found in his *Scito teipsum* and his *Commentary on the Epistle to the Romans*.

[2] By William, abbot of St Thierry, in Bernard. *Epist.* 326, al. 391. The ground of Bernard's opposition, which appears to have been first stated to Abelard in private, may be seen in his Letters (*Epp.* 188, 192, 193), and his *Tractatus de Erroribus P. Abælardi ad Innocent.* II.; *Opp.* I. 1441, ed. Paris, 1839.

[3] The charges brought against him were of the most serious kind, *e.g.* that he made 'degrees' in the holy Trinity, that he denied, or evacuated, the doctrines of grace, and divided the Person of our Lord like the Nestorians. All that is known respecting the proceedings of the council has been collected in Gieseler, III. 287, n. 24.

[4] In writing to Bernard and others, Innocent II. declares that he condemned the 'perversa dogmata cum auctore,' Mansi, XXI. 565; and afterwards commands, 'ut Petrum Abælardum et Arnaldum de Brixia [see above, p. 249], perversi dogmatis fabricatores et catholicæ fidei impugnatores, in religiosis locis...separatim faciatis includi, et libros erroris eorum, ubicumque reperti fuerint, igne comburi.'

[5] Respecting these and the spirit which suggested them, see Neander, VIII. 62, 63.

[6] By his influence a reconciliation was effected between Bernard and Abelard: see his *Epist.* lib. IV. ep. 4, in *Bibl. Patr.* ed. Lugdun. XXII. 907; Milman, III. 267.

errors bordering on Nestorianism¹. Convicted by a synod held at Paris in 1147, he disarmed his adversaries by recanting in the following year at Rheims² (March 21).

Western Church.

Our space will not admit a separate notice of the many other writers³, who in different ways attempted to pursue the philosophic methods of the Schoolmen in the study of theology. The impulse given in that direction by Abelard had been moderated for a time: the calmer views of Anselm having grown predominant, especially among the Victorines (surnamed from the abbey of S. Victor at Paris)—Hugo⁴, Richard⁵, and Walter⁶, all of whom combined the cultivation of the dialectics of the age with a more spiritual and mystic turn of mind⁷. It was through their endeavours more especially that men like Bernard were conciliated by degrees in favour of the general principles from which scholasticism had sprung.

Modification of Scholasticism.

Hugo of St Victor (d. 1141). Richard of St Victor (d. 1173). Walter of St Victor (circ. 1180). Robert le Poule, or Pullen (fl. 1150).

This combination was exhibited afresh in Robert le Poule (or Pullen), for some years distinguished as a

---

¹ The fourth proposition he was charged with maintaining is 'Quod Divina natura non esset incarnata:' cf. Capefigue, I. 357, 358. The following 'minor' points are also urged against him (Otto Frising. De Gestis Frider. lib. I. c. 50): 'Quod meritum humanum attenuando, nullum mereri diceret præter Christum: Quod Ecclesiæ sacramenta evacuando diceret, nullum baptizari nisi salvandum.' He wrote, among other subjects, on the Apocalypse (ed. Paris, 1512).

² See the 'Fidei symbolum contra errores Gilliberti Porretani,' in Mansi, XXI. 712.

³ e.g. John of Salisbury (d. 1180), a pupil of Abelard, but unlike him (Wright's Biogr. Brit. II. 230 sq.): Rupert of Deutz (d. 1135), a copious exegetical writer (Hist. Littér. de la France, XI. 422 sq.: Dorner, II. 389 sq.)

⁴ His chief works (ed. Rotomagi, 1648) are De Sacramentis Fidei and the Summa Sententiarum (assigned incorrectly, with the title Tractatus Theologicus, to Hildebert of Tours): see Liebner's Hugo von S. Victor und die theol. Richtungen seiner Zeit, Leipzig, 1832, and Hist. Littér. de la France, XII. 7. Neander (VIII. 65 sq.) gives a striking summary of his modes of thought.

⁵ Richard was of Scottish extraction, and wrote De Trinitate, De statu interioris hominis, etc. (ed. Rotomagi, 1650): cf. Neander, VIII. 80—82; Schröckh, XXIX. 275—290.

⁶ The opposition to Abelard and his school was strongest in this writer (otherwise called Walter of Mauretania; see above, p. 261, n. 5). His chief work is commonly entitled Contra quatuor labyrinthos Galliæ, being a passionate attack on the principles of Abelard, Peter Lombard, Peter of Poitiers, and Gilbert de la Porée. Extracts only are printed in Bulæus, Hist. Univ. Paris, II. 200 sq., 402 sq., 562 sq., 629 sq.

⁷ On this peculiarity, and the Greek influence it betrayed, see Dorner, II. 360 sq.

WESTERN CHURCH.

Peter Lombard, Master of the Sentences (d. 1164).

preacher¹ in Oxford, and at length a Roman cardinal (1144). His treatise called the *Sentences*² ('Libri Sententiarum') recognized the principle of basing every dialectic process on the Holy Scriptures and the Fathers. But the classical production of this kind is one by Peter Lombard, of Novara, who attained the greatest eminence at Paris³, where he died as bishop in 1164. His work was also termed *The Sentences*⁴ (or 'Quatuor Libri Sententiarum'). It consisted of timid arguments upon the leading theological questions then debated in the schools, supported always by quotations from the older Latin doctors of the Church; and since the whole is neatly and methodically put together, it was welcomed as a clear and useful hand-book by the students in divinity. Its fame, indeed, extended everywhere, and many able scholars both of that and future times wrote commentaries on it, making

---

¹ .... 'ibique scripturas Divinas, quæ per idem tempus in Anglia obsoluerant, præ scholasticis quippe neglectæ fuerant, per quinquennium legit, omnique die Dominico verbum Dei populo prædicavit, ex cujus doctrina plurimi profecerunt.' Quoted in Wright's *Biogr. Britan.* II. 182 (note). Another Englishman of distinction in the field of metaphysical theology was Robert of Melun, bishop of Hereford, who wrote a *Summa Theologiæ*. Ibid. p. 201. Copious extracts from this *Summa* are printed in Bulæus, *Histor. Univers. Paris.* II. 585—628.

² Published at Paris, 1655. He appears to have also written on the Apocalypse, and twenty of his Sermons are preserved among the Lambeth MSS. Wright, *Ibid.* p. 183.

³ He was opposed by Walter of St Victor (above, p. 263, n. 6), for his speculations touching the Incarnation (or 'Nihilianism,' as they were called); see Dorner, II. 379 sq.: but his work *On the Sentences* received the formal approbation of Innocent III. at the council of Lateran (1215), c. 2.

⁴ The first book treats 'De Mysterio Trinitatis,' the second 'De Rerum corporalium et spiritualium creatione et formatione,' the third 'De Incarnatione Verbi aliisque ad hoc spectantibus,' the fourth 'De Sacramentis et signis sacramentalibus.' See Schröckh's account of it and its author, XXVIII. 487—534; and an analysis of the work in Turner, *Middle Ages*, Part IV. ch. 1; and cf. Milman, *Latin Christianity*, Bk. XIV. ch. III. Peter Lombard had before him a Latin version of the great work of John Damascenus, περὶ ὀρθοδόξου πίστεως, and thus connected the Western with the Eastern scholasticism: Dorner, II. 257, 258. *Summæ* and *Sententiæ* were now multiplied in every quarter, the first being mainly devoted to the free discussion of doctrines and speculative problems, and the second more especially to the arrangement of passages derived from the writings of the Fathers. To the former class belongs the *Ars Catholicæ Fidei ex rationibus naturalibus demonstratæ*, of Alanus Magnus, a Parisian doctor (d. 1202), in Pez, *Thesaur. Anecdot.* I. pt. ii. 475 sq.

it the groundwork of more shrewd and independent speculations.

Hitherto the influence of the Aristotelic philosophy had been confined almost entirely to the single field of dialectics[1], where it served for the defence of Christian dogmas. Plato was the real favourite of the Church, although a concord[2] having been in part established between him and the Stagirite, the opinions of the latter had indirectly tinctured the theology of many writers in the west. It is remarkable, indeed, that when the other works of Aristotle, through the medium of the Arabs and Crusaders, were more widely circulated in the twelfth century, they were not only treated by the popes and councils with suspicion, but the physical and metaphysical books were actually condemned[3]. Yet this antipathy soon afterwards abated[4], and in the more palmy period of the Schoolmen, dating from Alexander of Hales, the blending of the Aristotelic processes and doctrines with the con-

WESTERN CHURCH.

Change of feeling with respect to Aristotle.

---

[1] Cf. above, p. 160, n. 2. The other works of Aristotle were, however, studied with enthusiasm in the Moorish schools of Spain, especially after the time of Avicenna (Ebn-Sina), who died in 1036. A new impulse in the same direction was given by Averroes (Ebn-Rashid), at the close of the twelfth century, who combined with his belief in the Koran an almost servile deference to the philosophic views of the Stagirite. See authorities in Tennemann's *Manual of Philosophy*, §§ 255—257: cf. Milman, VI. 265 sq. From the tenets of Averroes, when imbibed by Christian writers, grew the tendency to scepticism which the profound and ever-active Raymond Lull (above, p. 219) especially endeavoured to resist in his *Ars Generalis*.

[2] See Neander, VIII. 91, 92, 127; and Dr Hampden's *Thomas Aquinas*, in *Encyclop. Metrop.* XI. 804, 805.

[3] *e.g.* at the synod of Paris (1209 or 1210), and afterwards by a papal legate (1215). The 'statute' of the latter (Bulæus, *Hist. Univ. Paris*, III. 81) is as follows: 'Et quod legant libros Aristotelis de dialectica, tam de veteri quam de nova in scholis ordinarie et non ad cursum...Non legantur libri Aristotelis de metaphysica et naturali philosophia, nec Summæ de eisdem aut de doctrina magistri de Dinant aut Amalrici hæretici, aut Mauricii Hispani.' These persons were infected with the Pantheistic principles advocated by Erigena, and then spreading in the Moorish schools: see Dorner, II. 365, 366. The pope (1229) again forbids the introduction of 'profane science' into the study of Scripture and tradition: cf. Capefigue's remarks, II. 165, 166; and Milman, VI. 268.

[4] Thus Roger Bacon (*Opus Majus*, p. 14, ed. Jebb), writing fifty years later, says that Aristotle's treatises had been condemned 'ob densam ignorantiam.' Among the works of Robert Grosseteste (see above, p. 228) is a *Commentary* on parts of Aristotle (*in Libros Posteriorum*), ed. Venet. 1552.

WESTERN CHURCH.

troversies of the Western Church was almost universal[1].

Alexander of Hales (d. 1245), the Irrefragable.

Alexander of Hales (Alexius), after studying in the convent of that name in Gloucestershire, attained a high celebrity at Paris, where he was distinguished from the many scholars of the age as the 'Irrefragable Doctor.' His great work is a *Summa Universae Theologiae*[2], in which the various topics handled in the book of Peter Lombard are extended and discussed according to the strictly syllogistic method of the Schools.

He was a mendicant of the Franciscan order, and as such had taken part in the training of another schoolman (the 'Seraphic Doctor'), who was destined to effect a lasting hold upon the spirit of the Western Churches. This was John of Fidanza, or Bonaventura, in whom the rising order of Franciscans found an able champion[3] and a venerated head. Inferior in acumen to his fellow-countryman, archbishop Anselm, he was more than equal in the warmth and elevation of his feelings, though the mode in which they were too frequently expressed—the rapturous worship of the Virgin[4]—is a deep and startling blemish on his character. His works are very numerous[5], for the most part of a mystical, ascetic, and subjective kind.

Bonaventura (d. 1274), the Seraphic.

Contemporary with these two Franciscans, and no less distinguished, were the two Dominicans, Albert the Great and Thomas Aquinas, standing also in the same relation of tutor and pupil. Albert[6], born in Swabia (1193),

Albertus Magnus (d. 1280), the Universal.

---

[1] Cf. Milman's remarks on the era of Scholasticism, and the schoolmen; *Latin Christianity*, vi. 272 sq.; and Brewer's Preface to *Monumenta Franciscana*, pp. iii. sq., in *Chronicles and Memorials of Great Britain*.

[2] *Opp.* ed. Cologne, 1622, 4 vols.; see Schröckh (xxix. 9—54) for a sketch of his theological system.

[3] See above, p. 234; and, on his life and writings, *Hist. Littér. de la France*, xxix. 266 sq.; Schröckh, xxix. 209—282.

[4] When he became general of the Franciscans, he placed them under the peculiar patronage of the Virgin, and his works abound with extravagant and almost impious sayings in her honour (e.g. *Speculum de Laudibus B. Mariae*). It has been disputed whether the *Psalterium B. Mariae* be his or not, e.g. by Alban Butler in his *Life of S. Bonaventura* (July 14): cf. Schröckh, xxviii. 255, and Capefigue, ii. 40.

[5] The Vatican edition is in 8 vols. folio. Among the rest (vol. iv. v.) is a *Commentarius in IV. Libr. Sententiarum*. The first and second volumes contain expositions of the Holy Scriptures.

[6] See his *Works* in 21 vols. folio, ed. Lyons, 1651: and, for his Life,

educated at Paris and Bologna, and eventually settling at Cologne, exhibited all the marks of the genuine scholar. He was conversant with nearly every field of human thought, but most at home in physics, natural history, and ethics. His chief writings in divinity are *Commentaries*[1] on the Book of Sentences, and a *Summa Theologiæ*[2], in both of which, amid a crowd of metaphysical subtleties peculiar to the time, he manifests a clear conception of the leading truths of Christianity.

But Albert and indeed all others were eclipsed by his illustrious and profound disciple. Thomas de Aquino[3] (or Aquinas), honoured with the names of 'Universal' and 'Angelic Doctor,' and the founder of the able school of 'Thomists,' proved himself the master-spirit of scholasticism, and a most worthy representative of mediæval philosophy. He took his stand among the school of Realists, and was devoted strongly to the Aristotelian dialectics, which he used as the organ of investigation: but his independent genius urged him to dissent materially from other principles of Aristotle, and to graft upon the older system many foreign elements. A careful study[4] of the Bible and the Book of Sentences prepared him for the composition of those powerful works which occupied him till his death in 1274. The greatest of them is the *Summa Totius Theologiæ*[5], which, as it forms a clear exponent of

WESTERN CHURCH.

Thomas Aquinas (1224—1274), the Angelic.

General outline of his Summa Theologiæ.

Scriptores Ord. Prædicat. by Quetif and Echard, I. 162 sq., Schröckh, XXIV. 424 sq.

[1] Filling, vol. XIV—XVI.
[2] See Schröckh's Analysis, XXIX. 57 sq.
[3] See his *Life* in the *Acta Sanct.* Mart. I. 655 sq., and on his philosophico-religious system, Dr Hampden's *Aquinas*, in *Encycl. Metrop.* XL. 793 sq.; Schröckh, XXIX. 71—208; Ritter's *Gesch. der Christl. Philos.* IV. 257 sq.
[4] It is also mentioned in his biography (as above) that he never wrote, lectured, or disputed, without betaking himself to God in prayer for the Divine illumination, and he did the same when he was confronted by difficulties and doubts. The reason he assigned for the peculiar frequency of his devotions was the following: 'Quia frequenter contingit, quod dum intellectus superius subtilia speculatur, affectus inferius a devotione remittitur.'
[5] A good edition, with copious indexes, was published at Arras (Atrebati) in 1610. The whole works of Aquinas have been often reprinted. The best edition is that of Venice (1745 sq.) in 28 vols. 4to. His *Catena Aurea* (from the Fathers) has been translated into English (Oxf. 1843).

his views and is the most colossal work of that or any period, merits an especial notice[1]. It is divided into three great parts, (1) the Natural, (2) the Moral, (3) the Sacramental. In the first of these, the writer ascertains the nature and the limits of theology, which he esteems a proper science, based upon a supernatural revelation, the contents of which, though far transcending all the powers of human thought, are, when communicated, subjects for devout inquiry and admit of argumentative defence. Accordingly the writer next discusses the existence and the attributes of God, endeavouring to elucidate the nature of His will, His providence, the ground of His predestination[2], and the constitution of the Blessed Trinity in Unity,—a doctrine which, although he deems it incapable of logical demonstration, finds an echo and a counterpart in man. Descending from the Cause to the effects, he analyses the constituent parts of the creation, angels, the material world, and men, enlarging more especially upon the functions of the human soul, its close relation to the body, and the state of both before the Fall.

The second part is subdivided into the *Prima Secundæ*, and the *Secunda Secundæ*. The former carries on the general subject, viewing men no longer from the heavenly but from the earthly side, as moral and responsible agents gifted with a vast complexity of passions, sentiments, and faculties. The way in which these powers would naturally operate, if acting by themselves, is first considered, and the author then proceeds to shew how they are modified by supernatural agencies, or coexistent gifts of grace[3]. This leads him to compare the state, or the position, of mankind in reference to the systems (or economies) of

---

[1] Cf. Hampden, as above, p. 267, n. 3, and Kling's *Descriptio Summæ Theolog. Thomæ Aquin. succincta*, Bonn, 1846.

[2] On this point his views are rigorously Augustinian; Par. I. Quæst. XXIII. Anselm wrote a special treatise on it in a somewhat milder tone. The title is, *De Concordia Præscientiæ et Prædestinationis necnon Gratiæ Dei cum libero arbitrio*.

[3] He does not indeed suppose, as many of the Schoolmen did, that the communication of the gifts of grace was to depend upon the way in which mankind employed the simply natural qualities ('pura naturalia'). His view is, that grace was given from the first, and that the harmonious coexistence of the natural and the supernatural constituted man's 'originalis justitia.' The violation of this harmony ('inordinata dispositio partium animæ') is original sin. Cf. Neander, VIII. 193.

grace and nature, and, as the immediate consequence, to treat of our original righteousness, free-will, original sin, justification[1], and the various rules of life. In the *Secunda Secundæ*, the several virtues are discussed in turn, as they exist under the operation of Divine grace or that of nature only. They are seven in number. Three of them are 'theological,' or supernaturally infused and nourished,— viz. faith, hope, and love, while the remainder are the four cardinal virtues of justice, prudence, fortitude, and temperance, and are 'ethical' or purely human. The discussion of these virtues forms an admirable work on Christian morals.

<small>WESTERN CHURCH.</small>

The third part of the *Summa* is devoted to an exposition of the mysteries of the Incarnation and the efficacy of the Sacraments,—a class of topics which, according to the principles of all the mediæval writers, are essentially akin[2]. Aquinas traces every supernatural influence to the Person of the Word made flesh, who by the union of our nature with the Godhead has become the Reconstructor of humanity and the Dispenser of new life. This life, together with the aliment by which it is sustained, descends to man through certain outward media, or the sacramental ordinances of the Church: their number being seven, viz. Baptism, Confirmation, the Eucharist, Penitence, Orders, Matrimony, and Extreme Unction[3]. In the last division of the work we see the mighty influence of Aquinas in determining the scientific form and mutual action of those

<small>*Tertia Pars.*</small>

---

[1] This he makes to be primarily the infusion of grace, which operates (1) in the spontaneous movement of the will to God, (2) in the resistance to sin, and (3) to its forgiveness; although these effects are said to be produced simultaneously. *Prima Secund.* Quæst. CXIII. Art. 8: cf. Neander, VIII. 222 sq.

[2] 'Post considerationem eorum quæ pertinent ad mysteria Verbi Incarnati, considerandum est de Ecclesiæ sacramentis, quæ ab Ipso Verbo Incarnato efficaciam habent.' Quæst. LX. On the mutual relations and order of the sacraments in the theological system of Aquinas, see Quæst. LXV. Art. 1, 2. One of his reasons for assigning the chief place to the Eucharist is this: 'Nam in sacramento Eucharistiæ continetur Ipse Christus substantialiter, in aliis autem sacramentis continetur quædam virtus instrumentalis participata a Christo.' *Ibid.* Art. 3.

[3] The discussion of these points in detail was cut short by the author's death, before he reached the 'sacrament of orders:' but a Supplement containing his opinions on the rest was formed out of his Commentary on the *Book of Sentences*, and is appended to the Arras and other editions of the *Summa*.

WESTERN CHURCH.

doctrines which hereafter threatened to obtain complete ascendancy in all the western Churches.

John Duns Scotus (d. 1308), the Subtle.

The most powerful rival of Aquinas and the Thomists of this period was the English Franciscan, John Duns Scotus[1], whose acumen and success in the scholastic fields of war enabled him to organize the party known as 'Scotists.' He was termed the 'Subtle Doctor,' and although a realist in the dispute concerning universals and particulars, diverged on many topics from the system of Aquinas[2], and attracted a large number of disciples.

The peculiar opinions of his school.

In the narrower province of theology he is remarkable for his antagonism, in part at least, to the authority of St Augustine. He maintained the freedom of the human will, and stated other principles in such a way as to incur the imputation of Pelagianism[3]; while in his theorizing with regard to the conception of the Virgin he opposed, not only the more ancient teaching of the Church[4], but also that of Bernard[5] and the school of Thomists[6].

[1] Born at Dunston, near Alnwick; or at Dunse in Berwickshire; at 'Duns in the countrey of *Mers*, according to Spotswood (anno 1328),' p. 54. See *Life* of Scotus by Wadding (the Franciscan annalist) prefixed to his edition of the Works of Scotus, Lugdun. 1639, 12 vols. fol.

[2] Schröckh, xxiv. 435 sq.; Ritter, iv. 354 sq. Gieseler (iii. 305, n. 26) draws attention to an order in which all the Franciscan lecturers are commanded to follow Scotus 'tam in cursu philosophico quam in theologico.'

[3] *e.g.* on the question of original sin he argued that it was barely negative, a 'carentia justitiæ debitæ' (*In Lib. Sentent.* lib. ii. Dist. xxxii. § 7), discarding from his definition the idea of concupiscence (*Ibid.* Dist. xxx.) He questioned the absolute necessity of preventing grace, asserting 'quod ex puris naturalibus potest quæcunque voluntas saltem in statu naturæ instituta diligere Deum super omnia' (*Ibid.* lib. iii. Dist. xxvii. § 15): and while Aquinas made the heresy of Pelagius to consist in maintaining 'quod initium bene faciendi sit ex nobis, consummatio autem a Deo' (*Summa*, Part i., Quæst. xxiii., Art. 5), Scotus thought the root of it to lie in the position 'quod liberum arbitrium *sufficiat* sine gratia' *Ibid.* lib. ii. Dist. xxviii. § 1). These Pelagianizing tendencies of the Scotists were opposed by archbp. Bradwardine (of Canterbury), who died 1349, in his *De Causa Dei contra Pelagium*, etc., ed. Savile, Lond. 1618.

[4] Cf. above, p. 233, n. 5. Dorner (ii. 416, 417) connects the Mariolatry of Scotus with his peculiar views of the Incarnation.

[5] Bernard in his *Epist.* clxxiv. speaks of the doctrine of the immaculate conception as a novelty, 'quam ritus Ecclesiæ nescit, non probat ratio, non commendat antiqua traditio,' etc.

[6] In the *Summa*, Part. iii. Quæst. xxvii. Art. 1, as contrasted with Duns Scotus, *In Libr. Sentent.* lib. iii. Dist. iii. Quæst. i. §§ 9, 14 sq.; and *Rosarium B. Mariæ, seu Append. ad quæst.* 1. *dist.* 3: cf. Klee, *Hist.*

Passing by a crowd of minor writers[1] who adhered to one or other of these theological parties, our attention is arrested by the most original genius whom the thirteenth century produced. The Friar Bacon[2], born at Ilchester, in Somersetshire, **1214**, was trained in the universities of Oxford and Paris, where his time was for the most part devoted to scientific pursuits, and to the study of languages. His great proficiency in these had won for him the name of 'Doctor Mirabilis.' He entered the Franciscan Order, but the more fanatic members of that body, joining with unlettered clergymen and academics, put an end to his public lectures, and eventually procured his incarceration (**1278**), on the ground that he was prying too minutely into all the mysteries of nature. In the *Opus Majus de utilitate Scientiarum*[3],—a collection of his works addressed in **1266** to Pope Clement IV.,—the general object is to inculcate the need of a reform in the physical and other sciences: but he did not hesitate to push his principle of free inquiry into every sphere of human thought[4]. While indicating little or no love for the scholastic subtleties[5],

WESTERN CHURCH.

Roger Bacon (d. 1294), *the Wonderful.*

His general views in relation to theology.

---

of Dogmas, part II. ch. III. § 25, where it is mentioned that Duns Scotus so far carried his point in the University of Paris as to exclude all persons from degrees who did not pledge themselves to maintain the truth of the immaculate conception.

[1] William of Auvergne, bishop of Paris (d. 1248), deserves some mention as a theologian and apologist (*Opp.* Paris, 1674, 2 vols. folio), and as a sample of the scanty stock of writers who were not attached to one or other of the Mendicant Orders. Of the ritualists belonging to the thirteenth century the most eminent is Duranti (not to be confounded with a nominalistic schoolman, Durand de S. Pourçain), whose *Rationale Divinorum Officiorum* is a copious exposition of the principles supposed to be expressed in the structure, ornaments, the ministry, and ritual of the Church. It has been often published, *e.g.* Venet. 1609. On the other liturgical writings of the period, see Schröckh, XXVIII. 277 sq.

[2] Roger is to be distinguished from his contemporary *Robert* Bacon, the friend of Grosseteste. See Tanner's *Biblioth.* under the names: from which source a good account of Friar Bacon and his writings may be drawn. Some idea of his marvellous acquaintance with chemistry and other sciences is given by Dr Shaw, in Dr Hook's *Eccl. Biogr.* I. 450, 451: cf. Palgrave's *Merchant and Friar*, passim; and the Preface to the volume of Bacon's *Opera Inedita*, ed. Brewer, 1859, in the series of *Chronicles and Memorials of Great Britain.*

[3] Ed. Jebb, Lond. 1733.

[4] *e.g.* he points out errors in the writings of the Fathers (c. 12), arguing that 'in omni homine est multa imperfectio sapientiae, tam in sanctis quam in sapientibus.'

[5] He preferred Aristotle on the whole, but added very characteris-

he spoke in favour of the wider circulation and more earnest study of the sacred volume, tracing nearly all the evils of the times to want of personal acquaintance with this heavenly rule of life[1]. He proved the clearness and fertility of his convictions on these points by recommending a revision of the Latin Vulgate[2], and especially by urging the importance of recurring to the Greek and Hebrew texts. Indeed the mind of Roger Bacon was so greatly in advance of the period when he lived, as to have antedated much of what has only flourished since the reformation of the Western Church.

EASTERN CHURCH.

There was little in the mind of Eastern Christendom to correspond with the activity, enthusiasm, and almost universal progress we have noted in the sister churches of the West. Reposing with a vague and otiose belief on the traditional doctrines as they had been logically systematized by John of Damascus, the great body of the 'orthodox' (or Greek) communion were subsiding fast into a state of spiritual deadness and of intellectual senility. The rigours of Byzantine despotism, too prone to intermeddle with the articles of faith[3], the ill example of a

Deadness of the Greek communion.

tically, 'Posteriores ipsum in aliquibus correxerunt, et multa ad ejus opera addiderunt, et adhuc addentur usque ad finem mundi: quia *nihil est perfectum in humanis inventionibus:*' Ibid. part II. c. 8. The highest of all sciences (according to him) is the science that treats of divine things, and it is all contained in the Bible 'quæ in sacris literis tota continetur, per jus tamen canonicum et philosophiam explicanda:' as in the following note, p. 421: cf. Neander, VIII. 112, 113.

[1] See the remarkable extracts from his *Epistola de Laude Scripturæ Sanctæ*, in the additions made to Ussher's *Hist. Dogmat.* by Wharton (Lond. 1689), pp. 420—424. The MS. is in the Library at Lambeth: no. cc. fol. 38.

[2] This idea was carried out in part by Hugo de S. Charo (S. Cher), a Dominican (d. 1263), who by the aid of Hebrew, Greek, and Latin MSS. reformed the text of the whole Bible. He also composed a *Concordance* of the Scriptures (Schröckh, XXVIII. 331), and *Postillæ in Universa Biblia, juxta quadruplicem sensum* (Ibid. 368).

[3] Cf. above, p. 50, n. 4. In the present period Nicetas Choniates (*De Manuele Comneno*, lib. VII. c. 5) remarks that the emperors expected men to believe that they were, ὡς Σολομῶν θεόσοφοι καὶ δογματισταὶ θειότατοι, καὶ κανόνες τῶν κανόνων εὐθέστεροι, καὶ ἁπλῶς θείων καὶ ἀνθρωπίνων πραγμάτων ἀπροσφαλεῖς γνώμονες. The emperor here alluded to (1143—1180) excited a most violent controversy, by insisting on the general adoption of this

crowd of idle and unlettered monks[1], and the perplexities entailed upon the Eastern empire by the recklessness of the Crusaders[2], had contributed to this result. The literary spirit now and then revived, however; and if they in whom it wrought are often shadows in comparison of men like Chrysostom, or Basil, or the Gregories, they must be, notwithstanding, viewed as bright exceptions to the general dulness of the age.

Among the foremost scholars of the eleventh century is Michael Psellus, the younger, who besides composing multifarious treatises[3] on jurisprudence, physics, mathematics, and philosophy, displayed an aptitude for higher fields of contemplation in his *Chapters on the Holy Trinity and the Person of Christ*, and his *Paraphrases* on the Old Testament.

Contemporary with him was Theophylact[4], archbishop of Bulgaria, who achieved a lasting reputation by his *Commentaries* on the Gospels, the Acts, the Epistles of St Paul, and the Minor Prophets. They are based, however, for the most part on the corresponding labours of St Chrysostom.

Another exegetical writer was a monk of Constantinople, Euthymius Zigabenus[5], who commented on the Psalms, the Gospels, and the Pauline Epistles, in the style, and not

Michael Psellus (d. 1105?)

Theophylact (d. 1112?)

Euthymius Zigabenus (d. 1118?)

---

formula, τὸν σεσαρκωμένον Θεὸν προσφέρειν τε ὁμοῦ καὶ προσφέρεσθαι (*Ibid.*). Some of the bishops who resisted it, when sanctioned by a council, were instantly deposed: cf. Neander, VIII. 252, 253. On a later occasion, when the prelates made a stand against him, Manuel threatened to call in the pope, which ultimately led to a compromise: *Ibid.* p. 254. The despotism of Michael Palæologus (1259—1282) occasioned what is known as the Arsenian schism (1266—1312), by which the Church of Constantinople was for a time divided in itself and separated from that of Alexandria. See Neale, II. 311, 312.

[1] See the startling revelations of Eustathius, Ἐπίσκεψις βίου μοναχικοῦ ἐπὶ διορθώσει τῶν περὶ αὐτόν, *passim. Opp.* ed. Tafel, 1832.

[2] On the relations of the East and West at this period, see below, pp. 276 sq.

[3] See a list of them in Oudinus, *De Scriptoribus Eccl.* II. 646, and the article in Smith's *Biogr. Dict.* III. 563, 564. The work on the Trinity and some of the paraphrases have been published. Psellus also wrote an ecclesiastical treatise, Εἰς τὰς ἁγίας ἑπτὰ συνόδους, Basil. 1536.

[4] *Opp.* Venet. 1754—1763, 4 vols. fol.: cf. Schröckh, XXVIII. 315—318. The sober views of Theophylact on the separation of East and West may be gathered from his *Lib. de iis in quibus Latini accusantur.*

[5] Cf. above, p. 180, n. 1. Gieseler contends that he should be called Zygadenus. His valuable *Commentaries* on the Psalms and Gospels have

EASTERN CHURCH.

unfrequently the language, of the earlier doctors of the East. He also wrote a *Panoply*[1] in refutation of all forms of misbelief, deriving the great bulk of his materials from the same quarter.

Nicetas Acominatus (d. 1206 ?)

In the following century a kindred work[2], intended as the complement of this, proceeded from the learned pen of Nicetas Acominatus (born at Chonæ, formerly Colosse). The title is *Thesaurus Orthodoxiæ*, but only portions of it have been published.

Nicholas bp. of Methone (d. 1200 ?)

Nicholas, bishop of Methone (in Messenia) was a more original and able writer. He examined and rejected the philosophy of Proclus[3], the Neo-Platonist, whose principles appear to have survived in the Peloponnesus, and was also energetic in repelling the encroachments of the pope and in defending the peculiar tenets of the Greeks.

Eustathius archbp. of Thessalonica (d. 1198).

But all the Eastern scholars of this period are surpassed by the archbishop of Thessalonica, Eustathius. His gigantic commentaries[4] on the ancient poets, more especially on Homer, did not so engross his mind as to unfit him for the prosecution of his ecclesiastical studies. Some of his minor works[5], including *Sermons* and *Epistles*, have lately come to light, and we there see him treading in the

---

been often printed in Latin versions. The Greek text of that on the Psalms is in Theophylacti *Opp.* Tom. IV. 325 sqq.: that on the Gospels was printed at Leipzig, 1792, and Athens, 1840. The *Commentary* on the Epistles exists only in MS. Cf. Fabricius, *Bibl. Græca*, VIII. 328 sq.; Gieseler, III. 485, n. 4; and Schröckh (XXVIII. 306 sq.) on the character of his works.

[1] The full title is Πανοπλία δογματική τῆς ὀρθοδόξου πίστεως. Part only of the Greek original has been published (at Tergovisto, in Wallachia, 1711). A Latin translation appeared at Venice in 1555: but the thirteenth title, κατὰ τῶν τῆς παλαιᾶς Ῥώμης, ἤτοι τῶν Ἰταλῶν, on the doctrine of the Procession, is there dropped. See an interesting article (by Ullmann), in the *Studien und Kritiken*, for 1833, III. 665. Another work of this class (*A Collection of the Principles of Faith*) was composed for the Alexandrino Jacobites by Ebn-Nassal. It not only refutes the systems of paganism and Judaism, but makes an assault on the Nestorians and the Melchites. Neale, II. 304.

[2] Ullmann, *Ibid.* p. 680. The whole is extant in the Royal Library of Paris. The first five books appeared in Paris, 1569. On the historical writings of the author, see Smith's *Biogr. Dict.* II. 1183.

[3] The title of the treatise is Ἀνάπτυξις τῆς θεολογικῆς στοιχειώσεως Πρόκλου, ed. Vömel, Francf. 1825: cf. Ullmann, as above, pp. 701 sq. His treatises *De Primatu Papæ*, etc. are not published (Fabricius, *Bibl. Græc.* XI. 290).

[4] See Smith's *Biogr. Dict.* II. 120.

[5] Eustathii *Opuscula*, ed. Tafel, Franzof. 1832: cf. Neander, VIII. 248.

steps of Chrysostom, and waging war against the hollow- — EASTERN CHURCH.
ness, frivolity, and superstitions of the age.

Besides a multitude of long-forgotten writers on divinity, *Ebed-Jesu* (d. 1318).
and some who still enjoy considerable fame as jurists and
historians, others had continued to spring up beyond the
pale of the 'Orthodox' communion. Ebed-Jesu[1] metropolitan of Soba (Nisibis) was the most able and voluminous
writer of the Chaldæan (or 'Nestorian') body; and among
the Jacobites were Dionysius Bar-Salibi[2], bishop of Amida, *Bar-Salili* (d. 1171).
Jacob[3], bishop of Tagritum, and Abulpharagius[4] (Bar- *Jacob of Tagritum* (d. 1231).
Hebræus), maphrian or primate of the East. The kindred
sect of the Armenians also added many contributions to *Abulpha-ragius* (d. 1286).
the province of dogmatic and polemical theology, as well
as to the other fields of learning[5]. The best known and
most accessible are those of the Armenian catholicos, *Nerses* (d. 1173).
Nerses[6], who exhibits a decided predilection for the western
modes of thought.

Hated and occasionally persecuted by their Moslem conquerors, these sects had gradually been drawn more closely
to each other[7], though retaining their distinctive creeds.
The state of feeling was, however, different in the Greek
and Latin Christians, whom we saw diverging more completely and exchanging the most bitter fulminations at the
close of the previous period.

---

[1] Among other things (see Asseman, *Bibl. Orient.* III. part. I. 325) he wrote a treatise entitled *Liber Margaritæ seu de Veritate Christianæ Religionis*, printed in Maii *Script. Vet. Nova Collectio*, Rom. 1825, Tom. x. part. II. 317 sq.

[2] He wrote *Commentaries* on the whole Bible and many other treatises (Asseman, *Ibid.* II. 156). His *Liturgia* is published in Renaudot, *Liturg. Orient. Collectio*, II. 448 sq., ed. 1847.

[3] On his *Liber Thesaurorum*, see Asseman, *Ibid.* II. 237.

[4] Besides a very important historical work, *Hist. Dynastiarum*, of which versions have been printed entire (ed. Pocock, 1663), together with a portion of the original Syriac (Leipzig, 1789) and extracts from the rest in Asseman (*Ibid.* II. 244—463), Abulpharagius wrote many strictly theo-logical works, *e.g. Horreum Mysteriorum, Candelabrum Sanctorum de Fundamentis ecclesiasticis.* His *Nomocanon Ecclesiæ Antiochenæ* is pub-lished in a Latin version by Mai, as above, Tom. x. part. II. 1—268: and his *Liturgia* in Renaudot, II. 455—467, where see the editor's annotations, pp. 467—470.

[5] See Neumann's *Gesch. der Armenisch. Liter.* p. 148: cf. above, p. 175, n. 4.

[6] His works, with a Latin version, were published at Venice, in 2 vols. 8vo. 1833.

[7] Asseman (II. 291) quotes the following from Abulpharagius, who,

RELATIONS OF THE EASTERN AND WESTERN CHURCHES.

Relations of the East and West.

Prolongation of the schism.

The effect of the scholastic system, and still more of the development of papal absolutism, was to sharpen the great lines of demarcation which divided East from West. The Latin theory as to the mode of the Procession of the Holy Spirit, which has constituted, with some points of minor moment, an insuperable bar to compromise, was now more clearly stated and more logically urged into its consequences by a master mind like Anselm's[1]; while the towering claims of Hildebrand, content with nothing short of universal monarchy in every patriarchate of the Church, were met by indignation and defiance[2].

Reunion attempted 1098:

It is likely that the thought of widening the papal empire was a moving cause of the Crusades; and when the first of those enterprises was considered at the council of Bari[3] (in Apulia), **1098**, the Latin doctrine was distinctly

---

after censuring those who introduced absurd heresies into the Church, continues: 'Reliquæ vero quæ hodie in mundo obtinent sectæ, cum omnes de Trinitate et incolumitate naturarum, ex quibus est Christus absque conversione et commistione, *æque bene sentiant, in nominibus unionis solum secum pugnant:*' cf. *Ibid.* pp. 249, 266. The Armenians on more than one occasion made overtures to the Greek empire with a view to the establishment of union, and that union seemed to be almost completed in 1179. (Gieseler, III. 503, n. 9.) But subsequently (1199) fresh negotiations were opened with the popes, which led to a more permanent result (Schröckh, XXIX. 368 sq.). In 1239 it is recorded that the catholicos received a pallium from Rome (*Ibid.* 370). This truce was, however, ultimately broken in its turn. The powerful Latins also threatened at one period (1237—1247) to absorb the Jacobites and the Nestorians: see Raynaldus, *Ann. Eccl.* ad an. 1247, §§ 32—42; Schröckh, XXIX. 363—367.

[1] See his *De Processione Spiritus Sancti contra Græcos: Opp.* ed. Gerberon, pp. 49—61. The sober tone of this production may be estimated from the Prologue where he is speaking of his antagonists: 'Qui quoniam Evangelia nobiscum venerantur, et in aliis de Trino et Uno Deo credunt hoc ipsum per omnia quod nos, qui de eadem re certi sumus; spero per auxilium ejusdem Spiritus Sancti quia si malunt solidæ veritati acquiescere quam pro inani victoria contendere, per hoc quod absque ambiguitate confitentur ad hoc quod non recipiunt rationabiliter duci possint.'

[2] *e.g.* Anna Comnena, as quoted by Gibbon, ed. Milman, VI. 5, n. 11. Under Hildebrand (1075) the Western pontiffs made their first attempt upon the Russian church, 'ex parte B. Petri:' Mansi, XX. 183: Mouravieff, p. 362.

[3] Anselm happened to be present, and (adds William of Malmesbury) 'ita pertractavit quæstionis latera, ita penetravit et enubilavit intima, ut Latini clamore testarentur gaudium, Græci de se præberi dolerent ridiculum.' *De Gestis Pontif.* p. 100; ed. Hamilton. Out of this oration grew the treatise above mentioned.

—1305] *State of Religious Doctrine and Controversies.* 277

reaffirmed, and the anathema imposed afresh on all who ventured to impugn it. In the reign of the next pontiff (Paschal II.) a negotiation was set on foot (1113) by sending Peter Chrysolanus[1], archbishop of Milan, to the court of Alexius I. Comnenus, (1081—1118), who was trembling at the progress of the Seljuk Turks on one side and the wild Crusaders on the other. Terms of union were again proposed in 1115, Paschal writing a pacific letter to the emperor, but urging the submission[2] of the Eastern prelates as the foremost article of the concordat he was anxious to arrange. The project failed, however, as we learn from its revival in 1136, when Anselm, bishop of Havelberg. and ambassador of Lothair II., disputed with Nicetas, the archbishop of Nicomedia, at Constantinople. It is obvious from the extant record[3] of this interview, that the divergency of East and West had rather widened since the time of Cerularius; and the other writings of the age[4] bear witness to the fact. They shew especially[5] that the encroachments of the pope were now more keenly felt to

Margin: RELATIONS OF THE EAST AND WEST. and subsequently: but the effort unavailing.

---

[1] See his Oration in Leo Allatius, *Græcia Orthodoxa*, I. 379 sq. Rom. 1652. The treatise *De Eccl. Occident. atque Orient. perpetua Consensione*, by the same author, is an important, though one-sided, authority in this dispute.

[2] 'Prima igitur unitatis hujus via hæc videtur, ut confrater noster Constantinopolitanus patriarcha primatum et reverentiam sedis apostolicæ recognoscens...obstinatiam præteritam corrigat...Ea enim, quæ inter Latinos et Græcos fidei vel consuetudinum [diversitatem] faciunt, non videntur aliter posse sedari, nisi prius capiti membra cohæreant.' The whole of this letter is printed for the first time in Jaffé, *Regest. Pontif. Roman.* pp. 510, 511, Berolin. 1851. The independent bearing of the Russian Church at this period is well attested by a letter of the metropolitan of Kieff to the pope, in Mouravieff, ed. Blackmore, pp. 368—370.

[3] In D'Achery's *Spicileg.* I. 161 sq. Cf. the modern German essays, referred to by Neander, VIII. 256 (note).

[4] See the list in Gieseler, III. 491, n. 7. The popular hatred is graphically sketched by Gibbon, VI. 5 sq. At this period grew up the still pending controversy on the subject of the Holy Places at Jerusalem. After the capture of Jerusalem in 1187, the 'orthodox' or Greeks purchased from Saladin the church of the Holy Sepulchre; but Latin Christians, and even some of the Eastern sects (*e.g.* the Armenians), were allowed the use of chapels in it, to the great annoyance of the proper owners.

[5] Thus Nicetas, in the *Disputations* above quoted (lib. III. c. 8, p. 196): 'Si Romanus Pontifex in excelso throno gloriæ suæ residens nobis tonare, et quasi projicere mandata sua de sublimi voluerit, et non nostro concilio, sed proprio arbitrio, pro beneplacito suo de nobis et de ecclesiis nostris judicare, imo imperare voluerit: *quæ fraternitas, seu etiam quæ paternitas hæc esse poterit?* Quis hoc unquam æquo animo sustinere queat?' etc..

RELATIONS OF THE EAST AND WEST.

Foundation of a Latin empire at Constantinople.

be subversive of religious nationality, and that the 'Roman' Church was being substituted for the Catholic and Apostolic brotherhood which they were taught to reverence in the creed[1].

The founding of a Latin empire at Constantinople by the French and Venetians, and the brutal pillage that had been its harbinger (**1204**), could only deepen the hereditary hatred of the Greeks, and add fresh fuel to the flame[2]. It chanced, however, that the new political relations which this Latin dynasty effected, led the way to another series of attempts for binding the antagonistic churches into one. The Eastern emperors, who held their court at Nicæa, watching for an opportunity to stem the furious tide of western domination, ultimately sought to bring about this object by negotiating a religious treaty with the popes. The step originated in the able politician, John III. Vatatzes (**1222–1255**), who was seconded by two severe but on the whole conciliatory letters[3] from the pen of Germanus, the patriarch of Constantinople (**1232**). Gregory IX. attracted by these overtures dispatched his envoys to the East (**1233**). They were instructed to declare[4] that while he could not tolerate in any one the slightest deviation from the doctrines of the Roman Church, he

Its effect on the reunion of the Churches.

---

[1] *Ibid.*

[2] So deep had the aversion grown that at the date of the council of Lateran (1215), it was not unusual for the Greeks to rebaptize those who had been already baptized by the Latins; c. 4: cf. above, p. 186, n. 5. Other sweeping charges which polemics brought against each other may be seen in the *Tractatus contra Græcorum errores de Processione Spiritus S., de animabus defunctorum, de azymis et fermentato et de obedientia Rom. Ecclesiæ* (1252), in Canisius, *Lect. Antiq.*, ed. Basnage, IV. 29 sq. In the midst of these dissensions the French king, Philip Augustus, founded a 'collegium Constantinopolitanum' in Paris for the training of the Greeks who now and then embraced the Latin rite: Bulæus, *Hist. Univ. Paris.* III. 10.

[3] Preserved in Matthew Paris, A.D. 1237, pp. 386 sq.: but misdated. See an account of the life and writings of Germanus in Smith's *Biogr. Dict.* II. 264. He did not hesitate to trace the schism between the rival churches to the pride and tyranny of Rome: 'Divisio nostræ unitatis processit a tyrannide vestræ oppressionis [addressing the cardinals], et exactionum Romanæ ecclesiæ, quæ de matre facta noverca suos quos diu educaverat, more rapacis volucris suos pullos expellentis, filios elongavit:' p. 389.

[4] See the papal Letters in Matthew Paris, pp. 390 sq. The envoys were two Dominicans and two Franciscans, respecting whose negotiation, see Raynaldus, *Annal.* A.D. 1233, § 5 sq.

would allow the Orientals to retain a few of their peculiar usages, and even to omit, provided they did not repudiate[1], the expression *Filioque*, in their recitation of the Creed.

Although this effort shared the fate of many of its predecessors, an important school with leanings to the Western view of the Procession now arose among the Greeks. The leader of it was an influential ascetic, Nicephorus Blemmidas[2]; and when the policy of John Vatatzes was continued under Michael Palæologus, who drove the Latins from Constantinople (**1261**), the plan of a reunion was more widely entertained, and in so far as the Byzantine jurisdiction reached, was almost carried to effect. The emperor himself appears to have been forced into this negotiation by his dread of the crusade[3] which Urban IV. had organized against him, for the purpose of replacing Baldwin II., his Latin rival, on the throne. When every other scheme for warding off the danger failed him, he convened a synod at Constantinople, and enlarging on the critical position of affairs, attempted to win over the reluctant Clergy to his side. He argued[4] that the use of leavened or unleavened bread might be in future left an open question; that it was imprudent, and uncharitable also, for the Eastern Christians to require an absolute agreement in the choice of theological terms, and that they ought to exercise forbearance on such points, provided the antagonistic Latins would in turn expunge their *Filioque* from the Creed; that by agreeing to insert the

Marginalia: RELATIONS OF THE EAST AND WEST. Fresh attempts at union. The arguments of Michael Palæologus.

---

[1] They were even required to burn the books which they had written against the Latin doctrine of the Procession, and to inculcate it in their sermons.

[2] He wrote two works on the Procession, in the one maintaining the Greek doctrine, and in the other manifesting a decided preference for the Latin. Leo Allatius (*De Perpetua Consensione*, lib. II. c. 14) attempts to explain this variation. Both the treatises are published in that writer's *Græcia Orthodoxa*, I. 1—60. The firmness of Nicephorus in declining to administer the sacrament to Marcesina, an imperial mistress, is applauded by Neander, VIII. 263.

[3] See Gibbon, VI. 96 sq., ed. Milman.

[4] The best account is that of Georgius Pachymeres, who was advocate-general of the church of Constantinople, and wrote, among other things, an *Historia Byzantina*, containing the life of Michael Palæologus: see especially lib. v. c. 18 sq., ed. Bonn, 1835, and cf. Schröckh, XXIX. 432 sq.

marginalia: RELATIONS OF THE EAST AND WEST. — Resistance offered to them. — His deputation to the pope, 1273. — Reunion of Rome and Constanti-

name of the Roman pontiff in the 'diptychs,' they would not incur the charge of elevating him unduly, nor of derogating from the honour of the Eastern patriarchs; and lastly, that the exercise of papal jurisdiction in the matter of appeals, if such a claim as that should be in words asserted, could not, owing to the distance of the Eastern empire, be so harsh and burdensome as they were ready to forebode.

The patriarch of Constantinople, Joseph, who was ever an inflexible opponent of the compromise, had found a warm supporter in the chartophylax Beccus, or Veccus, (keeper of the records in the great church of Constantinople). But it seems that the convictions of the latter underwent a thorough change[1] while he was languishing in prison, as a penalty for his resistance to the wishes of the court; and afterwards we find him the most able and unflinching champion of the party who were urging on the project of reunion. Michael Palæologus now sent a message[2] to pope Gregory X., in which, ignoring the disinclination of the patriarch and the hostility of his own subjects at Constantinople, he expressed a strong desire for unity, and even ventured to hold out a hope of its immediate consummation (**1273**). In the following year a larger embassy[3] appeared in his behalf at what is called

---

[1] This change is ascribable, in part at least, to the writings of Nicephorus Blemmidas. Some have viewed it as no more than hypocritical pretence. But his subsequent firmness, notwithstanding all the persecutions he endured from the dominant party, is opposed to this construction. Many of his works are published by Leo Allatius, in the *Græcia Orthodoxa*.

[2] Neale, *East. Church*, 'Alexandria,' II. 315. The displeasure of the people at this movement of the court is noticed by Pachymeres, as above, lib. v. c. 22. Gibbon mentions, however, that the letters of union were ultimately signed by the emperor, his son, and thirty-five metropolitans (VI. 98), which included all the suffragans of that rank belonging to the patriarchate: yet (as Mr Neale remarks) they do not address the pope as 'œcumenical,' but only as the 'great pontiff of the Apostolic see.' *Ibid.* p. 316.

[3] The members of it were Germanus, formerly patriarch of Constantinople, Theophanes, metropolitan of Nicæa, and many other court dignitaries. In the letter which they carried with them (Mansi, XXIV. 67), Michael Palæologus, after he had made a statement of his faith according to a form drawn up by Clement IV. in 1267, preferred the following request: 'Rogamus magnitudinem vestram, ut ecclesia nostra dicat sanctum symbolum, prout dicebat hoc ante schisma usque in hodiernum diem;' but it seems that the delegates themselves had no objection to the

the 'general'[1] council of Lyons; and on June 29, 1274, the formal work of 'reconciliation' was inaugurated, in the presence of the pope himself, with unexampled grandeur and solemnity[2]. A later session of the prelates, on July 6, beheld the representatives of Michael Palæologus abjure the ancient schism, and recognize the papal primacy, as well as the distinctive tenets of the Roman Church.

On their return, the patriarch Joseph, who had previously retired into a convent waiting for the issue of negotiations he had vainly striven to retard, was superseded by his former colleague Beccus[3]: but the people of Constantinople viewed the union with unmixed abhorrence, and in many cases went so far as to decline religious intercourse with any one suspected of the slightest tenderness for Rome. The gentle pen of Beccus was in vain employed to soften the asperity of public feeling; and although he often interceded with the emperor in mitigation of the penalties inflicted by that heartless tyrant on the nonconforming party, his endeavours only tended to increase the general agitation. He resigned his honours, Dec. 26, 1282, convinced that he should never reconcile his flock to the unpopular alliance with the West[4].

The Roman pontiffs had in turn grown weary of the coldness, craft, and insincerity betrayed by Michael and his

Marginal notes: RELATIONS OF THE EAST AND WEST. *nople, at the council of Lyons, 1274. General disapprobation of the measure. Formal dissolution of the union, 1281.*

clause *Filioque*, as they chanted the creed with that addition on the 6th of July.

[1] The Council was not recognized as 'œcumenical' by Eastern churches: it contained no representatives of Athanasius the patriarch of Alexandria, nor of Euthymius of Antioch, nor of Gregory II. of Jerusalem. The last of these positively wrote against the union. Neale, *Ibid.* p. 317. The same repugnance to the union was felt in Russia. Mouravieff, p. 49.

[2] Five hundred Latin bishops, seventy abbots, and about a thousand other ecclesiastics were present, together with ambassadors from England, France, Germany, &c. The pope celebrated high mass, and Bonaventura preached. Aquinas, who had recently composed an *Opusculum contra Græcos*, was expected to take part in the proceedings of the council, but died on his journey thither.

[3] Pachymeres, as above, lib. v. c. 24 sq., and Neander, VIII. 270 sq. Banishment, imprisonment, confiscation of property, scourging, and personal mutilation were among the instruments employed by Michael Palæologus in forcing his subjects into an approval of the union with the Latins. On the other side, the ultra-Greeks were most unmeasured in their animosity and in the charges which they brought against their rivals.

[4] Pachymeres (lib. VI. c. 30) says that, with the exception of the emperor and patriarch, and a few of their immediate dependents, πάντες ἐδυσμέναινον τῇ εἰρήνῃ.

son in carrying out the terms of union. They accordingly allowed the crown of the Two Sicilies to fall into the hands of his powerful rival[1], Charles of Anjou (**1266**) : and when he instigated the revolt of those provinces in **1280**, pope Martin IV. restrained himself no longer, breaking up the hollow and unprofitable treaty by his excommunication of the Eastern emperor[2] (Nov. 18, **1281**). The speedy death of Michael Palæologus (**1282**) was followed by the overthrow and disappearance of the Latin party, and the formal revocation[3] of the acts in which the see of Constantinople had succumbed to that of Rome.

THE EASTERN AND WESTERN SECTS.

Rise and spread of the Bogomiles.

The most important of the Eastern sects who flourished at this period were the Bogomiles, or the Massilians[4], kindred (as we have already seen[5]) to the Enthusiasts or Euchites. Issuing in the early part of the twelfth century from Bulgaria, where they grew into a formidable body, they invaded other districts in the patriarchate of Constantinople, and soon afterwards obtained a footing in Egyptian dioceses[6].

At the centre of their theological system[7], which was

---

[1] Gibbon, VI. 100 sq.

[2] See the document in Raynaldus, *Annal. Eccles.* A.D. 1281, § 25. Earlier traces of displeasure are noted in Schröckh, XXIX. 449.

[3] The new emperor Andronicus II., although he had joined his father in negotiating the union on political grounds, was really opposed to it: see his *Life* by Pachymeres, lib. I. c. 2. He also was excommunicated, by Clement V., in 1307.

[4] That these names may be regarded as descriptive of the same body, is proved by the following passage, among others : 'Η πολυώνυμος τῶν Μασσιλιανῶν, εἴτουν Βογομίλων αἵρεσις ἐν πάσῃ πόλει, καὶ χώρᾳ, καὶ ἐπαρχίᾳ ἐπιπολάζει τανῦν. Euthymius Zigabenus, in his work entitled Ἔλεγχος καὶ Θρίαμβος τῆς βλασφήμου καὶ πολυειδοῦς αἱρέσεως τῶν ἀθέων Μασσαλιανῶν, τῶν καὶ Φουνδαϊτῶν καὶ Βογομίλων καλουμένων, καὶ Εὐχιτῶν, κ.τ.λ., edited by Tollius in his *Iter Italicum*, 1696, p. 112.

[5] Above, p. 187. The colony of the Paulicians at Philippopolis (above, p. 84, n. 4) was still thriving: but their influence was counteracted in a great degree by the foundation of the orthodox Alexiopolis in the reign of Alexius Comnenus (1081—1118). See the *Life* of that emperor ('Alexias') by his learned daughter Anna Comnena, lib. XIV.

[6] Neale, II. 240. According to this writer, a treatise, still in MS., was composed by the Alexandrine patriarch Eulogius against the Bogomiles.

[7] Our information on this subject is derived mainly from the work of Euthymius, above cited, n. 4, and the twenty-third title of his *Panoplia* (see above, p. 274, n. 1), which was edited separately by Gieseler,

—1305] *State of Religious Doctrine and Controversies.* 283

quasi-dualistic, stood a superhuman being whom they called Satanael, the first-born Son of God, and honoured with the second place in the administration of the world[1]. This Being (a distorted image of the Prince of Evil) was ere long intoxicated by the vastness of his power: he ceased to pay allegiance to the Father, and resolved to organize an empire of his own. A multitude of angels, whom he had involved in his rebellion, were ejected with him from the nearer presence of the Lord, and after fashioning the earth from preexistent but chaotic elements, he last of all created man. The human *soul*, however, had a higher origin: it was inspired directly into our first parents by the Lord of heaven Himself; the framer of the body having sought in vain to animate the work until he had addressed his supplications to the Author of all Good[2]. The very excellences now apparent in mankind inflamed the envy of Satanael. He seduced the mother of the human race; and Cain, the godless issue of that intercourse, became the root and representative of evil: while his brother Abel, on the contrary, the son of Adam, testified to the existence of a better principle in man. This principle, however, was comparatively inefficacious[3] owing to the crafty malice of the Tempter;

SECTS.
The main features of their creed.

Göttingen, 1842. The general truthfulness of Eastern writers on the Bogomiles has been established by the close agreement of their narrative with independent publications of the Western Church in refutation of the kindred sect of Cathari.

[1] Euthym. *Panop.* tit. XXIII. c. 6: cf. the apocryphal Gospel in Thilo's *Codex Apocryph. N. Test.* I. 885, and Neander's summary, VIII. 279 sq.

[2] Διεπρεσβεύσατο πρὸς τὸν ἀγαθὸν Πατέρα, καὶ παρεκάλεσε πεμφθῆναι παρ' αὐτοῦ πνοήν, ἐπαγγειλάμενος κοινὸν εἶναι τὸν ἄνθρωπον, εἰ ζωοποιηθῇ, καὶ ἀπὸ τοῦ γένους αὐτοῦ πληροῦσθαι τοὺς ἐν οὐρανῷ τόπους τῶν ἀπορριφθέντων ἀγγέλων: *Ibid.* c. 7. The same idea of supplying vacancies occasioned by the fall of the angels is mentioned elsewhere: *e. g.* by Scotus Erigena, *De Divisione Naturæ*, p. 304, ed. Oxon.

[3] Λέγουσιν, ὅτι τῶν ἀνθρώπων πικρῶς τυραννουμένων, καὶ ἀπηνῶς ἀπολλυμένων, μόγις ὀλίγοι τινὲς τῆς τοῦ πατρὸς μερίδος ἐγένοντο, καὶ εἰς τὴν τῶν ἀγγέλων τάξιν ἀνέβησαν. *Ibid.* c. 8. One of the acts of Satanael, according to this sect, was to delude Moses, and through him the Hebrew nation, by giving them the Law. The Bogomiles had consequently no reverence for the Pentateuch, although they used the Psalter and the Prophets, as well as the New Testament (c. 1). Neander thinks (VIII. 286) that they attributed a paramount authority to the Gospel of St John: and it is actually stated (c. 16) that a copy of that Gospel was laid upon the head of each on his admission to the sect.

Their false views respecting the Incarnation:

and at length[1] an act of mercy on the part of God was absolutely needed for the rescue and redemption of the human soul. The agent whom He singled out was Christ. A spirit, called the Son of God, or Logos, and identified with Michael the Archangel, came into the world, put on the semblance of a body[2], baffled the apostate angels, and divesting their malignant leader of all superhuman attributes, reduced his title from Satanael to Satan, and curtailed his empire in the world[3]. The Saviour was then taken up to heaven, where, after occupying the chief post of honour, He is, at the close of the present dispensation, to be reabsorbed into the essence out of which His being is derived.

and the Holy Trinity.

The Holy Spirit, in like manner, is, according to the Bogomiles, an emanation only, destined to revert hereafter, when His work has been completed, to the aboriginal and only proper source of life.

Other errors.

The authors of this scheme had many points in common with the other mediæval sects. They looked on all the Church as antichristian and as ruled by fallen angels, arguing that no others save their own community were genuine 'citizens of Christ'[4]. The strong repugnance which they felt to every thing that savoured of Mosaism[5] urged them to despise the ritual system of the Church: for instance, they contended that the only proper baptism

---

[1] This was said to be in the 5500th year after the creation of the world, which corresponded with the Christian era in the reckoning of Constantinople.

[2] σάρκα τῷ φαινομένῳ μὲν ὑλικὴν καὶ ὁμοίαν ἀνθρώπου σώματι τῇ δ' ἀληθείᾳ ἄϋλον καὶ θεοπρεπῆ, c. 8. The Incarnation and the Passion of the Christ were, therefore, equally unreal. *Ibid.*

[3] According to Euthymius (*Ibid.*) Satan was shut up in Tartarus (παχεῖ καὶ βαρεῖ κλοιῷ καταδῆσαι καὶ ἐγκλεῖσαι τῷ ταρτάρῳ); but it appears from other statements that the unredeemed were still, according to the Bogomiles, exposed to his malignity: cf. Neander's note, VIII. 281. The consciousness of this may have led them to propitiate the powers of darkness by a modified worship, which some of them actually paid; appealing in justification of their conduct to the language of apocryphal Gospels (*Ibid.* cc. 20, 21). On the devil-worshippers, cf. above, p. 187, n. 5.

[4] See Tollius, *Iter Ital.* p. 112. The word is χριστοπολῖται.

[5] See above, p. 283, n. 3. They spoke of churches as the habitation of demons (Euthymius, as above, c. 18), urging that the Almighty does not dwell in 'temples made with hands:' they condemned the sacrament of the altar (τὴν μυστικὴν καὶ φρικτὴν ἱερουργίαν), on the ground that it was θυσίαν τῶν ἐνοικούντων τοῖς ναοῖς δαιμόνων, c. 17. The only form of prayer which they allowed was the Lord's Prayer: c. 19.

is a baptism of the Spirit[1]. A more healthy feeling was indeed expressed in their hostility to image-worship[2] and exaggerated reverence of the saints, though even there the opposition rested mainly on Docetic views of Christ and His redemption[3].

SECTS.

Their opposition to images and saint-worship.

These opinions had been widely circulated[4] in the Eastern empire when Alexius Comnenus (d. 1118) caused inquiries to be made respecting them, and after he had singled out a number of the influential misbelievers[5] doomed them to imprisonment for life. An aged monk, named Basil, who came forward as the leader of the sect, resisted the persuasions of Alexius and the patriarch. He ultimately perished at the stake, in Constantinople, 1119. His creed, however, still survived and found adherents in all quarters, more especially in minds alive to the corruptions of the Church, and mystic in their texture[6].

Partial suppression of the sect, 1119.

The communication which existed now between the Eastern and the Western world, arising chiefly out of pilgrimages, commerce, and crusades, facilitated the transmission of these errors into Lombardy, the south of France, and ultimately into almost every part of Western Europe. All the varying titles, Bulgri[7], Pope-

The rise of the Cathari or Albigenses.

---

[1] c. 16. The baptism administered at church was in their eyes equivalent to John's, and therefore was a vestige of Judaism. Their own mode of initiation is described in the paragraph here quoted.

[2] Τοὺς Ἱεράρχας δὲ καὶ τοὺς Πατέρας ὁμοῦ πάντας ἀποδοκιμάζουσιν ὡς εἰδωλολάτρας διὰ τὴν τῶν εἰκόνων προσκύνησιν (c. 11). It is very remarkable that the Bogomiles cherished an esteem for Constantine Copronymus (above, p. 74).

[3] They abhorred the symbol of the cross ὡς ἀναιρέτην τοῦ Σωτῆρος (c. 14); they refused the title Θεοτόκος to the Virgin on the ground that it properly belongs to every holy soul, and not peculiarly to her who was unconscious even of the Saviour's birth (τῆς παρθένου μήτε τὴν εἴσοδον αὐτοῦ γνούσης μήτε τὴν ἔξοδον, c. 8). An Oration was composed by the patriarch of Constantinople, Germanus (d. 1254), *In exaltationem venerandæ crucis et adversus Bogomilos;* in Gretser, *Opp.* II. 112 sq.

[4] See the expressions in p. 282, n. 4.

[5] For an account of the stratagem employed by Alexius, see Schröckh, XXIX. 462 sq.

[6] See the sketch given by Neander of the two monks Chrysomalos and Niphon (VIII. 289—295). Several councils of Constantinople (*e. g.* 1140, 1143; Mansi, XXI. 551, 583) anathematized the principles of the Bogomiles.

[7] This name (with its varieties, Bulgares, Bougres, etc.) points at once to Bulgaria, the chief seat of the Bogomiles, and formerly infected with the cognate heresy of the Paulicians (Gibbon, V. 281 sq. ed. Milman).

licani¹, Paterini², Passagieri³, Cathari⁴, and Albigenses⁵, indicate, if not the very same, at least a group of kindred sects, all standing in relations more or less immediate with the Bogomiles, and holding certain points in common with the Paulicians and the Manichæans proper⁶.

At the basis of their speculative system lay the Eastern theories of dualism and emanation. But the former was considerably changed or softened, partly (as it seems) by contact with less impious sectaries, and partly by the independent action of the Western mind. One school⁷ of

---

¹ 'Popelicani' (= 'Publicani,' and in Flanders, 'Piphiles') seems to have been chiefly used in France. Ducange, *Gloss.* v. 'Populicani.' It is probably a corrupted form of Παυλικιανοί. See Dr Maitland's *Facts and Documents illustrative of the History, &c. of the Albigenses and Waldenses*, Lond. 1832, p. 91, and the same writer's *Eight Essays*, Lond. 1852, p. 172. The Greeks would pronounce their word Pavlikiani.

² See above, p. 189, n. 7. Matthew Paris, A.D. 1236, p. 362, writes, 'qui vulgariter dicuntur *Paterini* et *Bugares:*' and, A.D. 1238, p. 407: 'Ipsos autem nomine vulgari *Bugaros* appellavit (Robertus Bugre, the Inquisitor), sive essent *Paterini*, sive *Joviniani*, vel *Albigenses*, vel aliis hæresibus maculati.'

³ This name, with its equivalent 'Passagini,' is derived from 'Passagium,' the common word for a 'crusade' (Ducange, sub voc.); it therefore will suggest the channel by which Catharist opinions were conveyed at times into the west of Europe.

⁴ This name (= the Pure, or Puritans, and connected with 'Boni Homines' and 'Bons-hommes') was most current in Germany. It survives as a generic form in *Ketzer*. As early as Aldhelm (*Opp.* p. 87, ed. Giles) we read of heretics, 'qui se Katharos, id est, mundos nuncupari voluerunt,' but the reference is to the early Novatianists.

⁵ The name 'Albigenses' (meaning natives of the district Albigesium, or the neighbourhood of Alby) does not appear to have been used for marking out the members of this sect until some time after what is called the 'Albigensian' Crusade (Maitland, *Facts and Documents*, &c. p. 96). They were at first known by some one of the titles above mentioned, or others like them (see Schmidt, *Hist. et Doctrine de la secte des Cathares*, Paris, 1849, Tome II. pp. 275—284); and subsequently, as distinguished from the Waldenses, they bore the simple name of 'heretics:' Maitland, *Eight Essays*, p. 178.

⁶ See the works of Maitland and Schmidt above referred to; and especially Hahn's *Gesch. der Ketzer im Mittelalter*, Stuttgart, 1845—7; Gieseler, III. §§ 87—90, 96; and Neander, VIII. 297—330. The last writer has pointed out many particulars which shew the close affinity between the Cathari and Bogomiles, although he thinks (p. 297) that one class of the former may have sprung out of some other (Eastern) sect which differed in the details of its creed from Bogomiles or Euchites: cf. Schmidt's reply, II. 263—266, in which he contends that Bogomilism itself is rather a branch or modification of primitive Catharism.

⁷ Neander, VIII. 298. It is observable that some writers of this party appealed both to the Scriptures and Aristotle in favour of their views;

—1305] *State of Religious Doctrine and Controversies.*   287

Cathari continued, it is true, entirely *ditheistic*, cherishing the Manichæan view of two opposing Principles, which had alike subsisted from eternity in regions of their own (the visible and the invisible): but others[1], like the Bogo-miles, while tracing the formation of the present world to absolutely evil agencies, and looking upon matter as irreconcileably opposed to spirit, were nevertheless induced to recognize one only primal God, the Author of all true and permanent existence. The antagonistic powers of darkness had originally paid allegiance unto Him, and as their fall, with its results, at length necessitated the de-scent of Christ, who was a glorious emanation issuing from the Father in behalf of men, the fruit of His redemption will be seen in the eventual recovery of human souls and a return of the material world into the chaos out of which it had been shaped.

<small>SECTS.</small>

In noting the more practical phases of this heresy the modes of thought we saw prevailing in the Bogomiles continually recur. The Cathari rejected most of the pro-phetic writings of the Old Testament[2] as well as the dis-tinctive principles of the Mosaic ritual, on the ground that Satan was the author of them both[3]. Contending that the body of the Son of God[4], on His appearance among men, was an ethereal body, or was not in any way

<small>*Its more practical aspects.*</small>

but they indulged in the most extravagant flights of 'spiritual' inter-pretation. Among the chief of their dogmatic peculiarites they were pre-destinarians (p. 301), and represented the Virgin-Mother as an angel (p. 303).

[1] *Ibid.* p. 305; with which compare Schmidt's 'Appreciation Générale,' II. 167—173.

[2] The Dominican Moneta, who wrote his book *Adversus Catharos et Valdenses* about 1240, says (p. 218) that the Cathari at first rejected all the prophets except Isaiah: but they afterwards quote these writings in disputing with their adversaries.

[3] *e.g.* Peter, a Cistercian monk of Vaux Cernai (Vallis-sarnensis), whose *Hist. Albigensium* (as far as the year 1218) is printed in the *Recueil des Historiens de la France*, XIX. 1 sq.: 'Novum Testamentum benigno Deo, Vetus vero maligno attribuebant, et illud omnino repudiabant *præter quasdam auctoritates quæ de veteri Testamento novo sunt insertæ*,' etc. c. 2.

[4] Different views existed on this point. One school of Cathari ad-mitted the reality of our Saviour's body, but ascribed it to Satan, and affirmed that the genuine Christ ('bonus Christus') is purely spiritual and altogether different from the historic Christ (see Peter of Vaux Cernai, as in the former note): others held the same opinion as the Bogomiles; above, p. 283.

derived from the substance of His Virgin-mother, they repudiated every article of faith that rests upon the doctrine of the Incarnation. They agreed in substituting novel rites for those administered at church[1], denouncing with peculiar emphasis the baptism of unconscious children[2]. They were also most ascetic in their discipline; forbidding matrimony, and, at least in many districts, every kind of animal food. Nor should we deem this rigour hypocritical. The lives of the more spiritual or 'perfect' class[3] presented an example of simplicity, and sometimes even of moral elevation[4], higher than was commonly discernible in members of the Church; and to this circumstance should be ascribed at least some measure of the popularity and progress[5] of the Cathari as soon as they began to circulate their tenets in the West.

The Cathari most powerful in the south of France.

The ground in which those tenets were most deeply rooted was the south of France, from Béziers to Bordeaux, especially throughout the territories of the count of Toulouse, and in the neighbourhood of Alby. Here, indeed, among the haunts of gaiety, refinement, and romance, the morals both of court and people were most shamelessly

---

[1] Their hatred of the whole church-system is attested by contemporary writers, *e.g.* Ebrard and Ermengard, edited by Gretser (Ingolstadt, 1614), in a work bearing the incorrect title *Trias Scriptorum adv.* Waldensium *sectam:* cf. Gieseler, III. 405—407, n. 25, 26; and Maitland, *Facts and Documents,* pp. 372—391.

[2] Their own rite of initiation was called 'consolamentum' (cf. above, p. 189, n. 1), a 'baptism of the Spirit' ('Consolator'), which they administered by the laying on of hands and prayer. See Schmidt, II. 119 sq. respecting this and other rites. The best original authority is Rainerio Sacchoni (circ. 1250), whose work is analysed in Maitland's *Facts and Documents,* pp. 400 sq.; cf. pp. 525 sq.

[3] The Cathari were divided into (1) the 'Perfecti,' or 'Boni Homines,' and (2) the 'Credentes;' or 'Auditores:' see Schmidt, II. 91 sq. Neander, VIII. 315 sq. It is recorded that, although the number of the Cathari was immense in all quarters of the world in the first half of the thirteenth century, only four thousand belonged to the class of 'Perfecti.'

[4] The picture drawn by Schmidt (I. 194) may be somewhat too favourable, but the superiority of their moral character as compared with that of some of the prelates cannot be disputed. See the whole of the chapter, pp. 188 sq.

[5] *e.g.* William of Newburgh, *De Rebus Angl.* lib. II. c. 13, whose history closes in 1197, describes their rapid growth in France, Spain, Italy, and Germany. Some who found their way into England were suppressed as early as 1166, by a council at Oxford, (R. Diceto, ed. Twysden, c. 539. Wilkins, I. 438). They were so numerous in the south of France,

—1305] *State of Religious Doctrine and Controversies.* 289

relaxed[1]; but on a sudden the attention of the many, rich and poor alike, had been directed into other channels by the forcible harangues of 'Albigensian' preachers. With a few exceptions, all the barons of the neighbourhood became protectors of the heresy; some even ranking with its most devoted followers, the 'Perfect[2].' In a council held at Toulouse as early as July 8, 1119, a class of tenets such as those maintained among the Cathari[3], were solemnly denounced; and mission after mission[4] laboured to repress their wider circulation. It was not, however, until the pontificate of Innocent III.[5], that vigorous measures were adopted for the extirpation of the sect. The murder of the papal legate[6], Pierre de Castelnau, in 1208, which was attributed unjustly to count Raymond of Toulouse, a patron

SECTS.

Their violent repression; by Crusades,

Guienne, Provence, and the greater part of Gascony, that foreigners were told how heresy was rapidly infecting more than a thousand towns, and how the followers of Manes in that district were outnumbering those of Jesus Christ. Schmidt, I. 194. The same is mentioned with regard to Lombardy and the papal states (Schmidt, I. 142 sq.), where we may gather from the treatise of Bonacursus (circ. 1190), *Vita Hæreticorum, seu Manifestatio Hæresis Catharorum* (in D'Achery, I. 208 sq.), that the leaders of the sect ('Passagini') had so far modified their doctrines as to have betrayed a Judaizing tendency; cf. Neander, VIII. 332; Schmidt, II. 294.

[1] Abundant proofs of this are furnished in the 'chanzos' of the Provençal poets, collected, for example, by Raynouard in his *Poésies des Troubadours;* and in the *Fabliaux:* although these latter more commonly refer to the *north* of France.

[2] Schmidt, I. 195, 196.

[3] It denounces (can. 3) those, 'qui religionis speciem simulantes Dominici corporis et sanguinis sacramentum, puerorum baptisma, sacerdotium, et cæteros ecclesiasticos ordines et legitimarum damnant fœdera nuptiarum,' (Mansi, XXI. 225, where the date is incorrectly given: cf. Jaffé, p. 529). At this council an appeal was made to 'potestates exteræ,' in order to suppress the misbelievers. The decrees were echoed at the council of Lateran (1139): Mansi, XXI. 532. Other councils, *e.g.* Rheims (1148), c. 18, and Tours (1163) c. 4, adopted the same course. An important conference with the leaders of the Cathari was held in 1165 (Hoveden, *Chr.* II. 105, Mansi, XXII. 157) at Lombers, the residence of their bishop Sicard Cellerier, near Alby: cf. Schmidt, I. 70 sq.

[4] That in 1147 consisted of the legate Alberic and St Bernard: see Bernard. *Epist.* 241, from which we learn that the churches were deserted, the clergy despised, and nearly all the south of France addicted to the Cathari: cf. Schmidt, I. 44, 45. In 1181, Henry Cardinal bishop of Albano, who had before (1178) when abbot of Clairvaux endeavoured to reclaim the diocese of Alby in a gentler way, began to preach a crusade against it: *Ibid.* I. 83.

[5] See above, p. 233, on his patronage of Dominic, the founder of the Preachers.

[6] Schmidt, I. 217 sq.

M. A.   U

of the 'Albigenses,' led the way to an atrocious series of Crusades, at first conducted at the bidding of the pope by Simon de Montfort, earl of Leicester, and extending over thirty years[1]. By this terrific war the swarming misbelievers of Provence were almost literally 'drowned in blood.' The remnant which escaped the sword of the crusaders fell a prey to ruthless agents of the Inquisition,—the tribunal now established permanently by the council of Toulouse[2] (1229) for noting and extinguishing all kinds of heretical pravity.

The fears awakened at Rome and in the Western Church at large by the astounding progress of the 'Albigenses,' were increased by other movements, totally distinct in character, but also finding the great bulk of their adherents in the southern parts of France. The author of the earliest (1104—1124) was a priest of Bruis named Peter (hence the title *Petrobrusiani*), who, together with some startling traits of heterodoxy, manifested[3] an attachment to the central truth of Christianity, and a desire to elevate the tone of morals in the districts where he taught. He ultimately perished at the stake; but the impression he produced was much extended by a Cluniac monk and deacon, Henry[4]. After labouring sedulously

---

[1] See Barrau and Darragon, *Hist. des Croisades contre les Albigeois*, Paris, 1840, and Schmidt, as above, I. 219—293.

[2] Mansi, XXIII. 192 sq. The germ of this institution is contained in the decree of Lucius III. (1184), 'Contra Hæreticos,' (Maitland's *Facts*, &c. pp. 496—498); and its organization was advanced by the council of Lateran (1215), c. 3 (*Decret. Gregor.* lib. v. tit. 7, c. 13: in the *Corpus Juris Canon.*). On the general history see Limborch, *Hist. Inquisitionis*, Amst. 1692. It soon found other fields of duty in extinguishing the Cathari of Italy (Schmidt, I. 159 sq.), of Spain (*Ibid*. I. 372 sq.), of Germany (*Ibid*. I. 376 sq.), and also in suppressing (1234) a politico-religious sect, entitled 'Stedingers,' who had arisen in the district of Oldenburg: Gieseler, III. § 89, n. 37. *Friesisches Archiv*, ed. Ehrentraut, II. 265 sq., Oldenburg, 1854. They refused to pay tithes and tributes.

[3] Our chief information respecting him is derived from a contemporary Letter of Peter the Venerable, *Adversus Petrobrusianos Hæreticos; Opp.* p. 719, ed. Migne. It seems that Peter of Bruis and his immediate followers rejected infant baptism, on the ground that personal faith is always needed as a precondition, ere the grace of God can take effect ('nos vero tempus congruum fidei expectamus'). For this cause they rebaptized. They undervalued, if they did not absolutely set aside, the Eucharist. They burned the crosses, and denounced church-music and the ritual system of the age. They also censured and derided prayers and offerings for the dead: cf. Neander, VIII. 338—341.

[4] See *Gesta Hildeberti* among the *Acta Episcoporum Cenomanensium*

in the field which had been overrun by 'Albigensian' missionaries, and attracting many whom their doctrines did not satisfy[1], he fell (**1147**) into the hands of a papal legate, who had visited Provence in company with St Bernard for the purpose of resisting the further propagation of heretical opinions. Henry was sentenced at the council of Rheims (**1148**) to meagre diet and imprisonment for life.

and Henry the Cluniac monk (silenced 1148).

How far the influential sect, afterwards known as the 'Waldenses[2],' were allied with this reforming movement, is not easy to determine. They are certainly to be distinguished from the 'Albigenses[3].' In their creed we find no vestiges of dualism, nor anything which indicates the least affinity to oriental theories of emanation. What those bodies learned to hold in common, and what made them equally the prey of the Inquisitor, was their unwavering belief in the corruption of the Mediæval Church, especially as governed by the Roman pontiffs[4]. It has also been disputed whether the 'Waldenses' dated further back as a religious corporation than the twelfth century.

The Waldenses or Vaudés.

[*i.e.* of le Mans], in Mabillon, *Vet. Analect.* III. 312, and cf. Neander, VIII. 341—350; Gieseler, III. 391—393, n. 4.

[1] Schmidt. I. 40, 41.

[2] This name first occurs in an edict of Alfonso, king of Arragon (1194). (Maitland's *Facts and Documents*, &c., p. 181.) The 'Waldenses' are there associated with the 'Inzabbati' (*i.e.* persons wearing 'sabots' or wooden shoes), and with the 'Poor Men of Lyons.' Another of the names they bore was 'Leonistæ' (from Leonum = Lyons).

[3] This distinction has been questioned by two very different schools of theologians, one endeavouring to shew that the tenets of the Albigenses and Waldenses were equally false, and the second that they were equally true: but all dispassionate writers of the present day (*e.g.* Gieseler, Neander, Schmidt) agree in the conclusion above stated. Dr Maitland has discussed the question at length in his *Facts and Documents*, etc., and in his *Eight Essays* (1852), pp. 178 sq., he adduces evidence from a record of the Inquisition of Toulouse (1307—1323) which 'completely decides the question.' A new work, entitled *Die romanischen Waldenser*, etc. was put forth in 1853 (Halle) by Dr Herzog.

[4] In 1207 a pastor of the Albigenses maintained that the Church of Rome was not the Spouse of Christ, but the Apocalyptic Babylon. See the extract on this subject in Ussher's *De Christ. Eccl. Successione et Statu*, ch. x. § 23, *Opp.* II. 341, ed. Elrington. The Waldenses also ultimately urged the same objection (though at first their tone was different), 'Quod Ecclesia Romana non est Ecclesia Jesu Christi......... Quod Ecclesia Romana est ecclesia malignantium, et bestia et meretrix,' *etc.* See Rainerii *Summa de Catharis et Leonistis*, in Martène and Durand's *Thesaur. Anecdot.* V. 1775.

SECTS.

Their founder, Peter Waldo:

Although this view appears to have been current once with members of the sect[1], or had at least been confidently urged on some occasions when the adversary challenged them to prove the antiquity of their opinions, it is found to have no basis in authentic history.

The leader of the agitation out of which they grew (**1170**) was Peter Waldo (Pierre de Vaud), a citizen of Lyons, who renounced his property that he might give himself entirely to the service of religion. He began to circulate a Romaunt version of the Gospels and of many other books of Holy Writ[2], and with the aid of kindred spirits, laymen like himself, to preach among the populace; their object being, not to tamper with the creeds or revolutionize the ecclesiastical system, but rather to exalt the spirit and to purify the practice of the age. These warm and desultory efforts proved distasteful to the archbishop of Lyons, who compelled the preachers to desist. They carried an appeal to Rome (**1179**), exhibiting their version of the Bible to pope Alexander III., and suing for his appro-

---

[1] In the *Summa*, as above quoted, the Waldenses of the thirteenth century affirmed 'quod ecclesia Christi permansit in episcopis et aliis prælatis usque ad B. Sylvestrum [the contemporary of Constantine], et in eo defecit quousque ipsi eam restaurarunt: tamen dicunt, quod semper fuerunt aliqui qui Deum timebant et salvabantur.' But when it was argued, *e.g.* by the Dominican Moneta (circ. 1240) *Adversus Catharos et Valdenses*, ed. Ricchini, p. 402, that the Waldenses were not 'successores Ecclesiæ primitivæ,' and therefore not 'Ecclesia Dei,' some of them contended that the sect had lasted ever since the time of pope Sylvester, and others that it was traceable to the age of the Apostles: see the Additions to the *Summa* of Rainerio, in *Bibl. Patr.* ed. Lugdun. xxv. 264, and Pilschdorf, *Contra Waldenses* (circ. 1444): *Ibid.* xxv. 278. Schmidt (II. 287—293) has proved that history and tradition are both silent on this great antiquity until the 13th century, and that the sect was really no older than Peter Waldo. Neander (VIII. 368, note) thinks Dr Maitland somewhat too sceptical as to the genuineness of the *Nobla Leyczon*, a Waldensian summary of doctrines, claiming to belong to A.D. 1100. Schmidt, p. 290, supposes that it may have been written at the close of the 12th century, but the researches of Mr Bradshaw have shown that it cannot be earlier than the 15th (*The Books of the Vaudois*, p. 220; by Dr Todd, Cambridge, 1865).

[2] As he was himself no scholar, the version was made for him by two ecclesiastics. See a contemporary account by the Dominican Stephen De Borbone, extracted in D'Argentré, *Collectio Judiciorum de Novis Erroribus, qui ab initio xii sæc. usque ad an. 1632 in Ecclesia proscripti sunt*, Paris, 1728, I. 87. The same hands translated for him 'auctoritates Sanctorum multas per titulos congregatas, quas *Sententias* appellabant.'

bation both of it and of the new fraternity[1]. The papal licence was not given, although at present the Waldenses did not share in the anathemas pronounced on other bodies (Cathari included). They were afterwards condemned, however, in **1184**, by Lucius III.[2] But nothing could repress the sturdy vigour of the men who laboured at all costs to forward what they deemed a genuine reformation of the Church. Their principles were soon diffused in Southern France, in Arragon, in Piedmont, in Lombardy[3], and even in the Rhenish provinces[4]. Insisting as they always did on the desirableness of personal acquaintance with the Bible, which, in union with their claim to exercise the sacerdotal office[5], constituted the peculiarity in their original creed, they multiplied translations into the vernacular, and frequently surpassed the clergy in their knowledge of the scriptures[6]. Innocent III. endeavoured to unite them with the Church (**1210**), and he in part succeeded, forming his Waldensian converts into a society entitled *Pauperes Catholici*[7]; but the majority, estranged by persecution, zealously maintained a separate existence. At the close of the thirteenth century we find a number

SECTS.

fails to procure the papal sanction.

Rapid diffusion of his principles.

---

[1] See the important record of their conduct at the council of Lateran by one who was an eye-witness, Walter Mapes, afterwards archdeacon of Oxford (1196). The passage is in his *De Nugis Curialium*, Distinct. I. § xxxi. (ed. Wright, 1850), the title being 'De secta *Valdesiorum*.'

[2] 'In primis ergo Catharos et Patarinos, et eos qui se *Humiliatos* vel *Pauperes de Lugduno* falso nomine mentiuntur; Passaginos, Josepinos, Arnoldistas perpetuo decernimus anathemate subjacere.' Mansi, xxii. 477.

[3] See authorities at length in Gieseler, iii. § 88, n. 8, 9, 10.

[4] The following passage is an allusion to their progress in the neighbourhood of Trèves (1231): 'Et plures erant sectæ et multi earum instructi erant *Scripturis Sanctis, quas habebant in Theutonicam translatas.*' *Gesta Trevirorum*, i. 819, August. Trevir. 1836.

[5] *e.g.* They maintained (in the passage above cited, n. 4) that the Eucharist might be consecrated 'a viro et muliere, ordinato et non ordinato;' and both males and females preached on every side ('tam homines quam mulieres, idiotæ et illiterati, per villas discurrentes et domos penetrantes et in plateis prædicantes et etiam in ecclesiis, ad idem alios provocabant.' Stephen de Borbone (as above, p. 292, n. 2). They had a ministry, however, nominated by the brotherhood, and consisting of 'majorales' (= bishops?) and 'barbas' (= preachers?): see Gieseler, iii. 465, n. 29. Their ministers were married.

[6] Neander, viii. 360.

[7] Innocent III. *Epist.* lib. xi. epp. 196—198: lib. xii. epp. 17, 69: lib. xiii. ep. 78.

of them in the valleys of Piedmont[1], where after many dark vicissitudes they are surviving at the present day[2].

Their tenets, which were at the first distinguishable in but few particulars from those of other Christians, rapidly developed into forms antagonistic to the common teaching of the Mediæval Church[3]. The Vaudois were indeed to some extent precursors of the Reformation, more especially as it was often carried out in continental Europe.

The Apostolicals (1260—1307).

An allusion has been made already to the aberrations of the stricter school of the Franciscans[4], of the Beghards[5], and the Arnoldists[6] (or partisans of Arnold of Brescia). From the impulse which had been communicated by the authors of those movements, sprang another sect, entitled 'Apostolicals[7].' It was confined at first to Lombardy and

---

[1] See extracts from a record in the archives of Turin communicated by Krone in his *Frà Dolcino und die Patarener*, p. 22, Leipz. 1844.

[2] They maintained themselves in Provence until 1545, when by uniting with the Calvinists they were violently persecuted and expelled. For an account of their past sufferings and present condition, see Gilly's *Narrative*, &c. 4th edition, and Léger, *Hist. des Vaudois*. Their intercourse with Œcolampadius and other Swiss reformers, in 1530, is described by Herzog, pp. 333—376.

[3] They denied the sacramental character of orders, unction, confirmation, and marriage, and the efficacy of absolution and the Eucharist when these were administered by unworthy persons whether lay or cleric (cf. above, p. 293, n. 5). They did not accept the canon of the Mass, but were in favour of more frequent (even daily) communion. They did not invoke the saints, nor venerate the cross and relics. They did not believe in any kind of purgatory, and made no offerings for the dead. They repudiated tithes, the taking of an oath, military service, and capital punishment. They disparaged fasting, all distinction of days ('quod unus dies sit sicut alius'), and every kind of decoration in the ritual or the fabric of the church. With regard to baptism their opinions are not very clearly stated, but, owing to their strong belief in the necessity of actual preconditions on the part of the recipient, they seem at best to have esteemed it, when administered to infants, as an empty ceremonial ('quod ablutio, quæ datur infantibus, nihil prosit'): cf. Neander, VIII. 365. See on the Waldensian doctrines the authorities quoted above, p. 292, n. 1, and the *Extracts from Limborch's History of the Inquisition*, in Maitland's *Facts*, &c. pp. 229 sq.

[4] Above, p. 232.

[5] Above. p. 235. Gieseler, III. 469, 470, n. 35, has pointed out some features in which the Beghards, or, (as they described themselves) 'the Brothers and Sisters of the Free Spirit,' were akin to the Waldenses; and it will be shewn hereafter that they were progenitors of the German (not the English) Lullards, or Lollards.

[6] Above, pp. 249, 250.

[7] See Mosheim's *Gesch. des Apostel-ordens*, Helmstedt, 1748. A full,

certain districts of the Tyrol. Its main object was to realize the long-forgotten picture which the Bible seemed to furnish of a truly evangelic poverty, and of a Church where all the members, from the highest to the lowest, are united solely by the bonds of Christian love[1]. The exhortations of the Apostolicals were all, however, more or less distempered by fanatical and communistic theories[2], which, rousing the displeasure of the Inquisition and the civil power, at length consigned their hapless leader, Sagarelli[3], to the stake (1300). His able, but misguided follower, Dolcino, after braving almost every kind of danger, for the sake of his convictions, met the same unchristian treatment[4] (1307).

Sagarelli, and Dolcino.

but somewhat violent, description of the struggle which the 'Apostolicals' excited will be found in Mariotti's (Gallenga) *Frà Dolcino and his Times*, Lond. 1853.

[1] 'Sine vinculo obedientiæ exterioris, sed interioris tantum.'
[2] Mariotti, pp. 182 sq., pp. 213 sq. Extracts from two of Dolcino's circulars are given in Muratori, *Script. Rer. Ital.* IX. 450. The following views, among his other predictions, shew that he hoped to witness not only the purification of the papacy but also the founding of a native monarchy: 'Fredericus rex Siciliæ debet relevari in imperatorem, et facere reges novos, et Bonifacium papam pugnando habere et facere occidi cum aliis occidendis...Tunc omnes Christiani erunt positi in pace, et tunc erit unus papa sanctus a Deo missus mirabiliter et electus,...et sub illo papa erunt illi, *qui sunt de statu Apostolico*, et etiam alii de clericis et religiosis qui unientur eis,......et tunc accipient Spiritus Sancti gratiam, sicut acceperunt Apostoli in Ecclesia primitiva.' For Dante's view of Dolcino and his mission, see *Dell' Inferno*, cant. XXVIII. 55 sq.
[3] Mariotti, p. 102.
[4] *Ibid.* p. 296. In 1320 some branches of the sect of the 'Apostolicals' existed in the south of France, and traces of them are found in Germany as late as the year 1402. *Ibid.* pp. 314 sq.

CHAPTER XII.

ON THE STATE OF INTELLIGENCE AND PIETY.

Means of Grace and Knowledge.

New impulse given to the Western mind.

Confining our review to Western Christendom[1], in which alone the aspect of religion underwent a clearly measurable change, we must regard the present as an age of great activity and very general progress. The Crusades had opened a new world of intellectual enterprise; the fever of scholasticism arousing all the speculative faculties had urged men to investigate the grounds of their belief; while literary institutions, bent on furthering the spread of secular as well as sacred knowledge, and constructed after the illustrious models in the University of Paris, had sprung up on every side[2]. A somewhat novel feature in the works transmitted to us from the twelfth and thirteenth centuries should not be overlooked.

Literature not exclusively ecclesiastical:

The literature of Europe until then was almost everywhere exclusively 'religious,' or one might affirm at least that it was nearly always penetrated by a strong ecclesiastical element[3]. But afterwards a different class of works were published, which, if not entirely hostile to the Church, were calculated to impair its old ascendancy and to imperil the foundations of both faith and morals. Such were many

---

[1] On the torpor and monotony of the Eastern Church at this period also, see above, p. 272.

[2] See above, 234. Colleges began to be numerous in France, Italy, Spain, Portugal, and Germany (Möhler, *Schriften*, etc. II: 6). This impulse was transmitted as far as Iceland, on the copious literature of which, see Mallet's *Northern Antiquities*, pp. 363 sq. ed. 1847. The two 'general' councils of Lateran, A.D. 1179 (c. 18), and A.D. 1215 (c. 11), enjoin that a schoolmaster shall be provided in every cathedral church for teaching the poorer clerics and the young.

[3] Capefigue, *L'Église au Moyen Age*, I. 362.

of the amorous pieces[1] of the Troubadours, Trouvères, and Minnesingers. Soft and polished as they are, it is too obvious that their general tendency was to produce contempt for holy things and throw a veil upon the most revolting sensuality. The same is often true of mediæval romances[2], which, as may be argued from the copious list surviving at the present day, began to fascinate a very numerous circle.

The more earnest readers still preferred the ancient 'Lives of Saints[3].' These after some recasting were, as in the former age, translated into many dialects of Europe. Some acquaintance with the truths of Christianity might also be obtained from versions of the Bible, or at least of certain parts which were occasionally put in circulation[4]. But the most original method now adopted for imparting rudiments of sacred knowledge were dramatic exhibitions, called 'miracle-plays,' which grew at length into 'moralities.' The object was to bring the leading

MEANS OF GRACE AND KNOWLEDGE.

often very immoral.

Vernacular sources of religious knowledge.

Religious plays.

---

[1] See Sismondi, *Literature of the South of Europe*, c. IV.—c. VIII.; Taylor (Edgar), *Lays of the Minnesingers*, passim. It appears that one of the earliest of the amorous poets in the north of France was Abelard, the schoolman. Hallam, *Liter. of Eur.* pt. I. ch. I. § 36. On the swarms of romances that found their way into the monasteries at this period, see Warton, *Engl. Poet.* I. 80 sq. ed. 1840.

[2] See Ellis, *Specimens of Early Engl. Romances*, ed. Halliwell, 1848.

[3] The *Speculum Historiale* of Vincent of Beauvais (Bellovacensis), and the *Historia Lombardica sive* Legenda Aurea *de Vitis Sanctorum*, of Jacobus de Voragine (da Viraggio), were the favourite books in Western Europe. The popularity of the latter (the 'Golden Legend') continued to the time of the Reformation. A specimen of the vernacular hagiology of this period is furnished by a Semi-Saxon *Legend of St Catherine* (among the publications of the Cambridge Antiquarian Society). The date is the early part of the 13th century.

[4] *E.g.* before the year 1200, the English had translated into their own dialect, in prose, the Psalter and the Canticles of the Church; and towards the middle of the thirteenth century they seem to have possessed a prose version of the entire Bible. But most of the sacred literature at this period is *metrical*; *e. g.* the *Ormulum*, written perhaps about the commencement of the thirteenth century, and serving as a paraphrase of the Gospels and the Acts. Other instances are quoted in the *Preface* to the Wycliffite Bible, p. iii. Oxford, 1850. The *Historia Scholastica* of Peter Comestor (circ. 1190) was very generally circulated both in the original and in translations. It contains an abstract of sacred history, disfigured often by absurd interpolations and unauthorized glosses. A version of it, somewhat modified (1294), was known as the first French Bible. See Gilly's *Preface* to the *Romaunt Version of St John*, pp. xiv.—xvii. Lond. 1848.

facts of revelation and church-history more vividly before the ill-instructed mass. The infancy, the public life, and crucifixion of our Blessed Lord were the most favourite topics[1].

It is constantly complained, however, even with regard to the more enterprising class of scholars, that the Bible was comparatively thrust into the background[2], many of them seeming to prefer the study of the pagan writers or the civil law, and others giving all their time to lectures on the 'Book of Sentences.'

The Vaudois, on the contrary, like all the other mediæval sectaries who thought themselves constrained to wrestle with the evils of the times, appealed in every case directly to the Bible[3]; and although the meaning of the sacred text was often very grievously distorted in their efforts to establish a one-sided or heretical position, the fresh impulse which had now been given to scriptural inquiry was insensibly transmitted far and wide among the members of the Church itself[4]. At first, indeed, the use to which vernacular translations were applied

---

[1] See an abstract of one of them in Sismondi, *Lit. of the South of Europe*, I. 231 sq.; Mone's *Schauspiele des Mittelalters*, passim, Karlsruhe, 1846, and Warton's *Hist. of English Poetry*, II. 24 sq., ed. 1840. It is remarkable that a northern missionary (at Riga) made use of this vehicle in 1204, 'ut fidei Christianæ rudimenta gentilitas fide etiam disceret oculata;' Neander, VII. 52. One of the earliest, and in England the very first, of these theatrical pieces was a *Ludus S. Catharinæ*, performed at Dunstable about 1100: Dugdale's *Monast.* II. 184, new ed.

[2] Thus Robert le Poule (Pullen), as above, p. 263, read the Scriptures at Oxford, where, as well as in other parts of England, they had been neglected 'præ scholasticis:' cf. the remarkable language of Peter of Blois (Blesensis), archdeacon of Bath (cir. 1200), ep. LXXVI. The following words of Roger Bacon (quoted in Bulœus, *Hist. Univ. Paris.* III. 383) are to the same effect: 'Baccalaureus, qui legit *textum*, succumbit lectori Sententiarum. Parisiis ille, qui legit Sententias, habet principalem horam legendi secundum suam voluntatem, habet socium et cameram apud religiosos, sed qui legit *Bibliam* caret his,' etc.—But on the other hand numerous instances have been collected, more especially by Ussher (*Hist. Dogmatica:* Works, ed. Elrington, XII. 317—343), in which the ancient reverence for the Scriptures, as the rule of life, is very forcibly expressed.

[3] It was the principle of Peter Waldo to persuade all 'ut Biblia legerent, atque ex ipso fonte libentius haurirent aquam salutarem, quam ex hominum impuris lacunis. Soli enim Bibliæ scripturæ tot Divinis testimoniis ornatæ atque confirmatæ conscientias tuto inniti posse.' MS. quoted by Ussher, as above, p. 331.

[4] *E.g.* Roger Bacon, above, p. 271.

awakened the suspicions[1] of the prelates and the fury of the Inquisition. The endeavours to suppress them dated from the council of Toulouse[2] in 1229, reference being there intended more especially to the Romaunt translations circulated by the followers of Peter Waldo. But in spite of this repugnance on the part of the ecclesiastical authorities, the wish to draw instruction personally from the oracles of God continued to increase with the diffusion of intelligence.

The present age was also far superior to the last in the efficiency and number of its public teachers[3]. Every parish-priest, as heretofore, was bound[4] to inculcate on all the

MEANS OF GRACE AND KNOWLEDGE.

Attempted suppression of vernacular translations.

---

[1] Thus Innocent III. (1199), lib. II. ep. 141, after directing the attention of the bishop and chapter of Metz to the existence of a 'Gallic' version of the Psalter, Gospels, Pauline Epistles, *etc.*, proceeds as follows: 'Licet autem desiderium intelligendi Divinas Scripturas, et secundum eas studium adhortandi *reprehendendum non sit, sed potius commendandum;* in eo tamen apparent merito arguendi, quod tales occulta conventicula sua celebrant, officium sibi prædicationis usurpant, sacerdotum simplicitatem eludunt, et eorum consortium aspernantur, qui talibus non inhærent.' A like feeling was manifested in condemning the works of the pantheistic schoolman David of Dinant (see above, p. 265, n. 3). The prohibition was extended to all 'theological' works in the *French* language, David having used translations for disseminating his opinions: Neander, VIII. 131, 132.

[2] Can. 14. It forbids the laity to have in their possession any copy of the books of the Old and New Testament, except perhaps the Psalter and those parts of the Bible contained in the Breviary and the Hours of the Blessed Virgin, and most rigorously condemns the use of vernacular translations. See Fleury's apology for this injunction, *Hist. Eccles.,* liv. LXXIX. § 58. At the council of Tarragona (1234, c. 2), the censure is restricted to all versions 'in Romanico:' but in 1246 the council of Béziers (Biterrense), where the Cathari had been most numerous, absolutely urge the Inquisition (c. 36: Mansi, XXIII. 724) to take measures 'de libris theologicis non tenendis *etiam a laicis in Latino,* et neque ab ipsis neque a clericis *in vulgari.*' It is remarkable, however, that notwithstanding these local prohibitions, many parts of the Bible were still translated (*e.g.* into Italian and Spanish), and apparently authorized: Gilly, as above, pp. xvi., xvii. The reason given for putting out a new edition of the French 'Bible' (see above, p. 297, n. 4) in the reign of Charles V. of France (1364—1380), was to supplant the Waldensian versions: Gilly, p. xxii. Cf. Buckingham, *Bible in the Middle Ages,* pp. 43, 46. On the use made of translations of the Scriptures by the Roman missions to the East, see above, p. 218, n. 2.

[3] We may judge of the opportunities of instruction now afforded to the working-classes by the fact that all persons were enjoined to go to church (sometimes under a penalty, *e.g.* council of Toulouse, A.D. 1229, c. 25) on Sundays, on the greater festivals (see a list of them, *Ibid.* c. 26, or council of Exeter, A.D. 1287, c. 23), and on Saturday evenings.

[4] Cf. above, pp. 192, 193; see also the *Præcepta Communia* of Odo,

MEANS OF GRACE AND KNOWLEDGE.

Preaching,

often committed to the Mendicant Orders.

children of his cure at least some elementary knowledge of the Christian faith (by expositions of the Creed, the Lord's Prayer, the Ten Commandments, and at last the Ave Maria, in the vulgar tongue), as well as to be diligent in preaching to the rest[1]. But more was now effected through the voluntary labours of the Mendicants[2], whose zeal and learning were employed, as they itinerated here and there, in teaching simple truths of Christianity no less than in repelling what were deemed the shafts of misbelief. A prelate, such as Grosseteste[3], anxious for the spiritual advancement of his flock and painfully alive to the incompetence[4] of many of the seculars, occasionally invited Mendicants to aid him in his holy task; and even where they had no invitation, they considered that the papal licence was enough to warrant their admission into any diocese. The popularity of this abnormal method of procedure indicates the growing thirst for knowledge; and we must infer that, notwithstanding all the gross hypocrisy, fanaticism, and intermeddling spirit which the friars have too commonly betrayed in after times, they served at first as powerful agents in the hands of the Almighty for promoting intellectual culture and enlivening the stagnant pulses of religion[5].

---

bishop of Paris (circ. 1200), § 10, in Mansi, XXII. 681; the *Statuta Synodal.* of Richard of Chichester (1246), *Ibid.* XXIII. 714: and archbp. Peckham's *Constitutions* (1281), in Johnson, II. 282 sq.

[1] A mighty influence must have been exerted by the sermons of St Bernard, who often preached in the vernacular language. Specimens of this class are printed in the *Documens sur l'Histoire de France*, ed. Le Roux de Lincy, 1841. On the other famous preachers of this period, see Schröckh, XXIX. 313 sq. The sermons of Berthold, a Franciscan (d. 1272), are said to have produced a very deep impression on all kinds of hearers. Many of them (surviving in the vernacular) have been edited by Kling, Berlin, 1824. Specimens of early English Sermons of the 13th and 14th centuries have been edited for the Early English Text Society by Dr R. Morris, 1868.

[2] See above, pp. 230 sq.

[3] Above, p. 234, n. 2.

[4] This was also urged by the apologist of the Franciscan and Dominican orders. He regarded them as supernumeraries especially authorized by the pope in an emergency to remedy the sad defects of the parochial priests: cf. the language of Bonaventura and Aquinas quoted in Neander, VII. 398.

[5] The treatise of Humbert de Romanis (circ. 1250), general of the Dominicans, entitled *De Eruditione Prædicatorum*, is a fine proof of the earnestness with which men were enjoined to enter on the work

It was not until this period that the 'sacramental' system of the Church attained its full development[1]. The methodizing and complete determination of the subjects it involved is due to the abstruse inquiries of the Schoolmen. Previously the name of 'sacrament' was used to designate[2] a ritual or symbolic act in general,—Baptism, Confirmation, and the Eucharist belonging to a special class[3]. But in the twelfth century the ordinances which could claim to be admitted to the rank of 'sacraments' were found to coincide exactly with the sacred number seven[4]. The earliest trace of this scholastic limitation has been pointed out in a discourse of Otho the apostle of the Pomeranians[5] (1124); and from the age of Peter Lombard[6], Bonaventura, and Aquinas, members of the

CORRUPTIONS AND ABUSES.

Sacramental system of the Church.

Limitation of the sacraments to seven.

---

of preaching, though we trace in it a disposition to exaggerate the worth of sermons as compared with other means of grace. See a review of it in Neander, VII. 435—440. The following is the account given by the biographer of Aquinas (c. viii. s. 48, as above, p. 267, n. 3), respecting his style of preaching: 'Prædicationes suas, quibus placeret Deo, prodesset populo, sic formabat, ut non esset in curiosis humanæ sapientiæ verbis, sed in spiritu et virtute sermonis, qui, vitatis quæ curiositati potius quam utilitati deserviunt, in illo suo vulgari natalis soli proponebat et prosequebatur utilia populo.'

[1] See Hagenbach, *Hist. of Doctrine*, § 189 (vol. II. pp. 73 sq., Edinb. 1852), on the one side, and Klee, *Dogmengesch.* Pt. II. ch. vi., on the other.

[2] St Augustine's definition was 'sacræ rei signum,' or 'invisibilis gratiæ visibilis forma' (Klee, *Ibid.* § 1): but like Damiani (quoted above, p. 199, n. 3), he applied the word 'sacramentum' very generally. The same appears to have been the case with the word μυστήριον in the East, although the number of rites to which it was in strictness applicable, was at length reduced to six,—baptism, the Lord's Supper, the consecration of the holy oil (τελετὴ μύρον), priestly orders, monastic dedication (μοναχικὴ τελείωσις), and the ceremonies relating to the holy dead. Schröckh, XXIII. 127—129; XXVIII. 45.

[3] *E.g.* as late as Rabanus Maurus (*De Institut. Clericorum*, lib. I. c. 24), and Paschasius Radbert (*De Corpore et Sang. Domini*, c. 3), and Berengarius (*De Cœna Domini*, p. 153), the 'sacramenta' are restricted in this manner: and when Alexander of Hales (*Summa*, Pt. IV. Quæst. VIII. Art. 2) accepted the scholastic terminology he was constrained to allow that only two sacraments (baptism and the Eucharist) were instituted by the Lord Himself 'secundum suam formam.' The same appears to be the view of Hugo of St Victor, in his work *On the Sacraments* (above, p. 263, n. 4).

[4] See the varying theories on this point in Klee (as above), § 10, to which may be added the sermons of the Franciscan Berthold (as above, p. 300, n. 1), pp. 439 sq.

[5] Above, p. 208: cf. Schröckh, XXV. 227.

[6] *Sentent.*, lib. IV. Dist. I. sq., which practically settled the dis-

Western Church were taught to pay a large, if not an equal, share of reverence to all the 'sacraments of the new law,'—Baptism, Confirmation, the Eucharist, Penitence, Extreme Unction, Orders, and Matrimony. A distinction was, however, drawn among them in respect of dignity, specific virtues, and importance[1]. Preachers also were not wanting to insist upon the need of faith and other preconditions in all those, excepting infants[2], who were made partakers of the sacraments. Still it is plain that the prevailing tendency of this and former ages, as distinguished from the period since the Reformation, was to view a sacred rite far too exclusively in its objective character[3], (i.e. without regard to the susceptibility *of those to whom it was applied).*

These feelings were in no case carried out so far as in relation to the Eucharist. The doctrine which affirmed a physical 'transubstantiation' of the elements had, on the overthrow of Berengarius[4], gained complete possession of

---

cussion in the Western Church. The sects, however, still continued to protest against the elevation of a class of ordinances for which there was no express warrant in the Bible (e.g. the Waldenses, above, p. 294, n. 3).

[1] Klee, as above, § 11.

[2] See the remarkable passage in Peter Lombard, *Sentent.* lib. IV., Dist. 4, on the benefits of baptism in the case of infants. His language implies that the precise *amount* of spiritual blessing was disputed, and that some, who thought original sin to be remitted in the case of every child, contended that the grace imparted then was given 'in munere non in usu, ut cum ad majorem venerint [*i.e.* cuncti parvuli] ætatem, ex munere sortiantur usum, nisi per liberum arbitrium usum muneris extinguant peccando, et ita ex culpa eorum est, non ex defectu gratiæ, quod mali fiunt.' Aquinas discusses the same point, 'utrum pueri in baptismo consequantur gratiam et virtutes' (*Summa*, Pt. III., Quæst. LXIX., Art. vi.), determining it, for the most part, in the language of Augustine.

[3] The phrase 'ex opere operato' was now introduced to represent this mode of viewing sacraments; e.g. Duns Scotus (*Sent.* lib. IV. Dist. I., Quæst. 6, § 10) affirms, 'Sacramentum *ex virtute operis operati* confert gratiam, ita quod non requiritur ibi bonus motus anterior qui mereatur gratiam; sed sufficit, quod suscipiens non ponat obicem.' Aquinas, on the other hand (*Summa*, Pt. III., Quæst. LXII.) maintains that the sacrament is no more than the '*instrumentalis* causa gratiæ,' while the true agent is God: 'Deus sacramentis adhibitis in anima gratiam operatur:'... 'Nihil potest causare gratiam, nisi Deus.' Elsewhere, however (Pt. III. Quæst. LXXX. Art. 12), he argues that the 'perfection' of the Eucharist is not to be sought 'in usu fidelium, sed in consecratione materiæ.'

[4] See above, p. 173.

the leading teachers of the West[1]. Discussions[2], it is true, were agitated still among the Schoolmen as to the exact intention of the phrase 'to transubstantiate;' but the emphatic sentence of the council held at the Lateran[3] (1215), designed especially to counteract the spreading tenets of the Albigenses and some other sects[4], admitted of no casuistical evasion.

CORRUPTIONS AND ABUSES.

One effect of a belief in transubstantiation was to discontinue the original practice of administering the Eucharist in both kinds[5]; the reason being that our Blessed Lord existed so entirely and so indivisibly in either element that all who were partakers of the consecrated Host received therein His Body and His Blood[6]. This novel theory was called the doctrine of 'concomitance:' but notwithstanding all the specious logic which the schoolmen urged in its behalf, it was not generally accepted till the close of the thirteenth century.

Communion in one kind only.

Another consequence that flowed immediately from the scholastic dogmas on the Lord's Supper was the adoration of the Host. It had been usual long before to elevate[7]

Adoration of the Host.

---

[1] Gieseler (III. 315, n. 5) has pointed out an instance where the term 'transubstantiatio' occurs as early as Damiani in his *Expositio Canonis Missæ*, in Maii *Script. Vet. Collect.* VI., pt. II. 215, Rom. 1825). Other instances belonging to the twelfth century have been collected in Bp. Cosin's *Hist. Transubstant.* c. 7, new edit., which is an important authority on the whole question.

[2] See Klee, as above, § 25. One of the most independent writers on the subject was the Dominican, John of Paris (circ. 1300), whose *Determinatio de modo existendi Corporis Christi in sacramento altaris alio quam sit ille, quem tenet ecclesia* was edited by Allix, Lond. 1686: cf. Neander, VII. 473.

[3] 'In qua [*i.e.* Ecclesia] idem Ipse Sacerdos est et Sacrificium Jesus Christus, Cujus corpus et sanguis in sacramento altaris sub speciebus panis et vini veraciter continentur, transubstantiatis pane in corpus et vino in sanguinem potestate Divina', etc. c. 1. On the contemporary doctrine of the Eastern Church, see above, p. 95, n. 1; Schröekh, XXVIII. 72, 73; Hagenbach, § 197.

[4] Cf. Palmer's *Treatise on the Church*, part IV. ch. XI. § 2.

[5] Cf. above, p. 199, n. 3.

[6] Anselm (*Epist.* lib. IV. ep. 107) was the first who argued 'in utraque specie totum Christum sumi.' Others, quoted at length by Gieseler (III. 320—324, n. 11, 12), followed his example; though the cup did not begin to be actually *withdrawn* from the communicants till somewhat later. The steps by which the change was finally accomplished have been traced at length in Spittler (as above, p. 199, n. 3).

[7] Schröckh, XXVIII. 74: Klee, part II. ch. VI. § 32: L'Arroque, *Hist. of the Eucharist*, part I. ch. IX. We may gather the prevailing modes of

CORRUPTIONS AND ABUSES.

the holy sacrament with the idea of teaching by a symbol the triumphant exaltation of the Lord. A different meaning was, however, naturally imparted to the rite[1], where men believed that Christ was truly veiled beneath the sacramental emblems. These in turn became an object of the highest worship, which was paid to them not only in the celebration of the mass, but also when the Host was carried in procession to the sick. The annual feast of *Corpus Christi* (on the Thursday after Trinity Sunday) was the point in which these acts of worship culminated. It was authorized expressly in a bull of Urban IV.[2] (**1264**), and confirmed afresh by Clement V. at the council of Vienne[3] (**1311**).

Feast of Corpus Christi.

Practical result of a belief in transubstantiation.

Although we must acknowledge that the better class of minds may have been stimulated in their pious meditations[4] by thus realizing the immediate presence of the

thought from the 'Ancren Riwle,' written early in the 13th century (edited with translation by Morton; Camd. Soc. 1853): 'In the mass, when the priest elevates God's body, say these verses standing, *Ecce salus mundi, verbum Patris, hostia vera, Viva caro, deitas integra, verus homo:* and then fall down with this greeting, *Ave principium nostræ creationis,* etc.' p. 32.

[1] The first recorded instance of 'adoration' in Germany (*i.e.* of kneeling down before the host as an object of worship) is said to have occurred in the 13th century (circ. 1215). See Cæsarius of Heisterbach, *De Miraculis, etc., Dialogi,* lib. IX. c. 51 (quoted by Neander, VII. 474). In the *Decret. Gregor. IX.,* lib. III. tit. XLI. c. 10 (*Corpus Juris Canon.*), we find the following order of Honorius III. (circ. 1217): 'Sacerdos vero quilibet frequenter doceat plebem suam, ut, cum in celebratione missarum elevatur Hostia salutaris, quilibet se reverenter inclinet, idem faciens cum eam defert presbyter ad infirmum.' The Order of St Clara (above, p. 231, n. 2) devoted themselves especially to the adoration of the sacrament. Capefigue, II. 21.

[2] *Bullarium Romanum,* I. 146 sq. Lugdun. 1712. It seems to have existed somewhat earlier in the diocese of Liège, or at least the institution of it was suggested from that quarter. See *Gest. Pontiff. Leodiens.,* ed. Chapeaville, II. 293; Leodii, 1612.

[3] *Clementin.* lib. III. tit. XVI. (in the *Corpus Jur. Canon.*).

[4] *E.g.* the treatise *De Sacrament. Altaris,* Pt. II. c. 6 (wrongly ascribed to Anselm of Canterbury and printed in the old editions of his Works): 'Cum ergo, de carne Sua, amandi Se tantam ingerit materiam, magnam et mirificam animabus nostris vitæ alimoniam ministrat, cum dulciter recolligimus et in ventre memoriæ recondimus quæcunque pro nobis fecit et passus est Christus.' *Ancren Riwle,* p. 35 (Morton's translation): 'After the kiss of peace in the mass, when the priest consecrates, forget there all the world, and there be entirely out of the body; there in glowing love embrace your beloved [Saviour] Who is come down from heaven into your breast's bower, and hold Him fast until He shall have granted whatever you wish for.' Cf. Neander, VII. 467.

Crucified, the general effect of a belief in transubstantiation, and the doctrines in connexion with it, was to thin the number of communicants[1]. The Eucharist was commonly esteemed an awful and mysterious sacrifice of which the celebrant alone was worthy to partake, at least from day to day. His flock were present chiefly as spectators of the rite.

CORRUPTIONS AND ABUSES.

A grave delusion which had shewn itself already in the worship of the blessed Virgin was continued to the present age[2]. It now pervaded almost every class of Christians, not excepting the more thoughtful Schoolmen[3], and was one of the prime elements in giving birth to what are called the institutes of 'chivalry'[4]. The parallel indeed which was established at this time between the honours rendered to St Mary and to God Himself[5] is a distressing

Worship of the Virgin.

---

[1] The twenty-first canon of the Council of Lateran (1215) is evidence of this infrequency. It enjoins that all the faithful of either sex shall communicate at least once a year, viz. at Easter, on pain of excommunication ('nisi forte de consilio proprii sacerdotis ob aliquam rationabilem causam ad tempus ab ejus perceptione duxerit abstinendum'). Schröckh (XXVIII. 111 sq.) has collected other evidence, shewing that in France and England attempts were made to induce the people to communicate three times a year. Worthless priests now began to enter into pecuniary contracts, binding themselves to offer masses (say for twenty or thirty years) in behalf of the dying and the dead. The better class of prelates did not fail, however, to denounce the practice. *Ibid.* p. 113, and Neander, VII. 481. The practice of administering the Eucharist to *children* was discontinued from this epoch, scarcely any trace of it appearing after the twelfth century. It was actually forbidden at the council of Bordeaux (Burdegalense), A.D. 1255, c. 5, but is still retained in the Eastern Church.

[2] Buckingham, p. 255: 'In the 13th century the universal reverence of mankind found utterance in the establishment of that order, whose founders chose the title of Servites, or Serfs of Mary, as the expression of their joyful allegiance to *her sovereignty.*'

[3] *e.g.* Bonaventura, above, p. 266.

[4] See Miller's *History Philosophically Illustrated*, II. 14—16. A glance at the *Fabliaux* (ed. Le Grand) will shew the awful way in which the worship of the Virgin was associated with an almost diabolical licentiousness: see especially the *Contes Dévots*, in tome v.

[5] We see this feeling manifested strongly in the *Cursus B. Mariæ* (Neander, VII. 117, note), and in the compilation of the *Psalterium Minus*, the *Psalterium Majus B. Virginis Mariæ*, and the *Biblia Mariana*, which (whoever may have been the authors) were circulated at this period (cf. above, p. 266, n. 4; and Gieseler, III. 340—343, n. 9, 10, 12). Aquinas first employed the term *hyperdulia* (= 'medium inter latriam et duliam'), intending by it the peculiar veneration, short of supreme worship, which was due to the Virgin as distinguished from all other saints (*Summa*, Secunda Secundæ, Quæst. CIII. Art. iv.). He affirms elsewhere

CORRUPTIONS AND ABUSES.

proof that in the estimation even of her purest votaries she was exalted far above the human level and invested with prerogatives belonging only to her Son. A slight reaction may indeed have been occasioned through the partial failure of the effort, noticed on a previous page[1], when the Franciscans attempted to exact belief in the immaculate conception of the Virgin as an article of faith: but it is obvious that the party siding with Anselm, Bernard, and Aquinas was outnumbered by the rest, and that the general current of religious feeling had now set the other way.

Saint worship.

The number of factitious saints, already vast[2], was multiplied by the credulity of some and by the impious fraud of others, who on their return from Palestine were apt to circulate astounding tales among their countrymen, and furnish fresh supplies of relics to the convents on their way. These practices, however, were most warmly reprobated here and there[3].

Pilgrimages.

The rage for pilgrimages had not been diminished, even after the idea of rescuing the Holy Sepulchre was generally abandoned[4] on all sides. The less distant shrines were still frequented by a crowd of superstitious

---

(Part III. Quæst. xxv. Art. v.) 'quod matri Regis non debetur æqualis honor honori qui debetur Regi; debetur tamen ei *quidam honor consimilis* ratione cujusdam excellentiæ.'

[1] Above, p. 270. The *Feast of the Conception of the Virgin* (Dec. 8), corresponding with that of her *Nativity* (Sept. 8: cf. above, p. 92, n. 1) was introduced in the 13th century, but not made absolutely binding ('cujus celebrationi non imponitur necessitas;' Synod of Oxford, A.D. 1222, c. 8: Mansi, xxii. 1153). See, on the general question, Gravois, *De Ortu et Progressu Cultus ac Festi Immac. Concep. Dei Genetricis*, Luc. 1762. The Council of Basel (Sess. xxxvi.; Sept. 17, 1439) decreed that the doctrine of the Immaculate Conception was a pious opinion, agreeable to the worship of the Church, the Catholic Faith, and right reason. See the arguments against it in the great work of Torquemada, *Tractatus de Veritate Conceptionis B. M. V.* Rome, 1547; Oxford, 1869.

[2] Above, p. 196: see the very large *Catalogus Sanctorum*, compiled by Peter de Natalibus; fol. Lugdun. 1514. To this period belongs the famous legend of the 11,000 virgins of Cologne (perhaps a mis-reading of XI M. Virgines = XI Martyres, Virgines). The story was already current among our forefathers in the 14th century: see a *Norman-French Chronicle*, c. LIII. Cambr. Univ. MSS. Ee. I. 20.

[3] A fine specimen occurs in the treatise *De Pignoribus Sanctorum* of Guibert, abbot of Nogent-sous-Coucy (d. 1124): *Opp.* ed. D'Achery, 1651.

[4] Above, p. 253. The feelings of the more intelligent pilgrims may be gathered from a tract of Peter of Blois, *De Hierosolymitana Peregrinatione acceleranda*. See extracts of the same general character in Neander, VII. 425—427.

devotees, attracted thither, as of old, by an idea of lightening the conscience at an easy cost. Nor was the sterner and ascetic class of penitents extinct[1]: although it seems that in the West the spirit of religion had upon the whole become more joyous than was noted in the former period.

CORRUPTIONS AND ABUSES.

Extreme asceticism.

The influence of the Schools had shewn itself again in giving a more scientific shape to the conceptions which had long been current in the Western Church respecting penance. It is true that many popular abuses of an earlier date[2] were still too common both in England and the continent. They kept their ground in spite of all the efforts made by Gregory VII.[3] and other prelates to enforce a worthier and more evangelic doctrine. Peter Lombard, with the Schoolmen generally, insisted on contrition of the heart as one of three[4] essential elements in true repent-

Scholastic view of Penance.

---

[1] They frequently took refuge in some one of the religious Orders, or attached themselves to the third class of the Franciscans (see above, p. 231). In the Eastern Church the self-immolation of the monks assumed the most extravagant shapes. See Eustathius, *Ad Stylitam quendam*, c. 48 sq. (*Opp.* ed. Tafel). The pilgrimages of Italian 'Flagellants' (1260 sq.) are manifestations of the same spirit in the West (Muratori, *Script. Rer. Ital.* VIII. 712). The author of the *Ancren Riwle*, who is generally very stern, was under the necessity of giving such injunctions as these to the nuns of Tarent in Dorsetshire: 'Wear no iron, nor haircloth, nor hedgehog-skins; and do not beat yourselves therewith, nor with a scourge of leather thongs, nor leaded; and do not with holly nor with briars cause yourselves to bleed without leave of your confessor; and do not, at one time, use too many flagellations:' p. 419 (Morton's translation).

[2] See above, p. 201: and cf. council of York (1195) c, 4; of London (1237), c. 4: Wilkins, I. 501, 650; Johnson, II. 76, 154.

[3] His letter (1079) to the bishops and faithful of Brittany (lib. VII. ep. 10: Mansi, XX. 295) is very remarkable. He argues that true repentance is nothing less than a return to such a state of mind as to feel one's self obliged hereafter to the faithful performance of baptismal obligations. Other forms of penance, if this change of heart be wanting, are said to be sheer hypocrisy. See also the *Epistles* of Ivo of Chartres, epp. 47, 228; and the 16th canon of the synod of Melfi (1039): Mansi, XX. 724. The sober views of Hildebrand respecting monasticism may be gathered from his letter to the abbot of Clugny: lib. VI. ep. 17.

[4] The three-fold representation of penance, 'contritio (distinguished from *attritio*) cordis,' 'confessio oris,' and 'satisfactio operis,' dates from Hildebert of Tours, *e.g.* Sermo IV. in Quadragesima, *Opp.* col. 324. It is also found in Peter Lombard (*Sentent.* lib. IV., Dist. XVI.) and in the schoolmen generally. Peter Blesensis, *De Confessione Sacramentali* (p. 1086, ed. Migne) has the following passage: 'Christus autem purgationem peccatorum faciens, non in judicio, sed in desiderio, non in ardore, sed in amore, tria nobis purgatoria misericorditer assignavit,

ance;—the remaining parts, confession of the mouth and satisfaction, being signs or consequences of a moral change already wrought within. According to this view, humiliation in the sight of God is proved by corresponding acts of self-renunciation, by confession to a priest (a usage absolutely enjoined on all of either sex in the Lateran council[1], **1215**), and by performing, in obedience to his will, a cycle of religious exercises (fastings, prayers, alms, and other kindred works). The aim of these austerities, as well as that of penance in all cases, was to expiate the 'pœna,' or the *temporal* effect of sins which, it was argued, cleaves to the offender, and demands a rigorous satisfaction, even after the *eternal* consequences of them (or the 'culpa') are remitted freely by the pardoning grace of Christ[2]. As many as neglected to complete this satisfaction in the present life would find a debt remaining still to be discharged in purgatory,—apprehended by the Schoolmen as a place of discipline to which the spirits of the justified, and they alone, have access.

Peter Lombard also dealt a heavy blow on those who had exaggerated the effects of sacerdotal absolution[3]. He

cordis contritionem, oris confessionem, carnis afflictionem,' etc. On the names 'contrition' and 'attrition,' see Klee, part II. ch. VI. § 11.

[1] Peter Lombard (as above, Dist. XVII.) asserts the *necessity* of oral confession, 'si adsit facultas:' but the first conciliar authority absolutely demanding it of every one, 'postquam ad annos discretionis pervenerit,' is the *Concil. Later.* (1215), c. 21. See the arguments of Aquinas in the *Summa*, part III. Quæst. LXXXIV. sq. The practice of confessing to *laymen* was allowed in extreme cases, but in the 13th century such acts were judged to be non-sacramental: see Gieseler, III. § 83, n. 2: Klee, as above, § 19. On the violent controversy which sprang up at this period in the Jacobite communion respecting the necessity of auricular confession, see Neale, *Eastern Church*, II. 261 sq.

[2] *e. g.* Aquinas, (*Summa*, Pt. III. Supplement. Quæst. XVIII. Art. 2): 'Illi, qui per contritionem consequutus est remissionem peccatorum, *quantum ad culpam*, et per consequens *quantum ad reatum pœnæ æternæ*, quæ simul cum culpa dimittitur ex vi clavium, ex passione Christi efficaciam habentium, augetur gratia, et remittitur *temporalis* pœna, cujus reatus adhuc remanserat post culpæ remissionem: non tamen tota, sicut in baptismo, sed pars ejus,' etc.

[3] 'Hoc sane dicere ac sentire possumus, quod solus Deus dimittit peccata et retinet: et tamen Ecclesiæ contulit potestatem ligandi et solvendi. Sed aliter Ipse solvit vel ligat, aliter Ecclesia. Ipse enim per se tantum dimittit peccatum, quia et animam mundat ab interiori macula, et a debito æternæ mortis solvit. Non autem hoc sacerdotibus concessit, *quibus tamen tribuit potestatem solvendi et ligandi, i.e. ostendendi homines ligatos vel solutos.' Sentent.* lib. IV. Dist. XVIII. This view was, however, far from general: cf. Klee, § 8.

maintained that any sentence of the priest was valid only in so far as it accorded with the higher sentence of the Lord. But in the many a distinction of this kind was far too often disregarded, and the errors into which they fell would find abundant countenance in some proceedings of the Church itself. Indulgences, for instance, purporting to lessen the amount of satisfaction, or, in other words, to act as substitutes for penitential exercises[1], were now issued by the popes, in favour of all Western Christendom, when it was necessary to stir up the zeal of the Crusaders, or advance the interest of the Roman see. The earliest grant of 'plenary' indulgences is due to Urban II.[2] (1095). It was discovered also that a treasury of merits[3], rising chiefly out of Christ's, but partly out of those which others, by His grace, had been enabled to contribute, was now placed at the disposal of the popes, who could allot them to the needy members of the Church as an equivalent for uncompleted penance. A gigantic illustration of these principles recurred in 1300, which Boniface VIII. appointed as the year of Jubilee[4]. A plenary indulgence was thereby

CORRUPTIONS AND ABUSES.

Indulgences.

Treasury of merits.

---

[1] See above, p. 201.

[2] Council of *Clermont*, c. 2: 'Quicunque pro sola devotione non pro honoris vel pecuniæ adeptione, ad liberandam Ecclesiam Dei Jerusalem profectus fuerit, iter illud *pro omni pœnitentia* [ei] *reputetur:*' Mansi, xx. 816: cf. Gibbon, ed. Milman, v. 413 sq. The fearful relaxation of morals in the great bulk of the crusaders furnishes an instructive comment on this practice. See Aventinus, *Annal. Boiorum*, lib. vii. c. 3, edit. Gundling. Innocent III. himself (1215), in *Decretal. Greg. IX.*, lib. v. tit. xxxviii. c. 14, was obliged to limit the extension and number of indulgences, and Innocent IV. (1246), in Mansi, xxiii. 600, confesses that some of the Crusaders 'cum deberent ab excessibus abstinere, *propter libertatem eis indultam*, furta, homicidia, raptus mulierum, et alia perpetrant detestanda.' The inability of the populace to enter into the scholastic distinctions on this point is singularly illustrated by the language of William of Auxerre, who viewed the teaching of the Church about it as a kind of 'pious fraud.' Neander, vii. 486.

[3] 'Thesaurus meritorum,' or 'Thesaurus supererogationis perfectorum.' The first advocates of this notion were Alexander of Hales and Albertus Magnus (see extracts in Gieseler, § 84, n. 15—18). With regard to souls in purgatory it was contended that indulgences do not apply *auctoritative* but *impetrative*, i.e. not directly, but in virtue of the suffrages which are made in their behalf by the living. The question is discussed at length by Aquinas (*Summa*, Pt. iii. *Supplement*. Quæst. lxxi. Art. 10).

[4] See the *Bull* in the *Extravagantes Communes* (*Corp. Jur. Canon.*), lib. v. tit. ix. c. 1. The pope grants to all who are penitent, or shall become so, 'in præsenti et quolibet centesimo secuturo annis, non solum plenam, sed largiorem, imo plenissimam omnium suorum veniam peccatorum.'

held out to every Christian, who, for certain days, should punctually worship at the tombs of St Peter and St Paul. The news of this festivity was spread on every side, attracting a tumultuary host of pilgrims[1], male and female, who set out for the metropolis of Western Christendom, in search of what they hoped might prove itself a general amnesty, at least for all the temporal effects of sin, both present and to come.

Corruptions and abuses.

Year of Jubilee.

Contradictions in the general aspect of the age.

In that and other like events we see the characteristic features of the age. It was an age of feverish excitement, where the passions and imagination acted far more strongly than the reason, and accordingly it teemed throughout with moral paradoxes. Elements of darkness and of light, of genuine piety and abject superstition, of extreme decorum and unblushing profligacy, of self-sacrifice approaching almost to the apostolic model and of callousness that bordered on brutality, are found not only in immediate juxtaposition, but often, as it seems, amalgamated and allied. The courtly knight devoted to the special honour of the Virgin, but most openly unchaste, the grasping friar, the Inquisitor consigning to the faggot men whom he had just been labouring to convert, the gay recluse, the pleasure-hunting pilgrim, the Crusader bending on the blood-stained threshold of the Sepulchre and then disgracing by flagitious deeds the holy sign he had emblazoned on his armour,—these are specimens of the deplorable confusion to be traced in all the ruling modes of thought.

But on the other hand we should remember that anomalies which differ only in degree present themselves in every age of Christianity, nay, more or less, in every human heart; and that in spite of very much to sadden and perplex us in our study of the Middle Age, there is enough in men like Anselm, Bernard, Louis IX. of France, Aquinas, Grosseteste, and if we include the gentler sex, Elizabeth of Hessen, Hedwige of Poland, and a host of others, to attest the permanent influence of Christian truth and real saintliness of life.

[1] Capefigue, II. 142 sq.

Fourth Period of the Middle Ages.

THE CHRISTIAN CHURCH FROM THE TRANSFER
OF THE PAPAL SEE TO AVIGNON UNTIL
THE EXCOMMUNICATION OF LUTHER.

1305—1520.

CHAPTER XIII.

§ 1. *GROWTH OF THE CHURCH.*

MISSIONS.

THE Gospel of our Blessed Lord was now 'in truth or in pretence' accepted by the vast majority of European tribes, although in much of the Iberian peninsula, in Russia[1], and the modern Turkey[2], its ascendancy was broken or disputed by the adversaries of the Cross.

AMONG THE LITHUANIANS.

Introduction of the Gospel into Lithuania:

Almost the only district of importance which remained entirely in the shade of paganism was the grand-duchy of Lithuania[3], peopled by a branch of the Sarmatian family[4], in close relation to the Slaves[5]. As early as **1252** we read[6] that Mindove, the son of a Lithuanic chief, embraced the Christian faith, and Vitus, a Dominican, appears to have

---

[1] The Mongols were not expelled till 1462; see above, p. 121.
[2] Constantinople itself fell into the hands of the Muhammedans, May 29, 1453; the last refuge of the Christians being the church of St Sophia, which was afterwards converted into a mosque. Gibbon, VI. 312 sq., ed. Milman.
[3] Hither had fled a remnant of the Prussians, who still clung to heathenism: above, p. 215, n. 5.
[4] Numbers of their kinsmen in the East, instead of realizing the hopes of Catholic and Nestorian missionaries (cf. above, p. 216), shewed a stronger leaning to Muhammedanism. See Mosheim, *Hist. Tartar. Eccl.*, pp. 90 sq. In China also Christianity was well-nigh subverted in 1369 (above, p. 218, n. 3), and the subsequent irruptions (1370—1400) of Timur (or Tamerlane), an ardent patron of the Persian (anti-Turkish) sect of the Muhammedans, while they proved instrumental in curtailing the Ottoman power, were no less fatal to the propagation of the Gospel. See Gibbon, VI. 178 sq., ed. Milman.
[5] Dr Latham's *Ethnology of Europe*, pp. 154 sq., Lond. 1852.
[6] Döllinger, III. 285, 286: but cf. Schröckh, XXX. 496. Russian influences had also been exerted on the other side and in a milder spirit. Mouravieff, p. 42.

—1520]	*Growth of the Church.*	313

gone thither, at the bidding of pope Innocent IV., as missionary bishop: but ere long the influence he exerted was reversed, and scarcely aught is heard of Christianity in Lithuania until **1386**. In that year Jagal, or Jagello[1], the grand-duke, whose predatory inroads had been long the terror of his Polish neighbours, entered into an alliance with them, on condition that he should espouse their youthful monarch, Hedwige, and should plant the Church in every part of his dominions. Jagal was baptized at Cracow[2] (**1386**), by the name of Vladislav, and in conjunction with Bodzanta[3], the archbishop of Gnesen, and a staff of Polish missionaries headed by Vasillo, a Franciscan monk, he soon extinguished the more public and revolting rites of paganism. But, strange to say, the work of the evangelist was mainly undertaken by the duke himself[4], the missionaries having little or no knowledge of the native dialects. The change produced was, therefore, nearly always superficial[5], though, as time went on, the immediate neighbourhood of Wilna[6], where the bishops lived, was gradually pervaded by a knowledge of the truth.

MISSIONS.

through a Polish channel.

[1] The chief original authority on the conversion of Lithuania is the *Historia Poloniæ* of John Dlugoss (a canon of Cracow, who died 1480), ed. Lips. 1711, lib. x. pp. 96 sq.

[2] Some of his retinue who had been formerly baptized according to Greek rites could not be induced ' ad iterandum, vel, ut significantiori verbo utar, ad supplendum baptisma.' *Ibid.* p. 104.

[3] Wiltsch, II. 261.

[4] The following entry of the Polish chronicler is in many ways instructive: 'Per dies autem aliquot de articulis fidei, quos credere oportet, et Oratione Dominica atque symbolo per sacerdotes Polonorum, magis tamen per Wladislai regis [? operam], qui linguam gentis noverat et cui facilius assentiebat, edocta, sacri baptismatis unda renata est, largiente Wladislao rege singulis ex popularium numero post susceptum baptisma de panno ex Polonia adducto novas vestes, tunicas, et indumenta:' p. 110. The baptisms were performed by sprinkling a large mass of the people at once, to all of whom was given the same Christian name, *e.g.* Paul or Peter.

[5] In the middle of the fifteenth century, serpent-worship was still dominant in many districts (see Æneas Sylvius, *De Statu Europæ*, c. 26, pp. 275 sq., Helmstad. 1699): and traces of heathenism are recorded even in the sixteenth century (see Lucas David, *Preuss. Chronik.* ed. Henning, VII. 205).

[6] The see was founded in 1387, in which year, according to a chronicler (quoted by Raynaldus, ad an. § 15), Lithuania passed over 'ad ecclesiæ Romanæ obedientiam, optimi principis auctoritate inducta.' The bishop was placed in immediate subjection to the papal see, without a metropolitan.

AMONG THE SAMAITES AND LAPPS.

Missions.

Conversion of the Samaites:

The arms of the Teutonic knights[1] had forced a way into the region occupied by the tribe of Samaites (Samogitæ), which are probably to be connected with the savage and half-christian race of Samoieds[2], at present bordering on the Arctic circle. The slight impression thus produced was afterwards extended (**1413**) by the labours of a Lithuanian priest named Withold[3]. He was consecrated bishop of Wornie or Miedniki[4] (? **1417**), but numbers of his flock appear to have immediately relapsed. The date of their final conversion is unknown.

and Lapps.

The Lapps, a kindred tribe[5] inhabiting the northernmost extremity of Scandinavia, had submitted to the thriving state of Sweden in **1279**. From thence proceeded Christian missions, more particularly in the time of Hemming[6], primate of Upsala (**1335**), who founded the first church at Tornea, and baptized a multitude of people. It was not, however, till the sixteenth and two following centuries[7] that Christianity became the popular religion.

AMONG THE KUMANIANS.

Conversion of the Kumanians.

These were members of the Turkish family[8], who entered Europe at the close of the eleventh century upon the track of the Magyars. They settled more especially in Volhynia and Moldavia, where, unlike a number of their kinsmen who became Muhammedans, they clung to a degraded form of paganism[9]. In **1340** some Franciscan missionaries, who

---

[1] Above, p. 215.
[2] Schröckh denies this (xxx. 498), but assigns no reason. On the other hand it is indisputable that the Samoieds (a section of the Ugrian race) had formerly dwelt in more southern latitudes: cf. Latham, *Ethnology of Europe*, pp. 166 sq.
[3] Dlugoss, as above, lib. XI. pp. 342 sq.
[4] A bishopric had been planted here in 1387 (see Raynaldus, as above, p. 313, n. 6), but owing to the troubles of the period, was not actually filled until 1417: cf. Wiltsch, II. 262.
[5] Latham, as above, p. 147.
[6] See Scheffer's *Lapponia*, c. 8, pp. 63 sq., Francof. 1673.
[7] Guerike, *Kirchengesch.* II. 355, 356, Halle, 1843. On the earlier labours of Russian monks, see Mouravieff, pp. 70, 97.
[8] Latham, as above, p. 247.
[9] According to Spondanus, *Annales*, ad an. 1220 (*Continuatio*, I. p. 78), the archbishop of Gran had in that year baptized the king of

had been established in the town of Szeret (in Bukhovina), were assassinated by the natives. To avenge this barbarous wrong an army[1] of Hungarian crusaders marched into the district and compelled a large proportion of the heathen to adopt the Christian faith and recognize the Roman pontiff[2]. But as all Moldavia was ere long subdued by the Wallachians, the new 'converts' passed thereby into the jurisdiction of the Eastern Church[3].

MISSIONS.

IN THE CANARIES AND WESTERN AFRICA.

The enterprising spirit of the Portuguese had opened a new field for missionary zeal. Incited by the ardour of prince Henry[4], they discovered the important island of Madeira in 1420. Other efforts were alike successful; and in 1484 Bartolomè Diaz ventured round the southern point of Africa, which was significantly termed the 'Cape of Good Hope.' The ground-work of their Indian empire was established in 1508 by Alfonso Albuquerque. Meanwhile the authors of these mighty projects had secured the countenance and warrant of the pope, on the condition that wherever they might plant a flag, they should be also zealous in promoting the extension of the Christian faith[5]. This pledge, however, was but seldom kept in view throughout the present period; an immoderate lust

Influence of the discoveries of the Portuguese.

Apathy in regard to missions.

---

the Kumanians and some of his subjects: but it does not appear that Christianity was generally adopted till a later period: cf. Schröckh, xxx. 499, 500.

[1] See the native *Chronicle*, c. 46, in Schwandtner's *Script. Rer. Hungar.* I. 195.

[2] A Latin bishopric was placed at Szeret in 1370 by Urban V.: Wiltsch, II. 300, 340.

[3] *Ibid.* pp. 340, 349.

[4] See Mariana, *Hist. General de España*, lib. xxv. c. 11 (II. 166 sq., Madrid, 1678).

[5] The first arrangement of this kind was made by Henry of Portugal with Eugenius IV. in 1443. Other instances are cited in Schröckh, xxx. 501, 502. Mariana (lib. xxvi. c. 17) speaks as if it were a leading object of the expeditions 'Llevar la luz del Evangelio a lo postrero del mundo, y a la India Oriental.' Whenever missionary zeal was manifested, it was also turned against antagonistic forms of Christianity. Thus in India, the Portuguese laboured to repress the 'Syrian' Christians (above, p. 28) on the coast of Malabar (see Geddes, *Hist. of Church of Malabar*, p. 4, Lond. 1694); and the same spirit dictated the first interference of the Portuguese in the Church of Abyssinia, extending over half a century (1490 sq): Neale, *East. Church*, II. 343 sq.

Missions.

Conversion of the Canary Islands.

of wealth and territorial grandeur strangling for the most part every better aspiration. The Canary Islands are indeed to be excepted from this class. A party of Franciscans[1], about **1476**, attempted to convert the natives; and a letter[2] of pope Sixtus IV. attests their very general success, at least in four of the southern islands. The same missionaries penetrated as far as the 'western Ethiopians,' on the coast of Guinea[3]. And soon after, in **1484**, when traffic had been opened with the Portuguese, the seeds of Christianity were scattered also to the south of Guinea, in Congo and Benin[4]. But on the subsequent discovery of a passage round the Cape, the speculations of the western merchants were diverted into other channels.

Christianity on the coast of Guinea.

IN AMERICA.

Discovery of America.

Columbus, while engaged in the service of Ferdinand and Isabella, landed on the isle of San Salvador in **1492**; and five years later, a Venetian, Cabot or Gabotta, who had sailed from England, ranged along the actual coast of North America, and was indeed the first of the adventurers who trod the soil of the new continent[5]. In **1499** Brazil was also added to the empire of the Portuguese, and afterwards, in **1520**, Magalhaens achieved the circumnavigation of the globe. Yet owing to the unhappy policy of the Church in Spain and Portugal, these conquests did not lead at first to any true enlargement of her borders. What was done ostensibly for 'the conversion of the Indians' tended rather to accelerate their ruin[6]. The

Fanaticism of the Spanish conquerors:

---

[1] Raynaldus, ad an. 1476, § 21.
[2] 'Percepimus quod jam Divina cooperante gratia ex septem ipsarum Canariæ insulis habitatores quatuor earundem insularum ad fidem conversi sunt: in aliis vero convertendis tribus non pauca sed magna expectatur populorum et gentium multitudo converti; nam qui Deum hactenus non noverunt, modo cupiunt catholicam fidem suscipere, ac sacri baptismatis unda renasci,' *etc.* Quoted in Wiltsch, § 522, n. 1.
[3] Raynaldus, ad an. 1476, § 22.
[4] *Ibid.* ad an. 1484, § 82: Schröckh, xxx. 503.
[5] Cf. the interesting tradition noticed above, p. 110, n. 4.
[6] The title of the contemporary work of Bartolomè de las Casas, an eyewitness, is pathetically true: *Relacion de la destruicion de las Indias.* See an account of him and his writings in Prescott's *Conquest of Mexico*, I. 318 sq. Lond. 1850. He declares that in forty years his fellow-countrymen had massacred twelve millions of the natives of America.

fanatic temper of the Spaniard, maddened as he was by recent conflicts with the infidel at home, betrayed him into policy on which we cannot dwell without a shudder. Multitudes who did not bend to his imperious will and instantly renounce the ancient superstitions, were most brutally massacred, while slavery became the bitter portion of the rest[1]. Their only friend for many years was an ecclesiastic, Bartolomè de las Casas, who in sojourning among them (till 1516) drew a harrowing picture of the national and social wrongs he struggled to redress[2]. Some measures had indeed been taken for disseminating Christian principles and lightening the yoke of the oppressed. The pope already urged this point on making grants of territory[3] to the crowns of Spain and Portugal. At his desire a band of missionaries[4], chiefly of the Mendicant orders, hastened to the scene of action; and in many of the ordinances which prescribe the service of the Indians, it is stipulated that religious training shall be added. But these measures seldom took effect. In 1520 only five bishoprics[5] had been established, and the genuine converts were proportionately rare: although it should be stated that upon the final settlement of Mexico, the conqueror had begun to manifest a deep solicitude for the religious welfare of his charge[6].

MISSIONS.

somewhat modified.

Attempts to convert the Indians.

[1] The Tlascalans alone, at the recommendation of Cortes, were exempted from the system of *repartimientos* (or compulsory service). Prescott, as above, III. 218: cf. III. 284. At first the bondage of the conquered was most abject, but the emperor Charles V. consented to its mitigation, and allowed the Spaniards to transport a multitude of Negroes from the coast of Africa. Thus started the inhuman 'slave-trade.'

[2] Above, p. 316, n. 6. He finally retreated, almost in despair, to a convent in St Domingo. His dislike of slavery was, however, shared by the Dominican missionaries, who appear as the 'abolitionists' of that age.

[3] Alexander VI. affected to do this (1493), 'de nostra mera liberalitate ac de apostolicæ potestatis plenitudine:' Raynaldus, ad an. 1493, § 19: cf. Mariana, lib. XXVI. c. 3 (II. 184). In the same year he sent out missionaries to attempt the conversion of the natives, § 24.

[4] Prescott, III. 218 (note).

[5] Wiltsch, § 523, where a letter, addressed to Leo X. by Peter Martyr (an ecclesiastic of the court of Ferdinand), is quoted.

[6] Prescott, III. 219. He begged the emperor to send out holy men, not pampered prelates, but members of religious orders whose lives would be a fitting commentary on their doctrine. The result seems to have been eminently successful in this case, almost every vestige of the Aztec worship disappearing from the Spanish settlements in the course of the next twenty years.

COMPULSORY CONVERSION OF MUHAMMEDANS AND JEWS.

The Moors of Spain:

A series of reactions dating from an earlier period had confined the Moorish influence to a corner in the south of Spain; and when the royal city of Granada ultimately bowed beneath the arms of Ferdinand and Isabella, in **1492**, it was their ardent hope to Christianize the whole Peninsula afresh. The foremost agent they employed was Ximenes, archbishop of Toledo (**1495**). His arguments, however, did not always satisfy the audiences to whom they were addressed[1], and therefore he proceeded in the narrow spirit of the age, to which in other points he shewed himself remarkably superior[2], to advise the application of coercive measures[3], justifying them on grounds of policy. The copies of the Koran were immediately seized and burnt in public, while to gratify the rage of the fanatic populace, it was resolved at last, in **1501**, that every obstinate Muhammedan who did not quit the country should henceforward be reduced to the position of a serf. As one might naturally expect, a part of the Moriscos now conformed[4]; but many others, who were true to their convictions, crossed the channel into Barbary[5].

their conversion, or expulsion.

Persecution of the Jews,

The violence with which the Jews were handled by the other states of Europe[6] was intensified in the Peninsula, where they had long existed as a thriving and comparatively learned body[7]. The old story of their crucifying

---

[1] See Flechier, *Hist. du Cardinal Ximenes*, I. 136 sq. Paris, 1694. On the conquest of Granada, Ferdinand had positively pledged himself to tolerate the religion of the Moors. Mariana, lib. xxv. c. 16 (II. 176).

[2] He was, for instance, a great patron of learning, and contributed much to the editing of the Polyglott Bible which bears his name (Fleury, lib. cxix. § 142). A sketch of his ecclesiastical reforms is given in Prescott's *Ferdinand and Isabella*, II. 481 sq.

[3] On the different views that were taken of his conduct, see Schröckh, xxx. 518, 519.

[4] Mariana (lib. xxvii. c. 5) records many instances, where thousands were baptized together.

[5] *Ibid.*

[6] Schröckh (xxx. 551 sq.) has pointed out a number of cruelties committed on the Jews of Germany. One of the most inhuman persecutions, which he does not mention, happened in 1349, when they were charged with poisoning the wells and causing an unusual mortality (see Pezii *Scriptor. Rer. Austr.* I. 248).

[7] Their greatest theological luminary at this time was Rabbi Isaac Abarbanel, a distinguished exegetical writer, born at Lisbon (1437). His

children on Good Friday, gained a general currency at the beginning of the present period[1]. Laws were framed accordingly for their repression, and a superstitious rabble, stimulated, in the south of Spain particularly, by inflammatory preachers[2], vented their unchristian fury on the Jews, whom they despoiled of property and even life itself. More salutary influence was exerted here and there by magistrates or preachers of the better class[3]: and at the memorable disputation in Tortosa[4] which lasted several months (1414), a party of the most accomplished Rabbis owned their inability to answer their opponents, and, with two exceptions, instantly passed over to the Church. But although the conversion of their champions had disarmed to some extent the prejudice of others, it does not appear that the Hebrews as a body had been drawn more closely to the Christian faith. The thunders of the Spanish Inquisition, which began its course in 1480, were continually levelled at the Jews[5] and at a growing class of persons whom it taxed with Judaizing. Prompted by the same distempered zeal, or captivated by a prospect of replenishing the public coffers, Ferdinand and Isabella gave them

MISSIONS.

particularly in Spain.

Endeavours to convert them.

---

works on the Old Testament have been much used and valued by Christian commentators.

[1] Thus in Spain Alfonso X. enacted a law providing for the punishment of such offenders. A. de Castro, *Hist. of the Jews in Spain*, translated by Mr Kirwan, pp. 64, 65, Cambridge, 1851. At the same time all Jews were ordered to wear a red badge on their left shoulder, under heavy penalties.

[2] *e.g.* those preached at Seville, 1391, by archdeacon Martinez (*Ibid.* pp. 87 sq.), the effect of which was that many of his audience rushed into the streets and murdered all the Jews they met. He was restrained, however, by the king (John I.): but in the very next reign four thousand Jews were slain at once. *Ibid.* p. 92.

[3] The conversion (circ. 1390) of the learned Talmudist, Halorqi (afterwards known as Jerónimo de Santa Fé) is traced to the discourses of an earnest preacher, Vincente Ferrer. *Ibid.* p. 95. Pablo (afterwards bishop of Cartagena) was moved to follow his example by reading Aquinas *De Legibus*. *Ibid* p. 106.

[4] *Ibid.* pp. 96—100. The congress was held in the presence of the Spanish anti-pope Benedict XIII., who afterwards issued certain decrees condemnatory of Jewish tenets, and among other things requiring that Jews should listen every year to three sermons preached with the design of promoting their conversion: *Ibid.* p. 104. A similar decree was passed at the council of Basel in the sixteenth session (Feb. 5, 1434), where the necessity for founding Hebrew and other professorships in the Universities was strongly insisted on. Cf. above, p. 219, n. 4.

[5] *Ibid.* pp. 145 sq.

MISSIONS.

the alternative of baptism or expulsion[1]. Many, as we noticed in regard to the Moriscos, would be nominally Christianized in order to retain their property. A multitude of others fled for refuge chiefly into Portugal, but new calamities were thickening on their path. In **1493** the king of Portugal (John II.) ordered[2] that the children of the Hebrews should be forcibly abstracted and baptized; while such of the adults as were unwilling to be taught the truths of Christianity were in the following reign compelled to forfeit their possessions and to emigrate in quest of other homes.

[1] *Ibid.* p. 164. Accounts differ as to the actual number of the expelled. Mariana (lib. XXVI. c. 1) thinks it might be as great as eight hundred thousand.
[2] De Castro, as above, pp. 202 sq.

CHAPTER XIV.

CONSTITUTION AND GOVERNMENT OF THE CHRISTIAN CHURCH.

THE numerous changes that were supervening at this period on the constitution of the Western Church, internally regarded, had been so inextricably blended with ulterior questions touching its relation to the secular authority, that, in the narrow limits of a volume like the present, the two subjects will be most conveniently approached and carried on together.

Viewed by unobservant eyes, the form of government prevailing in the west of Christendom might often look as autocratic as it was in the palmy days of Gregory VII. or Innocent III.; but on a closer survey we shall find that while political events as well as public opinion had been hitherto conspiring almost uniformly to exalt the papacy, they now were running more and more directly counter to its claims. The very impulses which it had given for civilizing all the influential states of Europe were now threatening to recoil and overwhelm itself. From the commencement of the present period to the former half of the fifteenth century the consciousness of civil and of intellectual independence was awakening alike in kings, in scholars, and in legislative bodies. The important middle-class, now starting up on every side, had also grown impatient of the foreign bondage; and although the surface of the Church was somewhat smoother in the interval between the council of Basel (1443) and the appearance of Luther, it is obvious that a strong under-current of hostility to Rome had never ceased to work and rankle in men's bosoms. There was

THE PAPACY.

Growth of anti-papal feeling.

THE PAPACY.

Effect of the residence at Avignon (1305—1376).

still indeed no well-defined intention to revive the theory of local churches, or to limit, in things purely spiritual, the jurisdiction of the Roman see: but as one formidable class of its pretensions had intruded very far into the province of the civil power, the pontiffs daily ran the risk of weakening their sway in general by the arbitrary maintenance of some obnoxious point. The conflict, which at first is traceable in almost every case to the resentment of a crushed and outraged nationality, was easily extended to a different sphere of thought, till numbers of the more discerning spirits, keenly smarting under the injustice of the pope, had lost all real faith in his infallibility[1].

A heavy blow had been inflicted on the temporal supremacy of Rome when Clement V. submitted to the king of France and fixed his chair within the jurisdiction of a papal vassal, Robert of Anjou, at Avignon. The seventy years' captivity[2], as the Italians often called the papal sojourn in Provence, had tended much to weaken the prestige associated with the mother-city of the West. The pontiffs also, living as they now did far away from their estates, devised new engines of extortion[3] for replenishing their empty coffers. By this venal

[1] *e.g.* The following is the language of Marsilius of Padua, formerly rector of the University of Paris: 'sic igitur propter temporalia contendendo non vere defenditur sponsa Christi. Eam etenim, quæ vere Christi sponsa est, catholicam fidem et fidelium multitudinem, non defendunt *moderni Romanorum pontifices*, sed offendunt, illiusque pulchritudinem, unitatem videlicet, non servant, sed fœdant, dum zizanias et schismata seminando ipsius membra lacerant et ab invicem separant,' *etc.*; in Goldast, *Monarchia Roman.* II. 281, ed. Francof. 1668.

[2] 'L'empia Babilonia' is the phrase of Petrarch.

[3] *e.g.* the appropriation of rich benefices and bishoprics to the use of the pope or of his favourites, by what were known as 'reservations' or 'provisions.' Such benefices were held with others 'in commendam:' cf. above, p. 226, n. 4. The system in this form commenced under Clement V. (*Extravagantes Communes*, lib. III. tit. ii. c. 2, in 'Corpus Juris Canon.'), and was fully developed by his successor John XXII., who 'reserved' to himself all the bishoprics in Christendom (Baluze, *Vit. Paparum Avenion.*, I. 722; Hallam, *Middle Ages*, c. VII. pt. ii.: vol. II. p. 234, 10th ed.; where other instances are given). In England, where the papal mandates for preferring a particular clerk had been disputed long before, the system of 'provisions' was most strenuously repelled: see *Rot. Parl.*, 3 Ric. II. § 37, and especially the famous statute of Provisors (1351), 25 Edw. III., cap. 6. Other cases of resistance are cited in Twysden, *Vindication of the Church*, pp. 80, 81, Camb. ed. Annates, or first-fruits of Ecclesiastical benefices, were also instituted by John XXII.,

and rapacious policy the feelings of the Church were still more deeply irritated and more lastingly estranged[1].

In spite of the obsequiousness of Clement V. in dealing with the crown of France, he shewed as often as he dared that he inherited the domineering temper of the papacy[2]. But his pretensions were eclipsed by those of John XXII.[3] (1316), whose contest[4] with Louis of Bavaria, king of the Romans, was a prolongation of the mortal feud between the Ghibellines and Guelfs, to which allusion has been made above[5]. In 1323 (Oct. 8) a papal missive[6] called on Louis to revoke his proclamations, to abstain from the administration of the empire, and present himself, within three months, a suppliant at Avignon, if he wished his claims to be allowed. Meanwhile both laymen and ecclesiastics were commanded to withhold allegiance from him. Goaded by indignities like this, Louis put forth a counter-manifesto (Dec. 16, 1323), in which he did not hesitate to call his adversary a pretender and a fautor of heretical pravity. He also stated his intention of appealing to a General Council[7]. But his threats

Contest between John XXII. and Louis of Bavaria.

who accumulated in this way a prodigious treasure (Hallam, *Ibid.*; Twysden, pp. 104—107).

[1] *e.g.* Giovanni Villani (*Hist. Fiorent.* lib. IX. c. 58) draws the following picture of John XXII.: 'Questi fu huomo molto cupido di moneta e simoniaco, che ogni beneficio per moneta in sua corte si vendea,' *etc.*

[2] This was exemplified in his laying Venice under the interdict (1309), and even forbidding all commerce with it and empowering any one to seize the property or persons of its subjects. Raynald. ad an. 1309, § 6.

[3] Owing to a violent dispute between the French and Italian cardinals, the papal throne was vacant two years and nearly four months after the death of Clement (1314). It may here be noted that the last important contribution to the Canon Law (the *Libri Clementini*) was made by this pope in 1313: cf. above, p. 224, n. 1.

[4] One of the best accounts of this important struggle will be found in Öhlenschläger, *Staatsgesch. des röm. Kaiserthums in der erst. Hälfte des 14ten Jahrhund.* pp. 86 sq., Francof. 1755.

[5] p. 248. Dante was engaged in this controversy, taking the side of the Ghibellines. His book *On Monarchy* appeared in 1322.

[6] See the various *Processes* against the emperor in Martène and Durand's *Thesaur. Anecd.* II. 644 sq., and cf. Döllinger, IV. 106. The people, the jurists, and many of the clergy took the imperial side of the dispute.

[7] See above, p. 254. The document in Öhlenschläger, as above, *Urkundenbuch*, p. 84. Louis admits, however, that the Almighty has placed two great lights in the firmament of the Church, 'pontificalem videlicet auctoritatem et imperatoriam majestatem, illud ut praeesset diei, spiritualia disponendo, alterum ut praeesset nocti, temporalia judicando:' cf. above, p. 243, n. 2.

THE PAPACY.

Champions of the imperial interest.

and protests were alike unheeded, and the sentence of excommunication was launched against him in the following spring (March 21).

Amid the tumults which this controversy had produced, the Church was further startled by the publication of a treatise written by Imperialists[1] and levelled at the roots of papal, and indeed all other hierarchical supremacy. The title of it is *Defensor Pacis*. As the natural effect of a recoil from Hildebrandine principles, it manifests a disposition to exaggerate the privileges of the laity in matters that affect the Church, contending even that the power of the keys was delegated to the priesthood by their flock or by the emperor himself, who might be viewed as the representative of all[2]. In many points the authors of this work preserved a juster balance and may fairly take their stand with the precursors of the Reformation[3]. It is plain that nearly all the anti-papal writings of the age are tinctured with the principles of the extreme Franciscans, or the 'Spirituales[4],'

---

[1] The leading author was Marsilius of Padua, assisted by John of Janduno, a Franciscan: cf. Neander, IX. 35. The *Defensor Pacis* is printed in Goldast's *Monarch. Roman.* II. 154 sq. It was translated into English at the beginning of the Reformation, and included in a list of 'prohibited books:' Baker, *Notes on Burnet* (Brit. Mag. XXXVI. 395).

[2] *e.g.* Conclusio XVI., XVIII., XXIII., XXXVII. (These *Conclusions*, forty-one in number, are in the third Part of the treatise). The following is another indication of the same tendency (*Concl.* XXXIII.): 'Generale concilium aut *partiale* sacerdotum et episcoporum ac *reliquorum fidelium* per coactivam potestatem congregare, ad fidelem legislatorem aut ejus auctoritate principantem in communitatibus fidelium tantummodo pertinere, nec in aliter congregato determinata vim aut robur habere.' The *Defensor Pacis* also advocates the theory that priests and bishops were originally equal, and derives the primacy of Rome itself from a grant of Constantine ('qui quandam præeminentiam et potestatem tribuit episcopis et ecclesiæ Romanæ super cæteras mundi ecclesias seu presbyteros omnes'). As above, II. 243.

[3] Thus they plainly state, 'quod nullam scripturam irrevocabiliter veram credere vel fateri tenemur *de necessitate salutis æternæ*, nisi eas quæ canonicæ appellantur' (*Ibid.* p. 254); reserving, however, the first place in the *interpretation* of Scripture to general councils ('et ideo pie tenendum determinationes conciliorum generalium *in sensibus scripturæ dubiis* a Spiritu Sancto suæ veritatis originem sumere,' *Ibid.*).

[4] See above, p. 231. It was members of this school, headed by Ubertinus de Casali, who stigmatized the pope as a heretic for maintaining that our Lord and the Apostles 'in speciali non habuisse aliqua, nec in communi etiam.' See also the *Defensorium Wil. Occami contra Johan. papam XXII.*, in Brown's *Fascic.* II. 439—465.

who had long been halting in their loyalty to Rome. Another of that disaffected class is William of Ockham, the English schoolman, who had found a shelter at the court of Louis of Bavaria, and contended with a boldness hitherto unequalled for the dignity and independence of the empire[1]. He questioned the infallibility of the pope in judging even of doctrinal matters, and, unlike the great majority who shared his feelings on this head, he was unwilling to accept a General Council as the court of ultimate appeal.

The cause of John XXII. was defended, among others[2], by an Augustinian hermit of Ancona, Agustino Triomfi (Triumphus), who, in pushing ultramontane principles to their legitimate results, asserted that the pope alone could nominate an emperor, and therefore that the college of electors acted only at his beck or through his delegation[3]. But the hour was past when writers of this stamp could sway the general mind of Europe. Appealing to a future council[4], Louis braved the excommunication, and at last the interdict[5], of his opponent (1324). He confided in the loyalty of his dependents[6], and especially in the Franciscan order, one of whom he thrust into the

Defenders of the Papacy.

The papal threats inoperative.

---

[1] His *Disputatio de Potestate Ecclesiæ et Sæculi* and other kindred works are printed in Goldast, as above, II. 314 sq. His anti-popery is almost as hot as Luther's (*e.g.* p. 390): cf. Turner, *Hist. of England*, Middle Ages, III. 98.

[2] The principal was a Franciscan of a milder school, named Alvarus Pelagius, who composed his *De Planctu Ecclesiæ* about 1330 (ed. Venet. 1560). He maintains 'quod jurisdictionem habet universalem in toto mundo Papa *nedum in spiritualibus, sed temporalibus,* licet executionem gladii temporalis et jurisdictionem per filium suum legitimum imperatorem, cum fuerit, tanquam per advocatum et defensorem Ecclesiæ, et per alios reges...debeat exercere:' lib. I. c. 13.

[3] See the *Summa de Potestate Ecclesiastica* (ed. Rom., 1582), Quæst. XXXV. Art. 1 sq. The papal claims were seldom more offensively stated than in the following passage: 'Planum est autem, quod papa est omnis juris interpres et ordinator, tamquam architector in tota ecclesiastica hierarchia, vice Christi; unde quolibet jure potest, cum subest causa rationabilis, decimas laicorum, non solum subditorum, verum etiam regum, principum et dominorum recipere et concedere pro ecclesiæ utilitate, ac *eos, si noluerint dare, compellere.*' Quæst. LXXIII. Art. III.

[4] His formal appeal is given in Baluze, *Vit. Papar. Avenion.* II. 478.

[5] In Martène and Durand, as above, II. 660.

[6] We learn from the contemporary *Chronicon* of Johann von Winterthur (or Vitoduranus), that such of the clergy as observed the interdict were roughly handled by the people: see *Thesaurus Hist. Helveticæ* (Tiguri, 1735), I. 49.

place of John XXII. with the title Nicholas V., and from whom he received the imperial crown. These friars never ceased to tax the pontiff as a heretic, alleging, in addition to an older charge respecting his contempt of 'evangelical poverty,' that he had absolutely erred while preaching on the beatific vision of the saints[1].

Attempts at reconciliation.

The next pontiff, Benedict XII.[2] (1334), appears to have been anxious to reform his court, and even cancelled many grants of benefices which his predecessors had made over to themselves[3]. He also wished to bring about a reconciliation with Louis of Bavaria: but his efforts were resisted by the king of France, to whom he was in bondage[4]. For this cause the interdict of John XXII. long continued to disturb the peace of Germany. In 1338 a meeting of electors[5] held at Rense (on the banks of the Rhine) asserted the divine commission of the emperor, and laboured to emancipate him altogether from the trammels of the Roman pontiffs, venturing even to withdraw from them the ancient privilege of confirming his election. Clement VI. (1342) prolonged the controversy, and on finding the imperialists determined to maintain their ground, two other writs of excommunica-

Continuance and close of the struggle.

---

[1] According to the Continuator of the *Chronicon* of William de Nangis (D'Achery, III. 95), he had stated in a sermon (1331), 'quod animæ decedentium in gratia non videant Deum per essentiam, nec sint perfecte beatæ, nisi post resumptionem corporis:' cf. Döllinger, IV. 111 (note). The practical deduction from his view is thus stated by Giovanni Villani, lib. x. c. 230: 'Dicendo laicamente, come fedel Christiano, che *in vano si pregherebbono i santi*, ò harebbesi speranza di salute per li loro meriti, se nostra donna santa Maria...e li altri santi non potessono vedere la Deitade infino al dí del giudicio,' etc.

[2] Personally he was not a model for the clergy, being 'comestor maximus et potator egregius,' and the origin of the proverb 'bibamus papaliter:' see Neander, IX. 58.

[3] *e.g.* Baluze, *Vit. Papar. Avenion.* I. 198. Albert of Strasburg (Argentinensis), *Chron.* in Urstisii *German. Histor.* II. 125.

[4] Döllinger, IV. 116, 117.

[5] See the document in Öhlenschläger, as above, p. 188. This act was afterwards published (March, 1339) as a constitution of the empire (Goldast, *Constit. Imperial.* III. 111), and vigorously defended by Leopold of Bebenburg, afterwards bishop of Bamberg, and by William of Ockham. The last-mentioned writer took the part of Louis in another question, where he far exceeded his prerogative by trying to dissolve the marriage of Margaret of Carinthia, and granting to his son the dispensations necessary for contracting an alliance with her (1342). See Ockham, *De Jurisdictione imperatoris in causis matrimonialibus*, in Goldast's *Monarch.* I. 21, and the *Chronicon* of Vitoduranus (as above, p. 325, n. 6), p. 59.

tion¹, breathing curses hitherto unequalled in the manifestoes of the pope, were circulated in all quarters where adherents could be gained (1341, 1346). When Louis died in 1347, the prospects of his house and party had been darkened by the elevation of a rival candidate for the empire, Charles of Moravia, who had pledged himself² to carry out the policy suggested by the king of France and by the conclave at Avignon. Many of the violent Franciscans were now ready to conform, and even William of Ockham ultimately recognized, in words at least, the jurisdiction of the pope³.

But much as this important victory might seem to benefit the cause of Clement and to prop his sinking fortunes, they were damaged more and more by his rapacity, his nepotism, and the licentious splendour of his court⁴. He was succeeded by Innocent VI. (1352), who in a reign of ten years did something⁵ to produce a healthier tone of morals and to allay the ever-formidable spirit of remonstrance which was breaking out on every side, especially in parliaments and other public bodies. Urban V. (1362) attempted, notwithstanding the resistance of one faction in the conclave, to replace the papal chair in Italy (1367), but unpropitious circumstances drove him back⁶; and that desire could not be finally accomplished till the next pontificate (1370), when Gregory XI., relying on the influence of a nun, the able Catharine of Siena⁷, occupied

THE PAPACY.

Return of the Pope to Rome, 1376.

¹ In Raynald. ad an. 1343, § 43: ad an. 1346, § 3. For the intervening negociations with the pope, see documents in Öhlenschläger, pp. 226 sq.

² Raynald. ad an. 1346, § 19.

³ Döllinger, IV. 123.

⁴ See Albert of Strasburg (as above), p. 133, and Matteo Villani (who continued the *Historie Fiorentine* of his brother, Giovanni Villani), lib. III. c. 43: cf. Döllinger, IV. 124.

⁵ *e.g.* Baluze, *Vit. Papar. Avenion.* I. 357. Under his predecessor almost all the English benefices were reserved to the pope or other 'aliens,' which provoked the famous statute of Provisors (1350). Innocent VI. did not repeat his claims; and Urban V. issued a bull *Contra Pluralitates in beneficiis* (1365): Wilkins, III. 62.

⁶ Raynald. ad an. 1370, § 19. Petrarch (*Vie de Pétrarque*, by De Sade) was actively engaged in this dispute, contending for the claims of Rome as the metropolis of the popes, and eloquently denouncing the corruptions of Avignon, which he calls the third Babylon: see his *Epistolæ sine titulo*. A sketch of the rise and fall of Rienzi, and the civil revolutions of which Rome was now the theatre, will be found in Gibbon, ch. LXX.

⁷ Some of her works, including letters on this point, were printed

THE PAPACY.

The papal schism of forty years.

the old metropolis (1376). His death, which followed in 1378, gave rise to a dispute, which, next to the long residence at Avignon, tended more than other agencies to shake the empire of the popes, and stimulate a reformation of the Church[1]. The present schism, unlike convulsions of an earlier period[2], lasted almost forty years (1378—1417[3]), and therefore could not fail to give an impulse, hitherto unknown, in calling up the nationality of many a western state, in satisfying it that papal rule was not essential to its welfare, and in thereby adding strength to local jurisdictions. The dislike of 'aliens' and of Roman intermeddling was embittered at the same time by the fresh exactions[4] of the rival pontiffs, each of whom was

at Paris, 1644: see her *Life* in the *Act. Sanct.* April. III. 956. Bridget (Brigitta) of Sweden, also canonized, was equally urgent in promoting the return of Gregory: see her *Revelationes*, lib. IV. c. 139 sq., ed. Antverp. 1611.

[1] See Neander, IX. 67 sq. on the rise and important bearings of the papal schism. Henry of Hesse (*al.* Langenstein), in his *Consilium Pacis*, printed by Von der Hardt in the *Concil. Constant.* II. 1 sq., declares (1381) 'Hanc tribulationem a Deo non gratis permissam, sed in *necessariam opportunamque ecclesiæ reformationem* finaliter convertendam:' cf. Lenfant, *Concile de Pise*, lib. I. p. 51, Amsterd. 1724.

[2] See, for instance, p. 223, n. 3, 4, 5.

[3] In this year Benedict XIII. was deposed by the council of Constance, but he persisted in his claims until his death in 1424.

[4] See the treatise, written in 1401, *De Ruina Ecclesiæ* (al. *De Corrupto Ecclesiæ Statu*), attributed generally to Nicholas de Clémenges (Clemangis), and printed in Von der Hardt, *Concil. Constant.* tom. I. pt. III., and in Brown, *Fascic.* II. 555 sq. Neander (IX. 81 sq.) has reviewed this memorable work, together with a short treatise, *De Studio Theologico*, in D'Achery, I. 473 sq. The author traces the exile of the popes to their own 'fornicationes odibiles.' In speaking of his own time he writes: 'Adeo se et ecclesiam universalem eorum arbitrio subjecerunt atque dediderunt, ut vix aliquam parvulam præbendam nisi eorum mandato vel consensu in provinciis eorum tribuere ausi essent.' A second writer of the period, Theodoric of Niem (Nieheim), in his works, *De Schismate*, and *Nemus Unionis* (Argentor. 1629), has furnished ample evidence to the same effect. The English parliaments continued to resist, with more or less firmness, the increased exactions of the pope, and in 1389 the statute of Præmunire, 13 Ric. II. stat. II. c. 2 and 3, enlarged and reinforced by 16 Ric. II. c. 5, was levelled at the same offender. No one in future was to send or bring hither a summons or excommunication against any person for executing the statute of Provisors (cf. above, p. 327, n. 5), and the bearers of papal bulls or other instruments for the translation of bishops and like purposes, were subjected to the penalty of forfeiture and perpetual imprisonment. It is remarkable that the statute 16 Ric. II. was enrolled on the desire of the archbishop of Canterbury. Twysden, *Vindic. of the Church*, p. 111, Camb. ed.

clearly anxious to maintain his dignity at any cost whatever.

THE PAPACY.

The origin of this important feud appears to be as follows[1]. When the cardinals, of whom the great majority were French, had met to nominate a successor of Gregory XI., the Roman populace tumultuously demanded that their choice should fall on some Italian. Influenced by this menace they elected a Neapolitan, the archbishop of Bari, who at his coronation took the name of Urban VI. (April 18, 1378). The cardinals, however, soon repented of their choice, and, when the pressure of the mob had been withdrawn, endeavoured to annul the whole proceeding by the substitution of a member of their own conclave, and a Frenchman, who was crowned as Clement VII. (Oct. 31). Between these two competitors the Western Church was almost equally divided[2]. Urban, who remained at Rome, enjoyed the countenance of England, Italy, Bohemia, the German empire, Prussia, Poland, and the Scandinavian kingdoms: while his rival, who retreated to Avignon, was acknowledged in the whole of France[3], Scotland, Spain, Lorraine, Sicily, and Cyprus.

Its origin.

Balance of the two opposing factions.

Neither of the factions would consent to the retirement of their leader, and accordingly the quarrel was embittered and prolonged. The Roman conclave, after the death of Urban, nominated Boniface IX. (1389), Innocent VII. (1404), and Gregory XII. (1406); and Clement had an obstinate successor in the cardinal Pedro de Luna, Be-

Series of rival popes.

---

[1] Hallam, *Middle Ages*, II. 237, 238, 10th ed.: Maimbourg, *Hist. du grand Schisme*, Paris, 1678; and more especially Lenfant, *Concile de Pise*, who in the first and second books has fairly stated the evidence on both sides.

[2] Richard Ullerston (or Ulverstone), whose paper urging an immediate 'reformation of the church' was presented at the council of Pisa (1409), complains of this among the other consequences of the schism: 'Quod profecto exinde patuit, quod regna inter se prius divisa partibus a se invicem divisis et inter se de papatu contendentibus se pariformiter conjunxerunt.' See the whole of this remarkable document in Von der Hardt's *Concil. Constant.* I. 1126 sq.

[3] The university of Paris shewed its independence for some time by recognizing neither of the candidates, so that there were three parties in the Western Church, the Urbanites, the Clementites, and the Neutrals. The last party, who were looking to a general council for redress, were represented by Henry of Langenstein (cf. above, p. 328, n. 1): Neander, IX. 71, 72. The influential manifestoes issued at this crisis by the university are noticed in Bulæus, *Hist. Univ. Paris*, IV. 618 sq.

THE PAPACY.

Council of Pisa, 1409:

nedict XIII. (1394). Dismayed or scandalized by this unseemly struggle, the more earnest members of the Church[1] now looked in every quarter for redress. At length they seem to have been forced to a conclusion that the schism was never likely to be healed, except by the assembling of a general council[2], which (in cases where a reasonable doubt existed as to the validity of an election) nearly all the theologians deemed superior to the pope. The Council of Pisa[3] was now summoned in this spirit by the allied cardinals (1409), its object being to secure the unity, and stimulate the reformation, of the Church. During the sessions, which extended over many months (March 25—August 7), the rival pontiffs, on declining to present themselves for judgment, were pronounced contumacious (March 30), and at last were both formally deposed[4] (June 5) as guilty of schism, heresy, and perjury. The choice of the electors now fell on Peter of Candia (Alexander V.), who pledged himself to purify the Church[5],

---

[1] Others looked upon the question, it is true, in a very different manner, saying, 'nihil omnino curandum *quot papæ sint*.' Bulæus, *Hist. Univ. Paris*, IV. 700.

[2] Appeals had been occasionally made already to a general council in the case where Roman absolutism was peculiarly oppressive (see above, p. 254): but the coexistence of two rival pontiffs vying with each other in the magnitude of their exactions, led men to discuss the subject far more deeply. See, for instance, the remarkable treatise of Matthæus de Cracovia, bishop of Worms, entitled *De Squaloribus Romanæ Curiæ* (in Walch, *Moniment. Medii Ævi*, I. 1—100, Gotting. 1757).

[3] See Lenfant's *Hist. du Concile de Pise*, Amst. 1724: Mansi, XXVII. 1 sq. Among the very numerous prelates here assembled was Robert Hallam, bishop of Salisbury, who took an active part in the proceedings, and declared (April 30) that he had authority from the king of England to consent to whatever the council might determine for promoting unity: Mansi, *ib.* 125.

[4] 'Christi nomine invocato, sancta et universalis synodus universalem ecclesiam repræsentans, et ad quam cognitio et *decisio hujus causæ noscitur pertinere*...pronunciat...Angelum Corrario [*i.e.* Gregory XII.] et Petrum de Luna [*i.e.* Benedict XIII.] de papatu contendentes et eorum utrumque fuisse et esse notorios schismaticos, et antiqui schismatis nutritores, defensores,...necnon notorios hæreticos et a fide devios, notoriisque criminibus enormibus perjurii et violationis voti irretitos,' etc. On these grounds a definitive sentence is passed upon both, inhibiting them 'ne eorum aliquis pro summo pontifice gerere se præsumat,' *etc.*: Mansi, *ib.* 402: cf. Theodoric of Niem, *De Schismate*, lib. III. c. 44.

[5] Lenfant, I. 290. See the discourse of Gerson, preached before him, on this subject, in Gerson's *Works*, ed. Du Pin, II. 131. The text was Acts i. 6; from which he urged the pope to realize (as far as might

in head and members; but he died in the following year, when Balthassar Cossa (John XXIII.), notoriously[1] devoid of principle, succeeded to his throne. So far, however, was this council from allaying the religious conflicts of the west, that for a time it only added fuel to the flames. The whole of Spain and Scotland still adhered to Benedict; and as the Roman candidate (Gregory XII.) was not entirely unsupported, Christendom might gaze with horror at the spectacle of three antagonistic popes. A large majority, however, recognized the claim of John XXIII., upon the ground that he was nominated by the lawful conclave who presided in the council of Pisa. But this worthless pontiff afterwards consented, in an evil hour, to summon all the western prelates to another general council held at Constance (**1414–1418**), and intended, like its predecessor, to eradicate abuses, and to heal the papal schism[2]. The animus of the assemblage, numbering altogether eighteen thousand in ecclesiastics only[3], was displayed in the first session (Nov. **16, 1414**); where it was determined[4] that not only the prelates (bishops and abbots)

THE PAPACY.

ineffectual in repressing schism.

Council of Constance (1414–1418).

be) all the ends for which the Church of Christ was founded. But as many prelates hastened to depart, the question of reform was afterwards postponed until the year 1412, when Alexander was to call another council for that purpose ('reformare Ecclesiam in capite et in membris'). This delay was strongly censured by the ardent reformers, such as Nicholas de Clémenges: see his *Disputatio super materia Concilii Generalis* (written in 1416): *Opp.* ed. Lydius, 1613, p. 70. It is true that a synod was held at Rome in 1412, but, as the same writer complains (*Ibid.* p. 75), the time was merely wasted 'in rebus supervacuis nihilque ad utilitatem ecclesiæ pertinentibus.'

[1] Nicholas de Clémenges (*ibid.* p. 75) speaks of him in 1416 as 'Balthasar ille perfidissimus nuper e Petri sede (quam turpissime foedavit) ejectus:' see the *Life* of him by Theodoric of Niem in Von der Hardt's *Concil. Constant.* II. 336 sq.: and cf. Döllinger, IV. 152.

[2] See Lenfant's *Hist. du Concile de Constance*, Amst. 1727, and Von der Hardt, *Concil. Constant.* 6 vols. Francof. 1700 (additional volume containing *Index* by Bohnstedt, Berlin, 1742).

[3] Döllinger, IV. 155. In the train of this assemblage followed, it is said, no less than seven hundred 'mulieres communes.' See the statistical account of an eyewitness in Von der Hardt, V. pt. II. pp. 10 sq.

[4] The advocate of the inferior clergy was the cardinal Peter d'Ailly, bishop of Cambray. See the whole discussion in Von der Hardt, II. 224 sq. The Paris doctors, in suggesting the appeal to a general council (1394), had already urged the importance of introducing doctors of theology and law, or at least the representatives of cathedral chapters, monastic orders, &c. The prelates, as a body, were considered too illiterate for the decision of so grave a point ('quia plures eorum, proh pudor! hodie satis illiterati sunt'): see Bulœus, *Hist. Univ. Paris*, IV. 690.

Vote by 'nations.'

Deposition of John XXIII. 1415.

but inferior clergy, proctors for the universities, and others, not excluding jurists, should possess a deliberative voice. The princes and ambassadors of Christian states might also vote, except on articles of faith. And as Italian prelates, who were numerous and devoted to the interest of the pope, were not unlikely to impede the progress of reform, if suffrages continued to be taken by the head, it was arranged that all the members of the council should divide themselves into four 'nations[1],' the Italian, German, French, and English, each with equal rights, and that no proposition should be carried till it was separately discussed in all the nations, and then passed by a majority. Entrenched upon this vantage-ground, the members of the synod wrung a promise[2] of immediate abdication from pope John himself, by whom they were convened, and after he had violated his oath and fled[3] to Schaffhausen in disguise (March 21), they did not scruple to assert the paramount authority of the council, citing him (May 2) to appear before them, and at length completing his deposition[4] (May 12, 1415). To these acts indeed they were ostensibly impelled by a memorial[5], charging him with almost every species of depravity: but it is obvious that the real cause of their antagonism was a desire to limit

---

[1] See Lenfant, II. p. 45. After the renewed deposition of Benedict XIII. (July 26, 1417), a Spanish 'nation' was added.

[2] Von der Hardt, II. 240.

[3] He hoped that in his absence nothing could be undertaken to his detriment, and some of his adherents in the council argued 'quod concilium dissolutum esset propter absentiam et recessum dicti Balthasaris.' Theod. of Niem. *Vit. Joh. XXIII.* (as above), lib. II. c. 8.

[4] After stating that he had persevered in evil courses 'post monitiones debitas et caritativas,' and had shown himself altogether incorrigible, they proceed: 'Eum dicta sancta synodus amovet, privat et deponit, universos et singulos Christicolas, cujuscunque status dignitatis vel conditionis existant, ab ejus obedientia, fidelitate et juramento, absolutos declarando.' Von der Hardt, IV. 280; Mansi, XXVII. 716. In a former session (March 30) they had declared: 'Quod ipsa Synodus in Spiritu Sancto legitime congregata, generale concilium faciens et ecclesiam catholicam militantem repræsentans, *potestatem a Christo immediate habet*, cui quilibet cujuscunque status vel dignitatis, *etiamsi papalis*, existat, obedire tenetur in his, quæ pertinent ad fidem et ad exstirpationem dicti schismatis, ac *generalem reformationem* Ecclesiæ Dei in capite et in membris.' *Ibid.* IV. 89; Mansi, *ib.* 585. On this ground rest the famous 'Gallican Articles' of 1682.

[5] Theodoric of Niem, *Vit. Joh. XXIII.* lib. II. c. 3: cf. Hallam, *Middle Ages*, II. 240, 10th ed.

the supremacy of Rome and strangle the more daring of the papal usurpations. Two of the conspicuous leaders in the movement were Peter d'Ailly[1] (de Alliaco) and John Gerson[2], who had been successive chancellors of the university of Paris. They had warmly advocated the assembling of the Pisan council; and at Constance, the acute and fearless Gerson proved himself the soul of both the anti-Roman and reforming parties.

THE PAPACY.

Influence of Gerson.

Gregory XII. withdrew his claims (July 4, 1415), and measures were adopted for displacing Benedict XIII., who was accordingly degraded and deposed (July 26, 1417)[3]. In the forty-first session (Nov. 11, 1417), the cardinals, assisted for this turn by prelates of the different nations, elected a new pope. He took the style of Martin V. His earliest promise was to expedite the general reformation of the Church, a point on which the English, French, and German[4] deputies insisted strongly, and for which a plan[5] had been devised in the previous session; but ere long the council was dissolved by his authority (April

Election of a new pope, 1417.

---

[1] See, for instance, his *Monita de necessitate reformationis ecclesiæ* (in Gerson, *Opp.* II. 885 sq. ed. Du Pin), or his treatise *De difficultate reformationis in Concilio universali* (*Ibid.* 867 sq.).

[2] His works on this subject are too numerous for recital (*Opp.* tom. II. pt. II. *passim*). One of the most severe is entitled, *De Modis uniendi ac reformandi Ecclesiam in Concilio universali*. For a review of this memorable treatise, see Neander, IX. 136. On the flight of the pope, Gerson, in the name of the French ambassadors and the university of Paris, preached an energetic sermon (March 23) affirming the absolute superiority of the Council (*Opp.* tom. II. pt. II. 201 sq.).

[3] Von der Hardt, IV. 1373.

[4] The Germans, backed by Sigismund, the king of the Romans, were anxious to commence the work of reformation *before* they elected the new pope: but on this point they finally gave way (*Ibid.* IV. 1394 sq.). The following is their protest (p. 1424): 'Protestatur hæc natio Germanica coram Deo, tota curia cœlesti, universali ecclesia et vobis, quod nisi feceritis præmissa modo et ordine supra dictis, quod non per eam, sed per vos stat, stetit et stabit, quominus sponsa Christi, sancta mater ecclesia, suo Sponso inconvulsa, purior et immaculata reformetur, et reformata ad perfectam reducatur unitatem.' As early as June 15, 1415, a committee, termed the Reformation-college ('Reformatorium'), had been organized. On its resolutions, see Lenfant, II. 309 sq.

[5] Von der Hardt, IV. 1452. The points enumerated are nearly all of a fiscal and disciplinary character. The one most ultimately bearing on Christian doctrine is the question of indulgences, which in the time of the papal schism had been sold or distributed at random (cf. Von der Hardt, I. 1010).

22, 1418) without proceeding to redress the scandalous abuses[1] on which Roman despotism was fed.

Arrangements had been made[2], however, that a second council should be gathered at the end of five years to reconsider this gigantic task. It was convoked accordingly at Pavia (1423) by Martin V., who afterwards transferred it to Siena, where the barren sessions were prolonged into the following year. But owing to a further act of prorogation nothing was effected till the western prelates met at Basel (July 23, 1431), soon after the election of the new pope, Eugenius IV. The objects of this great assemblage[3], as enumerated in the outset, were (1) to extirpate all forms of heresy, (2) to reunite the Eastern and the Western Churches, (3) to promote instruction in the truth, (4) to check the wars then raging among Christian princes, (5) to bring about a reformation of the Church in head and members, (6) to re-establish, in so far as might be, the severity of ancient discipline. The president was the cardinal Juliano Cesarini[4], who had been selected for that office by Martin V. and confirmed in the appointment by Eugenius IV. It was plain, however, that the anti-papal spirit which prevailed at Constance had not ceased to animate the western prelates, and accordingly the Roman

---

[1] The only exceptions were a few decrees published March 21, 1418, for restraining simony, &c. (*Ibid.* p. 1535.) The unsuccessful termination of this council naturally shook men's faith in the probability of a reformation; *e.g.* Gobelinus Persona, a German chronicler, writing at the time (*Cosmodromium*, in Meibom. *Rer. German. Script.* I. 345, Helmæstad. 1688), complains as follows: 'Ego quidem jam annis multis statum pertractans Ecclesiæ, per quem modum ad universalis ecclesiæ reformationem, scandalis sublatis omnibus, pervenire posset curiosa mente revolvi. Quem quidem modum *Dominus fortasse ostendet*, cum in spiritu vehementi conteret naves Tharsis.' To abate the disaffection of the states who were most anxious for the remedy of some inveterate disorders, Martin entered into separate concordats with them, *e.g.* with the English, in Von der Hardt, I. 1079 sq.

[2] Von der Hardt, IV. 1546.

[3] See all the Acts and other documents relating to this council in Mansi, XXIX—XXXI.

[4] He was at the time engaged in trying to reclaim the Hussites (in Bohemia), and therefore opened the synod by means of two plenipotentiaries. In the following September he arrived at Basel, when he found only a small muster of prelates. The mode of voting in this synod differed from that which we have noticed at Constance. Here indeed, as there, the members were divided into four sections; but they were taken indiscriminately from any province of the Church.

curia eyed them with suspicion and alarm[1]. On the 12th of November, a bull was issued for transferring the council to Bologna[2], chiefly with the pretext that the Eastern Church was favourable to re-union, and preferred to hold their conference with the Latins in some town of Italy. But, notwithstanding this abrupt decision of the pope, the council of Basel, supported by the University of Paris[3] and emboldened by the arguments of Nicholas Cusanus[4] (of Cues, in the diocese of Trèves), proceeded with its arduous work; and in the second session (Feb. **15, 1432**) did not hesitate to reaffirm the most extreme decrees of Constance[5], which subordinated all ecclesiastical authority to that of universal synods. It was also now decided that the council could not lawfully be transferred, dissolved, or interrupted by any human power, without its own deliberation and consent. Relying on the countenance of Sigismund and other princes, the assembly warned, entreated, and required Eugenius (April 29) to present him-

---

[1] Capefigue, a consistent ultramontanist, sees the real ground of this alarm: 'Je considère les conciles de Constance, de Bâle, et la *Pragmatique Sanction*, comme les trois actes qui finissent le moyen âge de l'Eglise, *en ébranlant la forte et sainte dictature des papes:*' II. 335.

[2] Raynald. ad an. 1431, §§ 20, 21.

[3] See their *Epistle*, dated Feb. 9, 1432, in Bulæus, *Hist. Univ. Paris*, v. 412 sq. The university-men also acted the chief part in this assemblage: cf. Döllinger, IV. 184, 207.

[4] See his remarkable treatise, *De Catholica Concordantia*, written at this time, and printed with his other numerous *Works*, Basil. 1565. He afterwards (circ. 1437) went over to the papal side, and even did his utmost to discredit the proceedings at Basel. In the work above quoted, besides vindicating the supremacy of general councils, he threw suspicion on the Pseudo-Isidore decretals, the 'Donatio Constantini,' etc.

[5] Mansi, XXIX. 21. The president (Cardinal Juliano) felt himself constrained to write two energetic letters to the pope, his patron, (in Brown's *Fasciculus*, I. 54—67) deprecating the dissolution of the Council. He points out that by denying its authority, the pope rejected the council of Constance and ultimately destroyed his own title to the pontifical chair (p. 64). The following sentence is instructive: 'Si modo dissolvatur concilium, nonne populi Germaniæ videntes se non solum destitutos ab ecclesia, sed deceptos, concordabunt cum hæreticis [meaning the Hussites], et fient nobis inimiciores quam illi? Heu, Heu! quanta ista erit confusio! finis pro certo est. Jam, ut video, securis ad radicem posita est,' *etc*. p. 59. A like foreboding was expressed by a Spanish bishop, Andreas de Escobar (1434), writing to the same cardinal Juliano (see his *Gubernaculum Conciliorum*, in Von der Hardt, VI. 182): 'Et timendum est, quod ante diem judicii et in brevi, nisi super eam [*i.e.* the Roman Church] fiat reformatio et reparatio, desoletur et foras mittatur et ab hominibus conculcetur.'

THE PAPACY.

The pope declared contumacious.

self within three months[1], or send accredited persons who might give his sanction to the whole proceedings. Overtures of peace ensued, and for a while accommodation did not seem impossible: but in the following September, the promoters of the council moved that both the pope and cardinals should be pronounced contumacious, on the ground that the obnoxious bull which they had published for its dissolution was still unrevoked. At length the pope could not resist the urgent prayers of Sigismund and other advocates of peace: and as the council was now willing to withdraw its threats and censures, representatives, who swore[2] (April 8, 1434) that they would faithfully adhere to the decrees of Constance, and would labour to advance the objects contemplated by the present meeting, were deputed to attend in his behalf. But when, amid discussions for reducing the pecuniary tribute[3] to the pope (June 9, 1435), it was contended that in this respect he was amenable to their control, his emissaries bitterly protested. Other subjects of dispute arose continually, and in the end the papal nuncios, Juliano[4] with the rest, departed from the council. After their retreat the pope was censured even more emphatically for his backwardness in carrying out the work of reformation[5]; and in person or

His temporary recognition of the council.

Departure of his representatives.

---

[1] This threat was several times repeated, *e.g.* Sept. 6, 1432, Dec. 18, 1432, Feb. 19, 1433, Sept. 11, 1433. On Nov. 6, 1433 (the 14th session) a new respite of three months was granted to Eugenius, and at the same time were sent to him three forms of revocation. One of these he employed soon after in annulling all the bulls and other instruments which he had issued against the council. His letters to this effect were read Feb. 5, 1434.

[2] Mansi, xxix. 409. In the ensuing session (April 26) it was resolved that the legates should be permitted to preside in the council only on the condition that they should acknowledge their authority to be derived entirely from the council: *Ibid.* p. 90. The number of the prelates at Basel was now about one hundred.

[3] After abolishing first-fruits (Mansi, xxix. 104) it is added: 'Et si (quod absit) Romanus pontifex, qui præ cæteris universalium conciliorum exequi et custodire canones debet, adversus hanc sanctionem aliquid faciendo ecclesiam scandalizet, *generali Concilio deferatur.*' This was only one of a number of reforming acts which emanated from the council subsequently to July 14, 1433. The last decisions of the kind were made, Jan. 24, 1438: see Mansi, xxix. 159.

[4] He appears to have seceded in the twenty-fifth session (May 7, 1437), when his advice, touching certain Greek ambassadors who had come over to negociate a union, was rejected by the council.

[5] Mansi, xxix. 137 sq. They declared that nothing could induce him

by deputy was absolutely summoned to appear before the council within sixty days. But feeling his position stronger[1] than before, his tone was now proportionately changed. Instead of yielding to the summons, he put forth a document (Sept. 18, 1437) in which he sought to stifle the decrees of Basel, and urged the whole of Christendom to meet him in a council at Ferrara. The new leader of the Basel assembly was the cardinal l'Allemand[2], archbishop of Arles, who shewed himself unflinching in his struggles to promote a reformation of the Church. On March 29, 1438, the rival synod of Ferrara was condemned; and all who had frequented it, the pope himself among the number, excommunicated. In a later session he was formally deposed[3] (June 25, 1439). Into the place of Eugenius (Nov. 17) they elected an aristocratic hermit (formerly the duke of Savoy) who reluctantly assumed[4] the name of Felix V. (July 24, 1440). But from this very date the cause of the 'reforming' (anti-papal) party manifestly drooped[5]. The

THE PAPACY.

His bull convening a fresh council.

Counter movement at Basel.

Deposition of the pope.

'ut aliquam morum emendationem Christo placentem, aut notissimorum abusuum correctionem in ecclesia sancta Dei efficere satageret.'

[1] When he yielded to the wish of Sigismund and others, and acknowledged the assembly at Basel, his territory was in a state of revolution, and a prey to lawless condottieri (cf. Döllinger, IV. 188). This storm had now blown over, and Eugenius strengthened himself by dispatching nuncios to the several courts of Europe with his own ex-parte version of the subjects in dispute.

[2] Respecting him see Schröckh, XXXII. 65 sq. After the convocation of the synod of Ferrara he was the only cardinal who remained at Basel.

[3] Mansi, XXIX. 179. The synod decrees, 'Gabrielem prius nominatum Eugenium papam IV. fuisse et esse notorium et manifestum contumacem, mandatis seu praeceptis ecclesiae universalis inobedientem et in aperta rebellione persistentem,' *etc.* There was a small party at Basel, headed by Tedeschi, archbishop of Palermo (Panormitanus), which attempted to avert this crisis by maintaining that inferior clerics who constituted a large majority should be deprived of their deliberative voice. The bishops, it appears, were not disposed to go so far as the rest (cf. Döllinger, IV. 201, 202). Tedeschi himself, however, was a warm adherent of the council generally. See his work in favour of it (1439) in Mansi, XXXI. 205 sq. An answer was put forth by Johannes de Turrecremata, entitled *Summa de Ecclesia*, ed. Venet. 1561.

[4] See the *Letter* of Æneas Sylvius (August 13, 1440), giving an account of the coronation of Felix, in Brown's *Fasciculus*, I. 52—54. Felix was, however, recognized only in Savoy, Switzerland, Bavaria and some other parts of Germany.

[5] This was proved by the secession of the more influential members from the council. See the (one-sided) account of Johannes de Polemar

General reaction in his favour.

empire, Spain, and France were, for the most part, neutral, not renouncing their connexion with Eugenius, while they inconsistently professed to recognize the legitimacy of the council of Basel. The English people, with some others, took his side more warmly, and sent deputies to Florence, whither his new council of Ferrara was translated (**1439**). So vast indeed was the discomfiture now suffered by his adversaries, that upon the abdication of Felix V., ten years later, all attempts to limit his supremacy and purify the west of Christendom, by means of universal synods, were abandoned in despair.

Pragmatic Sanction of 1438,

The only country, where the principles which had been advocated in those synods gained a lasting hold upon the rulers both in Church and State, was France. In what is known as the *Pragmatic Sanction*[1] of Bourges, enacted under Charles VII. (**1438**), it was maintained distinctly, with some other kindred points, all adverse to the ultramontane claims, that General Councils are superior to the pope. This edict, which for half a century became the great palladium of the liberties of France, was afterwards repealed by Louis XI. for diplomatic reasons; but

finally exchanged for a Concordat.

as the Parisian parliament would not register his act, the 'Sanction' kept its ground until it was supplanted by a new Concordat in the time of Francis I.[2] (**1516**).

(1443), in Mansi, xxxi. 197 sq.; Æneas Sylvius, *Descriptio Germaniæ*, c. 10; and Hallam, *Middle Ages*, II. 244, 10th ed.

[1] Cf. above, p. 253: Gieseler, IV. pp. 369, 370. A history of this document is contained in the first volume of the well-known *Traités des Droits et Libertez de l'Eglise Gallicane*. Pope Pius II. said of it: 'The bishop of Rome, whose diocese is the world, has no more jurisdiction in France, than what the parliament is pleased to allow him.' Ranke, *Hist. of France*, I. 78, Lond. 1852. In Germany the pope (Nicholas V.) was able to obtain more copious concessions. The 'concordat of Aschaffenburg' (July, 1447), confirmed at Vienna (Feb. 17, 1448), replaced him nearly on his former ground (cf. above, p. 334, n. 1, and Gieseler, IV. p. 345). To the excesses which the Roman court afterwards committed we must trace the *Gravamina* of 1461, in Walch. *Moniment. Med. Ævi*, I. 101 sq., and the memorable *Centum Gravamina* drawn up by the German princes in 1522.

[2] Hallam, as above, p. 252. The following is the entry of the learned chronicler Genebrard (*Chronograph*. Paris, 1580), relating to this subject: 'Anno 1516 abrogata est in Galliis Pragmatica Sanctio, et Concordata, ut vocant, substituuntur, fremente *universo clero, scholasticis, populo, bonis denique et doctis omnibus*.' For the vigorous *Appellatio* of the University of Paris, reaffirming the principles laid down at the council of Basel, see Brown's *Fascic*. I. 68—71.

Amid the lull which rested on the surface of the Church at large for more than half a century anterior to the Reformation, the cupidity of Rome was far more generally confined within the papal states and their immediate circle[1]. Nearly all the line of pontiffs, Nicholas V. (**1447**), Calixtus III. (**1455**), Pius II. or Æneas Sylvius[2] (**1458**), Paul II. (**1464**), Sixtus IV. (**1471**), Innocent VIII. (**1484**), Alexander VI. (**1492**), Pius III.[3] (**1503**), Julius II. (**1503**), and Leo X.[4] (**1513—1522**), betrayed increasing love of pomp and worldly pleasures. Nepotism was the prevailing motive in their distribution of preferment, while the taxes of their chancery rose from day to day[5]. Too many also played a leading part in base political intrigues, which, even if successful, tended to destroy the influence and discredit the pretensions of the hierarchy at large. Nor may we pass in silence the appalling profligacy which too often stained the reputation of these later pontiffs, more particularly that of Alexander VI.[6], who is perhaps unequalled in the history of mediæval crime, except by Cæsar Borgia, his son An effort, it is true, was made

THE PAPACY.

Restriction of the influence of the popes:

their secularity,

and profligacy.

---

[1] Ranke, *Popes during the 16th and 17th centuries* (Bohn's ed.), I. § 4, pp. 25 sq. Sixtus IV. was the first to carry out this line of politics, and even favoured the conspiracy which led to the attempted assassination of Lorenzo dei Medici on the steps of the high-altar in the cathedral of Florence. 'Abuse followed abuse, and a dangerous confusion in the ideas of men on the nature of the ecclesiastical power and on the true position of the pope was the natural consequence.' Döllinger, IV. 220.

[2] He was formerly devoted to the anti-papal cause (see his important *Commentarius de Gestis Basiliensis Concilii*, in Brown's *Fascic.* I. 1—51), but under the influence of the great reaction that ensued, he joined the party of Nicholas V., and received a cardinal's hat from Calixtus III. (1456). He died of grief (1464) on finding that he could not stir the Church to join him in driving back the Turks who had now taken Constantinople (May 29, 1453), and occupied Bosnia and Slavonia. See the unsparing *Life* of him in Platina, *Vit. Pontif. Roman.*, and a more favourable one by Campani, in Muratori, *Script. Rer. Ital.* III. pt. II. 967 sq. His own *Epistolæ* (often printed) are the best original authority.

[3] The first word of this pope after his election (1503) was 'Reformation.' He died in twenty-six days. Döllinger, IV. 229.

[4] On the part taken by this pontiff at the outset of the Reformation, see Roscoe's *Life and Pontificate of Leo X.*, chap. xv.

[5] Ranke, p. 43. Döllinger (at the time of writing, an ultramontanist) is on these subjects too impartial for his English translator: see note at p. 228.

[6] Well might the cry be uttered that the pope was now preparing the way for Antichrist; and that he laboured to promote the coming of the kingdom, not of heaven, but of Satan. Ranke, I. 39.

OTHER BRANCHES OF THE HIERARCHY.

under Æneas Sylvius[1] and Julius II.[*] to resuscitate the Hildebrandine principles, and in the council of Lateran[2] (1512—1517) that effort was in part rewarded when the French, who had been hitherto the chief antagonists of ultra-papal claims, consented to abandon the Pragmatic Sanction[3]: yet, meanwhile, a different class of spirits breaking in tumultuously upon the guilty slumbers of the conclave, had begun to wrench away the time-worn pillars on which Roman despotism was reared.

Bishops of the period.

The other prelates of the west maintained their old relations to the papacy, with the exception that the lessening of its influence often added to the magnitude of theirs. This happened more especially throughout the forty-years' schism[4]. The pallium was, however, still procured by all the metropolitans: the Roman legate, where the office was not held by one of them, enjoyed precedence in ecclesiastical assemblies, and in cases where no obstacle[5] was

---

[1] See, for instance, his *Bulla Retractationum* (April 26, 1463; Raynald. ad an. § 114 sq.), in which he maintains that the pope has received supreme power over the whole Church directly from Christ Himself, and that all other ministers are his delegates ('per ordinem in omnem diffundit ecclesiam'). He assailed the French 'Pragmatic Sanction,' but Charles VII. (1460) met him by appealing to a general council: see *Preuves des Libertez de l'Eglise Gallicane*, c. XIII. § 10.

[*] It is of him Macchiavelli says (Ranke, I. 42) that 'time was, when no baron was so insignificant, but that he might venture to brave the papal power; now, it is regarded with respect even by a king of France.'

[2] Labbe, XIV. 1—346. In the year preceding the convocation of this synod, Louis XII. of France, quarrelling with pope Julius II., had instigated some of the cardinals to call a council at Pisa (Labbe, XIII. 1486 sq.). It met for several months (Nov. 1, 1511—April 21, 1512), and in the last session ventured to suspend the pope: but its members were then dispersed and nothing came of their denunciations. Louis XII. in the course of this dispute struck a coin with the legend 'Perdam Babylonis nomen:' see Thuanus (De Thou), *Hist.* I. 11.

[3] See above, p. 338, n. 2. 'La Pragmatique, véritable source de schisme et d'hérésie, fut heureusement révoquée par Louis XI.' Capefigue, II. 335 (note).

[4] Above, p. 328. On the other hand the growing system of papal 'provisions' (cf. above, p. 322, n. 3) tended to deprive them of a large portion of their former influence. This was confessed by Martin V. (1418), in striving to remedy some of the abuses generated by his predecessors, who exempted 'ecclesias, monasteria, capitula, conventus, prioratus, et personas' from the jurisdiction of the bishops 'in grave ipsorum Ordinariorum præjudicium:' Von der Hardt, IV. 1535.

[5] Such obstacles, however, did continually arise; *e.g.* in England, when Henry Beaufort, bishop of Winchester, was constituted legate by Martin V. (1426), he was admitted to the counsels of the sovereign only

made by kings and parliaments his influence was supreme. Appeals were also not unfrequently transferred from the diocesan and the provincial courts to what was deemed the chief tribunal of the west: but on this subject we observe a corresponding jealousy among the legislative bodies[1].

In appointing bishops there was much variety of usage, as the papal or imperial interest predominated. Theoretically every prelate was to be elected[2], in accordance with the ancient laws, and one of the most urgent stipulations of the council of Basel (July 14, 1433) related to this subject. It was meant to counteract encroachments[3] both of Rome and of the civil power. According to the German compact, made in 1448, these free elections[4] were to be continued, the appointment of a prelate lapsing to the pope, if the capitular election were not made within the legal time. But, for the most part, it is obvious that the crown was very loath to acquiesce in such arrangements, and contrived, while bent on humbling papal arrogance, to fix the right of nominating to the bishoprics and higher benefices absolutely in itself[5]. The French con-

OTHER BRANCHES OF THE HIERARCHY.

Their appointment:

---

on the condition, 'quod quotiens aliqua, materiæ, causæ, vel negotia ipsum dominum regem aut regna seu dominia sua ex parte una, ac sedem apostolicam ex parte altera concernentia .... idem cardinalis se ab hujusmodi consilio absentet, et communicationi eorundem, causarum, materiarum, et negotiorum *non intersit quovis modo*,' etc., *Rot. Parl.* 8° Hen. VI. c. 17. It is also worth observing that a charge brought against Wolsey was, that as legate he had transgressed the 'statute of Præmunire' (see above, p. 328, n. 4), by receiving bulls from Rome and acting on them without the king's leave. See the Articles against him in Herbert's *Hist. of Henry VIII.* pp. 294 sq. Lond. 1672.

[1] Cf. Twysden, *Vindication of the Church*, pp. 51 sq. Camb. ed.
[2] Above, pp. 151, 152, 237.
[3] See Sess. XII.; Mansi, XXIX. 61: 'Decretum de electionibus et confirmationibus episcoporum et prælatorum.' The prelates had their eye especially on the very numerous 'reservations' (electiones expectandæ) made by the pope in favour of some candidate of his own: but they proceed to exhort princes also to abstain from superseding, or intermeddling with, capitular elections. This indeed is only one of the measures they originated for securing the independence of the episcopate. Their president (the cardinal archbishop of Arles), after declaring that modern bishops were mere shadows ('umbræ quædam'), superior to the presbyters only 'habitu et reditibus,' goes on to state: 'At nos eos in statu reposuimus pristino...nos eos, qui jam non erant episcopi, fecimus episcopos.' Æn. Sylvius, *de Concil. Basil.* (in Brown's *Fascic.* I. 23).
[4] Schröckh, XXXII. 164, 165.
[5] Ranke, *Popes*, I. 31. The flagrant instances, that now meet us, of

OTHER BRANCHES OF THE HIERARCHY.

often made by the Crown.

cordat, for example, which restored the annates and some other privileges to Leo X., secured this right to Francis,— the nominee, however, being pledged to seek collation from the pope: and in this country, more particularly during the reign of Henry VII., the power of filling up the vacant sees had generally devolved upon the crown, which also was appropriating to itself one-half of the annates. Everywhere, indeed, the civil governments of Europe had become possessed of what were long regarded as ecclesiastical prerogatives. The secular element in the Church was threatening to suppress the spiritual or hierarchic, and accordingly throughout the earlier stages of the Reformation we shall have to notice the confusion of ideas which this new ascendancy produced[1].

Attempted reformation by means of diocesan synods.

In the attempt to reinvigorate episcopacy the council of Basel enjoined (Nov. 25, 1433) that each bishop should hold a diocesan synod once at least every year[2], and by his presence labour to advance the reformation both of pastors and of flocks. But owing to his sad unfitness, intellectual and moral, or his livelong absence[3] from the sphere to which his energies were due, the bishop very seldom gave effect to this injunction. It is true that fine exceptions are not absolutely wanting, but the bishops for

episcopal pluralities, are traceable, at least in some degree, to this dictation of the crown. Thus, the royal favourite Wolsey at the close of the present period was farming on easy terms the bishoprics of Bath, Worcester, and Hereford, the real owners being absentees: he also gained successively the bishoprics of Durham and Winchester, contriving to keep one of them along with his archbishopric: he also held in commendam the abbey of St Alban's and many other pieces of ecclesiastical preferment, besides enjoying the virtual patronage of most of the vacant benefices. Herbert, *Hist. of Henry VIII.* p. 57.

[1] See the just remarks on this point by Bp. Russell, *Church in Scotland*, I. 164, 165. The royal intermeddling with conventual and other church-property had in England begun some time before the Reformation; *e.g.* several monasteries were suppressed by Wolsey with the consent both of the king and the pope. Herbert's *Hist. of Henry VIII.*, pp. 146, 147, 163, 164, 251.

[2] Sess. xv.: 'Ad minus semel in anno ubi non est consuetudo bis annuatim celebrari.' Provincial synods were also ordered to assemble at least every third year, and in England we occasionally meet with a list of 'Reformanda in convocatione cleri;' *e. g.* A.D. 1444, Wilkins, III. 540.

[3] 'Multi ex eis qui pastorali apice potiuntur, perque annosa tempore potiti sunt, nunquam civitates suas intraverunt, suas ecclesias viderunt, sua loca vel dioeceses visitaverunt,' *etc.* Nicholas de Clémenges, *De corrupto Ecclesiæ Statu:* Brown's *Fascic.* II. 562. Passages might be multi-

the most part had grown ignorant, idle, and sensual, or were often occupied exclusively in search of honours and emoluments that bound them to the earth[1].

The monks, as we have seen already[2], gorged with the ecclesiastical endowments, lost the moral elevation[3] they had shewn throughout the early periods of the Church, and with it forfeited their hold on the affections of the people. Except the order of Carthusians[4] none of them adhered to the letter of their institute. Their intellectual vigour at the same time underwent a corresponding deterioration, insomuch that few if any works of merit, either in the field of science or in that of theology, proceeded in

<small>OTHER BRANCHES OF THE HIERARCHY.

Degeneracy of the monks.</small>

plied to the same effect, especially in reference to those cases where the pope presented his own courtiers to the foreign sees.

[1] *e.g.* in the *Defensor Pacis* (above quoted p. 324) we have the following complaint: 'Nunc vero propter regiminis corruptionem *plurima pars sacerdotum et episcoporum* in sacra Scriptura periti sunt parum, et si dicere liceat insufficienter; eo quod temporalia beneficiorum, quæ assequuntur officiosi, ambitiosi, cupidi, et causidici quidam obtinere volunt et obtinent obsequio, prece vel pretio vel sæculari potentia;' p. 258: cf. the frightful picture of the Spanish prelates, at the close of this period, drawn by the Dominican Pablo de Leon in his *Guia del Cielo* (extracts in De Castro, *Spanish Protestants*, Lond. 1851, pp. xxv. sq.). He traces many of the evils to the vile example of the Roman court, p. xxix. Other evidence is furnished by the decrees of the 'Reformation-college' at Constance: see Lenfant: liv. VII. s. 42 sq. John Sturmius (*ad Cardinales delectos;* Argentor. 1538) asserts: 'Per Germaniam in maximo numero episcoporum nullus est, qui, si canonum autoritas restituta esset, locum suum tueri possit. In Gallia quoque pauci sunt, sed tamen illa felicior est quam Germania. De Italia nihil affirmare possum. Anglia sola est quæ exemplo esse possit.'

[2] Above, p. 230. The Spanish writer, above quoted, while acknowledging that good and holy monks existed, urges their inconvenient wealth as a reason for some change. 'If left alone,' he says, 'every thing will very soon belong to the monasteries,' p. xx.

[3] See Nicholas de Clemènges (as above), p. 564. The same writer is equally severe in speaking of the nuns. He says that their convents were not 'Dei sanctuaria, sed Veneris execranda prostibula' (p. 566). And Gerson more than once advances the same charge; *e.g.* in a sermon preached before the council of Constance he declares, 'Et utinam nulla sint monasteria mulierum quæ facta sunt prostibula meretricum; et prohibeat adhuc deteriora Deus.' *Opp.* II. 550, ed. Dupin. The persecutions to which a nun of the stricter sort was subject are graphically described in a MS. belonging to the University of Cambridge (Dd. I. p. 372). The usages of a well-ordered nunnery are minutely described in the '*Ancren Riwle*' (Camd. Soc. 1853), ed. Morton.

[4] See the contemporary work of John Buschius, *De reformatione monasteriorum*, Lib. III. c. 82 (in Leibnitz's *Scriptores Brunsv.* II. 935). A healthier impulse was, however, given at the close of the 14th century to monasticism in Russia, by Sergius of Rostoff, on whom see Mouravieff, pp. 61 sq. and notes.

OTHER BRANCHES OF THE HIERARCHY.

Efforts to reform them.

this age from cloisters of the west. The councils of Constance¹ and Basel², in their endeavours to brace up monastic discipline afresh, produced some transitory changes, by insisting on the need of reformation and by authorizing a commission of inquiry into many of the German convents. But in spite of these remedial measures we are bound to argue, from complaints which rise in every quarter, that monasticism had grown almost incorrigible and was ripening daily for the scythe. As in the former period, numerous congregations, separating one by one from the degenerate Benedictines, organized themselves in fresh societies. Of these the principal were (1417) the congregation of S. Justina³, to which was afterwards united that of Monte Cassino. Offshoots⁴, in like manner, such as the Bernardines (1497), grew out of the Cistercian order.

New Congregations.

The condition of the Friars.

While the monks had thus degenerated step by step, the Mendicants retained their former influence. The great bulk of the religious endowments were now lavished upon them, until they rivalled the Establishment which they had bitterly attacked, in the magnificence of their foundations and the freedom of their mode of life⁵. Confiding in the patronage of popes⁶, of kings*, and noble ladies,

---

¹ On the orders made by the 'Reformation-college' at Constance, see Lenfant, liv. VII. s. 55.
² See Buschius, as above, pp. 476 sq., and elsewhere.
³ Helyot, *Hist. des Ordres Relig.* VI. 230 sq. Paris, 1714. The rise of other confraternities is mentioned in the same place.
⁴ *Ibid.* v. 56 sq. The Spanish 'Order of the Hieronymites' (hermits) had been founded as early as 1370; but they were at first devoted to the so-called rule of St Augustine. In 1424 they adopted another: see Holstein's *Codex*, III. 43 sq.; and Stirling's *Cloister-Life of the Emperor Charles V.*, pp. 77, 78.
⁵ See Nicholas de Clémenges, as above, pp. 564, 565; *The Vision of William concerning Piers the Plowman* (by William Langland, about 1362), ed. Skeat, Oxford, 1869; *The Creed of Piers Plowman*, ed. Skeat, London, 1867; and a still earlier satire *On the Times of Edw. II.*, edited by the present writer for the Percy Society, No. LXXXII. The author of the latter poem attacks the vices prevalent among all classes of the community, especially the 'Menours [Franciscans] and Jacobyn' [Dominicans], Carmes [Carmelites], and Friars of what was called the order of St Augustine: stan. 30 sq. In this particular he was a precursor of Wycliffe, on whose controversy with the Mendicants, see Vaughan's *Life*, pp. 82 sq., ed. 1853.
⁶ *e.g.* Sixtus IV. (himself a Franciscan) granted them enormous privileges in a bull entitled *Mare Magnum* (Aug. 31, 1474), which was confirmed in the 'Bulla Aurea' (July 26, 1479). The parish-priest who resisted them was threatened with the loss of his benefice. See the

they were able to surmount the opposition[1] of the Universities and the parochial clergy, who regarded them with mingled fear, abhorrence, and contempt. In spite of mutual jealousies and altercations[2], the four leading orders of Mendicants[3] (Franciscans, Dominicans, Carmelites, and Augustinians) held themselves together[4] and were almost absolute in the administration of the Western Church. Their learning and activity prevented them from forfeiting this prominent position, till the latter half of the fifteenth century, when all of them put forth the symptoms of decay[5].

OTHER BRANCHES OF THE HIERARCHY.

Their eventual decline.

While the Dominicans had been employed especially in

Bullarium Romanum, III. 3, 139. The subject was reopened in the 11th session of the council of Lateran (Dec. 19, 1516).

* See Turner's *Middle Ages*, III. 115 sq. The English Franciscans were most favoured by gentlewomen, the Dominicans by the nuns. *Ibid.* 116.

[1] Cf. above, pp. 233, 234. Pope John XXII. (*Extravagantes Communes*, lib. v., tit. iii. c. 2, in *Corp. Jur. Canon.*) took the side (1321) of the Friars against a doctor of the Sorbonne (J. de Poliaco); but the Sorbonne gained a victory in 1409; Bulæus, *Hist. Univ. Paris.* v. 189: cf. v. 522 sq. In Brown's *Fascic.* (II. 466—486) will be found a *Defensorium Curatorum contra privilegiatos* (1357), by Richard, archbishop of Armagh, who spent some years at Avignon, striving to interest the pope in favour of the parish-priests. The convocation of York (1466), under archbishop Nevil, condemned those Friars ('pardoners'), who went about raising funds by preaching (or selling) indulgences, in the name of the pope and other bishops: Johnson, *English Canons*, II. 521, 522.

[2] Cf. above, p. 233, and see Warton's *Engl. Poetry*, II. 87 sq., ed. 1840.

[3] Or, as they were now severally termed, the grey-friars, the black-friars, the white-friars, and the Austin-friars.

[4] Thus when they were attacked by the archbishop of Armagh (above, n. 1), the cause of all the four orders was defended in common: see Trithemius (John of Trittenheim), *Annal. Hirsaug.* II. 245.

[5] Such was plainly the case in England (see Warton, *Ibid.* pp. 92, 93). The Carmelites, who were once conspicuous in repelling Lollardism (Turner, III. 122), had lost their reputation both for scholarship and orthodoxy about 1460; and some time before, the Augustinians had ruined their cause by preaching seditious sermons. When Leland (circ. 1540) visited the ancient seat of the Franciscans at Oxford, he found in the library little more than empty shelves covered with dust and cobwebs ('inveni etiam et libros, sed quos tribus obolis non emerem'). The Observants (1425) were a reformed Order of Franciscans. The influence of the Mendicants was great, however, even at the end of the present period: for Erasmus (*Epist.* CCCCLXXVII., *Opp.* III. 515, ed. Lugd. Batav. 1703) declares that the world was then, among other evils, groaning under 'tyrannide Fratrum Mendicantium, qui cum sint satellites sedis Romanæ, tamen eo potentiæ ac multitudinis evadunt, ut ipsi Romano pontifici atque ipsis adeo regibus sint formidabiles.'

OTHER BRANCHES OF THE HIERARCHY.

Aberrations of one school of Minorites.

counteracting misbelief and guiding the machinery of the Inquisition, an important school of the Franciscans, as we noticed on a former page[1], were hostile to the see of Rome. The feeling which had prompted that hostility was equally aroused by other branches of the Church-establishment. In union with the Beghards[2], they continued to maintain that truly 'spiritual' persons would subsist exclusively on alms, that personal tithes were not due to the parochial clergy save by usage, and that deadly sin was fatal to the sacerdotal character[3]. They also propagated the Apocalyptic theories of earlier times[4], and one at least of their sodality laid claim to the prophetic office[5]. The more sober still adhered to the communion of the Church, reverting to the letter of their institute, and finally obtaining the approbation of the council of Constance[6] (**1415**). As distinguished from the laxer or conventual school of the Franciscans, they were called Friars-Regular.

Friars-Regular. The Beghards and Lollards.

But other groups, in which the Beghard influence[7] seems to have preponderated, now appeared in many countries of the west, especially in Flanders and some parts of Germany. One section of them, notwithstanding the indiscriminate censures[8] of pope Clement V., had manifested no desire to vary from the general teaching of the Church. They were religious brotherhoods and sister-

---

[1] Above, p. 324.

[2] Above, p. 235. They were condemned by John XXII. in 1317 (*Extravagantes Johan. XXII.* tit. VII., in *Corp. Jur. Canon.*), who declares that very many of them are persons, who 'a veritate Catholicæ fidei deviantes, ecclesiastica sacramenta despiciunt ac errores alios student multipliciter seminare.' Many of this class fell a prey to the Inquisition: cf. a contemporary account in Baluze, *Vit. Pap. Avenion.* I. 598.

[3] See, for instance, the proceedings against William Russell and other English Franciscans, in Wilkins, III. 433 sq.

[4] Above, pp. 332, 333. The *Postilla* of Oliva were still most popular among them. The Church of Rome was Babylon, the 'meretrix magna;' John XXII. was 'mysticus Antichristus, præparator viæ majoris Antichristi,' etc. See the *Liber Sententiarum*, p. 304, annexed to Limborch's *Hist. Inquisitionis*.

[5] See the *Copia Prophetiæ Fratris Joh. de Rupescissa*, etc. in Brown's *Fascic.* II. 494 sq. For other light on this interesting subject, consult Dr Maitland's *Eight Essays* (1852), pp. 206 sq.

[6] Von der Hardt, IV. 515.

[7] See above, p. 235, and Mosheim, as there quoted, pp. 244 sq.

[8] *e.g.* Clementin. *Constit.* lib. III. tit. xi. c. I. John XXII., on the contrary, in 1318, took the females commonly called *Beghinæ* under his protection. Mosheim, *Ibid.* pp. 627 sq.

hoods distinguished for their zeal in visiting the sick, or, in the case of those to whom the name of Lollards[1] (Lullards) was now popularly given, for singing at the funerals and for otherwise assisting in the burial of the dead. But it would seem that the title 'Lollard,' like the older one of Beghard, or Beguin, was at an early date synonymous with heretic[2], although the bearers[3] of them both were shielded, now and then at least, from the Inquisitor by missives of succeeding popes.

OTHER BRANCHES OF THE HIERARCHY.

Another confraternity, which ran the risk of being confounded with the Beghards, owed their origin to Gerhard Groot[4], a clergyman of Deventer, at the middle of the fourteenth century. They soon expanded, under the able patronage of the reformed 'canons of Windesheim,' into an order called the 'Fratres Vitæ Communis;' and while elevating in some degree the tone of personal religion, they contributed[5] to the more careful training both of

Common-Life Clerics.

---

[1] As early as the year 1309, we read of 'quidam hypocritæ gyrovagi, qui Lollardi, sive *Deum laudantes*, vocabantur,' in the neighbourhood of Liège: see the *Gest. Pontiff. Leod. Script.* ed. Chapeaville, II. 350. The derivation thus suggested is from the German *lullen* (='lull'), referring to the plaintive melody employed by them at funerals: cf. Gieseler, IV. p. 159, n. 4, and Maitland as above, p. 204. A ballad on Sir John Oldcastle, quoted by Turner (III. 144, note), appears to connect 'Lollardrie' with an English verb 'lolle.' See also Halliwell, *Arch. Dict.* s.v. 'Lollards.'

[2] See the last extract. In 1408, archbp. Arundel declares in his Constitutions against the Lollards (§ 10) that his province (of Canterbury) was 'infected with new unprofitable doctrines, and blemished with the *new* damnable brand of *Lollardy*' (Johnson, II. 470), which implies that the name was then somewhat fresh in England.

[3] Thus Boniface IX. (1395) recalls the exemptions which had been granted to persons of either sex ('vulgo Beghardi, seu *Lullardi* et Zuestriones, a se ipsis vero pauperes Fratricelli seu pauperes pueruli nominati' by himself or his predecessors, on the ground that heresies were lurking in the institute. Mosheim, as above, p. 409.

[4] See the deeply interesting *Life* of him by Thomas à Kempis (d. 1471) in the *Works* of the latter, III. 8 sq., ed. Colon.; and a *Chronicon* (circ. 1465) of the canons of Windesheim by one of their number, Joh. Buschius, ed. Antverp. 1621. This order had to defend themselves against a virulent attack of a Saxon Dominican (*Ibid.* pp. 547 sq.), and were supported by the leading men at the council of Constance. Lenfant, *Hist. du Concile*, liv. VI. §§ 64 sq. One of the grounds of objection to them was that they lived together without adopting monastic vows. They were afterwards protected for a time by Eugenius IV. (Mosheim, as above, pp. 668 sq.): but numbers, through their strong resemblance to the Beghards, were at last compelled to seek a shelter in the tertiary estate of the Franciscans (cf. above, p. 232).

[5] Their chronicler Buschius (as above, n. 4) asks with justice (p. 214):

OTHER BRANCHES OF THE HIERARCHY.

Degeneracy of the clerics.

laymen and ecclesiastics in the North of Europe. One of their most holy luminaries was Thomas à Kempis[1], who died in 1471.

It may be safely stated that the 'working' (parish) clergy had never been so debased as at the close of the present period. The corruptions we have marked already' were now threatening day by day to leaven all the lump. In Germany[2] and Spain[4] particularly, their unblushing licence, covetousness, pride, and secularity exposed them to the hatred of their flocks and to the satire of the whole community. Relieved on one side by exemptions from the jurisdiction of the civil courts, and on the other by the intermeddling zeal of Friars, on whom the actual cure of souls had very frequently devolved, they sank into luxurious ease and abject ignorance, or confined themselves to the mechanical performance of their sacred duties in the Church. Unchastity, the fruit of a mis-

'Quantæ in sæculo sunt personæ sexus utriusque, quæ amicitia his conjunctæ a sæculi vanitate per eas [congregationes] conversæ, et ad meliora...ipsarum exemplo inductæ et provocatæ, quamvis ad omnia evangelica consilia statim arripienda propter multa impedimenta nondum dare se valent, vitam tamen sanctam a peccatis alienam, ad earum informationem student observare, quis enumerabit?' Their scholastic and other institutions are described at length by Delprat, *Verhandeling over de Broederschap van G. Groote*, Utrecht, 1830 (translated into German, with additions, by Mohnike, Leipz. 1840).

[1] It has been disputed whether the *De Imitatione Christi* is to be classed among his warm-hearted writings (some assigning it to abbot Gersen, and others to Gerson, the Chancellor of Paris), but the evidence, external and internal, seems to point him out as the real author: cf. Gieseler, v. 73, 74, n. 12.

[2] Above, pp. 240, 241.

[3] *e.g.* The cardinal Cesarini (above, p. 335) makes the following report to Eugenius IV.: 'Incitavit etiam me huc venire [*i.e.* to the reforming council of Basel] deformitas et dissolutio cleri Alemanniæ, ex qua *laici supra modum irritantur adversus statum ecclesiasticum*. Propter quod valde timendum est, *nisi se emendent*, ne laici, more Hussitarum, *in totum clerum irruant*, ut publice dicunt:' in Brown's *Fascic.* I. 56.

[4] See especially De Castro's *Spanish Protestants*, pp. xvi. sq. Lond. 1851, and the original authorities there mentioned. The following proverb is a sample:

"*Clerigo,* fraile ó judio

"No lo tengas por amigo." p. xxxvii. For England the evidence that might be cited is overwhelming. Gower, for instance, who denounced 'Antichristes Lollardes,' is in the *Vox Clamantis* a stern censor of the vicious clergy. See the Preface: ed. by Mr Coxe for the Roxburgh Club, 1850. In this point he quite agrees with Wycliffe. The author of metrical Sermons [? Richard of Hampole], in the *Camb. Univ. MSS.*, Dd. I. pp. 188, 189, 283, has fine passages on the same subject.

guided rigour in ecclesiastical legislation, had been long the darkest blot upon their characters, and in the fourteenth and fifteenth centuries the proofs that it went on increasing are most lamentably rife. It had infected all the clerical estate, but seems to have been more especially notorious in cathedral-canons[1].

OTHER BRANCHES OF THE HIERARCHY.

To eradicate these old and ulcerating evils was a leading object in the great reformatory councils of Constance and Basel. One proposition there advanced was to annul the law enforcing celibacy[2]; but the common feeling, that of Gerson[3] with the rest, continued to incline the other way. The 'concubinary' priests (intending also by that name the clerics who might have been secretly married) were condemned with special emphasis at Basel[4] (Jan. 22, 1435). On their conviction they were sentenced, after a brief respite, to the loss of their benefices, and in case of new offences made incapable at any future time of holding Church preferment. Still, it is too obvious, from the cries of sorrow, indignation, and disgust which rise in every quarter, that these stern injunctions were comparatively

Attempts to repress the scandal:

unsuccessful.

---

[1] See the evidence with regard to Spain in De Castro as above, p. xxix. Nicholas de Cleménges, *De corrupto Ecclesiæ statu*, after declaiming against the ignorance and vices of the other clergy, characterizes the canons as 'indoctos, simoniacos, cupidos...adhuc etiam ebriosos, *incontinentissimos*, utpote qui passim et inverecunde prolem ex meretrice susceptam et scorta vice conjugum domi tenent,' *etc.* Brown's *Fascic.* II. 563, 564. At the same period the 'Reforming College' of Constance passed many regulations with a view to the improvement of these latter. See Lenfant, liv. VII. c. 54.

[2] *e.g.* Cardinal Zabarella, in Von der Hardt, I. 524. Platina (*Vit. Pii II.* p. 311) represents that pope as saying, that if there were good reasons for prohibiting the marriage of priests, there were stronger reasons for allowing it: cf. his language in Brown's *Fascic.* I. 50.

[3] See his *Dialogus Sophiæ et Naturæ super cælibatu ecclesiasticorum* (*Opp.* II. 617 sq., ed. Du Pin). Gieseler, V. pp. 15—18, has collected numerous instances of the other kind in which the marriage of the clergy was advocated by individual writers throughout the fifteenth century.

[4] Mansi, XXIX. 101. This decree also condemns a pernicious custom of some bishops, who accepted a pecuniary fine from clergymen without compelling them to put away their mistresses. A similar complaint had been already made by the House of Commons in 1372 (*Rotul. Parl.* 46° Edw. III. p. 313). They prayed the king for remedy against ordinaries who took sums of money from ecclesiastics and others 'pur redemption de lour pecche de jour en jour et an en an, *de ce que ils tiendrent overtement leurs concubines*.' The evil was however unredressed, as we may learn, among other evidence, from a monstrous anecdote in Erasmus, *Opp.* IX. 401: ed. Le Clerc.

OTHER BRANCHES OF THE HIERARCHY.

futile¹. Individuals² there would doubtl[ess be]
a bright exception to the guilty mass; bu[t men]
at length woke up and felt that some [ot]her system was imperatively needed, if [it was to retain] her hold on the affections of mankind[,] so generally confessed³ as that presente[d by] the parochial clergy.

¹ A long catalogue of authorities will be found [in chap.] 11.
² Such, for instance, were not wanting in Spai[n: see] above, p. xxxv.
³ The committee of cardinals appointed by pop[e ... to] consider what could possibly be done 'de emendar[.. ad]verted in the first place on the incompetence an[d vices of] priests and other clerics: 'Hinc innumera scand[ala in] ordinis ecclesiastici, hinc Divini cultus veneratio [minuta,] sed etiam prope jam extincta.' Le Plat, Monum[. Conc. Trid.] 598 sq., Lovan. 1782: cf. the present writer's Hist[ory, vol.] 1, 2; new edition.

CHAPTER XV.

ON THE STATE OF RELIGIOUS DOCTRINE AND CONTROVERSIES.

WESTERN CHURCH.

THE leading theologians of this period may be ranged in one of two great classes. They are either *speculative*, bent on reaching the solution of dogmatic problems through the aid of Greek philosophy; or *mystical*, reposing on the old foundations of belief and shrinking from all dialectic processes by which the former school had long been struggling to prove the truth and reasonableness of Christianity.

The spirit of inquiry which had been so powerfully stimulated in the two preceding centuries continued to be active in the present. Some indeed, as heretofore[1], employed scholastic weapons merely for the purpose of defence, for vindicating the established doctrines of the Church, and urging them in such a manner as to satisfy the systematizing genius of the age. On men of this kind, treading in the reverential steps of Anselm and Aquinas, the effect of disputation would be often salutary: it imparted a more definite and scientific shape to their convictions. But another train of consequences might result from the scholastic exercises. An acute and daring mind, unsobered by religious culture, might convert them into an arena for evolving its own scepticism, and thus philosophy would prove herself the parent and the nurse of misbelief. Examples of these rationalistic tendencies appeared at an early date among the Nominalists, in Roscellinus, and still more in the disciples of Abelard. It was not, however, till the four-

marginalia: WESTERN CHURCH. Two great classes of theologians. Continuance of scholasticism. Development of sceptical tendencies.

[1] See above, pp. 257, 258.

WESTERN CHURCH.

Durand de S. Pourçain (d. 1333), 'Doctor resolutissimus.'

teenth century that some objections which had hitherto been stated hypothetically in the mock-encounters of the schools were deemed unanswerable by the men who put them forth. In other words, scholasticism, which had been ever liable to this perversion[1], not unfrequently broke out at last into rebellion and derided supernatural truth.

The nominalistic school, from which these tendencies were mainly to proceed, was now revived under Durand of S. Pourçain[2] (de S. Porciano), a Dominican and formerly a Thomist. But the second founder of it was a provincial of the English Franciscans, William of Ockham, born in Surrey, and in earlier life addicted to the principles of Scotus[3]. He was aptly characterized as

---

[1] Fred. von Schlegel (*Phil. of Hist.* pp. 375 sq., ed. 1847) maintains that the basis of the Aristotelian philosophy is essentially 'rationalistic,' and that even the genius of Aquinas could not bring it into harmony with revelation. The remark that a principle might be true in philosophy, and yet false in theology, betrays the doubt which scholasticism felt with respect to its own intimate tendencies. Comte (liv. VI. c. 10) affirms that the growing triumph of scholasticism was actually working the destruction of the theological philosophy and authority. It should be borne in mind, however, that the worst forms of misbelief sprang up at the end of the fifteenth century, when Platonism had gained predominance afresh: see below, p. 355. Several glimpses of an older unbelief, arising from the false philosophy then prevalent, occur in the works of Petrarch: *e.g.* in his *De ignorantia sui ipsius et multorum*, he writes of the philosophers whom he encountered, 'Submotis arbitris oppugnant veritatem et pietatem, clanculum in angulis irridentes Christum, atque Aristotelem, quem non intelligunt, adorantes,' *etc.*, *Opp.* III. 1048. The frightful length to which these blasphemies were carried at the close of the present period is illustrated by the following extract from a letter of Erasmus (lib. XXVI. ep. 34, *Opp.* ed. Le Clerc): 'At ego Romæ his auribus audivi quosdam abominandis blasphemiis debacchantes in Christum, et in Illius Apostolos, idque multis mecum audientibus et quidem impune. Ibidem multos novi, qui commemorabant, se dicta horrenda audisse a quibusdam sacerdotibus aulæ Pontificiæ ministris, idque in *ipsa missa*, tam clare ut ea vox ad multorum aures pervenerit.'

[2] The freedom of his mind is indicated by his title, 'Doctor resolutissimus' (cf. Schröckh, XXXIV. 191 sq.). On many points, especially the doctrine of the sacraments, he ventured to depart from Aquinas. He arrived at the conclusion (*Opus super Sententias Lombardi*, Lib. IV. Dist. I. Quæst. 4), that there is in a sacrament no 'virtus causativa gratiæ,' the recipients, where they place no bar, deriving grace 'non a sacramento sed a Deo.' He also excludes matrimony from the number of sacraments 'properly so called' (Lib. IV. Dist. XXVI. Quæst. 8). Cf. Gieseler, IV. § 116, p. 168, n. 1.

[3] According to Dorner (II. 446, 447), it was the Scotist-nominalists, and not the Thomist-nominalists, who placed religion altogether on the same footing as philosophy, and gave an impulse to freethinking.

the 'Invincible' and 'Singular Doctor.' We have seen the intrepidity with which he vindicated the imperial interest in opposition to the pope[1], and this desire to question every species of traditionary knowledge made him sometimes overleap the common boundaries by which the doctrines of the Church were guarded and defined. An ardent speculator on the nature of ideas, he contended finally that thought itself is but subjective,— a conclusion which could hardly fail to give the most pernicious handle to freethinkers of the day. Indeed an under-stream of scepticism[2] pervades his own productions. Ockham was vehemently opposed by many of the Realists[3], but notwithstanding all their censures and the formal inhibition of his writings in the University of Paris[4], the ascendancy of Nominalism as modified by him was everywhere apparent, more especially in Germany and England[5]. One of the last influential schoolmen,

WESTERN CHURCH.

William of Ockham (d. 1347), the 'Invincible.'

Spread of Ockhamism.

---

[1] Above, p. 325. It is indeed remarkable, though easily explained, that what are called the 'orthodox' scholastics took the side of Roman despotism, and that the nominalists were very often in the ranks of anti-papists. Foxe (*Acts and Mon.* II. 659, ed. Lond. 1843) says of Ockham, that he was 'a worthy divine, and of a right sincere judgment, as the times then would either give or suffer.' His book, *Super potestate prælatis Ecclesiæ atque principibus terrarum commissa*, was printed in England, in the reign of Henry VIII., in Latin, and also in an English translation. On this ground we may understand why Ockham was at first a special favourite of Luther and Melanchthon, while in doctrine they were often quite antagonistic to him. See Laurence, *Bampt. Lect.* p. 59 (note) 3rd ed. He seems, however, favourable to the Lutheran view of consubstantiation: see his *Quodlibeta Septem una cum Tractatu de Sacramento Altaris*, lib. IV. Quæst. 35, ed. Argent. 1491. In the latter treatise (c. 3) he says that the Bible does not teach us to believe in the annihilation of the substance of the bread: cf. Schröckh, XXXIV. 195 sq., and, on the philosophical system of Ockham, as developed in his *Quæstiones in Lib. Sentent.* (ed. Lugdun. 1495), and his *Centiloquium Theologicum* (ed. Oxon. 1675), see Ritter, *Gesch. der Christ. Philos.* IV. 579 sq.

[2] See an essay by Rettberg, in the *Studien und Kritiken* for 1839, I. 69 sq.

[3] *e.g.* by Walter Burley, a scholar of Oxford, and formerly his fellow-student.

[4] Thus, while John Buridan, his pupil, was 'rector' of the university, the 'doctrina Gulielmi dicti Occam' was condemned (1339): see Bulæus *Hist. Univ. Paris*, IV. 257, and, for a sterner prohibition, *Ibid.* IV. 265. In 1473 the Realists obtained a fresh victory by means of a royal order (*Ibid.* V. 706 sq.), which commanded that the books of their opponents should be locked up. But the order was rescinded in 1481 (*Ibid.* V. 739).

[5] Cf. Mr Hallam's remark on this circumstance: *Literat. of Europe*, Pt. I. ch. III. § 69.

WESTERN CHURCH.

Reaction against the Aristotelian scholastics.

Gabriel Biel[1], who died in **1495**, adhered almost implicitly to him. A less extended notice of these writers[2] will suffice, particularly as their disputations do not fall so much into the province of theology as into that of metaphysics.

It was natural, when scholasticism had almost everywhere degenerated into lifeless subtleties, that a new period of reaction would commence. We saw the jealousy with which it was discountenanced by Bernard[3] at the first, and in proportion as its vices came to light, a multitude of others turned their arms against it[4]. Some of them indeed may have been actuated mainly by a wish to introduce a purer love of letters, which was certainly the case with not a few of the Platonic illuminati, who revived the study of the pagan classics in the

---

[1] His chief work is a *Collectorium ex Occamo in Lib. Sentent.* ed. Tübingen, 1501. His *Expositio Canonis Missæ*, important in a liturgical point of view, has been printed more than once. On his *protestantism*, see a dissertation entitled *De Gabriele Biel celeberrimo papista Antipapista*, by H. W. Biel, Viteb. 1719. Biel was succeeded by Cortesius ('the Cicero of dogmatists'), on whom see Schröckh, xxxiv. 217 sq.

[2] Some of the chief were Robert Holcot, an Englishman (d. 1349), Gregory of Rimini, or Ariminensis (d. 1358), Richard Swineshead (or Suisset), an Oxford man (circ. 1350), Henry of Hesse (d. 1397). But they were all surpassed by Peter d'Ailly (cf. above, p. 333), who was made a cardinal in 1411. He laboured to establish clear distinctions between theology and philosophy. See his *Quæstiones super Lib. Sentent.*, Argent. 1490, and a list of his other numerous works in Cave, *Hist. Liter.* ad an. 1396. A *Life* of him by Du Pin is contained in the first volume of Gerson's *Works*, ed. Du Pin.

[3] Above, p. 257, n. 2.

[4] This antagonism was shewn emphatically in Erasmus (b. 1486), whose *Moriæ Encomium* (1508), his *Ratio perveniendi ad veram Theologiam*, and other works, are full of severe critiques on the follies of the later schoolmen. He had been preceded by Laurentius Valla (*Opp.* Basil. 1543), who died in 1457, by Rodolph Agricola, or Hausmann, d. 1485 (*Opp.* Colon. 1539). One of his contemporaries who took the same side, was Ulrich von Hutten, d. 1523 (*Opp.* Berol. 1821—5). This German knight had a principal hand in the famous satires *Epistolæ Obscurorum Virorum* (ed. Münch, 1827), in which the stupidity and dog-Latin of the mendicant friars, and their loud outcries respecting the luxuries of the Humanists, are described so naturally and truthfully, that the Dominicans at first joined in circulating the book. See Gieseler, v. § 154, pp. 199 sq. Luther at the same time was able to rejoice that the 'lectiones sententiariæ' were despised, and that professors who wished to gain an audience must lecture on the Bible, St Augustine, 'aliumve Ecclesiasticæ auctoritatis doctorem.' See his *Letters*, ed. De Wette, I. 57.

second half of the fifteenth century[1]. They strove to banish the Stagyrite[2] and enthrone a more congenial philosophy in the affections of the Church. That movement failed, however, to revive the ancient truths of Christianity. Its general aim was heathenizing, more especially as it has been developed in the works of men like Marsilio Ficino, the favourite of the Medici, and others, who not only clothed the doctrines of the Gospel in the phraseology of Cicero and Horace, but were threatening to exalt their Grecian master into rivalry with Christ. So prevalent had errors of this class become, that in the eighth session of the Lateran council[3] (Dec. **19, 1513**) it was necessary to declare the immortality of individual souls (in opposition to the Platonic views of ultimate absorption), and to order all who might profess to teach the doctrines of the old philosophy that they should never hesitate to point out the particulars in which it differed from the Christian faith. The need of this injunction was peculiarly great in Italy[4], where learning in the fifteenth century, and, more than ever, at the dawn of Luther's reformation, threatened to assume an anti-christian character,—where wanton speculations had become most rife, and where indeed it was an index of good breeding to despise the mysteries of Holy Writ[5].

Western Church.

Revival of Platonism.

Its heretical tendencies:

especially in Italy.

But meanwhile other agents were at work in many parts of Germany. The studies of ecclesiastics had there taken a more distinctly biblical direction. Men who learned to know themselves were thirsting[6] after something more

Mystical school of theologians.

---

[1] See Roscoe's *Life of Leo X.* II. 87 sq., Lond. 1846; Hallam, *Lit. of Europe*, Pt. I. ch. II. § 64, and ch. III. § 85. Ficino, however, wrote an apologetic treatise, *De Religione Christiana*, analysed by Schröckh, XXXIV. 342 sq.

[2] Hallam, *Ibid.* ch. III. §§ 13 sq. Pico of Mirandola at one time would have fain established the consistency of the Aristotelian and Platonic systems: but his own leanings were towards the latter, which he blended with a multitude of wild opinions borrowed from the Cabbalistic writings of the Jews: see his *Heptaplus*, Basil. 1601.

[3] Labbe, XIV. 187.

[4] Cf. the extract from Erasmus, above, p. 352, n. 1, and others in Gieseler, v. § 154, pp. 181, 182, n. 8.

[5] 'In quel tempo non pareva fosse galantuomo e buon cortegiano colui che de dogmi della Chiesa non aveva *qualche opinione erronea ed heretica.*' MS. quoted in Ranke, *Popes*, I. 56, Lond. 1847.

[6] 'Nam quid potest ibi syncerum dici, ubi pro religione superstitio, pro divina sapientia hominum philosophia, pro Christo Socrates, pro

profound than the scholastic subtleties, more fervent than the cloudy reveries of Plato. Such was the new race of mystics. Here and there we find them swerving into serious errors[1], but more commonly they are distinguished by a simple and unreasoning adherence to the central doctrines of the faith, combining with it a peculiar earnestness and a desire to elevate the tone of personal religion. In the members, therefore, of this school (the 'Friends of God' as they were called) we may discern precursors[2] of a genuine reformation.

At the head of them is John Tauler[3], a Dominican of Cologne. He was originally captivated by the dialectic studies of the age, and the effect of them continued to be traceable in all his writings: but his intercourse with a Waldensian[4], Nicholas of Basel (1340), produced a thorough change in his convictions and pursuits. For twenty years he was an indefatigable preacher, stimulated[5], as it seems, by the political distractions of his country and the ravages of a terrific pestilence ('the black death'). His thrilling sermons[6], of which many were preserved in the vernacular dialects, are marked by evangelic tenderness and

sacris scriptoribus Aristoteles atque Plato in Ecclesiam irruperunt. Neque hæc ita intelligi velim, quasi reprehendam philosophiæ studium... sed sic se res habet, ut, nisi divinitatis cognitio præmonstratrix, mens ipsa hominis errans et vaga ad loca spinosa deviaque deducatur.' Sturmius *ad Cardinales delectos;* Argentor. 1538.

[1] *e.g.* Master Eckart (Aichard), a Dominican of Cologne, who died about 1325, and was one of a class of mystics who diverged into Neo-Platonism, affirming, for example, that our individuality would be forfeited at last on our reabsorption into the Divine essence. See Schmidt, *Etudes sur le mysticisme allemand au xiv*ᵉ *siècle*, à Paris, 1847, pp. 12 sq.; Neander, IX. 569 sq., and Ritter, *Christl. Philos.* IV. 498 sq. Some of the doctrines of Eckart were condemned in a bull of John XXII. (1329): see Raynald. ad an. 1329, §§ 70, 71.

[2] See Ullmann's *Reformatoren vor der Reformation,* Hamb. 1841 and 1842.

[3] See especially Schmidt's *Johannes Tauler von Strassburg,* Hamb. 1841, and his French Essay quoted in a previous note.

[4] On this point, see Neander, IX. 563 sq.

[5] *Ibid.* p. 588.

[6] The last (modernized) edition was printed at Frankfort, 1826, in 3 vols. octavo. Luther (1516) spoke of them as follows: 'Si te delectat puram, solidam, *antiquæ simillimam theologiam* legere in Germanica lingua effusam, Sermones Johannis Tauleri, prædicatoriæ professionis [*i.e.* a Dominican], tibi comparare potes...Neque enim ego vel in Latina vel in nostra lingua theologiam vidi salubriorem et cum Evangelio consonantiorem.' Luther's *Letters,* ed. De Wette, I. 46.

spiritual depth. They were peculiarly useful in resisting the general tendency to overvalue the liturgic element of worship.   *WESTERN CHURCH.*

Tauler will be found to have had numerous points in common with John Ruysbroek[1], prior of the Canons-Regular at Groenendaele near Brussels. He was equally desirous of conforming to the public institutions of the Church[2], although his language more than once excited a suspicion of his orthodoxy. Gerson[3] wrote (1406) against some chapters of a book in which the doctrine of eventual absorption into God appears to be maintained. The works[4] of Ruysbroek, in the Flemish language, were extensively circulated. They are characterized by thorough knowledge of the spiritual wants and aberrations of the age. He strove to wake afresh the consciousness of individual fellowship with God, in opposition to the modes of thought which prompted men to lean for help on outward union with the Church. The faults of Ruysbroek   *John Ruysbroek (d. 1381), 'doctor ecstaticus.'*

---

[1] See Schmidt, *Etudes sur le mysticisme*, etc. pp. 213 sq., Schröckh, xxxiv. 274 sq., and Neander ix. 579 sq. His works appeared in a Latin translation at Cologne, 1552, and subsequently.

[2] Extracts in Neander, pp. 556, 557.

[3] The title is *Epist. super tertia parte libri Joh. Ruysbroech de ornatu spiritualium nuptiarum*, Opp. I. 59, ed. Du Pin, where the remainder of the controversy will be found.

[4] They were translated into Latin (ed. Colon. 1552) and afterwards into German (Offenbach, 1701): cf. Schmidt, *Etudes* (as above), pp. 213 sq., Neander ix. 580 sq. A third writer of this school was Henry Suso (1300—1365), a Dominican of Swabia, on whom see Diepenbrock, *Suso's Leben und Schriften*, Regensburg, 1837. Many other Dominicans followed in his steps. Thomas à Kempis, one of the 'Common-Life' clerics (see above, p. 348, and Schröckh, xxxv. 302—339), may be added to the number, and so may the unknown author [? Ebland] of the famous treatise, *Eyn teutsch Theologia, das ist, eyn edles Büchlein vom rechten Verstand*, etc., edited by Luther in 1518. He says, in the Preface, that next to the Bible and St Augustine (his usual mode of speaking) there was no book he prized more highly. The best modern edition is that of Biesenthal, Berlin, 1842: another by Pfeiffer (Roman Catholic), Stuttgart, 1851. In England the mystical school, though far less influential, had a worthy representative in the hermit Richard Rolle, of Hampole, near Doncaster, who died in 1348. Very many of his writings are poetical. See Wharton's *Append.* to Cave, ad an. 1340, and Warton's *Hist. of Eng. Poetry*, II. 35—43, ed. 1840. The treatise *De Emendatione Vitæ* (printed at Paris, 1510) furnishes a good specimen of his teaching, *e.g.* cap. IX.: 'Si cupis ad amorem Dei pervenire et succendi in desiderio cœlestium gaudiorum, et induci ad contemptum terrenorum, non sis negligens ad meditandum et legendum sacram Scripturam.' Several of his English Treatises have been printed by the Early English Text Society.

marginalia:
WESTERN CHURCH.

John Gerson (1363—1429), 'doctor Christianissimus.'

Savonarola (1452—1498).

---

are the common faults of mystical writers, springing from undue development of the imaginative faculty.

John Charlies de Gerson, chancellor of Paris (1395), whom we have noticed as an adversary of the ultra-papal claims[1], and also as opposed in some degree to Ruysbroek, was himself upon the whole addicted to the principles of mysticism[2]. But many of his writings indicate especial aptness for discussing points of practical Christianity[3]. He was the most illustrious theologian of the time, and even now is generally revered. The part, however, which he played at Constance in promoting the condemnation of Huss[4] must ever be a grievous stain upon his character. He died in virtual exile[5] at Lyons, 1429.

Another mystic of a warmer temperament than Gerson, but deficient in his mental balance, was the Dominican, Girolamo Savonarola[6], born in 1452 at Ferrara. Some of his contemporaries, it is true, denounce him as a wild and visionary demagogue[7], but the majority bear witness

---

[1] Above, p. 333.

[2] See, for example, his *De Mystica Theologia*, and other kindred treatises in the collection of his *Works* by Du Pin, tom. III. pt. II. But he never failed to guard against the feverish illusions of enthusiasm: thus he wrote *Contra sectam Flagellantium;* and also *De probatione Spirituum*, giving rules for distinguishing false from true revelations. Cf. Schröckh, XXXIV. 291—302.

[3] On this account he was surnamed 'Doctor Christianissimus.' Schmidt has published an able *Essai sur Jean Gerson*, Paris, 1839.

[4] Lenfant, liv. III. § 5. It was of him that Huss wrote as follows: 'O si Deus daret tempus scribendi contra mendacia Parisiensis Cancellarii, qui tam temerarie et injuste coram tota multitudine non est veritus proximum erroribus annotare.' *Ibid.*

[5] Ibid. liv. VI. § 82: On his return from his asylum at Mölk, he exercised the humble office of catechizer of children, whom he collected daily in the church of St Paul at Lyons, and of whom he required no other reward than that they should repeat this simple prayer, 'God, have mercy on thy poor servant, Gerson.'

[6] A *Life* of him by Pico of Mirandola, his friend, is contained in the *Vit. Select. Virorum*, ed. Bates, Lond. 1681, pp. 108 sq. But the best accounts are that in Sismondi, *Hist. des Répub. Ital.* tome XII.; Meier's *Girolamo Savonarola*, Berlin, 1836; *The Life and Times of Girolamo Savonarola* (containing a complete catalogue of his writings), Lond. 1843; *Jérôme Savonarole, sa vie, ses prédications, ses écrits*, d'après les documens originaux, par F. T. Perrens, Paris, 1853; see also an Article on Savonarola in *Quart. Rev.* No. CXCVII.

[7] He laid especial stress on the Apocalypse, which, after 1485, he expounded at Brescia, Florence, and elsewhere to crowded audiences; denouncing the vengeance of heaven against Italy, and even claiming to himself a kind of prophetic mission (see *Life and Times*, as above, pp.

to his patriotism, his zeal, his learning, and his saintly life. The fiery eloquence of Savonarola was evoked[1] by the unparalleled corruption of the Roman see, as then administered by Innocent VIII. and Alexander VI. How many elements of superstition and fanaticism had been unconsciously blended with his nobler feelings is not easy to determine: but the freedom of his speech[2] in censuring the vices and disputing the infallibility of the pope has never been denied. In May, **1497**, when he was laid under the ban of excommunication[3], he answered the papal brief in letters full of vehement remonstrances, and even ultimately dared[4] to excommunicate the pope in turn (Feb. **18, 1498**). His capture, prompted by the rage of his political adversaries, followed on the eighth of April, and soon afterwards his ashes were thrown into the Arno at Florence (May **22**), with the sanction, if not through the instigation, of Alexander VI[5]. Savonarola has been called the Luther[6] of Italy: but his eventual implication in the quarrels of the Florentines proved fatal both to him and to his cause.

A truer prototype of Luther was John Wessel[7] (surnamed Basilius and also Gansfort), born at Gröningen

---

97 sq., and Savonarola's *Compendium Revelationum*). He became the head of the Frateschi, or republican, party at Florence, who endeavoured to avert the judgments of God by checking the fearful spread of immorality (*Ibid.* p. 155).

[1] Even Döllinger (IV. 227) admits this, and praises 'the eloquent and venerated Dominican.'

[2] *Life and Times*, as above, pp. 267 sq. His invectives were also directed generally against the prelates of the church. 'Illorum libidinem avaritiamque, illorum luxus simoniacasque labes insectabatur, publice privatimque monere solitus, a Babylone (Romam intelligens) fugiendum esse,' etc. *Vit. Select. Viror.* as above, p. 118.

[3] It was now that Pico of Mirandola wrote his *Apologia pro Hieronymi Savonarolæ viri prophetæ Innocentia*, which is printed in Goldast's *Monarch.* II. 1635 sq.

[4] *Life and Times*, pp. 320—322.   [5] *Ibid.* p. 354.

[6] Attempts have been made, but not successfully, to prove that he held the Lutheran view of justification, indulgences, &c.: cf. M'Crie's *Reformation in Italy*, p. 18, Lond. 1827.

[7] The best authority is Ullmann's *Johann Wessel, ein Vorgänger Luthers*, Hamb. 1834, and in the *Reformatoren vor der Reformation*, Hamb. 1842. The *Works* of Wessel (with a *Life* prefixed) were published at Gröningen, 1614. He is not to be confounded with his acquaintance *Johann von Wesel* (de Wesalia), called also Richrath and Burchardus, who was a professor of theology at Erfurt and afterwards a 'reforming' preacher at Worms. He died in prison (1482), as it seems, for

(1420). After studying and then lecturing in the universities of Heidelberg, Paris, Rome, and elsewhere, he grew dissatisfied with the scholastic theology, and took refuge in a warm but scientific mysticism. On almost every point, on justification, penance, purgatory, and even on the Eucharist, he has anticipated the conclusions of those earnest spirits[1] who were destined to commence the Saxon reformation of the Church. John Wessel was alike distinguished as a theologian and as a general scholar. He died in peace at Gröningen (1489), protected from the Inquisition by the bishop of Utrecht.

In Wessel, as in many of his predecessors, there had been awakened a fresh love for biblical studies. This alone had constituted in their hearts a bond of sympathy with men like Wycliffe and the Hussites, more especially perhaps in Germany, where versions of the Holy Scriptures had been made, and very largely circulated[2], in the latter half of the fifteenth century. Before that time the only critical works deserving notice[3] are the *Postills* of Nicholas de Lyra[4], a Franciscan, who applied his Hebrew knowledge

holding intercourse with the Hussites. For his *Paradoxa* and the proceedings against him, see Brown's *Fascic.* I. 325—333, and Ullmann, *Reform. vor der Ref.* I. 367 sq. His *Disputatio adversus Indulgentias* is printed in Walch, *Monim. Med. Ævi*, I. 111 sq. He denied the supremacy of the Roman Church, and asserted that of Holy Scripture: but, as John Wessel lamented (*Opp.* ed. 1614), p. 920, his 'eruditio et peracre ingenium' not unfrequently betrayed him into novelties. His 'reforming' principles were shared in some measure by the prior of a nunnery at Malines, John Pupper of Goch, near Cleves (d. 1475). Respecting him and others, see Ullmann, as above, and for some of his writings, Walch, *Monim. Med. Ævi*, II. pt. I. 1 sq., and IV. 73 sq.

[1] See, for instance, the extracts in Gieseler, v. § 153, pp. 172 sq., n. 18. Luther wrote the preface to a *Farrago* of his works, ed. Basil. 1522, and expressed himself in the following terms (which furnished Ullmann with a motto): 'Wenn ich den Wessel zuvor gelesen, so liessen meine Widersacher sich dünken, Luther hätte Alles vom Wessel genommen, *also stimmet unser Beider Geist* zusammen.'

[2] *e.g.* the old High-German version, printed first at Mentz, 1462, was reprinted *ten* times before the Reformation (see other evidence in Gieseler, v. § 146, p. 74, n. 13). In like manner an Italian version, printed at Venice as early as 1471, is said to have gone through *nine* editions in the fifteenth century (see M'Crie's *Reform. in Italy*, p. 53, Lond. 1827).

[3] Exceptions may be made in favour of the English Dominican Robert Holcot (d. 1349), on whose exegetical and other works, see Wharton's *Append.* to Cave's *Hist. Liter.* ad an. 1340; and of the Spanish prelate, Tostatus of Avila (d. 1454), on whom, see Schröckh, XXXIV. 147 sq.

[4] His *Postillæ Perpetuæ in Biblia* have been often published, first at Rome, 1471, in 5 vols. folio.

with effect to the elucidation of the Old Testament, and Gerson, who was led by corresponding works of St Augustine to construct a Harmony of the Four Gospels[1]. But on the resuscitation of the ancient literature and the discovery of printing, stronger impulses were communicated in this direction. The superior scholarship and taste of Laurentius Valla[2], cardinal Ximenes[3], Reuchlin[4], Erasmus[5], and others, indicated that a brighter period was now dawning on the field of scriptural hermeneutics. Though it be unfair to urge that men were wholly unacquainted with the Bible in the times anterior to the Reformation, we may safely argue that the Reformation was itself a consequence of the enlightenment which biblical inquiries had produced.

WESTERN CHURCH.

Gerson (d. 1429).

Laurentius Valla (d. 1451). Ximenes (d. 1522). Reuchlin (d. 1522). Erasmus (d. 1536).

EASTERN CHURCH.

As there was almost nothing in the Eastern Churches corresponding to the Middle Ages in the West, we meet with nothing like the healthy series of reactions just described. The present period was indeed more sterile and monotonous than all which went before it. Scarcely any theological writers[6] of importance can be traced excepting

Scarcity of great writers.

---

[1] This work is entitled *Monotessaron, seu unum ex quatuor Evangeliis:* Gerson, *Opp.* ed. Du Pin, iv. 83 sq. He looks upon the variations in the Sacred Writers as constituting a 'concordissima dissonantia.'

[2] His entire works were printed at Basel in 1540. The chief of them in this connexion (cf. above, p. 354, n. 4) is the series of *Annotationes in Novum Testamentum*, which display great critical ability. His work, *De Libero Arbitrio*, and still more the famous *Declamatio de falso credita et ementita Constantini Donatione* (cf. above, p. 254, n. 3), have laid him open to Bellarmine's charge of being a precursor of the Lutherans.

[3] Cf. above, p. 318. His sagacity and zeal in the preparation of the Complutensian Polyglott (1514—1517) were beyond all praise: see Schröckh, xxxiv. 81 sq. The papal sanction was, however, withheld until after the cardinal's death in 1522.

[4] Reuchlin's fame is mainly due to his restoration of *Hebrew* literature, in which he was bitterly opposed by many of the German monks. (See Maii *Vit. Reuchlini*, passim.) Against them are directed the most cutting satires of the *Epistolæ Obscurorum Virorum* (see above, p. 354, n. 4). Reuchlin's Hebrew grammar and lexicon were published in 1506: and in 1518 a fine edition of the Hebrew Bible appeared at Venice. M'Crie, *Reform. in Italy*, p. 40.

[5] His edition of the New Testament appeared at Basel in 1516: *Ibid.* pp. 47 sq. The mighty influence which his theological works exerted on the Reformation, more especially in England, where his caution was appreciated, belongs in strictness to the following period.

[6] To Church-history an important contribution was made by Nice-

those who figured in the controversy with the Latin Church.

The most distinguished of the biblical scholars was Theophanes[1], archbishop of Nicæa, who composed a *Harmony of the Old and New Testament*, and also an elaborate *Apology*, directing both of them against the Jews. A monk of Thessalonica, Simeon[2], wrote a *Dialogue against all Heresies*, and many other works in vindication of the 'orthodox' (or Greek) communion. George of Trebizond, a somewhat copious author[3], added to the stock of evidences in a book on the *Truth of Christianity*.

The state of feeling in the great majority of Eastern Christians was so torpid as to cause but few internal ruptures. The Strigolniks[4] of Russia, who in 1371 and afterwards obtained a host of proselytes at Novogorod, are the only formidable sect that sprang up in this period. They were bitterly opposed to all the members of the sacerdotal order, and their tenets, in some points at least, resemble those now current with the English 'Lollards.'

But another controversy[5], that broke out in the neighbourhood of Constantinople, also merits our attention, yielding as it does some insight into the prevailing modes of thought. A party of the monks who swarmed upon the 'Holy Mountain' (Athos)[6], in their contemplations on

---

phorus Callisti Xanthopuli (circ. 1333), whose work in eighteen books extends from the Incarnation to the death of Phocas (610): see Dowling's *Introd. to Eccl. Hist.* pp. 91 sq., Lond. 1838.

[1] See Wharton's *Append.* to Cave, ad an. 1347.

[2] *Ibid.* ad an. 1410. Leo Allatius (the Romanizer) writes, with reference to Simeon's *Dialogus*, that it is 'pius et doctus, dignusque qui aliquando lucem videat, *sed manuductus a Catholico.*' *De Simeonum Scriptis Diatriba*, p. 193. Another work of this Simeon is *On the Faith and Sacraments of the Church*, printed, according to Schröckh (xxxiv. 427), in Moldavia (1683) with the authority of Dositheus, patriarch of Jerusalem.

[3] Wharton, as above, ad an. 1440, and Leo Allatius, *De Georgiis Diatriba*, pp. 395 sq.

[4] See Mouravieff, ed. Blackmore, pp. 65, 379, 380. They maintained that all Christians are invested with the rights of priesthood, and elected their own teachers from among themselves. They also denied the necessity of confession, and made no prayers and offerings for the dead.

[5] On this controversy, see Schröckh, xxxiv. 431—451; Engelhardt, *Die Arsenianer* [cf. above, p. 272, n. 3] *und Hesychasten*, in Illgen's *Zeitschrift*, Bd. VIII. st. i. pp. 48 sq.; Dorner, *Lehre von der Person Christi*, II. 292—297.

[6] Since the 9th century Mount Athos has been covered with monas-

the blessedness of 'seeing God,' were led to argue that the Christian may arrive at a tranquillity of mind entirely free from perturbation, and that all enjoying such a state may hold an ocular intercourse with God Himself, as the Apostles were supposed to do when they beheld His glory shining forth in the Transfiguration of our Lord. These mystics bore the name of Quietists, or Hesychasts[1] ('Ησυχασταί). They were vehemently assailed[2] by Barlaam (circ. **1341**), a learned monk of the order of St Basil, and in all his earlier life a staunch defender of the Eastern Church[3]. His strictures roused the indignation of Gregorius Palamas[4], afterwards the archbishop-designate of Thessalonica; by whose influence several councils[5], held at Constantinople (**1341–1350**), were induced to shelter, if not absolutely patronize, the Quietists. Their censor, driven to revoke his acrimonious charges, instantly seceded to the Western Church[6], where he became the bishop of Gerace in Calabria. The Hesychastic school was thus enabled to achieve a triumph. They were generally supported by the eastern theologians[7]; among others by the celebrated mystic, Nicholas Cabasilas, archbishop also of Thessalonica (circ. **1350**). His important treatise on *The Life in Christ*[8] is now accessible to scholars.

opened by Barlaam (circ. 1341). Resistance of Gregorius Palamas,

and Nicholas Cabasilas.

teries. See their number and condition (in 1836) described in Curzon's *Visit to Monasteries in the Levant*, Lond. 1849, pp. 356 sq.

[1] Other names given to them by their opponents were Massalians (above, p. 282, n. 4), and Ὀμφαλόψυχοι (Umbilicanimi). The latter seems to have referred to their custom of sitting still and gazing on the pit of their stomach (not unlike some of the Hindu and other heathen ascetics).

[2] Joh. Cantacuzenus, *Hist.* lib. II. c. 39; Niceph. Gregoras, *Hist. Byzant.* lib. XI. c. 10.

[3] See, for instance, his Περὶ τῆς τοῦ Πάπα ἀρχῆς, ed. Salmasius, Lugdun. 1645.

[4] Joh. Cantacuzenus, *Ibid.* On his other writings, see Wharton's *Append.* to Cave, ad an. 1354.

[5] (1341), Mansi. xxv. 1147; (1347), xxvi. 105; (1350), *ib.* 127.

[6] Cantacuzenus, lib. II. c. 40; Niceph. Gregoras, *Ibid.* Some of the *Letters* which he wrote on the Western side of the controversy are printed in Canisius, *Lect. Antiq.*, ed. Basnage, IV. 361 sq. Other instances of secession to the Latin Church occur now and then.

[7] Cf. Schröckh, xxxiv. 449, 450.

[8] See Gass, *Die Mystik des Nicolaus Cabasilas vom Leben in Christo*, Griefswald, 1849: Wharton, as above, ad an. 1350. Among other works in vindication of the Greek Church, he wrote a treatise on the Procession of the Holy Ghost, in answer to Aquinas (cf. above, p. 281, n. 2).

RELATIONS OF THE EASTERN AND WESTERN CHURCHES.

Relations of East and West.

Eastern antipathy to the Latin Church.

The ancient resolution to maintain their freedom in defiance of the Roman court was still the general feeling of the eastern Christians. Some of them, for instance Nilus Cabasilas[1], who had preceded his nephew Nicholas in the archiepiscopal chair of Thessalonica, wrote with temper and ability. But in proportion as the Turks were menacing Constantinople, it became the policy of the enfeebled emperors to win the favour of the Latin Churches. This could only be effected by the healing of the schism.

Reopening of negotiations.

Negociations were accordingly reopened as early as 1333. In 1339 Andronicus III. Palæologus[2] dispatched a formal embassy to Benedict XII. at Avignon. The leader of this party was the monk Barlaam, who, as we have seen[3], immediately afterwards passed over to the Western Church. His mission was, however, fruitless in respect of his fellow-countrymen at large: and though another emperor, John VI. Palæologus, betook himself in person[4] to the court of Rome (1369), and by his abject homage to pope Urban V. endeavoured to awake the sympathy

Visit of John VI. Palæologus to Rome, 1369.

---

[1] His works, *De Causis Divisionum in Ecclesia* and *De Primatu Papæ* (translated into English, Lond. 1560), were edited by Salmasius, Hanov. 1608. He also wrote at great length *De Processione S. Spiritus adversus Latinos*: see Leo Allatius, *Diatriba de Nilis*, p. 49. Another Nilus (surnamed Damyla), circ. 1400, wrote several treatises on kindred subjects, but in a more bitter spirit: see Wharton's *Append.* to Cave, ad an. 1400.

[2] On the earlier correspondence, see Raynald. ad an. 1333, §§ 17 sq., and Gibbon, ch. LXVI. §§ 19 sq.) In 1339 (Raynald. ad an. §§ 19 sq.) the Greeks promise, 'Quæcunque a generali concilio determinata fuerint, omnes orientales libenter hæc recipient.' They also begged that the mode of stating the Procession of the Holy Ghost might be left an open question; but the Latins answered, that this would be to violate the unity of the faith ('quia in Ecclesia Catholica, in qua una fides esse noscitur, quoad hoc duplicem fidem minus veraciter esset dare'). With regard to the papal supremacy, Benedict intimated that the only way to 'auxilia, consilia, et favores,' was by cordially returning to 'the obedience of the Roman church.' A fresh embassy was sent to Avignon by Cantacuzenus (see his own *Hist.* lib. IV. c. 9), for the sake of negociating a union with Clement VI. (1348); but it also was fruitless.

[3] Above, p. 363.

[4] Raynald. ad an. 1369, § 1 sq. He had already (1355) bound himself by a secret oath to become 'fidelis, obediens, reverens, et devotus beatissimo patri et domino, domino Innocentio sacrosanctæ Romanæ ac universalis Ecclesiæ .... summo pontifici et ejus successoribus.' Raynald. ad an. 1355, § 34: cf. Gibbon, ch. LXVI. (VI. 217—220, ed. Milman).

of European princes, his defection from the Eastern Church produced no spiritual nor temporal results. His son, Manuel II., notwithstanding a fresh canvass for auxiliaries[1] in Italy, France, Germany, and England (1400 –1402), was unshaken in his predilections for the creed and worship of his fathers[2]. The invasions of Timur (or Tamerlane), who conquered Anatolia in 1402, and thus diverted[3] for a while the onslaught of the Turks, relieved the emperor from the necessity of forming an alliance with the west; but, danger having finally become more imminent than ever, a fresh series of negociations were commenced (1434) under John VII. Palæologus, his son.

This monarch, after some preliminaries, undertook to hold another conference with the Latin Church beyond the Adriatic; and when he was driven to determine[4] whether the true channel of communication were the Roman pontiff or the council of Basel, an accident eventually threw him into the arms of the former. He was carried off in triumph to the council of Ferrara (Feb. 28, 1438), attended by twenty-one eastern prelates, in addition to the patriarch of Constantinople[5]. The chief spokesmen on his side were

RELATIONS OF EAST AND WEST.

Anti-Roman bias of his son.

Fresh negociations under John VII. Palæologus. 1434.– 1438.

Council of Ferrara, 1438.

---

[1] Gibbon, *Ibid.* pp. 220—222. On account of the papal schism (above, p. 328) the emperor had studiously avoided committing himself to either party, and indeed that circumstance facilitated his application to the different courts.

[2] He even wrote twenty *Dialogues* in its defence: Leo Allatius, *De Eccl. Occident. et Orient. Perpet. Consensione*, p. 854. In 1418, however, he appears to have sent an embassy, headed by the archbishop of Kieff, to the council of Constance, where the Greeks were allowed to perform Divine Service according to their rite. See Lenfant, *Hist. du Concile de Const.* liv. VI. ch. 44.

[3] Cf. Miller's *History philosophically illustrated*, II. 371, 3rd edit.

[4] Both the council and the pope (cf. above, p. 337) had sent vessels to fetch the emperor from Constantinople, but the pope's galleys anticipated the other by a few days, and thus in all probability decided a most critical question as to the relations of the East and West in future ages. The admiral of the pope's galleys was his nephew, who had received instructions ἵνα πολεμήσῃ ὅπου ἂν εὕρῃ τὰ κάτεργα τῆς Συνόδου, καί, εἰ δυνήθῃ, καταδύσῃ καὶ ἀφανίσῃ. See on the whole subject the work of Syropulus (circ. 1444), *Vera Hist. unionis non veræ inter Græcos et Latinos*, ed. Creyghton, Hagæ Comitis, 1660, and the *Acts* of the councils of Ferrara and Florence, in Labbe, XIII. 1 sq.: cf. Schröckh, XXXIV. 413 sq.

[5] The Russian church at this time was governed by a metropolitan of Kieff, called Isidore, who had been appointed at Constantinople under Romanizing influences. He went to the council of Ferrara in spite of the misgivings of king Basil, and at length espoused the tenets of the

RELATIONS OF EAST AND WEST.

Mark of Ephesus, Dionysius of Sardis, and Bessarion of Nicæa. Legates also were accredited for the occasion by Philotheus of Alexandria and Dorotheus of Antioch; while Joachim of Jerusalem entrusted his subscription to Mark of Ephesus.

The pope (Eugenius IV.) was not generally present in the council, after the second session (March 15); but he left behind him two accomplished advocates, the cardinal Juliano[1], who had now retreated from the synod of Basel, and Andrew, the Latin bishop of Rhodes. The scheme of questions to be handled by the deputies consisted of the following heads: (1) the Procession of the Holy Spirit, (2) the addition of the clause *Filioque* to the Constantinopolitan creed, (3) Purgatory and the intermediate state, (4) the use of unleavened bread in the holy Eucharist, (5) the jurisdiction of the Roman see and the supremacy of the pope. A long delay occurred before the actual business of the conference was opened, owing to the thin attendance[2] of the western prelates at Ferrara. But in the following autumn (Oct. 8), when the vigour of the Basel assembly was declining, a debate[3] was held respecting the first point of controversy. It continued, with some interruptions, till the synod was at length transferred, by reason of the plague, to Florence.

Subjects of discussion.

Synod transferred to Florence, 1439.

There the sessions were resumed on Feb. 26, 1439, and with them the discussions as to the Procession of the Holy Ghost. The Latin arguments, adduced by the provincial of the Dominicans in Lombardy, were stigmatized at

---

western theologians. On his return, however, decorated with the Roman purple, he was for a while shut up in a monastery; but escaping thence took refuge with the pope. Mouravieff, pp. 76—78.

[1] See above, p. 334, and p. 336, n. 4.

[2] In the first session before the arrival of the Greeks there were present only cardinal Juliano, five archbishops, eighteen bishops, ten abbots, and some generals of monastic orders. Many of the European princes were in favour of the council of Basel (see above, p. 337), and Charles VII. of France, in particular, at first forbade any of his subjects to go to Ferrara.

[3] Andrew of Rhodes contended at great length in the 6th session (Oct. 20) that the clause *Filioque*, which the Greeks regarded as a mere addition, was in truth an explication, or necessary consequence, of what had been maintained from the beginning. In the next session (Oct. 25) he illustrated his remark by the enlargement of the Nicene Creed at Constantinople in 381.

length as absolutely heretical by Mark of Ephesus[1], but on the other hand Bessarion[2] owned himself a convert to the western doctrine, which he now proceeded to defend with vigour. A decree[3], embodying his conclusions, was put forward, pledging all who signed it to believe that the Holy Spirit is eternally from the Father and the Son, and that His essence is eternally from Both as from One principle, and by one only spiration ('tamquam ab uno principio et unica spiratione'): or, in different language, that the Son is verily the Cause, or principle, of the subsistence of the Holy Spirit equally with the Father. It was next conceded by the Easterns that unleavened bread as well as leavened might be lawfully and efficaciously employed in celebrating the Eucharist[4]. The Latin theories on purgatory also were admitted, the new definition being, that the soul of every penitent who dies in the love of God, before he has made satisfaction for his past misdeeds by bringing forth the fruits of penitence, is aided after death by prayers and other offerings which the faithful make in his behalf; while he himself is undergoing pains ('pœnis purgatoriis') in order to his final purification and reception into heaven[5]. Whether this effect be due to elemental fire or other agents, is

RELATIONS OF EAST AND WEST.

Secession to the Latin side.

Decrees on the Procession:

on unleavened bread:

on Purgatory:

---

[1] Respecting him and his numerous anti-Latin writings, see Wharton's *Append.* to Cave, ad an. 1436. His *Epistola de Synodo Florentina ad omnes Christianos* is printed, in the reply of Joseph, bp. of Methone, in Labbe, XIII. pp. 677 sq. Another Greek declared on this occasion, when a threat had been applied to make him surrender his belief: 'Mori malo, quam unquam Latinizare.'

[2] See Wharton, as above. Bessarion became a Roman cardinal, and on the death of Nicholas V. (1455) was on the point of succeeding to the popedom. His munificence and abilities contributed much to the diffusion of Greek literature in Italy.

[3] Labbe, XIII. 510 sq.

[4] The language is remarkable: 'In azymo sive fermentato pane triticeo corpus Christi veraciter confici [in Bessarion's version τελεῖσθαι ἀληθῶς]; sacerdotesque in altero ipsum Domini corpus conficere debere, unumquemque scilicet juxta suæ ecclesiæ, sive occidentalis, sive orientalis, consuetudinem.'

[5] *Ibid.* and cf. Schröckh, XXXIV. 429, 430. The other two cases, where the destination of the spirit is either heaven or hell, are put as follows: 'Illorumque animas, qui post baptisma susceptum nullam omnino peccati maculam incurrerunt, illas etiam, quæ post contractam peccati maculam vel in suis corporibus, vel eisdem exutæ corporibus, prout superius dictum est, sunt purgatæ, *in cœlum mox recipi*, et intueri clare ipsum Deum Trinum et Unum (cf. above, p. 326, n. 1), sicuti est, pro meritorum tamen diversitate alium alio perfectius; illorum autem

declared to be no matter for a synodal decision. As to the supremacy (τὸ πρωτεῖον) of the pope[1], the Greeks were willing to acknowledge it in all its latitude, unless indeed the final clause for saving the canonical order, rights, and privileges of the Eastern patriarchs were meant to circumscribe his power.

This memorable edict was published July 6, 1439, when it exhibited the signatures[2] of the emperor, the representatives of the patriarchs of Alexandria, Antioch, and Jerusalem, and of many others, not including Mark of Ephesus, nor the patriarch of Constantinople, who had lately died at Florence. The great object of so many conferences might seem to have been reached. But when the tidings of reunion were divulged in Russia[3] and the Eastern Church[4] at large, the synod was immediately repudiated by the several churches. The new patriarch of Constantinople, Metrophanes, became an object both of hatred and contempt to his own suffragans, who forced him in the end to abdicate his throne. All 'Latinizers' were regarded by the populace as abject traitors to the faith of Christ; and even the compliant patriarchs[5] who took a share in the proceedings at Ferrara, soon repented of their aberrations and openly reverted to the 'orthodox' belief.

animas, qui in actuali mortali peccato, vel solo originali decedunt, *mox in infernum descendere*, pœnis tamen disparibus puniendas.'

[1] 'Item diffinimus, sanctam apostolicam sedem et Romanum pontificem in universum orbem tenere primatum et ipsum pontificem Romanum successorem esse beati Petri principis apostolorum, et verum Christi vicarium, totiusque ecclesiæ caput et omnium Christianorum patrem ac doctorem existere,' etc. *Ibid.* The pope, however, it was added, is to act in accordance with the canons of the Church (καθ' ὃν τρόπον καὶ ἐν τοῖς πρακτικοῖς τῶν οἰκουμενικῶν συνόδων, καὶ ἐν τοῖς ἱεροῖς κανόσι διαλαμβάνεται).

[2] On the Latin side the persons who affixed their names were the pope, eight cardinals, the Latin patriarchs of Jerusalem and Grado, two episcopal ambassadors of the duke of Burgundy, eight archbishops, forty-seven bishops (nearly all Italians), four generals of monastic orders, and forty-one abbots. The Greeks, to the number of thirty, arrived at Constantinople, on their return, Feb. 1, 1440.

[3] See above, p. 365, n. 5.

[4] Neale's *Eastern Church*, 'Alexandria,' II. 337: and Gibbon, ch. LXVII. (VI. 260, 261, ed. Milman).

[5] See e.g. their synodal letter (1443) in Leo Allatius, *De Perpet. Consensione*, pp. 939 sq., in which they characterize the council of Florence as μιαράν, and threaten to excommunicate all who fraternize with the Latins. Their epistle to the emperor is quite as denunciatory: *Ibid.* pp. 942 sq.

—1520] *State of Religious Doctrine and Controversies.* 369

On the annihilation of Byzantine glory (**1453**) the reasons for soliciting the friendship of the Western Church had ceased to operate. The Christians of Constantinople were then permanently disengaged from their alliance with the civil power, and from that day to this, in spite of many proselytizing efforts, concentrated at the close of the sixteenth century against the Church of Russia[1], the inveterate quarrels of the East and West have never been composed.

The fears awakened at Constantinople by the Turks had acted in like manner on the court of Armenia. As early as **1317** an embassy[2] was sent imploring help from John XXII., and promising as an equivalent to bring about a cordial reconciliation with the Latin Church[3]. The briefs, however, which he circulated in the west of Europe with the hope of stirring up a new crusade were fruitless[4]: while, upon the other side, hereditary hatred of the council of Chalcedon[5] and a strong attachment to

RELATIONS OF EAST AND WEST.

Perpetuity of the schism.

Vain attempts to win over the Armenians.

---

[1] Mouravieff, p. 122.

[2] Raynald. ad an. 1317, § 35: cf. ad an. 1308, § 32, and above, p. 275, n. 7.

[3] *Ibid.* ad an. 1318, §§ 8—17. In the same year (§ 15) the pope sent a party of Dominicans to facilitate the union; but it never seems to have extended beyond the court and the nobles of Lesser Armenia: see (as below, n. 5) Art. XXXIV. Of course the little Latinized kingdom of Armenia (Cilicia) could not undertake for the Armenian Church, the bulk of which lay far off, and had been long under Turkish dominion.

[4] The patience of the Church was already well-nigh exhausted by the levying of tenths and other contributions with a similar pretext, for the benefit of the popes and the kings of France: cf. Twysden, *Vindication*, p. 103, Camb. ed. The pope, however, in the present case forwarded pecuniary help to the Armenians (Raynald. ad an. 1323, § 5: Schröckh, XXXIV. 453). There is some danger of confounding the Armenians of the little Christian kingdom which became extinct in 1393, with those of Greater Armenia, where the strength of the Armenian Church lay. The kingdom from its close connexion with the Crusaders was always more than half Roman.

[5] See a catalogue of errors alleged against them in 1341 by Benedict XII. (in writing to the Catholicos of Armenia); Raynald. ad an. 1341, §§ 45 sq. It is there stated (Art. III.) that they held a festival in honour of Dioscorus who was condemned at Chalcedon (Oct. 13, 451), themselves maintaining with him, or at least deducing from his theory, 'Quod sicut in Domino Jesu Christo erat unica Persona, ita erat una Natura, scilicet Divina, et una voluntas et una operatio' (cf. above, p. 64). They appear to have also held (Art. IV.) that since the Passion of our Lord original sin has been remitted to all the children of Adam ('pueri qui nascuntur ex filiis Adam non sunt damnationi addicti'). They did not believe in a purgatory ('quia, ut dicunt, si Christianus confiteatur peccata sua, omnia peccata ejus et *pœnæ peccatorum* ei dimittuntur,' Art. XVII.). They offered no prayers for the dead with the hope of procuring a remis-

M. A. B B

RELATIONS OF EAST AND WEST.

renewed at Florence;

extended to the Copts.

Latin party in Abyssinia.

Overtures to the Nestorians and the Maronites.

their semi-Jewish notions¹ swayed the bulk of the Armenian people to resist the tempting offers of the pope. In 1367 their country fell a prey to the Mameluke Turks, who threatened to erase all vestiges of Christianity². Yet even in the little kingdom a remnant survived. At the council of Florence, after the departure of the Greeks, a specious edict was drawn up (Nov. 22, 1440) for the purpose of embracing the Armenians in the general peace³. The kindred sect of Copts (or Jacobites) of Egypt, who had also undergone a frightful persecution at the hands of the Mamelukes⁴, were made the subjects of a like decree⁵ (Feb. 4, 1441). An emissary of the Coptic patriarch⁶ appeared in Florence, to facilitate this work. In neither case, however, did the overtures prevail except with individuals here and there. A firmer footing was at length obtained among the Christians of Abyssinia⁷. It proceeded from an interchange of salutations at the Florentine synod on the part of their king Zara Jacob and Eugenius IV. The ultimate effect of it was the formation of a Latinizing school, which flourished, for some time at least, under the auspices of the court of Portugal⁸. We gather also from the closing acts of the council of Florence, now translated to the Lateran (Sept. 30, 1444, and Aug. 7, 1445), that the prelates made a vigorous effort to win over the Jacobites⁹ ('Syrians'), and that numerous section of the Maronites¹⁰, who still

sion of sins ('sed generaliter orant pro omnibus mortuis, sicut pro beata Maria, Apostolis, Martyribus, et aliis sanctis, *ut in die judicii intrent in regnum cœleste.*' *Ibid.*). In Arts. LXXXIV., LXXXV., we are told that they absolutely denied the papal supremacy.

¹ Thus (Art. XLVI.) they observed the legal distinctions between the clean and unclean meats: cf. above, p. 187, n. 4.
² Raynald. ad an. 1382, § 49.
³ Labbe, XIII. 1197 sq.; Schröckh, XXXIV. 458.
⁴ Renaudot, *Hist. Patr. Alexand. Jacob.* pp. 602 sq.; Neale, II. 322, 323.
⁵ Labbe, *Ibid.* 1204 sq.: Schröckh, XXXIV. 416.
⁶ Neale, II. 336.
⁷ Neale, II. 336.
⁸ See above, p. 315, n. 5.
⁹ Labbe, XIII. 1222 sq. This decree states that Abdalla, archbp. of Edessa, had come to the synod in the name of Ignatius, patriarch of the Syrians.
¹⁰ *Ibid.* 1225 sq. (cf. above, p. 71). On the same occasion, deputies presented themselves in the name of Timotheus, metropolitan of the 'Chaldæans' (Nestorians) of Cyprus. By these proceedings, writes the Continuator of Fleury (ad an. 1445, s. 5), all the eastern sects would

adhered to the Monothelete opinions. Whether any kind of change resulted from these later manifestoes of the Western Church, it is not easy to decide.

CONTINUOUS EFFORTS TO WORK OUT A REFORMATION.

The name of Reformation[1] had been long familiar in the West of Europe. During all the present period, more especially the earlier half of the fifteenth century, it never ceased to vibrate in men's ears. A consciousness that the ecclesiastical system was diseased and lamentably out of joint, as well as a presentiment that things could not long continue as they were, had been awakened on all sides among the earnest and more thoughtful members of the Church. These feelings were occasionally shared by the chiefs of the Roman court[2] itself: but for the most part it had now become the centre of corruption and a rallying point for all the self-complacent and reactionary spirits. Hence the origin of the continued struggle made at Pisa, Constance, and Basel, to circumscribe the papal monarchy. The leaders in it felt that such a step was absolutely indispensable for healing the disorders of the age. The council-party, as we saw, enjoyed the patronage of kings and governments; it was supported almost uniformly by the lawyers and the more intelligent among the laity. We must, however, bear in mind that few reformers of this class had ever meditated critical inquiries into the established *dogmas* of the Church. One section of them were disposed to carry their reformatory principle no further than the temporal branches of the papal jurisdiction or the gross excesses in the lives of clergymen and monks. Accordingly the failure[3] of the

Reformatory efforts.

Reformers in the Church.

have been united to the Church of Rome, 'si ses decrets eussent été reçûs sur les lieux; mais par malheur ils n'eurent point d'effet:' cf. Gibbon, VI. 241, ed. Milman.

[1] See *e.g.* above, p. 21, n. 8; p. 251 n. 5.
[2] *e.g.* Pius III., above, p. 339, n. 3. The language of Hadrian VI. (by his Nuncio), at the diet of Nuremberg in 1522, is most emphatic: Raynald. ad an. 1522, § 66.
[3] See above, p. 334, n. 1. The cry for a general council was renewed, however, at the end of the fifteenth century, and prolonged by the Germans and English to the middle of the next. We gather from the following expressions that little hope was held out of a conciliar reformation: 'Quia ista deficiunt [*i.e.* obedientia principum, zelus fidei], quæso, ex conciliis cujusmodi reformatio proveniet .... Ecclesiam per concilium reformare non poterit omnis humana facultas: sed alium modum Altis-

REFORMA-
TORY
EFFORTS.

movement they had started, for convening general councils periodically, seemed a blow quite fatal to their projects of reform. But others who like them were anxious to preserve the outward unity of Christendom at almost any price, went further in applying sanatory measures. Chilled and wearied by the subtleties of a degenerate race of schoolmen, they reverted[1] for illumination to the Holy Scriptures, and the writings of the early Church. The great majority, indeed (for instance men like Gerson or Thomas à Kempis), were not conscious of antipathy to the established creed or ritual institutions of their country. Many doctrines[2] which have since been methodized in such a way as to present a sharper, a more startling and more systematic form, were tacitly allowed or even strenuously defended: yet meanwhile the general tone of their productions, as the use to which they were hereafter put by leaders of the Reformation shewed, was adverse[3] to the modes of thought and feeling which prevailed before that epoch.

simus procurabit, nobis quidem pro nunc incognitum, licet heu! præ foribus existat, ut ad pristinum statum ecclesia redeat.' The words are addressed by the Inquisitor Henry Institoris to the enthusiast (or impostor) Andrew archbishop of Crayn, who in 1480 summoned a general council on his own authority to Basel, and died in prison in 1484. Hottinger, *Hist. Eccl.* sæc. xv. p. 413; see also Farlati, *Illyricum sacrum*, vol. VII. pp. 437—448. Andrew was a Dominican friar, named Zuccomakehi, and his see was probably *in partibus;* he gave himself out as Cardinal of S. Sixtus. His whole history, which might be interesting, is unfortunately obscure. See Gieseler, v. pp. 154—156.

[1] See above, p. 356.

[2] Gerson, for example, reconciled himself to a belief in the Immaculate Conception of the Virgin, on the ground that it was a *development:* 'Doctores addiderunt multas veritates ultra Apostolos. Quapropter dicere possumus, hanc veritatem "*beatam Mariam non fuisse conceptam in peccato originali*" de illis esse veritatibus, *quæ noviter sunt revelatæ vel declaratæ*, tam per miracula quæ leguntur, quam per majorem partem Ecclesiæ sanctæ, quæ hoc modo tenet.' *Opp.* III. 1330, ed. Dupin. He also applies the remark to purgatory. Juster views are advocated in a Wycliffite treatise (1395) edited by Forshall (1851), the author asking (p. 79) in a parallel case: 'Bi what presumpcion bryngith in this synful man this *nouelrie*, not foundid opinli in the lawe of God neithir in roesun?'

[3] The *Catalogus Testium Veritatis, qui ante nostram ætatem reclamarunt Papæ* (ed. 1556), though constructed in a narrow, grasping, and, at times, in something like a disingenuous spirit, will furnish many illustrations of this remark. See also Field, *On the Church*, Append. to Book III. (II, 1—387, ed. 1849), who proves at length that the extreme opinions, stereotyped by the Council of Trent, were held only by 'a faction' in the age preceding Luther's.

—1520] *State of Religious Doctrine and Controversies.* 373

While the timid, calm, or isolated efforts of this kind were tending in the bosom of the Church itself to something more emphatic, other agencies external to it had been also urging on the work. In spite of the Inquisitors[1] who prowled in every part of Europe, many sects, retaining more or less of truth, and more or less antagonistic to the hierarchy and the ritual of the Church, continued to recruit their forces. Though the Cathari, or Albigenses, had been massacred[2] in all the south of France (except a miserable remnant[3]), they were at the middle of the fourteenth century so numerous[4] in Croatia, Slavonia, Dalmatia, Albania, Bulgaria, and especially in Bosnia, as to form a large proportion of the populace. The school of Peter Waldo had been similarly thinned by ruthless persecutions[5], but it still survived[6] in France, in parts of Germany, and even in Bohemia, as well as in the more sequestered vales and fastnesses of Piedmont[7]. The Beghards[8] also, with the German Lollards, or at least that section of them which had now revolted absolutely from the Church, including Fratricelli, 'Brothers and Sisters of the Free Spirit,' and a minor group of mystical and antinomian confraternities, appear at intervals on every side. They seemed to thrive not only in their earlier settlements, but also in the south of France, in

REFORMATORY EFFORTS.

Reformers out of the Church.

---

[1] Schröckh, xxxiv. 468 sq.
[2] See above, p. 289.
[3] Such are, possibly, the Cagots of the Pyrenees: Schmidt, *Hist. des Cathares*, etc. i. 360.
[4] *Ibid.* i. 125 sq. The inhabitants of Bosnia and Albania, where the doctrines of the Bogomiles were deeply rooted, afterwards became the champions of Islamism. Spencer's *Travels in European Turkey*, i. 303—312, Lond. 1851.
[5] The first of these, in the present period, was set on foot by John XXII. (1332), and many others followed: Schröckh, xxxiv. 488 sq.
[6] The numbers in Dauphiny, as late as 1373, are said to be 'maxima multitudo' (Raynald. ad an. § 20). Traces of them in different parts of Germany are noted by Gieseler to the end of the fourteenth century; iv. § 122, pp. 218, 219, n. 5. They are said to have entered Bohemia at the close of the twelfth (see *The Reformation and Anti-Reformation in Bohemia*, Lond. 1845, i. 5; and Krasinski, *Reform. in Poland*, i. 53).
[7] Above, p. 294.
[8] See above, pp. 232, 235, 294, n. 5, p. 346. In 1322, a person named Walter [Lollard?] was put to death at Cologne, for circulating heresy in the vernacular: see John of Trittenheim (Trithemius), *Annal.* ii. 155.

<small>REFORMATORY EFFORTS.</small>

Italy and Sicily¹. To these may be subjoined the Adamites, the Luciferians, the Turlupines (all independent offshoots from the Beghards²), the disciples of John Pirnensis³ in Silesia, and a party of Flagellants⁴, who, because they pushed ascetic principles to an intolerable length and flogged themselves in public several times a day, were finally restrained by Clement VI. (1349). They now seceded in great numbers from the Church.

<small>*John Wycliffe* (d. 1384), the '*Evangelic Doctor.*'</small>

A movement altogether disconnected⁵ from the rest had meanwhile been advancing rapidly in England. Its author was John Wycliffe, (or John of Wycliffe), born not far from Richmond, Yorkshire (? 1324). It is said that he

---

¹ John XXII. levelled a bull against them (Dec. 30, 1317), in the *Extravagantes Johan. XXII.*, tit. VII. ('*Corpus Juris Canon.*'). From it we gather that they sheltered themselves under the pretext of belonging to the tertiary order of Franciscans.

² See the literature respecting them in Gieseler, IV. § 122, pp. 224, 225, n. 10, 11, 12. Gerson (as there quoted) charges some of these sectaries with the most unbridled licentiousness.

³ The author of this sect appeared in 1341, maintaining among other kindred tenets that the pope was Antichrist, and more especially distinguished by his hatred of the clergy: Krasinski, *Reform. in Poland*, I. 55, 56. Perhaps they were in some way connected with the Russian Strigolniks (cf. above, p. 362), and many would at length pass over to the more extreme party of Hussites.

⁴ Cf. above, p. 201; and see Hahn, *Gesch. der Ketzer im Mittelalter*, II. 537 sq. The later Flagellants ('Bianchi') wore white garments, and on crossing the Alps into Italy (1399) produced a marvellous sensation. Benedict IX., however, finally apprehended the leader, and consigned him to the flames. Members of the sect were found in Thuringia and other parts of Germany at the outbreak of the Reformation. Another group of sectaries, entitled 'Dancers' (from their violent gesticulations under what they deemed the influence of the Holy Ghost), sprang up in Flanders about 1370: cf. Gieseler, IV. § 119, pp. 203, 204, n. 23, 24. Some of the phenomena presented by them may remind us of the modern 'electro-biology.'

⁵ 'It is a remarkable fact that the writings of Wycliffe never give us any reason to suppose that he was acquainted in any degree with the history of the Waldenses, the Albigenses, or with any of the continental sects:' Vaughan's *Wycliffe*, p. 46, ed. 1853. The predecessor whom he valued most was Grosseteste, bishop of Lincoln. 'Seith Robert Grosteed that this [pope's] bulles ben heresies' (MS. quoted in Turner, V. 148, n. 5)—is only one of a multitude of references which he has made to that prelate. In the Wycliffite treatise (1395) edited by Mr Forshall, with the title, *Remonstrance against Romish Corruptions* (Lond. 1851), there are no less than five such references to 'the worshipful clerk, Grosted, bisshop of Lincolne.' On Dr Maitland's theory for connecting the English Lollards with the political and other prophets of the continent (*e.g.* the abbot Joachim, above, p. 255, n. 1), see his *Eight Essays* (1852), pp. 207 sq.

was at one time a resident in Queen's College, Oxford[1], but as there were certainly two if not three persons at the university bearing the same name at this time, this is very uncertain[2]. The first fact distinctly known about him is that in 1361 he was master or warden of Balliol College[3]. Devoting his attention to scholastics, he is said to have outstripped[4] all others in that field of study: but his title *Evangelic* (Gospel) *Doctor* indicates that he was no less favourably known at Oxford for proficiency in biblical literature. Recent historical research has shewn that the theory once received, of the commencement[5] of Wycliffe's controversial labours[6] by an attack on the friars, is untenable.

REFORMATORY EFFORTS.

His early career.

[1] Even this statement about him is uncertain. Compare Shirley, *Fasciculi Zizaniorum*, pref. xii. xiv.; and the remarks of Mr H. T. Riley in the Second Report of the Historical MSS. Commission, 1871, pp. 141, 142.
[2] The John Wycliffe whose history is most frequently confounded with the reformer's, was in 1356 a fellow of Merton College, and afterwards rector of Mayfield in Sussex, who died in 1383. It is probable that this person was also Warden of Canterbury Hall. These preferments have frequently been assigned to the great Wycliffe, who however was a Doctor of Divinity at the time that his namesake was a Bachelor. The whole argument against the identity of the two is stated by Dr Shirley, *Fasciculi Zizaniorum*, pp. 513—528.
[3] He was also presented by this society (1361) to the rectory of Fylingham, in the archdeaconry of Stow, a benefice which he afterwards exchanged (1368) for Ludgershall, nearer to Oxford.
[4] Thus Henry Knyghton (in Twysden's *Scriptores X.*, col. 2644) is driven to admit, 'in philosophia nulli reputabatur secundus, in scholasticis disciplinis incomparabilis:' cf. Le Bas, *Life of Wiclif*, pp. 93, 944, Lond. 1832. He was a Realist,' and thus opposed himself to Ockham. For a complete list of his scholastic and philosophical writings (many of which are preserved in the Library of Trinity College, Cambridge, MSS. No. 326), see Shirley's *Catalogue of Wyclif's Original Works*, Oxford, 1865; *Select English Works of Wyclif*, ed. Arnold, III. xvii.; and Vaughan's *Wycliffe*, pp. 541 sq., ed. 1853.
[5] "That in 1356 he published his first work, *The Last Age of the Church;* that the same year he was one of the fellows of Merton, that in 1360 he took up the pen of the dying Archbishop Fitz Ralph of Armagh in his memorable controversy with the Mendicants, are facts only by courtesy and repetition. *The Last Age of the Church* has been assigned to him in common with half the English religious tracts of the fourteenth and fifteenth centuries, in the absence of all external, and in defiance of all internal evidence." Shirley, *Fasc. Zizan.* pref. xiii. On the authorship of the *Last Age of the Church*, see Shirley's Catalogue of Wiclif's Works, pref. p. xiii. It was edited by Dr Todd, Dublin, 1851.
[6] See *e.g.* his *Two Short Treatises against the Orders of Begging Friars*, Oxf. 1608; printed also in the *Select English Works of Wiclif*,

REFORMATORY EFFORTS.

His Objections to the Friars.

To whatever date however this hostility is to be referred, his works on the subject are the utterances of a man righteously indignant at the hollowness, the self-indulgence, and extortion of the papal volunteers. He seems to speak as if he had been personally thwarted by them in his ministerial labours: every scandal and disaster of the times was laid to their account. By them the working of the Church was said to have been so enfeebled and disorganized, that till they had been taught to understand the 'freedom of the Gospel' and the 'clean religion of Jesus Christ,' all other remedies would prove inefficacious. Wycliffe never paused nor faltered[1] in his declamations on this head, and therefore the hostility which he excited in a large and powerful section of his countrymen pursued him even to the grave. But on the other hand his zeal, his patriotism, and learning commended him to

ed. Arnold, Oxford, 1871; III. 366. Mr Arnold ascribes these tracts to 1382 and 1384, and even questions whether they are Wycliffe's. They contain however much of the teaching of his school on the subject. He had been preceded in this line by several writers (see above, p. 344, n. 5), especially by Richard Fitzralph, archbishop of Armagh, who had (in 1357) arraigned the Mendicants before the pope and cardinals at Avignon (above, p. 345, n. 1). The Friars, on the other hand, were not destitute of champions. See, for instance, *Wil. Wodfordus* (a Franciscan) *adversus Joh. Wiclefum Anglum* (in Brown's *Fasc.* I. 191 sq.), which is a full examination of the various errors charged on Wycliffe and his school.

[1] One of the few anecdotes preserved respecting him informs us that, when dangerously ill in 1379, he was visited by certain Mendicants who urged him to recal the accusations he had levelled at them. His reply was, 'I shall not die, but live, and again declare the evil deeds of the Friars:' Le Bas, p. 196. In the tract, *De Ecclesia et Membris suis*, written in the last year of his life (1384), and edited in 1851, with two other treatises by Dr Todd, and by Mr Arnold in the *Select English Works of Wyclif*, III. 338, he urges that 'for profit of the chirche shulden freris worche to quench this striyf.' 'But noon,' he adds, 'groundith here his word, as noon of thes newe ordris groundith, that he cam inne bi Crist, and but gif [*i.e.* unless] this groundyng be in dede, dremes and confermyngis ben nougt. On this maner shulden trewe men seke wisely the sothe, and purge our moder of apostemes, that ben harmful in the chirche. To this shulde the pope helpe, for to this dette weren apostlis boundun, and not to lordshipis of money but [*i.e.* except] in as myche as it helpide herto' etc., p. xlvii. (ed. Arnold, p. 353). The next treatise in Dr Todd's volume, *De Apostasia Cleri* (Arnold, p. 430), [*i.e.* their abandonment of their proper duties], shows that Wycliffe was not blind to failings in that quarter also; and the same is still more manifest in a work doubtfully attributed to him *Of Clerks Possessioners*: see an account of it in Vaughan, p. 526. Shirley, *Catalogue*, p. 41; Arnold, *Select Works of Wyclif*, III. xix.

Edward III., who made him one of the royal chaplains[1] and bestowed on him the prebend of Aust in the collegiate church of Westbury (Worcester) and the rectory of Lutterworth in Leicestershire[2] (1374). The favour of the crown had been already manifested in selecting him for one of the commissioners appointed to negociate at Bruges with certain papal envoys touching the pecuniary exactions of their master. Though the mission does not seem to have produced[3] a real mitigation of abuses, it would hardly fail to rivet the attention of an earnest soul like Wycliffe's on the manifold enormities prevailing in the papal court and the administration of the Church at large.

REFORMATORY EFFORTS.

Diplomatic mission to Bruges, 1374—1375.

His controversial career, so far as it can be dated by extant monuments, began about 1363, when on philosophical subjects he was engaged in a dispute with the Carmelite Kynyngham[4]. To Wycliffe's mind philosophical and practical questions presented themselves in close conjunction, scholastic, theological, and ecclesiastical abuses were too firmly allied to stand severally alone when once the reformer's hand was raised against any one of them. Still in 1366 we find him prepared to call himself 'a lowly and obedient son of the Roman Church[5];' as though the clearest

---

[1] This point is rather open to discussion, resting mainly on the way in which he speaks of himself as standing in a close relation to the crown ('peculiaris regis clericus'). As such he professed his readiness to maintain that the sovereign of this country may justly rule, though denying tribute to the pope: Vaughan, as above, p. 106.

[2] Le Bas, p. 155. He had meanwhile (before 1366) become a S. T. P. of Oxford, and as such lectured in Theology: see Shirley, *Fasc. Ziz.* pref. p. xvii.

[3] For instance, Wycliffe's coadjutor, the bishop of Bangor, was immediately afterwards translated (1375) by a papal bull to Hereford, although the issue of the conference was that the pope should desist from all 'reservations,' and that the king should no longer confer benefices by an arbitrary writ ('Quare impedit'): Le Bas, p. 154. The influence of the recent negociations may be seen, however, in the 'Rolls' of what is called the 'Good Parliament' (1376), which demanded among other things that no papal questor or collector should remain in England on pain of life and limb (see *Rot. Parl.* 50º Edw. III., § 114).

[4] Dr Shirley divides Wycliffe's literary career into three periods; the first lasting up to 1366 or 1367, including his logical, physical and scholastic works; the second including his attempts at constitutional reform in the church extending to the date of the great schism; the third from 1378 to his death, including his doctrinal writings. *Fasc. Ziz.* pref. pp. xxxix—xliii.

[5] Vaughan, p. 109. His views at this time on the question whether

REFORMA-
TORY
EFFORTS.

Attacks upon the papacy, 1376.

insight into its corruptions and its crooked policy were absolutely needed ere he could be roused to controvert the papacy itself.

His eyes were opened by the diplomatic mission to Bruges[1], and accordingly, soon after his return, the Romanizing party in the Church of England, stimulated as it seems by the emphatic warnings of the pope, and headed by William Courtenay, bishop of London, instituted measures for convicting him of heresy. He was cited to appear and vindicate himself before the convocation, which assembled at St Paul's Cathedral, 'Feb. 3, 1377'[2]. The charges brought against him were that he advanced, in lectures and elsewhere, a class of tenets like the following[3]:—that the Church of Rome is not the

the crown of England owe any feudal homage to the pope in consequence of the proceedings in the time of John (cf. above, p. 252) are stated in a *Determinatio*, printed in Lewis, *Life and Sufferings of John Wiclif*, pp. 349 sq., Oxf. 1820. In this treatise (p. 354) we may see the germ of a strange doctrine which afterwards became a reproach to him and his followers, viz. that power and property are held by the tenure of grace, and therefore liable to be forfeited by the 'mortal sin' of the owner. Mr Le Bas endeavours to relieve Wycliffe from this charge, pp. 350 sq.: cf. Vaughan, p. 460.

[1] He came from thence, persuaded that the 'proud, worldly priest of Rome' was 'the most cursed of clippers and pursekervers.' Lewis, p. 37.

[2] The chronology of these events is rather confusing, but according to the authorities at present accessible, the following appears to be the sequence. The Convocation at which Wycliffe first appeared was held at St Paul's for the purpose of granting a subsidy, Feb. 3, 1377, (Hody, p. 225). Wycliffe's appearance and the riot that broke up the sitting are placed on the 23rd of February. The pope's letters were issued on the 22nd of May. Of these the first is addressed to the University, and forbids the propounding of Wycliffe's opinions, (Wals. 346); the second to the archbishop and the bishop of London, bidding them admonish the king and nobles not to favour Wycliffe (*Ibid.* 347). The third to the same two prelates enjoining them to cite Wycliffe to Rome (*Ibid.* 348). The fourth to the same directing the arrest of the reformer (*Ibid.* 350), the fifth to the king desiring him to favour the prosecution. Edward died on the 21st of June. The letters of the archbishop and bishop addressed to the University, directing the appearance of Wycliffe at St Paul's in obedience to the papal mandate, are dated Dec. 28, 1377, (Wilkins III. 123). He is ordered to appear on the thirtieth day after citation. The place seems to have been changed, and probably the day also. The trial at Lambeth was the result, and it was broken up in much the same way as the former attempt at St Paul's. Compare Shirley, *Fasc. Ziz.* xxvi.—xxxiii., Vaughan, pp. 185 sq.

[3] All the nineteen propositions are given in Wilkins, as above, p. 123: cf. Massingberd's *Eng. Reformation*, p. 9, Lond. 1847. The last of the schedule must have been peculiarly offensive: 'Ecclesiasticus, immo

head of all Churches, nor has Christ committed larger functions to St Peter than to others of the Twelve; that the Roman pontiff has no powers of absolution different from those entrusted to all members of the priesthood; that ecclesiastical censures ought not to be used for gratifying individual spleen, and that an excommunicated person does not truly fare the worse unless he be already self-ejected from the fellowship of Christians; that the civil power, in certain cases, may both lawfully and meritoriously punish a delinquent church by appropriating its revenues; that the Gospel is sufficient as a rule of life for every class of Christians, and that other 'rules' (adopted by religious orders, for example) can add nothing of perfection to the law of God.

Summary of his opinions at this time.

When on the 23rd of February he appeared before the convocation he was accompanied by the earl marshal, Percy, and by John of Gaunt, the duke of Lancaster. The latter, as the head of a numerous party who were bent on lowering the pretensions of the English ecclesiastics, manifested a peculiar zeal in his behalf. Some verbal skirmishing that passed between the bishop of London and these powerful friends of Wycliffe, issued in a riot of the citizens, who could not brook what they esteemed the insult which was put on their diocesan, and who hated John of Gaunt. Amid this angry tumult the inquiry was suspended.

Proceedings against him. 1377.

During the few months that followed Wycliffe's enemies were busy at Rome. The king[1] died in June, but before this the pope had issued letters against the reformer, addressed to the king, the archbishop of Canterbury, and the chancellor of Oxford[2]. In pursuance of these orders

et Romanus pontifex, potest legitime a subditis et laicis corripi et etiam accusari.' In the accompanying instruments the pope associates Wycliffe with Marsilius of Padua (see above, p. 324, n. 1) 'of accursed memory.'

[1] Whether Edward, who enacted a statute of Præmunire (making the execution of all bulls, without the licence of the crown, a very grave offence), would have been likely to sanction the proceedings against Wycliffe, is not easy to determine.

[2] The following is part of Walsingham's entry at the year 1378, Riley's edition, vol. I. p. 345: 'Diu in pendulo hærebant [*i.e.* the Oxford authorities] utrum papalem bullam deberent cum honore recipere, vel omnino cum dedecore refutare ... Pudet recordationis tantæ imprudentiæ: et ideo supersedeo in hujusmodi materia immorari, ne materna videar

REFORMA-TORY EFFORTS.

Wycliffe appeared early in 1378 before the bishops at Lambeth; but on this occasion a fresh uproar stirred up, it seems by the partizans of the reformer[1], and supported by a message in his favour from the princess of Wales, determined the archbishop to dismiss him with a reprimand[2].

His line of defence,

It is important to remark the tone and tactics of the culprit while he was arraigned at this tribunal[3]. He examined all the several propositions which the papal rescript had alleged against him, urging in the outset that they were a puerile and garbled version of his real tenets, and declaring his willingness to acquiesce in the decisions of 'holy mother Church.' In proving that mankind had no power to make St Peter and his successors the political rulers of the world 'for ever,' he appealed to the admitted fact that temporal property could only last until the second advent. Other arguments alike evasive were applied to propositions on the subject of civil dominion and of civil inheritance: but when he finally

and the principles there enunciated.

approached the questions touching church-property, the power of excommunication, and the different orders of the ministry, his language was more candid and distinct. As tithes and all ecclesiastical possessions were but eleemosynary[4], he maintained that to withhold them, in some

---

ubera decerpere dentibus, quæ dare lac potum scientiæ consuevēre.' It appears also that Wycliffe carried with him a large party (even a majority) of the Londoners (Vaughan, pp. 189, 190), although the municipal authorities, and many of the citizens, who hated John of Gaunt, were active on the other side.

[1] Walsingham (p. 356) complains on this occasion, 'Non dico cives tantum Londinienses, sed viles ipsius civitatis se impudenter ingerere præsumpserunt in eandem capellam [*i.e.* at Lambeth], et verba facere pro eodem, et istud negotium impedire.'

[2] See Walsingham's indignant language on the cowardice or mildness of the prelates. He says, among other things, that they became 'velut homo non audiens, et non habens in ore suo redargutiones.' *Ibid.* p. 356. Their injunction charging Wycliffe to abstain from publishing his opinions, was altogether lost upon him.

[3] The same chronicler taxes him with dissimulation and crooked dealing in the interview at Lambeth; *Ibid.* pp. 356, 363: cf. Le Bas, pp. 178 sq.; Lingard, IV. 256 sq.; and Vaughan, pp. 207 sq., the last of whom makes merry on the occasion, it would seem to many readers, at Wycliffe's own expense.

[4] The payments to the papacy had always been spoken of as alms ('eleemosyna beati Petri'). Sir Thomas More, *Suppl. of Soules*, (Works, I. 296) describes Peterpence as 'ever payde before the conquest

instances at least, might be an act of duty and of genuine charity[1]. His statement was, however, somewhat modified by intimating that such revocations should be only made in cases where they had been authorized by civil and by canon law[2]. Respecting excommunications, he avowed that no effect was wrought by them unless the sentence of the Church accorded with the will of Christ. He followed several of the schoolmen[3] in regarding priests and bishops as of the same spiritual *order*, though different in rank or jurisdiction; arguing on this ground, that each of the seven sacraments might be lawfully administered by any of the sacerdotal class. He also reaffirmed his earlier statement, that ecclesiastics, nay the pope himself[4], might be on some accounts impleaded and corrected by their subjects, whether clerical or lay[5].

The death of Gregory XI. in the spring of 1378 was followed, as already noticed[6], by the schism which paralysed the vigour of the Roman court. Its jealousy

to the apostolike sea towarde the mayntenance therof, but only by way of gratitude and *almes*.' On the *Responsio magistri Johannis Wycliff* (1377) respecting this question, see *Fasciculi Zizaniorum*, pp. 258 sq., in *Chronicles of Great Britain:* cf. Twysden's *Vindication*, p. 96. Camb. ed.

[1] Wycliffe, like the abbot Joachim, Hildegard, and the more rigorous school of Friars, now arrived at the conviction that the secularity of the Church was mainly due to its abundant property. On this account he would have gladly seen ecclesiastics destitute of temporal possessions except the scantiest portion by which life could be sustained: cf. Le Bas, p. 194.

[2] It is manifest, however, from the proceedings of the synod of London (1382) that Wycliffe was still charged with holding more extreme opinions on this subject: 'Item quod decimæ sunt puræ eleemosynæ, et quod parochiani possint propter peccata suorum curatorum eas detinere, et ad libitum aliis conferre.' Wilkins, III. 157.

[3] See Palmer's *Treatise on the Church*, part VI. ch. iv. sect. 1.

[4] He does not even shrink from the supposition 'Si papa fuerit a fide devius.'

[5] After his escape from his enemies at Lambeth, Wycliffe had a controversy on the same topic with an anonymous divine called 'mixtus theologus.' He there carries his opinions out more fully: see Le Bas, pp. 190 sq.; Vaughan, pp. 216 sq.

[6] Above, p. 328. In Wycliffe's treatise, *Schisma Papæ* (1382), (*Select English Works of Wyclif;* ed. Arnold, Oxford 1871, p. 247,) he thus writes of the dissension: 'Trust we in the help of Christ on this point, for he hath begun already to help us graciously, in that he hath *clove the head of Antichrist*, and made the two parts fight against each other. For it is not to be doubted that the sin of the popes which hath been so long continued, hath brought in this division.' Quoted in Vaughan, p. 374.

REFORMATORY EFFORTS.

Wycliffe attacks the dogma of transubstantiation, 1380.

was thus diverted from the struggles of the English Church, and Wycliffe gathered strength and courage for his work. He had been hitherto endeavouring for the most part to suppress the evils that grew out of maladministration[1]. If he called the papacy an 'antichristian' power, he only meant, as did a host of earlier writers who had used a similar expression, to denounce the practical corruptions then abounding in the see of Rome. But after 1380 many of his protests went far deeper[2]. He repudiated the prevailing dogmas on the nature of the

[1] Thus in the one of his three manifestoes issued at this time, which Shirley fixes in October 1377, and Lewis after the Lambeth examination, his protest runs as follows: 'Hæ sunt conclusiones, quas vult etiam usque ad mortem defendere, ut per hoc valeat *mores Ecclesiæ* reformare.' (Lewis, p. 389, *Fasc. Ziz.* p. 245.) Wycliffe, in other words, had hardly exceeded many of his predecessors in the area and vehemence of his critiques. See for instance, *A Poem on the Times of Edward II.* (circ. 1320), edited by the present writer for the Percy Society, No. LXXXII., or the *Vision and Creed of Piers Plowman*, passim; although the Creed may have been itself a Wycliffite production.

[2] The following are five of the twelve theses which he is charged with maintaining at Oxford on this subject (1381): 1. 'Hostia consecrata quam videmus in altari nec est Christus nec aliqua Sui pars, sed efficax ejus signum. 2. Nullus viator [*i.e.* Christian] sufficit oculo corporali, sed fide Christum videre in hostia consecrata. 3. Olim fuit fides Ecclesiæ Romanæ in professione Berengarii, quod panis et vinum quæ remanent post benedictionem sunt hostia consecrata. 4. Eucharistia habet virtute verborum sacramentalium tam corpus quam sanguinem Christi vere et realiter ad quemlibet ejus punctum. 5. Transubstantiatio, idemptificatio, et impanatio, quibus utuntur baptistæ signorum in materia de Eucharistia, non sunt fundabiles in Scriptura.' *Fasc. Ziz.* pp. 105, 106. These views are fully stated in the fourth book of Wycliffe's *Trialogus* (in 1382), a work which embodies many of his academical lectures. It was printed in 1525, at Basel, with the title *Jo. Wiclefi viri undiquaque piissimi Dialogorum libri quatuor*; and has been republished at Oxford under the editorship of Dr Lechler of Leipzig, in 1869. In an English *Confession*, of the same date, preserved in Knyghton (inter *Scriptores X.,* col. 2649), he deems it 'heresie for to trow that this sacrament is Goddus body and no brede; for it is both togedur.' He also draws a sharp distinction between his view and that of 'heretykes that trowes and telles that this sacrament may on none wise be Goddus body.' Cf. also a Latin *Confessio*, in Vaughan, pp. 564 sq.; *Fasc. Ziz.* 115—132, where Wycliffe taunts his adversaries on the ground that they are 'secta cultorum accidentium,' and expresses his belief 'quod finaliter veritas vincet eos.' He also adduces seven witnesses from the Fathers of the Church 'ad testificandam Ecclesiæ judicis hujus sententiam,' ascribing the establishment of transubstantiation to Innocent III. and the Friars: cf. above, p. 302, Wycliffe's *Trialogus*, p. 263 (ed. Oxon.), and the Wycliffite *Remonstrance*, edited by Mr Forshall (Lond. 1851), p. 79. Neander (IX. pp. 218 sq., Bohn's edition) has investigated the opinions of the reformer on these topics.

Presence in the Eucharist. According to his view there is no physical conversion of the elements; they do not lose their proper substance after consecration: yet in some mode or other which he does not rigidly define, it is contended that the sacramental bread is simultaneously and truly the Body of Christ. In different language, Wycliffe seems to have revived the doctrine of Ratramnus, Ælfric, and Berengarius[1].

When these tenets had been advocated for some time in Oxford[2], they excited the hostility of William Berton, the chancellor (**1381**), who, calling to his aid twelve other doctors, eight of whom were members of religious orders and on that account the bitter enemies of Wycliffe, instantly pronounced the views of the reformer contrary to the determinations of the Church. They censured[3] him, and with him all who were unwilling to confess that after the consecration of the Eucharistic elements 'there do not remain in that venerable sacrament the material bread and wine which were there before, each according to its own substance or nature, but only the species of the same, under which species the very Body and Blood of Christ are really contained, not merely figuratively or tropically, but essentially, substantially, and corporeally,—so that Christ is there verily in His own proper bodily presence.' Silenced by the academical authorities, the fearless culprit next endeavoured to confound his adversaries by appealing to the king[4]; but he

His teaching on this subject condemned at Oxford.

[1] See the previous note, and cf. above, pp. 168, 169, 173.
[2] The *Diffinitio contra Opiniones Wycliffianas*, here alluded to (Vaughan, pp. 561—563; *Fascic. Ziz.* p. 110), complains that by the publication of 'pestiferous documents' at Oxford, 'fides Catholica periclitatur, devotio populi minoratur, et hæc universitas mater nostra non mediocriter diffamatur.'
[3] Vaughan, p. 562: cf. Twysden's *Vindication*, p. 234. They also appended a prohibition, 'ne quis de cætero aliquem publice docentem, tenentem vel defendentem præmissas duas assertiones erroneas aut earum alteram in scholis vel extra scholas in hac universitate quovismodo audiat vel auscultet, sed statim sic docentem tanquam serpentem venenum pestiferum emittentem fugiat et abscedat sub pœna excommunicationis majoris,' etc. (*Fasc. Ziz.* 112.) To set himself right with his friends and followers at large, Wycliffe now published (1381) his well-known tract entitled *Ostiolum* or *Wyckett* (printed first at Nuremberg in 1546). See Shirley's *Catalogue*, p. 33. He seems to have retreated from the University at the same time, but, according to Dr Vaughan (pp. 571 sq.), he was there again in the following year (1382).
[4] See the extract from archbp. Sudbury's *Register* in Wilkins, III.

was driven to suspend this measure by the intervention of John of Gaunt, who seems indeed to have been losing all his confidence in Wycliffe, when the latter animadverted on the doctrine, as distinguished from the practical corruptions and the secular encroachments, of the Church. A communistic outbreak of the English peasants and villeins, headed by Wat Tyler and John Balle[1], occurred at this very juncture; and although it was not instigated[2] or fomented by the new opinions, it could hardly fail to prejudice the civil power against all further movements; more especially when, as in Wycliffe's, little or no tenderness was shewn to the Establishment and other constituted authorities of the realm.

The primate had been murdered in the recent tumults. To his throne succeeded Courtenay, the old antagonist of the reforming party, who availed himself at once of the alarms now generally felt in England for suppressing what was deemed by many of his school the surest provocation of God's anger[3]. By his influence a new synod[4]

171, where the language is remarkable: '...appellavit non ad papam, vel episcopum, vel ordinarium ecclesiasticum; sed hæreticus adhærens sæculari potestati in defensionem sui erroris et hæresis appellavit ad regem Richardum, volens per hoc se protegere regali potestate, quod non puniretur, vel emendaretur, ecclesiastica potestate.' In the autumn of 1382, however, Wycliffe carried 'his appeal to Cæsar,' in a *Complaint* which he addressed to the king and parliament (printed at Oxford in 1608, with other pieces under the editorship of Dr James; ed. Arnold, III. 507). It is divided into four articles, three of which relate to the vows of religious orders, the relations of the clergy to the civil power, and the withholding of tithes and offerings from unworthy curates; while the fourth re-states the theory of Wycliffe on transubstantiation.

[1] Of this person, who was a priest, Knyghton (col. 2644) says that he was a 'precursor' of Wycliffe, but never intimates that the two were acting in concert: cf. Wilkins, III. 152, 153.

[2] This fact is well established by the author of a *History of England and France under the House of Lancaster* (Lond. 1852), pp. 16 sq., and notes: cf. Vaughan, pp. 260, 261. Mr Hallam, (*Middle Ages*, III. 178, 179, 10th ed.) leans to the other side. That incendiary principles were not uncommon at this period may be gathered from the condemnation of John Petit, a doctor of Paris, by the synod of Constance (July 6, 1415).

[3] *e.g.* The zealot, Walsingham (vol. II. p. 11), who never charged the Wycliffites with stimulating the insurrection, looks upon it as a judgment of heaven upon the prelates for not prosecuting the new heresy.

[4] Wilkins, III. 157. One of the prelates was William of Wykeham. It is remarkable that, among the other accusations here brought against the reformer, one is to this effect, that after the death of Urban VI. no pope ought to be recognized, but that the people should be, *like the Greeks*, governed by their own laws: § 9. See the contemporary history of these proceedings in *Fasciculi Zizaniorum*, ed. Shirley, pp. 272 sq.

was convened at the house of the Black Friars, London, (May 19, 1382), in order to deliberate respecting certain strange opinions which were said to have been widely circulated among both the nobility and the commoners of England. The proceedings had the sanction of eight prelates, with a sprinkling of canonists, civilians, and divines. Of twenty-four propositions[1] there attributed to Wycliffe, ten were branded as heretical, and all the rest as execrable and erroneous. Some of Wycliffe's more distinguished partisans, especially Nicholas Hereford, Philip Repington, and John Aston[2], were now called upon to disavow those tenets, or to suffer heavy penalties,—an ordeal which it seems but few of them had still sufficient constancy to meet[3]. There was indeed no English law at present which inflicted capital punishment in case of heresy: but Courtenay had been able to procure a royal letter[4] (dated July 13) which authorized their banishment from Oxford and the ultimate imprisonment of all who might defend the new opinions. Lancaster himself enjoined the leaders of the movement to throw down their arms; and after

_{REFORMATORY EFFORTS.}

_{Condemnation of the Wycliffites.}

---

[1] Many of these were statements, somewhat garbled, of what Wycliffe really taught. The most preposterous of them (§ 7) ran as follows: 'Quod Deus debet obedire diabolo,' an inference drawn perhaps from Wycliffe's rigorous views of predestination. Of the 'erroneous' conclusions one is thus expressed: 'Quod liceat alicui etiam diacono vel presbytero, prædicare verbum Dei absque auctoritate sedis apostolicæ vel episcopi catholici, seu alia de qua sufficienter constet.' This charge originated in the fact that some of Wycliffe's disciples, 'Simple Priests' or 'Poor Priests,' itinerated, like the Friars, in all parts of the country, often barefoot and in coarse raiment of a russet hue, inveighing against the corruptions of the Church, comforting the sick and dying, and expounding the Scriptures. They formed a kind of 'home-mission.' *Fasc. Ziz.* xl.

[2] Wilkins, III. 166. *Fasc. Ziz.* 289. The following passage from Walsingham (*Hypodigma Neustriæ*, in Camden's *Anglica*, &c. p. 535) appears to shew that Wycliffism was now most unpopular among the clergy. They granted the king a tenth in the autumn of 1382, but with the condition 'ut videlicet Rex manus apponat defensioni ecclesiæ, et præstet auxilium ad compressionem hæreticorum Wicklevensium, qui jam sua prava doctrina pœne infecerant totum regnum.'

[3] Vaughan, pp. 269 sq.; *Hist. of England under the House of Lancaster*, pp. 18—22, and note XII. How far Wycliffe was himself disposed at this time to modify his statements on the Eucharist may be gathered from the documents enumerated in p. 382, n. 2.

[4] Addressed to the Oxford authorities and also to sheriffs and mayors: see *Hist. of England*, as above, p. 360; and *Fascic. Zizaniorum*, pp. 312 sq.

Wycliffe's retirement and death, 1384.

His translation of the Bible.

Wycliffe had in vain endeavoured to excite the king and parliament in their behalf[1], he quietly resided on his benefice at Lutterworth, where he expired[2], in the communion of the English Church, Dec. **31, 1384**.

Meanwhile, however, he had occupied himself in labours that were destined to immortalize his name. The earlier of those versions of the Bible and 'Apocrypha,' which are known as 'Wycliffite[3],' was then completed. Not a few detached portions, as we have already seen[4], were rendered into English at an earlier date: but never till the present period was the whole of the sacred volume generally unlocked and circulated freely among all orders of society. Though it is probable that many who resisted Wycliffe's movement as unauthorized were still in favour of vernacular translations[5], others seem to have regarded

---

[1] See above, p. 383, n. 4: Vaughan, pp. 289 sq. His comparative impunity now stimulated Urban VI. (the rival pope acknowledged in this country) to cite him to the court of Rome. Wycliffe replied excusing himself in a half-sarcastic letter (printed in Vaughan, p. 576; *Select English Works*, ed. Arnold, III. 504; and in Latin in *Fascic. Zizan.* p. 341), upon the ground of bodily infirmity (a paralytic affection of which he died at last). Among other things he says: 'I suppose over this, that the pope be most oblished to the keping of the Gospel among all men that liven here. For the pope is highest vicar that Christ has here in erth. For moreness [i. e. superiority] of Christ's vicars is not measured by worldly moreness, bot by this, that this vicar sues [i. e. follows] more Christ by vertuous living: for thus teches the Gospel.'

[2] He was taken ill at mass on the feast of Thomas à Becket (Dec. 29) and died on the feast of pope Silvester, from which his enemies argued that his death was a Divine judgment for the violence with which he had assailed both these prelates.

[3] See on this subject the able *Preface* to the *Wycliffite Versions of the Bible*, published at Oxford, 1850, p. vi. The later and more popular version is mainly due to John Purvey, the second champion of the English Lollards; *Ibid.* p. xxxii.; Vaughan, p. 359, note.

[4] Above, p. 297, n. 4. Sir Thos. More (*Works*, p. 233, ed. 1549) actually asserts that Wycliffe's version of the whole Bible into English was not the oldest: but no one has ever verified the assertion: cf. Vaughan, p. 334. The extract given in Ussher (*Hist. Dogmat.*, Works, XII. 346, ed. Elrington) states that an earlier version was put forth by John of Trevisa, chaplain to Lord Berkeley; but this theory is also untenable; *Pref.* to the *Wycliffite Bible*, p. xxi.

[5] Even archbishop Arundel (*Constitutions against Lollards*, § 6; with notes in Johnson, II. 466, 467, Oxf. 1851) does not absolutely forbid such translations (in 1408), but requires that they shall first be submitted to the diocesan, or if need be, to a provincial council. He also praises Anne of Bohemia (the queen of Rich. II.), 'quod quamvis advena esset et peregrina, tamen *quatuor Evangelia in linguam Anglicam* versa et doctorum commentariis declarata assidue meditaretur.' Quoted in Ussher,

them in every case with horror and alarm[1]. In putting forth their work it is quite obvious that the authors were anticipating the most active opposition[2]. An attempt was made accordingly, soon after it appeared, to check its circulation[3]: but no measures of that kind were carried out till twenty years later, in a synod[4] held at Oxford (1408).

The general views of Wycliffe on dogmatic questions may be gathered partly from the evidence adduced above, and partly from the multitudinous tracts[5] he composed at Lutterworth immediately before his death; but none of these are so distinct and comprehensive as the more scholastic work entitled his *Trialogus*[6]. Accepting the conciliar definitions of the ancient Church[7] as they related to the central truths of our religion, he professed to be desirous of reverting in all other points to Holy Scripture and the early standards of belief[8]. The prominence

REFORMA-
TORY
EFFORTS.

Summary of his theological opinions:

as above, p. 352. Richard of Hampole's version of the Psalms (circ. 1340) was not prohibited.

[1] Thus Knyghton, the anti-Lollard, has the following characteristic passage (col. 2644): 'Hic magister Johannes Wyclif evangelium, quod Christus contulit clericis et Ecclesiæ doctoribus, ut ipsi laicis et inferioribus personis secundum temporis exigentiam et personarum indigentiam cum mentis eorum esurie dulciter ministrarent, transtulit de Latino in Anglicam linguam, non angelicam, unde per ipsum fit vulgare et magis apertum laicis et mulieribus legere scientibus, quam solet esse clericis admodum literatis et bene intelligentibus: et sic evangelica margarita spargitur' etc.

[2] For their mode of defence, see *Preface* to the *Wycliffite Bible*, pp. xiv, xv. note: Vaughan, p. 338. The title of Wycliffe's own treatise on this point is sufficiently startling: *How Antichrist and his clerks travail to destroy Holy Writ.*

[3] See the remarkable protest of John of Gaunt, when an attempt was made to suppress it by act of Parliament (1390), in Ussher, as above, p. 352.

[4] Wilkins, III. 314; Johnson, II. 457.

[5] Vaughan, p. 405. The number of them (see the Catalogue, *Ibid.* pp. 525—544) appears almost incredible.

[6] Above, p. 382, n. 2. It is analysed in Turner's *Hist. of Engl.* 'Middle Ages,' v. 185—193, ed. 1830.

[7] See the extracts in Massingberd, *Engl. Reformation*, pp. 127, 128, 2nd ed. The Wycliffite *Remonstrance* (ed. Forshall) occupies the same ground. It contends that the doctrine of transubstantiation is not expressed in Holy Writ and is unproved by 'kyndeli [*i.e.* natural] reesoun,' and experience. 'Also holi doctouris bi a thousand yeer and more taughten not this opinli, but expresli the contrarie, as it is opin of seynt Austyn, Jerom, and Chrisostom:' p. 78.

[8] The following prophecy in the *Trialogus* (ed. Oxon. p. 349) is very remarkable: 'Suppono autem, quod aliqui fratres, quos Deus docere

REFORMA-
TORY
EFFORTS.

*especially
on the sa-
craments.*

awarded in his system to the Incarnation and Atonement of the Saviour[1] led him to renounce all trust in human merit, to suspect, if not to discontinue invocations of the saints, and more especially to fulminate against the impious sale of 'pardons,' or indulgences. Though he persisted to the last in speaking of the 'sacraments' as seven in number[2], he arrived at clear distinctions with regard to their necessity, importance, and effect. The Eucharist, according to his view, while it is 'sacramentally the Body of Christ' is also 'in its nature truly bread[3];' and consequently the supreme worship of the Host appeared to him idolatrous[4]. In baptism, which he thought was properly administered to infants, he could recognize the ordinary channel instituted by the Lord Himself, and therefore commonly required, in order to the remission of sins[5]. He was in doubt as to the scripturalness of confirmation[6], shocked by an excessive ritualism with which it had been loaded and obscured. The ministerial 'orders,' he contended, were originally two[7]; on which account the bishop ought to be included in a category with the pope, the cardinals, and others, who had no existence in the apostolic age. The first step in genuine penitence[8], according to his view, is thorough change of heart, and though

dignatur, ad religionem primævam Christi devotius convertentur, et relicta sua perfidia, sive obtenta sive petita Antichristi licentia, redibunt libere ad religionem Christi primævam, et tunc ædificabunt ecclesiam sicut Paulus.'

[1] *Trialogus*, pp. 310, 356 sq.: cf. Le Bas, pp. 321, 322. He is most emphatic on the subject of indulgences in his treatise *On Prelates*, (1383): Vaughan, pp. 428—430.

[2] *Trialogus*, pp. 245 sq.

[3] *Ibid.* pp. 249 sq.: cf. above, p. 382, n. 2.

[4] See Neander's remarks on this point, IX. 225.

[5] *Trialogus*, pp. 281 sq.

[6] *Ibid.* p. 292: cf. Le Bas, p. 340.

[7] Cf. above, p. 381. The passage in the *Trialogus* (p. 296) runs as follows: 'In primitiva Ecclesia .... suffecerunt duo ordines clericorum, scilicet, sacerdos et diaconus .... Tunc enim adinventa non fuit distinctio papæ et cardinalium, patriarcharum et archiepiscoporum, episcoporum et archidiaconorum,' etc. In his treatise on *Obedience to Prelates* (1382), he defends the irregularities of 'poor priests' (cf. above, p. 385, n. 1) by urging that the 'worldly' bishops had no right to prevent them from instructing the people: Vaughan, pp. 424 sq.

[8] *Trialogus*, pp. 326 sq. Of confession he adds: 'Sed non credat aliquis, quin sine tali confessione auriculari stat hominem vere conteri et salvari, cum Petrus injunxit generalem pœnitentiam.'

he did not question the established usage of auricular confession, he denied its absolute necessity in every case. *REFORMATORY EFFORTS.*

His speculations on the nature and intent of matrimony[1] are peculiarly erratic. On the one side he conceived it to have been ordained for the filling up the vacancies occasioned in the court of heaven by the apostasy of Satan and his angels[2]: on the other, he regarded stipulations which forbid the marriage even of the nearest kindred as deriving all their force from human maxims and decrees[3]. The last in order of the 'sacraments,' extreme unction, was verbally retained: but he had looked in vain for traces of its institution in the Holy Scriptures[4].

While diverging thus at numerous points from the tradition of the Mediæval Church, it is remarkable that Wycliffe still continued to believe in purgatory[5], and at least to some extent in the effects producible on saints departed by the prayers and alms of holy friends surviving, and the service of the mass. A late, if not his very latest, publication[6] represents the family of God in three divisions: (1) the holy angels and beatified men, (2) the saints in purgatory, who are doomed to expiate the sins *Purgatory.*

Tripartite division of the Church.

---

[1] See the *Trialogus*, pp. 315—325, and Le Bas, pp. 342, 343.
[2] Cf. above, p. 283, n. 2.
[3] After speaking of the marriage of brothers and sisters in the infancy of the world, he adds: 'Nec superest ratio, quare non sic liceret hodie, nisi humana ordinatio, quæ dicit non solum ex cognatione, sed ex affinitate, amorem inter homines dilatari; et causa hæc hominum est nimis debilis' (p. 318). More sober views, however, are expressed in *An Apology for Lollard Doctrines*, attributed to *Wycliffe*, pp. 70, 71, ed. Todd, 1842.
[4] See the brief discussion in the next chapter of the *Trialogus* (lib. IV. c. 25). He maintains that St. James (v. 14) is not speaking of 'infirmitatem finalem, sed consolationem faciendam a presbytero, dum aliquis infirmatur, et quia per viam naturæ oleum abundans in illis partibus valet ad corporis sanitatem. Ideo talem meminit unctionem, non quod illud oleum agat in animam, sed quod oratio effusa a sacerdote devoto medicat quemquam, ut Deus infirmitati animæ suffragetur,' (p. 333).
[5] In his treatise *On the Curse Expounded* [*Select English Works*, III. 286, 287 (1383)], he says that saying of mass, with cleanness of holy life and burning devotion, pleaseth God Almighty, and is *profitable to Christian souls in purgatory*, and to men living on earth that they may withstand temptations to sins. Vaughan, p. 438: cf. Le Bas, pp. 327, 328.
[6] *De Ecclesia et Membris ejus*, edited by Dr Todd (Dublin, 1851), and in the *Select Works*, III. 338 sq.

REFORMA-
TORY
EFFORTS.

Absolute reprobation.

committed in the world[1], and (3) the remnant of true-hearted Christians who are following while on earth the footsteps of the Lord. As a result of his belief in absolute predestination[2], he confined the members of the Church to those who will eventually be saved[3]. The reprobate he held to form a class essentially and irreversibly distinct; although as long as men are in the body none (it was maintained) could feel assured of his eternal destination[4].

Development of his principles by the Lollards.

Many germs of error and extravagance may be detected in the theories of Wycliffe, much as those were overbalanced by the noble witness he had borne to long-forgotten truths and by the virtues of his private life. The anti-social principles avowed by some of his successors (known as early as the year 1387 by the opprobrious name of 'Lollards')[5] had been logically drawn from his extreme positions on the nature of property and the inherent vice of all ecclesiastical endowments. Part, indeed, of the success[6] attending his own labours would be due to this peculiarity of his creed: but there we also find an element conducing more than others to its premature decline. The upper classes of society were alienated[7], and a number

---

[1] The words are remarkable, particularly as indicating a distrust of prayers for the dead: 'The secound part of this chirche ben seintis in purgatorie; and thes synnen not of the newe, but purgen ther olde synnes: and many errours fallen in preiying for theis seyntis; and sith thei alle ben deede in body, Christis wordis may be takun of hem, Sue [follow] we Crist in our liyf and late the deede bérie the dede;' *Select Works*, III. 339.

[2] See Neander's investigation of this point, IX. 240 sq. One of the charges brought against Wycliffe at the council of Constance (1415) was, that 'omnia de necessitate absoluta eveniunt:' cf. Lenfant, *Hist. du Concile*, liv. II. ch. 59, Art. xxvii.

[3] 'This chirche is modir to ech man that shal be saaf, and conteyneth no membre but oonli men that shal be saved;' *De Ecclesia*, as above (*Select Works*, III. 339).

[4] *Ibid.* p. 339. He adds, that 'as ech man shal hope that he shal be saaf in bliss, so he shulde suppose that he be lyme of holi churche.'

[5] See above, p. 347, n. 1; and Turner, *Middle Ages*, v. 198, where the bishop of Worcester (1387) denounces the 'Lollards' as 'eternally-damned sons of Antichrist,' &c.

[6] This was so marked, that Knyghton, in speaking (coll. 2661, 2666) of knights, counts, and even dukes among the 'Wycliviani sive Lollardi,' adds: 'Secta illa in maximo honore illis diebus habebatur et in tantum multiplicata fuit, quod vix duos videres in via quin alter eorum discipulus Wyclefi fuerit.'

[7] *Hist. of England under the House of Lancaster*, pp. 36, 37.

of the more distinguished clerics, who had joined the movement in its earlier stages, now withdrew and took the other side[1]. Soon after Wycliffe's death complaints were made that the 'Lollards' advocated tenets like the following[2]: They regarded absolution as sinful and even impious: pilgrimages, invocation of saints, the keeping of saints'-days, and the use of images they branded as idolatry: they questioned[3] the lawfulness of oaths, and, undervaluing all episcopal jurisdiction, went so far as to ordain their ministers[4] and organize an independent sect. On more than one occasion members of it were obnoxious to the charge of stirring up sedition[5]; and the English court, at length relieved from other adversaries, entered on a vigorous course of action for repressing every kind of misbelief. The same repressive policy was followed out by Henry IV., who on dethroning Richard (Sept. 29, 1399) had found it more than ever needful to secure the aid of the ecclesiastics, monks, and friars[6]. At this epoch, it would

---

[1] Instances are given in Le Bas, pp. 386—390. The same occurred, and for similar reasons, in the great convulsion of the sixteenth century. Heath, for instance, an especial favourite of Melanchthon (1535), became the Marian archbishop of York (1555).

[2] See the catalogue of these 'novi errores' in Knyghton, col. 2707.

[3] The words are 'Quod non licet aliquo modo jurare:' cf. the charges brought against the Waldenses, above, p. 294, n. 3.

[4] Walsingham, *Hypodigma Neustriæ*, p. 544, alludes to this feature of their system in the following terms: 'Lollardi sequaces Johannis Wicliff in tantam sunt evecti temeritatem, ut eorum presbyteri, more pontificum [*i.e.* bishops] novos crearent presbyteros, asserentes quemlibet sacerdotem tantam habere potestatem conferendi sacramenta ecclesiastica quantum papa:' cf. the *Apology for the Lollards*, pp. 28 sq., and Dr Todd's remarks, 'Introd.,' pp. xxviii, xxix.

[5] *e.g.* they placarded the churches in London with scurrilous attacks upon the priests. *Hist. of England*, as above, pp. 29, 30. The boldness of their tone at this period is attested by the remonstrances which they addressed to the parliament of 1395 (Wilkins, III. 221). The substance of their manifesto was then expanded and published in the English language; and Mr Forshall has apparently identified the larger treatise with the *Ecclesiæ Regimen*, or so-called *Remonstrance*, which he edited in 1851: see his Pref. pp. ix, x. In the following year (1396), eighteen propositions taken from Wycliffe's *Trialogus* were condemned by a synod held in London (Wilkins, III. 229), and answered in the treatise of Woodford above cited, p. 375, n. 6.

[6] Soon after his accession he put forth a proclamation with the sanction of the House of Lords, directing the seizure and imprisonment of all persons who dared to preach against the Mendicants (March 21, 1400): Rymer's *Fœdera*, VIII. 87. Henry V. (Nov. 6, 1413) made a grant of 25 marks per annum to the Warden and Convent of Friars Minors in the

seem, the tenets of the Lollards[1] were expressed with greater boldness and pursued more generally into their logical results. They lost all reverence for the sacraments administered at church, and characterized the mass itself[2] as the watch-tower of Antichrist. They absolutely rejected the doctrine of purgatory[3], though retaining, with conditions, certain prayers and offerings for the dead[4]. They carried out their views of matrimony so far as to require that monks and nuns should marry, lowering at the same time its importance by dispensing with the intervention of the priest. Their strong antipathy to saints' days now extended to the weekly festival of the resurrection, which they treated as a merely Jewish ordinance[5]. Of other features now developed, none was practically more important than the circulation of a host of semi-political prophecies[6], suggested by extravagant ideas respecting the secularization of the Church.

It was to meet these later forms of Lollardism that Henry and his parliament devised the sanguinary statute[7] *De hæretico comburendo*. Trial in the civil courts was hereby superseded; for certificates from any bishop or his commissary, stating that a person was convicted or was vehemently suspected of heresy, constrained the

---

University of Cambridge for the support of the Catholic faith: *Documents relating to the University*, I. 38, ed. 1852.

[1] See *Hist. of England*, as above, p. 32.

[2] Wycliffe himself is charged (but, as it seems, unfairly) with disparaging 'the Mass and Hours.' Thus, in the *Articuli Joh. Wiclefi* condemned at Constance (in Brown's *Fascic.* I. 276), we read among others of this kind: 'Utile foret ecclesiæ poni in pristina libertate: et sic cessarent missarum superadditarum solennia et orationes cum horis canonicis adinventæ. Licet enim istæ tres adinventiones humanæ *per accidens prosint ecclesiæ, non tamen tantum quantum peccatum diaboli*.'

[3] Cf. above, p. 389.

[4] *e.g.* in one of the *Conclusions* (§ 7), addressed to Parliament (as above, p. 391, n. 5), they speak as follows: 'Quod spirituales orationes pro animabus mortuorum factæ in ecclesia nostra [*i.e.* the Church of England which they distinguish (§ 1) from its 'noverca,' the Church of Rome], præferentes unum per nomen magis quam alium, est falsum fundamentum eleemosynæ.'

[5] Cf. above, p. 294, n. 3; where the same charge is brought against the Waldenses.

[6] See Dr Maitland's 8th essay (1852) on *The Lollards*, pp. 216 sq. These 'prophecies' continued to be circulated until the very dawn of the Reformation.

[7] 2 Hen. IV. c. 15; Wilkins, III. 252. On the doubts respecting the authority of this act, see *Hist. of England*, as above, Note xvii.

sheriffs and their officers 'forthwith in some high place, before the people, to do him to be burnt.' An early victim of the spirit which presided in the framing of this merciless enactment was William Sawtre[1], a parish-priest, who had already manifested what were deemed heretical opinions, and had been driven to recant; but on reiterating his denial of transubstantiation[2], he was publicly burnt at Smithfield (Feb. 26, 1401). Another victim was Lord Cobham[3] (Sir John Oldcastle), a person of extraordinary merit. He had always set the highest value on the works of Wycliffe[4], and his mansion at Cowling Castle in Kent had often furnished Lollard preachers with a shelter and a home. Suspected of a leaning to the new opinions, he was now, on his appeal to Henry V.[5], transferred into the court of archbishop Arundel, his most implacable opponent[6] (Sept. 1413). The charges brought against him were that he impugned the jurisdiction of the English Church and propagated misbelief, particularly on the Eucharist, the merit of pilgrimages, relics, image-worship, and the papal monarchy. The trial ended in a sentence which proclaimed

REFORMA-
TORY
EFFORTS.

William Sawtre
(d. 1401).

Lord Cobham
(d. 1417).

---

[1] Vaughan, p. 486. The royal mandate for his execution (*Rot. Parl.* 2 Hen. IV. § 29) orders it to be made conspicuous 'in abhorrence of his crime and as an example to all other Christians.'

[2] This was the gravamen of the case against him. A MS. Chronicle of the period (Cambr. Univ. Libr. Dd. xiv. 2, fol. 305), in recounting similar persecutions, states the crime of one of the sufferers in these terms: 'bicause that he said that godys body myȝt nat be grounde in a mulle, and that he kept counseil in huyding of lollardis boks.'

[3] One of the best accounts of him is given in the anonymous *Hist. of England*, as above, pp. 60—87.

[4] Copies of them were diffused at his expense: Vaughan, p. 495.

[5] This monarch is praised by a contemporary as 'Christo et mundo commendatissimus inter reges,' for raising a standard 'contra Wiclevistas hæreticos.'

[6] In the convocation held at Oxford, 1408, and apparently adjourned to London, he had published his violent *Constitutions against Lollards* (Johnson, ii. 457—475, Oxf. 1851, where see the editor's notes). The first of these enjoins that 'no one preach to the people or clergy in Latin or in the vulgar tongue, within a church or without it, unless he present himself to the diocesan of the place in which he attempts to preach and be examined,' &c. In § 4, scholars are forbidden to dispute 'publicly, or even privately, concerning the Catholic faith or the sacraments of the Church.' Arundel was now supported by a Carmelite friar, Thomas Netter, of Walden, whose *Doctrinale Antiquitatum Fidei Eccl. Cathol.* (not unfrequently printed) is aimed at the Lollards. He is also generally regarded as the author of *Fasciculi Zizaniorum magistri Johannis Wyclif*, (above, p. 380, n. 4): see Shirley's Introd., pp. lxx. sq.

REFORMA-
TORY
EFFORTS.

him a 'pernicious and detestable heretic;' but in the respite granted with the hope of wringing from him a confession of his guilt, he found an opportunity of escaping into Wales[1], where he continued till **1417**. He was then recaptured, sentenced to the stake, and most barbarously executed in St Giles's Fields on Christmas-day[2].

The Council of Constance denounces Wycliffe, 1415.

A heavier blow had meanwhile been inflicted on the Lollards by the council of Constance[3] (**1415**). However cordially the bulk of the ecclesiastics there assembled might rejoice in the attempt of Wycliffe to repel the arrogance of Rome, to banish all administrative abuses, and to elevate the tone of morals in the Church at large[4], they could not tolerate those branches of his system where he meddled with the order of society and questioned the traditionary faith of Christians. Five-and-forty articles[5], extracted from his writings, were accordingly denounced (May **4, 1415**). Another list, extending to no less than

---

[1] Walsingham (ed. Riley, II. 306, 307) ascribes the rumours of disturbances in the following January to a secret conspiracy of the Lollards: but there is every reason to believe that Cobham was still in Wales: cf. Vaughan, pp. 503—505. In 1430, however, some of them *did* rise into actual rebellion: Turner, *Middle Ages*, III. 14, 15.

[2] Many other executions followed (Wilkins, III. 394 sq.) to the joy of men like Thomas Netter, who says (in the *Proem.* to his *Doctrinale*) that they were all consigned 'duplici poenæ, incendio propter Deum, suspendio propter regem.' Elmham, a Latin poet of the time, discovers Sir John Oldcastle in the apocalyptic number 666: *Liber Metricus*, I. cap. II. l. 89, 90.

'Nomine sexcenti sunt, sexaginta simul sex:
Extrahe quot remanent, his sua vita datur.'

Memorials of Hen. V., edited by Cole, in the series of *Chronicles and Memorials of Great Britain*, p. 96.

[3] The University of Oxford had deputed twelve persons in 1412 to examine the works of Wycliffe, and the result was that no fewer than two hundred and sixty-seven conclusions were branded as 'guilty of fire:' Wilkins, III. 339 sq. A fact like this appears to militate strongly against the genuineness of the *Publike Testimonie given out by the Universitie of Oxford* in honour of Wycliffe, and bearing date Oct. 5, 1406 (*Ibid.* III. 302): cf. Le Bas, pp. 309 sq. His writings were also condemned by pope John XXIII. in 1412: Mansi, XXVII. 505.

[4] We may estimate the strength of these feelings from the fact that the University of Oxford, which condemned the Lollard tenets in 1412, drew up in 1414, and by the king's express command, a series of *Articles concerning the Reformation of the Church* (Wilkins, III. 360—365).

[5] See Von der Hardt, *Concil. Constant.* IV. 150 sq., and Lenfant, *Hist. du Concile de Const.* liv. II. ch. 59. The proceedings were prefaced by a sermon from the bishop of Toulon, in which it is remarkable that the pope himself was handled in the roughest way.

sixty articles[1] was added in a further session (July 6); nearly all of them agreeing in the main with accusations that had been already urged against himself or some of his early followers in England. On the same occasion it was ordered that the bones of Wycliffe, if discernible from those of other persons, should be burnt,—a fulmination which, however, was suspended till the time of pope Martin V. (**1428**). The prelate whom he charged to see it executed was Fleming, bishop of Lincoln, once an ardent champion of the new opinions[2], who proceeded to exhume the body of his former friend, and after burning it, directed that the ashes should be thrown into the Swift, the stream which flows by Lutterworth[3].

The only writer who applied himself in earnest to convert the Lollards, by the use of candid argument and by diffusing tracts in the vernacular, was Reginald Pecock[4], who had been translated from the bishopric of St Asaph to that of Chichester in **1449**. His moderation was, however, almost fatal to him. He could not insist upon the absolute infallibility of the Church[5]; and after a vexatious controversy with his brother-prelates, he was driven by a threat of punishment for heresy to make a solemn recanta-

marginalia: REFORMATORY EFFORTS. *Burning of his bones,* **1428**. *Reginald Pecock,* (silenced **1457**).

---

[1] Von der Hardt, IV. 408 sq.; Lenfant, liv. III. ch. 42. Chicheley, who succeeded Arundel at Canterbury, in the following year (1416) followed up these censures in the same spirit (Wilkins, III. 378), aiming more especially to prevent the Lollards from holding 'secret conventicles.'

[2] See Le Bas, p. 390.

[3] Lyndwood (*Provinciale*, p. 284, Oxon. 1679) mentions these barbarous proceedings with apparent satisfaction.

[4] See Lewis, *Life of Pecock*, passim: and Wharton's *Append.* to Cave, ad an. 1444. His chief book against the Lollards is entitled *The Repressor of overmuch blaming of the Clergy;* printed (1860) in the series of *Chronicles and Memorials of Great Britain.* In the first part he discusses at great length the principal objection of the nonconformists, that nothing is to be received as true, or obligatory on the Christians, if it be not fully and expressly stated in the Bible. He maintains (Pt. I. ch. v. p. 25), 'if eny semyng discorde be bitwixe the wordis writen in the outward book of Holi Scripture and the doom of resoun, write in mannis soule and herte, the wordis so writen withoutforth ouȝten be expowned and be interpretid and brouȝt forto accorde with the doom of resoun in thilk mater;' &c.

[5] His obnoxious statements had appeared in his *Treatise of Faith*: see Mr Babington's *Introduction* to Pecock's *Repressor*, pp. xxxii. sq., and p. xxxix. n. 1. The second book, in which he shews that Scripture is the only perfect and substantial basis of belief, was published, London, 1688.

REFORMA-
TORY
EFFORTS.

Ulterior influence of the Lollards.

tion, and was finally imprisoned in Thorney abbey where he died[1].

Although it is not easy to trace out the fortunes of the Lollards during the political convulsions from which England suffered in the fifteenth century, nor to determine whether they were still surviving at the outbreak of the Reformation[2], we can scarcely doubt that strong predispositions were excited in its favour, by their preaching and their works. John Wycliffe may indeed be taken as the prototype[3] of one important school of English, and still more of Continental Church-reformers. In the natural bias of his mind, in the unwonted clearness of his moral intuitions, in his rude but manly style, and in the fearless energy with which he struggled, almost single-handed, to eradicate the gross abuses of the times, we see an agent qualified to censure and demolish errors rather than to strengthen the dismantled fortress of the Church, and beautify afresh the ancient sanctuary of truth: while some of his opinions, even where he was not conscious of the slightest wish to foster insurrection, were too easily convertible for such an end by over-heated crowds or by less scrupulous disciples. It is found, accordingly, that *the* Reformers who at last succeeded in the sphere of labour where his patriotic piety had failed, drew little, if at all, from his productions[4]: and in Germany, the Lutheran,

---

[1] He was allowed no writing materials, and 'no books to look on, but only a portuous [*i.e.* breviary], a mass-book, a psalter, a legend, and a Bible.' Harleian MS. quoted by Turner, III. 143, n. 47: cf. *Repressor*, Introd. p. lvii, and note 3. Leland (*Collectanea*, III. 410, ed. Hearne) extracts a passage from an old chronicle which throws light on the condemnation of Pecock: 'male sensit *de Eucharistia* et de sanctionibus Ecclesiæ.' The suspicion with which he was regarded is further seen in a supplemental statute of King's College, Cambridge (founded 1441); provision being then made that every scholar, at the end of his probationary years, should abjure the errors or heresies 'Johannis Wiclif, *Reginaldi Pecock*,' etc.: Lewis, as above, p. 173.

[2] Traces of their influence are found in the Acts of the Convocation of 1536: see Hardwick's *Hist. of the Articles*, pp. 34, 35, 2nd edition.

[3] See Prof. Blunt's remark on the affinity between the Lollard and the Puritan, in his *Sketch of the Reformation*, pp. 87 sq., 6th edit.

[4] Dr Todd, in the 'Advertisement' prefixed to his edition of Wycliffe's treatise *De Ecclesia et membris suis*, quotes a passage from Aylmer's *Harborough for faithful subjects*, printed at Strasburg, 1559, and launching censures at the prelates on account of their temporal possessions. The author seems to have been stirred to make this onslaught by reading 'Wicliefe's boke, which he wrote *De Ecclesia*:' but when he

as distinguished from the Swiss divines, appear to have regarded Lollardism with positive distaste[1].   *REFORMATORY EFFORTS.*

The feverish impulses, however, which that system had communicated to the general spirit of the age were soon transmitted to a distance. They not only tended to enlighten England, but 'electrified' Bohemia. Some indeed of the reaction there produced is traceable to other causes[2], for example, to the freer element in the original Christianity of the district; to the old antagonism between the Slavic and Germanic families, of whom the latter was in close alliance with the pope; and even more to individual preachers[3], who, anterior to the age of Huss or Wycliffe, started independent measures for the exaltation of their mother-Church.   *Simultaneous movement in Bohemia.*

Of these precursors, three at least deserve a special notice. Milicz, a Moravian of Cremsier, was the archdeacon of Prague, and secretary to the emperor Charles IV., the king of Bohemia. Anxious to devote himself entirely to the spiritual benefit of others, he resigned his large emoluments (**1364**), and during several years perambulated the country as an earnest preacher of repentance[4]. He was more and more oppressed by a conviction that   *Milicz (d. 1374).*

---

was at length promoted to the see of London, he 'changed his mind,' pp. 6—8: cf. Nicolas's *Life and Times of Hatton*, p. 237, Lond. 1847. The twenty-sixth of the *Articles of Religion*, if not others also, may have had an eye to errors of the Lollards; although in the *Remonstrance* edited by Mr Forshall, the writer of it grants that sacraments and other ordinances may be truly administered by 'evil men' (p. 123), but that in cases where the lives of priests are openly scandalous, their flocks are bound to keep aloof from their communion (cf. *Apology for Lollard Doctrines*, pp. 37—40, ed. Todd).

[1] Some of their antipathy was due to the aberrations mentioned in the previous note: e.g. *Apologia Confess. August.* (by Melanchthon), p. 149, in the *Libri Symbolici*, ed. Francke, Leipz. 1847: cf. other instances in Gieseler, IV. § 125, p. 257, n. 31, and Le Bas, pp. 320, 321.

[2] See above, pp. 111—115.

[3] The best modern authorities on this subject are Palacky's *Gesch. von Böhmen*, Prag. 1845, and Jordan's *Vorläufer des Husitenthums in Böhmen*, Leipz. 1846.

[4] At first his influence was impaired by his want of familiarity with the native tongue, or the strangeness of his accent ('propter incongruentiam vulgaris sermonis'); but afterwards he made a deep impression, more especially on the female auditors ('inceperunt mulieres superbæ pepla alta et gemmis circumdata caputia et vestimenta auro et argento ornata deponere'): see a *Life* of Milicz (by a disciple) in Balbinus, *Miscell. Hist. Bohemiæ*, Decad. I., lib. IV., pp. 45, 46; Prag. 1682.

<small>REFORMA-
TORY
EFFORTS.</small>

the Church had sunk into the grasp of Antichrist[1]. He treated on this topic in St Peter's at Rome[2] (1367), but was immediately silenced by the Inquisition[3]. Urban V., however, who attempted at that very juncture[4] to reoccupy the old metropolis, released the culprit from his chains and sent him back to Prague. He there resumed his work; but certain Friars, envious of his popularity and writhing under his rebukes, commenced a fresh attack upon him. He expired at Avignon in 1374, while the judicial process they had instituted was still pending[5].

<small>Conrad of
Wald-
hausen
(d. 1369).</small>

One of his contemporaries was an Austrian, Conrad of Waldhausen[6], who adopted a like method in Vienna for awakening all classes of society. He was at length invited by the emperor Charles IV. to aid the holy movement in Bohemia[7]; and the sermons which he there delivered seem to have produced a marvellous effect. Like Milicz, he had also proved himself peculiarly obnoxious to the Mendicants[8], who strove to silence him (1364). Their opposition failed, however, and he died in peace (1369).

Among the numerous followers of Milicz none acquired

---

[1] With this feeling he composed a *Libellus de Antichristo*, on which see Neander, IX. pp. 256 sq., Jordan, p. 29.

[2] He there announced 'quod Antichristus venit' (*Life*, as above, p. 51): feeling himself constrained to pray and labour 'pro domino nostro papa et pro domino imperatore, ut ita ordinent ecclesiam sanctam in spiritualibus et temporalibus, ut securi fideles deserviant Creatori:' Neander, IX. 259. Another of the charges subsequently brought against him was for strenuously maintaining 'quod omnis homo tenetur de necessitate saltem *ad minus bis in hebdomada* sumere Corporis Dominici sacramentum:' Jordan, p. 39, where all the twelve articles are given.

[3] This engine was now worked by Mendicants, to whom Milicz, like Wycliffe, made himself peculiarly obnoxious. On his apprehension some of them announced to their congregations in Prague, 'Carissimi, ecce jam Militius cremabitur:' *Life*, as above, p. 51.

[4] See above, p. 328.

[5] This point does not seem to be very clearly established: see Jordan, p. 27, and Neander, IX. p. 263.

[6] Sometimes called 'von Stiekna' through an error of the press which confounded him with another of the same class. Sczekna is said to have also distinguished himself by preaching 'contra clericos:' Neander, p. 264, note.

[7] On his labours there and heretofore, see Jordan, pp. 3 sq. He also was persuaded that the Antichrist was rampant in the Church.

[8] According to Balbinus (as above, p. 397, n. 4), p. 406, Conrad composed a large treatise entitled *Accusationes Mendicantium:* cf. Neander, pp. 268 sq.

so high a reputation as Matthias of Janow (in Bohemia), who, proceeding on the same conviction that the Church would decompose if it were not immediately reformed[1], appears to have anticipated many of the views afterwards cherished by the Lutheran divines. A six years' residence at Paris (hence his title of 'Magister Parisiensis') made him an accomplished scholar and philosopher: but holier aspirations were excited in him as he listened to the fervent preachers now arising in his native country. In 1381 he was collated to a stall in the cathedral church of Prague. The scandals there laid open to his gaze impelled him to rebuke the monks and clerics, in a work[2] *On the Abomination of Desolation in the Church*. A more important work[3], however, is entitled *Rules of the Old and New Testament*, in which, amid a number of prophetic theories, he handles the corruptions of the age with terrible severity. Among the remedies on which both he and Milicz had insisted, one was greater frequency in the reception of the Lord's Supper[4]; but a synod held at

REFORMA-TORY EFFORTS.

Matthias of Janow (d. 1394).

---

[1] He went so far even as to despair of the corrigibility of the Church in its present state: 'Dei Ecclesia nequit ad pristinam suam dignitatem reduci, vel reformari, nisi prius omnia fiant nova.' *De Sacerdotum et Monachorum Abominatione Desolationis*, etc. c. 37 (published in the *Hist. et Monument. Joh. Hus*, Norimb. 1715, I. 473 sq.). In an extract (given by Jordan, p. 68), he thinks it essential to a reformation that the ritual system of the Church and some of its dogmatical excrescences should be curtailed: 'Quapropter apud me decretum habeo, quod ad reformandam pacem et unionem in universit..te Christiana expedit omnem plantationem illam eradicare, et *abbreviare* iterum verbum super terram, et *reducere Christi Jesu Ecclesiam ad sua primordia salubria et compendiosa*.' The work has been ascribed sometimes to Wycliffe and also to Huss; but it is, no doubt, by Matthias.

[2] As in the previous note.

[3] The whole is still in MS., but extracts from it are supplied in Jordan, as above, pp. 59 sq.: cf. Neander's review, IX. pp. 280—335. In one passage (p. 313) it is manifest that Janow, had he followed out his argument, would have insisted on the necessity of communion in *both* kinds. His words are, 'Propter quotidianam frequentiam et propter dualitatem utriusque speciei, panis et vini, a quibus hoc sacrificium *integratur*.' cf. p. 333. According to his view, the Eucharist was the crowning act of worship (p. 323), and the Bible the great source of Christian joy and knowledge. On the latter point he spoke with a peculiar emphasis (Jordan, p. 30); 'Unde cum vidi quam plurimos portare semper reliquias et ossa diversorum sanctorum, pro defensione sua quilibet et sua singulari devotione...ego elegi mihi Bibliam, meam electam sociam meam peregrinationi, gestare semper mecum,' etc.

[4] See above, p. 398, n. 2. Janow thus expresses himself in the unpublished work reviewed by Neander (p. 329): 'Absit autem hoc a Chris-

REFORMA-TORY EFFORTS.

John Huss (d. 1415).

Prague¹ in **1388** discountenanced the practice, by forbidding laymen to communicate more frequently than once a month².

The ground had thus been broken for the sedulous but ill-requited labours of John Huss³ (Hus), who saw the light at Husinecz, a market-town of Bohemia, July 6, **1369**. His place of training was the newly-founded University of Prague, where he became professor (*i.e.* public tutor) in philosophy (**1396**). Soon afterwards, in (**1400**), he was chosen as the spiritual director of the queen Sophia; and his popular discourses at the chapel of Bethlehem⁴ in Prague (**1401**) were instrumental to the spreading of his influence from the court and university to all the humbler grades of life. His 'orthodoxy' at this time was unimpeachable: we find him bearing a commission from the primate Sbynco (Lepus) and conducting an inquiry into the genuineness of a reputed miracle at Wilsnack⁵.

Transmission of Wycliffe's writings to Bohemia.

Huss had grown familiar with the Sacred Writings, with the doctors of the Western Church, especially Augustine, and with modern authors of celebrity, including Grosseteste⁶ of Lincoln and his own fellow-countryman, Matthias of Janow, when the theological as well as other tracts of Wycliffe found their way as far as Prague and caused a general fermentation in the academic circles⁷.

---

tianis quod debeant solum semel in anno agere memoriam Dominicæ passionis, quæ continuis momentis debet in ipsorum pectoribus demorari.' He was in favour of *daily* communion.

¹ Jordan, p. 55.

² In the *Ancren Riwle* (Camd. Soc. 1853), p. 412, it is enjoined that, as men undervalue what is frequently administered, the laity should communicate only fifteen times in a year.

³ See especially, the *Historia et Monumenta Joh. Hus atque Hieron. Pragensis*, Norimb. 1715; Palacky, *Gesch. von Böhmen*, as above; Neander, IX. 339—537; and Daun's *Magister Johannes Hus*, 1853. *Documenta M. J. Hus vitam, doctrinam, causam in Constantiensi concilio actam*, &c. *illustrantia;* ed. Fr. Palacky, Prag. 1869.

⁴ The founder of this chapel states, in his deed of gift (Gieseler, v. § 150, p. 103, n. 1), that he called it 'Bethlehem quod interpretatur *domus panis*...hac consideratione, ut ibidem populus communis et Christi fideles pane prædicationis sanctæ refici debeant.'

⁵ See the particulars in Neander, pp. 342 sq.

⁶ This may be concluded from references to Grosseteste in the works of Huss.

⁷ According to Huss himself (*Contra Anglicum Joan. Stokes:* Opp. I. 108), who informs us that as early as 1381 some of the Wycliffite tracts

The exchange of sentiments promoted in this age by wandering scholars was facilitated in the case of England and Bohemia by the marriage, in 1382, of the princess Anna, daughter of Charles IV., to our Richard II. We are also told[1] that Jerome of Prague, who stood to Huss in a relation similar to that in which Melanchthon stood to Luther, sojourned for a time at Oxford (circ. **1398**), and on returning home imported numerous copies of the Wycliffite tracts to circulate among the students in Bohemia. Huss had not been favourably impressed with some of these productions; but a change[2] at length appears to have come over him, and he stood forth as Wycliffe's pupil and apologist. The ground-tone of their minds, however wide they may have been apart on isolated topics, was the same: they were both Realists[3], and both intensely anxious to promote the reformation of the Church[4].

A numerous party[5] now began to cluster in the chapel

Quarrel of

were known in Prague, and that he was acquainted with them before 1391. These, however, may have been chiefly philosophical in their character..

[1] The authority on which this statement generally rests is Æneas Sylvius (*Hist. Bohem.* c. 35), whose hatred of the Hussites will be gathered from the following extract: 'Imbutus jam ipse [*i. e.* vir quidam genere nobilis] Wiclevitarum veneno et ad nocendum paratus, tum quod erat familiæ suæ cognomen, Putridum Piscem, *i.e.* fœtidum virus, in cives suos evomuit.' Palacky, however, seems to think that the noble here mentioned was Nicholas von Faulfisch, a less distinguished follower of Wycliffe (III. pt. 2, 192, n. 245).

[2] Vaughan's *Wycliffe*, p. 509. Yet it is obvious from the language used by Huss himself (*Opp.* I. 330) that he did not acquiesce in some of Wycliffe's opinions even at the close of his career. He says that he holds to the 'sententiæ veræ' of the English reformer, 'non quia ipse dixit, sed quia Divina Scriptura, vel ratio infallibilis dicit. Si autem *aliquem errorem posuerit*, nec ipsum, nec quemcunque alium intendo in errore, quantumlibet modice, imitari.' On the other hand, Æneas Sylvius, as above, declares that Huss carried his admiration of Wycliffe to the highest pitch, asserting of his books that they contained all truth, 'adjiciensque crebro inter prædicandum, se postquam ex hac luce migraret in ea loca proficisci cupere, ad quæ Wyclevi anima pervenisset, quem virum bonum, sanctum, cœloque dignum non dubitaret.'

[3] Neander, IX. p. 349. The German students, on the contrary, were Nominalists, which introduced another element of strife.

[4] Huss (*Opp.* I. 109) mentions this as the great bond of sympathy with the English reformer: 'Movent me sua scripta, quibus nititur toto conamine omnes homines ad legem Christi reducere, et clerum præcipue, ut dimittendo sæculi pompam et dominationem vivat cum apostolis vitam Christi.'

[5] Neander, pp. 352 sq. Æneas Sylvius (as above, c. 35) puts the

M.A.   D D

margin:
REFORMA-
TORY
EFFORTS.

the German and Bohemian academics.

Huss attacks the corrupt ecclesiastics, **1407:**

---

and the lecture-room of Huss. In him the natives saw an able type of the Bohemian as distinguished from the other class of students; and accordingly the advocacy of the new opinions in religion was ere long identified with nationalism in politics, and irritated by the national dislike of every thing Germanic. In the midst of this unhappy war of races, nearly all the foreigners withdrew from Prague (**1409**), transfusing into other seats of learning the antipathy which most of them now cherished for both Wycliffe and the new reformers in Bohemia.

One of the most glaring evils on which Huss insisted from the opening to the close of his career, was the degeneracy of the ecclesiastics[1]. His invectives roused the anger of his former friend, archbishop Sbynco[2], who, imputing the sensation thus produced to the diffusion of the Lollard tracts, commanded them to be collected and committed to the flames[3] (**1408**). A series of complaints were also lodged at Rome[4], which finally evoked a bull of Alexander V. (Dec. 20, **1409**). He there enjoined a fresh inquiry, in the hope of burning all the other books of Wycliffe and suppressing every form of Lollardism.

---

matter thus: 'Rexerunt scholam Pragensem usque in ea tempora Teutones. Id molestissimum Bohemis fuit, hominibus natura ferocibus atque indomitis.' After the secession of the Germans, who are said to have numbered, at the least, five thousand (others have it *forty-four* thousand) students, there were only two thousand left in Prague. The malcontents established themselves at Leipzig.

[1] Cf. above, p. 401, n. 4. In 1407 he preached before a diocesan synod from Eph. vi. 14 (*Opp.* II. 32 sq.), and betrayed his leaning to the views of Wycliffe and Matthias of Janow with regard to the ecclesiastical endowments. He also inveighs against the dissolute habits of many of his audience ('prælati, canonici, plebani, et alii presbyteri,' p. 38).

[2] Neander, pp. 361 sq. A formal treatise ('Antiwickleffus') was composed at this juncture (1408) by Stephen, prior of the Carthusians of Dolan near Olmütz. It is printed in Pez, *Thesaur. Anecdot.* IV. part. ii. 149 sq. where the *Antihussus* and other cognate pieces may be found (pp. 361 sq.).

[3] Two hundred copies, of which many had been richly bound, were thus destroyed: cf. Vaughan's *Wycliffe*, p. 404. The University of Prague declared (June 15, 1410) that it was not a consenting party to the act of archbishop Sbynco and the rest 'in combustionem librorum magistri Johannis Wicklef:' Gieseler, v. § 150, p. 109, note 9. Neander (p. 377) places this combustion in the summer of 1410.

[4] Another ground of complaint was that the new reformer exercised pernicious influence by his sermons. This was to be obviated by forbidding any one to preach in a *private* chapel, such as the Bethlehem. See Alexander's bull in Raynald. ad an. 1409, § 89.

But Huss, like his precursor, was at first in favour with the court[1]; and this advantage, added to a keen perception of the weakness and injustice of the papacy, induced him to appeal from the decision of 'a pontiff ill informed' to one 'to be better informed[2].' So confident was he in his integrity, that on receiving news of Alexander's death (May 3, 1410) soon afterwards, he promptly brought his case before the new pope[3], the monster John XXIII. The culprit was now cited to attend in person at Bologna; but his friends, who knew the danger he was in, dissuaded him from such a step[4], and on his failing to appear, the sentence of excommunication (Feb. 1411) was launched immediately against him, notwithstanding all the interest employed on his behalf by Wenceslaus and the queen[5]. Their influence was, however, more successful in promoting an accommodation between him and the archbishop; Huss avowing his respect for the ecclesiastical authority and his determination to adhere in all things to the will of Christ and of the Church[6].

But in the following autumn Sbynco breathed his last, and when a legate was despatched from Rome with the accustomed pallium for the new archbishop, John XXIII. annexed to it a parcel of indulgences, which purported to be at once available for all persons who might volunteer to execute the ban that had been issued for dethroning his opponent, the king of Naples. The enormity of this procedure stirred the vehemence of Huss[7] and of his col-

REFORMATORY EFFORTS.

appeals to a pope better informed:

is excommunicated, 1411:

but reconciled to the archbishop.

Indulgences sent into Bohemia:

---

[1] Stephen, the prior of Dolan (as above), p. 390, ascribes the protection of Huss to the 'popularis vulgi favor et sæculare brachium.'

[2] 'A papa male informato ad papam melius informandum:' see Neander, p. 376.

[3] His *Appellatio ad sedem Apostolicam* is printed in the *Hist. et Monument.* I. 112. Respecting John XXIII., see above, p. 331.

[4] The following is part of his own version of the matter: 'Citatus autem personaliter ad Romanam curiam optabam comparere humiliter; sed quia mortis insidiæ tam in regno quam extra regnum præsertim a Teutonicis sunt mihi positæ, ideo multorum fretus consilio judicavi, quod foret Deum tentare, vitam morti tradere, profectu Ecclesiæ non urgente. Igitur non parui personaliter, sed advocatos et procuratores constitui, volens sanctæ sedi apostolicæ obedire.' See the rest of this *Confession of Faith*, correctly given in Pelzel, *Lebensgeschichte des Königs Wenceslaus*, Documents, No. 230; Prag. 1788.

[5] Neander, pp. 392 sq.

[6] *Ibid.* p. 396. He now put forth the *Confession*, quoted above, vindicating himself in the eyes of the University.

[7] He justified his resistance on the following grounds: 'Ego dixi quod

league, Jerome, to the very highest pitch. The latter, hot and sanguine, lost no time in propagating his enthusiasm among the students, who, in order to exact a kind of vengeance for the seizure of Wycliffe's writings, organized a mock-procession in the streets of Prague and burnt the papal instruments[1]. Though Huss had not directly sanctioned this irregularity, and though he afterwards regretted its occurrence, the most formidable censures of the Church alighted on his head[2]. He could no longer prosecute his public mission, but addressing an appeal to Jesus Christ Himself[3], the only righteous Judge, retreated from the theatre of strife.

The works[4] which he composed in his retirement have

---

affecto cordialiter implere *mandata apostolica* et ipsis omnino obedire, sed voco mandata apostolica doctrinas apostolorum Christi, et de quanto mandata pontificis concordaverint cum mandatis et doctrinis apostolicis, secundum regulam legis Christi, de tanto volo ipsis paratissime obedire. Sed *si quid adversi concepero* non obediam, etiamsi ignem pro combustione mei corporis meis oculis præponatis:' Neander, p. 400. His views on indulgences may be seen at length in a remarkable *Quæstio* devoted to that subject (1412): *Hist. et Monument.* I. 215 sq.

[1] See Pelzel, as above, II. 608 sq. It seems that the violence connected with this act estranged the king from Huss. According to Stephen of Dolan (in Pez, *Thesaur. Monument.* IV. part ii. 380), he published a decree, 'ut nequaquam aliquis audeat rebellare et contradicere occulte vel publice, sub capitali pœna, indulgentiis papalibus.' Three youths were afterwards executed for interrupting preachers who invited their flocks to purchase indulgences; see Neander, pp. 417 sq., and Lenfant, *Hist. du Concile de Constance,* liv. III. c. 11.

[2] He was excommunicated afresh, and all the place in which he lived was stricken by the papal interdict. Even the chapel in which he preached was to be levelled with the ground: Palacky, III. pt. i. 286.

[3] See the *Hist. et Monument.* I. 22.

[4] One of the most important, and indeed his very greatest work, is the *Tractatus de Ecclesia* (in the *Hist. et Monument.* I. 243 sq.). His division of the Church, like that of Wycliffe (see above, p. 389), is tripartite. The 'ecclesia dormiens' he defines (c. 2) to be 'numerus prædestinatorum in purgatorio patiens.' By recognizing some of the finally condemned as members of the Church on earth, he shews that he did not follow Wycliffe blindly (cf. above, p. 390, n. 4). The following are his words (c. 3): 'Dupliciter homines possunt esse de sancta matre Ecclesia, vel secundum prædestinationem ad vitam æternam, quomodo omnes finaliter sancti sunt de sancta matre Ecclesia; vel secundum prædestinationem solum ad præsentem justitiam, ut omnes, qui *aliquando* accipiunt gratiam remissionis peccatorum *sed finaliter non perseverant.*' He insists upon the fact (*e.g.* c. 4, c. 13 sq.) that Christ and He alone is the 'Head of the Church,' but also urges the importance of obeying the pope and cardinals (c. 17) 'dum docuerint veritatem juxta legem Dei.' Another source for ascertaining his opinions at this juncture are his *Letters (Ibid,* L 117 sq.: cf. Palacky, III. pt. i. 297, 298).

enabled us to mark the final stages in the growth of his belief. To many of the characteristic dogmas then prevailing in the Church he yielded his unwavering assent[1], confining his denunciations mainly to those points which he regarded as excrescences, abuses, or distorted forms of truth. His principles[2], indeed, had they been logically apprehended and consistently applied, must have constrained him to relinquish some of the positions advocated by the western schoolmen: but, unlike his English fellow-worker, Huss had not been largely gifted with the logical faculty, and therefore he continued all his life unconscious of his own divergencies. So far was he indeed from meditating the formation of a sect, that he had hoped to renovate the Western Church entirely from within. A reference to these facts may well explain the readiness[3] he shewed to vindicate himself before the council of Constance, whither he was now invited to proceed. That great assembly constituted in his eyes the lawful representative of Christendom; and as he had no longer any hope of finding justice at the papal court, he went in search of it elsewhere. We see him starting for the council[4] (Oct. 11, 1414) armed with testimonials of his 'orthodoxy' from the primate of Bohemia (Conrad), and the titular bishop of Nazareth, who was officiating as the inquisitor of heresy in the diocese of Prague[5]. He also bore the passport (or 'safe-conduct') of the king of the Romans, Sigismund[6], which guaranteed his personal

REFORMATORY EFFORTS.

gious opinions at this time.

He proceeds to the Council of Constance, 1414;

---

[1] See Lenfant's *Hist. du Concile de Constance*, liv. III. c. 50—55; and cf. liv. I. c. 27.

[2] Neander, pp. 429 sq.

[3] After his arrival at Constance he stated that he came with joy, and added, that if he were convicted of any error he would immediately abjure it. Lenfant, liv. I. c. 36.

[4] *Ibid.* liv. I. c. 24.

[5] In this document (*Hist. et Monument.* I. 3) the inquisitor declares, among other things, 'Collationes plures [*i. e.* with master John Huss] de diversis sacræ scripturæ materiis faciendo, nunquam aliquem in ipso inveni errorem vel hæresim, sed in omnibus verbis et operibus suis ipsum semper verum et catholicum hominem reperi.'

[6] *Ibid.* I. 2. The violation of this promise was subsequently justified (Sept. 23, 1415) by a decree of the council (in Von der Hardt, IV. 521), on the ground that Huss, by impugning the 'orthodox faith,' had rendered himself 'ab omni conductu et privilegio alienum; nec aliqua sibi fides aut promissio de jure naturali, Divino vel humano, *fuerit in præjudicium catholicæ fidei* observanda.'

REFORMA-
TORY
EFFORTS.

*where he
is treache-
rously im-
prisoned,*

protection in the very strongest terms. He reached Constance[1] on the third of November, attended by a party of his fellow-countrymen, especially the noble John of Chlum, his pupil and unwavering friend. But others, who were labouring to repress the holy movement in Bohemia, had arrived before him[2]. One of them, Palecz[3], his former colleague in the university of Prague, was actively engaged in circulating rumours to his disadvantage: and as many of the clerics there assembled had been prejudiced against him, partly through his recent quarrel with the German students, partly through his firmness in declining to pronounce an indiscriminate condemnation of Wycliffe and the Oxford school of church-reformers, he was treacherously taken into custody[4] (Nov. 28). The scenes that followed are the most revolting in the annals of the Western Church. The oral explanations[5] of the prisoner, even as reported by his adversaries, and the tracts[6] which he composed while languishing in chains, shew that to the last his own opinions coincided in almost every point with those professed by members of the council. *They were zealously employed in limiting the power and in denying the infallibility of Rome*[7]: they all of them ex-

---

[1] According to Lenfant (liv. I. c. 26) Huss immediately notified his arrival to pope John XXIII., who promised to lend him every help in his power.

[2] Lenfant, liv. I. c. 35: Neander, IX. p. 465. They had been alienated from him chiefly by his vigorous opposition to the papal indulgences.

[3] In a formal reply, *Ad Script. Steph. Paletz*, he had been constrained to speak as follows: 'Amicus Paletz, amica veritas, utrisque amicis existentibus, sanctum est præhonorare veritatem.'

[4] Neander, pp. 472 sq. Some of the loose charges brought against him may be seen in Lenfant, liv. I. c. 42. One of them was, that he taught the necessity of administering the Eucharist in both kinds; but we shall see hereafter that the accusation was groundless: cf. his own replies in *Hist. et Monum.* I. 15 sq. Gerson, the famous chancellor of Paris, also extracted nineteen articles from the treatise *De Ecclesia*, and called upon the council to condemn them (*Ibid.* pp. 29 sq.): cf. above, p. 358, n. 4. His fellow-countrymen expressed their indignation at the imprisonment of Huss (*Hist. et Monum.* I. 9 sq.), and they were seconded by the Polish nobles who were present at the council (Krasinski, *Reform. in Poland*, I. 62).

[5] *e.g.* in his three public hearings before the council (Lenfant, liv. III. c. 4 sq.; Neander, pp. 495—515). On the second of these occasions (June 7) he actually spoke of the view of Berengarius on the Eucharist as 'magna hæresis.'

[6] Lenfant, liv. I. c. 43.

[7] See above, pp. 331 sq.

—1520] *State of Religious Doctrine and Controversies.* 407

hibited a wish to elevate the morals of the clergy, and advance at least in some degree the reformation of the Church,—the very measures that lay nearest to the heart of Huss: yet so infatuated were they by their national prejudices, or so blinded by their hatred of a man who would not disavow all sympathy with Wycliffe[1] (much as he receded from the *doctrines* of the Lollards), that they sentenced him to perish at the stake[2]. As soon as the executioner had done his barbarous work, the ashes of the victim were all flung into the Rhine, 'that nothing might remain on earth of so execrable a heretic' (July 6, 1415).

<small>REFORMA-TORY EFFORTS.</small>

<small>and put to death, 1415.</small>

The ardent Jerome of Prague, who shared his sentiments, and who appeared at Constance hoping for a prosperous issue, was at first so panic-stricken by the fate of Huss that he consented to abjure the errors which the council charged against him[3] (Sept. 23). But his courage afterwards revived. He publicly revoked his abjuration (May 16, 1416), in so far as he had offered violence to truth or had defamed the memory of Huss and Wycliffe. He was therefore handed over to the civil power, and several of his most infuriated enemies were struck by the unearthly joy that swelled his bosom even in the flames[4] (May 30).

<small>Martyrdom of Jerome of Prague, 1416.</small>

The ashes of these two reformers lighted up a long

<small>Rise of the Hussite war.</small>

---

[1] A charge on which the council placed peculiar emphasis related to this point: 'Quod pertinaciter articulos erroneos Wicleffi docuisset in Bohemia et defendisset.' On his reply, see Lenfant, liv. III. c. 5, and Neander, p. 501. The former of these writers (liv. III. c. 57) shews that partial sympathy with Wycliffe was the ground of his condemnation; and it is remarkable that the order of the council for burning the bones of the English reformer immediately preceded the examination of Huss: cf. above, p. 395.

[2] *Hist. et Monum.* I. 33 sq., and Lenfant, liv. III. c. 45. The following passage indicates a hope that reformation would come at last: 'Prius laqueos, citationes et anathemata Anseri [a play on his own name, Hus = Goose] paraverunt, et jam nonnullis ex vobis insidiantur. Sed quia Anser, animal cicur, avis domestica, suprema volatu suo non pertingens, eorum laqueos [? non] rupit, nihilominus aliæ aves, quæ Verbo Dei et vita volatu suo alta petunt, eorum insidias conterent.' *Hist. et Monum.* I. 121.

[3] Lenfant, liv. IV. c. 31. See also the *Narratio* in the *Hist. et Monum.* Johan. Huss, II. 522 sq.

[4] Lenfant, liv. IV. c. 85. As he went to the place of execution he recited the Apostles' Creed, and at the stake his voice was heard chanting the Paschal Hymn, 'Salve, festa dies,' *etc.* The astonishment of Poggio,

REFORMA-
TORY
EFFORTS.

*Jacobellus
de Misa.*

The *Calix-
tines,* or
Utraquists.

and furious war¹. Their countrymen had already expostulated with the council, in the hope of rescuing the martyrs from its grasp; and when the tidings of their execution reached Bohemia, hostility to the Germans and to Sigismund expressed itself anew in revolutionary acts. Another element of strife had also been contributed. It seems that Huss, who held the mediæval doctrine of concomitance², had acquiesced in the propriety of the communion in one kind: but his disciple, Jacobellus de Misa (Jacob of Mies), incited probably by some expressions in the works of Matthias of Janow³, had begun as early as the autumn of 1414 to lay unwonted stress on the importance of administering the chalice to the laity⁴. The other side was taken quite as absolutely by the council of Constance⁵ (June 14, 1415), and 'The Chalice,' therefore, grew at length into a watch-word of that numerous party in Bohemia who revered the memory of Huss. For several years the forces of the empire were completely kept at bay: but the development of the religious differences among the Hussites was afterwards fatal to their arms. One section of them, the *Calixtines*⁶ or *Utraquists*⁷, may be called the moderate party. They adhered to Huss

the Florentine scholar, on listening to his defence before the council, is expressed in a letter to Leonardo Aretino, translated in Lenfant, c. 86.

¹ See Lenfant, *Hist. de la guerre des Hussites*, etc. Amsterdam, 1731, with a *Supplement* by Beausobre, Lausanne, 1785.

² Above, p. 303. The question is fully investigated by Lenfant, *Hist. du Concile de Const.* liv. II. c. 74 sq.

³ Cf. Neander, p. 488.

⁴ That he was the first to administer in both kinds is expressly stated in the *Apologia veræ Doctrinæ* drawn up in 1538 by the 'Moravians' (in Lydii *Waldensia*, II. 292, Dordreci, 1617): 'Magister Jacobellus primus omnium communionem utriusque speciei in Bohemia practicare cœpit:' cf. Æneas Sylvius, *Hist. Bohem.* c. 35.

⁵ See the decree in Von der Hardt, III. 646, where the modern practice is defended on the ground that it serves 'ad evitandum pericula aliqua et scandala.' The doctrine of concomitance is also affirmed in the strongest terms ('cum firmissime credendum sit, et nullatenus dubitandum, integrum corpus Christi et sanguinem tam sub specie panis quam sub specie vini veraciter contineri'). For the *Apologia* of Jacobellus in reply to this decree, see Von der Hardt, III. 591 sq. He was supported by the university of Prague (March 10, 1417), whose manifesto is printed in the *Hist. et Monum.* II. 539.

⁶ From Calix = chalice.

⁷ From the phrase 'sub utraque specie.'

—1520] *State of Religious Doctrine and Controversies.* 409

and Jacobellus, claiming[1] that the Word of God should be freely preached in all the kingdom of Bohemia, that the Eucharist should be administered according to the terms of the original institution, that the incomes of the clergy should be lowered, and a more rigorous discipline enforced on all the members of the Church. This section of the Hussites, after many sanguinary struggles with the empire and their brethren, were eventually absorbed into the Western Church, negociations with them having been conducted through the medium of the council of Basel[2] (1433). But the resistance was kept up much longer by the Taborites (so called from a Bohemian mountain, Tabor, where they pitched their earliest camp). While they adopted many theories like those now current in the sect of the Waldenses[3], they diverged at other points into a gloomy and morose fanaticism[4]. They ventured to destroy all sacred literature, with the exception of the Bible; to denude religion of all pomp and every kind of ceremonial; to deprive the clergy of their property; to pillage the religious houses; and, confiding in the hope that Christ would soon return in person as their king, they bade defiance to their constituted rulers in both church and state. They were suppressed, however, in the end, by the Bohemian government (circ. **1453**), or forced to sue for toleration as a sect. From their communion, after its fanatic

REFORMATORY EFFORTS.

The Taborites.

Origin of the Moravians, or United Brethren (circ. **1450**).

---

[1] See the whole document in Brzezyna (al. Byzynius), *Diarium Belli Hussitici* (in Ludewig's *Reliquiæ Manuscr.* VI. 175 sq.).

[2] See the documents in Martène and Durand, *Ampl. Collect.* VIII. 596 sq. The *Compactata* now drawn up concede the points on which the Calixtines had insisted, but with many stringent limitations: for instance, the priest who ministers in both kinds is nevertheless to teach the people that 'sub qualibet specie est integer et totus Christus:' cf. Mansi, xxx. 692. In 1462, Æneas Sylvius (Pius II.) declared the *Compactata* invalid, but they kept their ground in spite of his denunciation: Gieseler, v. § 152, pp. 145, 148, notes 10, 17.

[3] Members of this sect existed in Bohemia at this time: see above, p. 373, n. 6.

[4] On their actions and opinions, see Brzezyna (as above, n. 1), pp. 145 sq., 190 sq., and the *Reformation and Counter-Reformation in Bohemia*, I. 14 sq. Lond. 1845. Their chief leaders were Ziska (d. 1424) and Procopius (see Brown's *Fascic.* II. 632 sq.): but after 1453, when they had been defeated by the Calixtines, they disappear as a political body. About the same time (1450) they seem to have opened negociations with the patriarch of Constantinople: *Ibid.* p. 29. A section of the Taborites were now entitled 'Picards' (*i.e.* Beghards), a name of reproach already given to Milicz, and to the early followers of Huss.

*REFORMA-
TORY
EFFORTS.*

*Reforming
party in
Poland.*

*Appearance of
Luther
(1483–
1546).*

element had been expelled, arose the peaceful and still thriving confraternity[1] entitled the Moravians, or United Brethren, who thus constitute the chief historic link between the times of Huss or Wycliffe and our own.

It seems that efforts had been made to propagate the Hussite doctrines in the neighbouring state of Poland. As early as 1431 a public disputation[2] was held at Cracow between the doctors of the university and certain deputies from Bohemia; and in 1450, a Polish senator[3] proposed to expedite a reformation of the Church by calling in the aid of the secular authority. But further indications of this spirit are not clearly traceable until the partisans of Luther made some converts at Dantzig[4] and Thorn[5] about the year 1520.

He it was who carried out the principles[6] which Huss had perished in attempting to diffuse. Their characters,

---

[1] A complete history of them will be found in Carpzov, *Religionsuntersuchung der Böhmischen und Mährischen Brüder*, Leipz. 1742: see also Lydii *Waldensia*, II. 1 sq. Dordreci, 1617. They separated entirely from the Church in 1457, not 'propter cæremonias aliquas vel ritus ab hominibus institutos, sed propter malam et corruptam doctrinam.' They denied transubstantiation and condemned the adoration of the Host, affirming that Christ is not in the Eucharist 'corporaliter' but 'spiritaliter, potenter, benedicte, in veritate.' See the *Responsio Excusatoria Fratrum Waldensium* (1508), in Brown's *Fascic.* I. 184. Other doctrinal peculiarities are enumerated in two kindred documents (*Ibid.* pp. 162–172). Mosheim regards the modern Moravians, or United Brethren, rather as imitators than as representatives of the United Brethren of the sixteenth century, remarking especially that but a very small fraction of them is Bohemian or Moravian. (*Eccl. Hist.* III. 479.)

[2] Krasinski, *Reform. in Poland*, I. 79.

[3] *Ibid.* I. 92 sq.

[4] *Ibid.* p. 113.

[5] *Ibid.* p. 124. When the papal legate came to this place, and was proceeding to burn a portrait of Luther, he was pelted away by the crowd.

[6] See the striking words of Luther in the *Preface* he contributed to the *Works* of Huss, ed. Norimb. 1558 (quoted by Lenfant, *Hist. du Concile de Constance*, liv. I. c. 21). He speaks of his 'incredible astonishment' on reading a copy of the Sermons of John Huss, which he found (circ. 1506) in the convent at Erfurt: 'I could not comprehend,' he adds, 'for what cause they burnt so great a man, who explained the Scriptures with so much gravity and skill.' In 1519 Luther exchanged letters with some of the Utraquists of Bohemia, one of whom addressed him as follows: 'Quod olim Johannes Huss in Bohemia fuerat, hoc tu, Martine, es in Saxonia. Quid igitur tibi opus? Vigila et confortare in Domino, deinde cave ab hominibus:' see Gieseler, v. p. 246; Fourth Period, § I, n. 50. The connexion between Huss and Luther is strongly stated in a contemporary ballad, edited by Soltau (Leipzig, 1845), pp. 278, 279.

indeed, had many traits in common¹. Both were strongly indisposed to vary from the standard teaching of the Church²: yet both were ultimately driven into a posture of hostility by struggling to suppress the sacrilegious traffic in indulgences. Their conscience sickened and revolted at the spectacle. A power that authorized proceedings so iniquitous, and did not scruple to employ its engines for exterminating all whose moral nature had impelled them to protest, could hardly (so they reasoned) be of God. Although the Saxon friar had not anticipated the ulterior bearings of this thought while he was posting up his theses on indulgences³ (Oct. 31, 1517), his later interviews⁴ with Cajetan, Eck, and others tended to develope his opinions, and convinced him more and more that something must be done to purify the Western Church. When cited to the court of Rome, he entered an appeal⁵, as Huss had done before him, to a future and more evangelic pontiff (Oct. 16, 1518), and soon after indicated his intention of applying for redress to what he deemed the first tribunal of all Christendom, a general Council⁶ (Nov. 28):

REFORMATORY EFFORTS.

---

¹ One of the most important *differences* was in their philosophic modes of thought. Huss (we saw above, p. 401) was a determined Realist; while Luther seems to have inclined in early life to Nominalism. His favourite authors were Peter d'Ailly, Gerson, William of Ockham (cf. above, p. 353, n. 1), and Gabriel Biel, preferring them to Thomas (Aquinas) and Duns Scotus. He was marked, however, like his great Bohemian prototype, by an intense love for biblical studies ('fontes doctrinæ cælestis avide legebat ipse;') while they both were strongly Augustinian. Melanchthon says of Luther (*Vita Lutheri*, p. 7, ed. Heumann), after mentioning the above particulars: 'Sed omnia *Augustini* monumenta et sæpe legerat et optime meminerat:' cf. above, p. 357, n. 4.

² They were also ardently devoted to the pope. Luther has informed us that in early life he was so infatuated by the papal dogmas, 'ut paratissimus fuerim omnes, si potuissem, occidere aut occidentibus cooperari et consentire, qui papæ vel una syllaba obedientiam detrectarent.' *Pref.* to his Works, dated 1545.

³ See them (ninety-five in number) in Löscher, *Reformations-Acta und Documenta*, I. 438, Leipz. 1720. One thesis (§ 27) ran as follows: 'Hominem prædicant, qui statim ut jactus nummus in cistam tinnierit, evolare dicunt animam' [*i.e.* out of purgatory]. The papal bull enforcing the generally received doctrine of indulgences is dated Nov. 9, 1518: see it in Löscher, II. 493.

⁴ An account of these discussions is reserved for a future volume, when the gradual change in Luther's views will be exhibited more fully.

⁵ 'A papa non bene informato ad melius informandum.' See the document in Löscher, as above, II. 484.

⁶ *Ibid.* II. 505. He renewed this appeal Nov. 17, 1520.

_{REFORMA-TORY EFFORTS.}

A further series of discussions, held at Leipzig[1] (June 27, —July 16, 1519), ended in his formal condemnation by the pope (June 15, 1520): yet Luther, differing from a host of his precursors who had not been able to withstand the thunders of the Vatican, intrepidly arose to meet the danger, pouring forth a torrent of defiance and contempt. The bull of excommunication which had branded him as a heretic was publicly burnt[2] at the eastern gate of Wittenberg, together with a copy of the Decretals and other obnoxious writings[3] (Dec. 10, 1520).

A new epoch in Church-History.

Every chance of compromise and reconciliation[4] vanished at this point: it forms one of the most momentous epochs in the history of Europe, of the Church, and of the world. The deep and simultaneous heaving that was felt soon afterwards in Switzerland[5], in Spain, in Poland, and in Scandinavia, in the British Islands and in Hungary,

---

[1] *Ibid.* III. 215 sq. Luther was supported on this occasion by Carlstadt (Bodenstein); their chief antagonist was Eck. Immediately afterwards Melanchthon wrote his *Defensio contra Johan. Eckium:* Opp. I. 113, ed. Bretschneider. In the following year Eck betook himself to Rome in order to stir up the pontiff (Leo X.). The bull against Luther (in Raynald. ad an. 1520, § 51) was due to his exertions.

[2] See the reasons he assigned for this act (*Quare Pontificis Romani et discipulorum ejus Libri a Doctore M. Luthero combusti sint*) in his *Works,* ed. Walch, xv. 1927: cf. Roscoe's *Leo the Tenth,* II. 218, 219, Lond. 1846. On the following day he told his college-class, 'Nisi toto corde *dissentiatis a regno papali,* non potestis assequi vestrarum animarum salutem.' His treatise *De Captivitate Babylonica Ecclesiæ,* which was prohibited as early as Oct. 20, 1520 (De Wette, I. 517), shews that on the doctrine of the sacraments he had now broken altogether from the Mediæval Church.

[3] 'Omnes libri Papæ, Decretum, Decretales, Sext., Clement., Extravagant., et Bulla novissima Leonis X.; item Summa Angelica [a work on casuistry], Chrysoprasus Eccii [a treatise on predestination], et alia ejusdem autoris, Emseri, et quædam alia, quæ adjecta per alios sunt:' *Luthers Briefe,* ed. De Wette, I. 532.

[4] The nearest approximation to it, so far as the Saxon reformers were concerned, was at the diet of Ratisbon (1541): see the present writer's *Hist. of the Articles,* pp. 29, 30, 2nd edit.

[5] According to a statement of Capito (1536) in Hottinger's *Hist. Eccl.* sæc. xvi. pt. II. 207, the Swiss reformation sprang up more independently: 'Antequam Lutherus in lucem emerserat, Zuinglius et ego inter nos communicavimus de Pontifice dejiciendo, etiam dum ille vitam degeret in Eremitorio. Nam utrique ex Erasmi consuetudine et lectione bonorum auctorum qualecumque judicium tum subolescebat.' In Switzerland also it was the scandalous traffic in indulgences that fired the soul of Zwingli (*Ibid.* part iii. p. 162): cf. De Félice, *Hist. of the Protestants of France,* Introd. pp. xxix., xxx. Lond. 1853.

in France, in Belgium, and the Papal States themselves, as well as in the German provinces extending from the Baltic to the Tyrol, proved that all things were now fully ripe for some gigantic change; THE Reformation had arrived.

REFORMATORY EFFORTS.

CHAPTER XVI.

ON THE STATE OF INTELLIGENCE AND PIETY.

MEANS OF GRACE AND KNOWLEDGE.

Transitional character of this period.

ENOUGH has been already urged to warrant us in saying that this period in the lifetime of the Western Church is eminently one of twilight and transition. It may altogether be esteemed a sort of border-province that unites the Mediæval to the Modern history of Europe. Many of the old traditions, whether social, civil or religious, had been rudely shaken in the conflicts of an earlier date; but it was only in the fourteenth, and still more the fifteenth century, that we behold them tottering to their fall, or actually dethroned. Then also that romantic ardour,—the enthusiasm so characteristic of the Middle Age, producing its phantastic modes of thought and action, and diffusing over it an irresistible charm,—was more and more exhausted[1]. Popes and preachers, for example, sought in vain to organize a fresh crusade: their motives were no longer thought to be above suspicion, and accordingly, when armies of the 'paynim' hovered on the confines of the Western Church itself and made the potentates of Hungary and Poland tremble for their safety, few could now be stirred to raise a hand in their behalf. The spirit of religious chivalry was dying, or at least had forfeited the strong predominance it once possessed: it yielded to the cold, and often contemptuous, voice of reason or the maxims of prudential statecraft; while the failure of the public faith in the Roman system was tending to produce lukewarmness in the many, and in some a rabid unbelief. A different but no less portentous revolution had come over all the other faculties of man: he grew more con-

---

[1] The chief exceptions will be found in Spain: cf. above, p. 319.

scious of his freedom, of his personality, and of his power. The dim and circumscribed horizon of his thoughts, which heretofore he never dared to pass, and which his fathers deemed impassable, was every day expanding on all sides. A prospect wider, grander, and more full of hope seemed stretching at his feet.

MEANS OF GRACE AND KNOW-LEDGE.

The causes that had been conspiring to produce this mighty change were various, and were also acting through a multitude of independent channels. Some may be enumerated thus:—the bold discussions of the later Schoolmen[1], which, however heartless, had not failed to sharpen and evolve the intellectual powers; the restoration of a purer taste[2], exemplified in literature by men like Dante, Petrarch, Boccaccio, and Chaucer, and in art by Giotto, Michael Angelo, and Raphael; the frequent intercourse[3] between the Eastern and Western Christians, more particularly in negociating a reunion of the Church; the conquest of Constantinople by the Turks (**1453**); the westward flight of scholars bearing with them Greek and other manuscripts; the spread of commerce; the discovery of unknown and long-forgotten Continents, unveiling wider spheres of intellectual enterprise; the cultivation of the modern languages, and the invention (or at least extended use) of paper[4] as the common vehicle of writing. But the mightiest agent was the press; typography, or printing by the aid of moveable metallic types[5], originating at the middle of the fifteenth century. By means of it the ancient sources of instruction had been multiplied indefinitely; reading had become more easy and inviting, while the rapid diminution thus effected in the price of

Causes of the change.

Printing one of the most important.

---

[1] See above, pp. 351 sq.
[2] Miller's *History philosophically illustrated*, Bk. II. ch. XIII., XIV. Hallam (*Lit. of Europe*, Pt. I. ch. I. § 92) regards Petrarch as the restorer of polite letters. The reanimation of Architecture had preceded that of the other fine arts by many centuries. (See Hallam, *Europe during the Middle Ages*, ch. IX. pt. II.). Indeed it was the renaissance of heathenizing influence in the age preceding the Reformation that led to the departure from the ancient types in Italy and other countries of the West, and interfered with the development of Christian architecture in the unreformed as well as in the reformed communities.
[3] F. von Schlegel, *Phil. of History*, pp. 386, 387, ed. 1847.
[4] See Hallam, *Lit. of Europe*, Pt I. ch. I. §§ 59 sq.
[5] *Ibid.* ch. III. § 19; Miller, II. 446 sq. Tabular or block-printing was much older.

MEANS OF GRACE AND KNOWLEDGE.

Scholastic institutions and their results.

books¹ had made them more accessible to every grade of life. We may compute the influence of the new invention by considering that in thirty years, from **1470** to **1500**, more than ten thousand editions of books and pamphlets issued from the press².

The number of these publications may be also taken as an index to the growth of schools and other kindred institutions. It is true that as the monks degenerated³ many of the old establishments connected with religious houses were involved in their decline; and the same, though in a less degree, is often visible among the different ranks of Friars⁴: but meanwhile a considerable compensation had been made in every part of Europe by the founding of colleges and universities as well as minor seats of learning. Not a few indeed of these were planted on the very site of convents which had been legally suppressed for the purpose. At the time when Luther was engaged in giving lectures at Wittenberg, as many as sixty-six universities were organized in different parts of Europe, sixteen of them in Germany itself⁵; and even in the fourteenth century we know that such as then existed literally swarmed with students⁶. It is symptomatic of the influence exercised by institutions of this class

---

¹ The price was immediately diminished four-fifths: Hallam, *Ibid,* § 147.

² See the statistics, *Ibid.* § 142. More than half of these appeared in Italy. The editions of the Vulgate were 91. In England all the books printed in this interval amounted to 141.

³ See above, p. 343.

⁴ Above, p. 345.

⁵ Möhler's *Schriften*, etc. II. 6: Schröckh, xxx. 64—127.

⁶ It is said, but the statement is quite incredible, that before the plague of 1348, no less than thirty thousand students were congregated at Oxford in nearly four hundred seminaries. The following is a portion of the statement made by Richard, archbishop of Armagh, an Oxford man, in Brown's *Fascic.* II. 473, 474: 'Item consequitur grave damnum in clero, in hoc, quod jam in Studiis [*i.e.* the scholastic institutions] regni Angliæ propter talem substractionem a suis parentibus puerorum [*i.e.* their absorption into the Mendicant orders], laici ubique retrahunt suos filios ne mittant eos ad Studium, quia potius eligunt eos facere cultores agrorum eos habendo quam sic in Studiis eos taliter amittere: et sic fit quod ubi in Studio Oxoniensi adhuc meo tempore erant triginta millia studentium, non reperiuntur sex millia his diebus; et major hujus minutionis causa sive occasio, præmissa puerorum circumventio [*i.e.* by the Friars] æstimatur:' cf. Vaughan's *Wycliffe*, pp. 32, 33; and on the vast number of students who seceded from Prague in the time of Huss, see above, p. 401, n. 5.

that they invariably produced the chief antagonists of Roman absolutism[1]; Wycliffe, Huss, and others being numbered with the foremost academics of the age[2]. In very many, doubtless, no desire of reformation was awakened by the subtle exercises of the schools; and it is certain that no aim was further from the thoughts[3] of those who in the latter half of the fifteenth century were loud in advocating a return to every class of pagan models and were eagerly engaged in studying the æsthetics and philosophy of Greece: yet even there we must remember that the critical faculty was stimulated in a way unknown to former ages. Some at length were bent on turning this new light directly to the Church. The copies of the Holy Scriptures and the Earlier Fathers were sought out, collated, and in certain cases printed, more especially by scholars like Erasmus[4], who were thus unconsciously supplying food as well as armour to the champions of a later day. Men needed little penetration to discern that Christianity, at least in its ordinary manifestations, had receded far from its ideal; and although by some these changes were explained on what has since been termed the theory of development[5], another class of minds[6] would labour to retrace their steps, in bringing back the creed and ritual of the Church into more perfect harmony with those of Apostolic times.

MEANS OF GRACE AND KNOWLEDGE.

[1] This, we have seen, was remarkably the case in the model-university of Paris: and accordingly writers like Capefigue (*e.g.* II. 169) always regard it as professing 'une théologie équivoque et un catholicisme mixte, osant quelquefois la négation partielle de l'autorité du pape.'

[2] Even Gerson, while deploring the abuses of the period, turned with comfort to the thought that education might eventually uproot them: 'A pueris videtur incipienda Ecclesiæ reformatio.' *Opp.* II. 109, ed. Du Pin.

[3] See above, p. 355: and cf. M'Crie's *Reformation in Italy*, pp. 12. sq.

[4] See above, p. 361. It was indeed a characteristic of the reforming party, that they encouraged learning and carried with them the chief scholars of the time, at least in earlier stages of the movement (Roscoe, *Life of Leo X.*, II. 103, 104, ed. 1846). Yet, on the other hand, we must remember that the anti-reformation school was by no means destitute of learning. For instance, the decree which condemned Luther as a heretic was drawn and signed by the elegant pen of cardinal Sadoleti.

[5] Such, for instance, was the way in which Gerson reconciled himself to one prevailing doctrine of the age: see above, p. 372, n. 2.

[6] This was the conviction of archbishop Hermann of Cologne, among others: see his *Simple and Religious Consultation*, 'Epistle,' A, iii. Lond. 1547.

M. A.   E E

MEANS OF GRACE AND KNOWLEDGE.

Study of the Bible.

Continued use of vernacular translations.

The growing taste for purely biblica[l]
noted in a former page. That taste
not altogether fostered by the anti-Ro[man]
Church itself[2] by those who urged th[e]
tion, and still more by sectaries who
abnormal acts by combating the erro[rs]
had long been festering in Christend[om]
were the many absolutely destitute o[f]
and of access to the oracles of God.
had been aimed at the vernacular
thirteenth century had ceased to opera[te]
evaded, in all quarters. Several, it is
more gifted ecclesiastics, looked upon
an ill-concealed distrust[4], and some
monious partisans of Rome denounced

---

[1] Above, p. 360.
[2] *e.g.* by Nicholas de Clémenges (in the *D*
above, p. 828, n. 4), who, after urging the stud[y]
principle that they are streams which bear us up
has remarked in reference to the Sacred Writings
Divina sunt nihil debemus temere definire, n[ec]
oraculis approbari; quæ divinitus enuntiata de
sunt necessaria, aut ad salutem opportuna, si dil[igenter]
nos sufficienter instruunt' (p. 476). Dr Abendo[n]
preached at the council of Constance (1415), ex[horts]
particular to cultivate this study (Lenfant, liv. IV.
ing cardinal D'Ailly, in like manner, recommends
'ipsum fundamentum Ecclesiæ' is 'ipsa Sacræ
Brown's *Fascic.* II. 510). We see the effect of t[his]
the following passage of Pico of Mirandola (c
XII. 366, ed. Elrington): 'Ad hanc notitiam D[ivinam]
veteres theologi omnes exhortantur. Huic juniore
Gerson, aliique nonnulli assidue monent incum
his qui *ex officio* ad id negotii sunt obnoxii, ut s[i]
omnibus cujuscunque gradus et ordinis extiterint.

[3] See above, p. 299. To the instances there
may be added that an English *prose* version of th[e]
certain Canticles was made (circ. 1320) by Will[iam]
that another was contributed by Richard of Ham[pole]
n. 4), who added a brief commentary: see *Pr[eface]*
Bible, p. v.

[4] Even Gerson is to be reckoned in this cla[ss]
105, ed. Du Pin) 'prohibendam esse vulgarem
sacrorum nostræ Bibliæ, *præsertim extra moralita[tem]*
'claras rationes ad hoc plurimas invenire facile
urged by the anti-reformation writer, Cochlæus, in
Laicis legere novi Testamenti libros lingua vern[acula]
'*Ormulum*' (above, p. 297, n. 4) was received wit[h]
tion: see White's *Pref.* p. lxxv. Oxf. 1852.

[5] See, for example, the offensive language o[f]

—1520]   *State of Intelligence and Piety.*   419

yet in spite of this occasional resistance, they could never be displaced. In England numerous copies of the Wycliffite Bibles[1] were long cherished, even as it seems by many who did not embrace the Lollard doctrines; and in all the second half of the fifteenth century[2] translations of the Scriptures found a multitude of readers, in both Germany and northern Italy, and some in Spain itself.

We should remember also that a larger fraction of the whole community were educated at this period, having learned to write[3] as well as read. The operation of the Crusades had proved most favourable to the growth of civil liberty: they had relaxed the trammels of the feudal system[4]. Artisans and traders had sprung up on every side, and the inhabitants of towns, supplying the prolific germ of the important middle-class, were far more numerous than in all the earlier ages of the Church. Amid the humblest order of society, the peasants, where the bulk appear to have been scarcely above the state of villenage, some scanty tokens of amelioration and refinement[5] were discernible. The powers of thought had been more commonly aroused, and, as the natural effect of such awakening, the masses had grown conscious of their own importance.

Means of grace and knowledge.

Intelligence more widely diffused.

---

antagonist), above, p. 386, n. 1. In an anti-Lollard song, printed by Ritson, it is said to be 'unkyndly for a knight' to 'bable the Bibel day and night.'

[1] See above, p. 385, and the *Preface* to the Oxford edition, p. xxxiii. In the *Constitutions* of archbishop Arundel (Johnson, II. 466), the reading of such versions is prohibited, under pain of the greater excommunication, at least until they have been formally authorized.

[2] The numerous editions of the German and Italian Bibles have been mentioned above, p. 360: cf. Buckingham, *Bible in the Middle Ages*, pp. 60 sq. Attempts were made, however, to suppress all vernacular translations, for instance, by the archbp. of Mentz in 1486 (quoted in Gieseler, v. § 146, p. 75, n. 14). In Spain the lovers of the Sacred Books evaded the Inquisitor by translating portions of them into Castilian verse (*e.g.* Job, Psalms, Proverbs, and the Life of Christ, drawn from the Evangelists): A. de Castro, *Spanish Protestants*, p. lxii., Lond. 1851. On the importance attached to the vernacular dialects and to the general diffusion of the Scriptures by the Waldenses, see Neander, IX. 565. The price of the Sacred Books, however, would be long a serious bar to their progress in the lower orders of society. Thus a copy of Wycliffe's Bible, at the beginning of the 15th century, cost four marks and forty pence (=£2. 16s. 8d. of present money): Blunt's *Sketch of the Reformation*, p. 69, 6th edit.

[3] Hallam, *Liter. of Europe*, Pt. I. ch. I. §§ 54 sq.
[4] See Sir J. Stephen, *On the History of France*, Lect. VI.
[5] *History of England and France under the House of Lancaster*, p. 10.

MEANS OF GRACE AND KNOWLEDGE.

They were often most impatient of the yoke which both in secular and in sacred matters goaded them at every point and bowed them to the earth. The strength of such convictions was peculiarly betrayed in all the fourteenth century, when it is easy to observe the rapid growth of self-assertion, breaking out into political discontent[1].

Other books of devotion and religious instruction.

Besides the other tracts and ballads that were circulated for the gratifying of these intellectual wants, there was a constant issue of 'religious' publications. Thus in England a vernacular book of devotion for the laity was furnished by 'The Prymer[2].' The authors or translators of religious poetry[3] were also very numerous, choosing, for example, as their subject, an affecting passage in the life or sufferings of our blessed Lord, expounding Psalms or Canticles, or not unfrequently embellishing the passion of some primitive or mediæval saint. A deep impression must also have been produced by tracts like those contained in the 'Pauper Rusticus' or 'Poor Caitif,' which were now disseminated far and wide in English, with the hope of leading 'simple men and women of good will the right way to heaven[4].' The same idea was exten-

---

[1] *e.g.* in England, as early as 1275, it was found necessary to repress a number of ballads and other pieces tending 'to cause discord betwixt king and people' (Warton, *Engl. Poetry*, I. 45, ed. 1840); and in the time of Wycliffe and subsequently (see above, p. 384, n. 3) the spirit of disaffection shewed itself in the most violent forms (cf. the *Preface* to a Poem *On the times of Edw. II.*, ed. Percy Society, No. LXXXII., pp. vii. sq.).

[2] Edited, with a preliminary Dissertation, and an Appendix of some other vernacular forms of prayer, confession, &c., in Vol. II. of Maskell's *Monumenta Ritualia*. The contents are: the Matins, and Hours of our Lady; the Evensong; the Compline; the seven Psalms; the fifteen Psalms: the Litany (containing the germ of the English Litany now in use); the Placebo, and Dirige (the Office of the Dead); the Commendations; the *Pater noster*; the *Ave Maria*; the Creed; the Ten Commandments; the Seven deadly Sins. See the Contents of other copies of '*the* Prymer,' *ib.* pp. xl. sq.; Procter, *Hist. of the Prayer-Book*, pp. 12 sq.

[3] The Cambridge University Library is rich in this kind of literature. A remarkable instance occurs in MS. Dd. I. 1, § 7, entitled 'Memoriale Credentium,' which is said to be 'wreten in englisch tonge for lewid [lay] men, that nought understond *latyn* ne *frensch*, and is drawn out of holi writte and of holy doctors beforn this tyme.' It contains an account of the plagues of Egypt and the giving of the law, expositions of the Ten Commandments, the seven deadly sins, penance, transubstantiation, the Lord's prayer, the four cardinal virtues, the seven sacraments, the seven gifts of the Holy Ghost, the seven works of mercy, the joys of heaven and the pains of hell. The date is about 1330.

[4] For an account of it see Vaughan's *Wycliffe*, p. 533, new edit.

sively adopted on the continent, especially[1], as it would seem, by the new order in which Thomas à Kempis had been reared. Indeed the unexampled popularity of his own treatise 'On the Imitation of Christ'[2] will furnish a delightful proof that thousands of his fellow-men could find a pleasure in his simple and soul-stirring maxims,— maxims which, in spite of their asceticism, are ever animated by the breath of genuine Christianity.

MEANS OF GRACE AND KNOWLEDGE.

The sermons preached at church on Sundays and saints'- days must have varied with the piety and knowledge of the curate or the friar who supplied his place. In England many of them in the fourteenth century were *metrical*[3], consisting, as a general rule, of paraphrases on the Gospels throughout the year, enforced by anecdotes or stories which the preacher borrowed from the Old and New Testament, from Legends, and from other sources. Some of these productions are both simple and pathetic; but the great majority are pointless, cold, and nearly always full of puerilities. If we may judge from the severe remarks of Gerson[4] in his

Sermons.

Shirley points out that it is not a work of Wycliffe, but of a mendicant friar, on the authority of bishop Pecock. *Fasc. Zizan.* xiii.

[1] See Delprat (as above, p. 347, n. 5), pp. 306 sq. The Mendicants opposed this practice of the 'Common-Life Brothers,' affirming 'quod laici libros Teutonicales habere non deberent, et sermones non nisi ad populum in ecclesia fieri deberent.' The chronicler, John Busch, in his *De reformatione Monasteriorum* (as above, p. 343, n. 4), II. 925 sq., did not justify the translation of the 'Canon' (of the Mass), and of books which he thought 'altos et divinos;' yet he adds, 'libros morales de vitiis et virtutibus, de Incarnatione, Vita, et Passione Christi, de vita et sancta conversatione et martyrio sanctorum Apostolorum, *etc.*; homilias quoque et sermones Sanctorum, ad emendationem vitæ, morum disciplinam, inferni timorem, patriæque cœlestis amorem provocantes, habere et quotidie legere *cunctis doctis et indoctis* utilissimum est.'

[2] Above, p. 348, n. 1. This work is said to have gone through 1800 editions: Hallam's *Liter. of Europe*, Pt. I. ch. II. § 63.

[3] Thus in the volume of sacred poetry above mentioned (p. 420, n. 3), there is a long series of metrical sermons belonging to this class (pp. 48— 402). They proceed, with two exceptions, in the usual course from Advent onwards. Many other copies exist; *e.g.* one in the same repository, Gg. v. 31, and a third in the Ashmolean collection, No. 42. Such also had been the *Ormulum* (ed. Oxon. 1852), a series of Homilies, composed in metre without alliteration (early in the 13th century): cf. White's Pref. pp. lxx., lxxi. A series of Expositions of the Dominical Gospels, in Romance, is preserved in the Camb. Univ. MS. Gg. I. 1, fol. 135—261: their author was Robert de Gretham. For specimens of the English *prose* sermons in the following century, see the *Liber Festivalis* printed by Caxton.

[4] Lenfant, *Hist. du Concile de Constance*, liv. VII. c. 8. Gerson adds,

CORRUPTIONS AND ABUSES.

Sacramental system.

sermon before the Council of Rheims in 1408, the office of preaching was now generally disparaged; bishops having almost everywhere abandoned it to their stipendiaries or to the vagrant friars. In the age anterior to the Reformation it was often made a subject of complaint[1], that preachers spent their strength on empty subtleties, or even interlarded their discourses with citations from the pagan authors rather than the Word of God. A better class indeed always existed, such as we have sketched[2] in Germany and Bohemia, but the evidence compels us to infer that members of it were comparatively few[3].

The observations made already on the ritual and the sacramental system[4] of the Church apply still further to

that there was no greater rarity than to hear 'good Gospel-preaching.' 'Seeds of error,' he continues, 'are scattered abroad, and the people are fed with impertinent and frivolous tales.' Richard Ulverstone (above, p. 329, n. 2) in like manner expresses a hope, that when abuses had been taken away the pontiff would preach the Gospel himself, and would depute sound preachers to all parts of Christendom: *Ibid.* c. 9. The language of John of Trittenheim, immediately before the Reformation (circ. 1485), shows that this hope had not been realized. After speaking of the secularity and vices of the clergy generally, he adds, 'Romana lingua scribere vel loqui nesciunt, vix in vulgari exponere Evangelia didicerunt. Quantos errores, fabulas et hæreses in Ecclesia prædicando populis enuncient, quis nisi expertus credere posset!' *Instit. vitæ sacerdotalis,* c. 4: *Opp.* Mogunt. 1605.

[1] See the last reference, and other passages in Gieseler, v. § 146, pp. 70—72, notes 2, 3. A like charge had been brought against the preachers of an earlier date by Nicholas de Clémenges, in his *De studio Theolog.* (as above, p. 328, n. 4). He writes, 'Hodie plurimi exercentur, quæ licet intellectum utcunque acuant, nullo tamen igne succendunt affectum, nullo alimento pascunt, sed frigidum, torpentem, aridum relinquunt:' p. 476. Many of the *Sermones de Tempore,* the *Sermones de Sanctis,* the *Sermones Quadragesimales,* etc. of the period amply justify this comment. Immediately before the time of Luther several mendicants adopted a sarcastic and quasi-comic style of preaching, *e.g.* Geiler of Kaisersberg, Menot, a Franciscan of Paris, Gabriel of Barletta, a Neapolitan: see, especially, 'Der Prediger Olivier Maillard,' by C. Schmidt, in the *Zeitschrift für die histor. Theologie,* 1856, pp. 489—542. Some preachers used to give a coarse flavour to their discourses. This was thought to be especially allowable during the Easter festival, when, according to a prevalent custom, the roughest jests were tolerated even in the pulpit, to excite what was called the Easter laugh.

[2] See above, pp. 355 sq. and pp. 397 sq.

[3] Even Bossuet allows that many of the preachers 'made the basis of piety to consist in those practices which are only its accessories,' and that they 'did not speak of the grace of Jesus Christ as they ought to have done.' Quoted in De Félice, *Hist. of the Protestants of France,* Introd. p. xvii. Lond. 1853.

[4] Pp. 301—305.

the present period. Much as individual writers[1] called in question the scholastic arguments on which that system now reposed, and much as others might protest[2] against the notion that a sacrament can operate mechanically, or without conditions on the part of the recipient, it is plain that Western Christendom[3] had, generally speaking, acquiesced in the conclusions of the earlier Schoolmen; or, in other words, adopted the positions that were afterwards fixed and stereotyped by the Council of Trent[4]. Almost the only symptom of resistance, on the part of those who held the other doctrines of the Church, related to communion in both kinds; but we have seen that the Council of Constance[5] strenuously adhered to the prevailing usage, and at length, when some apparent relaxation had been made at Basel, the non-necessity of such communion (or the doctrine of 'concomitance') was quite as strongly reaffirmed.

CORRUPTIONS AND ABUSES.

The worship of the Virgin, which had been developed in preceding centuries to an appalling height, was carried even higher by the sensuous and impassioned writers of the present period. She was invoked, not only as the queen of heaven, our advocate, our mediatrix, and in some degree the moving cause of our redemption[6], but as the

Worship of the Virgin.

---

[1] *e.g.* Durand de S. Pourçain (above, p. 352, n. 2), Wycliffe, *Trialogus*, lib. IV. c. 1 sq.

[2] *e.g.* John Wessel (Luther's prototype), in Ullmann's *Life* of him (Hamb. 1834), pp. 322, 323.

[3] The Eastern Church (cf. above, p. 301, n. 2) had also manifested a disposition to accept the Western view, at least the representatives whom it sent to the council of Florence were committed to that course; Mansi, XXXI. 1054 sq.

[4] Hence the phrase 'scholasticorum doctrina' in the English Articles of 1552='doctrina Romanensium' in the Articles of 1562: see Hardwick's *Hist. of the Articles*, pp. 304, 305, 2nd edit.

[5] See above, p. 408. A treatise was composed in the name of the council by Maurice of Prague (Lenfant, liv. VI. c. 19), in which the chief weight of the argument is made to rest on the authority of synods. The populace were easily reconciled to the withdrawal of the Cup, especially when stories of 'bleeding Hosts' were circulated afresh: see Gieseler, V. § 145, p. 63, n. 9, where Nicholas Cusanus (1451), as papal legate, denounces the fabricators of this 'miracle' for their profaneness and cupidity. In the MS. volume referred to above (p. 420, n. 3) there is a story of an abbot who argued that 'the bred in the awter is not kyndeliche [naturally] Goddis body but a tokne thereof' (p. 522). He is confuted by a miracle, in which appeared 'in the awter a child ligging beforn the prest,' &c.

[6] These expressions were used even by John Huss, in 1414; see Lenfant, *Concile de Const.* liv. 1. c. 27.

CORRUPTIONS AND ABUSES.

all-powerful, the single, and the all-prevailing intercessor[1]. High and low, the scholar and the peasant, generally esteemed an 'Ave Maria' as equivalent to a 'Pater Noster'[2]. It was therefore easy to predict that the hostility[3] evoked by efforts which had long been seeking to exact belief in the immaculate conception of the Virgin, had grown feebler every day.

Although the spread of scholarship[4] had frequently ex-

---

[1] Instances occur, not only in poets like Chaucer, whose *Priere de Nostre Dame* contains the line 'Almighty and all merciable queene,' but also in the *Mariale* of an Italian Franciscan, Bernardinus de Bustis, on whose works see Wharton's *Append.* to Cave, ad an. 1480. One extract (Part. XII. Sermo II.) will suffice: 'A tempore quo virgo Maria concepit in utero Verbum Dei, quandam ut sic dicam jurisdictionem seu auctoritatem obtinuit in omni Spiritus Sancti processione temporali, ita ut *nulla creatura aliquam a Deo obtineat gratiam vel virtutem, nisi secundum Ipsius piæ matris dispensationem.*' 'In her the penitent beheld the Mother and the Mediatrix, the loving parent and the potent intercessor, eager to bless *as she was all-powerful to* save.' Buckingham, p. 255.

[2] See examples in Gieseler, §145, p. 65, n. 13. It is painful to observe an archbishop of Canterbury (Sudbury) enjoining his clergy (1377) to supplicate ('devotissime exorent') in one breath God, His Mother, and the Saints: Wilkins, III. 121. Two new festivals were instituted about the same date (1372, 1389) in honour of the Virgin, the former called *Festum Præsentationis*, the latter, *Festum Visitationis*. Another indication of the blindness with which the worship of the Virgin was now practised is supplied by the currency of the fable respecting a miraculous transfer of her house from Palestine to Loretto: see Gieseler, v. § 145, pp. 64, 65, n. 12.

[3] See above, p. 306. The way in which the credit of St. Bernard and other writers was now saved is indicated by the following extract from Gabriel Biel, the schoolman (*Collectorium*, lib. III. distinct. III. quæst. I. art. 2): 'Auctoritas Ecclesiæ major est auctoritate cujuscunque Sancti, *saltem* post canonicos Scriptores....Nec propter hoc culpandus est D. Bernhardus, sed nec S. Thomas, S. Bonaventura, cæterique Doctores cum magno moderamine opposita opinantes, quoniam *eorum tempore hoc licuit*, quoniam nulla determinatio vel Concilii vel Apostolicæ sedis facta fuit.' The conciliar authority to which he alludes is that of the synod of Basel (Mansi, XXIX. 183); yet even the decree there issued, owing to the quarrels of the council and the pope, was not regarded as a final settlement of the question. The Dominicans still protested, and went so far as to charge the advocates of the immaculate conception of the Virgin with the name of heretics; see a bull of Sixtus IV. (1483) in the Canon Law (*Extravagantes Commun.* lib. III. tit. XII. c 2).

[4] Thus Gerson preached a striking sermon at Constance on the canonization of St Bridget (cf. above, p. 327, n. 7, and Lenfant, liv. I. c. 70). The title is *De Probatione Spirituum* (*Opp.* I. 37 sq.). Jacobellus, the Hussite (Lenfant, liv. II. c. 73), disparages without absolutely rejecting some of the Legends; for instance, that of St Catharine of Alexandria. Gobelinus Persona (circ. 1420), and after him Nicholas Clopper (1472), were still more sceptical respecting her, although her name in some places was admitted into the 'Canon of the Mass.' See *An Historical Inquiry*

cited men to criticize the older Legends, and on more than one occasion to dispute the title even of the favourite saints of Christendom, their worship, generally speaking, had continued as before. They occupied the place of tutelar divinities[1], however much the holier class of Christians shrank from their complete association on a level with the King of saints Himself. It was indeed a gross exaggeration of the reverence paid to them in earlier times that stirred the zeal of Wycliffe[2]. Not content with placing them in a subordinate position, he impugned the custom of observing special festivals in honour of the saints: but few if any members of the Church were now disposed to follow his example.

This repugnance may have been increased in him by witnessing the multiplicity of such observances; for it is remarkable that in the present period indications of a wish to simplify the public ritual frequently occur and are betrayed by earnest men of very different schools of thought. They felt that true devotion ran the risk of being suffocated[3], and the memory of Christ Himself obscured, by

CORRUPTIONS AND ABUSES.

Worship of the saints.

Reaction against the ritualism of the age.

respecting her, by the present writer, among the Publications of the Cambridge Antiquarian Society (1849).

[1] Gerson admits (*Opp.* III. 947) that some Christians whom he terms 'simpletons' worshipped the very images of the saints, but he excuses this impiety on the ground of their invincible ignorance, or because they intend to do what the Church does in the honour she bestows on images. Huss, though censuring such worship, did not object to certain marks of outward reverence ('licet possint homines genua flectere, orare, offerre, candelas ponere,' etc.): *Opp.* II. 343.

[2] *Trialogus*, lib. III. c. 30. The 'reforming' party at Constance (including D'Ailly and Gerson) were in favour of abolishing all festivals 'not instituted by the old law and the decrees of the Fathers, especially the inferior holy-days,' on the ground that they were generally devoted to drunkenness and every species of excess: Lenfant, liv. VII. c. 62. A catalogue of the feasts which were rigorously observed by the Church of England in 1362, will be found in Wilkins, II. 560 (cf. Johnson's Notes, II. 346, 428, 429). The first in order is the Lord's Day ('ab hora diei sabbati vespertina inchoandum, non ante horam ipsam præveniendum, ne Judaicæ professionis participes videamur'). The festival of Trinity Sunday, or at least its universal observance on the octave of Whitsunday, also dates from the present period: see Guerike, *Manual of Antiquities*, ed. Morrison, p. 161.

[3] See the remarkable extract from Jacobus de Paradiso, a Carthusian (d. 1465) in Gieseler, § 145, vol. v. p. 59, n. 1, and the whole of another of his treatises, *De Septem Statibus Ecclesiæ*, in Brown's *Fascic.* II. 102—112. The same point is urged by Nicholas de Clémenges in his *De novis celebritatibus non instituendis* (*Opp.* pp. 143 sq., ed. Lydius). Matthias of Janow in like manner, in the *De Sacerdotum et Monachorum abomina-*

CORRUPTIONS AND ABUSES.

a complexity of rites that were too often altogether unintelligible to their flocks. These rites they also felt were celebrated only for filthy lucre by a multitude of hypocritical and sacrilegious priests[1]. The mind of Western Christendom had thus been predisposed for the avenging outbreak of the sixteenth century, which shewed its vehemence in nothing so distinctly as in the abolishing of 'dark and dumb ceremonies,'—prelates not uncommonly included in the number.

Penance.

But a darker blot, and one that was almost ingrained into the constitution of the Mediæval Church, is found in the prevailing theory of penance. At the basis of it lay the thought, that, notwithstanding the forgiveness of sins, a heavy debt is still remaining to be paid by the offender as a precondition to his ultimate acceptance with the Lord. The liquidation of this debt, according to the Schoolmen, is advanced not only by the self-denial and the personal afflictions of the sinner, but on his removal hence may be facilitated more and more through various acts of piety which others undertake in his behalf[2]. Among

---

tione (as above, p. 399, n. 1), c. 60, complained as follows: 'Multiplicata sunt ad hæc mandata et ceremoniæ hominum infinitæ, et ut tantum essent tremenda et tantæ auctoritatis, quemadmodum Dei summi præcepta, prædicantur et docentur et cum magna districtione imperantur.' The gentler influence of the 'Friends of God' (above, p. 356) was tending to the same result. Even the papal champion (cf. above, p. 325, n. 2), Alvarus Pelagius (*De Planctu Ecclesiæ*, lib. II. c. 5), is forced to acknowledge: 'Nostra autem Ecclesia plena et *superplena* est altaribus, missis, et sacrificiis.'

[1] *e.g.* Alvarus Pelagius, as in the previous note: 'Tot enim hodie dicuntur missæ quasi quæstuariæ, vel consuetudinariæ, vel ad complacentiam, vel ad scelera cooperienda, vel propriam justificationem, quod apud populum vel clerum sacrosanctum Corpus Domini jam vilescit.' And Jacobus de Paradiso (in Brown, II. 110), after inveighing against a number of superstitions, adds, 'Altaria aut ecclesias in conventiculis locorum, *sub spe miraculorum aut sacrorum erigentes propter turpem quæstum.*' The conclusion of the paragraph is very striking: 'Et quis omnia enarrare ac enumerare sufficiat, quibus Ecclesia modernis temporibus cernitur deformata? Putamusne hæc omnia aliquando posse *reformari?*' cf. the observations *Concerning the Service of the Church* and *Of Ceremonies*, prefixed to the English Prayer-Book.

[2] Gabriel Biel, *Expositio Missæ* (see above, p. 354, n. 1), Lect. LVII. states the question thus: 'Cum enim defuncti implere non possint opus, pro quo dantur indulgentiæ, dum illud pro eis fit ab alio, *jam opus alterius suffragatur eis,* ut possint consequi indulgentias, non minus quam si ipsi per se opus illud implevissent.' So far was this idea of substitution carried, that some of the Franciscans thought every member of their own Order safe, expecting that St Francis would descend annually and rescue

the more intelligent[1] it was asserted that relief is only possible to those who have already manifested true repentance and are truly justified before their death. The soul which has not in the present life been made a subject of this holy change will pass immediately into the prisons of the lost, where it can profit neither by its own compunction nor by the suffrages of other men. But in the popular discourses of the age we look in vain for such discrimination in the handling of these awful subjects; penance is too generally confounded with repentance, while the commutation and vicarious fulfilment of it are at least *assumed* to be available for all, however hardened or corrupt, and whether numbered with the living or with the dead[2].

CORRUPTIONS AND ABUSES.

A penance was awarded either publicly in case of flagrant and notorious sin, or privately in the confessional; its nature and degree depending on the customs of the diocese, or on the will of the spiritual adviser[3]. But the work of penitence was prosecuted by the several classes of delinquents in a very different spirit. Some, exceeding the most harsh requirements of the Church, endeavoured to allay the consciousness of guilt by various methods of self-torture, stimulated[4] now, as heretofore, by apprehensions, that the end of all things was at hand, particularly by the frequent wars, by famine, pestilence,

Ascetic view of it.

---

all who had died that year in the habit of the Order. See the account in Eccard, *Corpus. Hist. Med. Ævi*, II. 1101.

[1] Cf. above, pp. 307, 308.

[2] *e.g.* a plenary indulgence is said to be effectual 'pro vivis et defunctis,' and its common definition is 'omnium peccatorum et pœnarum, quas quis in purgatorio deberet pati, remissio.' Although the metrical preacher (*Camb. Univ. MSS.*, Dd. I. p. 361) condemns praying for those who are in hell on the ground that it is 'unskilful' and 'unworthy to God to hear,' he admits that such prayer *might* be answered.

[3] In the MS. volume, above quoted, p. 515, three 'degrees of penance' are enumerated: (1) 'beforn the busschop in the begynnyng of Lentone, in the cathedral chirche,' (2) 'dryuyng about the sinner, about the chirche or market, or other pilgrimage, with tapres and candelis,' &c., (3) 'beforn the prest whanne a man schryueth him of his synne and taketh his penaunce therfor.'

[4] Guerike, *Kirchengesch.* I. 820, 5th edit. A more healthy form of piety had shewn itself in others of this period, many of both sexes and of all ranks devoting at least an hour every day 'summum humano generi impensum beneficium, Christi Passionem, meditari ac repetere, ut exinde Deo grati mala mundi ferant patientius et virtutes operentur facilius.' See Neander, IX. p. 595.

CORRUPTIONS AND ABUSES.

Self-indulgent view of it.

or other national calamities, and by the desolating inroads of the Turk. By none had this conception of the penitential discipline been carried to so terrible a length as by the 'Flagellants[1],' who, although eventually excluded from the Church, were faithful to its real principles, and in respect of their unnatural austerity, had won the admiration[2] of both scholars and the more enthusiastic of the crowd. The gloom, however, which had been diffused in every quarter by the rigorous theory of penance was now dissipated, partly through the wider spread of knowledge, partly by a wish to substitute less onerous kinds of 'satisfaction' for the discipline exacted in the ancient canons of the Church. A favourite remedy was that of vowing pilgrimages to the shrine of some pre-eminent or wonder-working saint. The crowd of devotees that travelled to and fro on errands of this nature was prodigiously[3] enlarged; while it is obvious that the Years of Jubilee[4], as often as they revolved, would keep

---

[1] See above, p. 374: Gieseler, III. § 84, p. 378, n. 21; and IV. § 123, pp 227—232: Milman, *Latin Christianity*, IV. pp. 396, 397. Two outbreaks of this religious phrenzy occurred; in 1260, when the great pilgrimage of Flagellants started from Perugia; and in 1348 and following years, on the breaking out of the 'Black Death:' the practice lasted into the 15th century, until it was disapproved by the Council of Constance.

[2] On the reasons which influenced the council of Constance to deal gently with this sect, see Lenfant, liv. v. c. 50—55. It found a patron in the Spanish worthy Vincente Ferrer (above, p. 319, n. 3).

[3] *e.g.* the number of royal licences granted in the first seven months of 1445, to authorize the exportation of English pilgrims to the shrine of St Iago of Compostella in Spain (cf. above, p. 200, n. 2) was 2200: see the statistics in Turner, *Middle Ages*, III. 138, n. 28. Of domestic pilgrimages which stood in high repute in all the fifteenth century, the most popular was that to Becket's shrine at Canterbury, to Winifrith's Well, and to the image of Our Lady of Walsingham. On the continent multitudes resorted to Loretto, Einsiedeln, the Seamless Coat of Trèves, &c. &c.

[4] Cf. above, p. 310. Clement, in 1343, had fixed the recurrence of the Jubilee at the end of fifty years (see the *Extravagantes Communes*, lib. v. tit. 9, c. 2), esteeming it an act of amnesty to all who were 'vere pœnitentes et confessi.' Urban VI., however, in 1389, shortened the period to thirty-three years; but died soon afterwards. It was the sight of the enormities connected with the jubilee of Boniface IX. in the following year that roused the indignation of Theodoric of Niem (see his oft-quoted treatise *De Schismate*, lib. I. c. 68). He declares that the papal quæstors realized immense sums of money by the sale of indulgences, 'quia *omnia peccata* etiam *sine pœnitentia* ipsis confitentibus relaxarunt.' This conduct of his agents was, however, soon repudiated by Boniface himself: Raynald. ad an. 1390, § 2.

alive the public prepossessions by attracting an enthusiastic stream of pilgrims out of all the countries of the west to worship at the 'tomb of the Apostles.'

One of the chief baits by which the multitude were captivated at this period was the grant of fresh indulgences (remission of unfinished penance). But these grants could also be procured in other instances by money-payments, and without submitting to the dangers and discomforts of a lengthened tour. The 'pardoner'[1] had in the middle of the fourteenth century become a recognized official of the Roman pontiffs, and as such he introduced himself at every turn among the numerous chapmen of the age. The merit of his wares may have been sometimes questioned[2], while the purchaser had no explicit warrant of their universal applicability,—that is, in favour of the dead as well as of the living. But this point was definitely ruled in the affirmative[3] by Sixtus IV. (1477): and during all

CORRUPTIONS AND ABUSES.

Pardons from the pope.

---

[1] See Chaucer's well-known picture (or, in some respects, caricature) of the 'pardoner.' He also dealt in charms and relics, palming on the simple many bones of which the genuineness was more than questionable: cf. the *Secreta Sacerdotum* of Henry of Langenstein (quoted by Gieseler, IV. § 119, p. 200, n. 14), who, after speaking of the sale of precious relics, adds 'forte est os alicujus asini vel damnati.' Many timid efforts were made to put down unlicensed traffickers, and those quæstors who had exceeded their commission: cf. above, p. 345, n. 1, and Lenfant, *Concile de Constance*, liv. VII. c. 64.

[2] The affirmative side was generally taken (above, p. 309, n. 3), but Gerson, *Sermo II. pro defunctis*, still denies 'indulgentias acquiri posse pro mortuis.' Gabriel Biel, in like manner, had once doubted (*Lect.* LVI.) 'utrum indulgentiæ prosint defunctis;' but, cf. above, p. 426, n. 2. It was, in fact, esteemed a heresy (in 1479) to advocate the other side, 'Romanum pontificem purgatorii pœnam remittere non posse:' Raynald. ad an. 1479, § 32.

[3] See his *Declaratio*, with many other facts relating to this question, in Amort, *De origine, progressu, valore, et fructu Indulgentiarum*, II. 292, August. Vindel. 1735. His argument is the following: 'Quoniam orationes et eleemosynæ valent tanquam suffragia animabus impensa, nos, quibus plenitudo potestatis ex alto est attributa, de thesauro universalis Ecclesiæ, qui ex Christi sanctorumque Ejus meritis constat, nobis commisso, auxilium et suffragium animabus purgatorii afferre cupientes supradictam concessimus indulgentiam, ita tamen, ut fideles ipsi pro eisdem animabus suffragium darent, quod ipsæ defunctorum animæ per se nequeant adimplere.' When it was demanded why the pope, who claimed a kind of ownership in this treasury of merits, did not make more copious grants to Christians generally, the answer was, that as the minister of God he must dispense the good things of the Church with judgment and moderation ('discrete et cum moderamine') Luther revived this question in the 82nd of his theses on indulgences, as above, p. 411, n. 3.

CORRUP-
TIONS AND
ABUSES.

the next half-century the traffic in ind
into the most gigantic evil of the tim
ble supply of pardons¹, unrestrained b
their distinctive import and effects, w
commissaries², chiefly friars, like so m
or food: 'redemption for the sins' not
but of families and even districts, b
sale by public auction, and at last m
advance.

*Contro-
versy re-
specting
their ef-
ficacy.*

How many and how tangled were
impiety is gathered from a judgment
faculty³ at Paris in 1518. Those doc
found themselves unable to concur in
that *all* souls indifferently escape fror
instant when a contribution of ten 't
been made on their behalf, to funds cc
able object, or for instituting fresh cr
other hand their judgment clearly rec
principle on which the system of indu
They leave the full adjudication of the
of God, who it is argued will assuredly
according to a stated law or graduate
is disbursed, in aid of living or depar
superfluous treasure of the Church.

*Reaction
against
the whole
system of
Church
penance:*

It was however quite impossible th
could look upon this doctrine of vic;
the impious traffic it produced, with a
or respect. Too many poured contem

---

¹ Gabriel Biel accounts for their prodigious
fact that charity having waxed cold, 'nec satisf;
guntur, nec modice injunctæ perficiuntur.' *Exp*
² See, for instance, Luther's theses, § 21 sq
and cf. De Félice, *Hist. of the Protestants in*
The diplomata with which Tetzel was furnishe
forms with blank spaces for the names of th
filled up with his own hand, as occasion requ
preserved in Gerdes, *Scrinium Antiquarium* (dc
Reformation), I. 73, Groning. 1748. For the r
gences at Alcalá, see *L'Espagne Pittoresque*, b
Téréal, pp. 265—268.
³ *Ibid.* p. 113: cf. Smedley's *Reformed Reli*
Lond. 1832. The Sorbonne had in 1483 rejectec
souls in purgatory are 'de jurisdictione papæ,' a1
evacuate the whole region: see D'Argentré, *Colle
Erroribus*, I. part ii, 305.

terial office generally when they were told that a certificate of absolution could be purchased at their pleasure. Others of a graver mood, like Huss[1], or John of Wessel[2], viewed the subject differently; they brought it to the touchstone of antiquity and grew persuaded that indulgences, at least as they were sanctioned by the popes and schoolmen, were not able to abide the test. A way had thus been gradually prepared for Luther and his colleagues; and as soon as the half-hearted pontiff, Leo X., was urged to reaffirm the modern theory[3],—declaring that the temporal effects of sin may be remitted to the living and the dead alike, by means of the indulgences which he had been empowered to distribute as the almoner of Christ and of the saints,—the friar of Wittenberg restrained himself no longer. He rushed forward to denounce an antichristian and demoralizing traffic, and at first he carried with him nearly all the better spirits of the age[4]. For Luther had betrayed no wish to criticize the general teaching of the Church, to meddle with the continuity of her existence, to subvert her ancient ritual, or disparage her collective voice. The ground which he had occupied was moral rather than dogmatic. He had sought to reinvigorate

CORRUPTIONS AND ABUSES.

more especially in the time of Luther.

---

[1] Above, p. 408.

[2] See the whole of his *Adversus Indulgentias Disputatio*, in Walch, *Moniment. Medii Ævi*, Fasc. I., pp. 111—156. While granting that the pope was able to commute the penalty which human law may have in any case attached to sin, he absolutely denies the scripturalness of the pretension to relax a penalty imposed by God Himself ('non est in sacro Canone scriptum'). Durand de S. Pourçain, *In Sentent.* lib. IV., distinct. xx., quæst. 3, had long before suggested that the Bible said nothing of indulgences expressly ('expresse'), and that Ambrose, Hilary, Augustine, and Jerome were all equally silent: while Gabriel Biel (himself an advocate of indulgences) allows in Lect. LVII., quoted above, that, before the time of Gregory the Great, 'modicus vel nullus fuit usus indulgentiarum.'

[3] The document is printed in Löscher, as above, II. 493. After defining that the 'culpa' which attached to sin was graciously forgiven through the 'sacrament of penance,' he proceeded to discuss the 'temporalis pœna.' The following clause is unmistakeable: 'Ac propterea omnes tam vivos quam defunctos, qui veraciter omnes indulgentias hujusmodi consecuti fuerint, *a tanta temporali pœna* secundum Divinam justitiam pro peccatis suis actualibus debita liberari, *quanta concessæ et acquisitæ indulgentiæ æquivalet*.'

[4] Even F. von Schlegel (*Phil. of History*, pp. 400, 401, Lond. 1847) admits that the strong necessity of some regeneration was then universally felt, and that Luther seemed to numbers the very man for the work.

CORRUPTIONS AND ABUSES.

in man the consciousness of personal responsibility, while he insisted, with an emphasis unequalled since the time of St Augustine, on the need of individual fellowship with Christ.

If it appear that in the following stages of the movement which he headed some of his disciples pushed reforming principles to revolutionary lengths; if his iniquitous extrusion from the Western Church became the signal for igniting long-extinguished controversies, and the origin of feuds that vibrated in every corner of the Christian fold, those evils, it should never be forgotten, are less chargeable on the impetuosity of Luther than on the fierce antagonism of Rome. The pride, the worldliness, the arbitrary and exclusive temper of the papal court, as well as the unholy craft by which it undermined the liberty and threatened to eclipse the light of Christendom, had long been tending more than other causes to provoke inquiry and necessitate the crisis that ensued. All projects of reform, suggested either from within or from without, had consequently grown distasteful to the Roman pontiffs: it was so with hardly an exception in the fourteenth and the fifteenth centuries; and in the sixteenth we shall find them concentrating all their virulence to blast alike the Foreign and the English Reformations in the bud.

INDEX.

ABBOTS (lay), 147; 148, and n. 2.
ABELARD, the Nominalistic schoolman, his life and writings, 260—262; an amorous poet, 297, n. 1.
ADENDON, Oxford doctor, 418, n. 2.
ABSALOM (bp. of Roskild), 211.
Absolution, Peter Lombard on, 308, and n. 3.
ABULPHARAGIUS (maphrian of the Jacobites), writings of, 275, and n. 4.
Abyssinia, interference of the Portuguese, 315, n. 5; 370; negociations respecting, at Florence, 370.
ADALBERT (an anti-Roman prelate), 22.
ADALBERT, German missionary in Bohemia, 115; his attempts to convert the Prussians, 115, n. 3.
ADALBERT (first archbp. of Magdeburg), 118.
ADALBERT (archbp. of Bremen), 107, n. 1; 119, n. 2.
ADALDAG (archbp. of Hamburg-Bremen), 106.
ADALGAR, northern missionary, 106.
Adamites, sect of, 374.
ADAMNAN, 14, n. 4; his writings, 59, n. 3.
ADELMANN (bp. of Brescia), on the Eucharist, 169, n. 3.
Adoptionist controversy, 61—64.
ADREVALD, on the Eucharist, 168, n. 4.
ÆGIDIUS (archbp. of Bourges), on the limits of the papal power, 254, n. 3.
ÆLFHEAH (archbp. of Canterbury), 131, n. 2.
ÆLFRIC, on the Eucharist, 168, n. 2; his other writings, 174; difficulty of distinguishing between the 'Ælfrics,' 174, n. 4; his 'Lives of Saints,' 195.
ÆTHELBERHT, 7, 8.
AGATHO (pope), endeavours to settle the Monothelete controversy, 69.
AGIL (Aile), missionary, 17, n. 5.
AGRICOLA (Rodolph), 354, n. 4.

AGOBARD (archbp. of Lyons) writes on the Adoptionist controversy, 64, n. 2; on 'Ordeals,' 155; his other works, 157; protests against image-worship, 157, n. 5; tries to reform the service-books, 196, n. 2.
AIDAN (Irish missionary), 12, 13 n. 1.
ALANUS (Magnus), a Parisian schoolman, 264, n. 4.
ALBERT THE GREAT, life and writings, 266, 267.
ALBERT (priest of Bremen), employs force in converting the Lieflanders, 213.
Albigenses (see *Cathari*), import of the name, 286, n. 5.
ALCUIN, opposed to compulsory conversions, 24; 26, n. 4; his language to the pope, 41, n. 4; and to the emperor, 54, n. 2; on the study of Holy Scripture, 56, n. 3, his character and writings, 60, 61, n. 4; 62, n. 2, 3; 63.
ALDFRITH (king of Northumbria), his conduct towards Wilfrith, 15, n. 3.
ALDHELM, his writings, 59, n. 4; 89.
ALEXANDER VI. (pope), his heinous crimes, 339.
ALEXIUS COMNENUS (emperor), opposes the Paulicians, 282, n. 5; and represses the Bogomiles, 285.
ALFRED (king of England), 86, n. 1; 131; his patronage of learning and religion, 173; his works, 173, n. 4; his coadjutors, 174, n. 1.
All Saints, feast of, instituted, 92, 93, n. 1.
All Souls, feast of, instituted, 203.
ALLEMAND, reforming cardinal, 337; and n. 2; 341, n. 3.
AMALARIUS (of Metz), on the triplicity of the Body of Christ, 168, n. 1.
AMANDUS, missionary, 18, n. 4; 23, n. 5.
America, tradition respecting, 110, n. 4; discovery of, 316; attempts to convert the natives, 317; eventual success, 317, n. 6.

M. A.

F F

AMULO (archbp. of Lyons) engages in the Predestinarian controversy, 163.
Anathema, 202.
ANDREAS (archbp. of Lund), 213, n. 1.
ANDREW (of Rhodes), defends the Latin Church, 366, and n. 3.
ANDRONICUS III. PALÆOLOGUS, negociates with the Latins, 364.
Anglia (East), conversion of, 11, 12.
Anglo-Saxons, their settlement in England, 6; their mythology, 7, n. 2.
ANNA (of Bohemia), Queen of Richard II. of England, 386, n. 5; 401.
Annates, papal, 322, n. 3; 336, n. 3; 342.
ANSELM (archbp. of Canterbury), 159, n. 6; was the 'Augustine' of the Middle Age, 258, a Realist, 259, 260; writes against Roscellinus, 259, n. 3; against the Greeks, 276, and n. 3.
ANSELM (of Laon), 260, n. 2.
ANSELM (bp. of Havelberg), 277.
ANSKAR (Ansgar), his missionary life, 101—105; receives the pallium, 140, n. 4.
Anthropomorphists, 192, n. 5.
Apocrisiarius, what, 39, n. 1; 50, n. 3.
Apostolicals (sect of), 294, 295; later traces of, 295, n. 4.
Appeals (to Rome), 226, 227; peculiarly obnoxious to the English, 227, n. 2; to a general council, 330, n. 2.
Aquileia, archbps. of, suspend their communion with Rome, 38, n. 2.
AQUINAS (Thomas), life and writings, 267; analysis of his 'Summa,' 267—269.
Archbishops, their peculiar functions, 35; their influence weakened by the papacy, 35, 140, 141; metropolitans appointed in England, 36, 37, and in Germany, 36; how consecrated in England, 36, n. 6; vow obedience to the pope, 140; their rights defended at Milan, 141, n. 1.
Archdeacons, 46; exorbitance of, 239, and n. 6.
Archicapellanus, what, 45, n. 3; 143, n. 2.
Archpresbyters, 46, n. 3.
ARDGAR, missionary in Sweden, 104, and n. 1.
ARIALD, a Milanese preacher, 144, n. 2.
ARISTOTLE, his influence in the Western Church, 160, n. 1; 352, n. 1; change of feeling in regard to him, 265, 267, 354.

Armenians (church of the), their flourishing condition, 175, n. 4; their judaizing turn, 187, n. 4; attempts to reunite them to the Church, 275, n. 7; renewed with greater chances of success, 369, 370; their tenets in the 14th century, 369, n. 5; 370, n. 1.
ARNO (archbp. of Salzburg), 26, 111.
ARNOLD (cleric of Brescia), his movement against the hierarchy, 249; associated with Abelard, 262, n. 4.
ARNULPH (archbp. of Orleans), his 'reforming' tendencies, 138, n. 4.
Arsenian schism, 272, n. 3.
ARUNDEL (archbp. of Canterbury) opposes the Lollards, 393, n. 6.
Ascetics, 200, 201, 307.
Asia (Central), missions to, 27, 28, 128, 129.
ASSER, Alfred's coadjutor, 174, n. 1.
ASTON (John), 385.
Athanasian Creed, 57, n. 1.
Athinganians, sect of, 187, n. 4.
ATTO (bp. of Vercelli), 142, n. 2; 174, n. 2.
AUDOMAR (Omer), missionary 18, n. 4.
AUGUSTINE, ST (of Hippo), his canonical institute, 44, n. 3; influence of his theology on the Middle Age, 57 sq.; 156 sq.; 258; and especially on Luther, 357, n. 4; 411, n. 1.
AUGUSTINE (of Canterbury), 6; 7, n. 4; 8, 9, 11; 43, n. 3.
AUGUSTINIAN CANONS, 156, 257.
Augustinian friars, 344, n. 5; 345, and n. 5.
AUTBERT, missionary in Denmark, 102.
AUVERGNE (Wm. of), his writings, 271, n. 1.
Avares, mission to, 26.
AVERROES, his philosophy, 265, n. 1.
Avignon, papal residence at, 254, 322; effects of, 322, 323.
AYLMER (bp.) on Wycliffe, 396, n. 4.
Azymes, dispute respecting, 186, n. 2; 279, 366, 367.

BACON (Roger), life and writings, 271, 272.
BALLE (John), who, 384, n. 1.
BARDANES (emperor) revives Monotheletism, 70, and n. 3.
BARLAAM (eastern monk), opposes the Quietists, 363, and secedes to Rome, 363; his negociation for unity, 364.

Index.   435

Baptism, infant, 24, n. 2; 80; 164, 165; 189, n. 1; 192, n. 5; 288, 290, n. 3; 294, n. 3; 302, n. 2.

Basel, council of, its leading objects, 334; struggle with the pope, 334—337; conduct of the Greeks respecting, 365.

BASIL I. (emperor) persecutes the Paulicians, 84.

BASIL (monk), leader of the Bogomiles, 285.

Bavaria, conversion of, 18 sq.; presence of an anti-Roman party, 20, 21.

BEATUS, a writer in the Adoptionist controversy, 63, n. 1.

BECCUS (chartophylax at Constantinople), his Latinizing tendencies, 280, 281.

BECKET (archbp. of Canterbury), his contest with the crown, 249, 250; his influence in consolidating the papal power, 250, 251, n. 1.

BEDE (Venerable), on the increase of the episcopate, 46, n. 2; his theological writings, 59, 60; his devotion to biblical learning, 60, and n. 1; 89; on preaching in the native dialects, 87, n. 5.

Beghards (and Beguins), their rise and progress, 235; 346; remains of, 373, 374.

BENEDICT (of Monte Cassino), his order, 43.

BENEDICT (of Aniane), his monastic reforms, 148, and n. 3.

BENEDICT BISCOP, his influence, 59, n. 5; 94, n. 3.

BENEDICT IX., one of the most profligate of the popes, 139, n. 5.

BERENGARIUS, defends the ancient doctrine of the Eucharist, 169—173; extreme opinions of some of his adherents, 170, n. 4; 406, n. 5.

BERNARD (a Spanish priest), his failure in Pomerania, 207, 208.

BERNARD (of Clairvaux), his influence in extending the fame of the Cistercians, 230; his writings, and the character of his theology, 257, 270; his opposition to Abelard, 257, n. 2; 262.

BERNO, founder of the Cluniacs, 148.

BERTHOLD, a distinguished preacher, 300, n. 1.

BERTHOLD, a missionary in Livonia, invokes military aid, 212, 213.

BERTON (Wm.), chancellor of Oxford, 383.

BESSARION, convert to the Western Church, 367; his patronage of letters, 367, n. 2.

Bible (see *Scripture*).

BIEL (Gabriel), last of the schoolmen, 354, and n. 1.

BIRINUS, 10.

Bishops (diocesan), their functions, 34; their visitations, 45, 46, and n. 1; 97; election of, sometimes tumultuary, 50, n. 3; discontinuance of the practice, 51, 151, 341; its partial revival, 52, 151, n. 3; 341; usage in England, 53, 342; their general character, 142, 143; regarded as mere feudatories of the crown, 150, 151; their encroachments on the state, 153, exceptions, 154, 155, and n. 1; fettered by the papal power, 227, 228; their vow of servitude, 227; titular and suffragan bishops, 238, 239; object of the Basel council to elevate the western bishops, 341, and n. 3.

BODZANTA (archbp. of Gnesen), 313.

Bogomiles, rise of, and main features of their heresy, 282—285; repressed in part, 285, and n. 6; connexion with western sects, 285, 286, and n. 6.

Bohemia, conversion of, 114—116; ascendancy of German influence, 116; suppression of the Slavonic ritual, 116, n. 2.; reformatory movements in, 397—410.

BONAVENTURA, life and writings, 266; promotes the growth of Mariolatry, 266, n. 4.

BONIFACIUS (Winfrith), extensive missionary labours, 19—23; his writings, 59, n. 4; his Romanizing tendencies, 19, and n. 8; 35, and n. 4, 36, and n. 1, 2.

BORGIA (Cæsar), 339.

BRADWARDINE (archbp. of Canterbury), writes against the Scotists, 270, n. 3.

Bremen (see of); united with Hamburg, 104, and n. 3; point of departure for northern missions, 119, n. 2.

BRIDGET (of Sweden), 327, n. 7; her canonization, 424, n. 4.

British Church, 6, and n. 4; 7, n. 4; 8, n. 6; 14, n. 4; 15, n. 1; 20, n. 4.

BRUNO (bishop of Angers) favours Berengarius, 170.

FF 2

BRUNO, founder of the Carthusians, 229, and n. 1.
BRUNO, perishes in attempting to convert the Prussians, 115, n. 3.
Bulgaria, conversion of, 121—124; its temporary union with the Church of Constantinople, 124; controversy respecting, 183, 185.
BULGRI, 285, n. 7; 286, n. 2.
Byzantinism, what, 50, 51, and 50, n. 4; 272, and n. 3.

CÆDMON, his *Metrical Paraphrase*, 89, n. 4.
Cagots, who, 373, n. 3.
Calixtines, Hussite party, 408, 409.
Canary Islands, conversion of, 316.
CANDIDA CASA (=Whithern), 7, n. 1; 15, n. 2.
Canon law, its component parts, 224, n. 1; 323, n. 3.
Canons, order of, 44; their degeneracy, 144, 237; Dunstan's quarrel with them, 146; their right of electing the bishops, 237, and n. 5; attempts to reform them, 238; distinction between 'canons-regular' and 'canons-secular,' 238, n. 3.
Canonesses, 44, n. 3.
Canterbury, 8; 9, n. 5; province of, 15, n. 2; primacy settled in it, 36, n. 5.
CARINTHIA, conversion of, 25.
CARLOMAN, 42, n. 1.
Carmelites (white-friars), 229, n. 1; 344, n. 5; 345, and n. 5.
Carthusians, order of, 229, 343.
CASALI (Ubertinus de), a 'spiritualist' Franciscan, 232, n. 4; 324, n. 4.
CASAS (Bartolomé de las), friend of the American Indians, 317, and n. 2.
Catenæ, age of, 179.
Cathari, their rise, 286; principles of the sect, 286—288; their rapid growth and violent suppression, 289; remains of, 373.
CATHARINE (of Alexandria), relics of, introduced into the west, 198, n. 2; legend of, disputed, 424, n. 4.
CATHARINE (of Siena), her political influence, 327, and n. 7.
CEDD, 10; 14, n. 4.
CERULARIUS (patriarch of Constantinople) fixes the schism between East and West, 185, 186; his attack on the Latins, 186, n. 2.

Chaldæans (see *Nestorians*).
CHAMPEAUX (Wm. de), a schoolman, 260, and n. 4.
Chaplains, 45, and n. 3; their abject position, 144, and n. 1.
Chapters (rural), 45.
CHARO (Hugo de S.), a biblical scholar, 272, n. 2.
CHARLES THE BALD (emperor), 137, n. 1, 2; 154, n. 2.
CHARLEMAGNE, adopts coercive measures in the propagation of the Gospel, 24; his coronation by the pope, 40, n. 6; enforces the payment of tithes, 48; his extensive power in matters ecclesiastical, 54, n. 2; 154; on the study of Holy Scripture, 56, n. 2; his moderation respecting images, 77, and n. 5; his zeal in founding schools, 86; his coadjutors, 86, n. 3; publishes a *Homiliarium*, 88, n. 4. opposes many superstitions, 90, n. 2.
Chazars, partial conversion of, 124.
CHICHELEY (archbp. of Canterbury), on papal legates, 225, n. 6; persecutes the Lollards, 395, n. 1.
China, early traces of Christianity, 27, 218; its decline, 218, n. 2, 3.
CHINGHIS-KHAN, 216.
Chorepiscopi, 46, n. 2; 142, n. 1.
CHOSROES (Kesra) persecutes the Eastern Church, 29.
CHRISTIAN (monk), missionary labours in Prussia, 214.
CHRODEGANG (bp. of Metz) 44, and n. 5; 88, n. 1.
CHRYSOLANUS (Peter), archbp. of Milan, 277.
Church-building, 93, 204.
Cistercians, order of, 229.
CLARA, ST, order of, 231, n. 2; 304, n. 1.
Clarendon, Constitutions of, 250, and n. 2.
CLAUDIUS (bp. of Turin), his 'protestantism,' 158.
CLEMENGES (Nich. de), his 'reforming' works, 328, n. 4; 330, n. 5.
CLEMENT VII. (pope), his connexion with the forty years' schism, 329.
CLEMENT (anti-Roman prelate), 22.
Clergy, proper, 47, and n. 2; their marriage, 47; 145; 241; 349, and n. 2, 3; their concubinage tolerated, 349, n. 4; their income, 48; effects of their close alliance with the state, 54, 55; their intellectual qualifica-

tions, 86, and n. 3; 192, n. 5; their degeneracy, 142—144; 240—243; 348—350; extension of the law of celibacy to the minor orders, 241; the right of inferior clerics to vote in synods, 331, n. 4.
Clergy, itinerant, 45, and n. 2; 143.
Clerici conductitii, 238, n. 2.
Clugny, monks of, 148.
CNUT (Canute the Great), interest in northern missions, 106, and n. 8.
COBHAM (Lord), opinions and martyrdom, 393, 394.
Cœlestine-Hermits, 232.
COIFI, 12, n. 3.
Colleges, 235, n. 1; 278, n. 2; 296, n. 2; 416.
COLMAN (bishop of Lindisfarne), 14, and n. 7.
COLUMBA (Irish missionary), 6, n. 1; 7, n. 1.
COLUMBANUS (Irish missionary), his labours and opinions, 16.
Common-life Brothers, order of, 347, 348; their salutary influence, 347, and n. 5.
Communicants, number of, 85, n. 2; 96, n. 1; 305, n. 1; laymen forbidden to communicate more than once a month, 400.
Communion of children, discontinued in the west, 305, n. 1.
Communion in one kind, 303; controversy reopened, 399, n. 3; 406, n. 4.
Concomitance, doctrine of, 303.
Confession (auricular), generally practised, 97, 202; made absolutely binding, 308, and n. 1.
CONRAD (of Waldhausen), a 'reformer,' 398.
CONRADIN, last of the Hohenstaufen, 253.
Consolamentum, what, 288, n. 2.
Constance, council of, history and effects, 331; presence of Greek envoys, 365, n. 2.
CONSTANS II. (emperor), a Monothelete, his *Type of the Faith*, 67; forces compliance with it, 68.
CONSTANTINE, author of Paulicianism, 79.
CONSTANTINE COPRONYMUS (emperor), his proceedings against images, 74, 75; his personal character, 74, n. 2; respected by Bogomiles, 285, n. 2; and Petrobrusians, 290, n. 3.
Constantini Donatio, 254, n. 3.

Convocation (see *Synods*, provincial).
Copts (see *Jacobites*).
Corpus Christi, festival of, 304.
CORBINIAN (missionary), 18.
CORTES (conqueror of Mexico), his final wish to evangelize the natives, 317, n. 6.
CORTESIUS, a scholastic, 354, n. 1.
Councils (see also under *Synods*): of *Aix-la-Chapelle* (799), 64; *Ibid.* (816), 44; of *Arles* (813), 45, n. 4; 46, n. 7; of *Arras* (1025), 188, n. 2; of *Auvergne* (533), 51, n. 7; of *Barcelona* (599), 51, n. 6; of *Bari* (1098), 276; of *Basel* (1431—1440), 334—337; of *Béziers* (1246), 299, n. 2; of *Bologna* (1431), 335; of *Bordeaux* (1255), 305, n. 1; of *Braga* (675), 48, n. 5; of *Cashel* (1172), 87, n. 4; of *Cealchyth* (785), 46, n. 5; 57, n. 1; *Ibid.* (816), 141, n. 2; of *Châlons* (649), 45, n. 3; 88, n. 2; *Ibid.* (813), 44, n. 3; 141, n. 2; of *Clarendon* (1164), 250; of *Clermont* (1095), 246, n. 6; of *Clovesho* (747), 21, n. 8; 46, n. 1, 5; 56, n. 2; of *Cologne* (873), 145, n. 1; of *Constance* (1414—1418), 331 sq.; of *Constantinople* (680), 40, n. 2; *Ibid.* (754), 74; not œcumenical, 74, n. 4; *Ibid.* (867), 183; *Ibid.* (869), 183; not œcumenical, 183, n. 7; *Ibid.* (1054), 186, n. 6; *Ibid.* (1140 and 1143), 285, n. 6; of *Cordova* (852), 133; of *Coyaco* (1050), 195, n. 4; of *Douzi* (871), 137, n. 1; of *Eanham* (1009), 145, n. 4; 195, n. 4; of *Ferrara* (1437), 337, 338; 365; of *Fismes* (881), 148, n. 1; 154, n. 2; of *Florence* (1439), 338, 366—370; of *Frankfort* (794), 63. 78; of *Gran* (1114), 241, n. 2; of *Hertford* (673), 15, n. 2; of *Ingelheim* (948), 106, n. 3; of *Kiersy-sur-Oise* (849), 162; *Ibid.* (853), 164; of *Lateran* (1059), 146, n. 3; *Ibid.* (1123), 248; *Ibid.* (1139), 289, n. 3; *Ibid.* (1179), 239, n. 6; 293, n. 1; 296, n. 2; *Ibid.* (1215), 239, n. 7; 242, n. 2; 264, n. 3; 278, n. 1; 296, n. 2; 303; 305, n. 1; 327, n. 8; *Ibid.* (1444), 370; *Ibid.* (1512—1517), 340; 344, n. 6; 355; of *London* (1107), 247, n. 1; *Ibid.* (1108), 241, n. 4; *Ibid.* (1237), 307, n. 2; *Ibid.* (1382); 385; *Ibid.* (1396), 391, n. 5; of *Lombers* (1165), 289, n. 3; of *Lyons* (1274),

not œcumenical, 281, and n. 1; of *Mentz* (813), 88, 91; *Ibid.* (847), 192; n. 2; *Ibid.* (848), 162; of *Melfi* (1089), 307, n. 3; of *Metz* (859), 154, n. 2; *Ibid.* (863), 136, n. 4; *Ibid.* (888), 142, n. 1; *Second Council of Nicæa* (787), 76; *Sixth Œcumenical Council* (680), 69, 70; of *Orleans* (611), 48, n. 5; *Ibid.* (1022), 188, n. 2; of *Oxford* (1160), 288, n. 5; *Ibid.* (1408), 393, n. 6; of *Paris* (557), 51, n. 7; *Ibid.* (615), 52; *Ibid.* (825), 176, n. 1; *Ibid.* (829), 142, n. 1, 3; of *Pavia* (850), 142, n. 3; 143, n. 5; 199, n. 2; of *Pisa* (1409), 330; *Ibid.* (1512), 340, n. 2; of *Poitiers* (1076), 171, n. 6; of *Prague* (1388), 399, 400; of *Ratisbon* (792), 63; of *Ravenna* (1311), 238, n. 6; of *Rheims* (624), 52; *Ibid.* (991), 138, n. 5; *Ibid.* (1148), 289, n. 3; of *Rome* (595), 46, n. 8; *Ibid.* (601), 42, n. 5; *Ibid.* (649), 68; *Ibid.* (680), 69; *Ibid.* (731), 73, n. 6; *Ibid.* (745), 22; *Ibid.* (769), 74, n. 4; *Ibid.* (799), 63, n. 6; *Ibid.* (826), 150, n. 3; 192, n. 5; *Ibid.* (853), 150, n. 3; *Ibid.* (863), 182; *Ibid.* (869), 183, n. 7; *Ibid.* (1050), 169; *Ibid.* (1059), 238, n. 3; *Ibid.* (1075), 244; *Ibid.* (1079), 172; of *Savonières* (859), 165, and n. 3; 191, n. 1; 193, n. 3; of *Seligenstadt* (1022), 200, n. 1; of *Sens* (1140), 262; of *Seville* (618), 46, n. 5; of *Soissons* (744), 22; *Ibid.* (1092), 260; *Ibid.* (1121), 261; of *Spalato* (1069), 194, n. 3; of *Tarragona* (1234), 299, n. 2; of *Toledo* (633), 46, n. 4, 7; 47, n. 1; 48, n. 4; 56, n. 3; *Ibid.* (653), 46, n. 7; 47, n. 5; *Ibid.* (675), 47, n. 1; *Ibid.* (681), 53; of *Toulouse* (1119), 289; *Ibid.* (1229), 290, 299; of *Tours* (813), 88, n. 4; *Ibid.* (1163), 289, n. 3; of *Trosli* (909), 148, n. 2; 154, n. 2; 193, n. 1; *in Trullo* (691), 38, n. 2; 47; of *Valence* (855), 151, n. 3; 155, n. 3; 164; 192, n. 3; 193, n. 3; of *Whitby* (664), 14; of *Winchester* (1076), 241; of *Worms* (1076), 244, n. 5; of *York* (1195), 307, n. 1.

Courland, temporary conversion of, 213.

COURTENAY (bp. of London), Wycliffe's antagonist, 378, 384.

CRACOVIA (Matthæus de), reforming work, 330, n. 2.

Croats (Chrobatians), conversion of, 124.

Cross, reverenced even by Iconoclasts, 73, n. 5; 80, n. 3; festival in honour of, 93, n. 3; 'adoration' of, 158, n. 2; abhorred by the Bogomiles, 285, n. 3.

Crusades (eastern), 218; 246; 276, 277.

Crusades (Albigensian), 233.

Culdees, a Scotch order of canons, 237, n. 5.

CUNIBERT (bp. of Turin), 146, n. 1.

Cup in the Eucharist, withdrawal of, 199, n. 3; 303, n. 6, 304.

CUSANUS (Nicholas), his writings, 335, and n. 4.

CUTHBERT (archbp. of Canterbury), 21, n. 8; 36, n. 1.

CYRIL (a Greek missionary), 111; translates the Scriptures, 112, n. 1; evangelizes the Chazars, 124.

CYRUS (patriarch of Alexandria), a Monothelete heretic, 65.

D'AILLY (De Alliaco), reforming cardinal, 331, n. 4; 333, and n. 1; his theological writings, 354, n. 2.

DAMASCUS (John of), 57; his theological system, 71; vehement defender of images, 72, n. 1; 73.

DAMIANI (Pet.), the ally of Hildebrand, 146, n. 2.

Dancers, sect of, 374, n. 4.

Danes (see *Northmen*)

DANIEL (bp. of Winchester), 19, 23, n. 6.

DANTE, 255, n. 2; 323, n. 5.

Deans (rural), 46, n. 3.

Decretals (Pseudo-Isidore), 41, n. 1; origin of, 134, n. 1; their influence in extending the papal power, 134, 135; 152; quoted with this object, 136, n. 5; 137, n. 1; 182, n. 6.

Denmark, mission to, 102, 104—106; 108; mythology of, 18, n. 3; 105, n. 3; conflicts with the Germans in propagating the Gospel, 213.

DEUTZ (Rupert of), 263, n. 3.

Devil-worshippers, 187, n. 5.

DIDACUS (bp. of Osma), co-founder of the Dominicans, 232, 233.

DINANT, David of, a heterodox philosopher, 265, n. 3; 299, n. 1.

DINOOT (British abbot), 6, n. 4; 8, n. 6.

Index. 439

DIONYSIUS (Pseudo-), influence of his writings, 64, n. 4.
DIONYSIUS (the Areopagite), 160, n. 3.
DIONYSIUS (Bar-Salibi), a Jacobite author, 275.
DIUMA (bp. in Mercia), 13.
Dobrin, Knights-brethren of, 215.
DOLAN (Stephen of), anti-Hussite writer, 404, n. 1.
DOLCINO, 295.
Dominicans (see also *Mendicants*), rise and progress of, 232.
DRUTHMAR (Christian), work of, 159; views on the Eucharist, 168.
DUNSTAN (archbp. of Canterbury), the nature of his policy, 146; 153; 200, n. 1.
DURAND (de S. Pourçain), the Nominalistic schoolman, 352; some of his peculiarities, 352, n. 2; on indulgences, 431, n. 2.
DURANTI (Durandus), the liturgical writer, 271, n. 1.

EADBALD, 9.
EADWINE, 12.
Easter, modes of reckoning, 7, n. 4; 13, n. 1, 4.
EBBO (archbp. of Rheims), 101; 103, n. 5.
EBED-JESU, Nestorian writer, 275.
EBLAND, 357, n. 4.
EBN-NASSAL, work of, 274, n. 1.
ECGBERHT (archbp. of York) his patronage of letters, 60; writings, 60, n. 4.
ECGFRITH (king of Northumbria), his conduct towards Wilfrith, 15, n. 3.
ECKHART, a Neo-Platonist, 356, n. 1.
EDDIUS, 59, n. 4.
ELFEG (archbp.): see *Ælfheah*.
ELIGIUS (Eloy), missionary bishop, 18, n. 4.
ELIPANDUS (archbp. of Toledo), his part in the Adoptionist controversy, 61, 63.
ELMHAM, Latin poet, 394, n. 2.
EMMERAN (missionary bishop), 17, 18.
England, growth of the Church in, 6—16; its comparative civilization before the incursions of the Northmen, 86.
English missionaries to the Continent, 18—25; 106, n. 8; 107, 108; 109, n. 2; 110, and n. 3; 206, n. 2.

ERASMUS, his opposition to the schoolmen, 354, n. 4; his edition of the Greek Testament, 361, n. 5.
ERIC IX. (of Sweden), labours to extend the Church, 206.
ERIGENA (see *Scotus*).
ERIMBERT (northern missionary), 105.
Essex, conversion of, 9, 10.
Esthland, conversion of, 213.
ETHERIUS (bp. of Osma), 63, n. 1.
Eucharistic controversy, 165—173.
Euchites, sect of, 187, 282.
EULOGIUS (patriarch of Alexandria) writes against the Bogomiles, 282, n. 6.
EUSTASIUS (missionary), 17, n. 5.
EUSTATHUS (archbp. of Thessalonica), writings of, 274.
EUTYCHIUS (patriarch of Alexandria), 180.
Excommunication, 202.

Faroe Islands, conversion of, 110, 111.
Fasts, annual, 91, n. 4.
FELIX (bishop of Dunwich), 11.
FELIX (bishop of Urgel), leader in the Adoptionist controversy, 61—64.
Ferrara, council of, 365; presence of the Greeks, 365; transferred to Florence, 366.
Ferrer (Vincente), 319, n. 3; 428, n. 2.
Festivals, 91, 92, 178, 203; 299, n. 3; 304.
FICINO (Marsilio), a Christian Platonist, 355, and n. 1.
Filioque (clause so called), 57, n. 1; 184, n. 4; 279; 366, and n. 3.
FINAN (Irish missionary), 10, 13.
Finns, conversion of, 206, 207.
FITZ-RALPH (Richard, archbp. of Armagh), defends the clergy against the Mendicants, 345, n. 1, 4.
Flagellants, 201, and n. 2; 307, n. 1; sect of, 374; their number and extravagances, 374, n. 4; 428.
FLEMING (bp. of Lincoln), 395.
Florence, council of, 366—370; translated to the Lateran, 370.
FLORUS (deacon of Lyons), engages in the Predestinarian controversy, 163; views on the Eucharist, 168.
FRANCIS (of Assisi), 219, 231.
Franciscans (see also *Mendicants*), their rise and progress, 230, 231; third

estate of, 231; growth of an extreme, and anti-papal party, 231, 232; 346; their extravagant notions respecting purgatory, 426, n. 2.
Fratricelli, 232, 373.
Fredegis, 159.
FREDERIC I., Barbarossa, his struggle with the popes, 249, 251.
FREDERIC II. (emperor), continues the struggle, 251, 252; appeals to a general council, 254, n. 2; his personal character, 252, n. 6.
Friars (see *Mendicants*).
Friars-regular, 346.
FRIESLAND, conversion of, 18 sq.
FULBERT (bp. of Chartres), 175.
FURSEY (Irish monk), 11, 12; 95, n. 5.

GALLUS (Irish missionary), 17.
GAUNT (John of), his connexion with Wycliffe, 379, 384.
GAUZBERT (or Simon), missionary in Sweden, 103; 105, n. 1.
GEGNÆSIUS, a Paulician leader, 82.
GEORGE (of Trebizond), writing of, 362.
GERALD (count of Aurillac), 196, n. 1.
GERBERT (see *Sylvester II*.).
GERHARD, a 'Manichæan' leader, 190, n. 1.
GERHOH (of Reichersberg), 240, n. 4.
GERMANUS (patriarch of Constantinople), deposed for advocating image-worship, 73; his theory of 'relative' worship, 73, n. 2.
Germany, conversion of, 16 sq.; its heathen mythology, 18, n. 3.
GERSON (John), chancellor of Paris, his reforming efforts, 330, n. 5; 333, and n. 2; his theological writings, 357, 361; his theory of development, 372, n. 2.
GEZO (abbot of Tortona), on the Eucharist, 169, n. 1.
Ghibellines, conflict with the popes, 248 sq.
GISLEMAR (missionary to Denmark), 102.
Goslar (chapter of), stronghold of the German imperialists, 244, n. 5.
GOTTSCHALK (king of the Wends), his martyrdom, 118, 119.
GOTTSCHALK (monk of Fulda), revives the Predestinarian controversy, 160 —162; his firmness and violence, 162,
n. 2; defended by Remigius of Lyons and others, 164; his controversy respecting the phrase *Trina Deitas*, 165, n. 4.
GOWER (English poet), 348, n. 4.
GRATIAN, his 'Decretum,' 224, n. 1.
GREGORY VII. (pope), his 'reforming' tendencies, 139; 143, n. 2; 144, n. 3; endeavours to restrain the marriage of the clergy, 145, 146; attacks 'lay-investitures,' 152; symbolizes with Berengarius on the Eucharist, 170, and n. 4; 171, 172, n. 3; his leading principles as pope, 222, 223; 243; exasperates the people against the clergy, 223, and n. 2; his struggle with Henry IV. of Germany, 244, —245; his sober views on penance, 307, n. 3.
GREGORY (of Utrecht), missionary abbot, 23.
GREGORY THE GREAT (pope), 6; controversy with John the Faster, 38; enlarges the dominion of the papacy, 39, and n. 2, 3; his writings on theology, 57—59.
GREGORY (of Tours), 89, n. 5; 92.
Greenland, the Gospel in, 110; suppression of it by the Esquimaux, 110, n. 4; reintroduced by Moravian missionaries, *ibid*.
GROOT (Gerhard), founder of the 'Common-life Brothers,' 347, and n. 4.
GROSSETESTE (bp. of Lincoln), opposes the pope, 226, n. 4; warns him of his tendency to produce a schism, 228, and n. 2; his conduct with regard to the Mendicants, 234, n. 2; his complaint of the corruptions of the clergy, 240, n. 4; his commentary on Aristotle, 265, n. 4; influences on Wycliffe, 374, n. 5; and Huss, 400.
GUALBERT, founder of the Cœnobites of Vallombrosa, 149.
Guelphs, allies of the pope against the emperor, 248.
GUIBERT (abbot of Nogent), on relics, 306, n. 3.
Guinea, coast of, partly Christianized, 316.
GUISCARD (Robert), 245, and n. 6.
GUITMUND (archbp), on the Eucharist, 170, n. 4.
GUTHLAC (hermit), 90, n. 1.

HACON (Hagen) introduces Christianity into Norway, 108.
HADRIAN I. (pope), his activity in favour of images, 76, 78.
HAIMO (bp. of Halberstadt), writings of, 159; views on the Eucharist, 168, n. 5.
HALES (Alexander of), life and writings, 266.
HALITGAR (bishop of Cambray), 96, n. 5; 101.
HALLAM (Robert), bp. of Salisbury, at the council of Pisa, 330, n. 3.
HAMBURG (archbishopric of), 100, 103; 104, n. 2.
HAMPOLE (Richard Rolle of), his writings, 348, n. 4; 357, n. 4.
HARTWIG (archbp. of Bremen), 211, 212.
Heathenism, remnants of, 46, n. 1; 87, n. 1.
HENRY IV. (emperor), his struggle with Gregory VII., 243—245.
HENRY (of Upsala), an English missionary, 206.
HENRY (the Cluniac monk), propagates the Petrobrusian tenets, 290; is condemned, 291.
HEMMING (archbp. of Upsala), 314.
HERACLIUS, eastern emperor, drives back the Persians, 29; favours the Monothelete heresy, 65; his *Ecthesis*, 66.
HEREFORD (Nicholas), partisan of Wycliffe, 385.
HERIGAR (abbot of Lobes), on the Eucharist, 169, n. 1.
HERMANN (of Cologne), a converted Jew, 220.
HESSE (Henry of), 328, n. 1; 329, n. 3.
HESSIA, conversion of, 20 sq.
Hesychastic controversy, 362, 363.
Hieronymites, order of, 344, n. 4.
HILDEBERT (archbp. of Tours), his works, 258, n. 4; 263, n. 4.
HILDEBRAND (see *Gregory VII.*).
HILDEGARD (abbess), prophecies of, 254, 255.
HINCMAR (archbp. of Rheims), opposed to the ultra-papal claims, 136, 137, 140, n. 4; 141; and also to encroachments of the crown, 151, n. 3; his activity in the Predestinarian controversy, 162 sq.
HINCMAR (bishop of Laon), 137, n. 1; 140, n. 2.

Hirschau, monks of, 149, n. 3.
HOLCOT (Robert), 354, n. 2; 360, n. 3.
Holy Places (at Jerusalem), controversy respecting, 277, n. 4.
Homiliarium, what, 88, n. 4.
HONORIUS I. (pope), a Monothelete heretic, 64, n. 4; 69, and n. 4.
Hospitallers, Knights, their rise and fortunes, 236, 237.
HOWEL THE GOOD (of Wales), 173, n. 2.
HUMBERT (cardinal), his fierce opposition to Berengarius, 171; his mission to Constantinople, 186; and his attack on the Eastern Church, 186, n. 2.
HUMBERT (de Romanis), on preaching, 300, n. 5.
Hungarians, antiquities of, 126, and n. 1; inroads into Europe, 106, 126; evangelized, 126—128; their union with the Western Church, 128; their bishops appointed by the crown, 150, n. 1.
HUSS (John), life and writings of, 400—407; his early influence and repute, 400; studies the Wycliffite tracts, 400, and n. 7; his general sympathy with Wycliffe, 401, and n. 5; his quarrel with the German students, 401, and n. 5; appeals to a pope 'better informed,' 403; his excommunication, 403; reconciled to archbp. Sbynco, 403; condemns the papal indulgences, 403, 404; his religious opinions, 405; his reputed 'orthodoxy,' 405; proceedings against him at Constance, 405—407.
Hussites, war of the, 407—409.
HUTTEN (Ulrich von), chief contributor to the ' Epist. Obscurorum Virorum,' 354, n. 4; 361, n. 4.

Iceland, conversion of, 109; remnants of heathenism, 110, n. 2.
Iconoclastic controversy, 72—78; revived, 175—179.
IGNATIUS (patriarch of Constantinople), deposed, 182; controversy with Photius, 182, 183; assisted by the pope, 183; 183, n. 7.
ILDEFONSUS (of Toledo), 59, n. 2; 91, n. 3.
Images (see also *Iconoclastic Controversy*), how used in the time of Gregory the Great, 72, n. 3; opposite decrees respecting, 75, and n. 1; 76,

77; views of the English Church, 78, and n. 3; of the French, 78, 176, n. 3; worship of, established permanently in the east, 178; its extravagancies, 178, n. 1; prevailing theory, 197, 198, n. 1.

India, early traces of Christianity, 27, 28.

Indulgences, 201, 309, 333, n. 5; 345, n. 1; condemned by Huss, 404, and n. 1; by Luther, 411, 431; ultimate development of the doctrine, 429—431.

Infidelity, rife in Italy before the Reformation, 352, n. 1; 355.

INNOCENT III. (pope), carries the papal power to a climax, 221, 222, and n. 1; 224; his immense influence in temporal matters, 251, 252; on reading the Bible, 299, n. 1.

Inquisition, origin of, 290; its early labours, 290, n. 2.

Interdict, 202, and n. 4.

Investiture, confused ideas respecting, 150; right of lay-investiture denied, 243, 244; how the controversy was settled in England, 247, n. 1; and on the Continent, 247, 248.

Iona, 7, n. 1; 12; 14, n. 4; 131, n. 3.

Ireland, conspicuous for its learning, 10, n. 6; 17, and n. 2; 19, n. 1; 59, n.3.

IRENE (empress), an ardent image-worshipper, 73.

Irish missionaries, 7, and n. 4; 9—13; many of them withdraw from England, 14; their orders disputed, 15, n. 1; later traces of their influence, 87, n. 4; 141, n. 2; some penetrate to Iceland, 109, n. 4; 110.

ISIDORE (of Seville), his writings, 59; see also *Decretals* (Pseudo-Isidore).

Ivo (Ives), bishop of Chartres, 145, n. 2.

JACOB (bishop of Tagritum), a Jacobite author, 275.

Jacobites (of Egypt), their missionary efforts, 28; patronized by the Muhammedans, 32, n. 2; attempts to reabsorb them into the church, 275, n. 7.

JACOBELLUS (of Misa), contends for communion in both kinds, 408; questions some of the legends, 424, n. 4.

JANOW (Matth. of), a Bohemian 'reformer,' 399.

JARUMAN (bp.), 10, n. 4.

JEROME (of Prague), 401, and n. 1; 404; his martyrdom, 407.

Jews, forcible conversion of, 29, n. 3; 220; condemned by some, 220, n. 3; their copious literature, 220, and n. 2; 318, n. 7; their abhorrence of images, 72, and creature-worship, 220; occasional conversions, 220; 319, n. 3; 320; writings against, 220, n. 5; fresh persecutions, especially in Spain, 318, 319.

JOACHIM (abbot), prophecies of, 254, 255.

JOAN (the female pope), fable of, 136, n. 1.

JOHN THE FASTER, controversy with Gregory the Great, 38; his *Pœnitential* work, 59, n 4.

JOHN THE CHANTER, introduces Roman psalmody, &c. into England, 87, n. 4.

JOHN THE GRAMMARIAN (patriarch of Constantinople), opposes image-worship, 178.

JOHN (king of England), abject submission to the pope, 252, and n. 3.

JOHN (a Dominican of Paris) writes on the regal and papal power, 254, n. 3.

JOHN, a monk of Old Saxony, at Alfred's court, 159, n. 3; 174, n. 1.

JOHN III. VATATZES (emperor), endeavours to unite the Eastern and Western Churches, 278.

JOHN VI. PALÆOLOGUS, submits to the pope, 364, and n. 4.

JOHN VII. PALÆOLOGUS, negociates with the Western Church, 365.

JOHN IV. (pope), opposes Monotheletism, 66.

JOHN VIII. (pope), his policy in the case of Photius, 184, 185, n. 1.

JOHN XXII. (pope), his contest with the German emperor, 323—326; taxed with heresy, 326, n. 1.

JOHN XXIII. (pope), appointed by the council of Pisa, 331; deposed at Constance, 332.

JONAS (bp. of Orleans), on images, &c., 158, n. 2; on penitence, 200, n. 3.

JOSEPH (patriarch of Constantinople), opposed to reunion, 280, 281.

Jubilee, year of, 309, 428, and n. 4.

JULIANO (cardinal) 334, 336, n. 4; 366.

JUSTUS (bp. of Rochester), 9; 10, n. 2.

Jutland, mission to, 101.

KARBEAS, a Paulician leader, 84.
KEMPIS (Thomas à), 347, n. 4; a 'Common-life Brother,' 347; author of the 'De Imitatione Christi,' 348, n. 1; 421; his mystical tendency, 357, n. 4.
Kent, conversion of, 8, 9.
KILIAN (Irish missionary), 17.
Kumanians, conversion of, 314, 315; united with the Eastern Church, 315.

Laity, their right to elect bishops denied, 237, n. 5; their influence in synods, 324, n. 2.
Lamaism, what, 217.
LANFRANC (archbp. of Canterbury), his controversy with Berengarius, 159, n. 6; 169—171.
LANGENSTEIN, Henry of (see *Hesse*).
Languages, variety of, 87.
Lapps, partial conversion of, 314.
Latins, effect of their empire at Constantinople, 278, 279.
LAURENTIUS (of Canterbury), 9, and n. 4.
LEBWIN (missionary monk), 23, n. 7.
Legates (papal), their vast influence, 225, 226; peculiarly obnoxious to the English, 225, n. 6; 340, n. 5.
Legends (see *Saints, Lives of*).
LEIDRAD (archbp. of Lyons), 64; 86, n. 3.
LEO THE ARMENIAN (emperor), opposed to images, 176, 177; persecutes the Paulicians, 83.
LEO THE ISAURIAN (emperor), opens the image-controversy, 72, 73; his advisers, 72, n. 5; patronizes the Paulicians, 82.
LEO IV. CHAZARUS (emperor), opposed to images, 75.
LEO X. (pope), 339, n. 4; on indulgences, 431, and n. 3.
Libri Carolini, account of, 77.
Lieflanders, conversion of, 212, 213.
Lindisfarne (or Holy Island), 12, 14; 15, n. 2.
Lithuanians, nominal conversion of, 312, 313; through a Polish channel, 313; dependence on Rome, 313, n. 6; traces of heathenism, 313, n. 5.
LIUDGER (missionary), 25, 100.
Lollards, English, followers of Wycliffe, 390; their number, 390, n. 6; their development of Wycliffe's principles, 390, 391; incur the hatred of the crown, 391; their persecutions, 391 sq.; attempt to reclaim them, 396; remains of, 396.
Lollards, foreign, their origin and office, 347; meaning of the word, 347, n. 1; suspected of heresy, 347, n. 3.
LOMBARD (Peter), his 'Book of Sentences,' 264.
LOUIS OF BAVARIA, conflict with the popes, 325, 326; grants a divorce, 326, n. 5.
LOUIS THE PIOUS, his interest in northern missions, 101, 102, n. 4.
LOUIS IX. (of France), his unconscious limitation of the papal power, 253, and n. 4.
Luciferians, sect of, 374.
LULL (Raymond), life and labours, 219, 265, n. 1.
Lullards (see *Lollards*).
LUTHER, on the decline of scholasticism, 354, n. 4; recognizes many of his precursors, 356, n. 6; 357, n. 4; 360, n. 1; his early career, 410—412; his original moderation, 431.
LYRA (Nicholas de), biblical writings 360, 361.

MACARIUS (patriarch of Antioch), adheres to Monotheletism, 69.
Magna Carta, 252.
MAHOMET (see *Muhammed*).
Mainotes, conversion of, 125, n. 1.
Manichæans, so called, 188, 189; 188, n. 2.
MANUEL II. (emperor), visit to the west, 365; his firm adherence to the Eastern Church, 365, n. 2.
MARK (of Ephesus), defends the Eastern Church, 367, n. 1.
Maronites, account of, 71; fresh attempt to reabsorb them into the church, 370.
MARTIAL (St), controversy respecting, 198, n. 2.
MARTIN I. (pope), his opposition to Monotheletism, 67, 68; his banishment, 68.
MARSILIUS (of Padua), 322, n. 1; his 'Defensor Pacis,' 324; associated with Wycliffe, 378, n. 3.
MARY, ST (see *Virgin*).
Masses (for the dead), 95.
Masses (private), 95; condemned, 96, n. 2.
Massilians (see *Bogomiles*).

MATILDA (countess of Tuscany), 245.
MAURETANIA (Walter de), 261, n. 5; 263, n. 6.
MAURICE (of Prague), on communion in one kind, 423, n. 5.
MAXIMUS (the Confessor), strenuous opponent of the Monotheletes, 67; his barbarous fate, 68; the character of his theology, 67, 71; his works, 67, n. 3.
MEINHARD (canon), missionary in Livonia, 212.
Melchites, Egyptian catholics, 32, 65.
MELLITUS (bp. of London), 9; 10, n. 2.
MELUN (Robert de), an English metaphysical writer, 264, n. 1.
Mendicants, mutual jealousies of, 233, n. 5; their amazing progress, 234; their conflicts with the university authorities, 233, 234; their zeal as preachers, 300; their ultimate decline, 344, 345; Erasmus respecting, 345, n. 5.
Mercia, conversion of, 13.
Merits, treasury of, 309, and n. 3.
METHODIUS (a Greek missionary), 111, and n. 9; misunderstanding with German missionaries, 113; vindicates himself at Rome, 113, 114; his influence in Bohemia, 114; and perhaps in Bulgaria, 122, n. 2.
Metropolitans (see *Archbishops*).
MICHAEL II. (emperor), tolerates the image party, 178.
MICHAEL PALÆOLOGUS (emperor), tries to unite the east and west, 279—282.
MILICZ, Bohemian 'reformer,' 397, 399; insists on very frequent communion, 399, n. 4.
Minors (see *Franciscans*).
Miracle-plays, 297, 298, and n. 1.
Mirandola (Pico of), 355, n. 2; 386, n. 3.
Missi, what, 54, n. 2.
Mongols, their invasion of Russia, 216; attempts to convert them, 217, 218.
Monks, importance and privileges of, 42; great varieties of in the East, 43, n. 2; order of St Benedict, 43, and n. 3; peculiarly ardent in defending images, 74, n. 1; degeneracy of, 147, 229; exemptions of, 42, 148, n. 1; 228, n. 5; the favourites of the pope, 228; how ill-adapted to the wants of the 13th century, 230; state of the eastern monks, 272, 273, n. 1; 343, n. 4; further degeneracy of the western, 343; their superabundant property, 343, n. 2; vain attempts to reform them, 344.
Monotheletism (heresy), 64—71.
MONTE CORVINO (John de), missionary in eastern Asia, 218.
MONTFORT (Simon de), 290.
Moors, attempts made to repel them from Spain and Africa, 219; successful with regard to Spain, 318, 319; projects for converting them, 219.
Moravia, conversion of, 111—114; by Greek influence, 112, 113; final ascendancy of the Germans, 114.
Moravians (or United Brethren), their origin, 409, 410.
MUHAMMED, origin and character of his religion, 29—31; its rapid conquests, 33; and thus augments the papal power, 37.
Muhammedans, persecute the Spanish Christians, 132, 133; their literary labours, 33; 156, n. 2.
Mystics, western school of, 356.

Nations, vote by, at the Council of Constance, 332.
NERSES (Armenian catholicos), writings of, 275.
Nestorians (Chaldæans), their vast missionary settlements, 26, 27; 128, 129; 216; 218; patronized by the Muhammedans, 27; 32; and Mongols, 216, 217; their internal condition, 217, n. 3; attempts to reabsorb them into the church, 275, n. 7.
NETTER (Thomas, of Walden) writes against the Lollards, 393, n. 6; 394, n. 2.
Nicæa, second council of, 76, 77; *not* œcumenical, 76, n. 2.
NICEPHORUS (Callisti), historical work, 361, n. 6.
NICEPHORUS (patriarch of Constantinople), advocates image-worship, 176.
NICEPHORUS (Blemmidas), a Latinizer, 279, and n. 2.
NICETAS (Acominatus), writings of, 274, and n. 2.
NICETAS (Studite monk), writes against the Latins, 186, n. 2.
NICETAS (archbp. of Nicomedia), 277.
NICHOLAS I. (pope), quarrel with the Greek missionaries respecting Bulgaria, 123, 124; his instructions to the natives, 123; commences a new

epoch in the papacy, 136, 153; approves the ultra-predestinarian synod of Valence, 165, n. 1; conduct in the case of Photius, 182.
NICHOLAS (Cabasilas), writings of, 363, and n. 8.
NICHOLAS (bp. of Methone), writings of, 274, and n. 3.
NIEM (see *Theodoric*).
NILUS (Cabasilas), writes against the Latins, 364.
NILUS, a Calabrian recluse, 149.
NILUS (Damyla), an Anti-Latin writer, 364, n. 1.
Nisibis, Nestorian seat of learning, 27, n. 6.
Nominalists, what, 259, 260.
NORBERT, founder of the Præmonstratensians, 237.
Northmen (Danes and Norwegians), ravages of, 103, 105, 106, 129, 130, 131.
Northumbria, conversion of, 12.
Norway, converted, 108, 109; through English influence, 108, 109, n. 2.
NOTKER (a monk of St Gall), 194, n. 5.
NOTTING (bp. of Verona), engages in the Predestinarian controversy, 161, n. 2, 3.
Nubia, partly Christianized, 28, 29.

OCKHAM (Wm. of), his anti-popery, 325, and n. 1; 327; his views on divorce, 326, n. 5; founds a school of theology, 353; how far approved by Luther, 353, n. 1; condemnation of Ockhamism, 353, n. 2; but in vain, 353.
ŒCUMENIUS, his writings, 180, and n. 1.
OFFA (of Mercia), regulation respecting tithes, 48, n. 9.
Officials, 239.
OLAF (the Holy) demolishes Paganism in Norway, 109.
OLAF TRYGGVASÖN, reintroduces Christianity into Norway, 108.
OLDCASTLE, Sir John (see *Cobham*).
OLGA, Russian Princess, 120, and n. 4.
OLIVA (John Peter de), leader of the 'spiritualist' Franciscans, 232, n. 2; 346, n. 4.
Ordeals, 155, and n. 3.
Orders (religious), 228 sq.; 343.
Orders (military), 235 sq.
Orkney, conversion of, 110, 111.
Ormulum, 297, n. 4; 418, n. 4; 421, n. 3.
OSWALD (bp. of Worcester), patron of the monks, 146, n. 6.

OSWIU (of Northumbria), 10, 13; joins the Roman party, 14, and n. 6.
OTHO (bp. of Bamberg), missionary labours in Pomerania, 208, 209.

PALAMAS (Gregorius), writings of, 363.
Pallium, its nature, 37; worn by all eastern bishops, 37, n. 1; oath exacted at the conferring of, 140, 141.
Pardons (see *Indulgences*).
Paris, university of, 234; its independence during the papal schism, 329, n. 3; 331, n. 4; 335; and generally, 338, n. 2.
Parishes, 45, n. 1.
PASCHAL II. (pope), his humiliation in the investiture controversy, 247.
Passagieri, 286, n. 3; 288, n. 5.
PATARENI, or Paterini, who, 189, n. 7; 286, n. 2.
Patriarchs, eastern, how affected by Islamism, 37, 38; those of the Nestorians, 27, 37, n. 2; of the Jacobites, 29; 37, n. 2; original limits of the Roman, 37, n. 3; title Œcumenical Patriarch, 38; mostly nominated by the emperor, 50.
Patronage, right of, 45, and n. 4; how abused, 150, and n. 3.
Paulicians, history and creed of, 78—84; their vitality, 187; 282, n. 5; 286, and n. 1.
PAULINUS (patriarch of Aquileia), writes on the Adoptionist heresy, 64, n. 1
PAULINUS (Roman missionary), 12, n. 3, 4.
Pauperes Catholici, who, 293.
PECOCK (Reginald), opinions of, 395, and n. 4, 5; 396, n. 1; his troubles, 395, 396.
PELAGIUS (Alvarus), a Franciscan, 325, n. 2.
Penance, doctrine of, 96; 200, 201; commutation of Penances, 97, n. 1; 201; systematized completely, 307, 308 sq.
Penda, 12, 13.
Persia, Christianity of, 27; almost eradicated, 217, n. 5.
PETER (Comestor), his 'Scholastic History,' 297, n. 4.
PETER (Patriarch of Antioch), mediates between the east and west, 186, n. 7.
PETER (the Venerable), 230, n. 4; 262, and n. 6.
PETER (Cantor), treatise of, 240, n. 4.
Peter-pence, 380, n. 4.

PETIT (John), condemned at Constance, 384, n. 2.
PETRARCH, 322, n. 2; 327, n. 6; 352, n. 1.
Petrobrusiani, sect of, 290; opinions of the founder, 290, n. 3.
PHILIP THE FAIR (of France), humbles the papacy, 253, 254; appeals to a general council, 253, n. 5.
PHOCAS, establishes the papal primacy, 39, n. 1.
PHOTIUS (patriarch of Constantinople), his co-operation in missions to Bulgaria, 122; his quarrel with Pope Nicholas I., 123; his literary labours, 180; his controversy with Ignatius and the Western Church, 182—184.
Picards (=Beghards), 409, n. 4.
Pictures (see *Images*).
Pilgrims, 41, n. 3; 94, n. 2; sober views respecting, 94; to Rome, 199, 200; and n. 1; to the Holy Sepulchre, 200, 203, n. 5: and elsewhere, 200, n. 2; 306; 428, and n. 3.
PILIGRIN (of Passau), a missionary in Hungary, 127.
Piphiles, 286, n. 1.
PIRNA (John of), founder of a Silesian sect, 374, and n. 3.
Pisa, council of, its history and effects, 330, 331.
PIUS II. (see *Sylvius*).
PLATO, favourite of the church 265, revival of his philosophy, 352, n. 1; 354, 355.
Pluralists, 143, n. 2; 240; 341. n. 5.
Pœnitentiaries (officers), 239, n. 4.
Poland, conversion of, 116, 117; final ascendancy of German influence, 117; reforming party in, 406, n. 4; 410.
POLO (Marco), Venetian traveller, 218.
Pomeranians, conversion of, 207—209; gradually Germanized, 209.
Poor-priests, followers of Wycliffe, 385, n. 1.
Popelicani, 286, n. 1.
Popes (see *Rome*), entire series of, 38—41; 135—140; 222—225; 322—339.
PORRETANUS (bp. of Poitiers), an erratic schoolman, 262, 263, n. 1.
Portuguese, effect of their discoveries, 315; their interference in the church of Abyssinia, 315, n. 5.
Pragmatic Sanction, 253, n. 4; 335, n. 1; 338.

Præmonstratensians, order of, 237.
Præmunire, statute of, 328, n. 4.
Predestinarian controversy, 160—165.
PRESTER JOHN, who, 129, and n. 5; 216.
Primates (see *Archbishops*).
Printing, invention of, its effect on the Reformation, 415.
Procession of the Holy Ghost, controversy respecting, 181; 279; 364, n. 2; 366, 367.
Provisions, papal, 322, n. 3; 340, n. 4; English statute respecting, 327, n. 5; 328, n. 4.
PRUDENTIUS (bp. of Troyes), engages in the Predestinarian controversy, 163.
Prussians, conversion of, 115, n. 3; 213—216; mythology of, 214, n. 2; gradually Germanized, 215.
Prymer (English), what, 420, n. 2.
PSELLUS (Michael, the younger), writings of, 273.
PULLEN (Robert), an Oxford preacher and writer, 263, 264.
PUPPER (John), a 'reformer,' 359, n. 7.
Purgatory (doctrine of), 58, n. 6, 8; 94, 95; effects of a belief in, 202, 203; how defined at Florence, 367.
PURVEY (John), second leader of the Lollards, 386, n. 3.
PYRRHUS (patriarch of Constantinople), a Monothelete, 66, 67, n. 2.

RABANUS MAURUS (archbp. of Mentz), his writings and influence, 157; takes part in the Predestinarian controversy, 161, 163; opposes transubstantiation, 166, and n. 3.
RADBERT (Paschasius), 101; introduces the theory of transubstantiation, 166, 168, 169; maintains the miraculous delivery of the Virgin, 166, n. 2.
RATHERIUS (bp. of Verona), 138, n. 2; 144, n. 2; 146, n. 2; 174, n. 2; 197, n. 2.
RATRAMNUS (monk of Corbey), engages in the predestinarian controversy, 163; opposes the theory of Paschasius Radbert on transubstantiation, 167.
Realists, what, 260.
Recluses, 42, n. 2; 199.
Reformation-college, what, 333, n. 4.

Index. 445

epoch in the papacy, 136, 153; approves the ultra-predestinarian synod of Valence, 165, n. 1; conduct in the case of Photius, 182.
NICHOLAS (Cabasilas), writings of, 363, and n. 8.
NICHOLAS (bp. of Methone), writings of, 274, and n. 3.
NIEM (see *Theodoric*).
NILUS (Cabasilas), writes against the Latins, 364.
NILUS, a Calabrian recluse, 149.
NILUS (Damyla), an Anti-Latin writer, 364, n. 1.
Nisibis, Nestorian seat of learning, 27, n. 6.
Nominalists, what, 259, 260.
NORBERT, founder of the Præmonstratensians, 237.
Northmen (Danes and Norwegians), ravages of, 103, 105, 106, 129, 130, 131.
Northumbria, conversion of, 12.
Norway, converted, 108, 109; through English influence, 108, 109, n. 2.
NOTKER (a monk of St Gall), 194, n. 5.
NOTTING (bp. of Verona), engages in the Predestinarian controversy, 161, n. 2, 3.
Nubia, partly Christianized, 28, 29.

OCKHAM (Wm. of), his anti-popery, 325, and n. 1; 327; his views on divorce, 326, n. 5; founds a school of theology, 353; how far approved by Luther, 353, n. 1; condemnation of Ockhamism, 353, n. 4; but in vain, 353.
ŒCUMENIUS, his writings, 180, and n. 1.
OFFA (of Mercia), regulation respecting tithes, 48, n. 9.
Officials, 239.
OLAF (the Holy) demolishes Paganism in Norway, 109.
OLAF TRYGGVASÖN, reintroduces Christianity into Norway, 108.
OLDCASTLE, Sir John (see *Cobham*).
OLGA, Russian Princess, 120, and n. 4.
OLIVA (John Peter de), leader of the 'spiritualist' Franciscans, 232, n. 2; 346, n. 4.
Ordeals, 155, and n. 3.
Orders (religious), 228 sq.; 343.
Orders (military), 235 sq.
Orkney, conversion of, 110, 111.
Ormulum, 297, n. 4; 418, n. 4; 421, n. 3.
OSWALD (bp. of Worcester), patron of the monks, 146, n. 6.

OSWIU (of Northumbria), 10, 13; joins the Roman party, 14, and n. 6.
OTHO (bp. of Bamberg), missionary labours in Pomerania, 208, 209.

PALAMAS (Gregorius), writings of, 363.
Pallium, its nature, 37; worn by all eastern bishops, 37, n. 1; oath exacted at the conferring of, 140, 141.
Pardons (see *Indulgences*).
Paris, university of, 234; its independence during the papal schism, 329, n. 3; 331, n. 4; 335; and generally, 338, n. 2.
Parishes, 45, n. 1.
PASCHAL II. (pope), his humiliation in the investiture controversy, 247.
Passagieri, 286, n. 3; 288, n. 5.
PATARENI, or Paterini, who, 189, n. 7; 286, n. 2.
Patriarchs, eastern, how affected by Islamism, 37, 38; those of the Nestorians, 27, 37, n. 2; of the Jacobites, 29; 37, n. 2; original limits of the Roman, 37, n. 3; title Œcumenical Patriarch, 38; mostly nominated by the emperor, 50.
Patronage, right of, 45, and n. 4; how abused, 150, and n. 3.
Paulicians, history and creed of, 78—84; their vitality, 187; 282, n. 5; 286, and n. 1.
PAULINUS (patriarch of Aquileia), writes on the Adoptionist heresy, 64, n. 1
PAULINUS (Roman missionary), 12, n. 3, 4.
Pauperes Catholici, who, 293.
PECOCK (Reginald), opinions of, 395, and n. 4, 5; 396, n. 1; his troubles, 395, 396.
PELAGIUS (Alvarus), a Franciscan, 325, n. 2.
Penance, doctrine of, 96; 200, 201; commutation of Penances, 97, n. 1; 201; systematized completely, 307, 308 sq.
Penda, 12, 13.
Persia, Christianity of, 27; almost eradicated, 217, n. 5.
PETER (Comestor), his 'Scholastic History,' 297, n. 4.
PETER (Patriarch of Antioch), mediates between the east and west, 186, n. 7.
PETER (the Venerable), 230, n. 4; 262, and n. 6.
PETER (Cantor), treatise of, 240, n. 4.
Peter-pence, 380, n. 4.

PETIT (John), condemned at Constance, 384, n. 2.
PETRARCH, 322, n. 2; 327, n. 6; 352, n. 1.
Petrobrusiani, sect of, 290; opinions of the founder, 290, n. 3.
PHILIP THE FAIR (of France), humbles the papacy, 253, 254; appeals to a general council, 253, n. 5.
PHOCAS, establishes the papal primacy, 39, n. 1.
PHOTIUS (patriarch of Constantinople), his co-operation in missions to Bulgaria, 122; his quarrel with Pope Nicholas I., 123; his literary labours, 180; his controversy with Ignatius and the Western Church, 182—184.
Picards (= Beghards), 409, n. 4.
Pictures (see *Images*).
Pilgrims, 41, n. 3; 94, n. 2; sober views respecting, 94; to Rome, 199, 200; and n. 1; to the Holy Sepulchre, 200, 203, n. 5: and elsewhere, 200, n. 2; 306; 428, and n. 3.
PILIGRIN (of Passau), a missionary in Hungary, 127.
Piphiles, 286, n. 1.
PIRNA (John of), founder of a Silesian sect, 374, and n. 3.
Pisa, council of, its history and effects, 330, 331.
PIUS II. (see *Sylvius*).
PLATO, favourite of the church 265, revival of his philosophy, 352, n. 1; 354, 355.
Pluralists, 143, n. 2; 240; 341. n. 5.
Pœnitentiaries (officers), 239, n. 4.
Poland, conversion of, 116, 117; final ascendancy of German influence, 117; reforming party in, 406, n. 4; 410.
POLO (Marco), Venetian traveller, 218.
Pomeranians, conversion of, 207—209; gradually Germanized, 209.
Poor-priests, followers of Wycliffe, 385, n. 1.
Popelicani, 286, n. 1.
Popes (see *Rome*), entire series of, 38—41; 135—140; 222—225; 322—339.
PORRETANUS (bp. of Poitiers), an erratic schoolman, 262, 263, n. 1.
Portuguese, effect of their discoveries, 315; their interference in the church of Abyssinia, 315, n. 5.
Pragmatic Sanction, 253, n. 4; 335, n. 1; 338.

Præmonstratensians, order of, 237.
Præmunire, statute of, 328, n. 4.
Predestinarian controversy, 160—165.
PRESTER JOHN, who, 129, and n. 5; 216.
Primates (see *Archbishops*).
Printing, invention of, its effect on the Reformation, 415.
Procession of the Holy Ghost, controversy respecting, 181; 279; 364, n. 2; 366, 367.
Provisions, papal, 322, n. 3; 340, n. 4; English statute respecting, 327, n. 5; 328, n. 4.
PRUDENTIUS (bp. of Troyes), engages in the Predestinarian controversy, 163.
Prussians, conversion of, 115, n. 3; 213—216; mythology of, 214, n. 2; gradually Germanized, 215.
Prymer (English), what, 420, n. 2.
PSELLUS (Michael, the younger), writings of, 273.
PULLEN (Robert), an Oxford preacher and writer, 263, 264.
PUPPER (John), a 'reformer,' 359, n. 7.
Purgatory (doctrine of), 58, n. 6, 8; 94, 95; effects of a belief in, 202, 203; how defined at Florence, 367.
PURVEY (John), second leader of the Lollards, 386, n. 3.
PYRRHUS (patriarch of Constantinople), a Monothelete, 66, 67, n. 2.

RABANUS MAURUS (archbp. of Mentz), his writings and influence, 157; takes part in the Predestinarian controversy, 161, 163; opposes transubstantiation, 166, and n. 3.
RADBERT (Paschasius), 101; introduces the theory of transubstantiation, 166, 168, 169; maintains the miraculous delivery of the Virgin, 166, n. 2.
RATHERIUS (bp. of Verona), 138, n. 2; 144, n. 2; 146, n. 2; 174, n. 2; 197, n. 2.
RATRAMNUS (monk of Corbey), engages in the predestinarian controversy, 163; opposes the theory of Paschasius Radbert on transubstantiation, 167.
Realists, what, 260.
Recluses, 42, n. 2; 199.
Reformation-college, what, 333, n. 4.

Reformation, general cry for, 371 sq.
Relics, 93, and n. 2; traffic in, 198 and n. 2; other abuses, 198.
REPINGTON (Philip), 385.
Reservations, papal, 322, n. 3; 341, n. 3; 377, n. 3.
REUCHLIN, restorer of Hebrew literature, 361, and n. 4.
RIMBERT, northern missionary, 105, 107.
ROBERT, founder of the Cistercians, 229.
ROLLE (see *Hampole*).
ROLLO, 131, 132.
Rome, church and bishop of, their ascendancy in England, 13, and n. 3; 14, 41; occasionally checked, 15, and n. 3; rebuked by Columbanus, 17, and n. 1; their power extended to Germany, 19 sq., 35, 36; Spain and France, 39; and augmented by the Saracenic conquests, 37; rivalry of the church of Constantinople, 37, 38, n. 1; rapid progress of the papacy under Gregory the Great, 39, 40; and Hadrian I., 41, n. 3; popes often Greeks and Syrians, 40, n. 3; their temporal possessions, 40, n. 6; how long dependent on the eastern empire, 50; struggle with the emperor respecting Monotheletism, 68, 69, n. 4; temporary suspension of communion between Rome and Constantinople, 69, n. 1; the pope defies the imperial edict, 73, and n. 6; fresh quarrel between Rome and Constantinople, 122, 123; extension of the papal power under Nicholas I., 136, 182, 183; resistance to it still offered, 140, 141, n. 1, 2; the nomination of the pope wrested from the civil power, 151; his temporal encroachments, 152, 153; 242—252; permanent breach with the Eastern Churches, 183, 184, 186; culmination of the papal power, 221, 222; introduction of the phrase 'court of Rome,' 226; last instance of the pope's 'confirmation' by the emperor, 243, n. 1; papal power augmented by the Crusades, 246; commencement of reaction, 252 sq.; negociations with the Eastern Church, 278—282; fruitless, 282; fresh negociations, 364—368; ultimately disappointed, 368; general growth of anti-papal feeling, 321, 322; struggles with the German emperors, 244—254; 323—327; effects of the residence at Avignon, 322; and of the forty years' schism, 328; recognition of the papal power at Florence, 368.
ROMUALD, founder of the Camaldulensians, 149.
ROSCELLINUS, author of the Nominalistic philosophy, 259; abjures, 260, n. 1; opinions on clerical marriage, 241, n. 3.
ROSWITHA, Latin poetess, 174, n. 5.
RUBRUQUIS (William de), missionary in Tatary, 217, n. 3.
Rügen, isle of, stronghold of Slavonic heathenism, 211.
RUPRECHT (missionary bishop), 18.
Russia, conversion of, 119—121; by Greek influence, 120; intimate union with the church of Constantinople, 121, n. 1; incursion of the heathen Mongols, 121; 216, and n. 5; position of the monks, 148, n. 1; relation of the church to the state, 149, 150, and n. 1; attempt of Hildebrand against, 276, n. 2; its independence, 277, n. 2; 281, n. 1; repudiates the council of Florence, 365, n. 5; more recent attempts to win over to Rome, 369.
RUYSBROEK (John), life and labours, 357, 358; opposed by Gérson, 357.

Sacraments, lax usage of the word, 199, and n. 3; restricted to seven rites, 301; doctrine of, systematized, 269; 301; 423; eastern enumeration of, 301, n. 2; 423, n. 3; introduction of the phrase 'ex opere operato,' 302, n. 3.
SADOLETI (cardinal), 417, n. 4.
SAGARELLI, 295.
Saints (see also *Virgin*), exaggerated honour of, 91, and n. 1; 195, 196; 306; prevailing ideas, 197; 'apocryphal' saints, 196, and n. 2; 306; canonization, 197, and n. 3.
Saints ('Lives of') very numerous and influential, 89, 90; their general character, 90; attempts to suppress apocryphal stories, 90, n. 2; 'Golden Legend,' 297, n. 3.

SALISBURY (John of), 263, n. 3.
Samnites, conversion of, 314.
SAMSON, Irish opponent of Boniface, 22, n. 4.
SANCTO AMORE (William de), writes against the Mendicants, 234, n. 5.
Sanctuary, right of, 54, and ,n. 5.
SAVONAROLA (Girolamo), sketch of his life and writings, 358, 359.
SAWTRE (Wm.), his opinions and execution, 393.
Saxons (continental), conversion of, 19, n. 5, 23, n. 7; coercive measures of Charlemagne respecting, 24.
SBYNCO (archbp. of Prague), 400, 402, 403.
Schism, Papal, origin of, 328; divides the Western Church into equal factions, 329, and n. 3.
Schism of East and West, 181 sq.
Schleswig, conversion of, 106; remnants of heathenism, 107, n. 1.
Schola Saxonum (English college at Rome), 41, n. 3.
Scholasticism, 159, n. 6; its general drift, 258, 259; its chief luminaries, 258—271; 351—353; development of sceptical tendencies, 351, 352, and n. 1.
Schools, 86, and n. 5; 156, n. 2; 191, n. 1; 192, n. 5; 193; 296, n. 2; 415.
Scotists, 270.
Scotland, conversion of, 6; 7, n. 1; 12, n. 6; 15, n. 1; Norwegian influence in, 131.
SCOTUS (John Erigena), the character of his theology, 159, 160; takes part in the Predestinarian controversy, 163; his writings condemned, 163, n. 7; views on the Eucharist, 168; his work confounded with that of Ratramnus, 168, n. 3; 169, n. 2.
SCOTUS (Duns), life and writings, 270; some peculiarities of his school, 270, n. 3.
Scripture (Holy), continued reverence for, 56; 193; 399, n. 3; vernacular translations, 89; 194, and n. 3, 5; 297, and n. 4; scarcity of copies, 194, n. 1, 2; decline in the study of, 195, and n. 1; 298, and n. 2; Roger Bacon's views respecting, 272, and n. 1; vernacular translations prohibited, 299, and n. 4; but not universally, *ibid*.; 360, n. 2; 418, 419, and n. 2; revival of Scriptural studies, 360, 361; 418; Wycliffite versions, 386.
Semgallen, temporary conversion of, 213.
Sends (? synods), 46, n. 1.
Serfs, manumission of, 55.
SERGIUS (patriarch of Constantinople), a Monothelete heretic, 65.
SERGIUS, second founder of Paulicianism, 82, 83.
Sermons in the vernacular, how frequent, 87, 88, and n. 4; 192, and n. 2, 3; 300, and n. 5; 421, 422.
SERVATUS LUPUS (abbot of Ferrières), engages in the Predestinarian controversy, 163.
Servians, conversion of, 125; their ecclesiastical independence, 125, and n. 6.
SEVERINUS, a German missionary, 16, n. 1.
Shetland, conversion of, 110, 111.
SIGEBERHT (the Good), 10.
SIGEBERHT (of East Anglia), 11, and n. 5.
SIGEBERT (of Gemblours), against the ultra-papal claims, 247, n. 2.
SILVESTER (see *Sylvester*).
SIMEON (monk of Thessalonica), writings of, 362, and n. 2.
SIMEON (Metaphrastes), his writings, 179, n. 5; the influence of his 'Lives of Saints,' 195.
Simony, crime of, 143, and n. 2; 144, n. 2; 150, n. 2.
SIXTUS IV. (pope), his political turn, 339, n. 1; his special patronage of the friars, 344, n. 6.
Slave-trade (Negro), how commenced, 317, n. 1.
Slavic races, 111; 127; 207 sq.; antiquities of, 111, n. 5.
SOPHRONIUS (patriarch of Jerusalem), a champion against the Monotheletes, 65, 66.
Spain, persecutions in, 132, 133.
Stedingers, sect of, 290, n. 2.
STEPHEN (king of Hungary), his zeal in propagating the Gospel, 127.
STEPHEN (see *Dolan*).
Stercoranism, what, 168, n. 1.
STIEKNA, mistake respecting the name, 398, n. 6.
STRABO (Walafrid), writings of, 159, and n. 2; views on the Eucharist, 168.

Strigolniks, Russian sect, 362; 374, n. 3.
STURM (of Fulda), missionary abbot, 23, 25.
Styria, conversion of, 25, 26.
Sunday, rigorous observance of, 88, 195, n. 4.; 425, n. 2; how regarded by the Waldenses, 294, n. 3; and the Lollards, 392.
SUSO, a mystical writer, 357, n. 4.
Sussex, conversion of, 11.
SVENO (or Svend), scourge of Christianity, 106.
SVENO (Estrithson), a zealous propagator of the Gospel, 107, n. 1.
Sweden (mission to), 102—105; imperfect conversion of, 107, n. 3; 206, n. 2; mythology of, 18, n. 3; 105, n. 3.
SWINESHEAD (Richard), 354, n. 2.
SWITHBERHT, missionary, 19.
Sword-brothers, military order, 213.
SYLVESTER II., a 'reforming' pope, 138, n. 4; on the Eucharist, 169, n. 1; 175.
SYLVIUS (Æneas), his popedom, 339, n. 2; 340, n. 1.
Synods (diocesan), 46; regulations of the Council of Basel respecting, 342.
Synods (provincial), action of the Frankish revived, 21; 35, n. 3; of England, 46, n. 4; of Spain, 46, n. 4; nature of their acts, 46; combined with civil courts, 50, 53, 54; by whom convened, 53; to be held every year, 239, n. 7; 342, n. 2; in England called 'convocations,' 240; early traces of the representative principle, 240, n. 1.
Synods (œcumenical), 57, n. 1; 239, n. 7; sixth of this class held at Constantinople, 69, 70; declared superior to the pope, 332, n. 4; 333, n. 2; 335.

Taborites, a Bohemian party of reformers, 409.
TAJO (of Saragossa), 59, n. 2.
TARASIUS (patriarch of Constantinople), 76, and n. 1.
TATWIN (archbp. of Canterbury), 40, n. 5.
TAULER (John), life and labours, 356, 357.
Templars (Knights), their rise and dissolution, 235—236; charges brought against them, 236, n. 3.

Teutonic knights, influence of in Prussia, 215, 216.
THEODORA (empress), restores image-worship, 178; persecutes the Paulicians, 84.
THEODORE (the Studite), an ardent advocate of images, 177; other works, 177, n. 1; his repute as a theologian, 179.
THEODORE (Archbp. of Canterbury), 14; his writings, 59, n. 4.
THEODORE (bp. of Pharan), author of the Monothelete heresy, 64, and n. 4.
THEODORIC (of Niem), 328, n. 4; 428, n. 4.
Theopaschites, 192, n. 5.
THEOPHANES (archbishop of Nicæa), writings of, 362.
THEOPHILUS (emperor), represses image-worship, 178.
THEOPHYLACT, writings of, 273, and n. 4.
Thomists, 267.
Thontrakians (sect of), 187.
Thuringia, conversion of, 20, 21.
TIMUR (Tamerlane), 312, n. 4; 365.
Tithes, 48.
TOSTATUS (of Avila), 360, n. 3.
Transubstantiation, doctrine of, not held in the 7th century, 95, n. 1; established, 171 sq., 302, 303; practical results of this belief, 303, 304; Wycliffe's attack upon it, 382.
Treviæ, or *Treugæ Dei*, what, 155.
Trinitarians, order of, 229, n. 3
Trinity Sunday, festival of, 425, n, 2.
TRIUMPHUS (Augustinus), defends the papacy, 325.
Troubadours, 242, n. 3; 289, n. 1; 297.
Trullan Council (see also *Councils*), its importance, 85.
Turlupines, sect of, 374.
TYLER (Wat), 384.

ULFILAS, 89.
ULLERTON (or Ulverstone), his 'reforming' paper, 329, n. 2.
Unction (extreme), gradual elevation of, 199.
Universities, number and influence, 416, 417.
URBAN II. (pope), stimulates the first crusade, 246.
URBAN VI. (pope), his connexion with the forty years' schism, 329.
UROLF (archbp. of Lorch), 111.

VALLA (Laurentius), 354, n. 4; 361, and n. 2.
VASILLO, a Franciscan missionary in Lithuania, 313.
Vaudois (see *Waldenses*).
VECCUS (see *Beccus*).
Vicars-general, 239.
VICELIN (bp. of Oldenburg), missionary labours among the Wends, 210, 211.
Victorines, school of theologians, 263.
Vikings (northern pirates), 103.
VIRGILIUS, Irish opponent of Boniface, 24, n. 4.
VIRGIN (the blessed), story of her assumption, 92; festival in honour of it, *ibid.* and 92, n. 4; and of her birth, 92, n. 1; other festivals, 306, n. 1; excessive veneration of, 196, 197; 306; 423, 424; Hours and 'Psalter' of the Virgin, 196 and n. 5; 305, n. 5; dispute respecting her immaculate conception, 233, n. 5; 270; 306, n. 1; 423, n. 3.
VLADIMIR, promotes the spread of Christianity in Russia, 120, and n. 5.

Waldenses, different from Albigenses, 291, and n. 3; founded by Peter Waldo, 292, and n. 1; fail to procure the papal sanction, 293; peculiar tenets, 293, and n. 5; 294, n. 3; their rapid diffusion, 293; after-fortunes of the sect, 293, 294, and n. 2; 373 and n. 6.
Waldensis (see *Netter*).
WALDHAUSEN (see *Conrad*).
WAZO (bp. of Liège), opposed to persecution, 189, n. 4.
Wends, conversion of, attempted, 117; but in vain, 119; new attempts, 210; more successful, 210, 211.
WESALIA (John de), a 'reformer,' 359, n. 7; on indulgences, 431.
WESSEL (John), life and writings, 359, and n. 7, 360.
Wessex, conversion of, 10.
WIGHEARD (archbp. elect of Canterbury), 14, n. 6.
WILFRITH, 11, 14, 15; his appeals to Rome, 15, n. 3; foreign missionary labours, 18.
WILLEHAD (English missionary), 25; 100, n. 1.

WILLEBRORD, his missionary labours, 18, 19; sanctity, 93, n. 2.
WILLIAM (the Conqueror), his independent language to Hildebrand, 243, n. 4.
WILLIBALD (English traveller and missionary), 23, n. 1.
WILLIRAM (schoolmaster at Bamberg), 194, n. 5.
WINFRITH (see *Bonifacius*).
WITIZA 'reforming' king of Spain, 39. n. 6; 47. n. 5.
WOLSEY (cardinal), 340, n. 5; 341. n. 5; 342, n. 1.
WOODFORD (Wm.), defends the friars against Wycliffe, 375, n. 6.
WULFRAM, missionary bishop, 19.
WULFSTAN (English bishop), 174.
WULFSTAN (monk), 174, n. 5.
WURSING, missionary, 19.
WYKEHAM (William of), 384, n. 12.
WYCLIFFE (John), life and writings of, 374—390; his movement unconnected with others, 374; his profound respect for Grosseteste, 374, n. 5; assails the friars, 375, 376; diplomatic mission to Bruges, 377; summary of his earlier opinions, 377; especially on church property, 377, n. 5; proceedings against him, 378, 379; his line of defence, 380; his 'Poor Priests,' 385, n. 1; assails the dogma of transubstantiation, 382, 383, and n. 1; his teaching condemned at Oxford, 383; 394, n. 3, and London, 385; his version of the Bible, 386; his theological opinions, 387—390; his death, 386; condemned afresh at Constance, 394; his bones burnt, 395; Oxford testimonial respecting him, 394, n. 3; influence of his writings in Bohemia, 400, 401; (see *Lollards*, English).

XIMENES (cardinal), 318; his biblical studies, 361, and n. 3.

York, regains its archiepiscopal rank, 12, n. 6.

ZIGABENUS (Euthymius), writings of, 273, n. 5; 274, n. 1.
ZWINGLI, early projects of reform, 412, n. 5.

CAMBRIDGE: PRINTED BY C. J. CLAY, M.A. AT THE UNIVERSITY PRESS.

WORKS BY THE SAME AUTHOR.

A History of the Christian Church during the Reformation. Revised by W. STUBBS, M.A., Regius Professor of Modern History in the University of Oxford. Third Edition. Crown 8vo. 10s. 6d.

Christ and other Masters. A Historical Enquiry into some of the Chief Parallelisms and Contrasts between Christianity and the Religious Systems of the Ancient World. New Edition, revised with a Prefatory Memoir by the Rev. F. PROCTER, M.A. New and cheaper Edition, revised, in the press.

Twenty Sermons for Town Congregations. Crown 8vo. 6s. 6d.

MACMILLAN AND CO. LONDON.

THEOLOGICAL WORKS.

A Companion to the Lectionary. Being a Commentary on the Proper Lessons for Sundays and Holy Days. By the Rev. W. BENHAM, B.D., Vicar of Margate. Crown 8vo., 7s. 6d.

A History of the Book of Common Prayer. With a Rationale of its Offices. By the Rev. FRANCIS PROCTER, M.A. Ninth Edition, revised. Crown 8vo., 10s. 6d.

An Elementary Introduction to the Book of Common Prayer. By the Rev. F. PROCTER, M.A., and the Rev. G. F. MACLEAR, B.D. With an Explanation of the Morning and Evening Prayer and the Litany. Fourth Edition. 18mo., 2s. 6d.

The Psalms of David Chronologically arranged. An Amended Version, with Historical and Critical Introductions and Explanatory Notes. By FOUR FRIENDS. Second and Cheaper Edition, enlarged. Crown 8vo., 8s. 6d. Student's Edition, with Briefer Notes. 18mo., 3s. 6d.

The Book of Isaiah Chronologically arranged. An Amended Version, with Critical and Historical Introduction and Explanatory Notes. By T. K. CHEYNE, M.A., Fellow of Balliol College, Oxford. Crown 8vo., 7s. 6d.

Twelve Discourses on Subjects connected with the Liturgy and Worship of the Church of England. By C. J. VAUGHAN, D.D., Master of the Temple. Fcap 8vo., 6s.

The Church of the First Days. By C. J. VAUGHAN, D.D. Second Edition. 3 vols. Fcap 8vo., 4s. 6d. each.

    Vol. I.—The Church of Jerusalem.
      ,, II.—The Church of the Gentiles.
      ,, III.—The Church of the World.

MACMILLAN AND CO. LONDON.

www.ingramcontent.com/pod-product-compliance
Lightning Source LLC
Chambersburg PA
CBHW051848300426
44117CB00006B/311